A HISTORY OF
ENGLISH DRAMA
1660–1900

A HISTORY OF
ENGLISH DRAMA
1660-1900

BY
ALLARDYCE NICOLL

VOLUME I
RESTORATION DRAMA
1660–1700

FOURTH EDITION

CAMBRIDGE
AT THE UNIVERSITY PRESS
1965

PUBLISHED BY
THE SYNDICS OF THE CAMBRIDGE UNIVERSITY PRESS

Bentley House, 200 Euston Road, London, N.W. 1
American Branch: 32 East 57th Street, New York, N.Y. 10022

First Edition   1923
Second Edition revised 1928
Third Edition revised 1940
Fourth Edition revised 1952
Reprinted   1961

Issued as Volume I of
A History of English Drama 1660–1900
Reprinted   1965

Printed in Great Britain at the University Printing House, Cambridge
(Brooke Crutchley University Printer)

PREFACE

A History of Restoration Drama, published in 1923, was intended as the first of a series of volumes designed to trace the fortunes of English dramatic literature from the accession of Charles II to the close of Victoria's reign. There is, therefore, every reason for the appearance of the present completely revised and considerably expanded text of this book as volume one of a general stage history covering the years 1660 to 1900.

Restoration Drama had been partly revised in 1927 and again in 1939, but the amount of scholarly attention devoted to the subject during the past twenty-five years has now called for something of further reach. The lengthy appendix dealing with purely theatrical history has been entirely rewritten and the handlist of plays has not only been reviewed in the light of recent specialist studies but there has been added in summary form the basic information by which the performance and printing dates may be determined. In this connection, I should note that the original "handlists" in this book and in its successors have happily succeeded in accomplishing what they were designed to accomplish. Since no effort had previously been made to make complete catalogues of productions and published texts during these years, I fully realised that my work must be tentative merely; but I hoped that the "handlists" would encourage others to indicate errors and to make additions. This is fortunately being done for all the periods covered by the present history of the drama, from the carefully detailed bibliography of Restoration plays now being compiled by Fredson Bowers to the invaluable articles on "Early XIXth Century Plays" which Allen Wade and St Vincent Troubridge are currently contributing to *Theatre Notebook*.

So far as the main text of the present volume is concerned, an effort has been made, at the request of the publishers, to retain as many pages of the original as possible, in order to avoid entire resetting. It has proved feasible to rewrite some of these and to insert many references to recent books and articles, yet still some important material could not satisfactorily be included in this way. Consequently, I have added to the three main sections of the book supplementary pages which survey certain aspects of the subject and present additional references not fully dealt with in the text itself. By this means I have endeavoured to make this volume a critical record of all the significant contributions to its theme during recent years.

Like many students, I have been greatly aided in my task by the never-failing courtesy of the officials of the British Museum, the Bodleian Library and the Public Record Office —and to these I should add those of the London Library and of several American libraries where part of my work has been carried out. For particular advice and assistance I wish to thank Professor Emmett L. Avery, Dr William Van Lennep and Dr James G. McManaway—all of whom have so materially assisted, by their researches, every student of the Restoration drama.

ALLARDYCE NICOLL

The University
Birmingham

CONTENTS

CHAPTER ONE

THE THEATRE

I. *Introductory*

PARADOXICALLY, at a time when the last vestiges of ancient aristocratic life are rapidly vanishing and democracy is the watchword of the age, the predominantly aristocratic drama of the reign of Charles II has once more come into its own again. True, voices have been raised occasionally to champion the claim that the comedy of this period is "insufferably dull" and to protest that

the criticism that defenders of Restoration comedy need to answer is not that the comedies are "immoral," but that they are trivial, gross and dull.[1]

Such warnings are salutary when we think of the pronouncements of some among the more eccentric defenders of the Restoration theatre, but the charge of dulness is perhaps sufficiently met by pointing to the truly extraordinary interest displayed during recent years in stage revivals of these late seventeenth-century plays. We might be prepared to set aside the various productions of the Phoenix Society as having had appeal only to a special and limited audience, but we cannot ignore the way in which Congreve and his fellows have recently attracted the general public within the theatre's doors. The plays have come alive there and their wit has summoned forth the laughter they were intended to provoke. It is not without significance that only a few years ago appeared a "Playgoer's Handbook to Restoration Drama"[2]—

---

[1] L. C. Knights, "Restoration Comedy: the Reality and the Myth" (*Scrutiny*, 1937, VI. 122–43).

[2] Malcolm Elwin, *The Playgoer's Handbook to Restoration Drama* (1938).

in its title testifying to the widespread and theatrical interest in these works[1].

This theatrical interest has been accompanied by an energetic academic interest. After remaining largely neglected since their own times, or at least from the eighteenth century, numerous Restoration dramatists have had their plays edited during the past two or three decades, in volumes both sumptuously expensive and popularly simple[2]; and, apart from these collected "works," numerous single plays have received special attention[3]. A majestic bibliography of Dryden leads

[1] Before 1923, apart from chapters in general histories of literature, the only accounts of the Restoration drama appeared in the 1660–1700 sections of John Genest's *Some Account of the English Stage, from 1660 to 1830* (1832, 10 vols.), Sir A. W. Ward's *A History of English Dramatic Literature to the Death of Queen Anne* (1875; revised edition 1899, 3 vols.) and G. H. Nettleton's *English Drama of the Restoration and Eighteenth Century* (1914). To these might be added the important general study of literary conditions during the period, Alexandre Beljame's *Le public et les hommes de lettres au dixhuitième siècle* (Paris, 1897; issued in English translation only in 1948). The notes to the present volume indicate the wealth of studies since that time. In addition to the works on particular aspects referred to later, note may be taken of M. Ellehauge's *English Restoration Drama* (1933).

[2] Thus Montague Summers has prepared minutely annotated (although unfortunately rather erratically prepared) texts of Shadwell (1927, 5 vols.), Dryden (1934, 6 vols.), Wycherley (1924, 4 vols.), Congreve (1923, 4 vols.), Behn (1915, 6 vols.) and Otway (1926, 3 vols.). H. F. B. Brett-Smith has an admirable Etherege (1927, 2 vols.), J. C. Ghosh an Otway (1932, 2 vols.), Bonamy Dobrée a Vanbrugh (1927, 4 vols., in collaboration with G. Webb) and a Congreve (1925–8, 2 vols.), F. W. Bateson a Congreve (1930), Charles Stonehill a Farquhar (1930, 2 vols.), W. S. Clark an Orrery (1937, 2 vols.), John Hayward a Rochester (1926), V. de S. Pinto a Sedley (1928).

[3] For example, Buckingham's *The Rehearsal* (ed. Montague Summers, 1914), Kirkman's *The Wits* (ed. J. J. Elson, 1932), Tuke's *The Adventures of Five Hours* (ed. Montague Summers, 1927; and E. H. Swaen, 1927), Shadwell's *Epsom Wells* and *The Volunteers* (ed. D. M. Walmsley, 1930), Wycherley's *The Country Wife* (ed. U. Todd-Nayler, 1931; and, with *The Plain Dealer*, G. B. Churchill, 1924), Banks' *The Unhappy Favourite* (ed. T. M. H. Blair, 1939), Sir William Killigrew's *The Siege of Urbin* (ed. I. E. Taylor, 1946). Several anthologies also testify to the interest in the drama of the period—*Restoration Comedies* (1921) edited by Montague Summers, *Types of English Drama, 1660–1780* (1923) edited by D. H. Stevens, *Five Restoration Tragedies* (1928) edited by Bonamy Dobrée, *British Plays from the Restoration to 1820* (1929, 2 vols.) edited by M. J. Moses, *Plays of the Restoration and Eighteenth Century* (1931) edited by D. MacMillan and H. M. Jones, *Twelve Famous Plays of the Restoration and Eighteenth Century* (1933) edited by C. A. Moore, *English Plays, 1660–1820* (1935) edited by A. E. Morgan.

the van in a series of studies designed to chart the hitherto unexplored territory of Restoration play-publishing[1]. Basic contemporary texts have been issued with appropriate annotations[2]. Theatrical history of the period 1660–1700, which thirty years ago had been seriously dealt with only in a few articles devoted to particular problems, has now been more widely reviewed[3]. And at the same time numerous studies

[1] References to these studies are given in the Handlist of Plays. Montague Summers' *Bibliography of Restoration Drama* (1937), while useful as a list, but one to be treated with caution, is of course not in any respect a bibliography in the technical sense of the term. This is referred to later as "Summers, *Bibliography*". A much closer approach towards a bibliography is the excellent *Check List* prepared by Gertrude L. Woodward and James G. McManaway (1945): an elaborate bibliographic study of the drama from 1660 to 1700 is being prepared by Fredson Bowers.

[2] Especially important are *The Dramatic Records of Sir Henry Herbert* (ed. J. Q. Adams, 1917), referred to hereafter as "Herbert"; John Downes' *Roscius Anglicanus* (ed. Montague Summers, 1929), referred to as "Downes"; *A Comparison between the Two Stages* (ed. S. B. Wells, 1942), referred to under its title. It may be noted here that several early basic texts are generally referred to in the present volume simply by the names of their authors: thus "Langbaine" refers to Gerard Langbaine's *An Account of the English Dramatick Poets* (1691), "Gildon" to Charles Gildon's continuation of this work as *The Lives and Characters of the English Dramatick Poets* (1698), "Jacob" to Giles Jacob's *The Poetical Register* (1719), "Whincop" to *A Compleat List of all the English Dramatic Poets* contributed (apparently by John Mottley) to T. Whincop's *Scanderbeg* (1747), "*Biographia Dramatica*" to the edition of that work prepared by Stephen Jones in 1812. "Cibber" refers to *An Apology for the Life of Mr Colley Cibber*, edited by R. W. Lowe in 1889 (2 vols.). The reports of the Historical Manuscripts Commission are cited as "*HMC*."

[3] By far the most important volumes are Leslie Hotson's *The Commonwealth and Restoration Stage* (1928) and Eleanore Boswell's *The Restoration Court Stage (1660–1702)* (1932)—referred to as "Leslie Hotson" and "Eleanore Boswell" respectively. Both of these present many new documents culled from the Public Records Office. Montague Summers' *The Restoration Theatre* (1934) and *The Playhouse of Pepys* (1935)—referred to as "Summers, *Theatre*" and "Summers, *Playhouse*" respectively—give an account of theatrical conditions in this age. Emmett L. Avery has an invaluable "Tentative Calendar of Daily Theatrical Performances, 1660–1700" (*Research Studies of the State College of Washington*, XIII. 1945, 225–83)—referred to as "Emmett L. Avery"; and Alfred Harbage's *Annals of English Drama, 975–1700* (1940) forms a serviceable complement. Very useful, too, are the two collections of Sybil Rosenfeld, "Dramatic Advertisements in the Burney Newspapers, 1660–1700" (*PMLA*, LI. 1936, 123–52) and "The Restoration Stage in Newspapers and Journal, 1660–1700" (*Modern Language Review*, 1935, 445–59). The same author's publication of interesting Norwich records is referred to in Appendix A.

of individual playwrights have illuminated the practice of dramatic composition during these years[1].

Most important of all, however, are the many books and articles devoted to an attempt at reassessment of the Restoration drama. These may more appropriately be mentioned individually in those sections of the present book to which they have reference; but it may be advisable here to emphasise that through these diverse studies we have indeed come near to securing a balanced attitude towards the comedy and the serious drama of the age. Neither are we likely now to neglect the solid virtues of the heroic drama and the delicacy of the comic, nor are we tempted to over-praise because of a surrounding atmosphere of indifference. And, above all, we are better equipped now to see the Restoration stage and the dramatic literature to which it gave birth as the interesting and indispensable link between Shakespeare's Globe with its poetic plays and the modern theatres with their combination of realism and spectacle. Although this age seems at first to be a strange world of its own, separated alike from the eras dominated by Elizabeth on the one hand and by Victoria on the other, we are coming more and more to recognise that it does not stand alone. The excesses of its courtiers may momentarily persuade us of its isolation, but the deeper we search the surer becomes our realisation that the playwrights who

[1] Among these, apart from the numerous Dryden studies, are the following: *Aphra Behn* (by V. Sackville-West, 1927); *Colley Gibber* (by F. D. Senior, 1928; by D. M. E. Habbema, 1928; by R. H. Barker, 1939); *Congreve* (by D. Protopopesco, 1924; by Sir Edmund Gosse, revised edition 1924; by D. C. Taylor, 1931; by John C. Hodges, 1941); *Cowley* (by A. H. Nethercot, 1931; by Jean Loiseau, 1931); *Crowne* (by A. F. White, 1922); *D'Avenant* (by Alfred Harbage, 1935; by A. H. Nethercot, 1938); *Dennis* (by H. G. Paul, 1911); *D'Urfey* (by R. S. Forsythe, 1916); *Etherege* (the *Letterbook*, edited by Sybil Rosenfeld, 1928); *Farquhar* (by Willard Connelly, 1948); *Gould* (by E. H. Sloane, 1940); *Killigrew* (by Alfred Harbage, 1930); *Lee* and *Otway* (by R. G. Ham, 1931); *Mountford* (by A. S. Borgman, 1935); *Motteux* (by R. N. Cunningham, 1933); the Duke and Duchess of *Newcastle* (by H. Ten Eyck Perry, 1921); *Katherine Philips* (by P. W. Souers, 1931); *Sedley* (by V. de Sola Pinto, 1927); *Settle* (by F. C. Brown, 1910); *Shadwell* (by A. S. Borgman, 1928); *Southerne* (by J. W. Dodds, 1933); *Rochester* (by J. Prinz, 1927; by V. de Sola Pinto, 1927; by Charles Williams, 1935); *Vanbrugh* (by L. Whistler, 1938); *Wycherley* (by Charles Perromat, 1921; by Willard Connely, 1930).

fluttered around Drury Lane and Lincoln's Inn Fields were the descendants of Shakespeare and the ancestors of Shaw.

Thus, the interest we take in the stage and drama which flourished during the reigns of Charles II and his successors must perforce be motivated partly by historical considerations, partly by the intrinsic excellence to be discovered in at least a few plays of these times. Were we concerned merely with such comedies and tragedies as seemed to possess qualities of an enduring sort or such as might appear to merit revival on the modern stage, then most of the plays recorded here would necessarily find no mention: but, since the interest is a double one, it is obviously essential to bring under review not only the few which are permanently worthy but also the many which succeeded merely in arousing a little flutter of contemporary approval and their less fortunate companions which failed to attract even the audiences of their own days. Any account of Restoration drama must, accordingly, consider both the masterpieces of the time and the failures: only by taking these together can we properly assess either the virtues of the one or the defects of the other.

II. *The Audience*

All dramatic art depends ultimately for its form and content on the audience. The spectators of 1590 gave birth to *As You Like It*: the spectators of 1600 to *Hamlet* and to *Every Man in his Humour*: the spectators of 1670 to *The Conquest of Granada* and to *The Man of Mode*. Fundamentally, independent genius counts for less in the world of the theatre than does the general atmosphere of the time: "the drama's laws the drama's patrons give" is a rule which, it seems, may never be broken. Less than any other art is the drama ahead of its time. It reflects, very rarely prophesies: its basis is the world of sentiment around, not before, it.

Of all audiences, the audience of the years 1660 to 1700 is perhaps the easiest to analyse. Save for the very first year or two of the Restoration, two theatres, and for over twelve years, one theatre, supplied the wants of the London play-going public of the time[1]. Instead of cries that admittance was unobtainable, we meet with lament after lament that the managers and promoters could barely make ends meet[2]. If one theatre had a new play by a well-known author the other was as if deserted, sometimes summoning barely sufficient spectators to make a performance either advisable or even possible[3]. Outside of London, except for several strolling

[1] See, for the history of the theatres, Appendix A.

[2] References to small audiences are frequent in prologue and in epilogue from the earliest to the latest period. The first, probably, is that which appears in D'Avenant's prologue to the second part of *The Siege of Rhodes*:

> "*Oh! Money! Money! if the* WITS *would dress*
> *With Ornaments, the present face of Peace;*
> *And to our Poet half that Treasure spare,*
> *Which Faction gets from Fools to nourish War;*
> *Then his contracted Scenes should wider be,*
> *And move by greater Engines, till you see*
> (*Whilst you securely sit*) *fierce Armies meet....*"

About 1675-6 the T.R. seems to have been in a peculiarly bad way. See the prologue to a revival of *Every Man out of His Humour* (July, 1675) in Duffett's *New Poems, Songs, Prologues and Epilogues, Never before Printed* (1676), p. 72, and the epilogue to Lee's *Gloriana* (D.L. 1676):

> "*They told me at t'other House y'had left us quite...*
> *Good faith I'm very glad to see you here!*
> *'Tis well you can at a New Play appear.*"

About the year 1667 Pepys has many references to paucity of audiences. On Wed. 17 April, 1667, the King's house for *Rollo* was empty: it was "mighty empty" on Thurs. 1 Aug. for *The Custom of the Country*: it was poor on Mon. Aug. 26 for *The Surprisal*: and "not one soul" was in the pit by three o'clock on Mon. 16 Sept. The Union of 1682, when the two theatres amalgamated, was really the result of financial failure, and no one appears to have been inconvenienced because only one playhouse was open. When Betterton had seceded to the long disused L.I.F. house in 1695, the old complaints started again. Thus Jo. Haynes spoke the epilogue to Farquhar's *Love and a Bottle* (D.L. 1699) "*in Mourning*":

> "*I Come not here, our Poet's Fate to see,*
> *He and his Play may both be damn'd for me:*
> *No, Royal Theatre, I come to Mourn for Thee.*
> *And must these Structures then untimely fall,*
> *Whilst th'other House stands, and gets the Devil and all?*"

[3] Pepys found the T.R. empty on Thurs. July 4, 1661, at *Claracilla* because of the recent opening of D'Avenant's "opera": on Mon. Mar. 7, 1663-4, he found L.I.F. empty because of a new play at the T.R.: the emptiness of the T.R. on Mon. Aug. 26, 1667, was due to the production of *Sir Martin Mar-all* at L.I.F.: on Mon. Sept. 16, 1667, Pepys noted that L.I.F. was full for *Tu Quoque* but the T.R. empty for *The Scornful Lady*: on Sat. 5 Oct. 1667, the T.R. was empty for *Flora's Vagaries* because of a "new play" at L.I.F.: on Thurs. 14 May, 1668, the T.R. house was

companies and for visits of the London companies to Oxford and Cambridge[1], plays were unknown, and in the metropolis itself only a very small proportion of the people favoured the theatre. Charles had been restored with practically the full consent of the nation, but the Puritan tenets which had made possible the eighteen years duration of the Commonwealth régime could certainly not have vanished with the mere restoration of a king to his throne. Had the courtiers been less debauched, had Charles been less the slave to his passions, had the playwrights maintained a more sedate attitude towards life, the citizens might, too, have flocked to the playhouses as in Elizabethan times. Of direct reference to the middle classes in the theatre we have practically no record[2]. During the Dutch wars when a certain number of the gallants and the beaux were gone to sea, an appeal might be made from the stage to the citizens "of *Lombard*-street," but in the main those who were engaged in business, unless they were younger sons of the nobility, were ridiculed in plays, undesired among the spectators. The courtiers made of the theatre a meeting-place of their own, with licence of all kinds, bringing there their dubious loves, so that those citizens who still retained some of their Puritan convictions shunned the place like a plague[3]. More personal motives may have entered in as well. In the comedies, and the

small for *The Country Captain* because of *The Sullen Lovers* at L.I.F.: "not £10" was in the T.R. for *The Faithful Shepherdess* on Fri. Feb. 26, 1669, because *The Royal Shepherdess* had been performed for the first time at L.I.F. the day before.

[1] See Appendix A.

[2] The presence of citizens in the theatre was four times noted by Pepys and always as an exception, on Sat. Dec. 27, 1662 (second part of *The Siege of Rhodes*), on Thurs. Jan. 1, 1662–3 (*The Villain*), on Wed. 1 Jan. 1667–8 (*Sir Martin Mar-all*), on Sat. Dec. 26, 1668 (*Women Pleas'd*). It is noticeable that all of these were at the Duke's theatre, and all round the Christmas or New Year season. It is possible that the citizens visited the playhouse only on special occasions such as this, and that the "show" of D'Avenant's house particularly appealed to them.

[3] See Wright, *Historia Histrionica*, p. 6; he avers that "many of the more Civilised Part of the Town are uneasy in the Company, and shun the Theater as they would a House of Scandal." Tom Brown in his *Play-house* makes a similar remark that "Men of *Figure* and Consideration are known by seldom being there, and Men of *Wisdom* and Business by being always absent" [*Works*, 1708, III. 41].

comedies are but a reflex of real life, the citizens' wives are made fair game for the debauched sparks, their husbands the mere butts for ill-placed wit and buffoonery. It must certainly have appeared to many that the introduction of their women-folk into this place of ogling eyes and significant leers was a proceeding injudicious, to say the least[1].

The spectators, then, for whom the poets wrote and the actors played were the courtiers and their satellites. The noblemen in the pit and boxes, the fops and beaux and wits or would-be-wits who hung on to their society, the women of the court, depraved and licentious as the men, the courtesans with whom these women of quality moved and conversed as on equal terms, made up at least four-fifths of the entire audience. Add a sprinkling of footmen in the upper gallery, a stray country cousin or two scattered throughout the theatre, and the picture of the audience is complete.

All of these took their cue from the king. Charles returned from his exile with a very definite love of the drama and of literature in general. The theatre became with him a particular hobby. Of the two licensed houses, one, that which included the actor Mohun, was styled the Theatre Royal, its players, His Majesty's Servants, the other, that which included Betterton, was called the Duke's Theatre, from the fact that it was patronised by the brother of the King, the Duke of York. Charles was the first English sovereign to attend in any frequency a public playhouse, his initial appearance there being, according to Downes, at the opening of the new Duke's Theatre on Friday, June 28, 1661[2]. He had, of course, his own private playhouse at Whitehall, and there performances were given occasionally[3], but his

---

[1] "*The City neither likes us nor our Wit*," says Shadwell in the epilogue to *The Lancashire Witches* (D.G. 1681).

> "*They say their Wives learn ogling in the Pit;*
> *They'r from the Boxes taught to make Advances,*
> *To answer stolen Sighs and naughty Glances.*"

[2] Downes, p. 20, gives the date as "Spring, 1662," but a reference in Pepys shows that this is an error. In general, it should be noted that Downes, while providing an invaluable account of the stage, is not to be trusted where dates are concerned.

[3] On the various court theatres Eleanore Boswell's study is the prime

main interest seems to have been in the public theatres. He acted as judge whenever anything happened to disturb the equanimity of the management, even going so far as to allot shares which had fallen vacant[1], and governing the actions of the players[2]. He had his favourites among the actors, Lacy in particular, whom he caused to be painted for his palace. He had his loves among the actresses, the children of Nell Gwyn becoming Dukes and Lords. He it was who set the fashion for rimed plays, as Roger Boyle, Earl of Orrery, expressly informs us. He ordered Tuke to write *The Adventures of Five Hours* and Crowne to pen *Sir Courtly Nice*. He it was who provided vestments for the actors on special occasions, passing his state robes over to Mohun or to Betterton as the case might be. For a revival of D'Avenant's *Love and Honour* at L.I.F. sometime before 1665 the royal coronation suits were worn in the theatre[3], and the same suits apparently were lent again to the Duke's playhouse for the production of Orrery's *Henry V* in 1664[4]. On Dec. 11, 1667, Pepys heard that Charles was to give £500 for garments to deck up *Catiline* at the T.R., but seemingly the lending of state robes was an easier thing to get out of the merry monarch than a sum of money, however small. A month later the production of *Catiline* was being held over, the King's present not forthcoming.

From this royal countenance of the theatre the actors and the playwrights gained a certain amount of prestige. Of all artists they were nearest the court. They expressed in every way the sentiments of the court, and, unhappily, not only the wit they met with there in the persons of Rochester and

authority. A clear distinction must be made between this theatre and the Hall Theatre. Miss Boswell presents many documents from the Public Records Office relating to the structure and administration of both.

[1] That which lapsed owing to the death of Theophilus Bird was assigned by him (*Cal. State Papers, Dom. Series, Charles II*, 1663-4, p. 121).

[2] Thus in July, 1663, Henry Harris left the Duke's company for the royal troupe, but was forced by royal command to return (Pepys, July 22, 1663). The year before, in 1662, John Richards had similarly deserted for the Dublin theatre. The King thought fit to issue a warrant immediately, commanding the Lord Lieutenant to arrest him at once and ship him back to England (*Cal. State Papers, Dom. Series*, 1661-2, p. 455).

[3] Downes, p. 21.   [4] Downes, p. 27.

of Sedley or the exalted romance of Mdlle de Scudéry, but
also the profound royalism of the Stuart régime. The ultra-
monarchism which pervades this theatre may astound us
nowadays, but it must be remembered that, not only were
the dramatists and the actors cavaliers by necessity, the
Puritans condemning and decrying their very means of liveli-
hood, but that they were fettered by a fairly strict and pre-
judiced censorship. At first, certainly, some slight latitude
seems to have been allowed, as when the lost play of Howard's,
The Change of Crowns, was acted before the King, who flew
into a most uncharacteristic passion and ordered it to be
restrained—only, characteristically, to permit its revival in
a few days' time. Other plays, we know from contemporaries,
were regarded as attacks at the court, and were allowed, but
for the most part the office of censor, held in turn by Herbert
and by Killigrew, was rigidly exercised. An interdiction was
laid sometime or another on *The Maid's Tragedy*[1]. Crowne's
Henry the Sixth, part I (1681), because of some anti-Catholic
sentiments expressed in it, was suppressed[2]. Charles allowed,
but James disallowed, the acting of Dryden's *The Spanish
Fryar* (D.G. 1680)[3]. Shadwell suffered for some injudicious
remarks in *The Lancashire Witches* (D.G. 1681), Lee for
Lucius Junius Brutus (D.G. 1680)[4], Banks for *The Innocent
Usurper* (1694) and for *Cyrus the Great* (L.I.F. 1695)[5].

At several definite points in the history of this period,
however, a certain amount of criticism would seem to have
been tolerated, precisely because men did not know where
to stand. At first, naturally enough, all the "political" plays

---

[1] See Fowell, F. and Palmer, F., *Censorship in England* (1913), p. 101.
[2] Dedication to *The English Frier* (D.L. 1690).
[3] The order of suppression is in the P.R.O., L.C. 5/147, p. 239: it is
dated Dec. 8, 1686, and commands "that ye play called ye Spanish Friar
should bee noe more Acted."
[4] The order is dated Dec. 11, 1680 (L.C. 5/144, p. 28): "Whereas I am
informed that there is Acted by you a Play called Lucius Junius Brutus...
wherein are very Scandalous Expressions & Reflections vpon ye Government these are to require you Not to Act ye said Play again."
[5] Tate's *Richard II* was similarly banned on Dec. 14, 1680 (P.R.O.,
L.C. 5/144, p. 29). Dryden and Lee's *The Duke of Guise* on July 18, 1682
(P.R.O., L.C. 5/16, p. 101) and Crowne's *The City Politiques* on June 26,
1682 (P.R.O., L.C. 5/16, p. 83). See also Fowell and Palmer, *op. cit.* p. 103.

were violently monarchist, but later the indecision of the court in regard to religion led to a definite break of the dramatists into two camps, some, like Mrs Behn and D'Urfey, supporting the court as far as lay in their power, others, such as Settle and Shadwell, violently condemnatory of all but Protestant principles. The first era of keen political and religious controversy in the playhouses may be dated from 1679 to 1685, and in that era we do find a mass of conflicting satire, the dramatists carrying on what was literally a little verbal war of their own[1]. Another period of extreme excitement circles around the years 1689 and 1690, but then most of the political plays produced, such as *The Abdicated Prince*, *The Bloody Duke* and *The Royal Voyage* (all 1690), were either not meant to be acted, or were unable to secure a theatrical production.

This keen party and religious atmosphere, this intimate interest of the King in all affairs theatrical, this audience intent upon their own pleasures and upon court affairs rather than upon the plays themselves, were bound to produce a type of drama different from the drama of the former years. The theatre was their toy: they could do with it what they liked. They could appropriate a certain portion of the playhouse, that apparently between the front curtain and the outer edge of the stage, and stand there, conversing more or less wittily, picking their teeth and "oft combing their Hair[2]." This was no doubt between the acts, for, peculiarly enough when we think of Elizabethan example, no very great body of spectators, if any at all, would appear to have occupied seats on the stage itself until a comparatively late date in the century. In 1664 Sorbière particularly observed that this vice was not in practice then[3], and it is not until

---

[1] Considerable attention has recently been paid to the political elements in Restoration plays, especially in the late seventies and the eighties. Such political elements appear in the form of unacted "propaganda" pieces, in that of "parallels" in new tragedies or historical plays, in that of satirically conceived scenes in new comedies and in that of definitely tendentious prologues and epilogues. See *infra*, pp. 78–9.

[2] D'Avenant's *The Man's the Master* (L.I.F. 1668) epilogue.

[3] *Relation d'un Voyage en Angleterre* (Paris, 1664), p. 63.

about 1690 that we find many references to the custom. In 1674 it was apparently unknown, for Vincent saw fit to omit all references to gallants on the stage when he was re-writing Dekker's *Gul's Horn-Book*. On the other hand, in 1692, one of the characters in D'Urfey's *The Marriage-Hater Match'd* (D.L. 1692), declares of a lord: "I have seen him spoil many a Comedy, by baulking the Actors entrance, for when I have eagerly expected some Buffoon to divert, the first nauseous appearance has been my Lord[1]." In the next year Settle, if he be the author, issued an imploring prologue to *The Fairy Queen* (D.G. 1692) against those

> *new* Beau-Skreens,
> *That stand betwixt the Audience and the Scenes,*

while in 1693 Thomas Wright in his *The Female Vertuoso's* (D.G. 1693) emphasised the fact that *once* the stage had been "*kept free from* Beaux *and* Bullies[2]." The edict of William and Mary[3], made about this time, stating expressly that no person should either stand or *sit* upon the stage, evidently had no effect, the habit persisting on to the time of Garrick.

In this theatre, this toy of the upper classes, gentlemen apparently could enter without payment for a single act, or could rely on credit if they had not sufficient money to pay the door-keeper. Of the latter custom there is ample proof in the playhouse scene in Shadwell's *A True Widow* (D.G. 1678)[4]. Even as early as Dec. 30, 1667, Pepys thought it "a shame" that Sir Philip Cartaret was known at the theatre

---

[1] II. i.

[2] Prologue. Similar references are to be found in the epilogue to Scott's *The Unhappy Kindness* (D.L. 1697), "a *Beau-crowded* Stage": in the epilogue (by Motteux) to Mrs Pix' *The Innocent Mistress* (L.I.F. 1697):

> "*Then all thus stor'd, tho Money's scarce this Age,*
> *We need not fear t'have a* Beau-crowded *Stage:*"

and in IV. i of Motteux' *Love's a Jest* (L.I.F. 1696) where Airy declares "I can easily believe you've been...Side-boxing at the Play-house, Acting in the Pit, nay on the Stage too." Gildon, in *A Comparison between the Two Stages*, p. 32, in mentioning the great success of *A Trip to the Jubilee* states that "at that play" he had seen "the Pit, Box, and Stage... crowded."

[3] *Cal. State Papers, Dom. Series, William and Mary*, Feb. 1689–April, 1690, p. 321.

[4] Act IV.

"and do run upon the score for plays," and as late as 1693 F. P. in some verses prefixed to Higden's *The Wary Widdow* (D.L. 1693) could mention gallants who at the "*Playhouse judge on tick.*" The free act was regularly satirised by the poets, and attempts were made to put an end to it, but apparently not until about 1690 was it in any way limited[1]. D'Avenant murmured against the fashion in the epilogue to *The Man's the Master* (L.I.F. 1668) and with perfect justice, if we may take Pepys as a typical spectator. On Jan. 7, 1667/8, for example, the latter "to the...two playhouses, in the pit, to gaze up and down, and there did by this means, for nothing, see an act in 'The Schoole of Compliments' at the Duke of York's house, and 'Henry the Fourth' at the King's House." Even as late as 1693 Wright in the prologue to *The Female Vertuoso's* (D.G. 1693) had some satire on the "One-acters," and Farquhar in his *Essay on Comedy* (1700) has satiric reference to the "saucy impudent Fellows...call'd Door-Keepers, that can't let a Gentleman see a Play in Peace without jogging and nudging him every minute. *Sir, will you please to pay?...Sir, the Act's done, will you please to pay, Sir?*"[2] On the other hand, gentlemen who objected to disbursing their money to the ordinary door-keeper were often-times not unwilling to pay more than the simple half-crown in order to have access to the "tyring-room" where they might chat with the actresses. Whether a fixed charge was made for this or not, we know that some sort of payment was made. In spite of the fact that the actresses may not have been averse to this easy entrance to the tyring-house— the affability of a woman there was proverbial[3]—it is almost certain that the managers of the theatres were careful to gain some profit by it.

Another frequent abuse, partly connected with the privilege of the free act, is referred to by Lacy in *Sir Hercules Buffoon*

---

[1] *Cal. State Papers, Dom. Series*, 1689–90, p. 321.

[2] The earliest warrant against the practice is dated Dec. 7, 1663 (P.R.O.. L.C. 7/1 and 5/138 last page). See also *Cal. State Papers*, 1664–5, Feb. 27, 1665, p. 223, and May 16, 1667 (*id.* 1667–8, p. 395).

[3] Wycherley's *The Plain Dealer* (D.L. 1676), II: see also the same author's *The Country Wife* (D.L. 1675), prologue, and *The Gentleman Dancing-Master* (D.G. 1672), epilogue.

(D.G. 1684) where he gives a satirical recipe for seeing plays
"for nothing—one act in the Pit, another in a Box, and a
third in the Gallery[1]." It seems that in the Restoration
theatre extra money for box and other seats was collected
after the performance had well begun, a general small charge
only being made at the doors. Thus men of an easy sense of
morality and a nimble pair of heels could dodge the attendants
as they came round, moving rapidly from box to pit and from
pit to gallery. "I'm told," says D'Urfey in his prologue to
The Bath (D.L. 1701),

> *I'm told that Beaus with Perukes cover'd o're,*
> *Make such strange shift to save poor shillings four[2],*
> *They'll in Side-Box three Acts for nothing sit,*
> *At last sneak down for Six-pence to the Pit.*

When we conjure up before our minds such an audience
and such a management fearful at every moment of offending
the slender clientele, we can understand that attention to the
play in hand was often grievously lacking. Women of doubtful
character, "vizard Masks" as they were euphemistically
styled[3], flocked the playhouses, sitting alongside of the highest
of the land in the side-boxes[4], in the pit[5], and in the upper
gallery, the last-mentioned gaining by reason of their presence
none too enviable a reputation[6]. So numerous did they become that in 1688 Crowne could declare that they made up
"half the Pit, and all the Galleries[7]." It was to meet these,

[1] I. i.
[2] The price of admission to the boxes.
[3] The habit of mask-wearing seems to have come in shortly after the
Restoration, and, although abandoned by "Civil Gentlewomen" by
1680, it was not suppressed entirely until the edict of Anne in 1704.
It rapidly became the recognised mark of a prostitute, although even
"ladies of quality," such as Mrs Behn's *Feign'd Curtizans* seem not to
have minded being taken by their gentlemen friends as *femmes d'amour*.
See *infra*, p. 23.
[4] Epilogue to Lee's *Gloriana* (D.L. 1676).
[5] Epilogue to Wycherley's *The Plain Dealer* (D.L. 1676).
[6] Etherege's *She Wou'd if she Cou'd* (L.I.F. 1668), III. iii. See also
the epilogue to Crowne's *Sir Courtly Nice* (D.L. 1685) which speaks of
the galleries "finely us'd of late, where roosting Masques sat cackling for
a Mate." The gallants often ascended "(*for dangerous Intrigues*) to th'
Gallery," we are told in the prologue to Shadwell's *The Woman-Captain*
(D.G. 1679).
[7] Crowne's *Darius* (D.L. 1688), epilogue.

to indulge in their own doubtful intrigues with courtesan or
with merchant's wife that the gallants flocked to the theatre.
The women, for their part, were equally eager. Little Gatty
in Etherege's *She Wou'd if she Cou'd* (L.I.F. 1668) laments
in a song,

> To little or no purpose I spent many Days,
> In ranging the Park, th'Exchange, and th'Plays;
> For ne'er in my rambles till now did I prove
> So luckie to meet with the man I cou'd love.

As a consequence noise seems often to have "drowned the
Stage's Wit[1]." The epilogue to Lee's *Sophonisba* (D.L. 1675)
says of the typical beaux that

> One half o' the Play they spend in noise and brawl,
> Sleep out the rest, then wake and damn it all.

General disregard of other's feelings appears to have characterised the audience of the time. The gallants, so we are
informed in Etherege's *She Wou'd if she Cou'd* (L.I.F. 1668)
are in the habit of moving

> From one Play-house, to the other Play-house,
> And if they like neither the Play nor the Women,
> They seldom stay any longer than the combing
> Of their Perriwigs, or a whisper or two with a
> Friend; and then they cock their Caps, and out they
> Strut again[2].

Sedley can hold loud and animated conversations in the pit
with ladies of doubtful propriety, even though Pepys tends
to believe that they are "virtuous" and "of quality," or can
pass witticisms on the action of an heroic tragedy.

> The Age is alter'd now, he that has Wit,
> Ne're uses it abroad, but in the Pit,
> There spreads it all, and e're one Scene does know,
> Calls friend aside, Cryes, Dammy Jack lets go,
>
>   *   *   *   *   *
>
> Others that want Wit, hither come to glean,
> Seem to find fault and cavil at a Scene,
> Because they understand it not, yet will
> Dislike, because 'tis Modish, and Gentile[3].

[1] Prologue to Lee's *The Rival Queens* (D.L. 1677).   [2] I. ii.
[3] D'Urfey's prologue to *The Siege of Memphis* (D.L. 1676).

Scenes of licence must have been frequent. Shadwell in the first act of *The Virtuoso* (D.G. 1676) speaks of those who "come drunk and screaming into a Play-House, and stand upon the Benches, and toss their full Periwigs and empty Heads, and with their shrill unbroken Pipes cry, *Damme, this is a damn'd Play*." Not only, therefore, did the actors play to empty houses[1], of which a fair proportion were gallants who did not pay and another fair proportion were "deadheads[2]," but the meagre audiences who did put in an appearance barely gave the actors leave to perform. Higden in the dedication to his *The Wary Widdow* (D.L. 1693) makes complaint of some who "with a barbarous variety of Noise and Tumult" so disturbed his play "that many of the well meaning Spectatours (for I am sure it had very few Hearers) must conclude it a very criminall performance." Only with

[1] D'Urfey in the epilogue to *The Fool turn'd Critick* (D.L. 1676) speaks of the nonconformist preacher melting

> "*in durance half his Grease away,*
> *To get, like us, poor thirteen Pounds a day.*"

In *The Theatrical Inquisitor and Monthly Mirror* of July, 1816, a document is printed purporting to be a list of takings at the T.R. for a performance of *All for Love* on Wed. Dec. 12, 1677. According to this £7. 4s. came from the boxes, £14. 12s. 6d. from the pit (117 spectators in all), £14. 14s. 6d. from the mid-gallery (63 spectators), and £1. 13s. from the upper gallery (33 spectators)—£28. 4s. altogether, from which rent took £5. 14s., leaving £22. 10s. for the actors and running costs. The total number of paying persons in the house was but 249. Almost certainly takings of over £50 must have been abnormal. The anti-Cibber pamphlet *The Laureat* and documents in the P.R.O. both agree that about 1692 the daily receipts were "often under £20 per diem" (see Appendix B, and consult A. Thaler, *Shakespeare to Sheridan*, pp. 241–244). Not much stress can be put upon Herbert's early estimates, which were based on probably imaginary evidence, but he asserts that in 1662 D'Avenant was getting £200 a week from the Duke's house. As D'Avenant had 10 out of 15 shares, this represents a weekly total of £300, or an average of £50 a night, possibly fairly near the truth, when we consider that in 1662 the theatres were in the hey-day of their prosperity (see Herbert, p. 120, and Leslie Hotson's study of playhouse finance).

[2] Farquhar, in his *Essay on Comedy*, imagines a gallant talking to himself: "Before gad, I'll be plagu'd with 'em no longer; I'll e'en write a Play my self; by which means, my Character of Wit shall be establish'd (and) I shall enjoy the Freedom of the House." As Farquhar observed, this gives "the Liberty of the House to him and his Friends for ever after." Possibly these dead-heads were no more intent on keeping quiet when the plays of other poets were produced than were the courtiers and the fops who paid for admittance.

a sort of pathetic gesture did the players make pretence that these gallants aided their productions.

> *He who comes hither with design to hiss*
> *And with a bum revers'd to whisper Miss,*
> *To komb a Peruke, or to show gay Cloaths,*
> *Or to vent antique Nonsense with New Oaths;*
> *Our Poet welcomes as the Muses Friend,*
> *For he'll by Irony each Play commend...*[1]

Such a declaration rings hollow: it has a note of pathos in it rather than a note of happy satire. For the actors, indeed, conditions must often have become well-nigh intolerable. Pepys has several references to irritating noises in the public playhouses, and Betterton declared that the voices of the spectators "put the very Players out of Countenance[2]."

On they went with their loves and their quarrels and their sallies, heedless of the play before them. It was at the theatre that Wycherley had his first conversation with his later mistress, the Duchess of Cleveland, she sitting in the first row of the King's Box and he standing in the pit[3]. It was at the Dorset Garden playhouse that Langbaine saw Mr Scroop killed by Sir Thomas Armstrong during a performance of *Macbeth*[4]. Quarrels, in point of fact, both among the actors and among the spectators, were of frequent occurrence. "*Scow'ring the Watch*," says Dryden in the prologue to his *The Spanish Fryar* (D.G. 1680),

> *Grows out-of-Fashion Wit,*
> *Now we set up for Tilting in the Pit,*
> *Where 'tis agreed by Bullies, chicken hearted,*
> *To fright the Ladies first, and then be parted.*

[1] Second prologue to *The Amorous Old Woman* (1674) repeated later as the prologue to D'Urfey's *The Fool turn'd Critick* (D.L. 1676) and printed as the prologue to Orrery's *Mr Anthony* (D.G. 1672, printed 1690).

[2] *The Amorous Widow* (L.I.F. *c.* 1670), II. ii. Even as early as June 23, 1660, Thomas Jordan could write "*A Speech by way of Epilogue to those that would rise out of the Pit at the Red Bull in the last Scene, and disturb the Conclusion, by going on the Stage*" (*A Royal Arbor of Loyal Poesie*, 1660, p. 19).

[3] Dennis quoted by Lowe, *Life of Betterton*, p. 33.

[4] Langbaine, p. 460. This was on Sat., Aug. 28, 1675. A newsletter of Aug. 31 mentions the incident (*HMC*, 12th Report, Appendix VII, 121).

Not always, however, were the disturbances in the theatre such mild affairs of craven-hearted hectors. There was a serious affray among some gentlemen who had gone to see *The Unfortunate Lovers* at Salisbury Court on Nov. 19, 1660[1]. On July 20, 1667, Henry Killigrew was sent to the Tower for an altercation with Buckingham in the playhouse[2]. A private quarrel which developed into a general fight entailed a temporary prohibition of acting in 1680[3]. On April 27, 1682, "Mr. *Ch*(arles) D(eering), son to Sir *Edw. D.*, and Mr. *V*(aughan), quarrell'd in the *Duke's* Playhouse, and presently mounted the Stage and fought, and Mr *D.* was very dangerously wounded, and Mr. *V.* secured lest it should prove Mortal[4]." In a newsletter contained in the State Papers there is mentioned a quarrel between a Captain Leinster and another, during which many swords were drawn in the pit[5], while in the *Post-Boy* of June 22–25, 1695, we read that "on *Saturday* last, Words arose betwixt Mr. *Cary* and Mr. Young in the Playhouse, about a Gentlewoman, and the next morning they fought a Duel in *Hide* Park, where they were both Wounded: the Former died in the Evening at the *Star Inn* in the *Strand*." The following year one of the Clerks of the Exchequer was killed at the playhouse in a quarrel which rose there[6]. In 1699 two men quarrelled "at the Playhouse about a Mistress" and later fought a duel[7]. Smith, the actor, succeeded in killing his man in the theatre[8], and Mrs Barry and Mrs Bracegirdle had an almost fatal struggle when playing "rival queens." The actors, indeed, were apparently not one whit better than the spectators. Whincop, for example, tells us that there was so much punch-drinking business in Higden's comedy of *The Wary Widdow* (D.L. 1693) that the players all got intoxicated and had to close the piece at the third act[9], while Vanbrugh, in a cynical preface to *The Relapse* (D.L. 1696) declares that, owing to the uproarious drunken-

---

1 *HMC*, 5th Report, Appendix, 200.
2 *Ibid.*, 12th Report, Appendix VII, 51.
3 *True News*, Feb. 4–7, 1679/80.
4 *Impartial Protestant Mercury*, April 28–May 2, 1682.
5 *Cal. State Papers, Dom. Series*, May 1690–Oct. 1691, p. 312.
6 *London Post*, April 19–22; *Post Boy*, April 23–5, 1700.
7 *Protestant Mercury*, March 8–10, 1698/9.
8 Pepys, Nov. 14, 1666.   9 Whincop, p. 247.

ness of Powell in the character of Worthy, he "once gave
Amanda (acted by Mrs Rogers) for gone."

Probably the only thing that could stay the din of noise
and of rowdy gaiety was the acting of Betterton, the charm
of Nell Gwyn as she ran forward with her risque sallies, or
else the sweet free grace of Mrs Bracegirdle. Undoubtedly
the only other thing that could have stayed them would be
the flashing wit of Congreve, or the rude bombast of the
heroic tragedy tricked out with what their

> *Palates relished most,*
> *Charm! Song! and Show! a Murder and a Ghost!*[1]

This audience looked for nothing more[2]. They expected
naught but brilliant colour, elegance and wit—a fit setting
for their own coloured and elegant lives.

III. *Influence of the Audience on the Drama*

None of these wits or fops or courtiers of the audience
were thinkers: hardly any of them had a faith beyond vague
attachment to royalty: every one of them was eager for the
day's pleasure, eager for love and cynical laughter and the
enjoyment of the senses. Their influence on the theatre and
on dramatic productivity, moreover, was twofold. It was not
limited solely to the influence they might exert from their
position as spectators, for they acted in that age in the double
capacity of audience and of playwrights. Art with them was
a gentleman's toy, and so long as a well-bred indifference
was displayed, the penning of a comedy and a tragedy or
two could but add to their renown. With them poetry and
the drama sank to the level of a playful essay, a game to be
indulged in for a brief hour or two, an easy method of
whiling away the time. Etherege thus amused himself with

---

[1] Dryden and Lee's *Oedipus* (D.G. 1678), epilogue.
[2] Motteux, in the preface to his *Beauty in Distress* (L.I.F. 1698),
apologizes for the fact that this play is "*divested of all the things that now
recommend a Play most to the Liking of the Many. For it has no Singing,
no Dancing, no Mixture of Comedy, no Mirth, no change of Scene, no rich
Dresses, no Show, no Rants, no Similes, no Battle, no Killing on the Stage,
no Ghost, no Prodigy; and whats yet more, no Smut, no Profaneness, nor
Immorality.*"

comedy: Sir Robert Howard with tragedy. Roger Boyle, Earl of Orrery, wrote his heroic dramas only when confined indoors with gout. There was, therefore, from these men no attempt to express great ideals, because there was no definite sincerity, no individuality of utterance, and unfortunately such professional authors as appeared in this age took their lead from these more aristocratic dramatists even as the latter invariably took theirs from the king. Dryden, D'Urfey, Shadwell to a certain extent, Settle, Lee, all on the fringe of the elegant circle, strove as far as they could, not to give utterance to any beliefs they might individually have held, but merely to reflect what had been said before them by others more fortunately born. Only a very few men, such as Otway in *Venice Preserv'd* and in *The Orphan*, seemed to find expression definitely their own.

To their own elegance these courtly playwright-spectators added an elegance taken from a study of certain periods of classic and of pseudo-classic art. They knew their Ovids and their Horaces certainly: they took from Tibullus and from Juvenal satiric elements and adapted those elements to their own time: they felt truly and appreciated the grace and the cynicism of the poetry of Augustan Rome. But even more, they appreciated the pseudo-classic grace of France. Many of them had been, for varying periods, exiles abroad, and they had captured some part at least of that style and finish which allowed of the growth, on the one hand, of Racine, on the other, of Molière. Not that they translated faithfully into London the spirit of Paris. Their harder, coarser, English temperament would not allow them to do that: but they certainly, from 1660 to 1680, came as near to that French ideal as any body of men in England before or after them. It must be confessed that what they most liked in French art and life were not always the best things in that art or life. They took often the outward instead of the inner: imitated the temporary and the ephemeral instead of the permanent and the truly classic. At the same time they were able to give to English literature exactly what at that time it needed— a body of common-sense opinion, a precision and a lucidity such as were lacking in the poetical rhapsodies of the Ford school in tragedy, in the blunt humours of the Jonson school in comedy, in the conceits of the Donne school in poetry.

The effect of this peculiar audience and of these special playwrights is to be seen in many directions. It caused the unutterable coarseness which distinguished so much of Restoration workmanship, and which has made the works of this period neglected during the past Victorian century. A discussion of that will be more fitting hereafter. Suffice it to be noted here that this immorality, this coarseness, call it what we will, extended from the very first years of the century to the very last: but that all through the forty years there were men who endeavoured in various ways to counter the tendency of the times by writing "moral plays," and that the more definitely "moral" tendency visible after 1690 was mainly outward. Thus D'Urfey in the dedication to the third part of *The Comical History of Don Quixote* (D.G. 1695) informs us that some ladies of the audience considered certain portions of it coarse, but not the portions which we to-day would consider unutterably indecent. Those same ladies who objected to Mary the Buxome, yet evidently found nothing wrong in the prologue between Horden and Miss Cross, who was at this time only about twelve years old, or the incredibly indecent "boy and girl" songs incorporated in the body of the play.

The atmosphere of the court of Charles was vulgar in the extreme, but it was a more open immorality than, as I shall endeavour to show later, distinguished the years 1690–1700. Not that we can go any way to condone the earlier immorality. The stories of Rochester's and of Sedley's hideous pranks are too well-known to be repeated. All sort of moral ties, all sense of decency had gone. Women had become as libidinous as the men: "common Women" were "publick grown...in this damn'd lewd Town": nothing was left to occupy the minds of this circumscribed clique but intrigue and sensuality. Every name and title given to a woman came during this period to have an evil significance. "Lady," as Pepys shows us[1], had thus become debased in meaning, as had "Mother[2]" and "Madam[3]," "Miss" and "Mistress[4]." The utter filth that marks many of the lyrics contained, for example, in such a collection as the *Poems on Affairs of State*, is but the ordinary speech of women of this type and of their men companions made a trifle more "poetical." As is evident from the dialogues in the comedies the conversation of men with men or of women with men reaches a freedom seen at no other period of our history. If we listen to the words of a couple of lovers of the time we wonder sometimes whether our ears be not deceiving us. Turn even to a work of one of the geniuses of the age, turn to Dryden's *Secret Love*, and read the words of Celadon and Florimel: in spite of the wit, we stand aghast. That such a conversation as appears in the fifth act of this play—and it is evidently realistic—could ever have taken place between two cultured persons in a civilised society, or that it could ever have been taken as representative of general behaviour, shows us probably as clearly as anything the peculiar temper of the age with which we are dealing. There was refinement in this time, but there was also sensuality: the minds of the wits were filled with a succession of images in which fancy and carnal thought alternated or became confused, clashed and grew into what we know as the comedy of manners. It is natural, perhaps, that with a man of the calibre of Rochester such thoughts and images should preponderate, but when we discover that the most serious, nay some of the ultra-religious writers, indulge in similar carnal images, we are reminded of the all-pervading influence of the time. The truth is, that, in the period of the Restoration, the love of pleasure which had come as a reaction to the restrictions of the Puritan régime, led towards a recrudescence of brutality. No one in that age could possibly conceive of such a thing as innocence. Miranda, in *The Tempest*, is reft of her modesty: Eve in *The State of*

---

[1] Pepys, May 30, 1668.
[2] Dryden's *Sir Martin Mar-all* (L.I.F. 1667), IV. i.
[3] See *The Poor-Whores Petition*, 1668.
[4] Flecknoe, *Euterpe Reviv'd* (1675).

Innocence is made a woman of quality in the garden of Eden. Very little separated the women of "virtue" and the women of vice. In Farquhar's *Love and a Bottle* (D.L. 1698), for example, Lucinda, who is presented to us as virtuous and modest, puts on a mask, goes out into the park, and, after some rather disagreeable talk with her maid, "*slaps*" a strange man "*o' th' Shoulder with her Fan*[1]." This lack of distinction between the women of quality and the others naturally led to an intensification of free speech[2]. Women in that age found nothing strange in such conversation: they themselves could pose to their lovers as courtesans[3], or delight in puzzling the poor brains of the gallants as to who and what they were[4].

Such notes on the general attitude of the time may prepare us for the scenes which in those days could find visible presentment on the stage itself. Men and women in Restoration comedies and tragedies could be shown rising from couch or bed. The stage directions are quite explicit about the matter: there is no opportunity for us to presume that such scenes were glozed over in the acting[5]. Every means was employed to make the immorality more striking. *The Parson's Wedding*, recognised even in this period as a work of flagrant indecency, was put on the Theatre Royal stage acted solely by women[6]. Actresses were given the most vulgar and suggestive epilogues to recite, casting out broad hints to an audience not uneager to accept them[7].

Nor did matters stop there. Sexual disease had been carried over from France, and this horrible thing was treated

[1] I. i.
[2] In Act III of Shadwell's *A True Widow* (D.G. 1678), Theodosia tells Carlos that he "must not talk with Vizors in the Pit; though they look never so like Women of Quality."
[3] See Mrs Behn's *The Feign'd Curtizans* (D.G. 1679).
[4] Pepys, Feb. 18, 1666–7.
[5] See Mrs Behn's *Sir Patient Fancy* (D.G. 1678), III. vii, and IV. iv. Similar scenes are to be found in Leanerd's *The Rambling Justice* (D.L. 1678), IV. iii; in Crowne's *City Politiques* (D.L. 1683), V. ii; in Rawlins' *Tom Essence* (D.G. 1676), IV. ii; in Shadwell's *The Volunteers* (D.L. 1692), V. i; in Vanbrugh's *The Relapse* (D.L. 1696), V. ii; and in D'Urfey's *The Campaigners* (D.L. 1698), V. ii.
[6] Pepys, Oct. 11, 1664.
[7] See Autrey Nell Wiley, *Rare Prologues and Epilogues, 1642–1700* (1940).

half as a joke, half as a glory[1]. Florio in Crowne's *City Politiques* (D.L. 1683) could pretend to a disease he had not, could flaunt it openly for his own immoral ends. Beyond even that did the age penetrate. Incest and similar relationships are referred to again and again, not only in secret pieces like the *Sodom, or, The Quintessence of Debauchery* which Rochester may have penned, but in ordinary comedies and tragedies. The presence of such seems to have added piquancy to many a play. In Dryden's *Aureng-Zebe* (D.L. 1675), for example, Indamora is loved by the old Emperor, by Aureng-Zebe, his son, and by Morat, the son of the wife of the emperor, Nourmahal, while Nourmahal is in love with her step-son, Aureng-Zebe. Here a father, his son and his step-son are all rivals in love. In *Oedipus* (D.G. 1678) Dryden again introduces the theme of incest, and touches upon it later in *Don Sebastian* (D.L. 1689). Crowne treats the subject tragically in *Thyestes* (D.L. 1681) and also comically in *City Politiques* (D.L. 1683). More thoughtful presentations may be given in the anonymous *Fatal Discovery* (D.L. 1698) and in Otway's *The Orphan* (D.G. 1680), but the majority of dramatists, like those mentioned above or like Mrs Behn in *The Dutch Lover* (D.G. 1673), used it merely to pander to the depraved tastes of the audience. Occasionally, even, the spectators were content, perhaps eager, to see more than mere themes of incest. Unnatural sex relationships certainly existed in that age, and these too were reflected in the dramas. Rochester, when he was rewriting *Valentinian* (D.L. 1684) saw fit to drag in reference to this, and there is more than a hint of the vice in the speech of Damocles to his page in Edward Howard's *The Usurper* (T.R. in B.St. 1664).

When we have thus passed over in review all these follies, these vices and these depravities, for a moment it would seem as if the Macaulays were in the right—that nothing possible of good could come from the study of such a theatre and of such an age. In this time of degenerate manners, which seems

---

[1] See the prologue to D'Urfey's *Madam Fickle* (D.G. 1676) and the epilogue to Duffett's *The Spanish Rogue* (L.I.F. 1673). Shadwell's *The Humorists* (L.I.F. 1670) might also be noted in a like connection.

separated as if by aeons from the more spacious days of
Elizabeth, it might be thought that neither gallants nor playwrights could have risen above the crudest expression of
carnal licence. Yet, as we have seen, this Restoration audience
could and did give something to the theatre. The spectators
might be thoughtless and depraved, but they were cultured,
and the grace and the wit and the elegance which they
brought into life and the playhouse was something quite new.
Nothing precisely like their ease and refinement of dialogue
appears in the preceding dramas. We feel that the characters
of the comedy of this time are true aristocrats, tutored to
ease and a kind of delicacy in language, if not in thought, of
which their forefathers never could know. If they have lost
the valour and the strength of Drake and of Ralegh, they
have captured the fine spirit of Etherege and of Congreve.
Almost all the writers of the time have something of it, from
Dryden and Shadwell to the greatest masters of the manners
school. If, again, the women of the Restoration court seem
to our eyes to have lost that modesty which was yet frank
and clear-eyed, the modesty of Miranda and of Rosalind, we
must bear in mind that their free relations with their men
companions provided the basis on which the true comedy of
life could be built. Aphra Behn may have been licentious,
but she was establishing a surer position for her sisters than
any of the Elizabethan women had succeeded in establishing.
This new position of women and the grace of the courtiers
are not things to be defined: they lie rather in suggestion
and in atmosphere than in particular scenes or forms. In all
the literature of the age, nevertheless, we feel their influence,
the spirit which separates off the comedy of Jonson from this
gay, witty, immoral comedy of Restoration manners.

IV. *The Theatre*

It is quite obvious that the small and mean audience of
the Restoration theatre could have, besides those mentioned
above, even more far-reaching effects on dramatic and theatrical productivity. Being few in numbers they made of the

theatres practically what our repertory theatres are nowadays. No play, however brilliant, however splendidly produced, however popular by means of poetic beauty or of immoral suggestion, could count on a run of over a few days. We know that the gallants did not object to coming once or twice to see the same performance[1], especially when, as in the case of Shadwell's *The Sullen Lovers* (L.I.F. 1668), there was personal satire that everyone was talking about, but, even if each member of the audience did visit the same play twice, a run of a week was about all that was possible. Many plays died on the first night: the majority of the others saw no more than three consecutive performances. A few, such as Tuke's *The Adventures of Five Hours* (L.I.F. 1663) or the rehashing of *Henry VIII* (L.I.F. 1663) may have seen upwards of a dozen nights[2], but they were exceptions. Constant change was what was necessary, if the playhouses were even scantily to be filled. Even when plays had a slightly longer run than was ordinary, we find that the management often deemed it advisable to break that run by the insertion of a revival or two. Thus *The Sullen Lovers*, which Downes says ran for twelve nights, was seen by Pepys on Sat. May 2, 1668, Mon. May 4, Tues. May 5, but at the same theatre on Thurs. May 7, the diaryist saw *The Man's the Master* and on Mon. May 11, *The Tempest*. Naturally, if new plays could be thus summarily dismissed, revivals of older productions were allowed to survive for barely a night or two. Here again the records of Pepys are for us invaluable[3]. At the Theatre Royal on four consecutive nights, from Mon. Aug. 12, 1667 to Thurs. Aug. 15, that playgoer saw *Brenoralt*, *The Committee*, *The Country Captain* and *The Merry Wives of Windsor*. A week later, on four similarly consecutive days, from Thurs. Aug. 22 to Mon. Aug. 26, *The Indian Emperor*, *The Maiden*

---

[1] Even Charles, who was easily tired of his pleasures, was at three of the first five nights of D'Urfey's *A Fond Husband* (D.G. 1677); see *The Guardian*, No. 82, June 15, 1713.

[2] Pepys, Jan. 1, 1663-4 and Downes, p. 24.

[3] We have also Herbert's records of performances at the T.R. where he notes 16 different plays on 16 consecutive nights from Th. Nov. 5, 1660 to Mon. Nov. 26, 1660, but at the first opening of the theatres such a variety is quite understandable.

Queen, The Cardinal and *The Surprisal* were performed. On Tues. Sept. 15, 1668 *The Ladies a la Mode*, or *Damoiselles a la Mode*, was given for the second time, on Thurs. the 17th *Rollo*, on Fri. the 18th *Henry IV*, on Sat. the 19th *The Silent Woman*; on Thurs. May 14, 1668, *The Country Captain* was performed, on the Friday *The Committee*, on the Saturday *The Sea Voyage*, on the Monday *The Mulberry Garden*.

This rapid change of programme quite obviously must have affected the theatre in several distinct ways. It made a very high standard of acting necessary, and, even although such did exist, we have frequent complaints from playwrights and from public that the players were not always word-perfect[1]. How they could even have attempted to learn half of their numerous parts must be our wonder now. Looked at from another point of view, this rapid change made for a constant demand for new plays, and, the demand being ever-present, the supply, although profits from playwriting in Restoration days were not over-great, naturally followed. The dramatic literature of the years 1660 to 1700 is fairly vast. There were, as Downes tells us, "plenty of new Poets" about the year 1670[2], professional writers and courtly poets all flocking to give their wares to the playhouse. Only during the period when the theatres were united between 1682 and 1695 was there such a "reviveing of the old Stock of Plays" that "the Poets lay dormant" and "a new Play cou'd hardly get admittance[3]." For that time "Union *and* Catcalls...*quite spoyl'd the Stage*[4]," there being no demand, and a consequent decline in the supply. The contemporary references to this dearth of new plays in the period of the union of the theatres is amply borne out by an analysis of the fresh plays printed during the years 1682 to 1695. Thus, in the five years from 1689 to 1694 fewer new comedies were produced than in the two and a half years from 1696 to 1698. The corresponding relations as regards tragedy display exactly the same pheno-

---

[1] Pepys, Sat. Mar. 1, 1661–2, and Higden in the dedication to *The Wary Widdow* (D.L. 1693). Cf. *infra* p. 63.

[2] Downes, p. 34.

[3] Powell's preface to *The Treacherous Brothers* (D.L. 1689).

[4] Prologue to Jevon's *The Devil of a Wife* (D.G. 1686).

mena. As soon as Betterton broke the united playhouse into two, the poets rushed again to write up their comedies and their tragedies and their farces and their operas. "*The Plague of Scribling's grown so rife of late*," says the prologue to *Timoleon* (unacted?, 1697), "*Player and Poet share one common Fate*[1]." Congreve the year before in his prologue to the young Dryden's *The Husband his own Cuckold* (L.I.F. 1696) noted that the season had "been Remarkable two ways" —for the number of new poets and of plays damned by the spectators.

We have, then, in this period two wholly antagonistic movements—one which seemed to tend towards a crushing out of all vital life in the theatre, and another which seemed to inspire towards increased dramatic productivity: just as, from a different point of view we discovered tastes that at one and the same time led towards the most debased of sentiments and towards the finest and the most perfect dialogue that might be conceived possible for the wittily comic drama. The truth is that, whatever way we look at it, this courtly audience and its theatre will be found to possess both grievous defects and outstanding merits. The spectators could appreciate fine things, both in comedy and in tragedy, but they also were swayed by external ephemeral things of no value or permanent consequence. For this latter reason, the arts which may be called contributory to the drama, and which, in all great productions, should be rendered subservient to the characters and to the dialogue, grew to assume a larger and larger place in the reigns of Charles II and of James. As the years advanced we find scenery, and all that goes along with scenery, playing a more and more important part in the success or failure of plays: we find managers impoverishing themselves to glut the eager tastes of a show-loving public.

The year 1642, as is well known, had left the theatres much in the same state as they had been in when Shakespeare wrote, that is to say, with an Elizabethan platform stage and no scenery. In the latter years of the reign of Charles I,

[1] See also the prologue to *The Unnatural Mother* (L.I.F. 1697).

certainly, we do meet more frequently with references to "scenes" than we do in the preceding years, a sign possibly that the Elizabethan theatre would have changed naturally even though there had been no break in the Commonwealth period and a subsequent revival of the drama in 1660. On the other hand, all these references to scenery, save one, point to private and not public productions. Thus the sum of £300 necessary for the scenes of *Aglaura* in 1637 was defrayed by Sir John Suckling, the author, while the then Lord Chamberlain paid for "the cloathes and scaenes" of Habington's *Queen of Arragon* in 1640[1]. Masques, of course, had always had gorgeous scenery, and that that scenery must have had a considerable influence on later theatrical endeavour admits of no doubt: but after all the masque was purely a private affair and lies outside the history of the drama proper. The one reference mentioned above which does not come under the "private" category, is that contained in the patent granted to Sir William D'Avenant in 1639, authorising him to build a playhouse for music, scenes and dancing. This last proves, at least, that D'Avenant had made his plans, to be carried out only in 1656 and in 1661, more than three years before the closing of the theatres. The first hint, however, that we have of anything definitely new on the stage, appears in the title-page to *The Siege of Rhodes*, "*made a Representation by the Art of Prospective in Scenes, and the Story sung in Recitative Musick,*" D'Avenant's "opera" of 1656, followed by *The Cruelty of the Spaniards in Peru* and by *The History of Sir Francis Drake*. The first was played originally "*at the back part of Rutland House, in Aldersgate Street,*" possibly in September 1656: the latter two at the Cockpit in Drury Lane towards the close of 1658.

The scenery employed in these pre-Restoration productions must have been of a sufficiently crude and elementary character but it formed nevertheless the origin of modern stage decoration in England. It is certainly true that the value of

---

[1] See, for this whole subject, W. J. Lawrence's *The Elizabethan Play-House*, 2nd ser., p. 121 ff., Lily B. Campbell's *Scenes and Machines on the English Stage during the Renaissance* (1923) and the present writer's *Stuart Masques and the Renaissance Stage* (1938).

the innovation was not at once perceived either by playgoers or by actor-managers, but by the year 1670 D'Avenant's enterprise had borne full fruit. The old Elizabethan theatres, of course, which were occupied by the hastily-gathered bodies of actors who started to play immediately on the King's return, were naturally innocent of scenery, and even Killigrew's first playhouse, that in Vere Street, save for its tennis court form, was different in no wise from the theatres in which Shakespeare and Burbage had exercised their histrionic talents. As soon as D'Avenant succeeded in getting his patent, it is true, he reintroduced the various innovations which he had heralded in 1656, but even then the effects must have been of the crudest and possibly displayed errors and weaknesses due to the haste of organisation. Pepys visited D'Avenant's "opera," as it was called, a few days after it had been opened and noted the "fine scenes," fine, because he had nothing with which to compare them[1]. A few days later, however, this "opera" was closed, to reopen on Aug. 15 with *The Witts*, and on visiting it during the run of that play Pepys again duly noted the "admirable scenes." The next month he saw *Twelfth Night* at the same theatre, which again was evidently closed to allow of "some alteracion of their scene[2]." It was open once more on Oct. 21 with *Love and Honour*. It is difficult and hazardous to build any fabric of theory on facts meagre as these, but we might, I think, legitimately deduce from these notes of the diaryist that D'Avenant's innovations were but experiments and needed a great amount of re-casting before they were fit for public displayal.

Still, however inartistic they may have been, however ridiculous they might appear to our eyes nowadays, they certainly must have come as a new ray of light to the audiences of the early sixties of the century. About six days after the opening of D'Avenant's house, Pepys visited the Theatre Royal and this he found empty as it had been since the opera had started. The spectators, as we have seen, were not sufficient

---

[1] July 2, 1661. He saw *The Siege of Rhodes*. See Downes, p. 20.
[2] Sept. 11, 1661.

to fill both the theatres, and it was the Duke's playhouse that they preferred. Betterton was there, of course, to swell the house with his acting, but far more than this it must have been D'Avenant's scenery that attracted the audiences away from the erst-while thickly-crowded Theatre Royal to the newer "opera." D'Avenant had been clever enough to divine the fresh tastes of the play-going public. His endeavours without a doubt were simply directed towards making his theatre pay, but by reason of these novelties he stands now as the father of the eighteenth, nineteenth and twentieth century theatres in England. He it was who, to employ the scenery which he had introduced, moved his stage half-way between the " platform " of the Elizabethans and the " picture-frame" of our own days. No longer did the spectators completely surround the actors on all sides; no longer was the scene of each play performed against curtains that concealed an inner stage. All that was gone and in its stead was born the modern theatre.

While we recognise this fact, however, we must be careful to remember that all the traditions of the older stage were by no means lost. In the world of the theatre customs and traditions are perhaps more difficult to eradicate than in any other branch of working life. Instead of regarding D'Avenant's L.I.F. house as the first modern theatre, we shall be nearer to the truth if we say that the play-houses of 1661–1700 represent a compromise between the Globe of 1600 and the Covent Garden of 1900, modern and ancient ideals meeting in one, tradition and innovation warring one with another.

The stage itself serves as well as anything for an illustration. If we glance at the engraving prefixed to the opera of *Ariane*, performed at the King's playhouse in March 1673–4, we note at once that, although the main part of the stage is as ours is to-day, a remnant of the platform is still to be discovered in the shape of an oval "apron" jutting out for a few feet into the pit. Or else we may glance at the plan drawn by Wren, possibly for the second T.R., where the long apron is plainly visible, fully 17 feet deep, almost as long as the space from the proscenium to the back-cloth.

There were therefore in the Restoration theatres two stages, one to the front of the proscenium, and the other behind, corresponding to the Elizabethan stage and inner stage[1]. The actors thus entered now into a space enclosed by the back-scene and the two side-wings: but that is not where the action of the play took place. Almost invariably the performers stepped onto the oval projection in front, not quite surrounded by spectators as before, but in a much more intimate position than the actors of modern times. Here lovers moaned and villains cursed, heroes fought and died. How great a part was acted on this apron may be seen by a reference to such a play as Vanbrugh's *The Confederacy* (Hay. 1705) where in Act v a stage direction occurs "*They come forward, and the Scene shuts behind them.*" From that direction to the end of the play, notwithstanding the fact that no less than eleven characters enter and speak, the whole of the action takes place on the forward part of the stage. Practically always in the dramas of the time when a person is "*discovered*" by a curtain rising or a scene drawing a stage direction instructs him or her to "*come forward*" before he or she begins to speak. Thus in Act iii. Sc. iv of Dilke's *The Lover's Luck* (L.I.F. 1695) the "scene *opens to Collonel* Bellair's *Chamber, and discovers* Bellair...*he rises and comes forward*[2]." In *The Rehearsal* (T.R. in B.St. 1671) it may be noted, much of the business takes place on the oval in front of the curtain while in Act ii ("*The Play-House*") of Dennis' *A Plot and no Plot* (D.L. 1697) Frowsy, Friskit and Brush are bidden to "*appear at the Curtain*" and take their stands in a similar position. Only after the gradual disappearance of the "apron" in the eighteenth century did the actors retire behind the footlights into the interior of the stage itself, abandoning their sense of kinship with the audience and becoming far-off figures set in a distant world.

---

[1] The Wren drawings are in the Library of All Souls, Oxford. They have been frequently reproduced and discussed: see *infra*, pp. 286, 323. The inner stage appears to have been known as the "House" in contrast to the "Stage" which is the apron.

[2] So in Hopkins' *Boadicea* (L.I.F. 1697), ii. i, where Camilla is discovered asleep.

The stage, however, is but one example out of many, and
we need not be surprised, as we examine the other appurtenances and conventions of this theatre, if we find on every
hand evidence of a similar clash between old and modern.
Scenery, as introduced by D'Avenant, was bound to have an
almost incalculable effect on the structure of plays, rendering
them less chaotic in the matter of scenes, moving from the
constant change of the Elizabethan theatres to the more stable
forms of the late eighteenth and nineteenth centuries; yet
even till 1690 plays could be found shifting easily from short
scene to short scene without the least regard to the new conditions surrounding them. In Settle's spectacular *The Empress
of Morocco* (D.G. 1673) a separate scene could be shown for
three single lines[1]. In Mrs Behn's *Sir Patient Fancy* (D.G. 1678)
at Act III. Sc. v there is "*A confus'd Noise of the Serenade, the
Scene draws off to La.* Fancy's *Anti Chamber.*" Isabella enters,
speaks five lines, and then the "SCENE *changes to Lady* Fancy's
Bed-Chamber." A similar swift alteration of the scenery occurs
in Tuke's *The Adventures of Five Hours* (L.I.F. 1663) where
in Act III. Sc. iii we find "*the City of* Sevil," a scene of five
lines, changing immediately to "*Don* Henriques *House.*"
Often the mere introduction of a table and chairs could alter
the locality of a particular scene, as in D'Avenant's *The Man's
the Master* (L.I.F. 1668). There at one moment we are in
Don Ferdinand's house: suddenly the characters leave and
"*Enter* Stephano, Sancho. *A Table spread with Linen Tren-
chers and Spoons are* (sic) *set out, and five Chairs.*" Apparently
no change of scenery accompanied this, for D'Avenant,
following Elizabethan custom, saw fit to make Stephano
explain—"This Room, standing in the Garden, at distance
from the House, seems built for our purpose." This is particularly interesting as appearing in a play of D'Avenant's
own acted at the Duke's house, after the introduction of the
"scenes" which Pepys so much admired[2]. In many early

---

[1] III. i. "*Scene the Palace*" and then, immediately following, "*Scene
a Bed-Chamber.*"
[2] With probably no change of scenery were presented IV. ii and V. iii
of D'Urfey's *Squire Oldsapp* (D.G. 1678). In the former the stage

comedies and tragedies of the Restoration period no attempt was made by the authors to mark separate scenes, and although this does not prove that different pieces of scenery were not utilised, it does show that the dramatists for some years at least failed to think out their plays in terms of the new theatrical conditions.

Gradually, however, the influence of D'Avenant's improvements drove its way home in stage affairs. Even in 1663 Flecknoe could speak of the "present heighth of magnificence" in decoration and in setting, which made plays "more for sight, then for hearing[1]." By 1667 a foreigner, Chappuzeau, accustomed to the gorgeous theatres of the continent, was able sincerely to compliment English stagecraft which "*réussit admirablement dans la machine, et...va maintenant du pair avec les Italiens*[2]." This is an important piece of evidence and shows that within six years of the opening of the "opera" the new art of the theatre in England had almost caught up the similar art of the continent, early as that had been introduced. Conservatives like Flecknoe might still continue to cry out, fed by old prejudices. Shadwell might exclaim—

> *Then came Machines brought from a neighbour Nation,*
> *Oh! how we suffered under Decoration!*

direction has merely " *Table, Chairs, and Wine,*" and in the latter, " *Table, Chairs, and Bottles of Wine.*"

[1] *A Short Discourse of the English Stage* appended to *Love's Kingdom* (unacted, 1664). He qualified the statement by the assertion that "Scenes and Machines...are no new Invention, our Masks and some of our Playes in former times (though not so ordinary) having had as good, or rather better then any we have now....Of this curious Art the Italians (this latter age) are the greatest masters, the French good proficients, and we in England only Schollars and Learners yet, having proceeded no further then to bare Painting...especially not knowing yet how to place our Lights, for the more advantage and illuminating of the Scenes."

[2] *L'Europe vivante* (Geneva, 1667). This was of the L.I.F. house, or, as Chappuzeau styles it, "*la Troupe de Monsieur...dans la place de Lincolne.*" Other foreign writers were equally laudatory. Sorbières remarked the "*beaucoup de changements et de perspectives*" of the T.R. in B.St. in 1663, while Monconys, writing of the same theatre on May 22, 1663, declares that "*les changements de Théâtre et les machines sont fort ingénieusement inventées et exécutées.*" "*Les Changements*" at L.I.F. pleased the latter equally well on June 5 (see W. J. Lawrence, "A Forgotten Restoration Playhouse" (*Englische Studien*, 1905, xxxv. 279–89).

Dramatists might recognise that a play unattractively put forward was almost bound to fail—as Banks

> *Who not one Plea for Favour can pretend,*
> *Song, Show, nor Dance, these Scenes to recommend:*
> *And Sirs full well you know where that must end,*

yet this new "Show" had come to stay, and for good or bad had duly to be reckoned with. In Italy, in France, and in England the dramatist only too often was forced to subordinate himself to the machinist. In all countries, wit, good sense and character drawing seemed continually sacrificed for nonsensical sound and voluptuous sight[1]. At the same time, the innovations were to form the basis of our modern theatre. By them the stage had advanced from medieval conditions into a fresh world.

At first the English theatres, naturally enough, must have had but a small stock of scenes, and as is evident from the designs of Webb for *The Siege of Rhodes*, the effects must often have been illustrative rather than realistic. Convention still ruled over a great part of the theatrical world. The old *chambre à quatre portes* may occasionally have served[2], while for a masque in Stapylton's *The Slighted Maid* (L.I.F. 1663) a "*Scene is discovered, over which in Capital Letters is writ* CAMPI ELYSII," a relic of ancient times. Apart from this, the actual painted scenes were no doubt extremely limited. We frequently find references in stage directions to new pieces introduced into the Theatre Royal or the Duke's house, and those new pieces must have served over and over again, in not particularly fitting situations. On other occasions dramatists intimately connected with the theatres undoubtedly wrote up plays to stock scenery in hand. Special scenic effects had been devised for Howard and Dryden's *The Indian Queen*, acted first in Jan. 1663–4. Pepys heard say on Wed. Jan. 27 that for show it exceeded the rival play at Lincoln's Inn Fields, *Henry VIII*, which itself had special scenery. On

---

[1] Preface to Edward Howard's *The Six Days' Adventure* (L.I.F. 1671). Although playwriting was not so grievously injured in Restoration England by scenes and machines as it was in seventeenth-century Italy, the complaints from the authors are remarkably similar in both lands.

[2] See Flecknoe's *The Damoiselles a la Mode* (printed 1667), preface.

Fri. Feb. 5 Evelyn went to see *The Indian Queen* and duly noted the "rich scenes." The managers quite evidently had expended a good deal of money on it, and the spectators were bidden to

> *See what Shifts we are inforc'd to try,*
> *To help out Wit with some Variety;*
> *Shows may be found that never yet were seen,*
> *'Tis hard to find such Wit as ne'er has been:*
> *You have seen all that this old World cou'd do,*
> *We therefore try the fortune of the new,*
> *And hope it is below your Aim to hit*
> *At untaught Nature with your practis'd Wit...*
> *'Tis true, y'have Marks enough, the Plot, the Show,*
> *The Poet's Scenes, nay, more, the Painter's too;*
> *If all this fail, considering the Cost,*
> *'Tis a true Voyage to the Indies lost.*

Such scenes, apparently, those particularly of the prison (IV. i), and the temple (v. i) could not be put aside as useless after the run of the play, and accordingly we find, about a year later, the production of *The Indian Emperour*, "*Being the Sequeal of the* Indian *Queen*," evidently written to order. That it was not penned to provide a sequel to the plot of the former play is proved by the facts that Dryden was forced to confess that "the Conclusion of the *Indian* Queen...left little matter for another Story to be built on" and that he therefore provided readers and audience with a "Connection of *The* Indian *Emperor* to *The* Indian *Queen*," in order to introduce them to the new characters he was compelled to supply. Of the persons in *The Indian Queen* there remained "but two alive." The prologue, moreover, was sent out to advise the audience that

> *The Scenes are old, the Habits are the same,*
> *We wore last year...*

and probably were to wear repeatedly again in the following decade or two. The temple duly appeared in Act I. Sc. ii, the prison in Act IV. Sc. i and iv and in Act v. Sc. ii, while the "*Pleasant* Indian *Country*[1]," the "*Magician's Cave*[2]," the

---

[1] I. i; II (iii).   [2] II. i.

"*Chamber Royal*[1]," the "*Camp*[2]" and the "*pleasant Grotto*[3]" had all no doubt appeared in the former play[4]. At the Theatre Royal later records of the prison scene are to be found in Settle's *The Female Prelate* (D.L. 1679)[5], in the same author's *Fatal Love* (D.L. 1680)[6] and in Harris' *The Mistakes* (D.L. 1690)[7], and of the grotto in D'Urfey's *Commonwealth of Women* (D.L. 1685)[8] and in Lee's *Sophonisba* (D.L. 1675).

Our most interesting materials, however, for a knowledge of Restoration scenery are obtained, not from the Theatre Royal plays, but from those of the house of D'Avenant. There the scenic influence must have been considerably greater, and possibly the fact that the spectators seem on the whole to have preferred that theatre permitted the managers to indulge more largely in show and in finery. From the seventies of the century onwards we find continually critical remarks in Theatre Royal prologues and epilogues to the expenditure of the other house and the comparative success of that expenditure. Indeed about 1673–1674 the management of the King's company appear to have engaged in a fairly extensive series of burlesques which hit directly at the operatic versions of *Macbeth* and *The Tempest* and at the gorgeous *Empress of Morocco*[9]. *The Siege of Rhodes*, produced in June 1661, we know had a number of ambitious scenes— Rhodes with the Turkish fleet, the town besieged, Mount Philermos and the storming of the city—and these were no doubt augmented by a series of interiors employed in *The*

---

[1] III. i; IV. ii; V. i.   [2] III. ii.   [3] IV. iii.

[4] In a similar way Shadwell's *Psyche* (D.G. 1675) and Gildon's *Phaeton* (D.L. 1698) were written expressly to show off scenery, in these cases brought over from France.

[5] III.   [6] IV.   [7] III. i.   [8] IV. ii.

[9] See the plays of Duffett. He had already made an attack on the rich scenery of the Duke's house in the prologue to *The Spanish Rogue* (L.I.F. 1673). Note may also be taken of Fane's epilogue to *Love in the Dark* (D.L. 1675) which hits at the success of *Psyche*:

"*For Songs and Scenes, a double Audience bring,*
And Doggrell takes, which Smiths in Sattin sing.
Now to Machines, and a dull Mask you run,
We find that Wit's the Monster you would shun,
And by my troth 'tis most discreetly done."

Witts, performed on Thursday, Aug. 15, 1661. Scenery, probably rather crude, was used for *Hamlet*, "done with scenes very well," played on Sat. Aug. 24, 1661. For the revival of *Love and Honour* in October of the same year D'Avenant was probably able to make use of some of the older scenes, as no doubt for *The Bondman* (November) and *Cutter of Coleman Street* (December). All this time, however, he was, almost certainly, adding to his collection of properties, "*the New Scene of the Hall*" which we find mentioned in Porter's *The Villain*[1] (L.I.F. Sat. Oct. 18, 1662) being assuredly only one of many. *The Adventures of Five Hours*, produced on Thurs. Jan. 8, 1662-3[2], was, according to Downes, "cloath'd Excellently Fine in Proper Habits[3]," and we know that in it appeared one or two novel scenic effects such as "*The Rising Moon*" of Act III[4]. "*The Dress, the Author, and the Scenes are new*," the prologue informs us, and from the stage directions we can make out that among these new scenes were "*Don* Henrique's *House*[5]," "*Don* Octavio's *House*[6]," "*Don* Carlos's *House*[7]," "*a Garden*[8]" and "*The City of* Sevil[9]." These we may presume were utilised later in other dramas, almost certainly for Stapylton's *The Slighted Maid* (Feb. 1662-3) and *The Stepmother* (possibly Nov. 1663). In plays such as Etherege's *Love in a Tub* (March, 1664) there was ample opportunity for employing the interiors already mentioned. About April 1665, *Mustapha* was set on the L.I.F. stage and there all the scenery was new[10], as was also that used for *Tryphon* (Dec. 1668). Possibly the most interesting stage directions in the whole of Restoration drama are those

---

[1] IV. i.

[2] Pepys marked this as the first performance, but Evelyn saw a rehearsal on Tues. Dec. 23. In the text we find that "*The Prologue enters with a Play-Bill in his hand, and Reads* This Day being the 15th of December, shall be Acted a New Play"—from which it seems that the initial rehearsal (semi-public) was even prior to that date.

[3] P. 22.

[4] G. C. D. Odell, *Shakespeare from Betterton to Irving* (1920, I. 150), marks other appearances of this moon which had escaped my notice: Mrs Behn's *Widow Ranter* (D.L. 1689), v. i; Mountford's *Greenwich Park* (D.L. 1691); *The Fairy Queen* (D.G. 1692), IV.

[5] I; III; **v** (ii).   [6] IV (i).   [7] v (i); v (iii).

[8] III. ii.   [9] II (i); III (iii).   [10] Downes, p. 26.

which are to be found in the same author's *Guzman* (April,
1669) where certain scenes of *Mustapha* and of *Tryphon* are
directly referred to. "*A Flat Scene of a Chamber*[1]" might
be any one of the preceding pieces, as might also "*The Scene
with the Chimney in't*[2]," reminding us of that used many
years after in Mrs Centlivre's *Marplot* (D.L. 1710)[3], but of
others we are particularly told their origin. "*The Scene a
Garden* (*The Garden in* Tryphon *as a Back Scene*)[4]" and "*The
Queen of* Hungary'*s Chamber*[5]" are taken directly out of the
former tragedies, the first from Act I. Sc. i of *Tryphon* and
the second from Act IV. Sc. i of *Mustapha*. In *Guzman*, moreover, there is mention, besides these, of "*The New Black
Scene*[6]," of "*The New Flat Scene*" representing a Piazza[7],
and "*The Scene a Grove of Trees* (*The Forest*)[8]."

The two theatres, as has been observed above, vied in
rivalry, and we can see at L.I.F. and later at D.G., not only
such new scenes as are given above, but others on the model
of the T.R. *Indian Queen* decorations. The Forest last mentioned was a great favorite, appearing in Mrs Behn's *The
Young King* (D.G. 1679) as "*A Flat Wood*[9]" and in the same
authoress' *The Dutch Lover* (D.G. 1673) as "*A Flat Grove*[10]."
A "*Wood*" was among the L.I.F. possessions in 1696[11].
Barren wastes were also much favoured in both theatres, as
in D'Urfey's *A Commonwealth of Women* (D.L. 1685), "*A flat
Rock*[12]" and "*A Barren Island*[13]." One of the spectacular
scenes presented by the Royal Academy of Music in their
production of *Ariane* (Mar. 1673-4) was "*A Desart or Wilderness*," possibly, however, a desert that blossomed as the rose,

---

[1] III.   [2] II and IV.   [3] I. iii.   [4] IV.
[5] II and V.
[6] II (iii). Probably that used for the "*Room hung all with Black*" in
Act V of Whitaker's *The Conspiracy* (D.G. 1680).
[7] III.   [8] V.   [9] IV. i.
[10] III. ii. The grove appears also in Settle's *The Conquest of China*
(D.G. 1675), IV. ii; V. iii: in the same author's *The Fairy Queen* (D.G.
1692), II: in Shadwell's *The Libertine* (D.G. 1675), IV: in Otway's *Alcibiades* (D.G. 1675), II. i: in D'Urfey's *Squire Oldsapp* (D.G. 1678) as
"*A Wood or Grove*," I. ii: in Powell's *Brutus of Alba* (D.G. 1696), III. i:
and in Scott's *The Mock Marriage* (D.G. 1695), III. i.
[11] Harris' *The City Bride* (L.I.F. 1696), III. i. "A Wood" is also to be
found at D.L. in Powell's *The Treacherous Brothers* in 1689.
[12] III. i.   [13] IV. i.

like that "*Wilderness or Desart*" given "on a Stage near St. Lawrence-Lane" during the performance of Jordan's pageant, *London Triumphant* (1672), which "doth consist of divers Trees, in severall sorts of green Colours, some in Blossom, others wealthily laden, with some green and some ripe and proper Fruits and Spices...inhabited with Tawny *Moors*, who are laborious in gathering, carrying, setting, sorting, sowing, and ordering the Fruits[1]." Prisons, too, were as common at D.G. as at the royal house. One appeared early in Settle's *Cambyses* (L.I.F. 1671)[2]. Later examples are to be discovered in Pordage's *The Siege of Babylon* (D.G. 1677)[3] and Hopkin's *Boadicea* (L.I.F. 1697)[4]. Settle's *Cambyses*, besides, shows us at the Duke's house a temple[5] precisely on the lines of Dryden's Temple of the Sun. More ornate effects, such as Eliziums[6], Heavens and Hells[7], occur fairly frequently, and fire scenes are common[8].

What exactly these scenes looked like we can hardly tell now. In the majority of cases they must have been crude enough, featuring a background rather than anything else. It is to be remembered that, even in the eighteenth century, actors were commonly presented in front of, rather than within, a set. The fundamental principle involved in the creation of a scenic effect was one which had been originally developed in Italy. After the experimentation with angled wings and prisms based on the Greek *periaktoi*, architects there had devised the flat wings and backdrops which for so

---

[1] Note may be taken in this description of the illustrative nature of the scenery referred to *supra* p. 35.

[2] v. i. 　　[3] II. ii. 　　[4] v. iii. 　　[5] v.

[6] Lacy's *The Dumb Lady* (T.R. in B.St. 1669), IV: Otway's *Alcibiades* (D.G. 1675), v.

[7] Shadwell's *Psyche* (D.G. 1675). Hell appears in Powell's *Brutus of Alba* (D.G. 1696), I. i and ii: a "*Poetical Hell*" is in Dryden's *Albion and Albanius* (D.G. 1685), II: and Heaven in D'Avenant's *Circe* (D.G. 1677), II. i.

[8] Pepys noted a fire scene in *The Island Princess* on Thurs. Jan. 7, 1668–9. One had already appeared at the same T.R. in Howard's *The Vestal Virgin* (before 1665), III. i. At D.L. there is one in Act IV of Settle's *The Female Prelate* (1679) and another in the last act of Crowne's *The Destruction of Jerusalem* (1677). At D.G. houses are on fire in Act III of Settle's *Love and Revenge* (D.G. 1674) and in Charles D'Avenant's *Circe* (D.G. 1677), II. i.

long were to remain standard theatrical appurtenances. The wings, of course, were habitually employed in association with "cloud-borders," suitably painted to represent aerial effects for exteriors and ceilings for interiors. The Wren design displays the usual grooves running crossways over the stage and on these must have run the innumerable "flats" and side-wings of the Restoration theatre. In all, there appear to be five separate grooves indicated in this drawing, which would give the requisite number of changes demanded in many a spectacular play of the time. These flats employed were probably of two kinds; the usual shutters meeting in the centre or running across the stage, and the "cut-outs" where some part was removed to reveal a distant prospect far behind. By means of all, the Duke's and King's companies sought to feed the public with new and gorgeous novelties, by all accounts succeeding fairly well in their attempt.

Two or three things may be noted in connection with these scenes of an ornate character. Their influence on the drama-tists has already been touched upon, but a glance at their origin and later development may not here be unfitting. They were destined to survive over the Restoration period, penetrating into the eighteenth century, being utilised then both for the ordinary drama and for the opera, until towards the year 1740 they were ridiculed out of existence. In origin, some at least were undoubtedly continental. In the Bodleian there is an interesting pamphlet entitled The Description of the Great Machines, of the Descent of Orpheus into Hell; Presented by the French Comedians at the Cock-pit in Drury Lane (London, 1661), the work, no doubt, of the same troupe which Evelyn saw at the court on Monday, Dec. 16, 1661. This pamphlet describes many scenes identically similar to those we have met with above. The Grotto appears in I. i, the Garden in II. ii, the Grove in V. i, barren rocks in I and in III. i, a "dismal Hell" in IV. i. The scenery employed by those French actors may well have been left at the theatre on their return to their native land, and in any case their example must have gone far to influence later English theatrical endeavour. We certainly know by name seven English scene-painters of this time, Webb, Aggas,

Streeter, Stevenson, Towers, Fuller and Robinson[1], and we may suspect that they were all influenced by the scenic devices of the continent. Many of the scenes detailed above are subsequent to the performance of *Psyche* in 1674–5, for scenes to which Betterton had journeyed across the Channel. In this art of scene-painting we in England were, according to Flecknoe, but as "schollars" and learners: we looked to France in almost every way for inspiration and for tutoring. Only towards the end of the century was it possible for a dramatist to declare that he had "thrown away all our old *French* Lumber, our Clouds of Clouts, and set Theatrical Paintings at a much fairer Light[2]." All the temples and the palaces, all the groves and the heavens and hells, all the scenes of spirits and of sorcery and of wonder such as in Tate's *Brutus of Alba* (D.G. 1678), were but the English tribute in the form of imitative flattery to the scenic art of Les Grands Comédiens who put on their stage

> *Des Mers, des Rivages,*
> *Des Temples, Rochers et Bocages,*
> *Des Concerts, Danses et Balets,*
> *Dragons, Démons, Esprits-folets[3].*

Alongside of the more spectacular "heroic" scenes, borrowed, I feel, largely from French example, must have been many which realistically depicted English scenes. One of

---

[1] Robert Aggas, or Angus, and Samuel Towers appear as petitioners to the Lord Chamberlain against the King's men for £40, "for worke done in ye Theatre Royall,' on Aug. 8, 1677: in another petition, dated Dec. 2, 1682, the two "Paynters" similarly petitioned for a payment of £32 (L.C. 5/190 and 5/191). Robert Streeter, who was responsible for much scenic work at court (Eleanore Boswell, pp. 208–11), did the scenes for *The Conquest of Granada* (Evelyn, Feb. 9, 1671, and *Cal. State Papers, Treasury Books*, 1669–72, pp. 1158 and 1330). Stevenson, or Stephenson, decorated Shadwell's *Psyche* (D.G. 1675) and Robert Robinson was occupied with Settle's *The Virgin Prophetess* (D.L. 1701). Concerning Isaac Fuller an interesting document has been published by Leslie Hotson, pp. 250–3: his petition to the Lord Chamberlain for £250 on Jan. 26, 1669–70 is in L.C. 5/187. The amounts asked for by the painters, in particular the £335 demanded by Fuller for a single set in *Tyrannick Love* (T.R. in B.St. 1669), presented before the operatic craze of the seventies, amply demonstrate the importance scenery had assumed.

[2] Settle, *The World in the Moon* (D.G. 1697), preface.

[3] J. Loret, *La Muze Historique* quoted in Charlanne, *L'influence française en Angleterre au xvii* siècle* (1906).

these, peculiarly enough, is to be seen in the above-mentioned frontispiece to *Ariane*. There we discover two rows of conventional palaces ending in a quite realistic picture of Thames Bridge obviously painted on a back cloth or shutter. A similar scene in which a street of palaces ends in a picture of the Royal Exchange is described to us in Dryden's *Albion and Albanius* (D.G. 1685). There "*the Scene is a Street of Palaces, which lead to the Front of the* Royal-Exchange; *the great Arch is open, and the view is continued through the open part of the* Exchange, *to the Arch on the other side, and thence to as much of the Street beyond, as could properly be taken,*" that is to say, the two lines of "palaces" as in *Ariane*, with a central "relieve" of the arches and a back shutter at the rear of the stage showing through them. Of London sights the Mall seems to have been a favourite subject. At D.G. "*the Mail*" occurs in Act III. Sc. iii of Etherege's *The Man of Mode* in 1676, and at L.I.F. in Act II. Sc. i of Granville's *The She-Gallants* in 1695. Etherege's *She Wou'd if she Cou'd* (L.I.F. 1668) has Mulberry Garden in Act II. Sc. i, and the "*New Spring Garden*" in Act IV. Sc. ii. "The Mulberry Garden" appears once more in D'Urfey's *The Fool turn'd Critick* (D.L. 1676)[1] alongside of Covent Garden[2]. In all probability these references to scenes taken from those very places where the audience loved to stroll and preen themselves could be multiplied an hundred-fold[3].

[1] v. iii (really iv).

[2] I. i; II. i; III. i; v. i. Covent Garden was a common setting at both theatres: cf. Mrs Behn's *The Town-Fopp* (D.G. 1676); D'Urfey's *Madam Fickle* (D.G. 1676), and Leanerd's *The Rambling Justice* (D.L. 1678).

[3] In the Public Record Office (L.C. 5/141, p. 551) is an interesting order regarding the alteration of the Royal Whitehall stage, evidently for the production of *Calisto*. It is dated Jan. 25, 1674–5 and instructs that the stage should be brought forward into the pit, then follows the orders "To widen the whole Stage by drawing Back the Side Sceenes & altering the frames & Groves accordingly, To alter all the Cloudes aboue suiteable to the same by heighthening them and ading to them, To make an openinge for a Heaven aboue with all the Sceenes of Cloudes & shutter of cloudes necessary, To make a new paire of shutters of Boscage, To make a new paire & (? of) releuies rep^rsentinge ye prosspect of Somersett-house & ye Thames, To make a Temple in the Cloudes with Sceenes of Varnished Silke & places for lights for ye same, To make Seates for ye Goddesses & diverse Releiues proper for that rep^rsentacõn, To fix a new Curtaine To make severall new partitions in ye Tireing roomes...."

As in the case of scenery proper, we find that the machinist's art during the Restoration times was also deeply influenced by the example of France and of Italy. Betterton, we are told, took many an idea from the former country, executing them with the aid of his chief man, Thomas Wright, who contributed one comedy to the theatre. Many startling effects seem to have been achieved, most of the more elaborate, however, not until after the opening and development of the new Duke's house in Dorset Garden. If we take up the text of Shadwell's *The Tempest* (D.G. 1674) we find sufficiently ambitious effects. In the very first scene there is "*a Tempestuous Sea in perpetual Agitation*" accompanied by "*many dreadful Objects to it, as several Spirits in horrid Shapes flying down amongst the Sailors, then rising and crossing in the Air. And when the Ship is sinking, the whole House is darken'd, and a Shower of Fire falls upon 'em. This is accompanied with Lightning, and several Claps of Thunder, to the End of the Storm.*" A transformation scene follows: "*the Cloudy Sky, Rocks and Sea vanish; and when the Lights return, discover a beautiful Part of the Island, which was the Habitation of* Prospero." "Miraculous Effects...marvellous Changes, and strange Metamorphoses" had characterised the French actors' *Descent of Orpheus into Hell* in 1661, and these no doubt gave the tone to future English performances. Those few directions taken from the opening scenes of *The Tempest* display to us how far even in 1674 the managers had reached in the ability to present wondrous panoramas before their audiences. All the operas of the age, however, are rich in descriptions of novelties in machine and stagery, some of the most interesting, perhaps, being found in Dryden's *Albion and Albanius* (D.G. 1685). These particular descriptions, Dryden tells us, he had from Betterton himself. They are, therefore, not a poet's dream of what might have been, but was not, accomplished, but an actor-manager's account of what he had actually put upon the boards of his theatre. I have already quoted the first scene of this play with its street of palaces and the "relieve" of the Royal Exchange. Outside of this, we are told, between the apron in front and the back "house" or stage behind, were a couple of statues on horseback, "*on Pedestals of Marble, enrich'd with Gold, and bearing the Imperial Arms of* England." One of these represented Charles I (it was taken from the famous statue now standing at Charing Cross) and the other, Charles II. The changes that take place within this setting are so important that I shall give them in full. First "*Mercury* descends in a Chariot drawn by Ravens" and approaches Augusta and Thamesis "*She attended by Cities, He by Rivers.*" Shortly after "*A double Pedestal rises: On the Front of it is painted in Stone colour, two Women.*" Democracy and Zeal fall asleep on this pedestal "*and it sinks with them.*" This probably took place in the centre of the back stage or house, through one of the numerous traps which we know cut up the boards there. A few lines further on "*The Clouds divide, and* Juno *appears in a Machine drawn by Peacocks; while a Simphony is playing, it moves gently forward, and as it descends, it opens and discovers the Tail of the Peacock, which is so Large, that it almost fills the opening of the Stage between Scene and Scene.*" As the width of the Dorset Garden stage was about thirty feet, this indicates an extent of well over twenty feet for the peacock's tail. Still further on in the same play, "*Iris appears on a very large Machine. This was really seen the* 18th *of* March, 1684. *by Capt.* Christopher Gunman, *on Board his R.H. Yacht, then in* Calais Pierre: *He drew it as it appear'd, and gave a draught of it to us. We have only added the Cloud where the Person of* Iris *sits.*" This scene continues for a time and then "*Part of the Scene disappears, and the Four Triumphal Arches erected at his Majesties Coronation are seen.*" Act II starts with the "*Poetical Hell*" already mentioned. "The Change is Total[1]. *The Upper Part of the House, as well as the Side-Scenes. There is the Figure of* Prometheus *chain'd to a Rock, the Vulture gnawing his Liver.* Sisiphus

---

[1] G. C. D. Odell relies on this stage direction to prove that in the Restoration theatre the side-wings of one scene were often left when another back-shutter was drawn in. Possibly, however, Betterton means only that this is a deep scene, not a poetical Hell shown by a shutter towards the front of the house, or else he is referring to cloud borders.

rowling the Stone, the Belides, *&c. beyond, Abundance of Figures in various Torments. Then a great Arch of Fire. Behind this three Pyramids of Flames in perpetual agitation. Beyond this, glowing Fire, which terminates the Prospect.*" When we consider the lighting arrangements of the late seventeenth century we must agree that this scene must have required very careful management on the part of the machinist, a good deal of thinking out, and a considerable expense. Yet this "*Poetical Hell*" is not allowed to remain for long. It soon "*changes to a Prospect taken from the middle of the* Thames; *one side of it begins at* York-Stairs, *thence to* VVhite-Hall, *and the* Mill-Bank, *&c. The other from the* Saw-Mill, *thence to the* Bishop's Palace, *and on as far as can be seen in a clear Day.*" This continues for some time, during which Mercury descends and ascends, then "*The farther Part of the Heaven opens and discovers a Machine; as it moves forwards, the Clouds which are before it divide, and shew the Person of* Apollo, *holding the Reins in his Hand. As they fall lower, the Horses appear with the Rays and a great Glory about* Apollo." This advances and eventually "*goes forward out of sight.*" Meanwhile "Neptune *rises out of the Water, and a Train of Rivers*, Tritons, *and Sea-Nymphs attend him.*" It is not stated how they retire, their singing concluding the act. One wonders whether perhaps the curtain may not have been utilised here to mark the break between this scene and the next. Act III opens with "*a View of* Dover, *taken from the Sea: a row of Cliffs fill up each Side of the Stage, and the Sea the Middle of it, which runs into the* Peer: *Beyond the* Peer, *is the Town of* Dover: *On each Side of the Town, is seen a very high Hill; on one of which is the Castle of* Dover; *on the other, the great Stone which they call the* Devil's drop. *Behind the Town several Hills are seen at a great distance which finish the View.*" Here Nereids "*rise out of the Sea*" and dance with Tritons, but this is not the most startling effect. Somewhat further on in the scene "*The Cave of* Proteus *rises out of the Sea, it consists of several Arches of Rock work, adorn'd with mother of Pearl, Coral, and abundance of Shells of various Kinds: Thro' the Arches is seen the Sea, and parts of* Dover

Peer : In the middle of the Cave is Proteus *a sleep on a Rock adorn'd with Shells, &c. Like the Cave.* Albion *and* Acacia *seize on him, and while a Simphony is playing, he sinks as they are bringing him forward, and changes himself into a Lyon, a Crocodile, a Dragon, and then to his own Shape again."* This rising of the Cave must have necessitated a very large trap in the floor of the "house": out of the same trap must have issued the "*Island*" which "*arises to a soft Tune*" in the last act of Dryden's *King Arthur* (D.G. 1691). The cave, however, is soon done with. Fire now bursts forth "*betwixt them and* Albion," then "*a Fire arises from behind : They all sink to-gether.*" A little later "*A Machine rises out of the Sea : It opens and discovers* Venus *and* Albanius *sitting in a great Scallop-shell, richly adorn'd :* Venus *is attended by the Loves and Graces,* Albanius *by* Hero's*: The Shell is drawn by Dolphins : It moves forward, while a Simphony of Fluts-Doux, &c. is playing till it Lands 'em on the Stage, and then it closes and sinks.*" Those who remember the *Ariane* engraving may well wonder whether this shell be not the very same one which is to be seen guided by dolphins from Thames Bridge to the floor of the Duke's Theatre. It is a piece of property which, in all probability, would be preserved.

Almost immediately, in *Albion and Albanius*, we pass from this sea machine to an aerial one. "*Whilst a Simphony is playing; a very large, and a very glorious Machine descends; The figure of it Oval, all the Clouds shining with Gold, abun-dance of Angels and Cherubins flying about 'em, and playing in 'em; in the midst of it sits* Apollo *on a Throne of Gold; he comes from the Machine to* Albion." After a few words Albion "*mounts the Machine, which moves upward slowly.*" And then the final transformation. "*The Scene changes to a Walk of very high Trees : At the end of the Walk is a view of that part of* Windsor, *which faces* Eaton: *In the midst of it is a row of small Trees, which lead to the Castle-hill : In the first Scene, part of the Town and part of the Hill : In the next the Terrace Walk, the King's Lodgings, and the upper part of St.* George's *Chappel, then the Keep; And lastly, that part of the Castle, beyond the Keep. In the Air is a Vision of the Honours of the*

*Garter ; the Knights in Procession, and the King under a Canopy :
Beyond this, the upper end of St.* George's *Hall.* Fame *rises
out of the middle of the Stage, standing on a Globe ; on which is
the Arms of* England : *The Globe rests on a Pedestal : On the
Front of the Pedestal is drawn a Man with a long, lean, pale
Face, with Fiend's Wings, and Snakes twisted round his Body :
He is incompast by several Phanatical Rebellious Heads, who
suck Poison from him, which runs out of a Tap in his Side.*"

So ends *Albion and Albanius*, with a not very pretty allusion
to the despised Shaftesbury. I have quoted the scenic directions here in full in order to give some idea of what could be
accomplished in the theatre even fifteen years before the close
of the century. The same machines, of course, would be
used in more operas than one. We find, for instance, similar
directions in D'Urfey's *Cinthia and Endimion* (D.L. 1696).
At the same time, we must not suppose that the wonders of
Albion and Albanius in any way reached the acme of the
machinist's art in this age. In the stage directions to *The
Prophetess* (D.G. 1690) we are informed that "*Figures come
out of the Hangings and Dance : And Figures exactly the same
appear in their Places : When they have danc'd a while they go
to sit on the Chairs, they slip from 'em, and after joyn in the
Dance with 'em*[1]." In the same play there are magic trans-
formations in Act IV, and in Act V there is a machine with
four separate stages. This last four-staged machine was sur-
passed in Settle's *The World in the Moon* (D.G. 1697) where
eight stages make their appearance. In the first act of the
same opera a "*Flat-Scene draws and discovers Three grand
Arches of Clouds extending to the Roof of the House, terminated
with a Prospect of Cloud-work, all fill'd with the Figures of
Fames and* Cupids; *a Circular part of the back Clouds rolls
softly away, and gradually discovers a Silver Moon, near
Fourteen Foot Diameter : After which, the Silver Moon wanes
off by degrees, and discovers the World within, consisting of
Four grand Circles of Clouds, illustrated with* Cupids, *etc.
Twelve Golden Chariots are seen riding in the Clouds, fill'd with
Twelve Children, representing the Twelve Celestial Signs. The*

[1] Act III.

*Third Arch intirely rolling away, leaves the full Prospect ter-
minating with a large Lanschape of Woods, Waters, Towns, etc.*"
There is no need to quote more. Reading one spectacular
piece after another, we come to realise that the machinist's
art in Restoration times had reached a very high pitch of
perfection, that one theatre vied with another in producing
more and more gorgeous shows, and that often the poet had
to be subordinated to the scene shifter. All of this, too, led,
naturally enough, towards increased expenditure on the part
of the theatres, and these increased expenses, coupled with
the small audiences, rendered more inevitable the Union of
1682. Already we have seen Dryden commenting on the cost
entailed by *The Indian Queen* in 1664. Wright in his *Historia
Histrionica* (1699) remarks upon the "great expense and
continual charge of the players" due to "the scenes" and
"curious machines" of Betterton and his rivals, and the
prologue to Shadwell's *Tempest* in 1674 betrays quite clearly
the condition into which the Duke's Theatre had then placed
itself:

> Wee, as the ffathers of the Stage have said,
> To treat you here a vast expense have made;
> What they (the King's players) have gott from you in
> chests is laid,
> Or is for purchas'd Lands, or houses paid,
> You, in this house, all our estate may find,
> Wch for your pleasures wholly are design'd.

As regards the costume employed on the Restoration stage,
considerable diversity would seem to have ruled. The comedy
of the time, of course, required nothing but contemporary
garments, or, as Flecknoe expresses it, "any *French* Cloaths
A la Mode[1]," but in tragedy such were hardly so suitable,
and there does seem to have been some attempt made to
gain an approach to a kind of historical accuracy. In point
of fact, in costume the theatre must have presented the same
phenomenon as it did in scenery and in other respects, modern
meeting with ancient on the same platform. Thus in the
fourth engraving (for Act II. Sc. ii) of Settle's *The Empress*

[1] Preface to *The Damoiselles a la Mode* (1667).

of Morocco (D.G. 1673) although the Moors dancing in the
foreground are black enough and sufficiently scantily dressed,
the Moorish heroes and heroines in the background are just
seventeenth century ladies and gentlemen of quality, attired
in the latest Parisian fashions. On the one hand, the old
careless, unhistorical traditions of the Elizabethan stage reigned
unchecked. Periwigs for all characters seem to have been
the order of the day, and Wilson appears to have discovered
nothing ridiculous in making Manuel's periwig fall off and
in causing that gentleman with most Shakespearian accents
to exclaim:

> Take up that, and help me
> To put it on again. So—so! 'Tis well!

The stage direction informs us that "PHILO *takes up his grey
Perriwig, and helps him on with it again.*" This occurs in
Act I. Sc. iii, of a play styled *Andronicus Comnenius* (1664).
Salome, in Pordage's *Herod and Mariamne* (D.G.? 1673),
similarly, disguising herself as a man, evidently made use of
a wig, for, in fencing, "*her Perriwig falls off in making a pass
at* TYRIDATES." The alternative of the wig for heroes would
seem to have been the hat of lofty feathers which preserved
its existence up to the time of Garrick[1]. These convention-
alities and inaccuracies must, we may well imagine, have
oft-times been sufficiently blatant, so blatant indeed that they
were taken note of by continental visitors to our theatre[2].

   On the other hand, from prints and from descriptions of
seventeenth-century costuming, there does seem to be evidence
of a certain tendency at least towards historical accuracy.
On Tues. March 8, 1664, Pepys saw *Heraclius* acted, "the
garments like Romans very well." The prologue to Howard
and Dryden's *The Indian Queen* speaks of "*our naked
Indians*" and already we have noted the Moors in *The
Empress of Morocco*. Mrs Behn informs us that the Indian
Queen's dress used at the playhouse was one she had brought

---

[1] T. Davies, *Dramatic Miscellanies* (1785), III. 97. See also the print
of Quin as Coriolanus.
[2] Muralt, *Lettres sur les Anglois* (written *c.* 1695, Geneva 1725), quoted
by Joseph Texte in *Jean-Jacques Rousseau* (London, 1899), p. 41.

from Surinam and which she had presented to the players[1]. A print of " *The Indian Queen* "[2] displays a variant of this[3]. How far these attempts at accuracy extended it is very difficult now to say: probably not far, merely registering the slight tendency towards a change of outlook on the part of managers and of audience. The theatres must have presented a mass of conflicting garments, Elizabethan meeting with Eastern, Roman with American Indian. As we have seen, what the managers most thought about was show and novelty: nor was there a body of critical opinion in the audience which was likely to force a change of orientation.

As we pass in review the various aspects of the Restoration theatre, indeed, we come more and more to the conclusion that that theatre owed its whole being to Elizabethan example. The changes made were tentative rather than anything else and we must beware against thinking that they were more far-reaching than they were in reality. In spite of the scenery, as we have seen, actors still did most of their speaking on the forward oval, only a few feet away from the front rows of the pit: and to reach this forward oval, entrances, as with us, from the back part of the stage, would have been both tedious and awkward. As a matter of fact, very few such exits or entrances occur in Restoration comedies and tragedies, the players coming in and leaving the stage through four ordinary doors fixed, obliquely or square, well to the front, just adjoining the end box of the first row[4]. References are frequent

---

[1] Mrs Behn, *Oroonoko*.

[2] Reproduced in Odell, *op. cit.* i. 206.

[3] In this connection there is an interesting paragraph in the Lord Chamberlain's order regarding the new Lincoln's Inn Fields theatre (P.R.O., L.C. 7/3). It is there stated that the sharing actors have been to great expense "for a variety of Cloaths *Forreigne-habitts* Scoenes Properties &c." Evidently these "forreigne-habitts" were deemed necessary for the success of any theatre.

[4] The much-vexed question of the number of doors in Restoration theatres has a little literature of its own, but citations of earlier articles and books dealing with the subject are unnecessary since at least the chief points of difference have been settled. For the Theatre Royal in Vere Street we have no evidence; but certainly both Lincoln's Inn Fields and the second Theatre Royal had four doors of entrance, and the Wren design seems to prove that four also were operative at Drury Lane. A direction

in the actual plays of the period to "*one Door*" and "*the other Door*" or "*another Door*," and from the fact that entrances "*through the Scenes*" (i.e. between the back scene and the wings) are both rarely mentioned and very detailed in stage direction, we are forced to conclude that such were exceedingly infrequent and required special notification. From the directions in one or two plays it would appear that both doors on each side were in regular use. Thus in Edward Howard's *The Man of Newmarket* (D.L. 1678) Luce, who is supposed to be overhearing a conversation, "*peeps out*" of one of the doors—so goes the stage direction. Four lines further down she "*peeps again*," and, on being called by name, she answers, whereupon follows immediately the command—"Luce *appears at another door*[1]." From the action of the piece, which depends upon her immediate appearance, it would manifestly have been impossible for her to move round behind the scenes to the other side of the theatre. What she actually must have done was to "*peep*" in at the "lower" door of entrance and then approach the stage from the "upper" door. A very similar position occurs in the tragedy of *Alphonso, King of Naples* (D.L. 1690) written by George Powell, the actor. There Cesario and Urania are attacked by banditti. He "*fights them off*" and she "*Ex. confusedly, at the wrong Door*." It would certainly have been a very unnatural action on her part if she had mistaken her side of the stage and departed by a door on the opposite side. Had there not been the double door on each side, the dramatist (who, be it remembered, was also an actor) could easily have commanded her to retire "*through the scenes*." Those two examples are further strengthened by the notes, which had apparently escaped notice hitherto, printed in a peculiar play of John Banks, entitled *The Albion Queens*:

in Edward Howard's *The Man of Newmarket* (D.L. 1678), calling for five separate entries, may perhaps be explained as referring to these doors and a central entry. At the Theatre Royal in Bridges Street, however, six doors would seem to have been at the service of the actors. There are two plays that seem to indicate this. In Lacy's *The Old Troop* "*six doors*" are specifically mentioned, while in James Howard's *All Mistaken*, Act II has a stage-direction, "*Enter six Ladies, one after another*," followed by an "*Exeunt at several doors*."   [1] III. ii.

or, The Death of Mary Queen of Scotland. This tragedy was originally written in 1684 as *The Island Queens* but was inexplicably banned the stage at that period. It was published then "only in Defence of the Author and the Play," and did not appear on the boards of the theatre until 1704 when it was reprinted with the amended title. The copy from which this reprint was taken seems to have belonged to the prompter, and it is this which contains directions invaluable for any student of Restoration stage conditions.

In this play, opposite the entries of various characters, occur combinations of letters, V.D.O.P., V.D.P.S., L.D.P.S., L.D.O.P. and O.P.P.S. Quite obviously P.S. is "prompt side," the actor's left, and O.P. is "opposite prompt side," the actor's right. L.D. and V.D. can hardly mean anything but "Lower Door" and "Upper Door": so that V.D.O.P. is the upper door on the left of the stage (from the point of view of the audience) and L.D.O.P. is the other door on the same side. O.P.P.S. occurs only once (III. i) and that after a double entrance. This no doubt indicates an approach from either of the two doors on each side of the stage.

The Wren design proves that the four doors did exist: the stage directions here prove as conclusively that all four were in constant use in the theatre. Over these doors were fixed two windows—likewise used in the progress of plays. There is quite a number of dramas in which these casements are made use of, one character knocking at the door below and another speaking to him above as from the upper part of a house. It is possible, of course, that these were but a couple of boxes sometimes seated with spectators, but they were employed so frequently in comedy and in tragedy that one cares to believe that they were reserved entirely for dramatic purposes. While they are mentioned in the course of many a play, the only reference to them outside of stage directions that I am aware of is in the prologue spoken by "Mrs Barrer" (Mrs Barry) before D'Urfey's *The Virtuous Wife* (D.G. 1679) where the "little windows" are duly noted.

With the doors to the front of the stage and the windows constantly utilised by the actors, it is perfectly obvious that our modern use of the curtain, with its drop after every scene, was quite impossible. References to the front curtain are few in Restoration dramatic literature, although there are signs that the playwrights were coming more and more to appreciate its use, especially for plays and operas of a spectacular character. It is almost certain that a lowering or raising of the curtain was not indicated every time it was employed. In Powell's *The Cornish Comedy* (D.G. 1696), for instance, "*Exeunt*" occurs as a finale to Act III (with no mention of the curtain), and yet the first scene of Act IV opens with "*Curtain drawn*." In the same play "*Exeunt*" appears at the end of Act IV. Sc. i and "*Curtain drawn*" at the start of Act IV. Sc. ii. It seems to me that we are, accordingly, permitted to presume that the front curtain was employed rather more frequently than one might have supposed from extant stage references. In the same way we know from Dilke, who in the dedication to his *The City Lady* (L.I.F. 1697) attributes the cool reception of that play "to the tedious waiting to have the Curtain drawn after the Prologue was spoke," that normally the curtain was raised after the delivery of the prologue: yet in only one or two plays do we find mention of the curtain at the commencement of Act I. D'Avenant's *The Siege of Rhodes* and *The History of Sir Francis Drake* (1658) do have such a mention, as have Payne's *Siege of Constantinople* (D.G. 1674), D'Urfey's *Siege of Memphis* (D.L. 1676), Ravenscroft's *Edgar and Alfreda* (D.L. 1677), Tate's *Brutus of Alba* (D.G. 1678), Banks' *Destruction of Troy* (D.G. 1678), Saunders' *Tamerlane the Great* (D.L. 1681) and Harris' *The City Bride* (L.I.F. 1696), but beyond these I question whether we could discover more than one or two plays with references to this initial use of the curtain. At the end of the play, a lowering of the curtain was evidently not usual, just as it was not regular at the close of individual acts, although here again we are bound to note that some dramatists at least had come to a realisation of the value of a sudden as opposed to an Elizabethan long drawn-out, conclusion, and that we cannot be perfectly sure that the curtain may not have been employed more frequently than is now

apparent[1]. Among the playwrights who did seem to use the
curtain for purposes of their art, Orrery is important because
of his influence on the heroic tragedy. It may be noted that
three plays of that writer, *The Black Prince* (T.R. in B.St.
1667), *Herod the Great* (1694) and *Tryphon* (L.I.F. 1668)
have "*The Curtain falls*" in the last act. Dryden's or Betterton's *The Prophetess* (D.G. 1690) and D'Urfey's *Massaniello*
(D.L. 1699) end in a similar manner. We shall not be wrong,
probably, in saying that the average dramatist worked along
the old Elizabethan lines, although some, particularly those
who indulged in the heroic tragedy and in opera, had at
least a faint idea of what could be done with the curtain.
Settle in *Cambyses, King of Persia* (L.I.F. 1671) has a curtain fall at the end of Act III, although at the beginning of
Act IV we have a stage direction as to a "*scene-drawing*" not
a curtain rising. Howard in *The Surprisal* (T.R. in V.St.
1662) employs the curtain to introduce a masque[2]: Mrs
Behn reveals a spectacular temple by this device in *The
Forc'd Marriage* (L.I.F. 1670)[3] and again the same authoress
in *The Young King* (D.G. 1679) causes the curtain to be "*let
down—being drawn up, discovers* Orsames.*"

Not always, however, as we have seen, was the curtain so
used. Scenes in the Restoration theatre were habitually
changed in full view of the audience, and if any spectacular
piece of scenery had to be "discovered," it was done usually
by "drawing" the two portions of a flat apart. Thus in Act IV.
Sc. i of Lee's *Lucius Junius Brutus* (D.G. 1680) "*The* SCENE
draws, showing the Sacrifice," and in Act IV. Sc. ii of Dryden's
An Evening's Love (T.R. in B.St. 1668) "*The Scene opens
and discovers* Aurelia." Here again, we can observe, in some
dramatists, a consciousness of the effect which could be produced by a spectacular discovery such as these; towards the
end of the century we find the "discoveries" increasing very

---

[1] For this question see an article by W. J. Lawrence, "Doors and
Curtains in Restoration Theatres" (*Modern Language Review*, 1920, XV.
414–19).
[2] III. i.
[3] G. C. D. Odell has noted references to the curtain also in Caryll's
The English Princess, Mrs Manley's *The Royal Mischief*, and Motteux'
The Island Princess (*op. cit.* I. 133).

rapidly. Not that the scene-drawing was reserved for this alone: over and above this it was employed in many peculiar ways, exhibiting conventions which quite clearly take us back to the Globes and Fortunes of Elizabethan days. One of these is the peculiar method of drawing a scene in order to indicate the opening of a door into an inner room, the actors being supposed by this simple means to have changed entirely their locality. A typical example is to be discovered in Act v. Sc. ii of Crowne's *City Politiques* (D.L. 1683) where the Governor enters, and crying "Force open the Door!" "*The Scene is*" obediently "*drawn*" to reveal an inner chamber within. Crowne and Dryden especially seem to have been particularly fond of this stage convention, although numerous instances can be quoted from other and less well-known authors[1].

In the footnote to this page an example is given of a vision presented by means of such a stage device, and this again

---

[1] The following examples may serve to show the scope of the convention. Dryden's *The Rival Ladies* (T.R. in B St. 1664), v. i, where the Captain says "Don *Rod'rick's* Door opens, I'll speak to him," and "*The* SCENE *draws, and discovers the Captain's Cabin*": *An Evening's Love* (T.R. in B.St. 1668), v. i, where Bellamy commands "Maskall, open the Door," "Maskall *goes to one Side of the Scene, which draws, and discovers*" several characters: later Bellamy asks Maskall to "shut the Door," "Maskall *goes to the Scene and it closes*": Crowne's *Juliana* (L.I.F. 1671), iv. iii, where Juliana asks where the Cardinal is and she is told "he is so near, torches may show him." "*The Scene is drawn, the* CARDINAL *presented dead in a Grotto*": *The Ambitious Statesman* (D.L. 1679), iii. The Constable, "Open these folding Doors!" "*The Scene is drawn,*" and iv, The Constable, "Now...open these Doors!" "*The Scene is drawn*": *Thyestes* (D.L. 1681), v. i, Atreus "Open the Temple Gates," "*The Temple is open(ed)*", Philisthenes *lies bloody*": *Sir Courtly Nice* (D.L. 1685), i, Leonora "Open the Door!" "*The Scene is drawn*" and v, Violante "Open the Door," "*The Scene is drawn*": *Regulus* (D.L. 1692), v. iv, Xantippus "Open the Door!" "*The Scene is drawn, and* REGULUS *is discover'd sitting in a Chair bloody.*" Somewhat similar is the stage direction in *The History of Charles the Eighth* (D.G. 1671), iv. ii, where Mompensier remarks that "The Gardens, Sir, are nigh," and "CHARLES *and* MOMPENSIER *go out, and the Scene is Drawn.*" In v. ii of the same play a vision is presented by similar means. This convention lasted throughout the century, appearing as late as 1697 in Dilke's *The City Lady* (L.I.F. 1697), iii. i, Lady Grumble "Here, will some of you open those folding Doors there?" and "*Scene opens*": and in Drake's *The Sham Lawyer* (D.L. 1697), iv. i: Homily "This is the Door of the Chamber where he lies," "Homily *knocks, the Scene opens.*" There are even a few stray examples which may be quoted from the early eighteenth century.

is paralleled in many another play. In Lacy's *The Dumb Lady* (T.R. in B.St., 1669), for instance, there is introduced a conjurer who talks of Elizium. Suddenly crying "Stand fast!" "*He whistles, Elizium opens; many Women's Voices sing...they draw up Squire* SOFTHEAD *with a Devil, and he cries out.*" But to give further quotations of this and kindred conventions were needless. The fact is abundantly evident that the new methods, the spectacular devices, the consciousness of a new art in the theatre, existed alongside of the Elizabethan traditions. Continually actors could shift their places without moving one step from the stage: even, by a similar device, a certain portion of the characters could be cut off by a scene-shutting, leaving one or two on the front apron to continue the action of the play. In Dryden's *The Duke of Guise* (D.L. 1682), for example, Malicorne moves forward with a servant.

> *Malicorne:* Bid him enter and go off thyself.
> [*Exit* SERVANT
> [SCENE *closes upon the Company*

leaving of course Malicorne alone in the front. Such a convention, indeed, is commoner even than those enumerated immediately above. It could go so far as to transport, as on a wishing carpet, the character who remained into quite a different locality or position. In Mrs Trotter's *The Fatal Friendship* (L.I.F. 1698) Castalio is in prison. Grammont has gone to visit him. The former "*goes within the Scene.* GRA. *Advances, the scene shuts representing the outside of a Castle*[1]."

The audience of the later seventeenth century were evidently not critical of those things which to-day would be

---

[1] As examples the following are typical. Leanerd's *The Rambling Justice* (D.L. 1678), v. v, where "*They go into the Scene, and sit down, the Scene closes,*" leaving others on the stage: anonymous, *Romulus and Hersilia* (D.G. 1682), IV. ii, where some "*come forward, and the Scene shuts upon* Feliciana": Mrs Behn's *The Rover*, Part II (D.G. 1681), I. ii, "*The Forepart of the Church shuts over, except* Will. Blunt, Aria. *and* Lucia": Mrs Trotter's *Agnes de Castro* (D.L. 1695), v. i, "Elvira *asleep on a Couch,* Bianca *weeping by her,* Alvaro *advances. The King enters to him, and the Scene shuts*": Southerne's *The Wives Excuse* (D.L. 1691), IV. i, " *They go in to Play, The Scene shuts upon 'em.* WELLVILE *and* SIGHTLY *stay.*"

noticed first. Their criticism, we may guess, was, as prologue and epilogue declared, "modish." Give them fine scenes, and they recked not what absurdities might ensue. Give them wit and gallantry or "high-astounding terms," and the characters could change position, and open doors, and see very material visions, without much comment on their part. During the first years of the period, moreover, we must remember the majority of the audience were those who had sat in the Blackfriars and the Cockpit watching scenes from Ford and from Shirley, and possibly they might have objected had too sudden an alteration been made. They were bound by indissoluble ties with the Cavaliers of the earlier age, and the little traditions and conventions which had appeared natural and right to their forefathers were bound to seem natural and right to them. Only as the structure of society altered towards the close of the century and in the age of Anne do we find any very marked changes in the theatre, and even then the changes were by no means complete or far-reaching. Even in tricks of dramatic construction traces of Elizabethan example are everywhere to be discovered. One instance will stand for many. The old Elizabethan habit of "labelling" or describing a person prior to his entrance was not forgotten when the theatres closed in 1642. It was a favourite custom of the Restoration playwrights and endured well into the eighteenth century. "My Lord," says the servant in Crowne's *City Politiques* (D.L. 1683), "My Lord! here's an old Counsellor, *Bartoline*..." to which the Podesta makes answer, "This old Lawyer is a strange Fellow: he is very old, and very rich, and yet follows the Term, as if he were to begin the World," whereat the Bricklayer chimes in, "He has lost all his Teeth, that he can hardly speak, and he will be pleading for his Fee; but he is of our side, and so we must not speak against him[1]." As late as 1697 there was decided point in Dennis' jibe: "But since this Gentleman is to be shown in the Play-house, pray do what is done in our Comedies, and let me know something of the Character,

---

[1] II. i: cf. also Otway's *Venice Preserv'd* (D.G. 1682), I. i.

before I see the Person[1]." Truly very little of the older stage was forgotten in the long eighteen years' silence of the theatres.

Most of the novelties, as we have seen, were rather developments of earlier dramatic or theatrical forms than customs or forms introduced for the first time. Music, song and dance were among other characteristics of the Restoration playhouse, but even in the first part of the seventeenth century Jonson had declaimed against the attention which the audience were giving to these and similar adjuncts to plays. Certainly music, song and dance had never usurped so much attention on the Elizabethan stage as they did on the stage of the Restoration, but we can never forget that they had been introduced long before and only saw their full development in this age and in the age of Anne, being taken up in 1660 from the plays of 1640 and thence carried to a nadir of absurdity. We notice the tendency first in the occasional songs placed, often quite dramatically, in the plays of Dryden and of D'Urfey; as the years advance, we can see it progressing until it reaches its culmination in the dramatic operas and in the numerous late seventeenth century comedies positively interlarded with diverse and frequently unsuitable ditties. Masques, too, moved from the stately atmosphere of the court to take their place in public tragedy and comedy, until hardly a play of any sort whatever could close without the joyous accompaniment of a dance. Foreign, mainly French, terpsichorean artists were brought over to London by various of the theatrical managers. Before that, of course, English artists had performed in plays:—Priest and Moll Davies in *Sir Martin Mar-all* (L.I.F. 1667), Channel and Priest in the operatic version of *Macbeth*. In spite of unlimited praise such as Flecknoe showers on "*M*(adam) *M. Davies*" for "*her excellent Dancing and Singing*":—

> How I admire thee, *Davies*!
> Who would not say, to see thee *dance* so *light*,
> Thou wert all *air*, or else all *flame* and spright[2]—

---

[1] *A Plot and No Plot* (D.L. 1697), II.
[2] *Euterpe Reviv'd* (1675), p. 64.

in spite of such praise, against her and the other dancers, English and foreign, prologue and epilogue, all through the years of the Restoration period, thundered or cajoled. As we know from play-bills of the eighteenth century these dancers and singers of occasional songs were not careful to make their shows harmonise with the subject of the play performed. In the very early years of the period D'Avenant in *The Cruelty of the Spaniards in Peru* (1658) had utilised dancing for dramatic effect as when a group of Indians enter "*and, gazing on the face of the Scene, fall into a Mimick Dance, in which they express the Argument of the Prospect,*" but by 1670 all such dramatic purpose in dance and superimposed song had been lost. The foreign artists brought from across the seas, many of them probably ignorant of the English tongue, could not be expected to adapt their performances to the play of the evening, and dramatists must have felt that they were ruining the theatre of London. In 1676 Etherege in *The Man of Mode* (D.G. 1676)[1] was moved to peculiar satire, declaring that the Russians "hearing the great respect we have for foreign Dancing, have lately sent over some of their best Balladines, who are now practising a famous Ballet which will be suddenly danced at the Bear Garden"—an unconscious prophecy of Diaghilev and the Russian dancers in the present century[2].

> *The way to please you is easie if we knew't,*

says D'Urfey in the epilogue to *The Injur'd Princess* (D.L 1682),   *A Jigg, a Song, a Rhyme or two will do't.*

"Scenes, Habits, Dancing, or perhaps an Actress," remarks Edward Howard in the preface to his *Six Days' Adventure*

---

[1] II. i.

[2] French dancers were brought over by Grabut for the *Ariane* of March 1673–4. Some of these were engaged by the Theatre Royal but somehow the agreement was broken (P.R.O., L.C. 5/140 last page). On May 6, 1674, the Lord Chamberlain ordered "Mr Pecurr Mr Le Temps Mr Shenan and Mr D'muraile ffrench Dancers in the late Opera" to attend Killigrew and perform in his theatre (P.R.O., L.C. 5/140, p. 472). In the masque of *Calisto* the following year eight French dancers (St Andrée, Le Duc, Lessant, Dumraille, Berteau, de Lisle, Hariette, Le Roy) and at least four English dancers (Isaack, Dyers, Smyth, Mottley) took part (P.R.O., L.C. 5/141, p. 197). See Appendix B.

(L.I.F. 1671), "Take more with Spectators, than the best Dramatick Wit," and the same author, in the preface to his *The Women's Conquest* (L.I.F. 1670) emphasises the fact that "serious Plays (now in use)" do not "wholly relie upon their Heroick Foundation" but on their "Scenes, Machines, Habits, Jiggs, and Dances." The rapid development of the scenical art, even ten years after the opening of the theatres, was having its inevitable result.

Symphonies, and the growth of the orchestra, also went along with the introduction of dances and songs. Symphonies, of course, had formed part of the structure of D'Avenant's musical plays of 1656 and 1658, but his efforts, by 1680 or 1690, would have appeared sufficiently trivial and ridiculous.

The whole age was undoubtedly musical. That love of singing and of lute-playing which Elizabethan England had was retained over the Puritanical barriers of the Commonwealth. Great and small, important and unimportant, all seemed to have within them a passion for expressing themselves through the medium of music. From Shakespeare to Killigrew, from Milton to Pepys, this is equally true: England shared to the full that interest in song and in symphony which was so marked a feature of contemporary Italy and France. The most complete expression of this interest is, naturally, to be sought for in the later opera of the eighteenth century: but, even for the very first years of the Restoration, Pepys has left on record how the patentee of the Theatre Royal, who could neither sing nor play, took pains to perfect his theatre in the matter of music. He it was who removed the orchestra to a new position, a position imaged for it as early as 1600 by Emilio del Cavaliere[1]. He it was who increased

---

[1] Preface to the *Rappresentazione di Anima e di Corpo* (Rome, 1600). As in former days the Restoration orchestra first performed above or at the side of the projecting stage, and probably did so even in D'Avenant's early theatre, but by Killigrew it was placed where it is now, in front of, or under, the stage and was later enclosed by a row of ominous-looking spiked railings. For D'Avenant's theatre Pepys' reference to the "Musique room" (Nov. 7, 1667) seems conclusive, and even Killigrew's innovation, when made, would not seem to have been popular. Pepys, certainly, did not like it (May 8, 1663), and in a contemporary ballad concerning the fire of Jan. 25, 1671–2 it is quite evident that the music-room must have been in its old position at the top of the house. In Villiers' *The Chances*

the number of its performers from two or three to almost a dozen[1]. He it was, too, who started to emulate Italy by the introduction of foreign eunuchs for treble singing[2].

We may trace, therefore, this development of musical accompaniment in several different ways. We can take note of the ever greater and greater number of foreign performers who found a happy home in England. Farquhar in the epilogue to his *Love and a Bottle* (D.L. 1698) mentions these singers, among them "*Seignior Rampony*," a eunuch, and "*Don Sigismondo Fideli*," the latter of whom, a note to the epilogue informs us, was receiving "£20. a time." We may note the gradual development of the orchestra. We may note the introduction of large choruses such as the Chapel Royal boys in Shadwell's *Tempest*[3]. In every way, the ground was being prepared for the introduction after 1705 of the Italian

(T.R. in B.St. 1667) there is a stage direction for "*Musick...above*," and similar directions occur in Orrery's unacted *Zoroastres* (*Dramatic Works*, ed. W. S. Clark, II. 656, 672). In the prints to Settle's *The Empress of Morocco* (D.G. 1673) the music-room is set right in the centre of the proscenium. The probability is that both the music-room and the recess in front of the stage could be utilised by the performers, and, in certain cases, the stage itself (cf. stage directions in Porter's *The Villain* (L.I.F. 1662), I and II, and note 3 below).

[1] Pepys, May 8, 1663. The 24 performers mentioned in Shadwell's *Tempest* (D.G. 1674) were no doubt specially augmented for the occasion. Chappuzeau mentions 12 as against 6 in Paris (*Europe Vivante*, Geneva, 1667).

[2] Pepys, Oct. 14, 1668.

[3] The musicians of the King were frequently employed in the theatres. A grant of £40 of silks "to cloath the Musick for the play called The Indian Queene" was made to Killigrew in Jan. 1663–4 (P.R.O., L.C. 5/138, p. 15). On March 20, 1664–5, a similar grant was made for habits to clothe 24 "violins" (*id.* p. 45), and on March 18, an order was issued "to make vp Habitts of seuerall coloured rich Taffataes for fower and twenty violins" (*id.* p. 46). It may be noted that these entries fully substantiate the supposition that the musicians often appeared, as an integral part of the performance, not under the stage or in the "music room," but on the projecting apron itself in full view of the audience. A further warrant, issued on Dec. 20, 1664, commanded Singleton, Clayton, Young, Fitz, Hudson, Strong, Staggins, Bannister and Brockwell "to attend at His Ma^tes Theatre whensoever Mr Thomas Killigrew shall desire" (*id.* p. 429). For some reason these musicians came into conflict with Charles Killigrew, so that we find, a decade later, "The humble petition of John Singleton Theop ffitz Hen. Brockwell Edmund fflower and Jos ffashion part of his Ma^ts Band of Violins ag^t Mr Charles Killigrew Master of the Reuells for dismissing them their attendance at the play house—May 8, 1677" (P.R.O., L.C. 5/190 and 5/138, p. 429).

opera in all its entirety. At the same time, the structure of tragedies and of comedies was being weakened Farces like Ravenscroft's *The Anatomist* (L.I.F. 1696) came into being solely for the sake of their musical entertainments. The dramatic operas, in the hands of Shadwell and D'Urfey were rapidly driving pure tragedy from the stage.

In every way we are watching the dramatic art in a period of change, ere it has swept off its older traditions: and the audience forms both the cause of its development and the reason for the retention of more primitive forms.

V. *The Actors and Actresses*

Before leaving the stage and passing to the actual dramatic works of this half-century, we must pause to take into account another highly determining influence on the nature of both tragedy and comedy, an influence itself not dissociated from that of the audience. I refer to the actors and the actresses of the time.

As I have indicated above, the noise in the playhouse and the fact that the spectators went to the theatre more for their own private affairs than to watch the scenes before them, necessitated a very high standard of acting if a play were to take even at all. The constant change of repertoire also must have demanded from the performers a considerable ability, if they were satisfactorily to carry through day after day. We do, certainly, hear of cases when the actors, as Pepys says, "were at fault," and one comedy at least, in the opinion of the author, was "damnably acted at the *Theatre Royal* in *Drury Lane*[1]," but for the most part the histrionic talent must have been remarkable. It is difficult now to recapture the tones of an actor long since dead, to revisualise his appearance and his gestures: it is sometimes unsafe to take on trust the comments of contemporaries: but, weighing one thing with another, we must come to the conclusion that the

---

[1] Drake's *The Sham Lawyer* (D.L. 1696). Etherege's *She Wou'd if she Cou'd* (L.I.F. 1668) was nearly damned because of the wretched acting. "We're always damn'd imperfect the first night," says an actor in the epilogue to Motteux' *Beauty in Distress* (L.I.F. 1698). See also Pepys, July 28, 1664.

revival of the theatres saw the growth and development of a most notable body of English actors. Betterton himself must have been a genius, holding himself from the grosser vices of the time, placing before himself a high and noble ideal of the histrionic art. Nor did he stand alone. The age teems with tragic and comic actors, who, judging from all accounts, were worthy of the highest praise the Restoration critic could give them—that they were able by their interpretation of the poet's lines to cause even the fops and the orange-girls to cease their chattering.

This group of notable actors, both of the King's and of the Duke's companies, affected the drama in diverse ways, for good and for evil. Betterton, for example, must have admirably interpreted Shakespeare to his age—we know that he played Brutus, Falstaff, Hamlet, Henry VIII, Hotspur, Lear, Mercutio, Othello, Pericles, Toby Belch, Timon, and Troilus: he was the original actor of Jaffier in *Venice Preserv'd* and of Castalio in *The Orphan*: but at the same time his undoubted ability enabled him to pass off with applause, not only these outstanding characters, but also "the furious fustian and turgid rants" of contemporary melodrama. "If I tell you," says Cibber in his chatty *Apology*, "There was no one tragedy, for many years, more in favour with the town than *Alexander* (of Lee), to what must we impute this its command of publick Admiration? Not to its intrinsick Merit, surely...(but) plainly, (to) the grace and harmony of the actor's utterance." Betterton in this was again not alone. Doggett could invest a tedious or a truly humorous old alderman with charm: and Mrs Barry could grace a witty *Love for Love* of Congreve or a weary *History of Charles the Eighth of France: or, The Invasion of Naples by the French* of Crowne. The audience would cheer at both and only the more penetrating prefer the admirable to the ridiculous character, could dissociate Mrs Barry or Doggett or Betterton from the parts they played.

On the other hand, in this intimate theatre of 1660 to 1700, dramatists were much more nearly related to the stage than they have been in later centuries. Of the various eminent actors whom Cibber found on the united stage in 1690, only one of the men and only two or three of the women had not been acting in the early Restoration period. That is to say, these particular players had become the familiar spectacles of audiences at the Duke's and King's houses, and spectators and dramatists alike had come to know their little idiosyncrasies and mannerisms. A story typical of the age is told of Sandford, "an excellent Actor in disagreeable Characters." Once, in a new play, he was cast for an honest man. The audience waited impatiently until he should throw off his mask of virtue and appear a villain, and then, disappointed of their hope and expectation, they finally damned the play altogether[1]. This meant, not only that the management was forced to cast Sandford always for evil parts, but that the dramatists writing for the stage were impelled to create "Macchiavellian" characters specially for him. Most of the actors of Restoration times were in Sandford's case: few, like Betterton, were all-embracing enough to take parts both grave and gay. The majority took up one line, and aided thus in establishing those "stock" characters which appear in comedy after comedy, in tragedy after tragedy, during those forty years. Very few *dramatis personae* could be taken by "Any-Body" as is Ample in *The Revenge, or, A Match in Newgate* (D.G. 1680).

Of them all, of course, Betterton is chief. Born in 1635, he was some 25 years old when first Rhodes engaged him in his Cockpit company of actors, and there apparently he attained at once to a pre-eminent position. On Nov. 5, 1660, his name appears at the head of the actors who entered into agreement with D'Avenant. In 1668 he was associated with D'Avenant and Harris in the management of the theatre in L.I.F. and for it invented several new stage machines[2]. At

---

[1] Cibber (ed. Lowe, I. 132 and cf. Tony Aston in same edition of Cibber, II. 306).

[2] Betterton first introduced French dancers and singers, according to Downes, and invented the machines for *Albion and Albanius* and other operas. It was he who "procur'd from abroad...*Monsieur L'Abbe, Madam Sublini, Monsieur Balon, Margarita Delpine, Maria Gallia* and divers others" (Downes, p. 46). "He was the first Innovator on our rude

the Union of 1682 he assisted in amalgamating the two companies, and in 1695 was the first to break with the patentees and to open the rival house at L.I.F. All through he was regarded as the chief theatrical figure of his time, and there are only one or two satirical notices of him by contemporaries—a rare thing in that lampooning age[1]. Not till the beginning of the eighteenth century, when he was upwards of seventy years of age, did his strength begin to fail, and even then he continued acting, if intermittently, until his death in 1710.

It is an undoubted fact that Betterton's histrionic art impressed itself upon the dramatic literature of his age, his dignified, graceful, yet somewhat heavy and florid form interpreting admirably those interminable heroic generals who abound in that period of Restoration melodrama. In Orrery's *Henry V* (L.I.F. 1664) he created the part of Owen Tudor: in the same author's *Mustapha* (L.I.F. 1665) that of Soliman: in Banks' *The Destruction of Troy* (D.G. 1678) that of Achilles: in Settle's *Cambyses* (L.I.F. 1671) and in Banks' *Cyrus* (L.I.F. 1695) the two heroes who give their names to those plays: and these, and such-like characters, we may presume, were written with more than half an eye to the distinguished figure who was to interpret them.

Like most great actors, however, Betterton did not confine himself to tragedy. Although his figure, which was "serious, venerable, and majestic" in spite of a somewhat "Pockfretten" face[2] and a short thick neck rather inclining to be corpulent, seemed best suited for heavy heroic parts, he was evidently equally good not only in a roistering Falstaff, but in gay, light-o'-love flirters like Wittmore and Fainall. Thus in Tuke's *The Adventures of Five Hours* (L.I.F. 1663) we find him creating the part of Don Henrique: in Etherege's *Love in a Tub* (L.I.F. 1664) that of Beauford: and in Shadwell's *Epsom Wells* (D.G. 1672) that of Bevil. If he has to be taken into account for the development of the "hero" in

Stage," says the author of *The History of the English Stage* (1741, p. 7), forgetting D'Avenant.

[1] One of these is the Epilogue to *The Fatal Discovery* (D.L. 1698).

[2] Tony Aston (in Lowe's edition of Cibber, II. 300).

tragedy, he is no less important for the development of the character of the contemporary gallant, easy, graceful and debonair.

Betterton, however, would not seem to have been the chief lover of the Duke's company. "Ayery" Henry Harris appears to have taken those parts which demanded pathos and amorous passion more than heroism or witty dalliance. Harris is somewhat of an ephemeral figure, but contemporaries have told us of his successful parts. Romeo he took on the revival of Shakespeare's play at L.I.F. in 1665, and he created the parts of Sir Frederick Frollick in Etherege's *Love in a Tub* (L.I.F. 1664), of Warner in Dryden's *Sir Martin Mar-all* (L.I.F. 1667), of Raines in Shadwell's *Epsom Wells* (D.G. 1672), and of Hector in Banks' *The Destruction of Troy* (D.G. 1678)[1].

Corresponding to these two at the rival Theatre Royal we find "Major" Michael Mohun and Charles Hart, "the *Roscius* and *Aesopus*" of that age according to Rymer[2], both of them pre-Commonwealth actors who had taken up their profession again on the opening of the theatres. Neither of them acted after the Union of the companies in 1682. Mohun appears to have been a slightly heavier actor than Hart, who, as Davies informs us[3], "shone in the gay gentleman, such as *Dorimant* and *Loveless*." Mohun it was who created Mithridates in Lee's play of that name (D.L. 1678) as well as Augustus Caesar and Hannibal in the same author's *Gloriana* (D.L. 1676) and *Sophonisba* (D.L. 1675). Hart characteristically played Caesario in *Gloriana* and Massinissa in *Sophonisba*. Downes mentions him as being especially good as Mosca in *Volpone*, Don John in *The Chances* and Wildblood in Dryden's *The Mock Astrologer*. He is the recipient also of some verses in Flecknoe's *Euterpe Revived* (1675) which compares him with Richard Burbage:—"Such—*Burbadge* was *once*, And such *Charles Hart* is now[4]."

The only other really great serious actor of the time seems

---

[1] He acted from about 1660 on to about 1681.
[2] *Tragedies of the Last Age* (1678).
[3] *Dramatic Miscellanies*, III. 279. Downes is high in his praise (p. 16).
[4] *Euterpe Reviv'd*, p. 78.

to have been Edward Kynaston, whom we first meet as impersonating the Duke's sister in *The Loyal Subject*, making, as Pepys assures us, "the loveliest lady that ever I saw in my life[1]." Later in the century he developed a kind of stately grace, which enabled him to play such parts as Morat in *Aureng-Zebe* (D.L. 1675) and Muley Moloch in *Don Sebastian* (D.L. 1689) with a fitting awe and majesty[2]. Save for such "majestic" parts, however, he probably did little in influencing the characters created by the dramatists. He was certainly the original Lord Touchwood in *The Double Dealer* (D.L. 1693), the original Valentine in *Love in a Wood* (T.R. in B.St. 1671) and the original Freeman in *The Plain Dealer* (D.L. 1676), but none of these impersonations appear to have been noted.

Much more important for their influence on the works of the dramatists are the comedians, both of the Duke's and of the Royal company. Of these James Nokes or Noke of the L.I.F. house must have been one of the most outstanding. Contemporaries say that no one could equal him in the interpretation of a grave English type of folly. Sir Nicholas Cully in Etherege's *Love in a Tub* (L.I.F. 1664), Puny in Cowley's *Cutter of Coleman Street* (L.I.F. 1661), Ninny in Shadwell's *The Sullen Lovers* (L.I.F. 1668)—characters such as these abound in contemporary comedy, and many of them must have been penned especially for this actor. His Sir Martin Mar-all became famous[3]: Dryden, says the author of *The History of the English Stage*[4], "wrote *Gomez*, in the *Spanish Fryar* in Compliment to him": he was the original of Sir Davy Dunce in Otway's *The Souldier's Fortune* (D.G. 1680) and Davies notes that the success of the same author's *The History and Fall of Caius Marius* (D.G. 1679) was largely due to the acting of Underhill as Sulpitius and that of Nokes as the Nurse[5]. Cave Underhill, Nokes' companion in low comedy, cultivated the stiff, heavy and stupid boobies rather

---

[1] Pepys, Aug. 18, 1660. Downes also refers to his success in women's parts. "He was a Compleat Female Stage Beauty," says Cibber (I. 121-6).

[2] Cibber, I. 125. [3] Cibber, I. 141-5.
[4] P. 32. [5] III. 191.

than the simple and foolish *nouveaux riches*. His First Gravedigger in *Hamlet* became famous, as did two of his other parts, Obadiah in *The Committee* and Sir Sampson Legend in *Love for Love* (L.I.F. 1695)[1], Pedagog in Orrery's *Mr Anthony* (D.G. 1672), Diego in Tuke's *The Adventures of Five Hours* (L.I.F. 1663) and Moody in Dryden's *Sir Martin Mar-all* (L.I.F. 1667) may well have been written for him.

Among the actors at the T.R. were several who likewise indulged in specialised types of low comedy. John Lacy, who was a dramatist as well as a player, excelled in "humours" of various kinds[2], his Teague in *The Committee* becoming famous. He was a noted Falstaff, and achieved success as Sawney in his own adaptation of *The Taming of the Shrew* (T.R. in B.St. 1667). On July 13, 1667, Pepys heard that he was dying, but he appears to have continued acting until about 1681. Of the other players, two only remain to be noted, Mountfort and Sandford, the first of whom gave life to the wondrous Sparkishes and Sir Courtly Nices of the comedy of manners[3], the other of whom, as we have seen, gave birth to the Machiavellian villains with which Restoration tragedy and tragi-comedy abounds. The first was the creator of Young Belfond in Shadwell's *The Squire of Alsatia* (D.L. 1688), Wildish in the same author's *Bury Fair* (D.L. 1689), Young Reveller in his own *Greenwich Park* (D.L. 1691) and acted the Rover in Mrs Behn's play of that name (evidently after the Union of the companies). Sandford of the Duke's company may have inspired Porter to write Malignii in *The Villain* (L.I.F. 1662) and Lee to create Creon in *Oedipus* (D.G. 1678). He was the original Jasper of Payne's *The Fatal Jealousie* (D.G. 1672) and the original Gonzalez of Congreve's *The Mourning Bride* (L.I.F. 1697).

When studying the personnel of the Restoration theatre, however, we find probably more of interest in the women than in the men. It is with the actresses that the Restoration

---

[1] Cibber, I. 154–6.
[2] Pepys, May 21, 1662, June 10, 1663. Langbaine, pp. 317–18.
[3] Cibber, I. 127–30; also II. 342–5.

made its most characteristic break-away from the traditions of the older theatre, although it is very hard to determine exactly how far women had been allowed to appear on the stage before the year 1642. We know, of course, of the French troupe which visited the Blackfriars, the Red Bull and the Fortune in 1629 and which received a not over-flattering reception from their Albion audiences, and we know of the women who regularly acted in the court masques of the early seventeenth century. It would appear very strange if no attempt had been made to introduce some actress or other in the later years of the theatre of Charles I. The very fact that we have found the theatre of 1660 basing itself in all ways on the theatre of 1640 would induce us to believe that D'Avenant and Killigrew before the outbreak of Civil War had both known the charm of seeing Rosalind and Ophelia played by persons of their own sex.

However this may be, the first appearance of an actress that we can discover is the personation by Mrs Coleman of Ianthe in D'Avenant's "opera" of 1656, and this appearance did not signify by any means that the older tradition of boy-actors was broken. I have already mentioned the fact that Kynaston appeared in the early years of the theatre as a girl, and there must have been others who, besides him, impersonated the heroines of tragedy and of comedy. At the same time, the tradition had been broken into by the long Commonwealth period. Thus actors who, in 1642, had been playing girls' parts at the Red Bull and Blackfriars were now fully adult; the training of the boys in the earlier years must have taken time; and now there were none of these on whom the managers might rely. The remedy was perfectly obvious and it is only surprising that it was not thought of sooner. Pepys saw women on the stage for the first time on Jan. 3, 1660/61, at the Royal Theatre. We must remember, however, that the diarist had attended the theatre only some half a score of times previous to this date, and that because he saw women for the first time then does not mean either that women were, in Jan. 1660/61, fully established on the stage, or that they had not appeared before that date. From the fact that Jordan in his *Royal Arbor of Loyal Poesie* has "*A Prologue to introduce the first Woman who came to Act on the Stage in the Tragedy, call'd* The Moor of Venice" and that Herbert noted a production of *Othello* on Dec. 8, 1660, it has been presumed that this precise date marks the appearance of our first woman actress. I shall not dwell here on the separate problem as to the identity of this "blue-stocking" nor shall I comment on the slight ambiguity in the title to Jordan's poem, but I may remark that as early as October, 1660, the Red Bull players in a petition addressed to the King, mention that they have come to an agreement with Killigrew to act under his management along with "woemen." The petition does not actually state that they were so acting, but at any rate we may presume from its wording that the appearance of women on the stage had been well-talked of and probably already experimentally tried by that time. The production of *Othello* on Dec. 8, 1660, was apparently not the first after the Restoration, as Herbert notes that play among the repertoire of the Red Bull players, and there is just the possibility that another poem in Jordan's book indicates a much earlier date for the advent of our primal actress. He has, immediately before the prologue for *Othello*, "*A Prologue to a Comedy call'd* The Tamer Tam'd, June 25. 1660" and a corresponding epilogue "*Spoken by the Tamer, a Woman*"— which may, or may not, refer to a particular actress.

Whenever the first woman appeared, whoever she was, the fact remains that from the erection of the first houses of D'Avenant and Killigrew we find the actresses fully established and the boy-actors vanished away. Again, as with most of the Restoration innovations or stage developments, we must distinguish here between a good and a bad influence, both of which were exercised by these actresses. They certainly made possible a more charming presentation of Shakespearian tragedy and comedy, shedding a fresh light on the Desdemonas and the Ophelias of the past: but the new audience which had called them into being did not, it is to be suspected, regard them always from this artistic point of view. From the King down to the fops, the male spectators looked upon these actresses as little better than prostitutes, and they themselves were certainly not slow in encouraging promising lovers. The gallants could go behind the scenes, easily, on the payment of a little extra fee[1]. In prologue and in epilogue broad hints were cast out to the audience that the ladies of the theatre were not to be sued in vain. Very few of those actresses lived chaste lives. Nell Gwyn, Moll Davis, Mrs Barry, Mrs Bracegirdle—all were stamped with the same die. It is perfectly exceptional to find one like Mrs Sanderson, later the wife of Betterton, against whom little scandal was cast. We have to recognise that some of these women had a true artistic genius for the stage: but, at the same time, we must be careful not to assume that they always aided unselfishly in the interpretation of the works of dramatic art. The majority must have thought more of a fine gown, or maybe of a coach and pair, than of a fine play. Mrs Barry, who, being the beloved idol of the hopeless and hapless Otway, was the model and the inspiration of Monimia and of Belvidera and who, by her sympathetic acting of the heroines of the heroic tragedy, aided in establishing that form of dramatic art in a place of popularity, was as debased and licentious as the commonest women of the town. A contemporary critic declares that she could spend the night with a man, take all his money, and refuse to recognise him the following morning unless he could scrape together another pitiful five guineas. The story of Nell Gwyn is too well known to require re-telling. She was the original Florimel, and almost certainly Dryden wrote his light airy parts for her: yet she left the stage to flaunt it in Whitehall, there to found some of the most illustrious of our aristocratic families.

The actresses, on the other hand, however low they succeeded in dragging down the playhouse, did, like the men, present to the theatre a series of stock types, and helped to keep alive species of drama which in less able hands would have had but a short existence. Mrs Sanderson, later Mrs Betterton, seems to have been noted in Shakespearian parts, and may have done something toward popularising the works

---

[1] See *supra* p. 13.

of that master in the first years of the Restoration. Mrs Anne
Bracegirdle, whose advent came somewhat later, gave life to
those Statiras and Millamants which mark the last years of
the century. She was the favourite of both Congreve and
Rowe. " In Tamerlane, Rowe courted her Selima in the person
of Axalla; in the Fair Penitent, he was the Horatio to her
Lavinia; and in Ulysses, the Telemachus to Bracegirdle's
Semanthe. Congreve insinuated his addresses in his Valentine
to her Angelica, in Love for Love; in his Osmyn to her
Almeria, in the Mourning Bride; and lastly, in his Mirabel
to her Millamant, in the Way of the World[1]."

Another actress of the same period, Mrs Leigh, ably per-
sonated those antiquated and odious specimens of old-
maidism or of wasted age such as the typical Lady Wishfort.
Still another, Mrs Verbruggen, played the "hoydens" that
appear in so many of D'Urfey's plays and in those of not a
few of his contemporaries.

Creation of characters, then, whether male or female, use
of scenery, structure of dramas, management of plot, dialogue
and aim—all these we find, in this narrow little playhouse
world where one class ruled and a king's laugh was the cue
for applause, more intimately connected with the stage than
in almost any other period of our dramatic history. For the
Restoration, we have always to think of the particular Duke's
theatre and Theatre Royal for which the plays were written.
The basis of the dramas, their structure, their aim, their very
being, is to be explained only by a reference to the playhouse
itself, the actors and actresses on the stage, and the audience,
which sat gallantly indifferent and cynical in pit and side-box
and galleries.

[1] Davies, *Dramatic Miscellanies* (1784), III. 337–8.

SUPPLEMENTARY TO
CHAPTER ONE

The Audience

The Restoration theatre was from first to last an aristocratic playhouse; from Dryden's *The Rival Ladies* in 1664 to Congreve's *The Way of the World* in 1700 the best plays of the time reflected the tone of a leisured society intent upon conversational ease and polished manners[1]. At the same time, we must assume that as the reign of Charles II ended, giving way to those of James II and of William and Mary, the composition of the audience typical of the earlier years gradually became modified.

Unquestionably, the influence of "The Ladies" began to become powerful from the seventies of the century and assumed formidable proportions towards the end of the century[2]. During these years we find several references to direct opposition organised by groups of female spectators against plays not quite to their liking: Ravenscroft, for example, specifically informs us that when his *The London Cuckolds* (D.G. 1681) was acted,

> *some squeamish Females of renown*
> *Made visits with design to cry it down*[3].

And the "Ladies" were not content merely to exercise their influence as spectators: they boldly attacked the work of the stage itself. It is true that from 1670 Mrs Behn pursued an active career as a playwright, but, save for such amateur authoresses as the "Matchless Orinda," she remained uncom-

---

[1] The importance of the aristocratic wits, both as playwrights and as spectators, is well presented by J. H. Wilson in *The Court Wits of the Restoration* (1948), particularly pp. 142–73.

[2] This has been well dealt with by John Harrington Smith in *The Gay Couple in Restoration Comedy* (1948), pp. 132–7: see also his "Shadwell, The Ladies, and the Change in Comedy" (*Modern Philology*, 1948, XLVI. 22–33).

[3] Prologue to *Dame Dobson* (D.G. 1683).

panioned in her efforts until the last decade of the century. In one single year (December 1695 to December 1696) audiences saw no less than five new plays by female writers— Mrs Trotter's *Agnes de Castro*, Mrs Manley's *The Lost Lover* and *The Royal Mischief*, and Mrs Pix's *Ibrahim* and *The Spanish Wives*. This single record is sufficient to stand as a symbol of a new spirit at work in the age.

The advent of the "Ladies" as an influential force both in the auditorium and on the stage coincides with an apparent slight increase in the influence of the citizens—although there is not evidence sufficient to assume either that the Duke's Theatre in Dorset Garden became a kind of citizens' house[1] or that the citizens came in such numbers as to exert any powerful force on the stage. It is true that in 1672 Dryden's prologue to *Marriage à la Mode*, after referring to the absence of the wits (who had departed on military service), remarks that

> *Our City Friends so far will hardly come;*
> *They can take up with Pleasures nearer home,*
> *And see gay Shows and gawdy Scenes elsewhere;*
> *For we presume they seldom come to hear.*

The epilogue to Wycherley's *The Gentleman Dancing Master* (D.G. 1672) addresses the "*good men o' the' Exchange*"—

> *on whom alone*
> *We must depend, when Sparks to Sea are gone,*

while during the same year Sedley's prologue to Shadwell's *Epsom-Wells* (D.G. 1672) specifically turns its remarks towards the "Citts." On the other hand, we note all these references belong to a time when many of the gallants were away from town and that, even if the Duke's Theatre was more conveniently situated for civic playgoers and was better equipped with machinery to delight their tastes, the citizens certainly did not give enough support to the stage to prevent those economic disasters that forced the players into the Union of 1682, nor were they numerous enough to persuade the joint

---

[1] As is asserted by Ned Bliss Allen in *The Sources of Dryden's Comedies* (1935), pp. 124-5.

management to abandon the Theatre Royal for Dorset Garden. Between 1682 and 1695 the former house seems to have been used much more frequently than the latter, and even after 1695 it was the favourite[1]. All we can say with any measure of reasonable assurance is that the citizenry are mentioned more frequently in the later years and that non-aristocratic authors begin to play a more prominent rôle during the last two decades of the century, but that before 1700 their force was not great enough to produce a complete change in theatrical conditions.

One thing, at any rate, is certain: we can detect no marked change in social conduct, so far as the playhouse is concerned, between the earlier period and the later. The disturbances in the auditorium at the end of the century are similar to those in the years immediately after 1660. To the examples already given may be added the "great disorder" of December 15, 1691, recorded by Luttrell[2], when two lords were knocked down and "2 other lords puncht with the butt ends of muskets." After this affair the theatre was shut for a week.

Influence of the Audience on the Drama

The prevailingly aristocratic air of the theatre is shown by the way in which the well-born authors professed to toy with the writing of such plays as they produced, and not less markedly is this affectation stressed in the similar protestations vigorously made by those among the dramatists who, not born to the purple, penned their pieces commercially. Shadwell became notorious for the several declarations he published concerning the short space of time he spent in the composition of his comedies; so Ravenscroft affirms that "*A fortnights sickness did this Play produce*" when he penned a prologue for *The Citizen turn'd Gentleman* (D.G. 1672), Revet assures his readers that *The Town-Shifts* (L.I.F. 1671)

---

[1] Leslie Hotson, pp. 308–9, calculates that between 1695 and 1704 there were only 50 performances at Dorset Garden as against 1800 at Drury Lane.

[2] *A Brief Relation of State Affairs* (1857), II. 313–16.

was "thought on, begun, and finished, in a fortnight," while Payne pretends that *The Morning Ramble* (D.G. 1672) cost him but "*nine days' work*[1]."

In considering the influence of this audience, we should do well to pay special attention to a subject touched upon only incidentally in the preceding chapter. It is thoroughly characteristic that no play of the time was regarded as complete without the provision of both prologue and epilogue, and that almost as much effort was devoted to securing novel variety in these pieces as was given to the devising of new scenes[2]. Through the prologue and the epilogue the dramatist-poets displayed their wit; through such means the stage was kept in close touch with the auditorium; in most of the verses the tone is a familiar one, as of friend talking to friend, or wit to wit; intimacy is of their very being. Among the various studies designed to demonstrate the kinship between the theatre of Charles I and the theatre of Charles II, it is strange that this social vogue of the prologue should have been largely neglected[3], for nothing could more aptly indicate the similar tastes expressed by the audiences of the two periods. Whereas the Elizabethan prologues and epilogues were definitely attached to particular plays and certainly were regarded as no more than introductions and afterthoughts to the drama with which they were connected, their later seventeenth-century counterparts, whether of the period 1625–1642 or of the years 1660–1700, tended to be independent essays in verse capable of being spoken before or after any play, esteemed for their own worth and often instrumental in damning or making successful the performance during which they were delivered.

[1] See A. S. Borgman, *op. cit.* p. 25; the examples given above are there cited.

[2] Diverse aspects of this subject have been dealt with accurately and entertainingly by Autrey Nell Wiley in her *Rare Prologues and Epilogues, 1642–1700* (1940). See also her "The English Vogue of Prologues and Epilogues" (*Modern Language Notes*, 1932, XLVII. 255–7).

[3] There is one rather out-of-date *Study of the Prologue and Epilogue in English Literature from Shakespeare to Dryden* (1888), by G. S. Bowen.

The Theatre

The general picture of the Restoration playhouse has been rendered materially clearer by many studies recently devoted to a number of its peculiarities. We see now more clearly how the theatrical history of the time divides itself into marked sections. First come the years from the time of Charles' return in 1660 up to the Plague and the Fire— a period of tentative endeavour; then follows the full flourishing of the new drama from 1666 until 1679. In 1679 came a change. During August of the preceding year Titus Oates had revealed the existence of the Popish Plot, the ensuing months were feverish with political excitement and the atmosphere of the playhouse altered[1]. Spectators were more interested in practical affairs than in plays and consequently the receipts fell sharply; when some dramatists turned to write political tragedies and comedies several of them fell foul of the censorship, while party opposition was directed at others. Characteristically, such an author as Dryden, in presenting *The Kind Keeper* (D.G. 1678) to the reading public in 1680, felt it incumbent upon him to apologise for publishing his work "at so unseasonable a time."

During the earlier years only a few pieces are known to have suffered from the attentions of the censor[2], but after

---

[1] George W. Whiting, in "The Condition of the London Theatres, 1679–83" (*Modern Philology*, 1927, XXV. 195–206) and "Political Satire in London Stage Plays, 1680–83" (*id.* 1930, XXVIII. 29–43); Virgil L. Jones, "Methods of Satire in the Political Drama of the Restoration" (*Journal of English and Germanic Philology*, 1922, XXI. 662–9). Reference may also be made to an article by the present writer, "Political Plays of the Restoration" (*Modern Language Review*, 1921, XXI. 224–42). Louis I. Bredvold has a study of "Political Aspects of Dryden's *Amboyna* and *The Spanish Fryar*" (*University of Michigan Essays and Studies in English and Comparative Literature*, 1938).

[2] By good fortune the original manuscripts of the two works recorded in this connection have recently come to light and have been printed. F. S. Boas has edited Edward Howard's *The Change of Crownes* from a prompt-copy in private hands (1949) and Milton C. Nahm has presented the Worcester College text of Wilson's *The Cheats* (1935).

1679 the number rapidly increases[1]. This is not surprising when we observe the strong "Whig offensive" in the theatre with Dryden's anti-Catholic *The Spanish Fryar* (D.G. 1680), Lee's *Caesar Borgia* (D.G. 1679), Settle's *The Female Prelate* (D.L. 1679), as well as the anonymous *Coronation of Queen Elizabeth*, acted at Bartholomew and Southwark Fairs. In opposition came Otway's *The Souldiers Fortune* (D.G. 1680) and Crowne's *The Misery of Civil-War* (D.G. 1680), while Lee's *Lucius Junius Brutus* (D.G. 1680) and Tate's *The History of King Richard the Second* (D.L. 1680) were suppressed. Shortly after, Crowne's *Henry the Sixth* (D.G. 1681) and Shadwell's *The Lancashire Witches* (D.G. 1671) came under official disapproval, and the "loyal" dramatists produced several new works—D'Urfey's *Sir Barnaby Whigg* (D.L. 1681), Behn's *The Roundheads* (D.G. 1681), Tate's *The Ingratitude of a Common-Wealth* (D.L. 1681) and Ravenscroft's *The London Cuckolds* (D.G. 1681). Next came a run of plays with rebellion as their main theme—D'Urfey's *The Royalist* (D.G. 1682), Behn's *The City-Heiress* (D.G. 1682), Otway's *Venice Preserv'd* (D.G. 1682) and Southerne's *The Loyal Brother* (D.L. 1682)[2].

The year 1682 brings us to the union of the theatres, when poor audiences led to the many revivals of old plays and a consequent dearth of new tragedies and comedies, and this area of theatrical endeavour was not ended until a new

[1] Arthur F. White has provided an excellent survey in "The Office of Revels and Dramatic Censorship during the Restoration Period" (*Western Reserve Bulletin*, N.S. 1931, XXXIV. 5–45): useful analyses are here given of various censored dramas—Lee's *Lucius Junius Brutus*, Tate's *Richard II*, Shadwell's *The Lancashire Witches*, Crowne's *Henry VI* and *The City Politiques*, Dryden's *The Duke of Guise*, Banks' *Cyrus the Great*, *The Innocent Usurper* and *The Island Queens*. It is possible also that in the seventies *The Maid's Tragedy* was suppressed. In 1692 Dryden's *Cleomenes* was temporarily stopped at the command of Queen Mary.

[2] On political elements in Shadwell's plays see Albert S. Borgman, *Thomas Shadwell: His Life and Comedies* (1928), pp. 52–74 and in Southerne's, John Wendell Dodds, *Thomas Southerne, Dramatist* (1933), pp. 33–40. J. Harold Wilson, in "Satiric Elements in Rochester's *Valentinian*" (*Philological Quarterly*, 1937, XVI. 41–8), argues that Valentinian is a portrait of Charles and Maximus an image of the author himself. John Robert Moore discusses "Contemporary Satire in Otway's *Venice Preserved*" (*PMLA*, 1928, XLIII. 166–81).

audience provided the conditions necessary for the success of Betterton's secession in 1695. During this time note may well be taken of the rather peculiar development of the actor-playwright tradition. Jevon, Carlisle, Harris, Underhill, Haynes, Powell, Mountfort all come forward with their own plays during these years—preparing the way for the advent of Colley Cibber at the very end of the century.

To the staging of Restoration plays and to the influence of scenery upon dramatic technique much exploratory research has been devoted during recent years, and perhaps there is little more to be discovered, unless of course new documents or designs come to light[1]. Concerning the influence of the court masques given during the reign of Charles I there is now no doubt, especially since the discovery of Webb's designs has been more fully explored. These explorations show that within the constricted space of Rutland House Jones' follower endeavoured to apply the principles adopted in the latest of the masques and that he carried on these principles in his designs for the production of *Mustapha* at court.

Fortunately for this period we do have some pictorial evidence to guide us. Apart from the designs mentioned above, the frontispiece to *Ariane* gives us a definite idea of what the Theatre Royal looked like in 1674, although we must use our imagination to carry the "apron" well out beyond the small curving line which was all that the artist knew how to draw[2]; Wren's cross-section is almost certainly of this theatre;

[1] Montague Summers' *The Restoration Theatre* (1934) quotes much relevant material. The relationship of Restoration stage methods to methods used elsewhere is dealt with by Lily B. Campbell in *Scenes and Machines on the English Stage during the Renaissance* (1923) and by George R. Kernodle in *From Art to Theatre* (1944). Invaluable documentary evidence is presented in Eleanore Boswell's *The Restoration Court Stage (1660–1702)* (1932), while some interesting comments appear in Liselotte Heil's *Die Darstellung der englischen Tragödie zur Zeit Bettertons* (Düsseldorf, 1936). Other articles on special subjects are noted below. Many interesting contemporary comments on theatrical affairs are gathered together in *Plays about the Theatre in England* (1936), by Dane Farnsworth Smith.

[2] Writing on "A Restoration Opera Problem" (*TLS*, Sept. 26, 1929), W. J. Lawrence endeavoured to prove that this opera was Evelyn's "Italian opera in musiq" recorded for Jan. 5, 1673/4, that it was presented at court and that the engraving represents the Hall stage in Whitehall. Eleanore Boswell, pp. 111–12, demonstrates that this theory is quite untenable.

and *The Empress of Morocco* engravings (1673) give a picture of the stage at Dorset Garden. Other information comes both from the stage-directions in printed dramas and from those in playhouse texts. From these we can reconstruct the activity back-stage when the prompter's bell and whistle gave the signals for the striking up of music or the changing of scenes[1]. By the end of the century, spectacular show dominated over all else. The quotations given in the text from Settle's *The World in the Moon* may be supplemented by the announcement in *The Post Boy* for June 12–15, 1697:

Great Preparations are making for a new OPERA in the Playhouse in Dorset-Garden, of which there is great Expectation, the Scenes being several new Sets and of a moddel different from all that have been used in any Theatre whatever, being twice as high as any of their former Scenes. And the whole Decoration of the Stage not only infinitely beyond all the Opera's ever yet performed in England, but also by the acknowledgment of several Gentlemen that have Travell'd abroad, much exceeding all that has been seen on any of the Foreign Stages[2].

Obviously, one of the greatest difficulties at this time (as it was until the nineteenth century) must have been the provision of adequate illumination for the stage. Unfortunately there is little information here regarding the precise methods employed. We may assume that there were candles in the auditorium; we know that the "apron" was lit by great rings or branches of lights hung in front of the proscenium; and we have every reason to believe that footlights were in regular use. Even so, the light cast on the actors must have been faint—although, as one of the most distinguished of our theatre artists has wisely reminded us, the richness of contemporary decoration must have added considerably in increasing the illumination. "The ceilings alone were marvels of carving,

---

[1] William S. Clark, "Restoration Prompt Notes and Stage Practices" (*Modern Language Notes*, 1936, LI. 226–30); Montague Summers, *Restoration Theatre*, pp. 114–15.

[2] Substantiation for the supposition put forward on pp. 35–6 of the present volume that scenes constructed for one play were frequently used for others appears in Thomas B. Stroup's "Scenery for *The Indian Queen*" (*Modern Language Notes*, 1937, LII. 408–9). The stage direction in *Tyrannick Love* (T.R. 1669), "an Indian cave," refers to a set in *The Indian Queen* (T.R. 1664).

gilded and coloured, which acted as reflectors to the candle-light. What wasn't a looking-glass was a lustre; what not a lustre a spangle[1]."

In most plays simulation of darkness was no doubt secured by the means used for that effect as far back as the days of Shakespeare's Globe: when an actor came on stage with a candle or a lamp he was supposed to be entering into a darkened area and if the candle or lamp was extinguished the imaginative darkness became complete. Thus, for example, in Wycherley's *The Plain-Dealer* (D.L. 1676), Olivia enters with a candle and puts it out: thereafter total darkness is presumed until a couple of sailors come in with torches. Here we have to do with a simple convention; but it seems impossible now to determine what Charles D'Avenant means when, in his *Circe* (D.G. 1677), he says "*The Stage is wholly darken'd*," when the text of the operatic *Tempest* (D.G. 1674) declares that "*the whole House is darken'd*," when that of *The Prophetess* (D.G. 1690) notes that "*The Stage is darkened on a sudden*." Even if the footlights could have been sunk or covered—and for that there is no evidence—the result would certainly not have produced any very appreciable diminution of light[2]. Here perhaps is an insoluble problem.

The comparatively rare use of the curtain in the Restoration theatre is perhaps to be explained partly by the declaration of Claude Perrault, in his *Les dix livres d'architecture de Vitruve* (1673), that the ancients were behind the moderns in their handling of stage scenery and that because they could not alter their sets sufficiently quickly they were forced to make use of a curtain, the *siparium*. More probably, however, the fact was that the late seventeenth-century playhouse was still too close to the old Elizabethan to be able to establish a new tradition. How close was that tie has recently been demonstrated, for it has been shown[3] that, in addition to the front curtain, some

---

[1] Edward Gordon Craig, *Books and Theatres* (1925), essay on "Candle-light," p. 140.

[2] See Summers, *Restoration Theatre*, pp. 270-6. He assumes that the floats were lowered.

[3] William S. Clark, "Corpses, Concealments, and Curtains on the Restoration Stage" (*Review of English Studies*, 1937, XIII. 438-48).

of the theatres at least had a kind of traverse placed among the wings, a relic of the traverse of former times. In Dryden's *The Duke of Guise* (D.G. 1682) this is specifically called the "Traverse"; in other plays, such as Ravenscroft's *Titus Andronicus* (D.L. 1686) it is named "a Curtain." Normally used for the revelation of dead bodies, these mid-scene hangings could be put to a variety of uses quite distinct from those for which the front curtain was employed.

If such a device points backward, the device of the drop curtain, described in *The Prophetess* (D.G. 1690) points definitely forward. In Act III of this opera "*A Curtain falls representing the entrance into the inner parts of a Magnificent Pallace*"; later, in Act IV, the same "*Great Curtain*" is used and, when a magic wand is waved thrice, rises to the sound of soft music, revealing another set behind[1].

During recent years another subject which has attracted a good deal of attention is that of the songs and musical interludes introduced so freely into plays of the time[2]. This is an important theme, since these were the days when the continental opera became established in England and when the model was being shaped for the native ballad opera.

[1] Noted by Summers, *Restoration Stage*, p. 101. Among other plays the texts of which indicate a curtain raising immediately after the prologue may be noted: Howard and Dryden's *The Indian-Queen* (T.R. 1664), Settle's *Cambyses* (L.I.F. 1671), Ravenscroft's *The Citizen turn'd Gentleman* (D.G. 1672), Rochester's *Valentinian* (D.L. 1684) and Dryden's *Love Triumphant* (D.L. 1694), Payne's *The Fatal Jealousie* (D.G. 1672), D'Urfey's *Don Quixote I* (D.G. 1694), Crowne's *The Destruction of Jerusalem* (D.L. 1677). And to those which record a curtain fall at the close may be added Behn's *The Amorous Prince* (L.I.F. 1671), Payne's *The Fatal Jealousie* (D.G. 1672), Pordage's *The Siege of Babylon* (D.G. 1677) and Banks' *Cyrus the Great* (L.I.F. 1695).

[2] Robert Gale Noyes, "Conventions of Song in Restoration Tragedy" (*PMLA*, 1938, LIII. 162–88); "Songs from Restoration Drama in Contemporary and Eighteenth-century Poetical Miscellanies" (*ELH*, 1936, III. 291–361); "Contemporary Musical Settings of the Songs in Restoration Drama" (*ELH*, 1934, I. 325–411); "Contemporary Musical Settings of the Songs in Restoration Dramatic Operas" (*Harvard Studies and Notes in Philology and Literature*, 1938, XX). Willard Thorp has prepared an anthology of this material, *Songs from the Restoration Theatre* (1934). Among the increasing library on Purcell and the early opera there may be noted here, in addition to J. A. Westrup's excellent study of that master's work (*Purcell*, 1937), an article by Roy Lamson Jr. on "Henry Purcell's Dramatic Songs and the English Broadside Ballad" (*PMLA*, 1938, LIII. 148–61). Summers, *The Restoration Theatre*, pp. 108–18, discusses the question of music in plays.

CHAPTER TWO

TRAGEDY

I. *Restoration Tragedy and Comedy: Introductory*

ON turning from the audience and the theatre to the actual dramatic works written during the reigns of Charles, James and William, we seem at first to meet with a totally different productivity from what we should have expected. The comedy of manners and the coarser comedy of humours were certainly reflexes of the gay immoral aristocratic life of the age. Nothing could more perfectly have mirrored the upper-class life of the time than the comedy of Etherege and of Congreve: nothing could have pictured more faithfully the debased standards of social existence than plays such as *The Squire of Alsatia*. Opera, also, we might have been prepared for, because in opera we see the quintessence of music, song, show and dance—precisely those things which, we found, appealed to a vast majority of the play-going public of the epoch. But neither opera nor comedy at all exhausts the dramatic productivity of these forty years: there is left out of account that most characteristic of all the Restoration theatrical species, the heroic tragedy. This heroic tragedy is obviously a thing entirely apart from the comedy of gay licentious manners. With its flaunting honour and its impossibly idealistic love passions, it seems indeed so far away both from that comedy and from social life as we have seen it displayed in the theatre that it would appear impossible to find any link between them. Our first impulse might rather be to dismiss the whole of the heroic tragedy as a foreign innovation, or at any rate as a forced half-artificial flower, raised by the false taste of Charles and dying a natural death about the year 1677.

There are, however, two or three things which must give
us to pause. Even although many critics have thus regarded
the heroic tragedy, we must remember that Charles was
intensely of his age. He rarely forced on his courtiers anything they did not want, probably he could not have forced
it upon them. In embracing the heroic species, therefore,
we may be sure that he was but reflecting the attitude and
expressing the desires of his time. This belief is further
strengthened when we notice the obvious popularity of that
tragedy, not only during its recognised reign (1664–77) but
even for many years after. Sedley might crack jokes at some
follies in Orrery's *The General*[1]: Arrowsmith in *The Reformation* (D.G. 1673) might write elaborate burlesque on
the species[2]: Shadwell, who was no tragic expert, might
ridicule the love and honour rants in prologue and in epilogue[3]:
Edward Howard, as early as Shadwell, might rate against
heroic rime and "the wresting in of Dances, when unnatural
and improper to the business of the Scene and Plot[4]":
Buckingham and others might plan a *Rehearsal* in 1665 and
bring it on the stage in 1671: Duffett might be commissioned
by the Theatre Royal to write a satire on *The Empress of
Morocco* acted by the Duke's company: others, not much

---

[1] Pepys, Wed. Sept. 28, 1664.
[2] Especially IV. i.
[3] The prologue to his first play, *The Sullen Lovers* (L.I.F. 1668) makes
fun of the "*Love and Honour Feast*": the epilogue to *The Miser* (T.R. in
B.St. 1672) attacks the school of rime: the epilogue to *The Virtuoso* (D.G.
1676) speaks of

"*A dull Romantick whining Play:*
Where poor frail Woman's made a Deity,
With senseless amorous Idolatry,
And snivelling Heroes sigh, and pine, and cry.
Though singly they beat Armies, and huff Kings,
Rant at the Gods, and do impossible Things;
Though they can laugh at Danger, Blood, and Wounds;
Yet if the Dame once chides, the Milk-sop Heroe swoons.
Those doughty Things nor Manners have, nor Wit;
We ne'er saw Hero fit to drink with yet":

and in *The History of Timon of Athens* (D.G. 1678) in I. i it is noticeable
that, in the person of the poet, Shadwell aims a direct attack upon the
supporters of the popular tragedy.
[4] *The Usurper* (T.R. in B.St. 1664), preface (written probably in
1667).

inclined to the heroic species, like Ravenscroft[1] and New-castle[2], might take up the anti-heroic cue: even definitely heroic writers such as Settle in his *Ibrahim* (D.G. 1676)[3] might show quite plainly their realisation that they were not suiting themselves, but simply giving the public what it wanted. We may marshal quite a small army of anti-heroic utterances from such diverse quarters, but none of them, not all of them taken together, can dispute the fact that the heroic tragedy was popular and that its characters, scenes and emotions were continued long after the year 1677 rang the death-knell of rime.

Nor is it possible, even, to make any sharp division between the tragic dramatists and the comic dramatists of the age. Some men, like Nat Lee, wrote nothing but tragedies: others, like Etherege, wrote nothing but comedies: but the most noticeable figures, Dryden, Otway, Congreve, even men like Crowne and D'Urfey, shared serious and light emotion, turning easily from one to the other world as if familiar with both. The two worlds are as utterly different as could possibly be imagined, that we must confess. In Elizabethan times romantic comedy and romantic tragedy, realistic comedy and realistic tragedy, had not been overfar apart. We can compare Rosalind and Juliet, even women of the realistic comedy and

---

[1] The preface to his *The Careless Lovers* (D.G. 1673) is directed against "*Siedges and Opera's*" and the epilogue is on the same theme:

> "*They that observe the Humors of the* Stage,
> *Find* Fools *and* Heroes *best do please this Age,*
> *But both grown so extravagant, I scarse*
> *Can tell, if* Fool *or* Hero *makes the better Farce:*
> *As for Example, take our* Mamamouchi,
> *And then* Almansor, *that so much did touch ye,*
> *That bully* Hero, *that did kill and slay,*
> *And conquer ye* Ten Armies *in one Day.*"

[2] See Act III of *The Triumphant Widow, or, The Medley of Humours* (D.G. 1674) where the Musician is made to say: "Come, Sir, go on, I love Tragedy, especially Heroick. Oh, it does chime, and make the finest noise, 'tis no matter whether it be sense or no, so it be Heroick."

[3] Epilogue:

> "*How many has our Rhimer kill'd to day?*
> *What need of* Siege *and* Conquest *in a Play,*
> *When* Love *can do the work as well as they?*"

Alice Arden, and feel that there are points of resemblance between them. Can the same be said for Florimel and Almahide? Yet our task is clear: the tragedy of the heroic sort cannot be dissociated from its age: it must be explained not as an isolated phenomenon, as a dramatic species out of touch with its time, but as an integral part of Restoration theatrical endeavour.

On a more close examination of the characteristics of tragedy and comedy during this period, the difficulties which at first seem to confront one from every side begin gradually to vanish. Not all the features of Restoration comedy and tragedy can be explained by a reference to the changed and changing spirit of the age, but the main basis of that comedy and of that tragedy ultimately depends upon the altered tastes and temper of the epoch. The Elizabethan age had been infused with an intangible but ever-present spirit of heroism, a heroism that displayed itself in the exploits of Drake and of Ralegh, in the ardour of those common seamen whose courage sent scattering the mighty pride of the Spanish Armada, in the noble chivalric conceptions of Spenser. The age, if coarse, was accustomed to see actions that were instinct with courage and with faith. The doughty temper thus developed penetrated through all ranks of society, from the aristocrats of the court down to the lower rabble who stood chattering in the pit of the theatres. That there was a gradual weakening of that spirit after 1600 is readily demonstrable, but it gave to our literature, from 1580 onwards to near the outbreak of the Civil War, a certain dignity and nobility of romance. With romance and nobility around them in real life, the audiences at the Blackfriars and at the Globe were content to witness romance and nobility in tragedy and in comedy, a romance and a nobility not far removed from that of their actual experience. The quiet courage of *As You Like It*, the awful nobility of *Othello*, the perfect gentlemanliness of *The English Traveller*—all these are but reflexes of ordinary life. Many an Elizabethan lady must have seen herself in Rosalind: the courage and the faith of Othello is mirrored in the lives of countless sixteenth century soldiers:

not all the gallants who returned from the continent were *inglesi italianati—diavoli incarnati.*

In Jonson on the one hand and in Beaumont and Fletcher on the other, however, we may trace the evidence of a weakening of this temper. Romance in Beaumont and Fletcher is not the earlier Shakespearian romance: it is removed one step further from real life: and Jonson's comedy of humours displays before us, not the dignity of happy lives, but all the follies and the vices which he may have seen gathering force around him. Already with these men a greater cleavage is being made between comedy and tragedy: the one growing more and more obsessed with lives not tinged by courage and nobility, the other moving to realms far distant from contemporary England. Shakespeare's Italy, Denmark and Scotland are real to us: his Bohemia, influenced by the later romance, as well as Beaumont and Fletcher's "Cicilie" are wholly unreal and imaginary.

By the time of the Restoration this cleavage was complete. The audiences were no longer noble in temper, and consequently the heroic tragedy, removed a further stage from the actual, may be regarded as the true child of the enervation that had come over England. The age was debilitated: it was distinctly unheroic: and yet it was not so cynical as to throw over entirely the inculcation of heroism. To present, however, heroism in real-life plays would have raised too sharp a distinction between what was and what might have been, and accordingly in the heroic tragedy heroism is cast out of the world altogether and carried to an Eastern or an antique realm of exaggerated emotions, mythical and hopelessly ideal. The heroic play is like a Tale of a Land of No-where. We are interested in that land, but we do not hope ever to enter therein. The persons who move and speak there are not our equals, nor do they even draw the same breath as we do. Drake might have felt more than a little of himself in Tamburlaine, in Othello: Rochester could never dream that he was Almanzor or Charles that he was Maximin. The heroic tragedy, then, may be regarded as the very symbol of its time, with, attached to it, many other subordinate aspects.

Opera was of its kin, and the fanciful adaptations of Shakespeare's plays—everywhere an endeavour to move from the ideally real to the hopelessly impossible. It is to be observed, also, that this contrast is to be noticed not only between the Elizabethan and the Restoration plays, but between the English Restoration characters and the persons of the corresponding plays of the continent. In this connection M. L. Charlanne has drawn an interesting parallel between Félix and Maximin, and between Bérénice and Pauline.

Au lieu de ces hommes (he says referring to Félix) *vraiment hommes, auxquels nous nous assimilons parfois et que nous voudrions pouvoir égaler toujours, nous n'avons plus, chez Dryden, que des héros sans âme, chaleur et sans vie, des automates enfin* (and of the heroines) *ni shakespeariennes, ni cornéliennes, raciniennes moins encore, ces héroines sont sans intérêt, parce que sans passions: leur sein est toujours froid, leurs sens sont toujours calmes, et leur cœur toujours maître de ces émotions....Ce sont des héroïnes de roman, ce ne sont pas des femmes*[1].

Much as the dramatists might make their heroes and their heroines unreal, however, they knew that the audience did not desire at the Theatre Royal or at the Duke's playhouse an entirely impossible drama alone. They had inherited from the earlier period, not only the heroic romance of Beaumont and Fletcher, but the Jonsonian realistic and satiric comedy of humours. In comedy, therefore, they demanded a reflex of their own gay immoral lives as well as a series of plays full of personal satire. The comedy of manners was the answer to this demand, faithfully reproducing the upper-class wit, licentiousness and social ideals of the time. Almanzor and Courtal are the two twin symbols of the age.

Lampoons flooded the town in the late seventeenth century. Men of the court could pen indecent verses even on the King, calling him "old Rowley" to his face and describing in grossest terms his intercourse with the Duchess of Cleveland and Nell Gwyn. There is no lack of evidence that inwardly the courtiers and the wits saw the evils of their own time, but probably they cared less about the evils than about the follies.

---

[1] *L'influence française en Angleterre au xvii⁰ siècle* (Paris, 1906), pp. 464–5.

Accordingly any play that satirised a contemporary silliness was almost sure of success. The would-be wits, the old gentleman who professed to admire the days of good Queen Bess, the virtuosi, the country bumpkins, all of these were ridiculed. Of all that was not fine, elegant and witty the gallants made free sport. On the other hand, of any satire which attacked themselves or their ways the gallants were suspicious. There are few *milites gloriosi* on the Restoration stage, precisely because at least some of the courtiers have come down in history with the stain of cowardice on their names. Dryden's *Mr Limberham*, because it attacked the "crying sin of keeping," was given as cold a reception by the audience as possible, in spite of the fun and the wit which some modern critics profess to find in it. Smerk in Shadwell's *The Lancashire Witches* was a satire of the characteristics of many Anglican clerics, and was banned the stage. Occasionally only was burlesque of the gallants permitted:—when the burlesque was exclusively personal, and even then the nobleman or knight who was thus singled out could take dire vengeance[1]. Shadwell's *The Sullen Lovers* owed its contemporary success to its portraits of the Howards, and, as the victims themselves did not protest, evidently no one else did.

Impossible heroics, faithful reflections of upper-class social life, satire of everything not associated with their own existence or satire of members of their own circle so long as that satire was purely personal and not general—such were the things demanded by the audience of the Restoration: such the tendencies which made up the heroic tragedy and the comedy of manners.

---

[1] Thus Kynaston was beaten for acting in *The Heiress* "in abuse of Sedley" on Sat. Jan. 30, 1668/9 (see Pepys, Mon. Feb. 1, 1668/9). On Thurs. Mar. 4 of the same year, Pepys heard that Buckingham and Sir Robert Howard were writing a play to abuse Sir William Coventry, who declared he would slit the nose of any actor who offended him (see also Sat. Mar. 6). On Nov. 4, 1675, the Lord Chamberlain issued an order declaring that Haines should be suspended because he had "with ill & scandalous language & insolent carriage abused Sir Edmund Windham." Mrs Slade was suspended similarly on Nov. 25 of the same year (P.R.O., L.C. 5/141, pp. 287 and 294).

II. *Elizabethan and Foreign Influences*

Although the spirit of the age does not explain everything, it explains a good deal, so that when we turn to the actual tragedies produced we find that it is the social atmosphere rather than anything else which interprets these works for us. On the other hand, we must never forget the influence of past literary models, of cognate forms of literature, of contemporary foreign plays and of current philosophies upon the cosmopolitan and intellectual courtier-poets who surrounded King Charles. "Perhaps at no period," remarks one writer justly [1], "was the English drama subjected to such a medley of influences as during the Restoration." The force of all of these must be duly assessed; the only trap into which we can fall is to assume that the serious drama of the time was created and fashioned by any one among these models to the total or virtual exclusion of the others.

When the theatres opened, naturally the repertoire was composed entirely of plays from the pre-Commonwealth era, and these inevitably set their imprint on the works of the new dramatists. Limiting ourselves to the few formative years between the re-establishment of the Stuart stage and its closure because of the Plague, we find a widely representative collection of such earlier tragedies and tragi-comedies [2], and to these theatrical records must be added evidence which points to even greater influence than that exercised by the performances in the theatre. Again and again we find Restoration dramatists turning to the printed texts of pre-Commonwealth plays for situations and characters, and there is good reason to believe that some authors at least freely exploited the treasury of unprinted manuscript material still extant in those years [3].

[1] Cecil V. Deane, *Dramatic Theory and the Rhymed Heroic Play* (1931), p. 221.

[2] For the repertoires of the individual companies see Appendix A.

[3] This has been demonstrated in a brilliant article by Alfred Harbage, "Elizabethan-Restoration Palimpsest" (*Modern Language Review*, 1940, xxxv. 287–319).

Shakespeare's influence may be taken for granted: the record of productions, the innumerable references to his works and, paradoxically, the many stage adaptations of his plays amply testify to the esteem in which he was held. It is true that, to a certain extent, Shakespeare's position must have been somewhat like his position to-day, when we flock to see his tragedies on the stage but never dream of imitating them in our modern plays; yet, when we observe that such an author as Granville, in the preface to his *Heroick Love* (L.I.F. 1697), conceives the Moor of Venice as a "Hero" in the Restoration sense of that word, we are compelled to believe that something at least of the magniloquent grandeur of Almanzor and Cambyses may have been drawn from observation of the Shakespearian tragic characters[1].

With Shakespeare come several other "Elizabethan" dramatists. Massinger is important, if only because of the contemporary success of *The Bondman* and *The Virgin Martyr*[2], and Jonson, even although his tragedies are of less significance than his comedies, is not to be neglected[3]. True, Jonson's classicism was not of the kind likely to appeal very strongly to Restoration taste and no doubt many during these years shared Pepys' views when he described *Catiline* as "a play of much good sense and words to read, but that do appear the worst upon the stage, I mean, the least diverting[4]": on the other hand, it must not be forgotten that this very production of *Catiline* seems to have been one sponsored by an influential body of wits and graced with costumes provided by royalty

[1] For references on the Shakespeare adaptations see *infra*, pp. 171–80.

[2] See James G. McManaway, "Philip Massinger and the Restoration Drama" (*ELH*, 1934, I. 276–304) and Charles E. Ward, "Massinger and Dryden" (*ELH*, 1935, III. 263–6). The latter discusses the indebtedness of *Tyrannick Love* to *The Virgin Martyr*. Alwin Thaler, in "Thomas Heywood, D'Avenant and *The Siege of Rhodes*" (*PMLA*, 1924, XXXIX. 624–41), demonstrates how *The Fair Maid of the West*, by Massinger's fellow-dramatist, Heywood, aided in fashioning the earliest of Restoration heroic operas. Louis B. Wright has "Notes on Thomas Heywood's Later Reputation" (*Review of English Studies*, 1928, IV. 135–44)—showing that he was by no means forgotten.

[3] See Robert Gale Noyes, *Ben Jonson on the English Stage, 1660–1776* (1935), and W. D. Briggs, "The Influence of Jonson's Tragedy in the Seventeenth Century" (*Anglia*, 1911–12, XXXV. 277–337).

[4] Dec. 19, 1668.

itself[1]. With these early dramatists, too, may be noted Webster and Ford; the revivals of *The Duchess of Malfi*, *The White Devil* and *'Tis Pity She's A Whore* remind us that the tragedy of blood also played its part in the formation of the heroic species.

Still more popular were the plays of Beaumont and Fletcher. Dryden tells us that their works were given stage representation far beyond that accorded to any other among the older authors[2]. In these plays dramatic romance was given a new turn, a fresh conception of tragi-comedy was introduced and the spirit of courtly convention was at least adumbrated. No doubt, the wits of 1660 felt a vast gulf yawning between themselves and the wits of 1620, yet nevertheless there was much in the Fletcherian drama which harmonised with their own aims and they freely borrowed from this source. It is characteristic that when that libertine rake, the Earl of Rochester, essayed a tragedy he turned to *Valentinian*, content to base his dramatic writing on Fletcher but heightening the love interest in heroic manner[3]; similarly in *Love Triumphant* (D.L. 1693) Dryden heroicised *A King and No King*[4].

Of even greater importance still is the kind of play which ultimately developed out of the "Beaumont and Fletcher" style. During those early years of the Restoration we find evidently popular revivals of many mid-seventeenth century dramas now almost completely forgotten. Here are *Argalus*

---

[1] On Dec. 11, 1667, Pepys was informed by Harris that the King was giving the company £500 "for robes"; this money was not forthcoming on Jan. 11, 1667/8, but probably had been secured for the production on Dec. 18, 1668, since Pepys specifically mentions that it was "most fine in clothes."

[2] This is confirmed by such stage records as we have. Dryden's comment appears in the *Essay of Dramatick Poesie*. Genest, VI. 39–62, computes that in 1668 two plays of Fletcher were acted to one of Shakespeare; in 1710 the proportion was about even; by the beginning of the new century barely a couple of Fletcher's dramas were on the acting list. An important study is A. C. Sprague's *Beaumont and Fletcher on the Restoration Stage* (1926). J. H. Wilson surveys *The Influence of Beaumont and Fletcher on Restoration Drama* (1928), and J. W. Tupper examines "The Relation of the Heroic Play to the Romances of Beaumont and Fletcher" (*PMLA*, 1905, xx).

[3] J. H. Wilson, "Rochester's *Valentinian* and Heroic Sentiment" (*ELH*, 1937, IV. 265–73).

[4] Edwin Schröder, *Drydens letztes Drama* (Rostock, 1905).

and *Parthenia, Love's Mistress, Brennoralt, Love and Honour, Aglaura*—and these tell a definite story. The Platonic mode, so ardently cultivated by Henrietta Maria and by the courtiers of Charles I, was being carried on, if in altered terms, into the world of the courtiers of Charles II[1]. The latter might look back with a certain contempt upon their immediate ancestors, yet nevertheless they felt an affinity in temper with them. They enjoyed what those forefathers of theirs had enjoyed: the romance that they sought was only a development of the romance that had already appeared on the stages of the earlier theatres. "The basis of Restoration tragedy," it has been wisely said, "is the Romantic idea[2]." The impossible Platonic love, the conflict of passion and honour, the distant scenes of countries unknown or idealised, all these were taken from the dramas produced at the court of Charles I.

On the other hand, we must avoid the error of assuming that influences apart from this were of small importance. If the basis of Restoration tragedy is the romantic idea, it is equally true that this romanticism was accompanied by a strong inclination towards the classic concepts. The severer sort of classicism did not largely appeal, but Seneca was taken over by Dryden and Lee for their *Œdipus* (D.G. 1678), and several translations of his works testify to his popularity. The atmosphere of blood and horror here, and the ghosts, which duly appeared in Restoration plays in free supernatural profusion, harmonised with native strains. Italian *melodramma*, itself

[1] The significance of this Platonic mode has been excellently stressed by Kathleen M. Lynch in *The Social Mode of Restoration Comedy* (1926). In this she traces the continuity between the drama of 1630–1640 and that of 1660–1680. W. S. Clark, in "The Platonic Element in the Restoration Play" (*PMLA*, 1930, XLV. 623–6) and "The Sources of the Restoration Heroic Drama" (*Review of English Studies*, 1928, IV. 49–63) takes issue with her views and emphasises the strong French influence on the later stage, but his arguments are challenged by K. M. Lynch in "Conventions of Platonic Drama in the Heroic Plays of Orrery and Dryden" (*PMLA*, 1929, XLIV. 456–71). Alfred Harbage, in his study of Thomas Killigrew, stresses the formative influence exerted by that author's early dramas, heavily coloured by Platonic sentiments. The same author has an excellent account of the early seventeenth-century stage—*Cavalier Drama* (1936).

[2] Bonamy Dobrée, *Restoration Tragedy, 1660–1720* (1929), p. 29. Mario Praz has an essay on "Il dramma inglese della Restaurazione e i suoi aspetti preromantici" (*La Cultura*, 1933, XII).

classical in inspiration if baroque in execution, contributed to the unreality of the themes and to the development of operatic features[1]. D'Avenant owed the inspiration for his Commonwealth productions indirectly at least to Italy, and although the development of "Heroique Story in Stilo *Recitativo*[2]" was not to be largely pursued until the eighteenth century, the influence of Italian music and of Italian operatic art was felt in England during the latter part of the Restoration period, both in dramatic operas and in spoken tragedies. Only one of Purcell's pieces, certainly, is in recitative[3], but *The Siege of Rhodes* was sung even when Evelyn heard it on May 5, 1659. Recitative was introduced by Bannister into Stapylton's *The Slighted Maid* (L.I.F. 1663), and *Ariane*, produced in French in 1673/4, was called by Evelyn an Italian opera in music[4]. Later, in 1686, Quinault's *Cadmus et Hermione* seems to have been presented at the Duke's Theatre[5]. Italian and French singers arrived year by year to teach English audiences something of continental charm long before the appearance of "Seignior *Rampony*" and "Don *Sigismondo Fideli*" at the turn of the century. Pepys informs us that "the Italian Signor Batista [Draghi]" had "composed a play in Italian for the Opera, which T. Killigrew do intend to have up[6]," while a few months later, on Oct. 12, 1668, at the Theatre Royal, we find the diaryist in raptures over "the Eunuch who, it seems, is a Frenchman, but long bred in Italy[7]." Thus Italian singers, Italian music, Italian scenery and the plots of Italian operas also played their part in the development of Restoration tragic endeavour.

Naturally, however, of all outside influences on the English theatre of this time that of France is most important, not only

---

[1] Edward J. Dent has a most useful study of *The Foundations of English Opera* (1928). See also C. L. Myers, "Opera in England from 1656 to 1728" (*Western Reserve University Bulletin*, 1906, IX) and W. J. Lawrence, "Foreign Singers and Musicians at the Court of Charles II" (*Musical Quarterly*, 1923, IX. 217–25). The most recent work is E. W. White's *The Rise of English Opera* (1951).

[2] *The Play-House to be Lett* (L.I.F. c. 1663).   [3] *Dido and Æneas* (1689).

[4] Presumably he was referring to a rehearsal of *Ariane*.

[5] See Appendix C, under Quinault.   [6] Feb. 12, 1666/7.

[7] See also Oct. 14, when this "Eunuch" appeared in *The Faithful Shepherdess*.

because Paris was in closer touch with London than any other continental capital, but also because of the greater ease in obtaining French books. The French romance, both the earlier kind of pastoral romance typical in Honoré D'Urfé's *Astrée* (1607–1627) and of the later heroic *romans*, is here of prime significance. Madeleine de Scudéry's *Artamène ou le Grand Cyrus, Ibrahim, ou l'illustre Bassa* (1641) and *Clélie* (1654–1660), Georges de Scudéry's epic *Alaric, ou Rome vaincu* (1654), Gauthier de la Calprenède's *Cassandre* (1642–1645), *Cléopâtre* (1645–1658) and *Pharamond* (1661), Marie-Madeleine de La Fayette's *La Princesse de Clèves* (1678), Armand Desmarets de Saint-Sorlin's *Ariane* (1643) and Maria Le Roy Gomberville's *Polexandre* (1641) all were widely read and all provided suggestions for plot and character[1]. Nor must we forget in this connection such English works as Orrery's *Parthenissa* (1654)—to which Lee went for material when penning his *Sophonisba* (D.L. 1675)—works not only influenced by French romances but almost indistinguishable from these.

This was the time, of course, when the new classical tragedy was being shaped in France, and naturally this also came to influence the English playwrights, even although hardly one

---

[1] I have been unable to obtain a copy of H. W. Hill's *La Calprenède's Romances and the Restoration Drama* (1911). On this subject see A. H. Upham, *The French Influence in English Literature* (1903), pp. 365 ff.; L. Charlanne, *L'influence française en Angleterre au dixseptième siècle* (1906), pp. 387–404; and Cecil V. Deane, *Dramatic Theory and the Rhymed Heroic Play* (1931), pp. 4–16. A. E. Parsons, in "The English Heroic Play" (*Modern Language Review*, 1938, XXXIII. 1–14), stresses the great use made of French romances before 1642. Alwin Thaler discusses *Ibrahim* in "Thomas Heywood, D'Avenant and *The Siege of Rhodes*" (*PMLA*, 1924, XXXIX. 624–41); Jerome W. Schweitzer, in "Another Note on Dryden's Use of Georges de Scudéry's *Almahide*" (*Modern Language Notes*, 1947, LXII. 262–3), denies that *The Conquest of Granada* owes anything to *Ibrahim* but shows its prime indebtedness to *Almahide*; Otto Auer (*Über einige Dramen Nathaniel Lees mit besonderer Berücksichtigung seiner Beziehung zum französischen heroisch-galanten Roman*, Berlin, 1904) examines Lee's use of *Clélie* for his *Lucius Junius Brutus*. The situations taken from these sources are numerous. Among the most important are: Dryden's *The Indian Queen* (*Polexandre, Cassandre, Cléopâtre*); his *The Indian Emperour* (from the same sources); his *Tyrannick Love* (*Alaric*); his *The Conquest of Granada* (*Almahide*); Banks' *Cyrus the Great* (*Artamène*); his *The Rival Kings* (*Cassandre*); Settle's *Ibrahim* (*Ibrahim*); Behn's *The Young King* (*Cléopâtre*); Lee's *Gloriana* (*Cléopâtre*); his *Lucius Junius Brutus* (*Clélie*); his *The Princess of Cleve* (*La Princesse de Clèves*); his *Theodosius* (*Pharamond*); and his *The Rival Queens* (*Cassandre*).

of them was prepared to construct his work absolutely on the Parisian model. Already in 1637 Joseph Rutter had produced a translation of *Le Cid*—within a year of its appearance across the Channel. This fact in itself shows how eagerly the courtiers of Charles I looked to what was being accomplished by their French fellows, and the eagerness was even the greater among their descendants, men who had had an opportunity, during their exile, of attending performances on the French stage and of discussing the new plays in their original home.

It must, however, be remembered that what the English dramatists knew when they started to work was not the tragedy of Racine but the experimental drama of Corneille. At the Restoration, the former was fifty-four years of age, with his greatest triumphs behind him; the latter's first play, *La Thébaïde*, was not to come until 1664. Thus during the formative period it was Corneille's example which was set up before the English dramatists; Racine's example only later came to be known, dimly appreciated and vaguely followed. To this must be added the fact that, although there were many Gallomanes in London, most authors preserved a severely critical attitude towards the French theatre. Even in 1663 D'Avenant could pick numerous faults in Parisian tragedy:

> The *French* convey their Arguments too much
> In Dialogue: their Speeches are too long.
> Such length of Speeches seem not so unpleasing
> As the Contracted Walks of their Designs[1].

Dryden's remarks, made somewhat later, follow the same line. While recognising both the "modishness" of the French drama and some of its unquestioned excellences, he maintains a stout patriotic front to the foreigner and acknowledges his indebtedness mainly to the English tradition.

The assimilation and popularisation of this French serious drama was accomplished in two ways—by direct translation and by free adaptation on the usual Restoration lines. The first was to aid in establishing the rimed couplet as the chief tragic medium for a period of some fourteen years; the other, with one or two exceptions, was destined largely to intensify

[1] *The Play-House to Be Lett* (L.I.F. 1663), Act I.

the elements taken over from the pre-Commonwealth stage. Rimed renderings of the *Pompée* (1643) of Pierre Corneille appeared in the early years of the Restoration age, one by Katherine Philips (Smock Alley, Dublin, 1663) and another by Waller and a group of aristocratic wits (L.I.F. 1664). Mrs Philips also left a translation of *Horace* (1640), a translation completed by Denham and produced at court in 1668 and at the Theatre Royal in 1669. *Héraclius* (1646) was Englished by Carlell and by an anonymous author (L.I.F. 1664); Dauncer issued his version of *Nicomède* (1651) in 1671[1]. All of these, particularly those of the sixties, must have exercised a definite influence on the developing Restoration serious drama, although unquestionably in their unadapted forms they were too chill to be popular on the stage. Philippe Quinault, perhaps, was nearer to the English temper than Corneille. *La généreuse ingratitude* (1657) had given name and plot to Lower's *The Noble Ingratitude* of 1659, and its central theme was utilised by Corye for *The Generous Enemies* in 1671. *Agrippa, roi d'Albe* (1660) was freely adapted by Dauncer in his *Agrippa, King of Alba* (T.R. Dublin, ?1674), and later Gildon's *Phaeton* (D.L. 1698) was taken directly from the similarly named French opera of 1683. The introduction of Racine to the English stage does not come until Crowne's *Andromache* (D.G. 1674), based on *Andromaque* (1667) and Otway's *Titus and Berenice* (D.G. 1676), similarly based on *Bérénice* (1671). For a serious attempt to develop an English tragic style on his model we must wait until the eighteenth century.

This French tragedy of the reign of Louis XIV, the *melodramma* of Italy, the heroic play of England, the French romance were but so many aspects of a general European movement; and while often we cannot disentangle the separate threads of influence, we shall not be far wrong in saying that the English theatrical representative of this wider movement results mainly from an extension of already existing English elements altered to suit the temper of the age,

---

[1] See A. Mulert, *Pierre Corneille in der englischen Übersetzungs-Literatur des xvii-en Jahrhunderts* (Erlangen, 1900); D. F. Canfield, *Corneille and Racine in England* (1904); F. Y. Eccles, *Racine in England* (1922).

modified a trifle by the example of the Italian theatres and by a recognition of the greatness and precision of the French rimed tragedy.

In this rapid assessment of the sources of the Restoration serious drama mention, too, must be made of the influence exerted upon at least some of the playwrights by contemporary scientific thought. Dryden was one of the first members of the Royal Society, and although attempts have been made to show that his interest was not an active or continuing one[1], there can be no doubt concerning the impress made on his mind by Hobbes' philosophy, while *The State of Innocence* (1677) pays the sincerest form of flattery to Descartes[2]. No doubt the writers of tragedies and comedies were not great thinkers, but there is sufficient evidence to make us believe that contemporary philosophical speculations aided in giving form to the content of at least some among their plays. Corneille and Dryden alike found justification for their magniloquent heroes in Descartes.

---

[1] Claude Lloyd, "John Dryden and the Royal Society" (*PMLA*, 1930, XLV. 967–76).

[2] On the influence of philosophical thought on the drama see Cecil V. Deane, *Dramatic Theory and the Rhymed Heroic Play* (1931), pp. 27–39. Louis I. Bredvold ("Dryden, Hobbes, and the Royal Society," *Modern Philology*, 1928, XXV. 417–38) notes Dryden's use of Descartes. This use was independently observed by H. O. White ("Dryden and Descartes," *TLS*, Dec. 19, 1929); Thomas B. Stroup ("Philosophy and the Drama," *TLS*, Jan. 19, 1933) draws attention to Southerne's echo of the same philosopher in *The Loyal Brother* (D.L. 1682) and to Robert Howard's paraphrase of Locke in *The Vestal-Virgin* (T.R. before 1665). Frank L. Huntley ("Dryden's Discovery of Boileau," *Modern Philology*, 1947, XLV. 112–17) finds the first suggestion of Boileau's influence in *The State of Innocence*. Baxter Hathaway ("John Dryden and the Function of Tragedy," *PMLA*, 1943, LVIII. 665–73), perhaps rather forcedly, attempts to assess Dryden's philosophical position. In "The Dramatic Use of Hobbes' Political Ideas" (*ELH*, 1936, III. 140–69) Louis Teeter traces the influence of that philosopher in *The Conquest of Granada*, *The Indian Emperour* and *Tyrannick Love*, as well as in Orrery's *Tryphon* and Crowne's *Calisto* and *Caligula*. This influence, however, he insists is almost entirely "theatrical"—introduced to give colour to the plays rather than to inculcate a particular set of philosophic principles. Mildred E. Hartsock ("Dryden's Plays: A Study in Ideas," in *Seventeenth Century Studies: Second Series*, ed. Robert Shafer, 1937, pp. 71–178) finds more direct ideological adaptation of Hobbes' concepts. Other related material appears in Basil Willey, *The Seventeenth Century Background* (1934); Louis I. Bredvold, *The Intellectual Milieu of John Dryden* (1934); and Clarence De Witt Thorpe, *The Æsthetic Theory of Thomas Hobbes* (1940).

III. *The Rimed Heroic Tragedy: 1664–1677*

The chief channel through which these streams of influence descended to the Restoration period was undoubtedly D'Avenant, although Roger Boyle may be esteemed the first to give the heroic play its definite form, and Howard and Dryden may be recognised as the popularisers of the species.

Before passing to an analysis of what these men did for the particular kind, it may not be unfitting to distinguish here the mere use of rime in plays from the heroic tragedy itself. In spite of the arguments that have been brought forward to the contrary by several writers[1], rimed couplets do not mark out plays as being heroic. All we can say is that, when the heroic type was being evolved, rime came to be utilised for tragic purposes. From 1660 to 1670 there were written about eighteen new plays in this measure, from 1670 to 1680 no less than twenty-four. Only one appeared in the following decade, although there was a slight reaction in their favour from 1690 to 1700 and even later—four appearing previous to the opening of the century and some half-a-dozen subsequently[2]. However, as Dryden noted in his dedication of *The Rival Ladies* (T.R. in B.St. 1664) to the Earl of Orrery, the employment of couplets in tragedies was "not so much a new Way amongst us, as an old Way new Reviv'd." It had been known in Elizabethan times: it was carried on spasmodically through the earlier part of the seventeenth century, and on into the Commonwealth period. Waller and Denham had rendered the couplet more precise and classic in its non-dramatic use, until it came to D'Avenant "who at once brought it upon the Stage, and made it perfect, in the Siege of *Rhodes*." Meanwhile, it had received a fresh impetus from the rimed translations of French tragedies mentioned above,

---

[1] See *infra*, pp. 168-9.

[2] Orrery's *Altemira* of 1702 is *The General*, acted in 1664: an unacted *King Saul* was published in 1703; in 1705 was issued a miserable tragedy by Alexander Fyfe, *The Royal Martyr, K. Charles I*. The last of the type was probably *The Battle of Aughrim, or, The Fall of Monsieur St Ruth* (Dublin, 1728), by Robert Ashton.

and evidently the French model, praised by the king, impelled Orrery to write his dramas in the same measure. The couplet developed into a thing "*à la mode*," was adopted by Dryden, and eventually formed a passport to tragic success on the stage. Because these rimed couplets, however, synchronised with Dryden's rants and with Settle's heroics, it is rather uncritical for us to mingle and confuse a distinct school of plot and of character with a certain technical form that had its ramifications far outside that school. There are plays in couplets which are not by any means heroic[1]: there are plays in blank verse which partake of the nature of the Drawcansir school[2]. Rime in tragedy was but a passing, external fashion in dramatic technique, which synchronised very largely with the main heroic period, but which had an influence slight when compared with the influence of the other characteristics of the heroic plays. Heroic verse in drama is really of very little account, historically or otherwise: the heroic play, although in its pure form ephemeral, is one

[1] Apart from the adaptations of Corneille mentioned above, there are comedies wholly or partly in rime, such as Duffett's *The Spanish Rogue* (King's company at L.I.F. 1673) and Bulteel's *Amorous Orontus, or, The Love in Fashion* (T.R. 1664); there are tragi-comedies, such as Etherege's *The Comical Revenge* (L.I.F. 1664), Weston's *The Amazon Queen* (unacted 1667), Mrs Behn's *The Forc'd Marriage* (L.I.F. 1670), Tuke's *The Adventures of Five Hours* (L.I.F. 1663) and Crowne's *Juliana* (L.I.F. 1671); there are pastorals, such as Settle's *Pastor Fido* (D.G. 1676) and the anonymous *The Constant Nymph* (D.G. 1677); and there are unheroic tragedies, such as Fane's *The Sacrifice* (unacted, 1686) and Stapylton's *Hero and Leander* (unacted, 1669); not to mention unclassifiable plays, such as Ecclestone's *Noah's Flood* (unacted, 1679) and William Johns' *The Traitor to Himself* (unacted, 1678).

[2] Among these may be named Mrs Behn's *Abdelazer* (D.G. 1676), which came just at the end of the riming fever. Settle in his *Pastor Fido* (D.G. *c*. Dec. 1676) and Ravenscroft in his *King Edgar and Alfreda* (D.L. *c*. Oct. 1677) both testify to its abatement at that time, prior, be it noted, to Dryden's recantation, who, in this case, followed the tendency of the time, instead of leading it (although, of course, Dryden had hinted at his weariness in *Aureng-Zebe*, which was produced at D.L. in Nov. 1675). Heroic plays, however, did not die with rime, as many produced from 1680 onwards can testify. Note many be taken in particular of the anonymous *Romulus and Hersilia* (D.G. 1682), Southerne's *The Loyal Brother* (D.L. 1682), and Settle's *The Heir of Morocco* (D.L. 1682), *Distress'd Innocence* (D.L. 1690) and *The Ambitious Slave* (D.L. 1694). There was a perfect galaxy of blank verse tragedies in the eighteenth century with most decided heroic characteristics.

of the most interesting and influential productions of our
theatre.

On the more general question of the rise of the heroic
sentiment in the drama[1], Dryden, in his *Essay of Heroick
Playes* prefixed to *The Conquest of Granada* (T.R. in B.St.
1670), is quite explicit:

> For Heroick Plays (he says) the first Light we had of them on
> the *English Theatre*, was from the late Sir *William D'Avenant*:
> It being forbidden him in the Rebellious Times to Act Tragedies
> and Comedies...he was forc'd to turn his Thoughts another way;
> and to introduce the Examples of Moral Virtue, writ in Verse,
> and perform'd in *Recitative Musick*. The Original of this Musick
> and of the Scenes which adorn'd this Work, he had from the
> *Italian Opera's*: But he heighten'd his Characters...from the
> Example of *Corneille* and some *French Poets*....He (then) re-
> view'd his Siege of *Rhodes*, and caus'd it to be acted as a just Drama.
> ...But as few Men have the Happiness to begin and finish any
> new Project, so neither did he live to make his Design perfect....
> There wanted the Fulness of a Plot, and the Variety of Characters
> to form it as it ought; and perhaps, something might have been
> added to the Beauty of the Style.

From this Dryden proceeds to argue that "an Heroick Play
ought to be an Imitation (in little) of an Heroick Poem; and
consequently that Love and Valour ought to be the Subject
of it." D'Avenant, in Dryden's opinion, had not done this:
he had made his *Siege of Rhodes* a unity but he had not
drawn "all Things as far above ordinary Proportion of the
Stage, as that is beyond the common Words and Actions of
Human Life," "he comply'd not enough with the Greatness
and Majesty of an Heroick Poem." His attempt was rather
"to show us ourselves in our ordinary Habits" than present
an exalted picture of extraordinary nobility. For Dryden,
on the contrary, "an Heroick Poet is not ty'd to a bare
Representation of what is true, or exceeding probable": he

---

[1] Up to 1923 very little attention had been paid to this subject, practically the only two essays being L. N. Chase's *The English Heroic Play*
(1906) and C. G. Child's "The Rise of the Heroic Play" (*Modern Language Notes*, 1904, XIX). More recent investigations of the heroic territory
are discussed *infra*, pp. 178–9.

may, indeed ought, to "let himself loose to visionary Objects."

The rest of Dryden's discourse is equally valuable. He defends the "frequent use of Drums and Trumpets, and the Representations of Battles" by an appeal to Shakespeare. He affirms Almanzor to be modelled on Achilles, Rinaldo and Artéban of Calprenède, but professes to love the first two rather more than the last. He casts over the punctilious honour of the French, trusting to magnanimous passion. He defends Almanzor's words to sovereign powers and to the gods by the example of Achilles and Rinaldo, even of Jonson's Cethegus.

From all of this several definite facts can be gleaned. D'Avenant is recognised as the first introducer of heroic motives. Dryden has observed his imitation of the Italian opera, his imitation of Corneille: he might have added that he was certainly one of the first to go for plot to the contemporary romance of Mdlle de Scudéry, and that in his *Love and Honour* he carried on the native romance tradition, removing it a step further towards the heroic ideal. On the other hand, several things are noted as lacking in D'Avenant's work: (1) fulness of plot; (2) variety of characters; (3) extraordinary incidents (magic and such like); and (4) almost supernatural nobility of characters. If we turn to *The Siege of Rhodes*, we can see exactly what Dryden felt was wanting[1]. The scene is all right—a nebulous Rhodes. There is a hero Alphonso and a heroine Ianthe, divided from one another: but, in spite of heroic self-sacrifice on the part of Christians and of pagans alike, there is a softer atmosphere than in any of Dryden's plays. Alphonso is not all-conquering; he is, in the first part, wounded, in the second, taken prisoner. Soliman is not a villain, but acts as magnanimously as any hero. What Dryden wanted was, first, some thrilling super-

---

[1] *The Siege of Rhodes* has, of course, supreme priority in this field. The first part was given at Rutland House in 1656 and both parts appeared at the Cockpit in 1659. References to D'Avenant are given elsewhere: here may be noted an essay by Friedrich Laig, *Englische und französische Elemente in Sir William D'Avenants dramatischer Kunst* (Emsdetten, 1924).

natural incidents, secondly, the presence of some greater
complication of plot and of emotions, and, thirdly, the
heightening of the character of the hero. The whole atmosphere of the play is weak; the characters are shadows; the
language is not so refined as in the dramas of Dryden. Moreover, although *The Siege of Rhodes* is written partly in
couplets, it is not so regular as the later heroic tragedies. Its
operatic origin is still seen in the varying measures employed,
and in the choruses, of which any Restoration lyrist might
have been contemptuous:

> Then the hug'ous great *Turk*,
> Came to make us more work;
> > With enow men to eat
> > All he meant to defeat;
> Whose wonderful worship did confirm us
> > In the fear he would bide here
> > So long till he Dy'd here,
> By the Castle he build (*sic*) on *Philermus*.

Dryden and the others wanted something more refined than
this, something decidedly stronger, more arresting and more
pronounced in utterance.

In point of fact, Dryden might have found what he was
seeking for, those more definite "heroic" elements, in a play
written almost contemporaneously with D'Avenant's, but,
because given no performance in the theatres, forgotten by
the men of the time. This is *The Heroick-Lover, or, The
Infanta of Spain* (printed 1661) by a certain George Cartwright, of whom all we know is that he was "of *Fullham*,
Gent." Scened in Poland, this tragedy is almost entirely in
rime, and beyond an amount of contemporary political reference not usual in the ordinary heroic tragedy[1], it presents
in the characters and in the language, the germs of the type
to be more fully developed later. Nonantious is the typical
magnanimous and loyal lover and friend of the heroic play,
exactly equivalent to the Acacis of Howard and Dryden. The
Prince of *The Heroick-Lover* courts Francina, who is passion-

---

[1] The part of the plot which deals with the king and the revolt of
Zorates and Selucious evidently refers to Charles I. It is possible that
this interesting play was written nearer 1650 than 1660.

ately adored by Nonantious, and the latter is cast into a swirl of conflicting emotions such as we meet with all through the course of this dramatic form.

> Do, or not do, criminal ev'ry way.
> Of evils, chuse the lesser of the two.
> They are so equal, I know not which to do.
> My love to fair *Francina*, bids me not;
> My duty to my *Prince*, can't be forgot:
> How both, the ballance hold, so just and true,
> That willing both, I know not which to do[1].

In such a speech is recognisable the sentiment that runs through all the tragedies of the next fifteen years. In the end, this Nonantious, so magnanimous he is, stabs himself to give the Prince freedom to gain his mistress, and his last words are the words of a later hero:

> Yet 'fore I die, here on my bended Knee,
> Do I bequeath *Francina*, willingly.
> All, all the interest, which I have in her,
> Henceforward I do give, unto you Sir...
> I know she is too poor, a gift for you,
> But I can do not more, then I can do.
> Since that my life to you, is so suspect,
> 'Tis fit my Death, shoo'd witness my respect.
> *(Stabs himself*[2].

Francina, somewhat like Orrery's Queen of Hungary, departs into a nunnery, rejecting the proffered crown, which, without explanation, is handed to the Princess Flora of Spain, no doubt dragged in for political reasons. In politics, too, this forgotten author reproduces the thoughts of practically every one of his followers. In his play, the Admiral, approached by the conspirators, bursts out in true cavalier wrath at their proposals:

> Your Doctrine is of Devils; I fear to name
> The words which you have utter'd, without shame.
> That I shoo'd help, for to correct the King,
> Were he the worst, of any living thing!
> Or were his Royal soul, more black then Hell,
> Far be't in me, such wickedness shoo'd dwell..

---

[1] II. ii. [2] IV. iv.

To us, who cannot judge of common things
Does not belong, the judgement of great Kings.
They shoo'd be like stars, seated in the sky,
Far from our reach, though seeming near our eye[1].

Apart from this play, however, and apart from the rimed translations of French dramas mentioned above, among which Mrs Philips's *Pompey* (Smock Alley, Dublin, 1663) was the first, but the *Pompey* (L.I.F. 1664) written by Waller, Buckhurst and Sedley[2]—perhaps a few others as well—was more famous—apart from these, we can number few plays which, prior to 1664, presented those elements which Dryden desired. He did not want such mere alterations: he wanted a native drama of heroic grandeur, different from the French, not dependent upon it.

There is no doubt but that Roger Boyle, Earl of Orrery, was first in the field, in so far as composition is concerned[3]. Early in 1662, having heard that the King favoured the French style in drama, he was engaged in writing a play and this appeared in October 1662 as *Altamira* in Dublin and, in Sept. 1664, as *The General* at London's Theatre Royal. Already, however,

---

[1] II. iii.

[2] See *Poems on Affairs of State...the fifth edition, Corrected and much Enlarged* (1703), I. 209—*The Session of the Poets, to the Tune of Cock-Lawrel*:

"*B----t* and *Sydley*, with two or three more,
Translators of *Pompey*, dispute in their claim;
But *Apollo* made them be turn'd out of door,
And bid them be gone like Fools as they came."

[3] For information on Orrery's plays and for the assessment of his position in the dramatic history of the time much is owed to William S. Clark's excellent edition of this author's *Dramatic Works* (1937). Previously Clark had contributed many articles bearing on his chosen theme. His researches seem to show that the hypothesis concerning an early performance of *The Black Prince* cannot be substantiated (see F. W. Payne, "The Question of Precedence between Dryden and the Earl of Orrery," *Review of English Studies*, 1925, I. 173–81; W. H. Grattan Flood, "Orrery's *Black Prince*," *id.* 1925, 341–3; W. S. Clark, "Further Light upon the Heroic Plays of Roger Boyle," *id.* 1926, II. 206–11). L. J. Mills discusses "The Friendship Theme in Orrery's Plays" (*PMLA*, 1938, LIII. 795–806) and C. William Miller ("A Source Note on Boyle's *The Generall*," *Modern Language Quarterly*, 1947, VIII. 146–50) shows that the earliest of these dramas was based on situations taken from the author's own novel *Parthenissa* and from *Romeo and Juliet*. An important letter regarding *The General* is discussed by Bernard M. Wagner in "Restoration Heroic Drama" (*TLS*, Sept. 2, 1946).

in Jan. 1663/4 the King's men had presented *The Indian Queen* by Howard and Dryden, thus anticipating the English production of Orrery's first-written play by some eight months and his *Henry the Fifth* (L.I.F. Aug. 1664) by seven. Taking all things into consideration, and particularly observing that *The General* failed to reach printed form at this time, we may perhaps be justified in saying that, while Orrery was the fore-runner and while his personal distinction added prominence to his writings, his efforts gave less direction to the progress of the heroic species than Dryden's. Without seeking to minimise Orrery's importance or neglecting the clear implication in his letters that he was engaged in the experimental task of attempting, at the King's desire, to fashion a new dramatic style, we may further suggest that these plays of his are to be regarded rather as academic essays which by royal persuasion were brought to the public stage than as works designed to capture the attention of a theatre audience.

Orrery's plays are divisible into two classes, *Henry the Fifth* and *The Black Prince* (T.R. in B.St. Oct. 1667) standing together in contradistinction to *The General* (issued later as *Altemira*, in an adaptation by the Hon. Charles Boyle), *Mustapha* (L.I.F. April 1665), *Tryphon* (L.I.F. December 1668), *Herod the Great* (printed 1694) and *Zoroastres*, preserved in manuscript and not printed until recently. Both groups, certainly, have certain things in common. Both are highly spectacular, both are more restrained than Dryden's productions, both dwell much with love, both tend to introduce the theme of passion opposed to friendship, a theme already noted in Cartwright's *The Heroick-Lover*, both approach more nearly to the French drama than do the more well-known heroic plays of the time, both are inclined towards tragi-comical conclusions. On the other hand, all of the second group deal with unreal worlds: *Henry the Fifth* and *The Black Prince* continue in an altered strain the native chronicle history tradition.

Orrery, then, is to be noted for his important influence along certain definite lines: he has taken up the English historical heroic tragedy; he has decidedly imitated Corneille

8-2

in many a character and scene; he has adopted that inde-
terminate realm of drama which, in England and abroad,
hovered between the tragedy and the serious comedy.
Henry the Fifth is not a tragedy: it is an heroic history with
plentiful love scenes and the introduction of a great deal of
argument on the subject of the conflicting claims of passion
and friendship. *The Black Prince* similarly introduces to us
a mass of antagonistic amatory sentiments, circling around
a widow heroine with four separate lovers. The eternal clash
of contrasting emotions is everywhere emphasised:

> Two Ills he offers, one he bids me choose,
> I must my Mistress, or my Father loose[1].

The unnatural scenes, in which Orrery tried to imitate the
French, are seen here in the long letter the reading of which
Pepys tells us nearly damned the play[2], just as they are exemplified in another way in *The General* (*Altemira*) where
Mellizer stands through five or six pages while his son is dying
"for they were not to be interrupted by an inferiour Actor[3]." In
The General the conflict of Love and Honour is placed mostly
in the heart of the character whose position gives the title
to the play. This second drama of Orrery's is another which
does not end disastrously. *Mustapha* is quite evidently derived from Georges de Scudéry's *L'Illustre Bassa*, and again
presents before us a love drama of tragic proportions which
in this case ends disastrously. In it the Queen of Hungary
is introduced in captivity, Zanger and Mustapha both in love
with her. Through false reports Solyman orders Mustapha
to be executed, and Zanger, who had sworn that he would
not live longer than his brother, dutifully commits suicide.
Roxalana, who had complicated the plot, is divorced and
the fatal captive queen retires to a nunnery. Naturally the
emotional battles of the mind are very pronounced. Mustapha
feels them most badly:

> Fortune did never in one day design
> For any Heart, four Torments great as mine;
> I to my Friend and Brother Rival am.
> She, who did kindle, would put out my Flame;

> I from my Father's anger must remove,
> And that does banish me from her I love[1].

Heroic follies there are in abundance, the eternal sophistry and argument inaptly imitated from the French theatre. Thus Zanger:

> Since Nature no Religion knows but Love,
> He that loves most, does most Religious prove[2]—

or the same character of the Queen of Hungary in grief:

> When she her Royal Infant did embrace,
> Her Eyes such Floods of Tears show'r'd on her Face,
> That then, oh *Mustapha*! I did admire
> How so much Water sprang from so much Fire:
> And to increase the Miracle, I found
> At the same time, my Heart both burnt and drown'd[3].

The same follies, the same sophistries, the same conflicts, occur in all Orrery's dramas. In *Tryphon*, the tyrant who gives his name to the piece loves Cleopatra, the beloved of Aretus, the unknown real king, and then shifts his affections to Stratonice. He bids his servant convey the good news to the latter, and remarks that

> While *Stratonice* you to my Throne invite,
> To *Cleopatra* my Excuse I'le write.

Stratonice, however, happens to be the beloved of Demetrius, his friend, and at the conclusion Tryphon and his tool Arcas commit suicide, leaving the good characters to a happy ending. The conflict here appears in the breasts of several *dramatis personae*. In Act IV Aretus is in the throes of it:

> "O Love, O Friendship, and O Fatal Vow!" he cries,
> "To which shall I pay my Obedience now?"

Love is just as mysterious and wonderful a thing as in the other plays. Demetrius comes to adore Stratonice and Aretus upbraids him:

> Was't fit this Love from me conceal'd shou'd be?

to which Demetrius' answer is straight and to the point:

> Alas 'twas till last night unknown to me.

---

[1] III. i. A comparison of these sentiments with those of *The Heroick Lover* almost induces one to believe that Orrery had seen that drama.
[2] II. i.   [3] II. i.

The follies of the Orrerian drama must have been evident
to all. Above has been noticed the disgust of the audience
at some of the unnatural scenes, and Sedley's satiric remarks,
chronicled faithfully by Pepys, have enabled us to identify
The General as the later *Altemira*[1]. On the other hand,
Orrery's plays have a strength that D'Avenant's lack. Their
refined language, their verse skill, their outstanding characters, this conflict, which, crude as it may be, is interesting
and appealing—all must have been noticed by Dryden when
searching for a model. Dryden, however, was no man to
write dramas that would bore an audience. He was writing
for money, and his heroic tragedies, marking a distinct type
of their own, are at once more stirring, more impossible,
more bombastic, and more popular in tone than any which
had gone before. The spectators could but laugh at some of
Orrery's sentences, they could but hiss at some chill Gallicised
scene, they could but be thrilled at Maximin's notorious
vaunt to the gods. In analysing the Dryden species, therefore,
we find that he has introduced a larger, fuller, more intricate
plot, characters rather more varied and all very much more
exaggerated in tone, numerous scenes of strife and battle and
murder, a touch of cynicism in the songs and occasionally in
the dialogue—an atmosphere, that is to say, rather more
"heroic" in the Restoration sense of the word than romantic.
The author of *The Conquest of Granada* is not wrong in
saying that he made his hero approach more nearly to
Rinaldo than to Artéban.

From the first to the last Dryden followed this plan. *The
Indian Queen*, staged at the T.R. in B.St. in Jan. 1663/4,
shows it no less clearly than his latest plays. It is impossible
now, perhaps, to disentangle in this first play the scenes
written respectively by Sir Robert Howard and by Dryden,
but the tragedy as a whole approaches so closely in temper
and in plan Dryden's after works that we may presume the
general outline and at least a fair proportion of the dialogue
to have been by him[2]. The heroic figure here is Montezuma,

---

[1] Wed. Sept. 28, 1664.
[2] Scott attributed the Montezuma and Zempoalla scenes, along with that

general of the Inca's forces. We are introduced to him just when he has defeated the Mexicans. Flushed with victory, he has asked for the hand of the Inca's daughter, Orazia (the heroic heroine), whom he, with true ardour, loves to desperation. He is refused, and the insult stings his mighty soul to madness. He offers to free Acacis (the heroic magnanimous rival), the Prince of the Mexicans whom he has taken prisoner, but who, full of honourable thoughts, rejects the proffered freedom[1]. Montezuma then joins the Mexican forces, and, by his prowess alone, defeats his erstwhile inconquerable army and takes prisoner both the Inca and Orazia. Here, however, his troubles are only to begin. Zempoalla (the vengeful woman-type) the usurping Queen of Mexico, falls in love with him, while Traxalla (the heroic villain) her former general and suitor to her hand, does the same with Orazia, who has also honourably smitten the heart of Acacis. From all this intricate mêlée of emotions ensue various scenes of love, honour, virtue and vice, interrupted by the entrance of the forces of the rightful queen, Amexia, who turns out to be Montezuma's mother. The hero therefore is now noble enough by birth to marry Orazia—which he promptly does. To clear the air of his sorrowful presence, the unhappy Acacis commits suicide, as does Zempoalla for shame, while Traxalla, the only other inconvenient character left, is slain by Montezuma, so that in very truth, as Dryden himself noted when he was writing his sequel *The Indian Emperour*, there remained "but two of the considerable Characters alive[2]." Noticeable, however, is the fact, that, as in Orrery's plays, it is only the evil and weaker characters who are thus summarily despatched, the play ending happily for the magnanimous Montezuma and the divine Orazia.

On this plan or a plan similar to this were based nearly

of the incantation, to Dryden (*The Dramatic Works of John Dryden*, ed. Scott, W. and Saintsbury, G., Edinburgh, 1882, II. 225).

[1] It is noticeable, particularly in the Dryden type of drama, that honour hardly enters into the actions of the hero, but sways the lives of the lesser characters.

[2] *Connection of the* Indian Emperor *to the* Indian Queen, dispersed among the audience in 1665.

all Dryden's later heroic plays, and the stock characters, so pronounced here, appear again and again, disguised as best the author might determine, but quite recognisable. Of the manner in which these characters are presented, not much need be said. Dryden took over enough from Orrery to make his psychological delineations of the same crude yet forceful type. When one hears Montezuma lament:

> Oh Tyrant Love, how cruel are thy Laws!
> I forfeit Friendship, or betray thy Cause[1],

or cry:

> Thou hast perform'd what Honour bid thee do;
> But Friendship bars what Honour prompts me to,

one recognises the voice of the Black Prince or of Aretus. When one listens to the monologue of Zempoalla:

> Whence shou'd proceed this strange Diversity
> In my Resolves?......
> Does he command in Chains? What wou'd he do
> Proud Slave, if he were free, and I were so?
> But is he bound, ye Gods, or am I free?
> 'Tis Love, 'tis Love, that thus disorders me,

one hears the authentic voices of those who, in the other dramas, had felt a similar torment in their hearts. Here are the same drivelling, unreal, passionless theorisings of un-imagined types and spurious emotions, yet types and emotions, which, as Dryden knew, were bound to appeal to his age. Pepys had found the street "full of coaches" for *The Indian Queen* on Jan. 27, 1663/4 and heard it was "a fine thing." When he saw it on Feb. 1, he thought it "a most pleasant show, and beyond my expectation."

Its success, no doubt, as well as the rich scenery which the actors had caused to be painted, led Dryden to write the sequel of *The Indian Emperour*, printed in 1667, but acted at the T.R. in B.St. about April 1665. This play marks no material advance in the development of the species. Not superior in poetic power, more involved in plot, wholly im-possible in its heroic magnanimity and its passionless, un-psychological love and hate, it is rendered more popular by

[1] IV. i.

a number of scenes of stress and struggle, glutting to the full
this new taste in the audience for spectacle and for show.
There are magic caves, and temples, and prisons—there are
visions and the loud thundering of cannon—everything, in
fact, that might make the play more of a popular success on
the stage.

In *Tyrannick Love, or, The Royal Martyr* (T.R. in B.St.
c. June 1669) there is, however, a slight change. All the
elements of the earlier plays are retained here. There are the
same rich scenes, the introduction of the supernatural in the
astral spirits, the same criss-cross affections, and many of
the same types. Maximin is the villain emperor, modelled
apparently on the Valentinians of the Jacobean period, with
a lust towards S. Catherine, who might be compared with
Dorothea of *The Virgin Martyr*, which, it may be noted, was
evidently a fairly popular play in the repertoire of the King's
comedians[1]. There is no magnanimous hero, but Porphyrius,
Maximin's general, is the sympathetic character of the piece,
loving Berenice, Maximin's wife, and beloved by Valeria,
who is in turn adored by Placidius. Again there is a general
carnage at the close which leaves Berenice and Porphyrius
to carry on. In *Tyrannick Love*, however, one new thing,
just hinted at in the former plays, is emphasised. It is here
that there occur for the first time those notorious rants which
were to become such an outstanding characteristic of the
heroic drama of the years 1670 to 1677. The Maximin to the
gods passage does not appear till near the close of the fifth
act, but countless others come down to the same standard of
idiotic, inflated and grandiloquent nonsense. In the very
first act Maximin shows his character. A messenger announces a misfortune to his son, whereupon this giant super-
man bursts out with tumid rhetoric:

> Some God now, if he dares, relate what's past;
> Say but he's dead, that God shall mortal be.

Nor, even in his last words, after he has stabbed Placidius
does he sink to a humbler strain:

---

[1] *The Virgin Martyr* was first acted on Sat. Feb. 16, 1661. It was
played again on Thurs. Feb. 27, 1667/8, Mon. March 2, Fri. March 20
and Wed. May 6, 1668. This last production was about a year before
the appearance of Dryden's play.

And after thee I'll go,
Revenging still, and following ev'n to the other world my blow.
                                        [*Stabs him again.*
And shoving back this Earth on which I sit,
I'll mount, and scatter all the Gods I hit.

Reading such passages now, one can hardly restrain one's
risibility, but Dryden was sufficiently a man of the time to
realise that such rants were precisely the things the audience
wanted, something exaggerated to force their attention and
to raise the whole above the levels of ordinary life.
    The Conquest of Granada by the Spaniards[1] (T.R. in B.St.
c. December 1670) is decidedly a much finer piece of work,
our sympathies being actually seized—as they are seized by
so few of the heroic tragedies—for the unfortunate loves of
the gallant hero and the loveable heroine. The poetry of this
play is beautiful, nor can we gain an idea of Dryden's true
worth until we compare such a play as this with one of a
writer like Crowne. Romance for dulness, poetry for mere
verse, interest, if peculiar, for flatulent bombast—this is what
we find: and, even if the play is poetically unreal, it does
take us to a world that even our sophisticated minds may
delight to dwell in for "a dream while or so." *The Conquest
of Granada* is prefaced by the famous *Essay of Heroique Plays*
and contains the no less famous epilogue on the poets of the
past age, as well as the *Defence of the Epilogue.* Altogether,
it and the critical matter which accompanies it, may be taken
as a grand vindication of this particular species. Here we
can see the magnanimous character of the hero, who sets his
vanquished enemies free:

    But, since thou threaten'st us, I'll set thee free,
    That I again may fight, and conquer thee—

the frail yet doughty heroine, the half-foolish, half-villainous
King Boabdelin, the evil woman character, Lyndaraxa, the
villain Zulema. As with the other dramas, this tragedy ends
with a universal massacre of the evil characters and the retention of the pair of lovers, Almanzor and Almahide. Again

---

[1] G. H. Nettleton has an instructive essay on "Author's Changes in
Dryden's *Conquest of Granada*" (*Modern Language Notes*, 1935, L. 360–4).

we get the ridiculous rants and the cynical songs. Again the continual atmosphere of war, forming a lurid setting for a plot that is full of exaggerated love and passion.

Dryden's last rimed tragedy followed at Drury Lane about November 1675. *Aureng-Zebe*[1] is his final word in the typical form of this drama, although he was to continue utilising heroic incidents until his death. Once more the characters are familiar—the noble and valorous Aureng-Zebe, son to the Emperor, loving the equally noble Indamora, a captive queen like the Queen of Hungary in Orrery's *Mustapha*, the foolish emperor and his evil consort, Nourmahal, the semi-villain Morat, son to Nourmahal, married to Melesinda, the pathetic lover, Arimant, left out in the cold. The complication of amatory emotions is greater in this play than ever. Indamora is loved by the father emperor, by his son Aureng-Zebe, by his step-son Morat and by Arimant, Governor of Agra, she loving Aureng-Zebe alone, and Aureng-Zebe for his part being adored in an evil way by his step-mother, Nourmahal. The plot is thus as intricate as, if not more intricate than, before, and these love passions are set in the midst of scenes of fighting, excitement and suspense. Morat is killed, and Nourmahal runs "distracted." Eventually the latter dies, leaving once more the pair of true lovers, after innumerable thrills, to marry and settle down in peace.

In *Aureng-Zebe*, which on the whole is one of Dryden's best plays, the most interesting features are the comparative lack of bombast and the singular freedom of the rimed verse. It would almost appear as if the author had been tentatively feeling his way towards the greater liberty of *All for Love*. It abounds in run-on lines, and there are passages scattered through it of a pre-eminent beauty. Truly Nettleton is right when he declares that "quotation has not staled the fine passage" in IV. i[2]:

> When I consider Life, 'tis all a Cheat;
> Yet, fool'd with Hope, Men favour the Deceit.

---

[1] The 1699 edition has the title *Aureng-Zebe; or, The Great Mogul.*

[2] G. H. Nettleton, *English Drama of the Restoration and Eighteenth Century* (1914), p. 68.

On the three lines noted above, the heroic tragedy developed, one branch tending towards Drydenesque rant, battle and heroics, another towards the Orrerian historical play, and still a third towards the stricter calm, precision and artificiality of the French style and aim.

Thus Caryl in *The English Princess, or, The Death of Richard the III* (L.I.F. March 1667) early took up the hints given in *Henry V* and presented an heroic tragedy with no outlandish setting of oriental scenery, a fact to which the prologue duly draws attention:

> You must today your Appetite prepare
> For a plain English Treat of homely Fare:
> We neither *Bisque*, nor *Ollias* shall advance
> From Spanish Novel, or from French Romance;
> Nor shall we charm your Ears, or feast your Eyes
> With Turkey-Works, or Indian Rarityes.

There are ghosts in this play, it is true, and there is scenical display of a very limited sort, but for the most part Caryl's tragedy is set on a lower key. It unites the English historical subject with a pseudo-classic calm, obviously imitated from Orrery. As Pepys contemporaneously expressed it, "there was nothing eminent in it, as some tragedys are." A similar play, the sole production of its author, Thomas Shipman, is *Henry the Third of France, Stabb'd by a Fryer. With the Fall of the Guise* (L.I.F. *c.* March 1672). Genest has made a condemnation of the first four acts of this drama, and modern readers might be inclined to extend that condemnation to the whole five. It is indeed a sorry attempt, even though the author, in his preface with its vigorous defence of rime, evidently thought that his work was a masterpiece. The English historical play with the elements of heroics or classic calm had a considerable importance later, as we shall see when we come to consider the tragedies of 1678–1700, but just for the moment it could not stand up against its more formidable because more thrilling and more spectacular rivals.

This spectacular kind was pursued energetically in the first experiment of Elkanah Settle, *Cambyses, King of Persia*

(L.I.F. *c.* Jan. 1671)[1]. Modelled somewhat on the Dryden plan, it was a huge success and ran to four editions before the close of the century. All the formulae for a popular heroic play are in it—the curtain-falls and dramatic risings[2], the overwhelming atmosphere of love, the prison scenes[3], the scenes of horror[4], of ghosts, of spirits, of supernatural phenomena[5], the outlandish country and names. There is the usual stock king, the stage villain, Prexaspes, the "young Captive Prince" Osiris, and the beautiful mistress, Mandana, who sets all hearts aflame. This, like Dryden's plays, is a tragicomedy, in the sense that it ends with the overthrow of the evil and the preservation of the good characters.

Settle in the following years was destined to become one of the principal masters of the "quality he professed." His next play, *The Empress of Morocco* (D.G. July 1673), when printed, was so far honoured as to be adorned with six "Sculptures. The Like never done before," illustrating scenes in the play. The drama, which had been first produced at court[6], must have been a tremendous success[7], or the Theatre Royal management would not have pilloried it in Duffett's burlesque: and certainly its success, in spite of obvious absurdities, was not quite unmerited. The show of the Dryden species is there, and the atmosphere is that of love and war. The characters are typical: Laula the Queen-Mother in conspiracy with Crimalhaz; the honest prince, Muly Hamet, who, after a world of fighting, settles down to marry his love, Marianne. The plot, however, is slightly modified from the Dryden type, a fact which gives the play a certain novelty, and the verse, although mostly pedestrian, occasionally trembles on the verge of poetry.

---

[1] For the date see Appendix C.

[2] Cf. Act i.   [3] Cf. Act v. i.

[4] iii. iv.   [5] iv and v.

[6] For the date see Appendix C. There seems every reason for believing that the extraordinary publication of this play, with its lavish illustrations, was due to aristocratic patronage of Settle. Roswell G. Ham, in "Dryden versus Settle" (*Modern Philology*, 1928, xxv. 407–16), shows that for a time contemporaries looked upon this mediocre author as a rival worthy of competing with Dryden for the poet's laurels.

[7] In the preface to Dennis' *Remarks upon Mr Pope's Translation of Homer* (1717), we are told that it ran "a month together."

His success in this play soon led Settle to follow on with similar productions, *The Conquest of China, By the Tartars* (D.G. May 1675), full of rant, again a tragi-comedy in that, although a love-lorn princess of China sacrifices herself for her love and a villain causes massacres all round, the hero and the heroine are left alive at the end, and *Ibrahim, the Illustrious Bassa* (D.G. *c*. March 1676), save for *Pastor Fido*, the last of his riming productions. Derived obviously from the romance of Madeleine de Scudéry or from the homonymous play by her brother Georges, the plot and the characters of this latter heroic play are on the same plan as before. Ibrahim is the typical prince "to whose Success the Sultan's Glory's due," and whose

> Wondrous Arms such Miracles had done,
> I came but to behold the Fields he won,

as the Sultan himself expresses it. The plot is fairly simple, and in a way is a direct complement or contrary to Dryden's *The Indian Queen*. Ibrahim, returning victorious from war, asks not but is offered as a bride, Asteria, the daughter of Sultan Solyman. Ibrahim, however, has other thoughts, and dares to refuse the proffered maiden in favour of Isabella, with whom in turn the Sultan falls in love. The monarch is eventually converted by her purity and restores her to Ibrahim. In the meantime, Roxalana, the emperor's wife, has poisoned herself through jealousy and shame. We may easily recognise Montezuma in Ibrahim, the usual Emperor in Solyman, the forsaken queen in Roxalana, Orazia in Isabella. There is nothing new but a slight juggling of their relations to one another. The heroic play always suffered from a lack of novelty in the conception of the situations. The other play of Settle's mentioned above, *Pastor Fido, or, The Faithful Shepherd* (D.G. *c*. Dec. 1676) may be noted here in passing as the last riming play of this author, and as one of the few pastoral "heroic" dramas of the time.

Many others followed in the same line of popularised, we might almost call them national, heroics. D'Urfey presented *The Siege of Memphis, or, The Ambitious Queen* (D.L. *c*. Sept.

1676), an unsuccessful play[1], in which Zemlura, Queen of Egypt, falls in love with the Syrian Moaron, who in turn adores Zemlura's sister, Amasis. This drama, it may be noted, had a definitely tragic ending, a possible cause of its cool reception on the stage. The absence of the magnanimous hero is likewise noticeable. Pordage also came forward with *Herod and Mariamne* (D.G.? Oct. 1673)[2] which we are informed in the prologue was written in 1661 or in 1662; as this date, however, carries the history of the species even beyond Dryden and Orrery, and as the play has many characteristics of the later heroic dramas, we may presume that the year of composition was nearer 1670 than 1660. The characters of this play are as stereotyped as those of the others, and the rants at the close remind us of Dryden's Maximin. Herod has murdered Mariamne, then stabs and is stabbed by his rival Tyridates: whereupon the latter cries out that, revenge having done its part, love will now go on:

> And finish what *Mariamnes* Eyes begun.
> Though it grows dark, my Ghost shall rove about,
> And never stop till it has found thine out.

At this the burly Herod is duly distressed. He had never thought of this contingency.

> "Ha!" he cries. "Into what Confusion am I hurl'd,
> Hee'l be my Rival in the other World,"

and then comes to him the remedy,

> If Souls can fight, I thee to Battle dare.

Pordage gave one other heroic drama to the theatre in *The Siege of Babylon* (D.G. *c*. Sept. 1677) wherein the "Love and Honour" emphasised in the very first line betray no marked modifications from other previous examples. Rants, badly imitated from Dryden, disfigure Banks' *The Rival Kings, or, The Loves of Oroondates and Statira* (D.L. *c*. June 1677), plainly derived from Calprenède's *Cassandre* and associated

---

[1] Cf. the dedication.

[2] On the staging of this play see the discussion and references in Appendix A. M. J. Valency has a study of *The Tragedies of Herod and Mariamne* (1940), in which various dramatic versions of the theme are examined.

with Lee's *The Rival Queens*, produced earlier in the year at the same theatre. Another play by Banks, *The Destruction of Troy* (D.G. *c*. Nov. 1678) was composed probably before the rimed fever gave over and was re-worked in a later strain: the same possibly is true of Mrs Behn's *Abdelazer, or, The Moor's Revenge* (D.G. *c*. Sept. 1676). This play, based on Marlowe's *Lust's Dominion*, connects us with a few plays by Otway and Sedley, where we find a very marked element of Elizabethan reminiscences in the midst of the heroic rants. Here the central figure, brave and bombastic but also half a villain, is Abdelazer, a moor, married to Florella and beloved by the Queen of Spain. Complications arise when the new king comes to adore the Moor's wife, who, along with the king, is murdered by the pair of guilty lovers. Abdelazer then for his own purposes strives to kill the Queen's other son, Philip, together with the Cardinal. There is a mass of fighting and intrigue, in the midst of which the Moor, after murdering the Queen and making love to Leonora, is betrayed by his own lieutenant, Osmin, and dies ranting. The plot is plainly not of the ordinary Drawcansir type, but the love and honour that pervades the whole is in the typical heroic strain. Even the Cardinal can tell us that "Love and Honour" he has "always made the Business" of his "Life[1]," or else feel "a Contest of Love and Honour" swelling his "Rising Heart[2]."

Among other plays which belong to this category, Sedley's *Antony and Cleopatra* (D.G. Feb. 1676/7), a tragedy which hardly is of the kind we should have expected from this companion of the wits, inevitably fails when placed alongside of Dryden's or of Shakespeare's masterpieces on the same theme, but Otway's *Alcibiades* (D.G. Sept. 1675) and *Don Carlos, Prince of Spain* (D.G. *c*. June 1676) merit fuller attention[3]. The first, possibly, has hardly the graces of the second, but is by no means negligible. *Don Carlos* is truly a triumph of the heroic species. The characters are all of the same stock type we have met with before—the artificial

[1] iv. iv.   [2] v. i.
[3] On Otway and Lee see the study by Roswell G. Ham (1931).

monarch, the machiavellian Ruy-Gomez and the Edmund-like villain Don John, but the language and the sentiments are much more natural and unaffected than those of the ordinary productions of this school, and Otway has an absence of rant which should gain our appreciative commendation.

Of all the authors of the Drydenesque tragedy, however, Lee takes precedence. An entirely tragic writer, he produced not a single line of comedy. His mind seemed too fixed on the gruesome side of life, on the hard and rocky paths of existence, ever to turn aside to happier and to more pleasant prospects. A magnificent reader of his own works, he yet seems to have been of that self-sensitive type of man who fails when the world's eyes are bent on him: so that, after a short period, he abandoned the actor's career in disgust. That his mind had a morbid turn cannot be denied: but it is equally impossible to deny that he possessed to no small degree the gifts of the true poet, felicity and enthusiasm. He dwelt too much on those periods of history when vice seemed to rise to abnormal heights—Rome of the Neros, Rome of the Borgias and Paris of Saint Bartholomew's Day—but in his finest plays he has captured our attention for themes which are odious in themselves and which do not always contain the requisites for a true tragic plot. Whether he sank to rime or rose with blank verse there are scattered through his works passages which can remind us only of the best of the later Elizabethans—of Webster and of Ford—and sometimes even of Shakespeare himself.

Lee's rimed heroic plays are only three in number, although we must remember that he, like many of the others, reproduced the atmosphere of heroism even after he had abandoned rime and adopted blank verse. His dramatic career he opened with *The Tragedy of Nero, Emperour of Rome* (D.L. May 1674), a play practically wholly written in rime[1], and thus tuning in with the popular fancy. So closely indeed has Lee followed the prevailing mood of the age, that his bombast is hardly to be matched even in the worst

---

[1] There is a little blank verse, and one or two passages in prose.

productions of the same cast[1]. Probably the finest scenes in
it are those where Brittanicus runs mad[2]—an early sign of a
fatal bent in Lee's own mind. These are indeed admirably
executed, although the horror of the whole piece is too continuous. There is no working up to a preconceived end, and
when we consider that it begins with a murder, we realise that
our interest must flag somewhat ere the end be reached.

Sophonisba, or, Hannibal's Overthrow (D.L. April 1675)
followed the next year, a decided success, not only in its own
time, but through at least the first half of the eighteenth
century[3]. Written in rimed verse, it does not reproduce the
slightly amateurish rants so visible in *Nero*, and is decidedly
thrilling in a melodramatic way. Valueless as are many of
the scenes, it does seem to contain characters and language
calculated not only to appeal to a poetic taste, but also to
arouse the highest emotions in an audience. Follies there are,
of course, as in that ridiculous first meeting of Rosalinda and
of Massina in Act II[4], but what seventeenth or eighteenth
century lady could refuse to cheer Hannibal at his last exit:

> Haste, haste, *Maherbal*, and fresh Levies make;
> Honour that did but now calm Slumbers take,
> Shall like the Ocean in a Tempest wake:
> We'll pass new *Alpes*, new Consuls overthrow,
> To *Rome* with far more dreadful Armies go...
> Nor stop till *Rosalinda*'s Statue, Crown'd,
> Sits in the Capitol with Gods enthron'd?[5]

---

[1] For example Nero's rants in II. iii:

> "When I look sad, whole *Hecatombs* should fall.
> Ha! who are they? my fretting blood does rise:
> Hands, rest: I'le try to blast him with my Eyes.
> Make me Basilisk, but one short hour,
> Some GOD, that would be *Nero*'s Emperour."

[2] IV and V.

[3] See G. Saupe, *Die Sophonisbatragödien in der englischen Literatur des
17. und 18. Jahrhunderts* (Halle, 1929).

[4] *Rosalinda:* "Who's there?
> *Massina:*   First instruct me what you are,
> And how you came to be thus Heavenly fair:
> What is it makes your Cheeks so fresh and bright,
> The Red of Roses, or the Lillies white?" and so on.

[5] V.

Undoubtedly, apart from the melodramatic atmosphere, apart from the extraneous trapping of visions and of portents[1], there remains in this play a force, an enthusiasm lacking even in the works of Dryden himself. It is the divine passion, the last of the madnesses of poetry, ere poetry of inspiration fell into its slumber of a hundred years.

The following year, in Jan. 1675/6, was produced at D.L. Lee's third tragedy, *Gloriana, or, The Court of Augustus Caesar*, his "worst Tragedy" as Genest styles it[2]. Genest's criticism must be accepted carefully. Those who have read this play will agree that in places at least it rises to a certain dramatic intensity by no means unconvincing. Such is that scene in the last act where Gloriana lies in the bed of Augustus, ready to slay him, and Caesario, her lover, comes to part the curtains:

> *Gloriana:* Who's this? am I awake or do I see?
>   *Caesario* here indeed, can this be he?
>   If thou be *Caesar*'s Son that did adore
>   The Blood of *Pompey*, speak, or love no more.
> *Caesario:* Love no more.
> *Gloriana:* Why dost thou thus with frightful Action gaze?
>   Or art thou but the Ghost of him that was?
> *Caesario:* The Ghost of him that was.
> *Gloriana:* Such by thy stedfast Eyes thou wou'dst appear,
>   Thy dread replies unusual horrour bear...
>   Who was thy Murd'rer, if thou murder'd be?
>   By *Caesar* slain, or wert thou kill'd by the...
> *Caesario:* Kill'd by thee.

These individual passages, wherein Lee rises truly to the heights of his art, make up for the lack of novelty in character drawing and the monotony of the conclusion. Lee was not the kind of man to love tragi-comic endings to his plays, and accordingly we find that the stage at the close of every fifth act is literally strewed with corpses. Deeply influenced by the tendencies of his age, he could not indulge in subtle studies of mind-states, and his characters at this time are simply the stock characters of the heroic tragedy. Augustus

---

[1] Note the "*Heaven of Blood*" and the "*Spirits in Battle*" in II. ii.
[2] I. 182.

is the ordinary lustful king, to be traced through Dryden
from Valentinian and other figures of the early seventeenth
century. He develops an evil passion for Gloriana, the
mistress of his son Caesario, who in turn is beloved by
Narcissa, the pathetic heroine. The last mentioned, as was
inevitable in these heroic plays, stabs herself for love.

The only other writer during this time who at all approached towards that third type of the heroic tragedy—the
duller, more artificial species which tried to imitate the rimed
plays of France—was John Crowne, the dramatist patronised
by Rochester when that nobleman had cast off Dryden from
his good graces. In all Crowne has contributed two heroic
plays to the theatre and another, written by an unknown
author, he touched up for the stage. *The History of Charles
the Eighth of France, or, The Invasion of Naples by the French*
was the first new play acted at the theatre at Dorset Garden
in 1671. In spite of its almost contemporary subject matter,
it is as heroic as any drama set in Peru or India or China[1].
The scene is one of war, but the main business of the plot
concerns Ferdinand's love for Cornelia and Charles' love for
Julia, the sister of Ferdinand. It is truly, what the epilogue
calls it, "*a dull Rhiming Play*," and is interesting only because
in type it stands midway between Orrery and Dryden. *The
Destruction of Jerusalem by Titus Vespasian* (two parts D.L.
Jan. 1676/7) is almost equally dull although its greater licence
and more numerous stirring scenes procured for it a greater
meed of contemporary approval. The other play, which
Crowne merely rendered fit for the stage, is a translation of
Racine's *Andromaque*[2], and has solely an historic significance.
In all of these plays Crowne was obviously trying to combine
popular elements with his natural leaning towards pseudo-
classicism. That leaning towards classicism is more clearly
seen in his later dramas, *Thyestes, Darius, Regulus* and
Caligula.

In thus passing over in review the actual heroic tragedies
of the years 1664–77, I have indicated so much of the plot
and structure of the dramas that little need now be said in

---

[1] See particularly III. i.   [2] *Andromache* (D.G. *c.* August 1674).

a general summary of the various characteristics of the species. All three types, as has been abundantly evident, had qualities in common, the only differences being, in the Dryden species a superabundance of rant and stirring scenes, in the Orrerian a more classic chill and chastened calm.

Love, as is perfectly obvious, was the prevading atmosphere of all three, a love that wrapped everything in its control and lost itself in ridiculous similes and nonsensical reasonings. "The Flame of Love," says Perdiccas in Cooke's *Love's Triumph* (unacted, 1678),

> The flame of Love no water can asswage,
> It makes it blaze, and roar with fiercer rage,

and although Statira informs him

> 'Tis cause you don't—
> Fling on fresh buckets at a faster rate:
> A close supply its fury would abate[1],

neither he nor any of his heroic companions took the advice, but let the conflagration proceed in merry crackling style. This love affects heroes and heroines, saints and sinners, in the strangest ways. Not only does it conquer and disturb the all-conquering warrior—"Frail Prince!" says Lelius in Lee's *Sophonisba* (D.L. 1675),

> Frail Prince, how wavering all his Actions be,
> By Passions toss'd in Love's Tempestuous Sea[2],—

but the characters are all afflicted by it with such a suddenness that they hardly know at first what it is. Part of Zempoalla's soliloquy in *The Indian Queen* I have already quoted[3], and that is but typical of the sentiments of many another character. Sometimes, even, according to their own words, these characters cannot distinguish the force of love from a physical wound. In Banks' *The Destruction of Troy* (D.G. 1678) Achilles is in the temple: Paris flings a dart and wounds him, whereat the hero, thinking of his mistress, cries out aloud:

> Ha! Ha! *Polyxena*...what ails my Heart!
> Sure 'twas not Love that gave that deadly smart—
> I'me hurt...O Gods! who can the Pain indure![4]

[1] I. viii.   [2] I. ii.   [3] *Supra*, p. 112.   [4] v.

It is quite obvious that, given a love of this kind, passion should take away from those whom it seizes all power of common sense. Sertorius, in Sir Robert Howard's *The Vestal Virgin, or, The Roman Ladies* (T.R. in B.St. before 1665), is going to a duel, and bids Caska do a last service for him:

> I have but one Thing more then to enjoin thee;
> If I shou'd fall by *Tiridates'* Sword,
> Carry the News thy self unto *Hersilia*,
> And watch her as thou would'st an Arrow shot,
> To see whether it hit or no.

Caska, who is not in love, sees the folly of this:

> "To what purpose, Sir?..." he asks,
> "How, Sir, shou'd I send you Word?"

This appears to come as an entirely new thought to Sertorius, who, meditatively gazing on his companion, can only murmur "'Tis true." Later he announces his fresh intention to Tiridates:

> I will be just to you; but if I fall,
> Carry no News of Love, nor me, at all;
> For I have thought upon't, and find it vain,
> To me no Message can come back again[1].

This wonderful love, as we have seen, is usually presented in violent conflict with what may be styled honour, which might be friendship or loyalty, but rarely the point of honour as in the French plays[2]. The more limited sense of honour appears in only one or two stray dramas of the period. Of the Love and Honour contests I have given sufficient examples above. In the breasts of all the heroes of this drama there proceeds a continual tempest of warring passions: each separate figure could endorse the words of Caesario in Lee's *Gloriana* (D.L. 1676):

> Revenge and Friendship in my Bosom clash'd,
> Like Mountain billows, each the other dash'd[3].

Love and honour both could serve towards the making of rivals temporary friends, as in *The Indian Emperor*, or as in

---

[1] II.

[2] The essential differences between the French love tragedy and the English are discussed in several critical studies: see *supra*, pp. 97–8 and *infra*, pp. 187–8.   [3] II.

Howard's *The Vestal Virgin* (T.R. in B.St. before 1665) where
Sertorius bids his enemy and rival join with him:

> Come, *Tiridates*,
> *Hersilia*'s Danger now our Quarrel ends,
> And when she is unsafe, we must be Friends:
> Our Action's some fantastic Planet guides,
> Ill-Fortune can unite whom Good divides[1].

Although love is mostly the dominating note in these plays,
even to the exclusion of honour, in some honour has decidedly definite claims. Thus in Tuke's *The Adventures of
Five Hours* (L.I.F. 1663) Octavio requests Antonio to retire:

> You from a Life of Perils hither come
> To find a Nuptial Bed, not seek a Tomb,

but Antonio will hear naught of it:

> My Friend ingag'd, it never must be said,
> *Antonio* left him so to go to Bed.

Even when Octavio reminds him that he is married, he
replies:

> Wedded to Honour, that must yield to none[2].

In the main, however, honour is subservient to love and to
individual passion. Montezuma and Almanzor can shift
about as pleases their fancies. The hero is above smaller
scruples such as might affect ordinary mortals:

> None but the Conquer'd should have sence of shame.
> Shall shows of Vertue darken (your) bright Fame?
> Success does cover all the Crimes of War,
> And Fame and Vertue still consistent are[3]—

these words of Rustan's in Orrery's *Mustapha* (L.I.F. 1665)
might be taken as a motto by all the heroes of the day. It is
not that they are frail, as Dryden points out in his defence
of Almanzor, but that they form worlds of honour and of
morality for themselves. It may indeed be conjectured
whether the tendency of the time did not give rise to this
aspect of their personalities. When men could shift easily
from Republicanism to adoration of monarchy, from a faithful

----

[1] II.   [2] II.   [3] I. i.

serving of the Catholic church to an embracing of the creed of the English church, from Whiggery to Toryism, it seems but natural that they should introduce their own characteristics into the figures of their idealising imagination. Man is decidedly anthropomorphic in his creative powers, and Almanzor is simply a god idealised from actual Wallers and Drydens.

These idealised heroes do not on any occasion hesitate to point out to others their majestic positions. "I shine above thee," remarks Scipio in *Sophonisba* (D.L. 1675),

> like a Star fix'd higher,
> Whom though you cannot reach, you may admire[1].

Araspes in *Gloriana* (D.L. 1676) tells Caesario he is but a man. The latter's reply is characteristic:

> Said you of me? 'Twas poor:
> A man! *Araspes*, I was always more.
> When me in Swadling-bands the Nurses rock'd,
> My Soul was full with God-like Courage stock'd;
> The Sounds which first my wondrous Voice did move,
> Were Father *Julius*, and grandsire *Jove*:
> E'en in my Childhood I was more than Man[2].

Nor did heroes share this self-esteem only among others of their own class: heroes and villains alike have the most exalted notions of themselves and of their actions. The Queen Mother in Settle's *The Empress of Morocco* (D.G. 1673) is as bad as Almanzor:

> From Springs so deep shall sink thee down to Hell.
> I shed my Tears, as Rain in *Egypt* falls,
> Sent for no common Cause, but to foretell
> Destructions, Ruins, Plagues, and Funerals[3],

and a character in the same author's *The Conquest of China* (D.G. 1675) can decide that

> Those few Millions we've yet vanquisht, are
> A bare dumb Shew of a poor Pageant War,
> Our Honour now for greater Action calls[4].

---

[1] II. i.   [2] II.   [3] III (v).   [4] I. i.

Even so late as 1694, Pembroke in Banks' *The Innocent Usurper* (1694) could remember sufficient of the rants of the heroes and the villains of 1670 to cry:

> Weep Heav'ns, fall Hail and Torrents from the Skye,
> And when y'ave drein'd the Briney Ocean dry,
> Weep on, and pour the watery Globe and Night,
> On the World's back, and quench this Orb of Light[1].—

all *à propos* of his own emotions.

These exaggerated emotions, as we have abundantly seen, led to a falsification of all psychology. Not one of the heroes, heroines or villains of the exalted tragedy acts rightly. Their psychology is hopelessly wrong. Whether it is love or war or death their actions and their words are the actions and the words of unreality. Their declarations ring hollow. Massinissa in Lee's *Sophonisba* (D.L. 1675) has already shown us the follies and the unnatural sentiments that this exalted temper could produce. The unreality of that meeting of Massinissa and of Rosalinda is paralleled in the same play in the death of Trebellius, who, as he expires, can find energy to pour out a torrent of heroic words:

> Cut off in my full growth! curse on your strife;
> To die thus, when I business had for Life!
> Just *Scipio* will revenge my Death, beware;
> I feel I'm going, though I know not where[2].

The constant straining after exaggerated effect even led the dramatists to create for their characters a special language. The unnatural sentiments and the ranting rhetoric poured forth by them found a counterpart in their marvellous oaths. "Zounds," the fashionable exclamation of real life, would have been too commonplace to appear on their lips. "Furies! and Hell!"[3] however, was quite in keeping with their personalities: or "Tortures! and Hell!"[4] or "Hell! Plagues! and Death!"[5] or "Hell! Furies! Fiends! and Plagues!"[6]

---

[1] iv. i.   [2] iv.
[3] Lee's *Gloriana* (D.L. 1676), i. i; *The Duke of Guise* (D.L. 1682), i. ii; Banks' *Vertue Betray'd* (D.G. 1682), i. i.
[4] Settle's *Ibrahim* (D.G. 1676), iii. i.
[5] Southerne's *The Loyal Brother* (D.L. 1682), iii. ii.
[6] *Id.* ii. i.

"Ravens! and Vultures!" occurs in Settle's *The Female Prelate* (D.L. 1679)[1] though Lee outshines them all with his "Night! Horror! Death! Confusion! Hell! and Furies!"[2] his no less inspiring "Death and Devils! Daggers! Poison! Fire!"[3] and his "Gods! Devils! Hell! Heaven! and Earth!"[4] These heroic exclamations, like the rants, as several among these references clearly demonstrate, endured long after the rimed fashion had passed away. "Hell! Scalding Lead! and Sulphures!" appears as late as 1694 in Banks' *The Innocent Usurper*.

From the presence of the exaggerated hero, also, and of the exaggerated villain, fed, too, from earlier Elizabethan founts, came the prevalence in the heroic drama of the Dryden school, of situations of horror, murder, torture and blood. Some of the scenes described in the stage directions to the heroic plays equal in bloody suggestion even some of the passages in *Titus Andronicus*. The sixth engraving to Settle's *The Empress of Morocco* (D.G. 1673) shows a dungeon filled with mutilated bodies impaled on stakes, the ground littered with the bones of former victims[5]. Indeed, the horrible presentments that are put forward in so many of the Restoration tragedies, heroic and otherwise, make us realise that, if the poetic spirit of Webster and of Ford was in many ways lost, certainly their love of blood and of riotous torment never was. From Ford and from Webster, too, came to the Restoration dramatists as a whole that dabbling in unnatural sex-relationships which I have taken note of above.

Just as the presence of the horrors and peculiar sex themes

---

[1] IV. iii.   [2] *Oedipus* (D.G. 1678), III. i.

[3] *Caesar Borgia* (D.G. 1679), IV, where also in V occurs "Racks, Rocks and Fire! Cauldrons of molten Lead!"

[4] *Nero* (D.L. 1674), III. i.

[5] Cf. also Settle's *Cambyses* (L.I.F. 1671), III. iv—"*The Body of* Osiris, *beheaded; & an Executioner with the suppos'd Head in a Vessel of Blood*": and *The Conquest of China* (D.G. 1675), where in V. iii is a "*Scene of Murdered Women*," and in which occurs a stage direction "*Dy omnes*." In Payne's *The Siege of Constantinople* (D.G. 1674) we have as a last scene "*a great Number of Dead and Dying men in several manner of Deaths. The* Chancellor, Lorenzo, *and* Michael *Empal'd*," while in *The Treacherous Brothers* (D.L. 1689) of Powell, "*The Scene drawn discovers* Men(aphon) *Executed, being flung from a Battlement upon Spikes.*"

was not due to the influence of Corneille or of Racine, but, taken from earlier Elizabethan example, was working in direct opposition to the French influence, so the multiplicity of action, the innumerable characters and the licence of stirring scenes acted *coram populo*, were all decidedly English ingredients in the cosmopolitan nature of the heroic drama. "Sieges" and "Conquests" abound, and "Destructions" are not uncommon—all titles, which, avoided on the continent, point to the difference of temperament between the audience of Paris and the audience of London.

As a fit background for these stirring scenes the public of the seventeenth century desired settings of rich gorgeous loveliness, full of a strangeness that should reave them away from the drabness of contemporary conditions. In this wise, the Oriental settings given to many a tragedy may be taken as indicating a desire to escape from conventional surroundings to a world of unrestrained bustle and turmoil and impossible romance. These scenes most frequently had some vague historical basis, but truth to history and truth to local customs was never insisted upon. To fit them in with the prevailing temper of the time, the characters, were they Romans, Arabians, Mexicans, Chinamen, even Englishmen of the earlier Tudor periods, were all warped out of their national characteristics and made to live in the one world[1]— the world of heroic ardour and of dauntless courage. Even Orrery, with his historical tragedies, has not more truth to nature than Dryden or Nat Lee has.

The heroic tragedy, on all sides, is to be explained by declaring it a conscious artificialising of early seventeenth century romantic drama, with elements introduced to please the tastes of the Restoration novelty-seeking audience, and all modified just a trifle to make it approach a little nearer to the heroic plays of France.

[1] Ilse Hecht has a useful study of the women characters in these plays— *Der heroische Frauentyp im Restaurationsdrama* (Leipzig, 1932). The Eastern settings and personages are discussed by L. Wann in "The Oriental in Restoration Drama" (*Wisconsin University Studies*, 1918, ii).

IV. *Other Types of Tragedy:* 1660–1677

In thus dealing at length with the characteristics of the rimed heroic play, it must not be presumed that that was the only type of serious drama put before the public during the years 1664–77. Native English influence led to a development of non-heroic tragedy also, and this, though less popular, must never be forgotten: the prevailing desire for novelty, show, music and dance, coupled with the undoubted influence of D'Avenant, tended towards the elaboration of the opera.

The germs of opera, certainly, may be traced back to native English example as well—in this case, directly to the masque. All through the seventeenth century the opera remained in its "English" form: it did not adopt the *recitativo* and *aria* of Italian productions, presaged though these had been by D'Avenant in *The Siege of Rhodes* and hinted at by Flecknoe in his early unacted *Love's Dominion* (1654) later brought out as *Love's Kingdom* at L.I.F. in 1664. The operas of the time were with a few exceptions all dramatic operas, composed of dialogue in prose or verse interspersed with fragments of song and with choruses. Anything indeed that was slightly more musical than ordinary and possessed an additional supply of airs appears in Restoration times to have gained for itself the title of opera. Thus for Downes Shadwell's play of *The Lancashire Witches* (D.G. 1681) because of its songs became "a kind of Opera[1]," and Granville in a preface to his *Genuine Works in Verse and Prose* (1732) reminds us that "to introduce Singing and Dancing, by Head and Shoulders, no way relative to the Action, does not turn a Play into an Opera: though that Title is now promiscuously given to every Farce sprinkled here and there with a Song and a Dance."

In spite of Flecknoe's and D'Avenant's early endeavours, and in spite of the fact that D'Avenant's house seems to have been known generally as the "Opera," we do not come to the definitely operatic period of the drama till the seventies of the century. Music was but slowly developing in the

[1] P. 38.

theatres, and Purcell, to whose influence may be attributed a fair amount of the interest in this form of theatrical production, did not apply his talents to the dramatic sphere until the year 1686. Purcell, certainly, was not alone in contributing to the popularity of the species. We find engaged in the writing of dramatic music not only Englishmen such as Matthew Locke, who collaborated with D'Avenant in pre-Restoration times and who later had an interest in composing the music for the operatic versions of *Macbeth* and of *The Tempest*[1], but foreigners as well. Battista Draghi aided Locke in setting the music for Shadwell's *Psyche* (D.G. 1674/5): Cambert arrived in England in 1673 and he and his pupil Grabut had a share in the more ornate performances at the Theatre Royal and at the court theatre. French troupes of opera singers were certainly performing in England several times between 1660 and 1700[2]. An early production was *The Descent of Orpheus into Hell* by Chapoton of which "the Description of the Great Machines" is still extant. This was no doubt performed by a company under Jean Channouveau, who received £300 from the king for his services on Dec. 2, 1661, and whom Evelyn records as acting at court on the 16th of the same month. I have also noted the performance of *Ariane, ou, Le Mariage de Bacchus* in March 1673/4. This was an opera originally written by Perrin and set to music by Cambert himself: it was produced by the newly founded Royal Academy of Music, organised by Cambert and Grabut. *Pomone*, set by Cambert, and performed at Paris in 1671, was very probably put on the English stage about the same time. In May 1677 appeared another opera, this time by Madame La Roche-Guilhen, entitled

---

[1] On the music for these operatic plays, and on the opera generally during the Restoration period, see Edward J. Dent, *Foundations of English Opera* (1928). Considerable controversy has raged concerning the extant music for *Macbeth* (*op. cit.* pp. 128–36): it has been variously ascribed to Locke, Purcell and Leveridge. John Bannister, Pelham Humfrey, Pietro Reggio, Matthew Locke and G. B. Draghi were all concerned with *The Tempest*, and later there came the Purcell score (*op. cit.* pp. 136–8 and 229–30).

[2] See D. M. Walmsley, "The Influence of Foreign Opera on English Operatic Plays of the Restoration Period" (*Anglia*, 1928, LII. 37–50).

Rare en Tout[1]. The foreign composers who got these operas
produced, the singers who took the leading parts and the
dancers who were imported especially from France, all worked
with the regular managements of the theatres. Grabut's later
collaboration with Southerne and with Dryden is well known.

The first step towards a fuller development of the English
opera was probably that made by D'Avenant and Dryden in
The Tempest (L.I.F. Nov. 1667) and by D'Avenant in *Macbeth*
(two versions, about 1664 and in 1673). The earlier *Tempest*,
however, is barely an opera: it has operatic features: it is
removed one degree further into the world of romance by the
introduction of a sister to Miranda, named Dorinda, and of
Hippolito, a youth who has never seen a woman, as well as
by its emphasis on show. It was left to Shadwell to move
the musical adaptation of Shakespeare still another stage, to
the full realms of the opera proper[2]. The description of the
orchestra in this opera of Shadwell's, the elaborate stage
settings, the machines and the songs—of which "Arise ye
Subterranean Winds" is a masterpiece—all mark out the
dramatic opera of the English type. *Macbeth*, also, by
D'Avenant, was carried a further stage into the operatic
world (D.G. Feb. 1672/3)[3]. This second *Macbeth* is not less
typical. The atmosphere is thoroughly operatic. The witches
enter and exeunt "flying[4]." There is thunder and lightning
to be heard[5]—that thunder and lightning which was so
satirised by Duffett in his epilogue "Being a new Fancy after
the old, and most surprising way of MACBETH, Perform'd with
new and costly MACHINES," appended to his burlesque *The
Empress of Morocco* (D.L. 1673). The ghost descends and
rises again at Macbeth's feet[6]. Every attempt is made to

---

[1] See Appendix B, and notes on the play lists given there in *The Times
Literary Supplement*, Sept. 21, 1922. Note should be taken in W. J. Lawrence's article on "Foreign Singers and Musicians at the Court of
Charles II" (*Musical Quarterly*, April 1923) of the reference to the *Ballet
et Musique pour le divertissement du Roy de la Grande Bretagne* (1674).

[2] On this question of the operatic treatment of Shakespeare see Hazelton
Spencer, *Shakespeare Improved* (1927), especially pp. 152–73, 192–209
and 318–28. For the arguments regarding authorship see Appendix C.

[3] See the text of the edition of 1674.

[4] I. i.   [5] I. i.   [6] III.

lower the tragic tension and to heighten the artificiality of the piece—a movement analogous to that we have seen in full force in the development of the heroic tragedy.

The first real non-Shakespearian opera was Shadwell's *Psyche* (D.G. Feb. 1674/5), largely derived from Molière and again satirised by Duffett. Here we have moved into what is truly the operatic realm of Restoration dramas. The tendency of the heroic play had been merely an exaggeration of the rational tragic endeavour—to raise and to generalise human qualities into an almost divine and infallible content. The tendency of the opera, on the other hand, was towards the completely unreal. It is this that Dryden felt when he declared that "the suppos'd Persons" of the opera "are generally supernatural, as Gods and Goddesses, and Heroes which at least are descended from them, and are in due time to be adopted into their number[1]." Thus, for the most part, while the heroic tragedy treated of distant oriental realms with a sham historical background, the opera dwelt on mythical episodes and with entirely fanciful scenes. The very title of this play of Shadwell's, or of Charles D'Avenant's *Circe* (D.G. 1677) or of Dryden's *Albion and Albanius* (D.G. 1685) and *King Arthur* (D.G. 1691) or of Settle's *The Fairy Queen* (D.G. 1692) and *The World in the Moon* (D.G. 1697) serve to display the vast chasm which lay between the pure tragedy and its musical contemporary.

Naturally, not many of these operas deserve any very lengthy literary mention. *Psyche* might be produced at the then enormous expense of £800, with vocal music by Locke and instrumental by Giovanni Battista Draghi, with dances by St André and scenery by Stephenson, but for us to-day the whole piece lacks inherent interest. Apart from a stray song or two, it is a thing dead and valueless. Of D'Avenant's *Circe* (D.G. May 1677) exactly the same may be said. Here again, packed into the limits of five acts, we find music, song and show, crowds of spirits and furies and syrens, "*A Dance of the Winds*[2]" and a dance of "*Pleasant Dreams*[3]." "*The*

---

[1] Preface to *Albion and Albanius* (D.G. 1685).
[2] II. i. [3] V. vi.

Heav'ns open" in one scene[1], and in the last the city suddenly bursts into flame. All such theatrical accompaniments
lacking now, we can barely summon up enough courage to
pass over the borders of the initial scene. Nemesis will
always follow the opera. One of the most appealing of stage
forms, its libretto is doomed to everlasting oblivion.

Apart from the opera there remain a certain number of
serious plays written between 1660 and 1677 still unaccounted
for. These, either complete tragedies or compounds of
tragedy and of comedy, may nearly all be styled Elizabethan
in tone. That is to say, they present reminiscences of one or
other of the older types of drama, Shakespearian, Websterian,
romantic or pastoral, without any marked developments of
heroic elements. These plays may be regarded as backwaters
in the forward rush of the drama, and yet must have played
no inconsiderable part in the future growth of that "Shakespearian" style which was heralded by Dryden in his *All for
Love*. Of all the Elizabethan models, naturally, the romantic
plays of Beaumont and Fletcher played a chief part, although
we can often trace the influence of other and different types
in plays that are definitely romantic in tone. Possibly next
in importance we might rank the influence of the school of
horrors.

Of the latter type, mixed with Shakespearian reminiscence,
is *The Villain* (L.I.F. Oct. 1662) by Thomas Porter, praised
by Young Killigrew on its first production[2]. Here Malignii
is another Iago and Charlotte goes mad in imitation of
Ophelia. Iago appeared again, ten years later, in *The Fatal
Jealousie* (D.G. Aug. 1672) of Nevil Payne, where he mas-
querades as Jasper, in opposition to a not ill-drawn Othello
in Don Antonio[3]. Of the same type is Henry Cary's tragedy
The Mariage Night (L.I.F. *c.* Sept. 1663) in which reminiscences of Tourneur's *The Revenger's Tragedy* are combined
with echoes from Shakespeare's works. Something of the

---

[1] II. i.

[2] Pepys, Oct. 20, 1662.

[3] On this playwright see the essay by Willard Thorp, "Henry Nevil
Payne, Dramatist and Jacobite Conspirator" (in the *Parrott Presentation
Volume*, 1935, pp. 347-81).

same note is struck once more in Killigrew's *The Imperial Tragedy* (unacted? 1669), which is one mass of coffins, black rooms, "*dismal Vaults*," ghosts, spirits and "satyres" and it finds reflection, also, in Ravenscroft's alteration of *Titus Andronicus*, acted at Drury Lane about 1679. In this connection it should be observed that Shakespeare's original *Titus Andronicus* is listed among the plays revived shortly after the Restoration. It is of course difficult now to determine whether the audience and the dramatists of the time took these and other horrors seriously. Edward Howard, Downes tells us, turned *Romeo and Juliet* into a tragi-comedy with a happy ending and this was played on alternate evenings with the Shakespeare original. Similarly Sir Robert Howard[1], in writing *The Vestal Virgin* (T.R. in B.St. before 1665), gave his play a double fifth act, in one of which a general scene of carnage is introduced, Artabaces entering with his eyes out, in the other the whole is ended in "*a Comical Way*" and Lacy, in speaking the epilogue, cracks jokes about the change of *dénouement*. The cynicism of the age so permeates the theatre of the Restoration that it is difficult indeed to determine precisely what was a genuine expression of emotion and what was a false sentiment uttered merely to satisfy a passing whim.

A few other plays in this period mingle in varying proportions elements taken from Shakespeare and elements taken from other sources. Sir Robert Howard's other tragic drama, *The Great Favourite, or, The Duke of Lerma* (T.R. in B.St. Feb. 1668) is one of the best of these[2]. There is no excess of bloodshed here, although poison is employed for effect, and the Machiavellian Duke of Lerma with his tool, Roderigo del Caldroon, the pure Maria with the complicated touches in her psychology, and the young king, make up a story that causes us to think more highly of Dryden's

---

[1] Peculiarly, Howard has so far remained without a biographer, although useful notes on his life have been contributed by Florence R. Scott (e.g. in *PMLA*, 1937, LIII. 1094–1100, and *Modern Language Notes*, 1940, LV. 410–6): see also E. S. de Beer in *NQ*, April 4, 1944, CLXXXVII. 214–15.

[2] Alfred Harbage almost definitely proves that this work, so much better than any of Howard's other serious writing, is based on a now lost play by Ford (see Appendix C).

collaborator, enemy and friend, than his other works would have warranted.

Most of the other Elizabethan-type plays merit but brief historical mention. Most of these are tragi-comedies, and a certain number of them are Arcadian in scene and in character. At the very first opening of the theatres, before the discovery of the heroic play, there seems to have been a slight flutter of interest in pastoral themes. Fanshawe's translation of *Il Pastor Fido* by Guarini (printed 1647) was reprinted in 1664. Flecknoe's *Love's Kingdom* (L.I.F. 1664), although scened in Cyprus, has an Arcadian atmosphere. Thomas Forde's *Love's Labyrinth* (printed 1660) boldly sets its "*scoene*" in "*Arcadia*," as does John Fountain's *The Rewards of Virtue* (printed 1661). This interest in the pastoral form would appear to have lasted erratically throughout the century. We have records of old pastorals revived, and a number of early Restoration pastorals were re-worked later. Fountain's drama gave Shadwell the basis for *The Royal Shepherdess* (L.I.F. Feb. 1668/9) and Fanshawe's translation provided Settle with the model for his *Pastor Fido* already mentioned. *The Constant Nymph*, written by "a Person of Quality" and staged at D.G. about July 1677, also attests to the popularity of the species during the acknowledged reign of the heroic play.

The majority of these plays, however, were rather romantic than definitely pastoral in tone. Edward Howard's two dramas, *The Usurper* (T.R. in B.St. Jan. 1663/4) and *The Women's Conquest* (L.I.F. *c.* Nov. 1670) are of this style. The first is set in Sicily and mingles in a peculiar manner allegoric political reference and romantic story. In it Damocles, Hugo de Petra and Cleomenes shroud under thin veils the figures of Oliver Cromwell, Peters and Monk. The scene of the other is Scythia, but a Scythia much alike to the Arcadia of Shadwell and others. The comic part here is sustained by Foscaris, a gentleman who has left his wife but who "longs for" her "after he has parted with her," and by Andrages, "another Husband, who loves his Wife so well that he cannot part with her, though she seems to provoke him to it."

Generally the plot is dull, but the language in places rises above the mediocre[1].

Of similar nature are Sir William Killigrew's three tragi-comedies. Sir William Killigrew, like D'Avenant, was of the older age, and his plays freely exploit and expand upon the strained, artificial emotionalism of the "cavalier" playwrights who flourished in the reign of Charles I. *The Seege of Urbin* (T.R. 1665) is one fantastic story of romance, villainy, duelling, fighting, jealousy and love. *Ormasdes* (1664), called later *Love and Friendship*, is scened in Cytherea, and is, unlike the former which is in prose, written in blank verse, with very occasional lapses into rime. It is a love tragedy in which complicated emotions arise out of the passion of Cleandra, Queen of Cytherea, for her general, Ormasdes, who is loved by and who loves Valeriana, Queen of Treconia (not the King, as in the list of *dramatis personae*). The sick scene in Act v is rather well conceived, where Ormasdes sleeps by the couch of Valeriana. *Selindra* (T.R. in V.St., March 1661/2) is set in Byzantium and is highly romantic. In it, Astella, princess of Hungary, disguises herself as Selindra, while her brother, Polinesso, likewise changes his personality, apparently by the use of a periwig and a patch over one eye.

The two tragi-comedies of Sir Robert Stapylton have also much of the same characteristics, *The Slighted Maid* (L.I.F. Feb. 1662/3) being scened in an exceedingly nebulous Naples, and *The Stepmother* (L.I.F. *c.* Nov. 1663) in a no less nebulous province of early Britain. In both the names of the *dramatis personae* are Arcadian, Iberio and Pyramena, Filamor and Pontia. Both plays are full of masques[2], and both are tricked out with musical additions, "The Instrumental, Vocal, and Recitative Musick" of the former being "composed by Mr *Banister*," one of the principal royal

---

[1] This play is interesting for the preface in defence of tragi-comedies, and against heroic dramas and end-stopped verse. This is indeed more "a Discourse, or Essay on Dramatick Poesie, then a Preface to a Play." There are in addition no less than three prologues—one spoken by Underhill, Angel and Nokes, in condemnation of "*Scaramouchos*, and *Jack Puddings*," a second by Jonson's shade, and a third more regular.

[2] There are at least three in each.

violinists. Both are very moral in tone, and both have an
entire absence of any psychological sense—the marvellous
conversion of the "stepmother" being typical of all the
characters represented in each.

Mrs Behn's *The Dutch Lover* (D.G. Feb. 1672/3) might
be taken as a tragi-comedy variant of the Spanish intrigue
type of comedy, but her *The Forc'd Marriage, or, The Jealous
Bridegroom* (L.I.F. Dec. 1670) may fairly be styled a romantic
serio-drama. The scene of the latter is laid in France, but a
France peopled with Philanders and Galateas—mythical as
Arcadia. The purpose of the play is a solemn one. It conveys
a moral precept, or thought at least—and for that is valuable
as a vague premonition of graver eighteenth century sentimental comedies to come[1].

A play of much less interest is *The Amorous Prince, or,
The Curious Husband* (L.I.F. *c.* May 1671) set in an equally
mythical Florence, and approaching again towards the pastoral style. It has a mixture of romantic sentiment and
intrigue, but has no dramatic or literary value when compared with *The Forc'd Marriage*[2].

Tragi-comedy was also touched in this period by Dryden
in *The Rival Ladies*, in *Secret Love* and in *Marriage a la
Mode*, but those three plays, although definitely connected
with the heroic drama, may more fittingly be considered
among this author's comedies. Crowne approached the type
more seriously in his *Juliana, or, The Princess of Poland*
(L.I.F. *c.* Aug. 1671). This play, in its dull manner, attempts
at emotion which, however, runs to nothing but rant. A single
example will suffice. "I'll run and kill him!" cries Alexey,
to which Paulina answers:

> No, let me alone!
> I'll kill him, but it shall be with Torments!
> Steel, Poison, Fire, Racks, Scorpions, Hell!
> Oh me unfortunate![3]

---

[1] It is based partly on the tale of the *curioso impertinente*. The romantic
plot deals with the love of the Prince of Florence for the fair (and high-
born) shepherdess, Chloris. The intrigue concerns Antonio, the jealous
husband, who sets Alberto, in love with Ismena, to tempt Clarina, his
wife. Of a familiar tone to this play is the worthless play of Mrs Boothby,
Marcelia, or, The Treacherous Friend (T.R. in B.St. *c.* Aug. 1669).

[2] See also *infra*, p. 267.   [3] II. iii.

Rant such as this fills the play, together with improbable incidents and unnatural valour and miraculous escapes, so that the whole appears to us as it does to the Landlord at the close of the piece:

What! I warrant this young Man is that young Man's Wife: why, sure my House was enchanted to Day, lodg'd Princes and Dukes, like Mummers and Masqueraders; and Women and Wenches in men's Cloaths, and Cloak-bags, and Scufflings, and they kill one another, and they're alive again, and this, and that, and I know not what. Here's work indeed!

A not unfitting close to this period of Restoration tragi-comedy.

V. *Tragedy and Opera:* 1678–1700

With the year 1678, as we have already noted, we move into a new era of dramatic productivity, the rimed tragedy dying a natural death of old age, and the pseudo-classic and Shakespearian elements rising gradually to a more dominant position. In studying, however, the tragedies written between 1678 and 1700, we must take due notice of the fact that, while Shakespeare adaptations and pseudo-classic plays were assuming ever a larger and a larger place in the repertoire of the playhouses, the older elements represented in the heroic tragedy were by no means dead. Opera still flourished, and was embraced by both pseudo-classicist and by Shakespearian alike. George Granville, first baron Lansdowne, could write plays noticeable for their chill and at the same time pen a purely operatic *British Enchanters* (Haymarket, 1706): Dryden could turn from more or less chastened productions to present an *Albion and Albanius* (D.G. 1685). Moreover, the heroic atmosphere proper by no means perished when the year 1677 saw the abandonment of rime. Not only did Lee, Settle and Tate continue to pour out plays which for all general purposes may be styled heroic, but even the classic Granville produced a tragedy which he styled by the symbolic title, *Heroick Love* (L.I.F. 1697).

New forces at the same time were already at work, chief among which may be numbered that pathetic type, which,

weak in the seventeenth century, was destined to join forces
with the sentimental theatre and dominate a great part of
the productivity of the eighteenth century stage. There is no
possibility, of course, of keeping all these various old and new
elements in water-tight compartments, but we can, largely,
determine the type of a particular play by a reference to the
pathetic, Shakespearian, operatic, heroic or classic school.

First in point of importance, probably, because it was to
develop along straight lines leading to Addison's *Cato* and
Johnson's *Irene*, is the pseudo-classic movement, but it must
be remembered that even in the chillest of late seventeenth
century tragedies some of the tendencies of the heroic drama
can usually be traced. We have already noted in the preceding decades the stricter type of French drama cultivated
in translations, and considerably "altered in its dress" by
Roger Boyle, Earl of Orrery. The influence of Orrery was
deeply marked on certain of the later classical plays, although
there were some men who preferred to abandon even his
example and pass to duller and less inspired realms. There
were men among the pseudo-classicists who demanded the
chillest of plot and of expression, who held frantically to the
unities, who would permit none but two speaking characters
on the stage at one time. Such ultra-classicism, however, was
evidently never very popular. Rymer could not get his *Edgar,
or, The English Monarch* acted, even although he called it
"An Heroick Tragedy." Filmer's *The Unnatural Brother*
(L.I.F. *c.* Jan. 1696/7) was a failure, and the author in his
preface definitely states his belief that this was due to the
lack of stirring scenes and to the fact that there were never
more than two or three speaking characters on the stage at
one time, things for which he prided himself and in condemning which he judged the audience showed a want of
taste. The truth seems to be, that whatever dulness fashion
may have cast on tragedy at any one time, the English
audiences always desired to be aroused by something more
than severe chill and classic calm. Dryden, Lee, Settle, Tate,
nay Otway himself, knew what they were doing when they
left the stricter classic school and chose rather to perpetuate

the atmosphere of heroics or the atmosphere of Shakespeare. Out of some thirty-six tragedies produced on the stage between 1678 and 1688 only one, the *Sertorius* (D.L. *c*. March, 1679) of Bancroft is at all classic in this limited sense. Its lengthy soliloquies and its lack of action give it a calmness which marks it out as unique in the period[1]. That it was not successful may be presumed from the fact that it was never reprinted and that we have no record of any revival of it in the later years of the century. Out of over forty tragedies in the period extending from 1689 to the end of the century barely three or four written in the same style as this can be counted. Edward Filmer's *The Unnatural Brother* has already been mentioned[2], but even that play betrays some reminiscences of the Elizabethan drama, just as does Congreve's *The Mourning Bride* (L.I.F. 1697) where, set as it were to a

[1] The first scene is one long soliloquy, which I quote here because it seems to me to present some of the best dramatic blank verse, outside of Dryden's, written in this age:

> " Cease, you Celestial Pow'rs, and give that Ease,
> Which, to obtain, I, with repeated Pray'rs,
> The bloud of *Hecatombs*, and Incense smoke,
> So oft have fill'd your Heav'ns; and bless the Man
> Which, from his Infancy to Autumn years,
> Subject to every Blast, has known the Fate
> Of greatness, or abjected Poverty.
> Oh, *Marius*, through what Paths Ambition led!
> But thou'rt no more; and Hell has left behind
> A *Janus* Fury, who, with Sword and Pen,
> Or Stabs, or to enevitable Fate thrusts on,
> Doom'd by Proscription, numbers to attend
> On gastly Death: while Slaughter, big with Blood,
> In Sanguine hue, and a Tyrannick Pace,
> Sweeps, like a Plague; and makes *Rome*'s Senate look
> Like Sons of Earth, scap'd from *Deucalion*'s flood...
> Yet, Gods, be kind, and *Sylla*'s brood shall know,
> He that, with Patience, can endure like Me,
> May weather out the Storm, and Victim make
> The over-daring Fool who hastes to meet
> (In *Pompey*) certain Fate; or Knowledge bought
> At dear Expence. Down, you rebellious wrongs;
> Incite me not to acts, that misbecome
> A *Roman* mind to bear: Take flight, my Soul,
> Into a Spere like thy essential make;
> That I may scatter into open Air
> The envious mischiefs which inviron me."

[2] One act of this tragedy was reprinted and performed in Motteux' *The Novelty.*

dim musical accompaniment, we have resuscitated before us all the incidentals which Ford and Webster drew upon to stir the minds of their audiences to horror. The air is dark and foreboding: there is the sound of tears behind the symphonies. In spite of what seems its calm, it inherits many of the tendencies of the older drama, and any worth that it may have for us to-day, any popularity it may have had in its own time, is due to these more native characteristics. We may say, indeed, looking upon the tragedy of 1678–1700 as a whole, that the theatre was in much the same position it held in 1590, pseudo-classicists like Rymer condemning the popular plays, yet themselves unable to capture the attention or the sympathy of the public. In speaking of the classic movement during this time, we must remember that such classicism was largely a super-imposition: that the basis of the characters and of the language was nearer to Elizabethan or heroic types than to the model of the French stage.

If we omit the Shakespeare adaptations, which obviously have a particular value of their own, the most outstanding thing in the tragic drama of 1678–1700 is the heroic note. By no means did Dryden throw off his rants and his stirring scenes when he deserted his long-loved mistress rime. In collaborating with Lee he chose *Oedipus* (D.G. *c*. Nov. 1678) as a subject, and in this drama, although he made use of the preceding plays of Sophocles, Seneca and Corneille, the scenic effects and the rants are connected more with *The Conquest of Granada* than with *Cato*. After a long silence, when in 1689 Dryden returned to the theatre with *Don Sebastian, King of Portugal* (D.L. Dec. 1689), he presented to the stage a theme of heroic "Love and Honour" replete with the usual ranting bombast. The preface indeed observes that "Love and Honour (the mistaken Topicks of Tragedy) were quite worn out" by the time of its appearance, but sufficient proofs remain to show that the elements of the heroic play lingered on in disguised but not unrecognisable forms. In this very same preface Dryden displays his indebtedness to former models. There is a "roughness of the Numbers and Cadences...not casual, but so design'd":

he has "not exactly kept to the three mechanick Rules of Unity" because "the Genius of the *English* cannot bear too regular a Play" and he has "observ'd that the *English* will not bear a thorow Tragedy; but are pleas'd, that it shou'd be lightned with Under-Parts of Mirth." There was no man more capable of analysing the tendencies of his age than Dryden, and he has here shown us in direct words the tendencies of the drama of 1689. This play of *Don Sebastian*, along with *Cleomenes, the Spartan Heroe* (D.L. April 1692), displays clearly in creative form the strength and the power of the older elements, showing how harmoniously these could be joined with the slight chastening tendency of the age. Dryden's last play, also, a tragi-comedy styled *Love Triumphant, or, Nature will prevail* (D.L. 1694) may be taken as representing a union of heroic valour[1] and of low comedy. It failed[2], not because of the inclusion of the former, but because the characters are unnaturally and artificially drawn. The critics have probably been too scathing on this drama, but truly the sudden change of Veramond's mood in the fifth act is nothing short of ridiculous. Only in single scenes does it rise to anything of a height of grandeur.

Very little chastening is to be seen in the works of the other tragic dramatists of the period. Lee, with whom Dryden collaborated in *The Duke of Guise* (D.L. Nov. 1682)[3], a political play[4] which stands out for hardly anything save its fine song, "Tell me, *Thyrsis*, tell your Anguish, Why you

---

[1] There are in it several scenes in rime.

[2] See Scott-Saintsbury edition of Dryden, VIII. 369–70.

[3] Anton Wülker examines *Shakespeares Einfluss auf die dramatische Kunst von Nathaniel Lee* (Münster, 1934).

[4] The political parallel gave rise to not a little controversy. In 1683 appeared *The True History of the* Duke of Guise, and a trifle later the same year *Some Reflections upon the Pretended Parallel in the Play call'd* The Duke of Guise, a work ascribed to Hunt and Settle. To this Dryden replied with *The Vindication or the Parallel of the* French *Holy League and the* English *League and Covenant turn'd into a seditious Libell against the King and his Royal Highness by* Thomas Hunt *and the Authors of the Reflections upon the Pretended Parallel in the Play call'd* The Duke of Guise (1683). See also the single page folio sheet entitled *Sol in Opposition to Saturn, or, A Short Return to the Tragedy call'd* The Duke of Guise (1683).

sigh and why you languish," almost certainly Dryden's, continued in blank verse the old themes of court corruption and of pure and impure love. *Caesar Borgia, the Son of Pope Alexander VI* (D.G. *c.* Sept. 1679) for which Dryden wrote the prologue and in which Betterton sustained the title-role, represents the refashioning from Lee's somewhat morbid imagination of the terrible court of renascent Rome. Externally it is but a gruesome murder drama, filled with the true "heroic" exclamations, with little to stay our attention. Bellamira, the innocent victim of this hotbed of lust and of bloodthirstiness, we somehow cannot feel for: she is too weak and ephemeral. In Caesar, however, Lee has evidently tried to present what is rarely seen in Restoration tragedies—a complex character. In him we see, not the nauseous struggle of love and honour, but of manliness and vicious influence, of conscience warring against the pernicious atmosphere in which he has been bred. This complexity in places is not badly worked out, particularly in the second act, where the action and the dialogue, from the scene between Orsino and Bellamira to that between Caesar and Machiavel, rise to very near true tragic heights.

Theodosius, or, The Force of Love (D.G. *c.* Sept. 1680) immediately followed this terrible tragedy. The dedication betrays Lee's natural sympathy towards a certain part of classic art, although in the body of the play there are numerous Shakespearian reminiscences.

> With Hounds that open'd like *Thessalian* Bulls,
> Like Tygers flu'd, and sanded as the Shore,
> With Ears, and Chests, that dash'd the Morning Dew...[1]

is quite obviously a direct imitation from a famous passage in *A Midsummer Night's Dream*. In the development of the plot, in which the weak-minded Theodosius leaves the care of his kingdom ever more and more in the hands of his sister, Pulcheria, Lee was evidently striving once again to devise a further opportunity for the displayal of complexity of character. Pulcheria, indeed, is one of the few really artisti-

------

[1] i. i.

cally-drawn women figures of Restoration tragedy, a character that inestimably raises in our eyes the worth of Lee as
a dramatic poet.

The same year saw *Lucius Junius Brutus, Father of his
Country* (D.G. Dec. 1680), a play, that, taken along with the
former one, displays well the onward development of the
author's dramatic skill. The plot is well-arranged, and fine
emotional situations are carried out with not a small touch of
genius. Tiberius and Vitellius enter in one scene:

> *Tiberius:* Hark, are we not pursu'd?
> *Vitellius:* No; 'tis the Tread
> Of our own Friends that follow in the dark...[1]

Such is a true touch of dramatic poetry, and it is merely one
of a number of hints of a brighter fire, circling chiefly around
the figures of Titus, Brutus and Teraminta. In spite of the
fact that love sways the whole piece, in the hard, excessive
person of Brutus, in the loyal and loving Titus, in the degenerate Tiberius and in the clinging Teraminta, we are
conveyed to a world that breathes of an inspiration far apart
from Settle's heroes and from Howard's rants. We are there
where poetry grips the sense, where the old Romans, even
if in a seventeenth century dress, walk again the stony streets
of a rock-built Capitol.

It is with something of a sigh that one turns from this real
triumph to the ineffectual and worthless *The Princess of Cleve*
(D.G. *c.* Sept. 1681). This play, the plot of which is chaotic
and the atmosphere corrupt, shows not the slightest hint even
of poetic and true dramatic sentiment. Turning to it from the
last-mentioned drama is like turning from a shaded but
beautiful grove to a rotting dung-heap. Unfortunately, also,
Constantine the Great (D.L. *c.* Nov. 1683) does not do much
to heighten Lee's position. Although it begins with a vision
of the Cross, it deals mainly with the threadbare theme of
the passion of a father and a son for one woman. Nor is this
theme well worked out: the only scenes that have in them
anything noteworthy are those few in which the unhappy
Fausta appears. Both Constantine and Crispus are ephemeral

[1] III. i.

figures, and Arius the villain is far too conventional to be considered worthy of detailed mention. *Constantine*, save for a poor *Massacre of Paris* (D.L. Nov. 1689)[1], was Lee's last drama. Three years after the production of *The Massacre of Paris*, he died, leaving behind him a broken reputation. He had struck the chord of the poetic lyre, but his hand was not sure and we hear continual discords in his music. We are appalled at the contrast between his rants and his most pathetic and poetic passages. We stand aghast at the wild outflowings of words which but a touch would render into effectively dramatic poetry. He had more enthusiasm than Dryden had, more, indeed, than had any writer since the death of Ford, but he lacked balance somewhere, lacked that power of control which lies behind all the highest art. I know of no more striking passage in the whole of Restoration tragedy than that scene, part of which has been already quoted above, in *Gloriana*, with its heart-dulled repetitions, yet *Gloriana* is not *Venice Preserv'd* precisely because it lacks the continued stress of the latter play. Lee flies to fall again, but Otway's flights are steady as an eagle's way. On the other hand, as I have endeavoured to show, Lee is of inestimable importance in any attempt to divine the quality of the tragedy of his age. He was not only one of the chief of the rimed-heroic dramatists, but he carried on the heroic tradition into his blank verse plays. He not only felt the touch of the classical movement, but went back for inspiration to Webster and to Ford and to Shakespeare. Above all we must bear in mind that his dramas were among the most popular of the time. Most of them were reprinted frequently, and, if we may judge by the numbers of copies now in existence, in fairly large editions. Next to Dryden, possibly, he was the most influential man of his age.

As in Dryden and in Lee, in Settle we can trace the continuance of the heroic characteristics with elements political introduced to arouse contemporary interest. *The Female*

---

[1] Several scenes of Acts I and IV appeared in Act II of *The Duke of Guise*. The only really tragic elements in it are the relations between Guise and Marguerite, which work at the end to really dramatic intensity.

Prelate, Being the History of the Life and Death of Pope Joan
(D.L. *c*. Sept. 1679) is a purely political or politico-religious
drama, accorded a clamorous welcome by the Whigs, worked
out, as far as such a thing could be, with fair skill[1]. In it
Settle not only continues his strain of popular heroic sentiment from *The Empress of Morocco*, but has evidently felt
the impress of the new pathetic movement. He has so developed the plot that we can feel a trifle of sympathy for the
unfortunate Duke of Saxony and the miserable Angeline. An
even poorer play is *Fatal Love, or, The Forc'd Inconstancy*
(D.L. *c*. Sept. 1680). Based according to Langbaine on a
Greek tale, it is interesting solely for the fact that it is a
tragedy of horror, closing with a universal massacre, Lysandra
alone remaining alive, apparently only for the purpose of
speaking the epilogue[2].

As a kind of blank verse sequel to *The Empress of Morocco*,
appeared about March 1682 at D.L., *The Heir of Morocco,
with the Death of Gayland*, a play decidedly of the heroic
species[3]. The prologue itself draws the attention of the
audience to the fact that the author "*has his Play with Love
and Honour cram'd.*" Altomar is a pure "hero," marvellous
in battle, tender in love, merciful, gracious, constant: Artemira
is a pure heroine: and Meroin a regular heroic villain. It is
interesting to notice along with Dryden's remark in the
preface to *Don Sebastian*, the statement made in the epilogue
to one of Settle's later plays, *The Ambitious Slave, or, A
Generous Revenge* (D.L. March 1693/4) that this was an "*Out-
of-Fashion*" drama. It is possible that all that Dryden and
Settle meant by these statements was that the cruder type of
heroics was passing away, was being tempered by the incroach
of pathetic motives. In any case the popularity of the heroic

---

[1] The piece is plainly anti-Catholic and unfair at that. It deals with
the tale of "Pope Joan," who for years was believed to have succeeded
Leo IV to the pontifical chair in 855. Regarding the authenticity of this
story, see Döllinger, J., *Fables respecting the Popes of the Middle Ages*
(English trans. pp. 3–36).

[2] "*In the Habit of a Nun.*"

[3] A record of Settle's life, literary relationships and dramatic career is
provided by F. C. Brown, *Elkanah Settle: His Life and Works* (1910).

species did not seem to decline. *Distress'd Innocence, or, The Princess of Persia* (D.L. Oct. 1690) and *The Ambitious Slave* may be taken as pure examples of the heroic drama in a blank verse dress. The former, which was a success[1], has some very good scenes between Hormidas and Cleomira, scenes which mingle the pathetic note with the heroic ardour. Unlike it, *The Ambitious Slave* was a failure—probably because, although written in 1682, its production was delayed until the mode had passed for the rimed outbursts of the second decade of the Restoration; by 1694 these perhaps seemed more than a trifle absurd and inflated. It was no doubt the lack of the pathetic that caused its want of appeal. Settle continued writing on into the second decade of the eighteenth century, but this was his last experiment in the heroic style.

Many others, however, in the eighties and the nineties of the century continued in the same strain. Crowne's works have no great literary value, but in this connection they have a very great historical interest. *The Ambitious Statesman, or, The Loyal Favourite* (D.L. *c.* March 1679) in spite of the fact that its author considered it "the most vigorous of all" his "foolish Labours[2]," did not really deserve anything more than the cool reception which was accorded it on the stage. Professedly based on history, it is purely unhistorical, filled with stock characters that hardly ever rouse us to even a momentary interest. *Thyestes* (D.L. *c.* March 1681) followed two years later, and received a very favourable welcome. As in the case of *Oedipus*, this reception no doubt manifests the vitiated state of the public taste. Even in a play such as this, anti-Catholicism had to be introduced[3], even here indecent sentiments had to be advanced[4], and what with these and with the bloody horrors of Senecan and of Restoration imagination, the play exceeds even the nightmares of John

---

[1] Cf. the dedication.
[2] Preface.
[3] Cf. the epilogue:
   "*We shewed you in the Priests today, a true And perfect Picture of Old* Rome *and new.*"
[4] Cf. "*The Song at* Atreus *his Banquet*" inserted in the play.

Ford and falls far below Ford's work in poetic and dramatic
power. Crowne seems to have been particularly attracted by
subjects taken from the lives of the Roman and other em-
perors, for he followed *Thyestes* with no less than three
similar themes, *Darius, King of Persia* (D.L. April 1688),
Regulus (D.L. June 1692) and *Caligula* (D.L. *c.* March 1698)[1].
All of these show the same characteristics—the attempt at
a classical calm and yet the retention of motives taken directly
from the heroic rimed tragedy of the past decades. *Darius*
is the weakest and least interesting of these three, in spite of
its Persian setting. *Regulus*, in blank verse, deals with the
various machinations of love and ambition in Carthage, and
ends with the death of Regulus and with the running mad
of his wife, Fulvia. As a whole it may be counted a dull late
heroic tragedy. *Caligula* has a special point of interest in
that it is written in rime and otherwise is a definitely heroic
drama in subject and in treatment, full of rants and bombast,
but not uninteresting if one can sufficiently disengage oneself
from the rather humpty-dumpty verse. Valerius here is the
usual noble general: Cesonia the typical heroine: Caligula
the weak king—all stock characters of the old stage. From
two other points of view this production is worthy of attention. In the first place, the preface shows the effect of the
moral change in the age, or at least of the conventional veneer
of morality which was but cloaking unbridled licence, for
there we discover Crowne valiantly defending himself against
the supposition that he had used "*Baudy*" to gain theatrical
success in his former plays and apologising at the same time
for the over-generous presentation of atheism in *The Destruction of Jerusalem*. In the second place, from a scenical
point of view, the play is noticeable for the fact that there
are five (or possibly only four) changes of scene throughout
the whole of the piece—a manifest sign of the influence both
of the new stage conditions and of the classic tendencies of
the time. Otherwise, however, the tragedy might have been

---

[1] These themes were evidently popular; cp. Dryden's *Cleomenes*. The
popularity was possibly due to the revivals of Shakespeare's *Julius Caesar*,
Coriolanus and similar dramas.

written in 1676 instead of 1698. All through the dialogue
there are scattered specimens of the true heroic diction. In
the first act Caligula mentions to Cesonia the subject of
tombs:

> *Cesonia:* Sir, why do you name Tombs?
> *Caligula:* Does it become
> A Heroine to startle at a Tomb?[1]—

a question which reveals the highly self-conscious and unnatural psychology of the doughty persons of the Drawcansir
theatre. Later in the play, Cesonia shows to us that she
truly has no such mean qualms:

> "The least offensive Vapour strikes me dead," she says,
> "I can endure no Sweets but what excel;
> Yet of dead Enemies I like the Smell[2]."

The tastes of some of these heroines are certainly peculiar,
to say the least. As for Caligula, he vaunts himself in true
heroic proportions, and classical legend is called in to support
his diction:

> Wou'd to the Gods all *Rome* had but one Neck,
> That I might cut off Millions at a Blow[3].

One of the few other rimed tragedies of the age is *Boadicea,
Queen of Britain* (L.I.F. 1697) written by Charles Hopkins[4],
of which the only scenes worth noticing are those between
Cassabelan and Camilla. These mingle the heroic with the
pathetic style so rapidly coming into fashion. Previous to
this tragedy, Hopkins had written one other, *Pyrrhus, King
of Epirus* (L.I.F. *c.* August, 1695). Composed in blank verse,
it is a very humanised heroic drama without any rants and
without much pother of mixed-up loves—turning as it does
mainly on the faithful passion of Pyrrhus for his wife.

Like *The Ambitious Slave*, the Earl of Orrery's *Herod the
Great*, although printed only in 1694, was certainly of earlier
vintage, rimed in the manner of an outmoded time. On the

---

[1] I. i.   [2] I. i.   [3] I. i.
[4] See Alice E. Jones, "A Note on Charles Hopkins" (*Modern Language
Notes,* 1940, LV. 191–4).

other hand, there seems to be no reason for doubting that Robert Gould's partly rimed *The Rival Sisters, or, The Violence of Love* (D.L. *c.* Oct. 1695) was written close to the time of its production. The latter, however, is not heroic, but rather more of a domestic play based on a theme not unlike that of Shirley's *The Maid's Revenge*. It deals with the forced, or rather cheated, marriage of Antonio to Catalina, whose sister, Berinthia, the husband really loves, and on the miseries consequent on that. The whole is very well executed, and the marriage scene with its accompaniment of thunder and lightning is excellently conceived and written. Unknown though it be to-day, this drama is decidedly one of the best tragedies of the end of the century and deserves more attention than hitherto it has received.

In blank verse the heroic note, mingled with the pathetic atmosphere coming into fashion, was struck once more by Thomas Southerne. His first play, *The Loyal Brother, or, The Persian Prince* (D.L. *c.* Feb. 1682), founded on a French romance, *Tachmas*, is spoilt by the political reference which seemed inevitable in any plays written about the years 1681 to 1685. Here Shaftesbury is but thinly disguised as Ismail, and the Duke of York even less thinly disguised as Tachmas. Otherwise the play is thoroughly heroic. Tachmas, the noble general and loyal brother, lives to enjoy Semanthe whom the Sophy freely gives him, and Ismail, the villain, meets a well-merited death. Ranting exclamations proper to the Drawcansir school fill the tragedy. The only part that breaks new ground is that scene in the second act, between Semanthe and Tachmas, which breathes an air of sylvan calm and of blissful peace foreign to the dramas of Dryden and of Orrery.

Most of Southerne's other serious plays are less heroic than this initial attempt, but in all the influence of Dryden and others of his school is to be felt. *The Disappointment, or, The Mother in Fashion* (D.L. April 1684) is styled a "Play": for the plot Southerne has borrowed from the tale of the *curioso impertinente* and from *Measure for Measure*. Although it deals mainly with the libertine captain Alberto and with the odious Mother-bawd, it is strangely lacking in scenes of indecency or vulgar suggestion. The chaste Erminia is a decidedly "moral" type, and, while from a modern standpoint we may censure Juliana, we feel pleased when we see that weak if venturesome lady creep back to Alberto's heart in the end. With this play, Southerne first made his great and definite break with the pure heroics, pointing forward to what was to be his great endeavour in the future, the development of a new type of sentimental, moral, problem dramas. Closely associated with the rising sentimental school we must also number *The Fatal Marriage, or, The Innocent Adultery* (D.L. *c.* Feb. 1693/4), another "Play" which won a continental celebrity through the French translation in *Le Théâtre anglais* (1746) and through the German rendering by Von Schröder in 1792[1]. Intrinsically it is a really fine serious drama, although to our modern taste it may appear a trifle artificial. The sentiment in places rings false and many of the actions do not seem to be motived sufficiently. The language, too, is peculiarly erratic. At one moment we may meet with the most execrable blank verse and at the next be confronted with bursts of passionate exclamation that remind us of Ford and Webster at their best. Such is that passage in the last act when Isabella in her misery cries out:

> Oh! they tear me! Cut off my Hands—
> Let me leave something with him—
> They'll clasp him fast.

In a strange and artistic manner here Southerne has united the spirit of the tragedy of blood with the spirit of the new sentimental and pathetic drama, still with a few reminiscences of the heroic stage. Sentiment rather than horror, however, looms over the fatal bride, tossed on a tormented sea of diabolically-human intrigue[2].

The same atmosphere is once more conjured up in *Oroonoko,*

---

[1] Garrick altered it in 1757 and Kemble in 1814.

[2] It is based on a novel of Mrs Behn—*The History of the Nun, or, The Fair Vow-Breaker.* This and other novels by the same authoress undoubtedly helped to colour the drama of the time. How far some of them

or, The Royal Slave (D.L. *c.* Dec. 1695). It, too, was based on a novel by Mrs Behn and enjoyed a success hardly less than that of *The Fatal Marriage*. In spite of a certain theatricality which is so apparent to us in all Restoration dramatic productions, this tragi-comedy is a decided triumph. It is true that Oroonoko himself is rather much of a stock love-and-honour hero, but even admitting that, the sense of tragedy, with the central figure and his one tragic flaw, if weakly carried out, reminds us strongly of the creations of Otway. Imoinda is a delightful picture of a poor Indian maid, a figure interesting as a premonition of those "noble savages" cultivated by the followers of Rousseau in the eighteenth century. She stands out as a frail flower bent by the rude winds of civilised perversion and vice. The sense of pathos in this play is so great, the cumulative effect is so fine, that it is indeed a pity that the final lines should destroy the spirit of the whole:

> And if he went astray,
> There's Mercy still above to set him right,
> But *Christians*, guided by the heavenly Ray,
> Have no Excuse if we mistake our Way.

Southerne, after the production of *Oroonoko*, wrote only three more plays, but these, although interesting, cannot be dealt with here, produced as they were in the eighteenth century. The fact that Southerne was one of the few dramatists whose work extends over the border of the two centuries and the fact that he mingled in such an artistic way the various elements heroic, Shakespearian and pathetic make him one of the most interesting figures of the tragedy of the time. He stands with Rowe as one of the chief influences on the development of the later theatre.

Numbers of other less well-known dramatists followed in the footsteps of Lee and of Southerne in adopting the heroic

were based on personal experience is a subject that has been much discussed recently: see Ernest Bernbaum, "Mrs Behn's Autobiography a Fiction" (*PMLA*, 1913, XXVIII. 432–53) and "Mrs Behn's 'Oroonoko'" (*Kittredge Anniversary Papers*, 1913), H. D. Benjamins, "Een koninklijke Slaaf in Suriname" (*De West-Indische Gids*, 1919, pp. 474–80), Wylie Sypher, "A Note on the Realism of Mrs Behn s *Oroonoko*" (*Modern Language Quarterly*, 1942, III. 401–5), H. G. Platt, Jr., "Astrea and Celadon" (*PMLA*, 1934, XLIX. 544–59).

drama, sometimes in its pure form, sometimes with the introduction of more novel elements. Whitaker's *The Conspiracy, or, The Change of Government* (D.G. *c.* March. 1680) has a certain interest as being the sole rimed play produced between the abandonment of rime in 1677 and the appearance of the little group of rimed plays mentioned above. It is a sort of Fordian variant of the heroic tragedy, "Death" in person making his appearance in the first and last acts, and rooms "*hung all with black,*" skulls and coffins being plentifully utilised. The anonymous *Romulus and Hersilia, or, The Sabine War* (D.G. August 1682) is no more valuable from an intrinsic point of view, but is interesting as being written for many scenes in prose (an anticipation of Lillo in that regard) although "*Plain Love and Honour,*" as the prologue informs us, is the theme. Other heroic plays of the time may be rapidly passed over. Saunders' *Tamerlane the Great* (D.L. *c.* March 1681) is of some importance because of its subject matter. It is interesting to note that the author appears to have been entirely ignorant of the famous work of Marlowe on the same theme, confessing only that he had heard mention of some "*Cock-pit* Play The *Scythian* Shepherd, or, *Tamerlane* the Great,*" which, he deemed, was of no great value. Of no interest as a play, but of value when we consider the other works of its author, is *Cyrus the Great, or, The Tragedy of Love* (L.I.F. *c.* Dec. 1695) by John Banks. In spite of the fact that Banks embraced the distinctly domestic drama of the time, and in spite of the fact that in the thunder and lightning and in the witches' song he has a clear imitation of *Macbeth, Cyrus* is just a blank verse variation of an heroic *motif* from *Le Grand Cyrus* of Madeleine de Scudéry. It is full of horrors. In the first scene is a battle-field with dead bodies lying around, one of which "*carkasses*" is revived by a witch, and in the last act is a terrible picture of a mutilated body—typical of the scenes contemporaries were prepared to endure. A slightly chillier play of a similar type is *The Treacherous Brothers* (D.L. *c.* Dec. 1689) by Powell the actor. This is a very ambitious tragedy, in would-be poetical language, but fails to catch our emotions. The action of Menaphon and of Orgillus in sending the Queen and Ithocles to sleep and thus stirring the King's jealousy against them is barely motived. Orgillus has no object for doing so at all, and Menaphon is merely angry because the Queen, Semanthe, had rejected his unlawful love. This tragedy and *Alphonso, King of Naples* (D.L. *c.* Dec. 1690) show well the chastening of the heroic element of the earlier years and the re-introduction of an Elizabethan atmosphere. *Alphonso* seems to aim at a saner tragic type. The pathos arising out of the misfortunes and the deaths of Cesario and Urania is well portrayed, and the author all through has evidently been striving to arouse our sympathies and our emotions. With *The Royal Mischief* (L.I.F. *c.* April 1696) of Mrs Manley, we are back again at the Fordian blood tragedy, again with elements of heroics, not only in the Eastern setting but in the language of the piece. It seems to have met with some opposition from "the warmth in it"—an opposition not ill-directed. Two other typically heroic plays must close this brief account. The first of these, *Victorious Love* (D.L. June 1698) by William Walker, is poor enough with its ghosts and its priest scenes, but the *Heroick Love, or, The Cruel Separation* (L.I.F. *c.* Dec. 1697) of George Granville, Lord Lansdowne, may not be dismissed so easily. Downes tells us that it was well acted and successful, and, indeed, for its type, it deserved to be. As a dramatic work of art it may seem to fail in many particulars and certainly wants that essential element of individuality, but, in a fairly calm kind of way, it presents a not unworthy or uninteresting development of the Drydenesque tragedy. It has no characters worth speaking of save Chruseis, yet the atmosphere of the whole, in which heroic ardour is softened by a classical influence, is well deserving of our critical attention.

Besides the pure type of heroic tragedy exemplified so well in this last play, besides the heroic play modified by elements taken directly from previous Elizabethan example, it is quite natural that there should be a number of dramas wherein heroics should be amalgamated with operatic tendencies. Of such a nature are the two dramas of Charles Gildon, a playwright who carried on his work into the eighteenth century.

Phaeton, or, The Fatal Divorce (D.L. *c.* March 1698) is based on Quinault and Euripides[1], with reminiscences of the English heroic species. The unities are preserved, but the spirit is romantic, with typical ghosts and groves and love-scenes. From the prologue we learn that many of its "Ornaments," that is to say scenery and costumes, had been brought over "from *France*" as in the case of earlier operatic productions. *The Roman Bride's Revenge* (D.L. *c.* Nov. 1696) is also of the heroic style. Martian may stand as the typical hero-lover: Portia as the usual heroine: and the Emperor as the wicked potentate of the early Restoration school: but classical and operatic elements are worked in here, too, so that the play differs little in atmosphere from the more decidedly operatic *Phaeton*.

Regular opera was, naturally enough, exceedingly popular among the audiences of the last years of the century, although the managers looked on it with suspicion because of the additional cost it entailed on the playhouses. Dryden's *Albion and Albanius* (D.G. June 1685), planned as a vast piece of royal flattery, is finest of these, although, because of political disturbances, it was something of a failure on the stage. Planned originally as a kind of symbolic history of the reign of Charles and in this form put on rehearsal, it was just about to be performed publicly when Charles died. It was then enlarged so as to embrace Albanius, who is James. On June 3, 1685, it was put on the stage, and was promising a lengthy run, when on the sixth night news came of the landing of Monmouth. Hurriedly the ill-fated thing was laid aside[2]. Nearly all the characters in this opera are allegorical. Augusta is London: Thamesis appears in person, as also does Democracy, symbolising the Republicans, while Zelota stands for the hypocritical "zealots" of contemporary times.

---

[1] The preface confesses that the author had started his scheme from the French and had finished by borrowing hints from the Greek. Quinault's opera of *Phaëton* appeared in 1683 with music by Lully. It was the first opera seen by Louis XV. Cf. Delandine, A. F., *Bibliographie Dramatique* (Paris, N.D.), p. 441. The music to the English version was by Daniel Purcell.

[2] It is possible that Dryden intended *The State of Innocence* for the stage: see P. S. Havens in *Parrott Presentation Volume* (1935), pp. 383–98.

Albion, clearly, is Charles, and Albanius has been already indicated as James. Monk is presented under the faint disguise of Archon. Compared with other operas of the age *Albion and Albanius* is a triumph: in the shorter measures of this play Dryden has excelled himself:

> See the God of Seas attends Thee,
> Nymphs Divine, a Beauteous Train;
> All the calmer gales befriend Thee
> In thy passage o're the Main;
> Every Maid her Locks is binding,
> Every *Triton's* Horn is winding,
> Welcome to the watry Plain.

This opera Dryden followed with another, *King Arthur, or, The British Worthy* (D.G. *c.* May 1691). His former work had been set by Grabut, but for the score to this he turned to Purcell. With Purcell's music and with the dances arranged by Priest, it gained a tumult of praise in its own day, praise that did not, for a hundred years, die away[1]. Written in blank verse that breaks at times into aria, it is much more beautiful as a whole than *Albion and Albanius*, although none of the lyrical measures rise to the level of a number in the former opera. The most lovely of these lyrical measures here is the song in the last act:

> *Fairest Isle, all Isles Excelling,*
>   *Seat of Pleasures, and of Loves;*
> Venus *here will chuse her Dwelling,*
>   *And forsake her* Cyprian *Groves.*
>
> Cupid, *from his Fav'rite Nation,*
>   *Care and Envy will Remove;*
> *Jealousie, that poisons Passion,*
>   *And Despair that dies for Love.*
>
> *Gentle Murmurs, sweet Complaining,*
>   *Sighs that blow the Fire of Love;*
> *Soft Repulses, kind Disdaining,*
>   *Shall be all the Pains you prove.*
>
> *Every Swain shall pay his Duty,*
>   *Grateful every Nymph shall prove;*
> *And as these Excel in Beauty,*
>   *Those shall be Renown'd for Love.*

---

[1] It was still played in the nineteenth century.

Had all operas such beautiful libretti as these two have, there would be small cause for complaint.

Another opera similar to *King Arthur*, is the *Brutus of Alba, or, Augusta's Triumph* (D.G. *c.* Oct. 1696), a play published by Powell and Verbruggen, not, as some have said, an alteration of Tate's similarly named play, but rather a sequel to that[1]. This opera has all the scenical devices dear to the machinist's heart. There is in it a magic wand that can call up a misty cloud and then change it into a great windmill from whence come millers and country wenches to dance, turn it again into a witch from whom issue devils to join in a romp with the aged beldame and finally cause the whole to vanish. While the general level of the dialogue and the songs is much lower than that of Dryden's opera, both blank verse and aria are by no means to be despised. *Brutus of Alba* is among the really interesting productions of the age.

The "moral" tone of the time found its way even into this species of dramatic production in the opera of Thomas D'Urfey, *Cinthia and Endimion, or, The Loves of the Deities* (D.L. *c.* Dec. 1696), which is a kind of "morality" play of gods and goddesses, "morally fashioning the Vertues and Vices of Human Nature." From the preface one learns that it was written some three years previously, but that its public exhibition was delayed by the death of Queen Mary. It is by no means contemptible, for D'Urfey had the true *flair* of the song-writer. He has presented here one truly beautiful lyric:

From the vast Empire of the Sea below[2].

Elements of disintegration are very visible in the kindred work of Elkanah Settle, who, besides adapting *Philaster* into an operatic shape, produced an interesting opera tending towards musical comedy, and possibly another, tending towards pantomime.

The Fairy Queen (D.G. May 1692), rather vaguely attributed to him, is derived from *A Midsummer Night's Dream*, but has such alterations that the original is completely trans-

---

[1] This was set to music by Daniel Purcell.
[2] Act II.

formed. There are masques of allegoric figures, such as Night and Sleep[1]: there are masques of Shepherds and of Shepherd-esses[2]: there are masques of the Seasons[3]: and there are "Chinese *Dances*," in which, among many other things, are introduced six monkeys. Likewise set by Purcell and with the dances arranged by Priest, it does not seem to have been such a success as the productions of Dryden and of D'Urfey, although why this should have been we cannot tell[4]. It certainly had all the scenic attractiveness of the other pieces, and even in modern times when revived was welcomed en-thusiastically[5]. From a stage point of view it is valuable as containing the earliest example of a "transformation scene," in the modern sense, of which I know. In the fifth act enters "*a Machine drawn by Peacocks*." These latter spread their tails until they fill the entirety of the stage: and then the whole suddenly vanishes and becomes transmogrified into some-thing quite different[6].

If pantomime saw a premonition in *The Fairy Queen*, comic opera took its rise with *The World in the Moon* (D.G. June 1697), set to music by Daniel Purcell and by Clark. Unlike the authors of *Psyche* and of *Circe*, Settle has here flung off all Gallic tradition in stage craft, and boasts of having "*thrown away all our old* French *Lumber, our Clouds of Clouts, and set Theatrical Paintings at a much fairer Light*[7]." Contem-poraries, including the author himself, seem to have been at a loss where to classify the play. Called an "opera" and a "comedy" by Settle himself[8], it was styled by Gildon a "comical opera[9]" and by Whincop a "dramatic-comic-opera[10]." In effect it is a kind of hybrid, alternating the most wondrous of scenic effects with scenes of real-life comedy.

---

[1] II.   [2] III.   [3] IV.   [4] Downes, p. 43.

[5] The music, edited by J. S. Shedlock, was published by the Purcell Society in 1903 (*Works of Henry Purcell*, vol. 12).

[6] The first Quarto was printed in 1692: another "*with Alterations*" appeared in 1693. The alterations consist mainly of the addition of a few songs. On the date and text of the work see F. C. Brown, *Elkanah Settle* (1910).

[7] Cf. dedication to Christopher Rich and the epilogue.

[8] The latter appears over the *dramatis personae*.

[9] Gildon's Langbaine, p. 124.

[10] *List of all the Dramatic Authors in Scanderbeg* (1747), p. 283.

For the former, apart from the examples given before in this
work[1], one may note the Dance of the *"Green Men"* in Act I,
the entertainment at Cinthia's Court in Act II and the scenic
wonders of Act IV (a *"Prospect of Terras Walks on Eight
several Stages"*). As regards the latter ingredient, the comic
scenes are decidedly interesting, taking the form of a "rehearsal" of the opera itself. In Act II Wildblood, Stanmore
and Tom sit with Jo Haynes on the stage watching the performance, their remarks being exceedingly interesting and
valuable from an historical point of view. Altogether the
piece deserved that success which, we are informed, it
received.

A consideration of Settle's operas has led us almost to the
bounds of pure comedy. It will now be necessary to turn
back from the musical drama to trace the development of
the more pronounced Elizabethan and pathetic plays of the
age. Both of these we have already met with, mingled with
elements heroic: my endeavour now will be to indicate, first
of all those tragedies which are more particularly to be
associated with the rise of sentimental drama and the bourgeois tragedy, and secondly those productions which seem
to be related more nearly either to Webster or Shakespeare
than to Orrery and Dryden.

The two groups are not mutually exclusive. It is quite
evident, even from a cursory glance at the domestic and
pathetic dramas of the time, that the authors of such tragedies
were influenced directly by a new reading of Shakespeare
and of other Elizabethan dramatists. The same men who
were chief in the school of pathos wrote also more distinctly
"Elizabethan" tragedies: Otway gave on the one hand *The
Orphan*, on the other, *Venice Preserv'd*.

A consideration of Otway's work shows us also that we
must not expect to find heroics entirely absent from the most
pathetic of tragedies. Otway, as we have seen, had started
in the heroic school. He passed on from that to deface
Romeo and Juliet by turning it into *The History and Fall of
Caius Marius* (D.G. *c.* Sept. 1679), and then, inspired pro-

---

[1] See *supra*, p. 48.

bably by the love which he bore towards the talented but morally vicious Mrs Barry, he created two of the finest tragedies of the time, revealing in them his appreciation of the work of the Elizabethans and his interest in domestic sorrows.

The Orphan, or, The Unhappy Marriage (D.G. *c.* March 1680)[1], "a very moving Tragedy" as Langbaine described it[2], is derived from a seventeenth century novel called *The English Adventures*. It deals with the love of two brothers for one girl, the orphan Monimia, that of one of them, Castalio, in a pure way, that of the other, licentious. Castalio marries her, but for several reasons has to retain his marriage a secret. While arranging to come on his marriage night to her room he is overheard by his brother: and the latter, deeming the whole matter but a libertine's jest, forestalls him and enters first the darkened and silent room. This theme, which is wrought to the end with considerable skill, may perhaps not be good material for tragedy, but there can be no doubt that the scenes are genuinely affecting. The plot undoubtedly presents a situation with untold possibilities for psychological and emotional development, and that Otway did not neglect those possibilities is evident from Mrs Barry's declaration that she never uttered that fatal and pathetic "*O Castalio!*" after the cheat is discovered, without the tears rising to her throat and to her eyes. Viewed from amidst the dull heap of expiring heroes and of banal heroines, this tragedy is one of utmost merit. It has brought true pathos into drama, pathos and sentiment, told in a manner at once vigorous and calm. It would have been noteworthy in any age: it was a triumph in its own[3].

Two years later, Dorset Garden saw the production of an even finer play, *Venice Preserv'd, or, A Plot Discovered* (D.G. Feb. 1681/2), a drama, which, like *The Orphan*, not only had

---

[1] This play reached a fifth edition by 1711. It was translated into French by Desclozeaux about 1822, and into German the same year.

[2] P. 398.

[3] Mrs Barry acted Monimia, and Betterton Castalio. Curll informs us that Mrs Bracegirdle, then six years old, acted the page. As is well known, the play long held the stage.

a lengthy and dignified stage career in England, but carried
Otway's fame to the most distant corners of the earth[1]. The
comic parts, mainly concerned with the character of Antonio,
which is in all probability a satiric portrait of Shaftesbury,
are the only marring features in it, not because these are
badly written, but because they do not harmonise well
with the general theme of the play. Nothing could better
illustrate the vitiating effect of the political interests which
dramatists at this time thought fit to include in their plays.
Yet Otway has succeeded in rising above the topical and has
firmly grasped the essentials. The impression the tragedy
leaves on the reader's mind is powerful, and that impression
is but intensified when it is seen well-acted upon the stage.
The characters are finely and delicately handled. The development of Jaffier's psychology, veering from hatred to
desire for revenge, from desire of liberty to active revolution,
is an almost perfect study—all confused as it is by his love.
Pierre, too, is a beautiful picture of the firm and clear-hearted
rebel, steady to the last: "And Liberty!" he cries, his words
expressing his inmost soul, to which Jaffier's "Revenge! Revenge!" forms a not unfitting and uninstructive counterpart[2].
What though the other characters are more conventional—
Priuli, Antonio, Aquilina and Renault—when we have these
two for ever before us? Particularly of note are the speeches
of Pierre, especially those at the beginning of the play: "So,
indeed, men think me..."[3] and "Yes, a most notorious

[1] It has been revived probably oftener than any other play save those
of Shakespeare. All through the eighteenth century it was kept on the
stage. Garrick played in it. Kemble's version appeared in 1795. It was
produced by Macready at Covent Garden in 1838, and by Phelps at
Sadler's Wells in 1845. Nor is its inspirational value for our own time
gone: Gordon Craig's impressionistic designs for scenery and the recent
Phoenix Society revival testify to that. A Dutch translation by G. Muyser
(*Het Gered Venetie*) appeared in 1755. La Fosse adapted it as *Manlius
Capitolinus* in 1698. It was translated into French by de la Place (*Théâtre
anglais*, tom. v) in 1746, and again by Baron A. G. B. Brugière de la
Barante (*Chefs-d'œuvre des théâtres étrangers*, tom. II) about 1822. In
German it made its appearance in 1847, and in Italian as *Venezia Salvata*
(translated by M. Leoni) in 1817. As early as 1764 a Russian translation was issued by Ia. Kozelski (Возмущеніе противъ Венеціи
трагедія).

[2] II. ii.   [3] I. i.

Villain..." and that fine outburst in Act III, when swords are
directed at Jaffier:

> Who talks of killing? Who's he'll shed the Blood
> That's dear to me? Is't you? or you? or you, Sir?[1]

And the ending of the play is magnificent, closing upon the
poor misguided Belvidera's madness and the noble release of
Pierre from the ignominy of the gallows. There is something
in a poet's heart always revolutionary, and even though Otway
was one of Dryden's persuasion—a monarchical absolutist—
in this play he shows his sympathy for souls who struggle
up out of the rut of life—out into the spacious sunlight of
rebellion. There are firm-hearted, single-spirited Pierres who
live to-day: there are cowardly Renaults, half-conspirators,
half-egotistical-libertines: there are Jaffiers who sway between
the ideal of revolution and other ideals: there are Belvideras,
too, who, unconscious of the fact, mar men's ideals and men's
lives. It is truly the highest art that is universal in this way
and for all time: and who will deny that Otway has reached
if not the summit, at least the lesser heights?

Another writer of undoubted merit who stands alongside
Otway in the imaging of emotional and pathetic scenes is
John Banks[2], whom we have already met with as an exponent
of the heroic tragedy. Like Otway's *Alcibiades*, *The Rival
Kings* of this writer and *The Destruction of Troy* were but
ephemeral things obviously produced simply to satisfy the
tastes of the public of the seventies of the century. By 1682,
like Otway again, Banks had completely turned round, and,
although to the end of his career he retained traces of the
heroic style, in all of his after works save the peculiar *Cyrus
the Great* of 1695, he pointed deliberately towards that type
of drama which was destined to be taken up in the eighteenth
century by Rowe and to form the basis of a new tragic productivity. *The Unhappy Favourite, or, The Earl of Essex*

---

[1] III. ii.

[2] A very useful study of Banks' work is given in the introduction to
T. M. H. Blair's edition of *The Unhappy Favourite* (1939). This author
was unfortunate in his relations with the stage, and had he not persistently
inserted political matter in his dramas we may well believe that his genuine
contributions to Restoration literature would now be more greatly esteemed.

(D.L. *c.* Sept. 1681) in its very title shows the tendency of his art. Evidently a popular success in its own times[1] and later[2], *The Unhappy Favourite* is interesting because, in the scenes between the Earl and the Countess of Essex there is struck a note rarely felt in Restoration drama, a note, however, that has its echoes in Otway and even in Southerne. In spite of follies in it, such as the numerous asides and as that first line ridiculed in *Tom Thumb*:

> Help me to raile, prodigious minded *Burleigh*,

it shows a decided attempt to produce a tragic spirit higher and more delicate than that of the heroic tragedy.

This attempt Banks continued in *Vertue Betray'd, or, Anna Bullen* (D.G. *c.* April, 1682)[3], again an historical work and again pathetic and emotional in tone. It is, in the words of the suppressed epilogue, a "*distrest Domestick Tale*," stressing most of all the truly affecting scenes between Piercy and Anna. In some ways it has affinities with the older heroic drama: it is purely a love play: Lady Blount cries "Hell and Furies!" in the time-honoured strain: Henry is but the typical monarch, Wolsey the typical villain and Lady Diana Talbot the typical love-lorn maiden who dies of a broken heart. These reminiscences of the popular drama of 1664–77, however, do not take from the fact that this is a sentimental tragedy, with close affinities to the school of pathos developing rapidly from the year 1682. It is also to be observed that it is the first of those "she-tragedies" made popular more than twenty years later.

A somewhat similar play is *The Island Queens, or, The Death of Mary Queen of Scotland. Publish'd only in Defence of the Author and the Play, against some mistaken Censures, occasion'd by its being prohibited the Stage* (1684), also a "she-tragedy" but evidently not so pleasing to the court faction as *Vertue Betray'd.* The latter had had a pronounced royalist

---

[1] See the dedications to *Vertue Betray'd* and to *Cyrus the Great.*

[2] It long held the stage in the acting version of Ralph (1731). It was translated into German in 1786.

[3] See Hazelton Spencer, 'Improving Shakespeare" (*PMLA*, 1926, XLI. 735–7).

note[1], but this following play, although it does not seem to our eyes a very dangerous piece of work, was suppressed. It was not seen on the stage until it had been altered into *The Albion Queens, or The Death of Mary Queen of Scotland* (acted at D.L. and printed 1704). As in the other productions of Banks, there is a poetic touch here, chiefly in the pitiful figure of Mary. Elizabeth's last words in *The Albion Queens* end on a despairing note heard seldom in the mouths of Restoration stage potentates. "O *Cecil*," she cries,

> O *Cecil!* Shall I never be at rest?
> We are but Gawdy Executioners at best;
> Fixt to our Crowns, we bear the galling Weight,
> Of censuring Fools, and flattering Knaves of State.

It was sentiments like this which in all likelihood the then monarch did not exactly appreciate.

Equally important and equally neglected is *The Innocent Usurper, or, The Death of the Lady Jane Gray* (1694). This tragedy was likewise prohibited by the censor, again for what reason is not made quite plain. *The Innocent Usurper*, the last of this series of historical plays, is as typical as any of Banks' productions. We meet here once more with the occasional heroic exclamations—"Hell! Scalding Lead! and Sulphures!"[2] is only one of them—and Pembroke's already-quoted soliloquy in Act IV:

> Weep, Heav'ns, fall Hail and Torrents from the Skye,
> And when y'ave drein'd the Briney Ocean dry,
> Weep on, and pour the Watery Globe and Night,
> On the World's back, and quench this Orb of Light,

reads as if it came from some tragedy of 1675. Again, however, the atmosphere of the play is not heroic but pathetic, and domestic sorrows are duly insisted upon. The tragedy of Lady Jane is very pitifully painted for us, and the Duchess of Suffolk is a figure at once vital and vigorously delineated,

---

[1] Henry VIII closes the play with the words:
    "*A Prince can do no Ill!*...
For Heav'n ne'er made a King, but made him just."
[2] v. i.

a kind of Restoration Lady Macbeth. "Go to —— Are you a Man?" she asks,

> Have you that Blood
> Yet left within you that your Birth created?
> Or did it only boast (hoping to mix
> With mine) that you were Noble and Ambitious?
> O Gods! that Woman should so far excel
> Mankind in ev'ry thing, yet be so curst
> To be born Slaves, and live in loath'd Subjection![1]

On the whole Banks merits a position much higher than that which is usually accorded to him. As a pioneer he stands alongside of Mrs Behn and of D'Urfey and of Otway and of Southerne in the development of the newer drama. In no way can one endorse the view that he is to be considered merely as "an admirer of Lee" and as one who "faithfully reproduced that author's worst characteristics[2]." Only of the earlier two dramas and of the later *Cyrus the Great* (which, the author informs us, was written before *The Unhappy Favourite*, most probably in the last years of the heroic fever) is this true, and all these plays stand quite apart from what were Banks' main works. As an artist he stands next to Otway: as a precursor of Rowe he stands almost unique in his age.

Connected with Banks in the adoption of historical themes mingled with pathos is John Bancroft, to whom in fair certainty may be ascribed the two plays of *King Edward the Third, with the Fall of Mortimer Earl of March. An Historicall Play* (D.L. *c.* Nov. 1690) and *Henry the Second, King of England; with the Death of Rosamond* (D.L. Nov. 1692)[3]. These two plays are both very Elizabethan in character. The

---

[1] 1. i. Banks was evidently greatly influenced by *Macbeth*. I have already drawn attention to other reminiscences in *Cyrus the Great*. The scene in *The Innocent Usurper* where the Duchess meets Suffolk and asks:

> "What has alarm'd my Lord
> To be thus early up? Is *Edward* dead?"

reminds us strongly of similar scenes in Shakespeare's play.

[2] See *C.H.E.L.*, vol. VIII.

[3] There is every reason, however, for believing that these two plays are largely reworkings of now lost Elizabethan originals. See Appendix C.

former is but a poor piece of work, in which the comic scenes moving around the person of Serjeant Eitherside, are infinitely superior to the serious portions of the play. *Henry the Second* on the other hand is a very fine historical tragedy. It betrays obvious reminiscences of preceding plays, but the blank verse is good and the characters fairly successfully worked out. The satire of priests and the person of Sir Thomas Vaughan, a kind of replica of Pandarus, recall to us *Troilus and Cressida* of Dryden, and the revengeful abbot seems a copy of Wolsey in Banks' *Vertue Betray'd*. The last words of Rosamond, however, owe more to Elizabethan example:

> I do. Thus I submit, and Drink the Bane of Life;
> The Bane of Love. Oh *Henry!* thus I fall thy Sacrifice,

and it was Elizabethan example that urged on this revival of plays dealing with English history.

The pathetic note merging in with Elizabethan imitation is to be seen in many tragedies of the later years of the century. Many instances of how it crept even into the heroic plays of the time have been noted above. Similarly there has been noted the insistence on what had already appeared in the rimed heroic dramas of 1664–77, the atmosphere of horror. Those dramatists, who in this later time, went in for such plays, seem to have been more successful on the whole than most other tragic dramatists. They are much more numerous, and obviously their productions made wide appeal to contemporary audiences. The main thing that separates them from those who had before introduced horror into heroic plays is that they all made a fresh return directly to Elizabethan sources. A play like Ravenscroft's *The Italian Husband* (L.I.F. *c.* Nov. 1697) betrays closer similarities to some Elizabethan and Jacobean dramas than to horror elements either in the heroic or in other plays written between 1660 and the date of its production. Possessed of a certain power of appeal and rather strikingly written, it leaves us aghast at the frightful scene at the end where the lover and the wife lie dead in the chamber, to remain there until the latter's father shall come. The husband has no doubt but that this scene will find the approbation of his father-in-law:

> I know 'twill greive his Heart, he lov'd her well,
> But Princes have noble Souls,
> His Sense of Honour will excuse the Deed.

Such a scene reminds us at once of Shirley or Ford or Webster. The attempt to raise the emotions, and at the same time the endeavour to achieve something of powerful calm, is truly fed directly from Elizabethan founts[1].

Most of the horror plays of this time are revenge dramas, and this theme again was in most cases taken over from older pre-Restoration sources. Thomas Scott's *The Unhappy Kindness, or, A Fruitless Revenge* (D.L. 1697) is but an alteration of Fletcher's *Wife for a Month*, and William Phillips' *The Revengeful Queen* (D.L. *c.* June 1698) betrays clearly the influence of D'Avenant's *Albovine*. Other dramas deal with kindred atmospheres. *The Fatal Discovery, or, Love in Ruines* (D.L. *c.* Feb. 1698), a play published by Powell[2], turns on the unwitting double incest of Cornaro, who is not only the father of his own sister, Eromena, but later falls in love with and marries her. It has a comic underplot which merely serves to intensify the disgust and horror the whole tragedy casts upon us. *Beauty in Distress* (L.I.F. *c.* April 1698) by Motteux is likewise interesting, as being still a further specimen of the tragedy of blood, although written "to a Moral[3]," with the external format of classic restraint. The duration of the tragedy is three hours, and the place remains fixed in an ante-chamber. Despite its keeping to the unities, it is as noisy as any swash-buckling Cockpit production, and is valuable precisely because of that.

Many plays of the period, of course, cannot be crushed into one or other of the separate schools, being like this last-mentioned work of Motteux. Brady's *The Rape, or, The Innocent Impostors* (D.L. Feb. 1691/2) with its theme of

---

[1] E. T. Norris ("The Italian Source for Ravenscroft's *The Italian Husband*", *Review of English Studies*, 1934, x. 202–5) traces its origin to Cicognini's *Il tradimento per l'honore*.

[2] Who, in his preface, makes a vigorous attack on Dryden for his "Praelude" to *Heroick Love*.   [3] Preface.

Goths and Vandals is thus difficult to classify, as well as plays like the anonymous *Timoleon, or, The Revolution* (unacted, 1697)[1] and *The Unnatural Mother* (L.I.F. *c.* Aug. 1697), the latter with an Eastern setting but no very decided heroic features[2]. On all, however, to some extent the seal of the heroic or of the Elizabethan drama was set. Shakespeare had been found again, and the age was slowly creeping away from Beaumont and Fletcher to a new appreciation of the master's works.

VI. *Adaptations of Shakespeare*

A consideration of the plays which present such marked features of Elizabethan imitation may well lead us to an examination of the definite adaptations of the period and that to a general summary of this rapid analysis of tragic endeavour in the age of the Restoration. Probably nowhere better than in these adaptations can we find the key to the whole dramatic productivity of the period. Nowhere better can we find expressed the likes and the dislikes of the time.

If we take Shakespeare and watch the Restoration attitude towards his work, we shall at once penetrate deeply within the hearts and the minds of the dramatists and of the audience. I shall not here refer to Pepys' critical strictures on *Romeo* or on *Hamlet*, because Pepys seems to me a highly unsatisfactory witness[3]. He was prone to express his thoughts in rather an exaggerated form, and he was often influenced unduly by external considerations. Sometimes he was breaking a vow not to enter the theatre for a period of months, sometimes he was disappointed in the company or in the acting. His value as a critic, moreover, is clearly enough displayed in his ludicrous comparison of *The Adventures of Five Hours*

[1] This has been attributed to Southby (cf. MS. note in the Bodl. ~opy, Mal. 116).

[2] A fairly worthless play is *Pausanius, The Betrayer of his Country* (D.L. 1696) written in strict imitation of the French school. It was brought on the stage by Southerne and has been ascribed to Richard Norton. It was esteemed by eighteenth-century classicists (see Garth, *The Dispensary*, p. 51 of the 1699 edition).

[3] Hazelton Spencer, in "Mr Pepys is Not Amused" (*ELH*, 1940, VII. 163–76), shows how often the diarist's judgments were coloured by external events.

and *Othello*. There are many other men in the period who can better be trusted. Dryden in some of his works might be ruled out as being a man far and away superior to his age, but after all Dryden, his life through, was trying to plumb the tastes of his time. We may take his word for certain things. And we may take Tate's, for Tate, as is evident from the prefaces to *The History of King Lear* and to *The Loyal General*, evidently thought a good deal of and about Shakespeare and was prepared honestly to like or to dislike as his mind bade him, not swayed by sudden fancies but basing his ideas on definite critical precepts.

Before we come to the adaptations and to the prefaces in particular we may briefly note what the age did not like in Shakespeare. The comedies for the most part were neglected by the men and women of the time, the reason being that in the early comedies there is too much romance and in the later too chaotic plots. Thus there were never seen in the Restoration *Love's Labour's Lost*, *The Two Gentlemen of Verona*, *The Comedy of Errors*, *The Merchant of Venice*, *All's Well*, *As You Like It*, and *The Winter's Tale*. *The Tempest* was taken and altered because it had a unified plot, as well as possibilities for operatic display. *Measure for Measure* was run in with *Much Ado* by D'Avenant, but apparently without success. *A Midsummer Night's Dream* was made into an opera. *The Taming of the Shrew* was sufficiently realistic to be a fair success in Lacy's adaptation, and *The Merry Wives*, similarly a realistic play, was performed as early as Nov. 9, 1660, and as late as Dec. 17, 1675. Of all the romantic comedies which now we adore, only *Twelfth Night* in an unadapted form was given a half-hearted show on the stage during those forty years.

With the histories and the tragedies it was different. The latter obviously appealed to the age, although there were many things that seemed to the Restoration courtiers indecorous in them. *Romeo*, the early lyrical tragedy, was made into a tragi-comedy by Howard and classicised by Otway. *Macbeth* was made into an opera by D'Avenant. *Lear* was made happy in Tate's version. *Antony* was rendered heroic and sedate in Dryden's famous tragedy. *Othello* and *Hamlet* escaped the hands of the adapter, why is not quite clear: they were presented in cut, but unadded-to, versions. Of the other tragic dramas, *Troilus* was heroicised by Dryden: *Coriolanus* made political by Tate: *Titus Andronicus* rendered more bloody by Ravenscroft: *Timon* turned "into a Play" by Shadwell: *Julius Caesar* feebly tampered with by an anonymous author: *Cymbeline* made pathetic by D'Urfey. *Pericles* apparently saw a solitary performance early in the Restoration period at the Cockpit: there is no record of any later revival.

The histories made their appeal in other ways. They were easily turned into political parallels, as in Crowne's *Henry VI* and Tate's *Richard II*. Sometimes, as in *Henry VIII*, they could well be utilised to set off the rich scenes then coming into fashion.

Even such a brief survey as this has shown us many of the likes and the dislikes of the age. The adapters, Dryden in particular, have pointed out still more clearly what they preferred and what they thought wrong in Shakespeare's works. Dryden, let us remember, had as great a veneration for Shakespeare as any man in his age. There is no hesitancy in his words in the preface to *Troilus and Cressida*, when he states that "our Reverence for *Shakespear* (is) much more just, than that of the *Grecians* for *Aeschylus*." He is filled with a glow of admiration for his great English predecessor. This glow of admiration, however, did not blind him to what appeared to be errors and weaknesses in Shakespeare; in this very preface we find four objections to Shakespeare's work clearly enunciated. First, he says, writing of the earlier *Troilus* but thinking of many other plays, much of the language is obsolete, coarse and too figurative. This is merely an echo of what almost everyone in that age was saying.

> That which the World call'd Wit in *Shakespeare*'s Age,
>   Is laught at, as improper for our Stage,

said a prologue written for a 1667 performance of James Shirley's *Love Tricks*, and in 1673 one Richard Ward, when looking about for a quotation to illustrate the use of "unprofitable and ineffectual Words," chose some ten lines from *The Merchant of Venice* as a prime example[1].

Dryden's second objection is that the whole play of *Troilus and Cressida* moves with a careless incoherent motion. Here again he was but expressing a common criticism of the age, the age that was growing rapidly classical, that disliked romantic incoherency and adored precision, mathematical though that might be.

Thirdly, "the latter part of the Tragedy is nothing but a confusion of Drums and Trumpets, Excursions and Alarms" —the words are Dryden's own. On turning to his own adaptation, one might think that he has increased the fighting and this "confusion of Excursions and Alarms"—but Dryden's criticism was directed rather at what seemed to him the purposeless confusion than at the confusion itself.

Finally, as a fourth objection, Dryden finds that "the chief Persons...are left alive: *Cressida* is false and is not punish'd."

We may, perhaps, looking over these statements and these facts, now tabulate briefly some of the things that the Restoration age saw in Shakespeare and some of the things which they whole-heartedly condemned. They liked the heroes of the tragedies, but as these were not sufficiently exaggerated, in their alterations they tried to make the Shakespeare figures approximate as closely as possible to the late seventeenth century standard; or else they took away from the reality of the types by the introduction of operatic features. *Hamlet* and *Othello* alone they permitted to be seen unadapted. *Hamlet*, hesitating, dallying, did not offend their susceptibilities, and in *Othello*, I have often suspected, the contemporary audience must have looked upon Iago as the central figure. Othello, I am certain, they could not have possibly

---

[1] A few of the sentences in this chapter I have taken from my own pamphlet on *Dryden as an Adapter of Shakespeare* (Shakespeare Association Pamphlets, No. 8, 1922). The subject of Shakespeare's fate during the Restoration has been thoroughly dealt with by Hazelton Spencer in *Shakespeare Improved* (1927), by G. C. D. Odell in *Shakespeare from Betterton to Irving* (1920) and by Montague Summers in *Shakespeare Adaptations* (1922). See also Arthur C. Sprague, *Shakespeare and the Actors* (1944).

appreciated. They liked, also, the settings of many Shakespeare plays, because they realised the possibilities in them of theatrical display, and they liked, in the later years, the scenes of pathos. They were conscious of the greatness of Shakespeare, but probably conscious of it in a vague way which defied analysis or definition.

On the other hand, they objected to Shakespeare's language. They objected to his romantic comedy. They objected to the too-great realism of his heroes. They objected to the chaos of his scenes. They objected to his lack of poetic justice and to the universal calamities which overwhelmed good and bad alike.

The adaptations, therefore, made of those plays they liked, followed certain very definite critical lines. There was practically no tampering with the text simply for the sake of tampering. The language was made easier and less involved. The heroes were made more heroic. Tragedies and comedies alike were turned into operas. The eternally changing scenes of the Shakespearian dramas were made more unified. The comedies and the comic scenes in the tragedies were made witty and vulgar in the Restoration way. Both tragedies and histories were rendered into political parallels.

It is impossible here to do more than glance at some of the more important of the adaptations as illustrating these various points.

The Tempest of Dryden and D'Avenant may be taken as displaying the tendency towards the introduction of "classically" regular, almost mechanically regular, groups of characters in the plays. Ferdinand and Miranda, Hippolito and Dorinda, Ariel and Milcha, Caliban and Sycorax pair off in a wonderful way. Our only surprise is that the happy thought did not come to D'Avenant of providing Prospero with a female counterpart. This comedy may be taken also as illustrating the introduction of political elements, the Duke Trincalo scenes, evidently the most popular parts in the play, satirising the Republican parties. The new spirit of vulgar wit and suggestiveness is to be noticed here, coarseness in the Duke Trincalo scenes and innuendoes in the dialogue between Miranda and Dorinda. This debasing of Shakespeare's humour is only part of what went on all through the age. Pandarus in Dryden's *Troilus and Cressida*, in a similar way, is made inexpressibly coarse. One might cite in the same connection the gratuitous indecencies introduced by Rochester into his alteration of Fletcher's *Valentinian*.

Two other alterations of D'Avenant's present equally entertaining features. *Macbeth*, as I have noted, was turned into an opera. This in itself is interesting, but there are other changes in it, more detailed changes, which have an even greater importance. The language is consistently simplified and made regular.

> "To us fair Weather's foul, and foul is fair!" say the witches,
> "Come hover through the foggy, filthy Air...."

The words of Lady Macbeth and of Macbeth himself are robbed of their strength in an attempt to make them be more readily understood.

> There wou'd be Musick in a Raven's Voice,
> Which shou'd but croke the Entrance of the King
> Under my Battlements,

or

> No, they wou'd sooner add a Tincture to
> The Sea, and turn the Green into a Red—

or

> She shou'd have Di'd hereafter,
> I brought her here, to see my Victimes, not to Die.
> To Morrow, to Morrow and to Morrow,
> Creeps in a stealing pace from Day to Day,
> To the last Minute of Recorded Time;
> And all our Yesterdays have lighted Fools
> To their Eternal Homes—

any of these is typical of the silent changes made throughout. Here, also, in this *Macbeth*, beyond the mere alterations made in order to use machine and scenery, we may trace the influence of the new stage conditions. Lady Macduff's part is enormously lengthened, purely for the sake, apparently, of giving opportunity to some rising actress of the Duke's Theatre.

The other plays present equally valuable and interesting

evidence of the tastes of the age. D'Avenant's *The Rivals*, made out of *The Two Noble Kinsmen*, is a tragi-comedy, with the same simplification of language, and with a reduction of the spirit of Thebes to the spirit of Arcadia. Of Theocles and Philander (Arcite and Palamon) we are told that

> they killed
> With such regret, as if they did embrew
> Their Swords in Blood to blush for those they slew.

Dryden's *Troilus and Cressida* shows us the attempt to make heroic those plays of Shakespeare which to the Restoration seemed to lack the exaggerated sentiment necessary for tragedy. Troilus here has become a hero, Cressida a heroine, just as in *All for Love* Antony is made the brother of Almanzor, Cleopatra the sister of Almahide, Dolabella the image of Acacis. *Troilus and Cressida* and *All for Love*, however, differ from most of the adaptations in ending seriously and tragically. *Romeo*, we remember, was given a happy conclusion, and Cordelia and Edgar were paired off in Tate's *Lear*. All these last-mentioned dramas display in common the tendency to make more unified and more symmetrical the romantically irregular plots of Shakespeare. While this was in general due to the pseudo-classic criticism of the time, it was probably urged forward by the changing conditions of the stage. Shakespeare's works, written for the platform of the Globe, were being adapted for performance in the picture-frame of the Duke's and the Theatre Royal.

In these adaptations, then, we may find the key to the age, an age, dependent on the old, but with new conditions and with new ideals: an age intent on its own wit, on its own ideas, on its own conceptions, able dimly to appreciate the great work of the past, but filled with an over-weening sense of its own importance and offended at any attempt to inculcate in a reasonable way honour or virtue: an age that has inherited great and noble things, yet debilitate and weak, nursing the degenerate descendants of a powerful race, glorious sometimes in its decay, but graceless, if debonair, corrupt, if airy and splendid.

SUPPLEMENTARY TO
CHAPTER TWO

The past two decades have seen much attention devoted to the tragedy and the heroic drama of the Restoration period, with a determined endeavour to appreciate what precisely was the effect at which the playwrights aimed. Despite the fact that contemporaries tended to identify the heroic play with the play in rimed couplets[1], we may still find ourselves justified in regarding the riming fashion as something distinct from the development of heroic themes. If we do not, then there is an ever-present danger of confusing medium and content. The fact remains that the couplet form was being shaped for rhetorical purposes by many writers before 1642[2] and that its adoption for dramatic purposes after 1660 was inevitable.

Dryden's achievements, of course, have attracted the majority of writers on this subject[3]. It was his example which aided Voltaire in the establishment of a new kind of heroic drama in France during the eighteenth century[4]. That an English author, contemporary with Racine, could thus fashion an independent tragic model testifies strongly to Dryden's dramatic gifts. The fact itself, however, is not so surprising as at first sight it appears. When we consider the already-quoted remark of a modern critic: "The basis of Restoration tragedy

[1] This is emphasised by W. S. Clark in "The Definition of the 'Heroic Play' in the Restoration Period" (*Review of English Studies*, 1932, VIII. 437–44). Clark declares that a contemporary definition might have taken the form of "a wholly serious play, composed in rimed verse, with a tone befitting heroic poetry, and concerned with the lofty sentiments of persons in high station." A very useful study is Cecil V. Deane's *Dramatic Theory and the Rhymed Heroic Play* (1931).

[2] See Ruth C. Wallerstein, "The Development of the Rhetoric and Metre of the Heroic Couplet, especially in 1625–45" (*PMLA*, 1935, L. 166–209).

[3] See W. Mann, *Drydens heroische Tragödien* (Württemberg, 1932) and B. J. Pendlebury, *Dryden's Heroic Plays: A Study of the Origins* (1923).

[4] T. W. Russell, *Voltaire, Dryden and Heroic Tragedy* (1946) and "Dryden, inspirateur de Voltaire" (*Revue de littérature comparée*, 1948, XXII. 321–8).

is the Romantic idea[1]," we recognise that the age of Charles II wore its classicism with a difference[2]. This has led at least one writer[3] to postulate a "comic" purpose in the penning of these scenes and in the creation of these characters, with a sceptical attitude distinct from Orrery's more serious purpose. Without endorsing this view, which seems to read into Dryden's heroic dramas something that does not belong to the seventeenth century, we may well agree that "in the character of Almanzor" there is "a mixture of the splendid and the grotesque."

Among the later plays *All for Love* (D.L. Dec. 1677), long dismissed as merely a poor imitation of Shakespeare's *Antony and Cleopatra*, has of late received considerable critical attention. It may, of course, easily be demonstrated that the inspirational fire which illuminates the earlier play has a warmth and a consuming power far beyond anything within Dryden's reach[4], and obviously the imagery which gives grandeur to the one finds no parallel to the other. Where Shakespeare's imagery is part of the fundamental concept, Dryden's

images do not spring naturally from his theme, as the leaves from a tree; they are improvised; and though they may illuminate separate ideas, feelings, and even characters and scenes, they serve to destroy rather than to create the unity of the whole. *All for Love* is a fine tragedy decorated with poetry. It is not a poetic tragedy in the truest meaning of the term[5].

[1] Bonamy Dobrée, *Restoration Tragedy, 1660–1720* (1929), p. 29. See *supra*, p. 94.

[2] See P. S. Wood, "The Opposition to Neo-Classicism in England between 1660 and 1700" (*PMLA*, 1928, XLIII. 182–97). On Dryden's critical position in relation to Rymer's see Fred G. Walcott, "John Dryden's Answer to Thomas Rymer's *The Tragedies of the Last Age*" (*Philological Quarterly*, 1936, XV. 194–214).

[3] D. W. Jefferson, "The Significance of Dryden's Heroic Plays" (*Proceedings of the Leeds Philosophical and Literary Society*, 1938–43, V. 125–39). It is rather difficult to accept Baxter Hathaway's thesis in "John Dryden and the Function of Tragedy" (*PMLA*, 1943, LVIII. 665–73) that Dryden passed from a neo-Stoic conception to a sentimental view of tragedy's purpose.

[4] F. R. Leavis, "*Antony and Cleopatra* and *All for Love*: A Critical Exercise" (*Scrutiny*, 1936, V. 158–69). There is an interesting discussion of this play also in Ruth Wallerstein's "Dryden and the Analysis of Shakespeare's Technique" (*Review of English Studies*, 1943, XIX. 165–85).

[5] Kenneth Muir, "The Imagery of *All for Love*" (*Proceedings of the Leeds Philosophical and Literary Society*, 1938–43, V. 140–9).

All this is true, yet perhaps the judgement of another student of the play may be allowed to modify this statement. Although "in the use of the lambent phrase, the metaphor that vanquishes or seduces, in the revealing word that lightens like a flash" Dryden falls far below Shakespeare, still "in its result, *All for Love* is more decisively a tragedy than any...except Shakespeare's best, and *Antony and Cleopatra* is not one of them[1]."

Dryden's eminence, certainly, was recognised in his own time, and his influence was potent, but we must not forget that contemporaries are not always able to make a clear distinction between genius and mere competence—nor must we neglect to bear in mind always that the Restoration was an age when the literary aristocrats were all-powerful and that their tastes were capricious. Even the uninspired Elkanah Settle, during the Battle of the Poets, was regarded by many as a worthy rival to Dryden[2]. Even such a play as *The Mourning Bride* (L.I.F. 1697), one of Congreve's mistakes and "a thriller rather than a tragedy[3]," could prove a popular success[4]. More comprehensible is the esteem in which both Lee and Otway were held; rightly, these two authors have always maintained their position in the roll of tragic writers, and the present age has not been without significant reassessments of their value[5].

[1] Bonamy Dobrée, *op. cit.* pp. 89–90.
[2] See *supra*, p. 117.
[3] Bonamy Dobrée, *op. cit.* p. 168.
[4] Elmer B. Potter discusses "The Paradox of Congreve's *Mourning Bride*" (*PMLA*, 1943, LVIII. 977–1001)—the contrast between its contemporary success and its later neglect. Emmett L. Avery has an account of "The Popularity of *The Mourning Bride* in the Eighteenth Century" (*Research Studies of the State College of Washington*, 1941, IX. 115–16).
[5] The lives of these two dramatists have been well told by Roswell G. Ham in *Otway and Lee: Biography from a Baroque Age* (1931), and Bonamy Dobrée (*op. cit.* pp. 110–48) has two excellent chapters on their achievements. To the studies listed in the preceding pages may be added Clifford Leech's "Restoration Tragedy: A Reconsideration", *Durham University Journal*, 1950, XLII. 106–15. This presents an acute study of the merits and defects of the heroic play.

CHAPTER THREE

COMEDY

I. *Introductory: Elizabethan and Foreign Models*

CONCERNING the origins of Restoration comedy, and of that particular kind to which has been given the title "comedy of manners," violently divergent views have been expressed. There have been many to argue that in effect these plays were inspired and largely moulded by the comic drama of Paris as that was fashioned into the peerless form it assumed in the hands of Molière; others have affirmed that what we have here is a unique artistic development, owing little either to the French theatre or to earlier English endeavour, a thing summoned forth from the society that took its cue from the Merry Monarch; still others have sought to prove that essentially the comic endeavour of dramatists from Dryden to Congreve shows a logical progress from the comic trends fully evident in the plays which were being produced in the decades before the theatres were closed by Puritan ordinance in 1642.

Fortunately, the past few years have seen the appearance of a number of specialised studies devoted to this subject, and through these not only have the basic facts been more clearly established but also a surer approach towards the interpretation of these facts has been rendered possible.

Of one thing there can be now not the slightest doubt: Restoration comedy owes a tremendous debt, indeed its greatest debt, to the drama produced in England from the time of Jonson to that of Shirley[1]. During those formative seasons between 1660 and 1665, when the younger dramatists were slowly feeling their way towards a form of expression adequate

---

[1] By far the most important study of this subject is that by Kathleen M. Lynch, *The Social Mode of Restoration Comedy* (*University of Michigan Publications in Language and Literature*, III; New York, 1926).

to their needs, they had the opportunity of seeing a rich array of their predecessors' works[1]. Among these, diverse comic styles were represented. True, Shakespeare's comedies fall far down in the catalogue of revivals. Apart from *The Merry Wives*, essentially a farce, only two such works are known to have been given during these years, and both were probably unsuccessful[2]. Far back in time lay the days of good Queen Bess, and the romantic dramas that had pleased her subjects now had lost their savour. It was different, however, with Jonson, whose classically inclined style, rich powers of observation, humorous types and satiric tendencies assuredly made strong appeal to the later seventeenth-century audience[3]. Although he showed but little interest in social manners and although his scenes may have seemed to many a trifle rough, he had in him qualities well suited to be welcomed by the age. Almost all felt the impress of his art. He gave to Dryden in his earlier dramas many a hint, sometimes well employed, sometimes rather blunderingly taken over[4]. He was the master in chief of Shadwell[5]. He presented to the comedy of manners, if not the main types, at least the background against which these main types moved. For Dryden and others a model had been set by his works and on that model other works, more appropriate for the later age, might be fashioned.

[1] Lists of these plays, presented by the "old" and the "young" actors, and by the troupes of Killigrew and D'Avenant, are given in Appendix A.

[2] Pepys' comments are likely to have been typical: for him *A Midsummer Night's Dream* was "the most insipid ridiculous play that ever I saw in my life" (Sept. 29, 1662) while *Twelfth Night* was "but a silly play" (Sept. 11, 1661 and Jan. 6, 1662/3).

[3] The importance of Jonson in this period is attested by Robert Gale Noyes in *Ben Jonson on the English Stage, 1660–1776* (1935), J. F. Bradley and J. Q. Adams in *The Jonson Allusion-Book* (1922), and Gerald E. Bentley in *Shakespeare and Jonson* (1945). C. B. Graham shows Jonson's enduring influence on later writers such as Mrs Behn and John Dennis ("An Echo of Jonson in Aphra Behn's *Sir Patient Fancy*," *Modern Language Notes*, 1938, LIII. 278–9), "The Jonsonian Tradition in the Comedies of John Dennis" (*id.* 1941, LVI. 370–2), "Jonson Allusions in Restoration Comedy" (*Review of English Studies*, 1939, XV. 200–4), and "The Jonsonian Tradition in the Comedies of Thomas D'Urfey" (*Modern Language Quarterly*, 1947, VIII. 47–52).

[4] Ned Bliss Allen, *The Sources of John Dryden's Comedies* (1935), pp. 10–21, 217–18, 202–3.

[5] Albert S. Borgman, *Thomas Shadwell: His Life and Comedies* (1928), especially pp. 38–43.

That process of refashioning, however, was itself not entirely new. During the early years of the seventeenth century Fletcher, in association with Beaumont and others among his playwriting companions, had adumbrated something new, and with good reason his plays proved by far the most popular when the theatres reopened in 1660. Although he displays comparatively little awareness of social standards, Fletcher definitely stands forward as a representative of aristocratic youth and lays prime stress on witty conversational ease. Such a play as *The Wild Goose Chase*, for example, a "famous play" as Pepys called it[1] and one destined to become the basis of Farquhar's *The Inconstant* (D.L. 1702), might, on the surface, almost be mistaken for the work of one of the writers of the manners school. The characters have both names and aptitudes similar to those given by Congreve to his stage figures—Mirabell, "a Travell'd Monsieur and great defyer of all Ladies in the way of Marriage, otherwise their much loose Servant, at last caught by the despis'd *Oriana*," Pinac "his fellow Traveller, of a lively Spirit, and Servant to the no less sprightly *Lillia-Bianca*," Oriana "a witty follower of the Chase," Rosalura and Lillia-Bianca "Airie Daughters of *Nantolet*." Except for the absence in it of any strong impress of a social code, here is the same subservience of the plot to witty dialogue, the same air of graceful abandon, the same careless disregard of more sober moral standards, as we find in the Restoration comedies[2]. Reading this and other kindred dramas in the "Beaumont and Fletcher" series we feel that we are indeed standing on the threshold of Charles' Whitehall or entering the gates of St James's Park.

Nor did Beaumont and Fletcher stand alone in modifying and shaping the comic form during these earlier years. Again, it is not without reason that several plays by Brome figured largely in the Restoration repertoires, for this author, while in some respects merely a faithful imitator of his master Jonson and not, like Fletcher, himself a well-born gallant, contributed

---

[1] Jan. 11, 1667/8.
[2] For references to the studies of A. C. Sprague and J. H. Wilson, see *supra*, p. 93.

materially to the social content of comedy. Precisely because he was of humble birth, perhaps, he showed himself fully aware of the rapidly growing separation in standards between the young aristocracy and the citizens; indeed, in several of his plays he deliberately sought to wrest laughter from the anxious, awkward endeavours made by those not born to the manner to capture the delicate wit which the gallants mastered so easily. When we think of the prominent place given to the would-be wits in Restoration plays and of the episodes in those plays which bear at least a general likeness to scenes in his comedies, we must unquestionably add the now almost forgotten Richard Brome to the list of earlier Caroline playwrights who paved the way for Congreve.

Then, too, there is Shirley, although here a puzzle confronts us. Some of his comedies, as we have seen, were revived at the Restoration, but peculiarly among them there is no record of the two plays, *Hyde Park* and *The Lady of Pleasure*, which most closely approach the later style, while for some extraordinary and hitherto entirely unexplained cause the author himself seems to have come to be regarded as a mere drudge, an uninspired poetaster. Despite this, however, there can be no question about two facts—first, that in these two plays Shirley came nearer than any of his companions to creating the formula upon which the comedy of manners was constructed, and, secondly, that because of this, his influence was extensive. His portraits of Celestina and Carol are limned in the style which created Floriwell and Millamant; his gallants are the direct ancestors of Celadon and Mirabell[1].

In recent studies of this subject of the indebtedness of Restoration comedy to the playwrights who wrote between 1600 and 1642, one important and hitherto almost wholly neglected source of influence has been brought to light. It has long been recognised, of course, that, with the insistent encouragement of Queen Henrietta Maria French *préciosité* became a recognised cult, that Honoré d'Urfé's *Astrée* was

---

[1] N. B. Allen, *op. cit.* pp. 34–6, points out that Dryden, notwithstanding his contemptuous remarks about Shirley, borrowed from *The Lady of Pleasure* and that Shirley's comic style clearly "anticipates the comedy of manners in several important ways."

regarded as a masterpiece and a model and that the Platonic mood was freely expressed by a group of courtly dramatists, sometimes sincerely and sometimes evidently with an underlying smile. Suckling thus used Platonic sentiment in his *Aglaura* and *Brennoralt*, while D'Avenant curried royal favour both in his masque *The Temple of Love* and in such tragicomedies as *The Platonic Lovers*, *Love and Honour* and *The Fair Favourite*. In itself, *préciosité* is far removed from the realm of laughter, but, as has been pointed out[1], it could and did contribute to Restoration comedy in two distinct ways. First, there is the fact that even the *Astrée* introduces in Hylas a character who exists for the purpose of making fun of the exalted sentiments expressed by his "Platonic" companions; and, secondly, there is the other fact that, even when the cult itself had been replaced by a code of manners the very reverse of the "Platonic," the style of the French romances could not be forgotten but suffered a sea change into another form of artificiality[2]. This means that, although the content of the "Platonic" philosophy so beloved of Henrietta Maria is totally different from the Restoration gallants' philosophy, the two came together in their belief that cultured social life required a tone and a style based on fineness of wit. In the one, this wit was applied to the subtle interpretation of love as a spiritual essence, not to be defiled by sensual desires; in the other, it was applied to the pursuit of love as the chief business for the young gallant and his ladies. Both agreed in viewing love as a force distinct from marital emotions; the "Platonic" mistress, if chaste, was sister to the Restoration mistress and the erstwhile devoted "servant" became the agreeable Restoration rake. Between Suckling and Sedley there is much in common, and Henrietta Maria is a royal ancestor for Millamant.

The recognition of this connection helps to explain not only the co-existence of the "love and honour" drama and the comedy of manners but also the otherwise perplexing appearance during the decade immediately after the theatres'

---

[1] Kathleen M. Lynch, *op. cit.* pp. 43–136; N. B. Allen, *op. cit.* pp. 100–6.
[2] Kathleen M. Lynch, "D'Urfé's *Astrée* and the 'Proviso' Scenes in Dryden's Comedy" (*Philological Quarterly*, 1925, IV. 302–8).

reopening of numerous plays wherein heroic episodes appeared alongside lightly comic scenes. Neither Dryden's *Secret Love* nor Etherege's *The Comical Revenge* is to be regarded as a peculiar admixture of diverse elements; rather are these works to be interpreted as plays in which two apparently divergent and opposed philosophies are set forth for what they are— independent developments of one common social mode.

In considering the impress of this "Platonic" tragi-comedy we have obviously been dealing with a force partly French and partly English. Now it is necessary to turn to the direct influence exerted upon the Restoration playwrights by contemporary Parisian comedy. That such influence existed no one can possibly doubt: the only question is how far the influence passed beyond the mere providing of comic episodes to a power inspiring comic attitudes.

Without doubt the people with whom the Restoration courtiers found themselves most in sympathy were the French —gay and cynical, living under a royalist régime and, after years of disturbance, creating a culture of classical precision. The Parisian stage would have attracted the English dramatists in any case, but that attraction was made the stronger and the more immediate by the personal relationships so many of the courtier-playwrights had formed during their years of exile.

By a coincidence, Molière's career occupied almost precisely the first years of the Restoration period in England. In November 1658 his *L'étourdi* was presented in Paris, followed by *Le dépit amoureux* the following month and by *Les précieuses ridicules* in November 1659. *L'école des maris* and *L'école des femmes* came in 1661 and 1662 respectively, *Le misanthrope* and *Le médecin malgré lui* in 1666, *L'avare* in 1668, *Tartuffe* in 1669[1], *Le bourgeois gentilhomme* in 1670 and *Les femmes savantes* in 1672. The rapidity with which these became known in London testifies to the close connections between the two stages. Already by 1663 *Sganarelle*, produced in 1660, appeared in D'Avenant's *The Playhouse to be Lett*, while the two years 1667–1668 saw *L'école des maris* turned into Flecknoe's *The Damoiselles a la Mode* (T.R. 1668), *L'étourdi* into Dryden's

---

[1] As a three-act piece this had been acted once in 1664.

Sir Martin Mar-all (L.I.F. 1667) and *Les fâcheux* (1661) into Shadwell's *The Sullen Lovers* (L.I.F. 1668).

These set the fashion, and even if we reject the innumerable doubtful claims that have been made by plagiary-hunters, the list of adaptations and borrowings is a lengthy one[1]. Apart from the plays mentioned above, *L'école des maris* gave something to Sedley for *The Mulberry-Garden* (T.R. 1668), to Wycherley for *The Country Wife* (D.L. 1675), to Otway for *The Souldiers Fortune* (D.G. 1680) and to Shadwell for *The Amorous Bigotte* (D.L. 1690), besides possibly influencing

---

[1] Nearly all the findings (or imaginings) of the earlier students of this subject have been rendered obsolete since the appearance of John Wilcox's *The Relation of Molière to Restoration Comedy* (1938) and of Ned Bliss Allen's work on *The Sources of John Dryden's Comedies* (1935). Since the publication of these books André de Mandach, in *Molière et la comédie de mœurs en Angleterre* (1946), has resurveyed the ground, making several fresh suggestions; his article on "Tartuffe chez les Anglais" (*Gazette de Lausanne*, Feb. 9, 1946) should also be noted. Among the earlier studies may be listed: J. E. Gillet, *Molière en Angleterre, 1660–1670* (*Mémoires de l'Académie Royale de Belgique*, N.S. 1913, IX); D. H. Miles, *The Influence of Molière on Restoration Comedy* (1910); W. Harvey-Jellie, *Les sources du théâtre anglais à l'époque de la Restauration* (1906); C. H. Humbert, *Molière in England* (1874); Henri Van Laun, "Les plagiaires de Molière" (*Le Molièriste*, 1880–1, II. 143–9, 235–40, 303–7; 1881–2, III. 52–62, 137–46); M. Besing, *Molières Einfluss auf das englische Lustspiel bis 1700* (Borna-Leipzig, 1913); Louis Charlanne, *L'influence française en Angleterre au xviiᵉ siècle* (1906). Besides these general studies, there are numerous special investigations, such as: Karl Hartmann, *Einfluss Molières auf Drydens komisch-dramatische Dichtungen* (Leipzig, 1885); Philipp Ott, *Über das Verhältniss des Lustspieldichters Dryden zur gleichzeitigen französischen Komödie, insbesondere zu Molière* (Munich, 1885); Paul Sandmann, "Molières *École des femmes* und Wycherleys *Country Wife*" (*Archiv für das Studium der neuren Sprachen und Literaturen*, 1884, LXVII. 153–82); Hans Ferchlandt, *Molières Misanthrop und seine englischen Nachahmungen* (Halle, 1907); A. Wernicke, *Das Verhältniss von John Lacys The Dumb Lady zu Molières Le Médecin malgré lui und L'Amour médecin* (Halle, 1903); A. Bennewitz, *Molières Einfluss auf Congreve* (Leipzig, 1889). Nearly all of these, as Wilcox and Allen demonstrate, err: (*a*) by failing to apply any definite method in their research, and (*b*) in imagining connections where none exist. The borrowings listed above are those which, after careful examination, Wilcox accepts as certain or highly probable. An interesting general assessment of the difference between the contemporary comedy of Paris and London appears in T. C. Macaulay's "French and English Drama in the Seventeenth Century: Some Contrasts and Parallels" (*Essays and Studies by Members of the English Association*, 1935, pp. 45–74): a similar short study, "Some Thoughts concerning Molière and the Restoration Drama," is contributed by W. M. Kerby to *Modern Languages*, 1941–2, XXIII. 120–31.

Wycherley in *The Gentleman Dancing Master* (D.G. 1672). Dryden's *An Evening's Love* (T.R. 1668) borrowed both from *Les précieuses ridicules* and from *Le dépit amoureux*; the former was also used by Flecknoe in *Les Damoiselles a la Mode* (T.R. 1668), by Mrs Behn in *The False Count* (D.G. 1681), by Crowne in *Sir Courtly Nice* (D.L. 1685) and by Shadwell in *Bury-Fair* (D.L. 1689)[1]. *L'école des femmes* (1662) gave much material to Caryl's *Sir Salomon* (L.I.F. *c.* 1669) and Wycherley's *The Country Wife* (D.L. 1675), besides offering something to Flecknoe's *The Damoiselles a la Mode* (T.R. 1668), Ravenscroft's *The London Cuckolds* (D.G. 1681) and possibly Otway's *The Atheist* (D.G. 1683). To *Le mariage forcé* (1664) Ravenscroft turned in his *Scaramouch a Philosopher* (D.L. 1677) and others may have borrowed from it. *Tartuffe* was adapted by Medbourne (T.R. 1670) and may have influenced Crowne's *The English Frier* (D.L. 1690). Wycherley's *The Plain-Dealer* (D.L. 1676) was inspired by *Le misanthrope*; Lacy's *The Dumb Lady* (T.R. *c.* 1669) came from *Le médecin malgré lui*; Molière and Plautus gave Dryden's *Amphitryon* (D.L. 1690). From *George Dandin* Mrs Behn or Betterton drew *The Amorous Widow* (L.I.F. *c.* 1670) and from *L'avare* Shadwell wrought *The Miser* (T.R. 1672). Ravenscroft seems to have used the same play for part of *The Citizen turn'd Gentleman* (D.G. 1672), a comedy based mainly on *Monsieur de Pourceaugnac* and *Le bourgeois gentilhomme*; he turned again to the former of these last two pieces in *The Careless Lovers* (D.G. 1673) and *The Canterbury Guests* (D.L. 1694) and to the latter in *Scaramouch a Philosopher* (D.L. 1677)[2]. *Les femmes savantes*, besides producing Wright's *The Female Vertuoso's* (D.G. 1693), was utilised by Shadwell in *Bury-Fair* (D.L. 1689), and *Le malade imaginaire* was the basis of Mrs Behn's *Sir Patient Fancy* (D.G. 1678)[3].

---

[1] Wilcox, *op. cit.* pp. 113 and 80, finds "a possible" but "not a certain" borrowing in Dryden's *Marriage A-la-Mode* (L.I.F. 1672) and in Etherege's *The Man of Mode* (D.G. 1676).

[2] This pot-pourri also owed to *Les fourberies de Scapin* (1671), which gave Otway *The Cheats of Scapin* (D.G. 1676).

[3] On Shadwell's sources for *The Sullen Lovers* (L.I.F. 1668) see Asmus Erichsen, *Thomas Shadwells Komödie "The Sullen Lovers" in ihrem Verhältnis zu Molières Komödien "Le Misanthrope" und "Les Fâcheux"* (Flensburg, 1906) and John Wilcox, *op. cit.* pp. 117-19.

This by no means exhausts the complete list of minor borrowings, but it is sufficient to demonstrate that Molière's plays
were eagerly seized upon as soon as they became available and
that, despite the condescending comments made by several
English dramatists and critics, his achievements were highly
esteemed. It is true that in many instances his influence was
rather in the direction of farce than in that of comedy and that
the Restoration authors almost always found his plots so thin
that they either huddled two or three of his pieces together or
associated his episodes with others borrowed from diverse
sources. Already in 1663 Southland, in his preface to *Love
a la Mode* (1663), noted that "the *French* are commonly content in their Comedies with one single Humour and Rime,"
in contradistinction to the English who delighted in complexity, while as late as 1741 Luigi Riccoboni, in *An Historical
and Critical Account of the Theatres of Europe*, observed how
in their adaptations of French dramas the English "Authors
have doubled the Intrigue."

Because of these facts and others connected with them,
there has been a recent trend designed to prove that in spirit
Molière offered little or nothing to Restoration comedy.
Undoubtedly such an attitude is more fully justified than
earlier attempts to explain this comedy by sole reference to
the work of the French master, but perhaps it is inclined to
ignore one important aspect. We may easily demonstrate that
the good social sense so dominant in Molière's works is utterly
different from the mood of Restoration comedy, and that his
wit is far removed from the kind of wit beloved by Etherege
and his companions. To proceed further from this to an assertion that therefore Molière gave nothing to the comedy of
manners is, on the other hand, completely unwarranted. In
the realm of literature influence may be strong, and shaping
inspiration powerful, even when the work so inspired is completely alien to the inspiring force. No one would claim that
Bernard Shaw's plays express the mood dominant in the plays
of Ibsen, yet we have ample testimony to the fact that in his
formative years Shaw owed much to his Scandinavian master.
Something of the same thing is true of Restoration comedy.
Molière provided a model which was used at least by some of

the English authors to produce dramas based on a different attitude to life yet intimately allied to his. Wycherley's wit and comic outlook have nothing in common with Molière's; at the same time there is every justification for the statement that "Wycherley...learned from Molière how to focus his implications"—and it was precisely by such focusing of implications that the comedy of manners showed its superiority to the earlier kindred dramas by Shirley and his companions.

By no means, of course, was Molière the only seventeenth-century French playwright followed during the period of the Restoration. When Dryden composed *Sir Martin Mar-all* (L.I.F. 1667) he took Molière as his model for the last three acts, but the first two were based on Philippe Quinault's *L'amant indiscret* (1654). Similarly Thomas Corneille's *Don Bertram de Cigarral* (1650) added to Quinault's *La généreuse ingratitude* (1654) gave Corye's *The Generous Enemies* (T.R. 1671)[1]. Borrowings from Corneille generally were numerous: Dryden's *An Evening's Love* (T.R. 1668), besides one plot suggested by Molière's *Le dépit amoureux*, has another taken from *Le feint astrologue* (1648), which, itself taken from Calderón's *El astrologo fingido* (printed 1633), was translated anonymously as *The Feign'd Astrologer* (1668). Another of his plays, *L'Amour à la mode* (1655), also taken from a Spanish original (*El amor al uso*, printed 1681, by Antonio de Solis), produced Bulteel's *Amorous Orontus, or, The Love in Fashion* (T.R. 1664) and no doubt provided Southland with the title for his *Love a la Mode* (1663). Similarly *Le Baron d'Albikrac* (1667), based on Moreto's *La tia y la sobrina* (printed 1654), gave part of the plot for Betterton's *The Amorous Widow* (L.I.F. c. 1670)[2]. From Pierre Corneille's *Le menteur* (1644) came the anonymous *The Mistaken Beauty, or, The Lyar*

---

[1] Pierre Legouis, "Quinault et Dryden: Une Source de *The Spanish Fryar*" (*Revue de littérature comparée*, 1931, XI. 398–415), shows that Dryden freely filched from *L'Astrate* (1665).

[2] John Harrington Smith, "Thomas Corneille to Betterton to Congreve" (*Journal of English and Germanic Philology*, 1946, XLV. 209–13). Smith thinks that thus Congreve was influenced in *The Way of the World*. In "A Possible Source of 'The Way of the World'" (*Modern Language Review*, 1938, XXXIII. 258–60) E. Millicent Pool draws attention to the likeness between the "proviso" scenes of that play and of Nolant de Fatouville's *Arlequin Jason*.

(D.L. 1684), and from *Crispin médecin* (1670) of Noel le Breton, sieur de Hauteroche, came Ravenscroft's *The Anatomist* (L.I.F. 1696)[1]. When Vanbrugh wrote his *Æsop* (D.L. 1696) he turned for inspiration to the *Ésope* (1690) of Edmé Boursault. Contemporary French novels, too, of a kind different from the laborious romances, provided scenes and characters. In addition to his plays[2], Paul Scarron's *Le roman comique* (1651–57) offered to Fane the plot of his *Love in the Dark* (D.L. 1675), to Otway and to Dryden episodes in *The Souldiers Fortune* (D.G. 1680), *The Rival Ladies* (T.R. in B.St. 1664) and *The Assignation* (L.I.F. 1672)[3]. So Wycherley owed something indirectly to *Le roman bourgeois* (1666) of Antoine Furetière in *The Plain Dealer* (D.L. 1676)[4]. Among other indebtednesses may be noted the use made of Jean Campistron's *L'amante amant* (1684) in Lord Lansdowne's *The She-Gallants* (L.I.F. 1695)[5], of Jacob de Montfleury's *La fille capitaine* (printed 1671) in Shadwell's *The Woman-Captain* (D.G. 1679) and his *L'école des jaloux* (1664) in Mrs Behn's *The False Count* (D.G. 1681[6]). No doubt further comparative studies will reveal other borrowings from these sources.

Closely allied to the influence of France, because of its own influence on the French dramatists, was the appeal made by the contemporary stage of Madrid. The question of Spanish influence on English drama at this time has, it is true, never fully been worked out, and perhaps the immensity

---

[1] Raymond E. Parshall, "The Source of Ravenscroft's 'The Anatomist'" (*Review of English Studies*, 1936, XII. 328–33); Edward T. Norris, "The Original of Ravenscroft's *The Anatomist*" (*Modern Language Notes*, 1931, XLVI. 522–6).

[2] D'Avenant in *The Man's the Master* (L.I.F. 1668) used his *Jodelet, ou le maître-valet* (1645) and *L'héritier ridicule* (1649).

[3] J. U. Rundle "The Source of Dryden's 'Comic Plot' in *The Assignation*" (*Modern Philology*, 1947, XLV. 104–11) argues that Dryden went, not to Scarron, but to Calderón's *Con quien vengo vengo*. He also gives evidence to show that *The Mock Astrologer* owes directly to *El astrologo fingido*.

[4] Edwin E. Williams, in "Furetière and Wycherley: 'Le roman bourgeois' in Restoration Comedy" (*Modern Language Notes*, 1938, LIII. 98–104) shows that Furetière's novel was translated in 1671 as *Scarrons City Romance*.

[5] J. H. Smith, *The Gay Couple in Restoration Comedy* (1948), pp. 164 and 189; W. T. Bandy, "French Sources for Six English Comedies, 1660–1750" (*JEGP*, 1948, XLVII. 390–7).

[6] E. G. Mathews, "Montfleury's *École des jaloux* and Aphra Behn's *False Count*" (*Modern Language Notes*, 1939, LIV. 438–9).

of the task might well dissuade any student from attempting
it. From what already has been done on this line, however,
we know that the influence was no slight one. Calderón,
mainly because he was a contemporary of Molière and
Etherege and Congreve, was eagerly looked to. Charles seems
to have known him well. At the advice of the king Sir
Samuel Tuke translated *Los Empeños de Seis Horas* as *The
Adventures of Five Hours* (L.I.F. 1663). Another courtier,
George, Lord Digby, rendered *No siempre lo Peor es Cierto*
as *Elvira* (L.I.F. 1662–5) and Downes mentions two other
comedies by the same writer, *'Tis Better than it was* and
Worse and Worse, which no doubt are from *Mejor esta que
estaba* and *Peor esta que estaba*. Part of Wycherley's *The
Gentleman Dancing-Master* (D.G. 1672) is taken from *El
Maestro de danzar*[1].

Calderón, along with Moreto, was the Spanish dramatist
probably with the nearest ties of kinship to the Restoration
playwrights. Lope de Vega, although he too was made use
of, lay further away with his over-strained intrigue, his
jealousy and his flagrant honour. It was Moreto's *No puede
ser* that gave birth to Crowne's finest comedy, *Sir Courtly
Nice* (D.L. 1685), a play which, like *The Adventures of Five
Hours*, was written at the command of the king. *No puede ser*
was also the source of St Serfe's earlier drama, *Tarugo's
Wiles* (L.I.F. 1667). Vega, Alarcón, Molina and the others
came to us mainly through the medium of the French,
although there are scores of plays of "Spanish extraction,"
the sources of which have never been discovered.

Italy, too, played its part in the development of the comic
types of Restoration drama, not so much through its intellectual plays, the *commedia erudita*, as through the *commedia
dell' arte*, the descendant of the old Roman drama and the
ancestor of modern farce and pantomime. Many of the most
brilliant plays of Italy, such as Macchiavelli's *Mandragola*,
appear at this time to have gone completely unnoticed.
Macchiavelli may have remained a type of evil and of great-

---

[1] On the sources of Ravenscroft's *The Wrangling Lovers* (D.G. 1676)
see H. C. Lancaster, "Calderón, Bourseult and Ravenscroft" (*Modern
Language Notes*, 1936, LI) and further comments by J. U. Rundle (*ib.*
1947. LXII. 382–4).

ness, may have retained the position he held during the Elizabethan period, may, through his tales, have inspired one or two plots in Restoration comedies, but his work for the Italian theatre was unknown and uncared for. The *commedia dell' arte*, on the other hand, seized powerfully on the fancies of the English audiences. It competed successfully with the comedy of manners. Its types were taken over into English dramas, and it itself gave impetus to that farcical element which becomes so pronounced in the last years of the century. A fuller consideration of its power and influence may well be left over to a later chapter of this book.

II. *Types of Restoration Comedy*

Out of Jonson and Fletcher, then, tempered by reminiscences of Molière, of the *commedia dell' arte* and of Calderón grew the comedy of the Restoration: and the study of the development of that comedy really resolves itself into a disentangling of such diverse founts of inspiration. It must, of course, be realised at the very start that Restoration comedy is something far wider than is connoted by the modern use of that term. We have been rather apt to make it include solely that group of major dramatists which is composed of the outstanding figures of Etherege, Wycherley, Congreve, Farquhar and Vanbrugh, to the almost complete exclusion of all those innumerable writers who supplied the Theatre Royal and the Duke's with their daily fare. It is perfectly true that that group of major dramatists undoubtedly represents English comedy at its highest, not only in its own age but probably in all ages, but the result of the over-treatment of these playwrights by scholars and enthusiasts has been to cast into comparative neglect a mass of lesser comic writers who stretch from the Shadwells and the Drydens down to the insignificant Ravenscrofts and Tates. To gain a true and an historical view of the complete development of comedy from 1660 to the close of the century one must include everything, good and bad, in one's researches, and not confine oneself to two or three outstanding figures. The spirit of the

Elizabethan age would but ill be realised if we limited ourselves to Shakespeare, or that of the Romantic Revival if we
read Wordsworth alone.

In the first place, by embracing more than those major
five dramatists of the Restoration mentioned above, we come
to realise that Restoration comedy is by no means a thing
wholly of the manners style. The manners style was in point
of fact too high to be attained by all the playwrights of the
age, who chose rather the humbler paths of pure Jonsonian
imitation. The strata of Restoration comedy, indeed, are
truly infinite, and any attempt at rigid classification is bound
to fail. At the same time, some classification is necessary, and
happily one can enumerate several divergent types which will
include almost if not quite all of the theatrical productions of
the epoch.

When the theatres opened in 1660 there were roughly four
distinct or semi-distinct schools of comic invention, that of
Jonson, described as the school of humours or of satire, that
of Shirley, adumbrating the school of manners, that of Shakespeare, which may be called the comedy of romance or of
humour, and that of Spanish intrigue. These represented
almost all the older styles of comic drama as inherited from
Elizabethan sources and were, of course, the first that were
ransacked by the band of new playwrights eagerly seeking for
models and plots. With *The Wild Gallant* (T.R. in V.St. 1663)
and with *Secret Love* (T.R. in B.St. 1667) of Dryden came in
a variation of the intrigue type, a more distinct tendency
towards the later manners school, more especially to be
noticed in the presence of the pair of lovers, witty, gay, anti-
moral and sprightly. Dryden's endeavour serves to register
a step in the direction of Etherege. With the latter we are
fully within the new reign, that reign which was to continue
through Congreve and Vanbrugh into far distant decades of
another century. For many years these five distinct types
remained the recognised schools in which the comic dramatists
worked, until, about the sixties and the early seventies of the
century, farce, derived largely from French and Italian

imitation, crept into favour and for a time dominated the theatres. Finally, in the last decade of the century, although hinted at as early as 1680 if not before even that date, there developed that still newer type of comic drama to which has been given the name of sentimental.

None of these seven separate schools can be wholly dissociated from another, and most often we see merely general mixtures of two or three of them more or less successfully welded together. Dryden, following Jonson and Fletcher in half a hundred ways, yet delineates the new type of comic hero in his Celadons and Lovebys. In a similar way, Shadwell, who, in *The Sullen Lovers* (L.I.F. 1668), condemns the new comedy of manners, the two chief persons of which, he declares, "are most commonly a Swearing, Drinking, Whoring Ruffian for a Lover, and an impudent, ill-bred *tomrig* for a Mistress," yet obviously gives many a hint to Congreve, as, for instance, in the Gartrude and Selfish scenes in *A True Widow* (D.G. 1678) which are quite clearly connected with the similar Miss Prue and Tattle episodes in *Love for Love* (L.I.F. 1695). In one of his later plays, too, *Bury Fair* (D.L. 1689), he introduces precisely that pair of lovers whom he had so inveighed against, twenty years previously. As a typical play of the period one might take Mrs Behn's *The Luckey Chance* (D.L. 1686) which has characteristics of the manners school in Bellmour, of the humours school in Sir Feeble Fainwood, all wrought into a complicated scheme of intrigue.

Again, the chronology of the period must, in any treatment of Restoration comedy, be carefully watched. Charles died in 1685, and before that date only two of the five major dramatists had presented any of their works before the public. Congreve did not produce his *Old Batchelor* until March 1693 and *The Way of the World* did not make its appearance till 1700. Farquhar's eight plays date from 1698 to 1707, Vanbrugh's eleven from 1696 to 1715. The school of manners, therefore, is by no means confined, as the school of rimed heroics had been, to a single decade or two. It was not a thing peculiar to the court of Charles. It flourished long after

Jeremy Collier's outburst of 1698, even after the fuller development of the sentimental comedy in the hands of Cibber and of Steele. At the same time, we are bound to recognise that the comedy of manners, brought to fulfilment only in the last years of the century, was in itself a relic of the licence and the wit and the ease instituted by Charles in his Restoration court.

This comedy of manners is a peculiar, intangible sort of thing. In plot and in character it was not much of an innovation. Fletcher's *The Wild Goose Chase*, as we have seen, contains a good deal of its atmosphere. Jonsonian personages abound in Etherege and in Congreve. The intrigue of the Spanish school is to be marked in almost every plot. Molière and his companions of the French stage gave merely a touch to the wit and to the theme. The title itself—Comedy of Manners—is rather difficult to explain, but here at least there are indications which point to the characteristics of the type. Schelling calls Jonson's comedy a comedy of manners: so perhaps it is, but obviously there is something in Congreve different from Jonson. Manners, in the mouths of the Restoration dramatists themselves, meant something quite apart from the modern meaning of the term. "A Manner?" cries Cynthia in *The Double Dealer*[1], "What's that, Madam?" and Lady Froth replies, "Some distinguishing Quality, as for example, the *Bel-air* or *Brilliant* of Mr *Brisk*...or something of his own, that should look a little *Jene-scay-quoysh*." This quotation seems to make the question easier. When we say that Jonson's comedy is a comedy of manners we are using the word manners in its ordinary sense of ways of men: when we say that Congreve's comedy is a comedy of manners we are using the word in its Congrevian sense, betokening something brilliant about a man or a woman, not a humour, but a grace or a habit of refined culture, something that "looks a little Jene-scay-quoysh." Genteel comedy—to employ Addison's phrase—is this late seventeenth century drama, not the ungenteel comedy of Jonson.

Even with these indications as to its inner nature it is

[1] II. ii.

difficult to hazard even an indistinct definition of the type. The manners school, after all, depends rather on an atmosphere which cannot be precisely analysed than on outstanding characteristics. Of a certainty D'Urfey's plays are not as Congreve's: but to lay one's finger on the exact point of departure is rather difficult. We may, however, disentangle some of what appear to be the true characteristics of the species. In the main, we may say, the invariable elements of the comedy of manners are the presence of at least one pair of witty lovers, the woman as emancipated as the man, their dialogue free and graceful, an air of refined cynicism over the whole production, the plot of less consequence than the wit, an absence of crude realism, a total lack of any emotion whatsoever. This, certainly, will not take us very far, but it may serve at least to indicate in some ways the differences between the comedy of manners and the other types of Jonsonian and sentimental dramas. It is assuredly true that Dryden presents to us a pair of lovers somewhat after the style of the manners heroes and heroines, and that Spanish intrigue could take part in the plays of Etherege and of Congreve: but Dryden after all, although he may be regarded as one of the fathers of the typical Restoration comedy, is yet divided from Etherege by the presence in him of a certain passion and enthusiasm, while Spanish or other intrigue, appearing though it does sometimes in the plays of manners, never usurps all of the attention as it does, for example, in Tuke's *The Adventures of Five Hours*. The comedy of manners could make use of the French and the Spanish theatres, could reproduce some of Dryden's scenes or some of Jonson's characters, but, by its intellectualism, succeeded in remaining something independent and separate.

Before passing to an examination of the diverse dramas of the various writers or groups, a few words may still be said concerning that eternally vexing problem of immorality in Restoration comedies. It is often hastily assumed and stated that the school of manners had a monopoly in this immorality, and that Jeremy Collier put an end both to vice on the stage and to the comedy of manners in 1698. The second part of this assumption, to be discussed fully, would have to be taken well into the eighteenth century, a task impossible in this book, but it may be stated fairly dogmatically that neither the first nor the second supposition has any foundation in fact.

That the Congrevian comedy, if translated into terms of real life, presents many scenes of dubious and "immoral" character is true, but the Jonsonian comedy was just as licentious, with brutality added thereto. Indeed, it is interesting to note that such a man as Shadwell in *The Squire of Alsatia* (D.L. 1688), where he more or less adopts the critical attitude he had expressed in *The Sullen Lovers*, is hopelessly and permeatingly vulgar, brutal and immoral—for reasons which will be seen presently—while in *Bury Fair* (D.L. 1689), where he succumbs to the influence of Etherege's manners, his dialogue is markedly more palatable. Neither the one type nor the other can be acquitted on the score of immodesty, but neither can the whole immorality of the age be foisted on one at the expense of the rest. Rather one might hazard the statement that the comedy of manners is less vicious and harmful than many other types of Restoration plays which, because less witty, escape scot free. Addison's and Steele's strictures on Etherege are well known. *The Man of Mode* for them is "a perfect Contradiction to good Manners, good Sense and common Honesty." It is allowed by them to be nature, "but Nature in its utmost Corruption and Degeneracy[1]." This may be true. The upper-class life of the days of Charles was not a very pretty life, and the comedy of manners certainly reflects certain aspects of that existence. The problem of the comedy of manners, however, hardly lies here: in reflecting this upper-class life it stands alongside of many other types of drama and of many other forms of literature. The problem, of course, has been deeply complicated by the exaggerated pronouncements, on the one hand, of Puritans who see all art through the dark spectacles of their own morality, and, on the other, both of moral perverts who take delight in pornographic literature of any sort, and of

[1] *Spectator*, No. 65, May 15, 1711.

fanciful enthusiasts who have out-Eliaed Elia in the weaving of airy dreams. A true judgment can be gained only by a strictly impartial critic, one who recognises that morality is a word of very indefinite meaning and yet that there is a line of vulgarity below which art ceases to be art and becomes mere vicious and vulgar writing.

The first point to notice, it seems to me, is that in the hands of Etherege and of Congreve, comedy is wholly intellectual and passionless. There is no "warmth" in their works, as a Restoration critic might have said. There is little of that deliberate propaganda for evil which marks out the works of Rochester. If there are vulgar scenes or sensual jokes they are dragged in not for the sake of the vulgarity or of the sensuality, but because they are witty and amusing. There is nothing amusing in vulgarity itself: art alone can make it so. The second point to be noted is not unconnected with this first. The life reflected in the comedies of Etherege and of Congreve is not the whole of life: it is rather the essence of the upper-class existence of the time. The world presented before us, then, is certainly not artificial in Lamb's sense, it is only too real: but it is not realistic to the extent of dragging in forcibly the cruder aspects of life. The best plays of the manners school have about them a species of inverted spiritual existence which takes away from them a part of that brutality which is so painfully evident in the more ordinary "realistic" plays of the age. Actual sensuality is not needlessly emphasised. One example, which I feel is typical, may be taken from *The Old Batchelor*. Vainlove there wanders carelessly after "*l'amour*," not for the "blisses" thereof, but for the joyous sense of the chase itself. A great deal of the intrigue of the age, a great deal of the free conversation of the men and of the women, was of this type: it was not necessarily carnal, but was indulged in purely as an intellectual stimulant. Flirtation in that time was an art: assignations were planned with subtlety: indelicate hints in conversation were devised with skill and precision and grace.

I am not here striving to defend Restoration life: far from it: but I am endeavouring to place the comedy of Etherege and of Congreve in a place by itself, where the question of morality hardly enters in, where licentiousness is an intellectual thing and is not always reduced to worldly essence. Wherever there is emotion, this whole airy fabric vanishes. *The Plain Dealer* is apt to disgust and appal precisely because Wycherley has in that play taken upon himself to display all of life as he saw it, not to rear delicate fancies in a spirit's name. In the comedy of Etherege and of Congreve no emotion can enter in: the dialogue of Millamant and of Mirabel is as cold and chill as Cinthia's beams.

This question of actuality and of emotion is well brought out in a study of Shadwell's plays. I think no one, reading this author's *The Squire of Alsatia* (D.L. 1688), but would feel, I should not say shocked, but disgusted. The realism of the play brings to the fore all our ideas of refinement, of delicacy, if not of actual morality. There is not wit enough to cloak the sheer vulgarity: and yet the strangeness of it all is that Shadwell imagined he had before him a moral purpose —to show how an indulgent father produces in his son good qualities and how an intolerant one produces the opposite. As soon as deliberate morality and emotion are introduced into the plays of the age, they become at once vulgar and disgusting: for what are we to say concerning the two Belfonts? The elder is a poor fool rooked by the audacious villains of Alsatia: the younger, who is the model of goodness, after abandoning a mistress, Mrs Termagant, who has had a child by him and who has loved him passionately, after despoiling, too, an attorney's silly little daughter, leaves them both for his future wife, Isabella, paying the wretched attorney for what he had done. Isabella, true to her age, shows no repulsion, although the hero is as heartless, as cruel and as cynical as he was before.

Fundamentally, there may be as much vice at the back of Congreve's or of Etherege's plays, but it is never so forced on our attention as here. With emotion gone, with only one side of life treated, we become for the moment pagan, without a thought of the morrow, existing solely for the joy of the hour. We are given a finely polished art of the intellect that gives us amply in return for the vulgarity. Congreve has taken the more ethereal, graceful, fantastic, joyous qualities of the time and has expressed them in perfect form: Shadwell and the others have taken the sensual brutality of the age, deadening, dulling, uninspiring. Both could feed the mind with the most revolting of thoughts, but the one could give something in atonement therefor and the other could not. What a difference between the wantonly vulgar "purge" scenes in James Howard's *All Mistaken* (T.R. in B.St. 1667) or the banalities of the drolls in *The Muse of Newmarket* and the double-entendres of the "china" scene in Wycherley's *The Country-Wife* (D.L. 1675)! Both could show most fulsome scenes of carnality: both could play with what they thought the humorous side of sexual disease: but somehow, in writers of Shadwell's calibre, all that filth seems exaggerated, seems dragged to our notice as it were, in writers of a more polished taste it comes in only as an incidental.

III. *The Jonsonian Element: Shadwell*

In any summary of the comic productivity of the Restoration period it is not unfitting to start with Jonson. Jonson was the first great classicist in our drama, and in his humours he succeeded in stamping his impress heavily and securely on all later dramatic endeavour. When the theatres opened in 1660, his plays, as I have indicated above, were exceedingly popular at the Theatre Royal. No one thought of adapting him. However rough he may have appeared to some of the refined wits ("Refin'd Wits?" cries Sir Thomas in Crowne's *The Countrey-Wit*, "With a pox: unrefin'd, lewd, debauch'd Fops, that scarce ever read a Book in their Lives, except it were a Play") his love of the Roman theatre, his satiric bent and his presentation of contemporary types must have endeared him to a certain section of the audience, if not to all. Some, like Shadwell, idolised him as a god, following him step by step: some, like Congreve, took over from him a certain amount but refined upon his manner and his style: some, like Dryden, professed a greater love for Shakespeare

than for him but still imitated and followed certain elements
in his art. By no one was he forgotten. In the mid-decades
of the period there might have been some controversy about
his actual position in the history of literature, but from 1660
to 1700 he remained one of the chief of the old dramatists in
the theatrical repertoires.

Although Jonson's style of comedy was taken up at an
earlier date by other writers, his chief disciple throughout
the entirety of the period was Thomas Shadwell. This
author, remembered mostly because he was at one time poet
laureate, and, greater distinction still, had quarrels with John
Dryden, is one whose achievements have been recently
better appreciated than they generally were in the past[1]. He
is coarse, it is true, but not coarser than many others of his
age. He is positively nauseating with his "humours," yet he
could be almost as witty as Etherege if he chose. He had
opinions of his own, and, if he did not always act up to them,
no one can deny that his plays have to a large extent that
artistic finish and workmanship which characterise the work
of a master hand. Dryden might call him "dull," echoing
the criticism made by Settle in the dedication to *Love and
Revenge* (D.G. 1674). Many might laugh at his idiosyncrasies, his love of beer and his habit of declaring that his
plays were written in unconscionably brief spaces of time,
but for all that he remains one of the chief of the comic
dramatists outside of the school of manners.

Shadwell's entry into the world of the theatre was a triumphant one. On May 2, 1668, there was produced at L.I.F.
The Sullen Lovers, or, The Impertinents, a play that at once
attracted attention, not only because of the easy development
of the plot and of the ludicrous scenes, but because of the
vast amount of satire in it. Sir Positive At-all was at once
recognised as a burlesque portrait of Sir Robert Howard, and
this, in the words of Pepys, did "take, all the Duke's and
every body's talk being of that, and telling more stories of
him, of the like nature, that it is now the town and country

---

[1] The publication of his dramatic works and the study by A. S. Borgman
have materially contributed to this.

talk, and they say, is most exactly true." Ninny, "a conceited Poet," was as obviously an attack upon Sir Robert's brother, Edward. Woodcock, Pepys heard on the 6th, was meant for St John.

Shadwell himself, at the appearance of this work, must have been about twenty-five or twenty-six years of age, evidently a young man sure of himself, spoiling for a fight and bent on rivalling that other young man who had only four years previously made his debut as a dramatist, John Dryden. Two things that Dryden had adopted he attacked stoutly— the new style in comedy and the new style in tragedy. The "Love and Honour Feast" is opposed in the prologue to this his first play, and in Act III, Sc. i, occurs a reference to a play of Sir Positive At-all's called "The Lady in the Lobster," wherein, as we are told, one hangs himself at the command of his mistress. This looks suspiciously like a direct hit at *The Indian Queen* with its pathetic, or would-be pathetic, figure of Acacis. The new style in comedy is likewise opposed in the preface, which, as a whole, is decidedly well-written and interesting. After referring to the success of his own comedy, the author condemns the "Composer and Dancing-Master" of the age, who, even in 1668, had evidently become the "best Poets." He praises the pseudo-classical rules, draws attention to the fact that he has observed faithfully the three unities, and gives rich praise to Jonson. Then he turns on the new style. Possibly here he was thinking chiefly of Dryden. Already I have quoted his criticism of the two chief persons of this new drama—"a Swearing, Drinking, Whoring Ruffian for a Lover, and an impudent, ill-bred *tomrig* for a Mistress"—these forming "the fine people of the Play." This is the first attack on the new style in comedy that I know of, and it is particularly interesting because Shadwell himself in later years came to be influenced by Etherege and by Dryden. It is observable, also, that Shadwell, in this play, and in others, did not confine himself strictly to Jonson as a master. Here he owes decidedly to Molière in *Les Fâcheux*.

Within a couple of years Shadwell had continued his comic

output. After providing a pastoral in *The Royal Shepherdess*,
he came forward, about December 1670, with *The Humorists*
(L.I.F.). That he had not been thinking of Etherege in the
preface to *The Sullen Lovers* seems to be proved by the
preface to this third play of his: for in it he declares that
She Wou'd if she Cou'd, which had appeared two months
before *The Sullen Lovers*, was "the best Comedy that has
been written since the Restauration of the Stage." Why precisely he approved of this particular comedy he did not make
quite plain—the rest of his preface being taken up with a
defence of Jonson's comedy of humours, a style which he
defines in the regular Jonson way:

> *A Humour is the Biass of the Mind,*
> *By which with Violence 'tis one Way inclin'd:*
> *It makes our Actions lean on one Side still,*
> *And in all Changes that way bends our Will.*

The Humorists is particularly noticeable for two things: one
has reference to the age, and the other to Shadwell's own
conception of drama. After the success of the satire in *The
Sullen Lovers*, he apparently repeated the experiment by
ridiculing a number of the follies and the vices of the age,
but, as I have already indicated, the Restoration strongly
objected to general satire, and evidently *The Humorists* fell
flat on the stage. The other point of interest is the appearance
here of the fairly pure Raymund and Theodosia, a pair of
lovers conceived evidently in opposition to Dryden's "Ruffian"
and "Tomrig." This pair of lovers Shadwell was to repeat
with many minor variations in later plays. Apart from these
two, *The Humorists*, with its Sneak, Crazy, Briske, Drybob
and others, is a regular comedy of humours.

Ridicule of the popular tragedy appears once more in the
epilogue to *The Miser* (T.R. in B.St. Jan. 1671/2) in the shape
of an attack on the riming drama then at the height of its
fame. *The Miser* is confessedly but an alteration of Molière's
L'avare[1], although Shadwell thought fit to "say without

---

[1] Genest points out that Shadwell's main alteration of the French play
consists in the introduction of eight additional characters—the action
in Molière not being sufficient to maintain interest on the English stage
(*op. cit.* I. 119).

Vanity, that *Moliere's* Part of it" had "not suffer'd in" his "Hands," and to add the words, significant for an understanding of that age, "nor did I ever know a *French* Comedy made use of by the worst of our Poets, that was not better'd by 'em." *The Miser* is not an entirely negligible play, and illustrates well Shadwell's probably unconscious movement towards the wit of the manners school, as when Theodore declares he is in love and Ranter is prompt with his repartee: "But it's in an honourable way, I hope: not at all inclining to Wedlock?"

This style of wit, with even more spice in it, is continued in *Epsom Wells* (D.G. Dec. 1672) which was not only one of Shadwell's best plays, but also one of his most successful ones[1]. While the coarseness of many of its scenes is distressingly obvious, one cannot fail to appreciate its manifest talent. It is true that marriage is at a premium, that nothing seems to exist in its world but the fine art of cuckolding, yet the conversation, on the whole, comes very near in refinement to the Congreve strain. One can only wish that the atmosphere of the piece were not so debased. In this atmosphere we see the reverse of the heroic. In the very years that heard the most glorious rants of love and honour, the same audience listened to the query of Raines:

Art not thou a Villain to cuckold this honest Fellow, and thy Friend, *Ned*?

and to the answer of Bevil:

Gad, it's impossible to be a man of honour in these cases.

Out of the two contrarieties must a picture of the time be wrought.

For the next few years, Shadwell busied himself with opera and with tragedy, producing the operatic *Tempest* in April 1674, the spectacular *Psyche* in Feb. 1674/5 and the blank verse *Libertine* in June 1675. In the latter he makes a violent attack upon Settle, a return for the rival dramatist's remarks in the preface to *Love and Revenge* (D.G. Nov. 1674), declaring that he "had rather try new ways to please, than to

---

[1] It continued on the stage till 1726.

write on in the same Road, as too many do." With *The Virtuoso* (D.G. May 1676) Shadwell returned to comedy. Again there is a lengthy epistle dedicatory discussing the aim of comedy and of the presentation of humours. The author informs us that he has "endeavour'd in this Play at Humour, Wit, and Satyr" and that "Four of the Humours are entirely new." He dismisses as unsuitable for comedy, humours based on mere word-affectations, on dress-fashions, and on Gallomania, as well as "unnatural Farce-Fools." He admits into his gallery of humour-portraits only a certain class: "the artificial Folly of those, who are not Coxcombs by Nature, but with great Art and Industry make themselves so," he tells us, "is a proper object of Comedy."

> *No one Man's Humour makes a part alone,*

he insists in the prologue,

> *But scatter'd Follies gather'd into one.*

In *The Virtuoso*, Shadwell has again given to us his pairs of pure lovers, here named Longvil and Bruce, adoring honestly Clarinda and Miranda. In these portraits he errs as far from Dryden as he does from his more illustrious contemporary, Congreve, marring his art, indeed, by them, for too frequently his plays are thus divided sharply into two atmospheres almost independent the one of the other. What Dryden thought of them may be seen by a reference to the line in *MacFlecknoe* concerning "Whole *Raymond* Families and Tribes of *Bruce*."

The satire in *The Virtuoso* is more subtly chosen. The Restoration gallants must have appreciated the picture of Sir Nicholas Gimcrack, the "Virtuoso," and of Snarl, who admires nothing but the things of a former age[1].

Shadwell's work in comedy was continued after this till towards the close of the century. About December 1678 ap-

---

[1] G. Blakemore Evans ("The Source of Shadwell's Character of Sir Formal Trifle in 'The Virtuoso'", *Modern Language Review*, 1940, XXXV. 211–14) traces Shadwell's indebtedness to D'Avenant's *News from Plymouth* (see also Florence R. Scott in the same journal, 1944, XXXIX. 183–5). Claud Lloyd ("Shadwell and the Virtuosi," *PMLA*, 1929, XLIV. 472–94) discusses the satire directed against amateur "scientists" and collectors of the time.

peared at D.G. *A True Widow*, which, because it showed up the "crying sin of Keeping," was a failure on the stage[1]. In this play Shadwell, who was evidently on friendly terms with Dryden, has indulged in no direct satire at any particular form of dramatic art, the whole being a pure comedy of humours with, even, a few touches reminiscent of the poet laureate. Some of these humours are "new," to use Shadwell's own epithet, Lump, "a methodical Blockhead" and a Christian by trade, being a distinctly novel type. The plot, however, is more confused than is Shadwell's usual, and the rather vulgar touch of the author is painfully visible in the character of Lady Busy, who, in spite of her title, acts precisely as a bawd.

The Woman Captain (D.G. *c.* Sept. 1679) is, intrinsically, a poorer play, although it was not unsuccessful on the stage. Mrs Gripe's male part, certainly, is a fine acting one, and the manner in which she escapes from her husband and her obtained freedom in the end are not without interest for us, and must have had a similar interest for contemporary audiences. It may be noted that Shadwell displays less of the direct influence of Jonson here than he does in any of his comedies.

The Lancashire Witches, and Tegue o Divelly the Irish Priest appeared at D.G. about Sept. 1681, and was followed by a sequel, *The Amorous Bigotte, with the Second Part of Tegue o Divelly* at D.L. about March 1690. The first of these two companion plays is interesting almost solely for its political element and for the presence in it of the witches. "Fops and Knaves," Shadwell informs us, "Are the fittest Characters for Comedy, and this Town was wont to abound with variety of Vanities and knaveries till this unhappy Division. But all run now into Politicks, and you must needs, if you touch upon any Humour of this Time, offend one of the Parties." Shadwell had analysed his difficulties aright, but he had not been able to avoid them. Again he was unfortunate in his satire. Instead of ridiculing the Roman Clergy alone, he turned on the Anglican church in the character of Smerk,

---

[1] See the dedication to Sedley.

with the result that the censor cut out vast scenes to the detriment of the play. In this, Shadwell had not the skill and the grace of a Dryden.

The witches are interesting as a relic of Elizabethan example. Whether Shadwell really believed in them is uncertain. Probably he was truly "somewhat Costive of Belief": possibly, on the other hand, he had a slightly greater faith in them than one might have expected[1]. In any case, the witches are fine spirity creatures acting according to the best recipes, the author appending to the first three acts voluminous "Notes upon the Magick," in an endeavour to find medieval authority for some of the not too savoury pranks of his weird sisters.

In his next comedy Shadwell turned away from politics, presenting in *The Squire of Alsatia* (D.L. May 1688) a picture of that underground existence of villains and rooks which Scott has repainted for us in *The Fortunes of Nigel*. Here Shadwell has turned from the upper-class life of the time, an aspect of life which after all he was less qualified to depict, and has displayed a realistic and valuable picture of middle-class citizens, of thieves, of rascals in the London of the seventeenth century. Severe as Langbaine is on this play as a plagiarised performance, there is no question that it is a real life—often too real life—picture of the times. It is very difficult, indeed, attempting to analyse our feelings on reading such a comedy as this is. With Congreve as we have seen we are in a comparatively artificial world, at least a world of the intellect, and it is almost with an effort that we relate the puppet figures of his stage to what we know of the author, of Dryden, of Rochester. With Shadwell, somehow, it is different. Congreve is the pure artist. Shadwell is something besides. He is a perverted moralist: and it is precisely his perverted morals—his relating of art to life—that causes us to shrink somewhat from the picture which he presents to us. That his audience felt no distaste is proved by the extraordinary success of this comedy, a fact which incidentally serves to

---

[1] E. Ammann (*Analysis of Thomas Shadwell's Lancashire Witches*, Bern, 1905) thinks he was sceptical.

emphasise the relationship it held to their own thoughts and to their own lives.

Shadwell's next few comedies hardly reach the level of those which went before. They reflect the new love of farce which was so rapidly taking possession of the comic stage in the last years of the century, and there is just the faintest touch in them of the disintegrating spirit of sentimentalism. *Bury Fair* (D.L. *c.* April 1689) is a well-written play, and, unlike most of Shadwell's, not too coarse. It has a great deal of tomfoolery in it, mainly concerned with the characters of Sir Humphrey and Oldwit, and there is the inevitable girl disguised as a boy as well as the improvised count: but even these farcical elements do not make *Bury Fair* a bad play. Wildish, one of the heroes of the piece, is not so vulgar as some others of his companions on the comic stage and Lord Bellamy, if a trifle priggish, is a living and vital character, who, in his "moral" aspect, indicates the change of tone visible after 1690. *The Scowrers* (D.L. *c.* Dec. 1690) followed in little more than a year, a comedy to which Langbaine paid the, for him, tremendous compliment of absolving it from any doubts as regards plagiarism. The prologue emphasises its "moral" tendency, and in the relations between Sir William Rant and his father we are already far away from the typical Restoration filial and paternal *rapprochements.* "Good Sir," says Sir William, "No more: you'll break my Heart. Gentle and kind Reproof I cannot bear." It is a speech that would have come but artificially from the mouths of any of the graceless rascals of the preceding decades. The conversion of the same gentleman and of his friend Wildfire by the pure love with which they are suddenly smitten for Eugenia and for Clara respectively has elements in it that also have relationships with the sentimental fashion[1].

The Scowrers was Shadwell's last comedy to be issued in his lifetime. His widow, however, published posthumously a still further, but not very brilliant one, *The Volunteers, or,*

[1] Although in II. i there is a sentence that ably sums up the philosophy of the manners heroes: "When a man is lewd with a *bon Grace* there's something in it, but a Fellow that is aukwardly wicked is not to be born (*i.e.* borne)."

The Stock Jobbers (D.L. *c.* Nov. 1692). Although there is more than one good character in this piece, General Blunt and Colonel Hackwell being most excellently drawn, this last comedy shows a falling off from the former two plays. It has almost the appearance of having been written earlier and laid aside until it was resurrected by the poet's relict. The sentimental style, save in Eugenia's country-loving propensities, is conspicuous by its absence, the whole comedy being taken up with an intrigue plot of doubtful propriety mingled with often undigested satire against affected ladies and beaux of the "Fantastick, Concited" type.

Notwithstanding the comparative neglect which has been accorded him by critics, it must be apparent, from even the short notices of his plays which I have given here, that Thomas Shadwell is an author by no means to be so lowly rated. No writer has so covered the entire Restoration period with his work as he has done. No writer has revealed with such a life-like touch the details of the society of his age. If, on the one hand, as Professor Saintsbury avers[1], he was in a way a father of the comedy of manners, although that claim be somewhat doubtful, in his old age he was one of the fathers of the comedy of sentiment. Undoubtedly, for sheer merit, as for historical importance, he stands next to Dryden after the great masters of the manners comedy.

The school of Jonson, while it saw its most pronounced disciple in Thomas Shadwell, had many other supporters in the age, some of them men who had already written comedies and tragedies in pre-Commonwealth days. Indeed, Shadwell himself may well have taken some of his inspiration from these early Restoration writers rather than always directly from Jonson, his master. On the other hand, we must remember that the majority of these humours dramatists do not display that type of comedy in its purest form. Their workmanship is frequently crude, and only too often their efforts descend to the levels of farce. It is, indeed, the debased comedy of humours and the debased imitations of Molière mingled with the influence of the *commedia dell' arte* tradition that produced

---

[1] Preface to the *Mermaid* Shadwell.

the farce type of drama proper in the latter years of the century.

Of these dramatists, first must be named Abraham Cowley, whose *Cutter of Coleman Street* was produced in 1661 by the Duke's company. This play was but a rehashing for changed conditions of the same author's *The Guardian* (1650) which had been acted at Cambridge in 1641 [1]. Its scene was altered to "*London*, in the year 1658" and its main purpose devoted to the lashing of the Puritans in the person of "Mistris *Fear-the-Lord Barebottle*." Save for a few touches of more refined wit, and in spite of Lamb's enthusiasm for it, it seems to be remarkable in no very particular way, although, as Elia has pointed out, the character of Puny does have a certain interest in that he was the ancestor of the "half-witted wits" of a later period [2].

A play of somewhat similar tendencies was *The Rump, or, The Mirrour of the Late Times*, written by John Tatham, an author who had already produced several plays both before the closing of the theatres and during Commonwealth times. This play was perhaps one of the first new dramas to be produced in the Restoration period [3]. Not very remarkable save for its political bias, much of its humour turns on the Scots dialect spoken by Lord Stoneware, a dialect that seems to have been a favourite with the author, as it had appeared also in Jocky and Billy, the two Scots beggars in *The Scots Figgaries* and in the "Scotch Mountebank" of *The Distracted State*. Possibly the play's best feature from a literary point of view is the portrayal of ambition and folly in the figure of Lady Lambert.

Another writer, thoroughly "loyal," who produced scenes after the old manner, was John Wilson, a native of Plymouth, who, besides a tragedy and a tragi-comedy, contributed two

[1] See G. C. Moore Smith, *College Plays* (1923), pp. 70 and 90.

[2] Arthur C. Nethercot, in *Abraham Cowley: The Muse's Hannibal* (1931), and in a series of articles, pleads for a higher evaluation of his work than that given above. See also the study by Jean Loiseau (1931).

[3] Virgil J. Scott, "A Reinterpretation of John Tatham's *The Rump: or The Mirrour of the Late Times*" (*Philological Quarterly*, 1945, XXIV. 114–18).

Jonsonian pieces to the stage. Both of these have received considerable praise. Wilson is certainly one of the best of those later Elizabethans who endured over the Commonwealth period, but hardly, one would imagine, deserves all the laurel that has been bestowed upon him. *The Cheats* (T.R. in V.St. March 1662/3) is but a would-be imitation of Jonson, with little to relieve its incoherent brutality save the rather good scene in III. iii where pedantic experts in etymology are satirised. It does, however, have very great interest, both for the fact that it is one of the earliest of Restoration comedies and for its chequered stage career[1]. *The Projectors* (unacted? 1665)[2] did not make its appearance till later. It, too, is an imitation, though not a slavish one, of Jonson's manner, but it has simplicity and coherency of plot and of style, which the other has not.

Boisterous and farcical plays of a like sort were produced by John Lacy, an actor at the Theatre Royal. The pupil of John Ogilby in dancing and in acting[3], he was the pupil, albeit a poor one, of Jonson in his dramatic art. His *The Old Troop, or, Monsieur Raggou* (T.R. in V.St. 1663) is remarkable for not whitewashing altogether the Cavaliers, but even ultra-loyal Tatham and Cowley had not done that[4]. It is but a poor farcical piece of work, although it held the stage for nearly sixty years. Lacy's adaptation of Shakespeare in *Sauny the Scott, or, The Taming of the Shrew* (T.R. in B.St. April 1667) has no more merit. The main humour is kept up by the title-character, whom Lacy himself played, the *vis comica* of whose personality seems to come from the fact that he habi-

---

[1] The Worcester College manuscript has been edited by M. C. Nahm (1935). F. S. Boas ("Sir Henry Herbert and 'The Cheats'," *TLS*, April 15, 1920) had previously shown how, after its suspension, it was "surveyed" by Denham and Waller, who were ordered by the King to report on it. For a general survey of Wilson's work see K. Faber, *John Wilsons Dramen: Eine Quellenstudie* (Wiesbaden, 1904).

[2] There is no satisfactory proof that it was ever acted.

[3] Aubrey, *Brief Lives* (ed. A. Clark, Oxford, 1898, II. 28).

[4] Cf. the "two Hectors" in *The Cheats*, Bilboe and Titere Tu, "the one usurping the name of a *Major*, the other of a *Captain*," as well as Cutter and Worm in *Cutter of Coleman Street*.

tually employs words not commonly mentioned in polite society. For his third play, *The Dumb Lady, or, The Farriar made Physician* (T.R. in B.St. 1669), Lacy travelled to Molière, forming his farcical comedy of humours out of *Le médecin malgré lui* and *L'amour médecin*. In spite of the fact that this, as well as his other comedies, has been favourably noticed by dramatic historians, Lacy's genius appears, on careful examination, to have been of the flimsiest sort. *The Dumb Lady* is hardly anything more than a mere farce and its dialogue is execrable. The characters are of no value either as psychological studies or as humours, and all that comedy rises to is a kind of miserable tom-foolery unrelieved by gracious sentiments or the presence of intellectual clarity. *Sir Hercules Buffoon, or, The Poetical Squire* (D.G. *c.* Sept. 1684) is equally poor, farcical elements being everywhere prominent. The most interesting portions of it have merely an historical significance. These are the little satiric touches on wits and on heroic poetry, touches which display a certain feeling abroad in the age, a surfeit of the glorious sentiment, a kind of boredom at those clamorous denizens of the pit[1].

The comedy of humours, with many variations into the other types of intrigue and of farce, continued through the whole forty years of the Restoration period. Sir Robert Howard, who holds such an important position in the development of the theatre in the years following 1660, presented one important specimen of the humours comedy in

---

[1] "To be witty now is to be more troublesome in a Play-house than a Butcher at a Bear-Garden....That's Wit to see Plays for nothing,—one act in the Pit, another in a Box, and a third in the Gallery—that's Wit." And again:

Squire: But, Father, which do you hold to be the most honourable, your comick or heroick Poet?

Hercules: Oh your Heroick without doubt because he comes nearer to the Romantick strain than the other.

Squire: Romantick! what signifies the word Romantick?

Hercules: Why it comes from the word Romance, and Romance is the *Arabic* word for a Swinger, and Swinger is the *Hebrew* word for a Liar.

Squire: By this you prove the Heroic Poets to be Liars?

Hercules: No, no, by no means, Romantically inclined, only."

The Committee (T.R. in V.St. Nov. 1662)[1]. This, undoubtedly
the most valuable of Howard's plays, is interesting for several
things, first, because it is a "political" comedy, with rancour
at the Commonwealth régime, and secondly, because, with
no very striking originalities, it yet catches somewhat of the
breezy air of Ben Jonson's characters. The "Committee" is
the Sequestration Committee, and the plot circles around the
hypocritical Mr and Mrs Day, their daughter Ruth, their
ward Arabella, and Colonels Blunt and Careless, the last being
a couple of idealised portraits of true Cavalier spirit and
honesty. Running through this plot, with a free and easy
broad comedy manner, goes Teague or Teg, Careless' Irish
servant, a character, taken from life it is said, which was one
of the favourites of the actor Lacy and did much to make
the play a permanent success throughout the whole of the
Restoration period.

Howard's other comedies, when placed alongside *The
Committee*, hardly merit much attention. *The Blind Lady*
(1660) was never acted in any theatre, and is a poor piece of
work, while *The Surprisal* (T.R. in V.St. April 1662), with
its Italian scenes, chockfull of asides and "drawings" of
swords and daggers, is almost entirely negligible.

Edward Howard, like his brother Robert, also wrote
comedies much in the same strain. *Six Days' Adventure, or,
The New Utopia* (L.I.F. *c.* March 1671) is one of the few
omissions of the patient Genest. In spite of a poor reception
on the stage it was ushered out in print by four sets of
laudatory verses, two of them by Aphra Behn and Ravenscroft respectively. It is a fair production, but in its sad
admixture of semi-classical and of modern names, it grates
on the edges of our more fastidious taste[2]. *The Man of
Newmarket* (D.L. *c.* April, 1678), Howard's other comedy,
has a certain interest of its own as being a kind of adaptation

---

[1] It was seen by Evelyn on Nov. 27, 1662. Genest gives the date wrongly
as April 10, 1665. Pepys saw it on June 12, 1663, and thought it "a merry
but indifferent play, only Lacy's part, as Irish footman, is beyond
imagination."

[2] Eugenia, Euphorbus, etc., alongside Franckman and Foppering. For
a similar admixture of names see Sedley's *The Mulberry-Garden*.

of the Jonsonian style to the race-course, but as a dramatic work of art it falls below the *Six Days' Adventure.*

During the early years of the period, William Cavendish, Duke of Newcastle, is to be remembered, partly for the fact that he took over some of Jonson's style, partly for the fact that he succeeded in fusing that style with something of novelty. *The Humorous Lovers* (L.I.F. March 1667) which appeared in the same year as his joint work with Dryden, *Sir Martin Mar-all*, is interesting for its "theatre" scene[1] and for the snatches of song and of masque, elements which the noble author was to develop more largely in his later play[2]. This later play, *The Triumphant Widow, or, The Medley of Humours*, produced at D.G. certainly by Nov. 1674, is a decidedly peculiar comedy, worth noticing, not only for its occasional flashes of wit and for its satire of heroic poetry[3], but also for its strange structure, a structure that reminds us forcibly, as Sir A. W. Ward has pointed out[4], of the later comic opera. Newcastle, no doubt, was simply developing suggestions left by the Elizabethans in that direction, but those developments of his effectually separate off the play from the average contemporary drama[5]. It is observable that some of the characters of this play of Newcastle's—Justice Spoil-wit and Sir John Noddy—gave to Thomas Shadwell suggestions for his masterpiece, *Bury Fair*.

The other humours plays of the Restoration period stand on a much lower level than those already mentioned. They are of value only from an historical point of view, as being fairly typical specimens of the ordinary fare of the theatres. A certain Rawlins, otherwise unknown, published anonymously two such comedies, *Tom Essence, or, The Modish*

[1] III. ii.

[2] The character of Boldman here and that of Comely in *The English Monsieur* no doubt did much to popularise the anti-love and marriage type that was so common during this period.

[3] Chiefly in the character of Crambo, but also in other scattered passages: cf. the Musician in III. i.

[4] *Op. cit.* III. 333.

[5] The play is full of Shakespearian reminiscences. The Footpad is Autolycus: Lady Haughty and her maid in one scene remind us of Portia and Nerissa: the Constable has touches of Shakespeare's clownish officials.

Wife (D.G. *c.* Aug. 1676) and *Tunbridge-Wells, or, A Day's Courtship* (D.G. *c.* March 1678). The former, which was a vacation production, seems to have taken part of its plot from Molière's *Le cocu imaginaire*. It is quite well worked out, but is too realistic in places where realism might conveniently have been omitted from a stage production. *Tunbridge-Wells* is a very similar play, with nothing particularly noteworthy in it save that, although greatly concerned with Jonsonian humours, particularly in the characters of Owmuch, Paywel and Parson Quibble, it pays tribute also to the manners style in Fairlove, Wilding, Alinda and Courtwit.

The Town-Shifts, or, The Suburb-Justice (L.I.F. *c.* March 1671) by Edward Revet, combines a sentimental plot with scenes of comic humours[1], wherein the author has aimed at reproducing certain Elizabethan tones in the characters of Clowt the Constable, Goody Fells and Mold the Sexton. A similarly summary dismissal may be given to the anonymous *The Woman turn'd Bully* (D.G. *c.* May 1675), an exceedingly dull comedy in spite of Langbaine's criticism of it[2], and of value only when considered with other plays, such as that of Revet, as forming part of the repertoire of the playhouses. Indeed, it is hardly worth while descending much further into the depths of the ordinary rank and file of Restoration workmanship in this style. By a brief mention of one or two other minor plays, memorable for certain definite points of interest, we may fitly close this account of the comedy of humours as it appeared in the Restoration.

Again for Shakespearian reminiscences, particularly in the scene of the Watch, we may recall *The Morning Ramble, or, The Town Humours* (D.G. Nov. 1672) ascribed by Langbaine to Nevil Payne. The plot of this play is exceedingly weak, but the dialogue moves easily and the author, Payne or

---

[1] J. Harrington Smith (*The Gay Couple in Restoration Comedy*, 1948, pp. 122–3) draws attention to the fact that this play has considerable historical interest in its emphasis on a pair of serious-minded young lovers. He further suggests that it possesses greater intrinsic value than is indicated above ("one of the most charming plays of the period"). See also C. M. Scheurer, "An Early Sentimental Comedy" (*Anglia*, 1913, XXXVII. 125–8).

[2] It was "A very Diverting Comedy," he thought (p. 556).

another, had some conception at least of the delineation of character. Laurence Maidwell's *The Loving Enemies* (D.G. *c.* March 1680) on the other hand, is to be remembered, not for any decided beauties in it, but for its promise. Its plot certainly is hopelessly artificial[1]; it is obviously the work of an amateur, but had Maidwell produced some other comedies he might have given something quite valuable to the stage. The character of Circumstantio, that "formal *Valet de Chambre* very troublesome with impertinent Rhetorick," is exceedingly well-drawn.

Besides these are a certain number of Jonsonian "political" pieces which may for a moment claim our attention. *Mr Turbulent, or, The Melanchollicks* (D.G. Jan. 1681/2) re-issued three years later as *The Factious Citizen, or, The Melancholy Visioner*[2], is one of the best of these. Another is *The Rampant Alderman, or, News from the Exchange* (printed 1685), a three-act piece, largely a farcical rendering of Marmion's *The Fine Companion*, with recollections of Jonson[3]. The appearance of this latter comedy in 1685 shows well the way towards which the Jonson comedy was tending in the last years of the century. After Shadwell, we may say, there are few of the rich rough, realistic comedies of the old style. Of the very few *The Lover's Luck* (L.I.F. *c.* Dec. 1695) by Thomas Dilke is probably the most noticeable. Rather coarsely written, it yet succeeds in presenting in a fairly fresh manner such well worn stock characters as Sir Nicholas Purflew, "a formal Herald and Antiquary" and Alderman Whim, "a Projector and Humourist." Than this, Dilke's other two comedies are considerably weaker, although of the

---

[1] Lorenzo and Marcello hate one another through a family feud, but Julia, Lorenzo's sister, loves Marcello without his ever having seen her. In exactly similar manner, Camilla, Marcello's sister, loves Lorenzo. Antonio loves Lucinda, old Paulo's daughter, while pretending to pay suit to the Widow, whom Paulo courts for himself. There is a scene of Camilla's coming to a duel, very similar to a situation in one of the plays of Mrs Behn.

[2] This fact seems to have been unnoticed by Genest, who does not mention *Mr Turbulent*, and enters *The Factious Citizen* as acted at D.G. in 1685.

[3] "Doctor *Oats*," *i.e.* Titus Oates, appears in person—"one who squeaks Sedition in the Coffee-House."

same spirit and style. *The City Lady, or, Folly Reclaim'd*
(L.I.F. *c.* Jan. 1696/7) appears, from the dedication, to have
been a failure on the stage, wherein it shared the fate of
many of these Jonsonian or Shadwellian pieces. *The Pretenders, or, The Town Unmaskt* (L.I.F. *c.* March 1698), with
its descriptive list of *dramatis personae*, shows clearly its indebtedness to the same source. *The Fortune-Hunters, or, Two
Fools well met* (D.L. *c.* March 1689), by Capt. James Carlisle[1],
ridiculous as some of its incidents are, is a comedy that
merits attention along with the first mentioned of Dilke's.
Unlike Dilke's, however, it appears to have been successful[2],
and was later heavily plundered by Cibber for *The Woman's
Wit*.

"Shadwellian" humours of a low type fill, likewise, *The
Wary Widdow, or, Sir Noisy Parrat* (D.L. *c.* March 1692/3)
the sole production of Henry Higden. Neither it nor the
somewhat similar anonymous comedy[3], *The Bragadocio, or,
The Bawd turn'd Puritan* (1691), presents anything very noteworthy.

The truth is, that, after 1680, the pure play of humours
appears to have made little appeal to the audiences of the
time. The comedy of humours thereafter passed away, and
the humours farce came to take its place. If pure humours
of a really comic standard appeared in the drama, they did
so not in Jonsonian plays but in the comedies of manners,
where the spirits of Jonson and of Fletcher seemed to meet,
or in the comedies of sentiment where often they were
introduced as a background for other more modern characters. Those who, like Shadwell, continued in the older
strain were deemed out of date, relics of a bygone age, unworthy the attention of an elegant and witty audience of
courtiers tutored to something more delicate and more refined.

[1] He fought in Ireland under William III. Captain is the title given
him in the advertisement of this play at the end of Shadwell's *The
Scowrers* (D.L. 1690).
[2] See Gildon's Langbaine, p. 16.
[3] The title-page states it was "by a Person of Quality."

IV. *The Comedy of Intrigue: Mrs Behn*

The same phenomenon may be seen, although in not so marked a degree, in the development of the comedy of Spanish intrigue. Here again the Restoration theatre borrowed wholesale from the older stage, adding to the earlier Caroline Spanish impress by direct translation or adaptation from Calderón and his compeers. Again, however, as with the comedy of humours, the pure comedy of intrigue failed to hold its own to the end of the century. Popular from 1660 to 1670, it rapidly drifted away into the types of manners or of farce, remaining in its pure form only in the hands of a few dramatists who, like Mrs Behn, retained a love for the particular species with which they had started their theatrical careers.

The popularity of the intrigue style in the earlier years of the period must have been influenced considerably by the tastes of Charles. He it was, as we have seen, who suggested to Sir Samuel Tuke the Spanish drama from which was fashioned *The Adventures of Five Hours* (L.I.F. Jan. 1662/3)[1], a comedy which proved one of the greatest successes of the first years of the new theatres. Like many of these "Spanish" plays, *The Adventures of Five Hours* is an admixture of fun and of seriousness. It is a regular intrigue play of love, revenge, and honour, alternating grave with gay, dignified Spanish manners with the ludicrous tomfooleries of serving men. From its pure style and its admirable workmanship one may well regret that it was the sole comedy which its author produced, even although one cannot now subscribe to Pepys' violently encomiastic criticism of it[2].

About the same date as the production of Tuke's play, Porter was composing his *The Carnival* (T.R. *c.* 1663), a well-

---

[1] It had been on rehearsal before that date, and seems to have been intended for a first production on Dec. 15, 1662.

[2] See Pepys for Jan. 8, 1662/3 when he thought it "the best...that ever I saw, or think ever shall." *Othello* became insipid to him after reading it. It was printed in 1663 and reprinted in 1664; "Revis'd and Corrected" in 1671. Several other editions followed in the eighteenth century.

written drama, although now completely forgotten. It, too, is a comedy of the Spanish intrigue class, cast in a kind of blank verse, very irregular, but not at all harsh. To Porter is also ascribed *A Witty Combat, or, The Female Victor*, apparently not the same play as that entitled *The German Princess* which Pepys saw at L.I.F. on April 15, 1664[1]. This latter play is interesting as being a more middle class drama than is typical of Restoration literature. The hypocritical parson and Mr King are two characters well-drawn, and there is a fresh little song in the third act that deserves remembering:

> *Away, away, flatter no more*
> *My easie Faith, for now I see*
> *What thou in me seem'd to adore*
> *Thou mak'st thy pleasures property;*
> *No more, no more will I believe*
> *The man that can so soon deceive.*

Like *The Carnival*, of Spanish extraction also is *Tarugo's Wiles, or, The Coffee-House* (L.I.F. Oct. 1667) by Sir Thomas St Serfe. Its coffee-house scene is particularly good, although probably not very germane to the plot. It, like *The Adventures of Five Hours*, had a great popularity in the first years of the Restoration, a popularity that continued till well on in the century. *The Adventures of Five Hours* as well as *The Carnival* and *Tarugo's Wiles* must have done much to fix the success of the Spanish comedy in the period 1660–70. From that date, however, this particular type was popularised chiefly by one writer, Mrs Aphra Behn, those others who adopted it mostly mingling it with manners or with farce. Mrs Behn, we may say, holds, in relation to the development of the comedy of intrigue, much the same position that Shadwell holds in relation to the development of the comedy of humours.

Of all the minor dramatists of the period, Mrs Behn is probably the best known, but not always in the best way. Although her works have been made readily available in reprint, it is to be questioned whether they are widely read,

---

[1] Genest (I. 51–53) assumed that these were identical.

and the general concept of the authoress' comedies is perhaps one largely determined by Puritanic strictures on her immorality. The fact is that she is no worse, and is often a great deal better, than the average playwright of her age. Indecent, free, sometimes positively vulgar, she was in several of her plays; but, on the whole, when we compare her works with similar productions of D'Urfey and Shadwell, even of Dryden, we must be prepared to admit the comparative purity of her dialogue. She has, moreover, on many occasions introduced thoughts and ideas which not only display her unconventional and modern attitude towards life's relations, but also formed the basis for not a few moralisations in the sentimental eighteenth century to come.

Modern she was, and in more senses than one. L. Whibley has noted that "her success depended on her ability to write like a man[1]," and in this assuredly there is some truth. She is the first of the modern women. The Renascence gave us women types who were the perfect complements of men— Vittoria Colonna, or even her frailer sister, Veronica Franco —the modern world has given us the ideal of woman's equality with man. It is the latter ideal which Mrs Behn represents. Her postal communication with Major Halsall is as between one man and another[2]: her secret service work was the work of a man: she was probably the first woman to earn her living by her pen. It is as such, if we are to be just, that we must think of her: not as the companion of the Restoration roué, more dissolute than he, but as the pioneer of our modern womanhood. She herself did not wish to outrival Dryden in his looseness of phrase, or Shadwell in his vulgarities:

> *Her humble Muse soars not in the High-rode,*
> *Of Wit transverst, or Baudy* A-la-Mode...

she cried in one play[3], and a fuller feminist apologia may be found in the epilogue to another[4].

---

[1] *Camb. Hist. Engl. Lit.* VIII. 142.
[2] See *Cal. State Papers, Dom. Series*, 1666–1667, pp. 44, 72, 82.
[3] Epilogue to *The Dutch Lover*.
[4] To *Sir Patient Fancy* (D.G. 1678).

Apart from her importance as an authoress, Aphra Behn acquires distinction because of the very great range and variety in her work. Her novels give her a secure position in the history of prose fiction: her verse, if not particularly excelling, puts her among the minor poets of the time; and her plays have interesting diversity. Here are tragedies and tragi-comedies; here are comedies of intrigue, influenced indirectly at least by the Spanish theatre; here are farces, confessedly written to catch the taste of the age; and here are plays of a "moral" or "problem" tendency. Thus she stands forward both as a companion of the Restoration rakes and as one who helped to establish the new sentimental drama.

Of the first type she has given us several examples. *The Dutch Lover* (D.G. Feb. 1672/3) is based it is said on a so-called Spanish novel of "De las Coveras" entitled *Don Fenise*, the same that furnished D'Urfey with material for his *Banditti* (D.L. 1686). This comedy depends entirely on intrigue for its effect; all the characters are Spanish save "myn heer *Haunce van Ezel*" and his man, who are comically Dutch. It reads well, but is too complicated, turning on ill-sorted lovers and almost incestuous attachments. Three separate characters in the play are found to be of different parentage from what they thought. Noticeable is the song in Act III, Sc. iii, which has a quality that gives it real distinction, and the soliloquy immediately following, very reminiscent as it is of Shakespearian phrasing.

A variant of the same species of comedy appears in *The Debauchee, or, The Credulous Cuckold* (D.G. *c.* Feb. 1676/7), which, however, can be described as little more than an adaptation of Brome's *The Mad Couple Well Match't.* *The Rover, or, The Banish't Cavaliers* (First Part, D.G. March 1676/7; Second Part, D.G. April 1681) is a decidedly better and more individual play. Again a comedy of intrigue, set this time in Naples and in Madrid, it divides itself naturally into two "camps" of characters—the Englishmen, circling around Willmore, the Rover, and the Spaniards. The characters of Willmore and of his mistress, Hellena, here recall to a certain extent the pair of lovers beloved by

Dryden. Hellena speaks exactly like Florimel in *Secret Love*. At the close of the First Part these two are united happily, but in the Second, which is inferior to the former, we meet with Willmore alone, he having lost her by death. "Ay, faith," he says, "And nothing remains with me but the sad Remembrance—not so much as the least Part of her hundred thousand Crowns." In that comment, for Mrs Behn had made us love Hellena, we truly feel at its worst the callousness of the age, a callousness that was more disastrous and soul-destroying than the vilest libertinism. The sole interest the Second Part can have for us to-day is in the introduction in it of Harlequin and Scaramouch, the former of whom, apparently, spoke extempore in Italian. Presumably here Mrs Behn, with her alert appreciation of audience tastes, was eagerly seizing on the contemporary interest in the *commedia dell'arte*, stimulated by the visit of the Modena company.

Sir Patient Fancy (D.G. Jan. 1677/8) is of the same intrigue school, but is much more indecent than the former plays already mentioned, and probably more so than any of those which were yet unwritten. This is the play, indeed, which, more than any other, has inclined the minds of the critics to attribute a systematic looseness to the works of Mrs Behn. That many of the scenes justify such critical opinion is certain, yet we should note that these episodes introduced by Mrs Behn into *Sir Patient Fancy* are no worse than the similar episodes in Dryden's *Mr Limberham*, produced almost at the same time. Without doubt she was here trying to satisfy contemporary tastes and, noting the success of other plays with definitely immodest plots, she must have decided that this was the way to win an audience.

Typically of the intrigue type as intrigue appeared towards the close of the century is Mrs Behn's next play, *The Feign'd Curtizans, or, A Night's Intrigue* (D.G. *c.* March 1678/9). Here can be seen very clearly the gradual tendency of this species towards the morass of farce. Genest has chosen to call it a good comedy[1], but to me it seems a poor and dull

---

[1] I. 270.

performance. There are no characters worth speaking of and
the plot is a sorry contrivance. There is much disguising
as men on the part of the women, and in the fifth act appears
Marcella "in Man's Cloaths" and meets Fillamour for a
duel in place of her brother, Julio, who stands behind—a
situation already utilised by Mrs Behn in *The Dutch Lover*.
Even a brief glance at the printed text of the comedy shows
clearly enough that new farcical "business" was coming to
take chief place in the building up of a comedy, the skill of
the performer taking precedence over the skill of the playwright.

This, indeed, is the last play of Mrs Behn's, except for the
"problem" dramas and a couple of "true-blue Protestant"
plays, *The City Heiress, or, Sir Timothy Treat-all* (D.G.
c. March, 1681/2) and *The Round-Heads, or, The Good Old
Cause* (D.G. *c*. Dec. 1681), the second merely a rehashing of
Tatham's *The Rump*, which can be styled by the name of
comedy. The rest are farces of the flimsiest description,
created purely to satisfy the particular tastes of the audiences
of 1680 onwards.

Intrigue seems, in this age, to have been peculiarly accept-
able to the women writers, Mrs Pix and Mrs Manley uniting
with Mrs Behn in presenting dramas of this type with,
running through them, threads of sentiment and of moralisation. *The Spanish Wives* (D.G. *c*. Sept. 1696) of the former,
which mingles Restoration licence with touches of sentimentalism[1], is set in Barcelona and deals mainly with the
Governor, "a merry old Lord," who gives his wife, but not
successfully for himself, more liberties than appear to have
been usual in contemporary Spain. *The Innocent Mistress*
(L.I.F. *c*. June 1697) appeared a few months later at the
rival house. In it the tone is changed considerably, there
being quite a definite sentimental tone running through it,
in spite of the fact that it borrows more than a little from
Etherege's final comedy. The epilogue is valuable for some

---

[1] James M. Edmunds ("An Example of Early Sentimentalism,"
Modern Language Notes, 1933, XLVIII. 94–7) stresses the features that
show a break with the Restoration code. J. Harrington Smith, *op. cit.*
p. 190, denies their sentimental quality.

historical references. *The Deceiver Deceiv'd* (L.I.F. *c.* Dec. 1697), published the year following, was entirely unsuccessful. It is distinctly less brilliant than the former two.

Mrs Manley's one comedy, *The Lost Lover, or, The Jealous Husband* (D.L. *c.* March 1696) is almost entirely negligible, being a hastily written comedy and exceedingly short. It belongs, however, to the same tradition, and for that is interesting.

Beyond the comedies of Dryden, which, as we have seen, form a special category of their own, very few of the intrigue plays of the period after 1675 merit special attention. John Corye's *The Generous Enemies, or, The Ridiculous Lovers* (T.R. in B.St. July 1671) is, in the words of the editors of the *Biographia Dramatica*, one "entire piece of plagiarism from beginning to end[1]," being derived from Quinault, Corneille, Randolph and Fletcher. The various elements are hardly amalgamated with any signal success. Mountfort's *The Successfull Straingers* (D.L. *c.* Dec. 1689) is more serious, and contains some blank verse that is moderately felicitous. It is, however, neither touching in its tragic portions nor over-witty in the comic. In spite of a prologue by Dryden and an epilogue by Tate, Harris' *The Mistakes, or, The False Report* (D.L. *c.* Dec. 1690)[2], another tragi-comedy of the same class, merits no greater attention. Scened in Naples, with Spanish characters, it does not rise to higher levels than does the comedy of Corye.

All these plays, however, bad as some of them individually may be, are valuable as showing the last relics of this style of drama existing alongside, but being rapidly submerged by, its debased farcical form. Intrigue comedy had a great influence on the theatre of the Restoration: intrigue plays a great part in the structure of the comedy of manners, and intrigue forms the largest element in the comedies of John Dryden. On the other hand, in its pure form, except for the

---

[1] *Biographia Dramatica*, II. 259.

[2] There seems to be no good reason for presuming that the play has been wrongly fathered on Harris. His name appears on the title-page, although the preface admits that Mountfort wrote one scene in the first act.

few odd dramas of Mrs Behn and the others, it ceased to be very popular on the stage, for much the same reasons that explain the disappearance of the Jonsonian drama.

V. *The Comedy of Dryden*

Dryden, in the progress of Restoration comedy, holds somewhat of a central position. In him appear the intrigue strain and the humours strain, alongside of suggestions which led on the one hand to the comedy of manners and on the other to the comedy of sentiment.

In general, it may be said that Dryden's comedy owes more than that of the majority of his contemporaries to the theatre of the pre-Commonwealth period. It is certainly true that, in many ways, the comedy of manners owes to him, if not its actual inception, at least its heralding, yet, on the other hand, the entire ensemble, the spirit of Dryden, is by no means similar to that of Congreve. Dryden introduces a kind of spurious romance into his comedies which Congreve never knew. Sometimes he is more given to humours: and nowhere did he know the fine sparkle and zest with which the masters of the new comedy irradiated their compositions. The heroes of Etherege and of Congreve, too, are more dilettante than Dryden's are: there is a certain intensity about the wild madcap flirtations of Dryden's Lovebys and Fainalls that is more emotional and more real, in the ordinary sense of that word, than the cynical intellectualism of the characters, let us say, of Etherege. The world of roués did not sit very well on Dryden. He had a heart and he showed it, and, although he could be more vulgar and more indecent than the worst of them, he sets our sympathies a-trembling for his lovers, wicked, frivolous, stupid creatures though they be. In their best plays neither Etherege nor Congreve ever touches our hearts. Herein lies the secret of their art.

Dryden's main contribution to the comic theatre was his lovers. These lovers, adumbrated in his first play, and undoubtedly influenced by Nell Gwyn and by Hart, were the prototypes of the heroes and the heroines of the comedy of

Etherege, however far the two may stand apart in essentials. In Dryden's very first play they make their appearance. *The Wild Gallant* (T.R. in V.St. Feb. 1662/3) is saved from utter imbecility only by the presence of Lady Constant and of Loveby. If, as has recently been argued, Dryden in this comedy is merely rewriting an older drama, we may hope that those creations at least are his: the other characters, too plainly borrowed from Jonson and from the followers of Jonson, are dull and monotonous. Surely no more tedious and clownish humour has ever been invented than that of the incessant jest-loving qualities of Bibber, the tailor. *The Wild Gallant* was unsuccessful, both in 1663 and when revived in an altered form in 1667, but it must have shown to the new dramatists of the first decade of the Restoration what could be done with the fresh wit and the realistic presentation of the gallants and their lady-loves.

Dryden's following three plays were two tragi-comedies and an heroic drama. These, taken together with *The Wild Gallant*, illustrate well the close relationship between the serious and the comic theatre of this time, since the first of the tragi-comedies, *The Rival Ladies* (T.R. in B.St. *c.* June 1684), very definitely has affiliations with *The Indian Emperour* (T.R. in B.St. 1665) and at the same time shows connections both with the comedy and the second tragi-comedy. Of particular interest in *The Rival Ladies* are the scenes of what George Saintsbury happily styled "amatory Battle-dore and Shuttle-cock[1]"—a serious counterpart to the cut and thrust of comic wit.

The pair of witty lovers, presented in *The Wild Gallant*, were repeated again, in a much finer form, in Dryden's next tragi-comedy, *Secret Love, or, The Maiden Queen* (T.R. in B.St. March 1666/7), a play derived from *Le Grand Cyrus* with hints from other exotic romances. By this time Etherege had produced his first play, but, because of *The Wild Gallant*, to Dryden must be given the credit of having invented first these lovers whom he has symbolically immortalised in

[1] W. Scott and G. Saintsbury, *The Dramatic Works of John Dryden* (Edinburgh, 1882), II. 128 and Ward, *op. cit.* III. 347.

Celadon and Florimel. It has been suggested that this pair
is a reflection of Charles II and Lady Castlemaine: if so, the
royal influence on comedy was indeed great.

From this date the history of Dryden's progress in comedy
is a history of repetitions of these themes of intrigue and
these characters of frivolous wit. *Sir Martin Mar-all, or,
The Feign'd Innocence* appeared at L.I.F. six months after
Secret Love (L.I.F. Aug. 1667). It would seem that this
comedy was merely a re-working by Dryden of a translation
made by the Duke of Newcastle of Molière's *L'étourdi*. Whatever the story of its composition, however, it is evident that
it was, as an early dramatic historian informs us, written
solely for that apparently inimitable comedian, Noke or
Nokes. No play proved more popular on the stage than *Sir
Martin Mar-all*: it is to be questioned whether Dryden was
better known in his own day by any play more than this.
It certainly is a clever piece of work, uniting the intrigue
loved during the early years of the Restoration, with French
characters rendered coarser and more English in the spirit
and the manner of Jonson.

On June 12, 1668 appeared, again with a reversion to the
T.R., *An Evening's Love, or, The Mock Astrologer*, once more
Spanish in scene and borrowed from a Spanish source,
Calderón's *El astrologo fingido* through *Le feint astrologue* of
Corneille. The scene is Madrid of the Carnival, anno domini
1665. Once more Celadon appears born again in Wildblood,
acted by Hart, and Florimel in Jacintha, acted by Nell Gwyn.
The more sedate character of Bellamy was taken by Michael
Mohun, who, the year before, had impersonated Philocles
in *Secret Love*. Not as beautiful or as striking as the comic
scenes in this earlier play, *An Evening's Love* does not give
one quite such a sense of flagrant immorality, and why Pepys
and Evelyn singled it out as "very smutty" and as "very
profane" one can hardly tell—although one can well imagine
the sense of shocked righteousness with which such a man as
Jeremy Collier must have read the chapel scene. One notable
feature is presented in *An Evening's Love*, and that is Dryden's
first important critical preface on comic themes, a preface

which reveals clearly enough his aim in dramatic art, showing plainly how broadly he stood at the parting of the ways of Jonson and of Congreve. Noting Jonson's lack of repartee, he yet praises his humours, and ends by desiring a comedy with "neither so little of Humour as *Fletcher* shows, nor so little of Love and Wit as *Jonson*." In those words the comedy of Dryden is defined: in those words is prophesied the comedy of manners.

For the next few years Dryden does not seem to have been particularly successful in the realms of comedy, partly perhaps because of the rise of new and promising dramatists, partly because of the fact that he himself was engaged on tragedies and on other non-dramatic literary works. By 1672, when, in all probability about April, there was acted by the King's Men at L.I.F. the comedy called *Marriage a la Mode*, Dryden was well known in the intellectual circle of London, but by that date as well, Shadwell had established himself as a master of humours, Mrs Behn as an expert in intrigue, Ravenscroft as an able producer of rough farces, Etherege and Wycherley as captains of a new comedy of manners.

Dryden, therefore, was by no means alone in the dramatic world of his day, but he continued, if not the most noted, at least one of the most popular writers of comedies. It is surprising to note how little, professional author as he was, he allowed himself to be influenced by the new styles coming into fashion. *Marriage a la Mode* is just such a play as *Secret Love*. One of the mixed species of romantic tragicomedies, it has serious portions which do not seem to merit the slightly qualified condemnation given to them by Sir Walter Scott, George Saintsbury and the editors of the *Biographia Dramatica*. They are reminiscences, certainly, of the Sicilian episodes in the former play, but have a decided beauty of their own. In the same way, Celadon and Florimel are recalled in the Palamede-Doralice, Rhodophil-Melantha couples. Doralice is a kind of married Florimel, a Restoration Rosalind. It is noticeable that this comedy, licentious as is so much of the dialogue[1], containing a song in Act IV

---

[1] See particularly the final scene.

indecent even beyond any of Dryden's earlier ones, flaunts
in the epilogue a kind of stage morality leading (by the
Rhodophil story) to "*the way to Reformation.*" So far,
possibly, Dryden felt faintly the impress of the rising reaction
to the flagrant manners of the early Restoration days.

A trifle later than *Marriage a la Mode*, appeared on the
same stage *The Assignation, or, Love in a Nunnery*, and some
six years later at D.G., *The Kind Keeper, or, Mr Limberham*
(March 1677/8). Both of these were unsuccessful, possibly
because of the lack in them of the graceless couples which
had dominated the early plays, possibly because of the indecencies which marked out at least the second of them. For
their failure, Dryden, as is the way with authors, blamed the
actors, but the reason of the non-success, one would suspect,
is to be sought for rather in the plays themselves. In *The
Assignation* Dryden obviously tried to repeat Celadon and
Florimel in Ascanio and Hippolita, but he has failed to give
them the life which animated his first creations. In *Mr
Limberham* he abandoned even any attempt to revitalise the
pair, and left a drama which has in it not one figure of outstanding excellence. *The Assignation* is dull: *Mr Limberham*
is indecent. It seems surprising that critics, from Langbaine
to Saintsbury, have professed to find the latter comedy one
of the best of Dryden's. Judged even by the standards of its
own time, it is terrible in tone. A sickening atmosphere of
sex and of animalism hangs over it; nor is that atmosphere
relieved by the presence of any airy wit. It may be a satire—
a satire on "credulous Cuckolds" and on "Keepers"—but
the satire passes little beyond the crudest realism. There is
nothing to atone for the foetid odour that seems to hang
about it. It is one of the truly immoral works of the period,
and its failure may have been partly due to the gradual rise
of sentimental feeling which subconsciously was filling the
hearts of some with horror at the licentiousness of the times,
which was driving others to hypocrisy and the concealing of
outward immorality.

For two years Dryden abandoned the lighter stage: no
other comedy of his appeared until *The Spanish Fryar* in

March 1680 at D.G. On this play opinion has been much
divided in the past. In its own day it was praised or condemned according as the critics were Protestants or Catholics.
In later times it found a defendant in Sir Walter Scott, an
opponent in George Saintsbury. To the average modern
reader it seems an unsatisfactory piece of work. Its serious
and comic portions are kept rather rigidly apart, and the
masses of supposed fathers and hidden sisters and kings
murdered only to be brought to life again, take from our
appreciation of any wit there is in it. Its atmosphere is false,
nor has it wit to bear it through. It has not the passion of
Otway's muse or the gaiety of Congreve's, and is hardly
likely ever to be resuscitated from the obscurity into which
it has fallen.

By 1680 Dryden's work in comedy was nearly done.
Amphitryon, or, The Two Socia's was yet to make its appearance at D.L. in October 1690, but *Amphitryon* differs in
almost all things from Dryden's other works. Confessedly
based on Plautus and Molière, it parts from both in the
introduction of the love of Mercury for Phaedra, a love that
reminds us again of Celadon and Florimel. It is Celadon
and Florimel, however, in another age, less witty, less gay,
more evilly suggestive. Mercury and Phaedra reflect in their
own way the changing spirit of the time, just as the carnal
love of Jupiter shows how the airy licentiousness of the court
of Charles was moving towards a Puritanical lewdity. *Amphitryon* is an amusing and an interesting play, but it has not
the charm which lingers over Dryden's early works.

On surveying the influence which Dryden exerted on the
tragedy of his time, and noting his large productivity in
comedy, it must seem surprising that the direct impress of
his art was not greater than in reality it was. Indirectly he
led the way towards the comedy of manners, yet the comedy
of manners, as we have seen, stands sharply separated from
his works. Of direct followers he had few. Mrs Behn, as we
have seen, has reproduced his pair of lovers in *The Rover*, and
Ravenscroft seemed to have *Secret Love* in mind when he
was writing *The Careless Lovers*, but possibly the only

dramatist who consciously imitated him was the Hon. James Howard, Dryden's own kinsman by marriage, author of *All Mistaken, or, The Mad Couple* (T.R. in B.St. Sept. 1667) and *The English Monsieur* (T.R. in B.St. July 1663). The second of these two plays, produced just after Dryden's first comedy, almost certainly owes much to *The Wild Gallant*. Loveby and Lady Constant are reproduced there in Wellbred and Lady Wealthy. The comedy differs in type only in that the other characters, Comely, Vaine and Frenchlove, are more strongly coloured humours than the majority of the *dramatis personae* of Dryden. The same mad couple reappears once more in the tragi-comedy, *All Mistaken*, in the persons of Philidor and Mirida, characters who call to mind at once Celadon and Florimel.

Beyond these, however, and a few plays which are more directly associated with Dryden's name, there is little that shows the definite impress of his style. Of the plays which are associated with him, two or three call for attention. About Sept. 1675 appeared at D.L. a play called *The Mistaken Husband*, said to have been given by a person of quality to Dryden but more probably an adaptation of a now-lost play by Brome. Considerable controversy has circled round this comedy, George Saintsbury denying any of it to the laureate[1], Swinburne postulating II. i and IV. iv as his[2]. The play, it must be admitted, has certain interesting and peculiar features. Mrs Manley has remained for nine years in her father's (Learcut's) house, her husband being gone abroad and she in mourning for his supposed death. Arrives an impostor, Hazard, and his friend, Underwit, who pretend that the former is in reality Manley, altered during the decade of his absence. Mrs Manley is wholly or partly deceived, and Hazard is accepted as the long-lost husband. In the interval Manley himself makes his appearance and proves his identity, but Mrs Manley has found out, on acquaintance, that she rather prefers Hazard. The real husband is paid off

---

[1] W. Scott and G. Saintsbury, *The Dramatic Works of John Dryden* (Edinburgh, 1882), VIII. 645–7.
[2] *Gentleman's Magazine*, N.S., CCLXIX. 416–55.

and a marriage between the wife and the impostor is arranged. This Mrs Manley and Hazard situation does not lack of a certain spicy wit which might well have come from the pen of the laureate, Mrs Manley being rather an interestingly drawn prototype of the Shavian heroine, such as Hypatia in *Misalliance*.

In 1663, when, we are told, Dryden was given this play by a person of quality, no dramatic works had come from his pen, so that it is probable that the unknown author was a friend, probably connected with the Howards, and it may be suggested that he may have been no other than T. Southland, brother-in-law of Sir R. Colbrand, who issued in 1663 *Love a la Mode* (acted at Middlesex House) and to whom might also be attributed *The Ungrateful Favourite* published as by "a Person of Honour" the following year. Both of these latter plays were printed by John Cotterel and both had the same Horatian motto on the title-pages, although only the first has the initials "J.S." which led to the identification of the author. Neither *The Ungrateful Favourite* nor *Love a la Mode* is as good a play as *The Mistaken Husband*, but both are fairly well written, and the latter, in especial, has touches in it that remind us of the witty passages of the Drydenesque play.

A somewhat similar controversy has arisen over another peculiar comedy, styled *The Mall, or, The Modish Lovers*, which appeared at D.L. about Jan. 1673/4, and was published a few months later with a preface signed "J.D." These initials have frequently caused the play to be attributed to John Dryden, but there would seem to be no reason why that poet should have failed to print his own name had he been the author: probably John Dover, author of *The Roman Generalls* (1667) was responsible. On the other hand, the Easy-Amorous scenes are very similar to several in *Sir Martin Mar-all*, Sir Martin being even referred to by name in III. i, and in the abandonment of his wife by Easy there is a situation which speaks highly for the individuality of the author, whoever he may be.

[1] *Op. cit.* VIII. 645.

Apart from these, the Dryden comedy as a separate type did not continue to exist in Restoration literature. It was the work of a single man, who, probably, with no very special bent towards the theatre, hammered out a path of his own, not by genius, but by sheer hard endeavour and painstaking effort. We can look for reminiscences of Dryden in many Restoration plays, from the comedies of manners to the farces, but we can nowhere find comedies, apart from those already mentioned, modelled directly on his own style, as we found tragedies modelled on *The Indian Emperour* and on *Almanzor and Almahide.*

VI. *The Comedy of Manners*

In some ways, of course, as I have already pointed out, Dryden may be regarded as a father of the comedy of manners, his pairs of lovers undoubtedly influencing greatly the work of Etherege, perhaps the work of Wycherley. Other writers, too, not usually associated with the main figures of the comedy of manners, both paid tribute to the strength of that type by direct imitation, or themselves wrote works which, partly manners in style, influenced the development of that species. One of these, Rawlins, with his *Tunbridge Wells* (D.G. *c.* March 1677/8), has already been noticed. Another, of still greater importance, is Sir Charles Sedley, who produced at the T.R. in B.St. in May 1668 *The Mulberry-Garden,* and at D.L. in May 1687 *Bellamira, or, The Mistress.*

These two plays are especially interesting as displaying the passage of the *Committee* type of humours to a more vivid, refined and courtly wit. *The Mulberry-Garden,* as a whole, is not a good comedy, being too sharply divided into two separate, distinct portions. Indeed, on reading it, one comes to the conclusion that one of these portions, that which is in rimed verse and includes the characters of Horatio, Eugenio, Philander, Althea and Diana, may have been written several years earlier than the other, which, in nervous prose, presents the real-life persons of Ned Estridge, Jack Wildish and Harry Modish—typical figures of Restoration comedy.

The play may not be as witty as might have been expected
from its author[1], but, when we note that it was "long
expected" and therefore likely to be of some influence on
contemporary drama, and when we place it alongside of *She
Wou'd if she Cou'd*, produced three months earlier, and of
The Sullen Lovers acted barely a fortnight previously, it
appears one of the most interesting plays of the first decade
of our period. It is not rendered negligible even when placed
alongside of *Bellamira*, which, based confessedly on the
Eunuchus, is a much more decisive play. Satirical, witty,
licentious, with that air of finesse which characterises the
comedy of manners, it well deserves to be placed alongside
of the works of Etherege and of Wycherley.

If Dryden, Shadwell, Sedley and Rawlins each presented
something to this particular type, however, it is Sir George
Etherege to whom must be given the credit of definitely
establishing the species. A typical Restoration beau and man
of letters, a roué and a wit, he infused into all his comedies
that air of the *beau-monde* which was later to be so clarified
and rendered gracious by the inimitable genius of Congreve.
The Comical Revenge, or, Love in a Tub (L.I.F. March, 1664)[2]
was really only a tentative effort. Marred by the introduction
of rimed verse, which, however, makes it of interest historically, and by several other crudities, it does not really grip
one as do so many other plays of the manners school. It has
wit, particularly in the person of Sir Frederick, whose
attitude towards the world is summed up in the *bon mot* that
"Men are now and then subject to those Infirmities in drink
which Women have when they're sober[3]." The wit, however,
is not on the whole of that sparkling variety which charms us
above the intricacy and the improbability of a complicated
plot.

With *She Wou'd if she Cou'd* (L.I.F. Feb. 1667/8), on the
other hand, we may say that the new age had fairly started.

---

[1] On Sedley see the study by V. de Sola Pinto (1927).

[2] Downes (p. 25) says it brought more profit and esteem to the house
than any other comedy.

[3] I. ii.

Probably due to the poor acting[1], it was not the success that one might have expected from that of *The Comical Revenge*; even in print it achieved only three editions by the end of the century to set against the seven or eight of the former play. It is interesting to note, in regarding the work of Etherege and later of Congreve, that the audiences of the time did not appear capable of separating the gold from the dross. They condemned *The Way of the World* even as they condemned this comedy of Congreve's predecessor. Whatever its reception, *She Wou'd if she Cou'd* is undoubtedly a much superior piece to *The Comical Revenge*. It captured completely that spirit of the fine world that had been merely hinted at in the former comedy. Instinct with life, it passed beyond mere humours and types to a realm of living human beings, representative probably of a class, but not caricatured out of all resemblance to their actual prototypes.

Very similar in general tone is *The Man of Mode, or, Sir Fopling Flutter* (D.G. March 1675/6), a play which has become, as it were, one of the very symbols of the comedy of manners[2]. Steele in *The Spectator* saw fit to condemn it as a sort of type specimen of its class, and others, who defend that class, have accordingly given it highest praise. This comedy, which, unlike the last-mentioned play of Etherege, was a tremendous success, displays, perfectly, that fine brilliancy of prose dialogue, that easy, cultured, heartless atmosphere which we must associate with the works of this school. How fine is Dorimant! He is the gentleman *par excellence*—but how heartless! He casts off Mrs Loveit for Belinda as easily as he casts off the latter for Harriet, whom he marries. How exquisite is the character of Sir Fopling, father of what an innumerable progeny of descendants, stretching from Sir Patient Fancy and Sir Courtly Nice to Cibber's beaux of the age of Anne and later! The plot is complicated, but, like

---

[1] Cf. Downes, pp. 28–9, and Shadwell, *The Humorists*, preface. See also Pepys' account of the first performance on Feb. 6, 1667/8, when he overheard Etherege "mightily...find fault with the actors."

[2] Several writers have presumed it to be a satire with Dorimant as Rochester and Young Bellair as Etherege (see Earl of Oxford's *Works*, II. 315 and note of Oldys to Langbaine. p. 187).

Congreve's, seems a part of life, life of a world far from ours, where hearts are atrophied and polite manners and graceful bearing cover a multitude of sins. The characters, some of them, are stereotyped[1], yet they are not overdrawn nor do they shadow the gayer, livelier figures of Dorimant and of Bellair. With *The Man of Mode* the comedy of manners came to its majority, just as with Cibber it sank to a shamefaced and emasculated old age.

The comedy of manners, meanwhile, had been taken up by others, in especial by William Wycherley, who, as an artist, falls far below Etherege, as a powerful force in contemporary life, rises far above him[2]. The lover of the Duchess of Cleveland, the tutor of the King's son, the husband of the Countess of Drogheda, the prisoner in the Fleet, was a quite different being from the airy ambassador, patron of a deserted *comédienne* in the Low Countries. John Palmer is not far wrong in styling him a Puritan with the external veneer of a Restoration gentleman[3]. He burst up the foetid air of the time with a force equal to that of Collier. He lashed the age with his plain-dealing pen, lading out his disgust upon a slightly fluttered world of roués and their mistresses. He has not the style of the greater masters of the manners school, polished and fine: his wit does not overshadow his plots as does the wit of Etherege or of Congreve: yet, in scenes where his moral horror is not aroused, he can be almost as delicate as they.

The whole of Wycherley's plays, it may be noted, fall within half a decade, his first comedy appearing in 1671 and his last in 1676. Living on to the age of Pope, he seems to have spent his energy in those few brilliant years. In *Love in a Wood, or, St James's Park* (T.R. in B.St. *c.* March, 1671) we are led into a world somewhat similar to that of Etherege,

---

[1] Such as Old Bellair, the lover of the past age.

[2] The effect which he had on his contemporaries may best be realised from the countless references to his chief play. "The Author of the *Plain Dealer*," thought Dryden, "Has oblig'd all honest and virtuous Men, by one of the most bold, most general, and most useful Satyrs which has ever been presented on the *English* Theatre" (Preface to *The State of Innocence*, 1677).

[3] See for this whole subject *The Comedy of Manners* (1913).

yet hardly so fine, and, as in the Alderman Gripe and Lucy scenes, tending to vulgarity. From the very first opening sentence of the play, however, we may see the masterly construction. The plot is ably and interestingly developed: but something remains indefinably incongruous. There is almost something of Shadwell in Wycherley's work. There is always the sense that the heart is struggling for entry into the world of the intellect.

Of like nature, though less successful, was *The Gentleman Dancing-Master* (D.G. *c.* Aug. 1672) in which the construction, with its opposed types of French and Spanish foppery, is even simpler than in the comedy preceding. *The Gentleman Dancing-Master* is interesting as being nearer in spirit to Etherege than almost any other of Wycherley's plays: it stands furthest in tone from *The Plain Dealer*.

In *The Country Wife* (D.L. Jan. 1674/5)[1] Wycherley has continued in the same free easy strain. *The Country Wife* is a bright and glorious farce, in which the innuendo so successfully employed in *The Gentleman Dancing-Master* is brought to a stage of utmost perfection. The famous "China" scene of Horner is probably unrivalled in our literature, and, much as it has been condemned by moralists, can be nothing but admired for its sheer cleverness and for its swift biting humour. Here the vulgarity so apparent in Shadwell's work is cast aside: this is a piece of intellectualism, wherein the wit takes from the harmful effect it otherwise might have had.

The name of Wycherley, however, "manly," "brawny"[2] Wycherley, stands not so much with these former plays, although they were enough to make the fame of any dramatist, but with a comedy almost unique in its age—*The Plain Dealer* (D.L. Dec. 1676). In it the roué joins hands with the

---

[1] On the dating of Wycherley's plays see Appendix C. The enduring popularity of *The Country Wife*, in the original and in altered form, is surveyed by Emmett L. Avery in "*The Country Wife* in the Eighteenth Century" (*Research Studies of the State College of Washington*, 1942, x. 142–58). This play, as is well known, has been brought back to the stage recently in its original form, after its place had for long been taken by Garrick's discreet treatment of it in *The Country Girl*.

[2] Dryden's and Rochester's epithets for him.

moralist, realism is mingled with artificial manners, emotions
with the intellect. It satirises perfectly the infidelity and the
foppishness of the time, at the very moments that it sinks
to the depths of carnal viciousness. There is only one pure
character in the whole of its five acts, and that is Fidelia,
devoted Fidelia who follows her rough and faithless lover
with a tenderness that almost draws the tears from our eyes.
Everyone else is swallowed up in sense. The chief figure is,
of course, Manly himself, a pessimistic hater of man's
hypocrisy, and one who owes not a little to the Alceste of
Molière's *Le misanthrope*. Beside him and Fidelia, with the
possible exception of Olivia, Manly's former mistress, all the
other characters seem mere shadows of personified qualities.
Lord Plausible is simply the typical fop with nothing individual in his composition, just as Novel is the representative
of the would-be wits, and Widow Blackacre of the law-mad
amateurs. On women, fops, wits and lawyers indiscriminately
the satire falls, intermixed with that loathsome description of
passion which only men like Shadwell and Wycherley among
the Restoration dramatists could give to us. Wycherley, says
Congreve, was sent "to lash the crying Age," but he has
lashed its sores into more fulsome aspects, until we have
naught to do but turn our eyes away in misery and in
disgust.

   In Wycherley's *Plain Dealer*, then, we see inherent all the
elements which were to lead towards the complete decay of
the species of comedy which he had adopted in his first
dramas. The reality of the mind, in this comedy, has been
replaced by the reality of the body: the airiness of the
liberated cavalier has given way to the moral horror of the
sinning Puritan. By 1676 the age was moving steadily in the
direction of sentimentalism, pure intellect was being banished
by feeling; emotion was taking the place of wit. This change,
certainly, is not felt with any strength till after the year 1680
and Congreve, writing in the last decade of the century, felt
little more than a touch of it, but we can note the first hints
of it, in so diverse forms as *The Plain Dealer*, the plays of
Dryden and the plays of Mrs Behn. The age was rapidly

undergoing a transformation: even in the time of Charles the spirit was not quite the same as it had been in 1665. After the Revolution a new era commences.

It is peculiar to note that in Wycherley, in Dryden, in Mrs Behn and in others the elements of sentimentalism could exist alongside of humorous qualities which might well be thought entirely contrary to their aim. In this respect the three comedies produced by Thomas Southerne have a special interest. Southerne is probably best known to-day for his tragedy, *The Fatal Marriage*, and for his "play," *The Disappointment*, dramas in which he definitely took his stand with Otway and with Cibber in an endeavour to introduce the problem play and the bourgeois tragedy. In his own time, however, he was no doubt more famous for his three comic pieces, each with rich elements of the manners style.

Sir Anthony Love, or, The Rambling Lady (D.L. *c.* Dec. 1690) is a "she-comedy," Sir Anthony Love being none other than Lucia, a former kept mistress, now in love with Valentine. It is worth noting that he or she gives vent to the same theory concerning a certain class of women chasers, who pursue the chase for the mere pleasure of the hunt, as is to be found in Congreve's *Love for Love*. This play, which was a success in its own days, is a fair specimen of mannerised comedy, its dialogue being good and witty, although marred by Southerne's prevailing weakness—the over-use of theatrical broken sentences, wherein the meaning of one speaker is continued or perverted by another. This mannerism, which Southerne occasionally employs effectively, becomes wearisome and monotonous by the end of the play. *The Wives Excuse, or, Cuckolds make themselves* appeared at the same theatre precisely a year later (*c.* Dec. 1691). It was a failure, and the author, possibly because of that, obtained some congratulatory verses from Dryden which he inserted in the printed edition of the text. These verses liken the author to Terence, a somewhat exaggerated comparison. *The Wives Excuse* is not a very good play, although it is of the same class as *Sir Anthony Love*. Probably its main point of interest for us is an historical one—the introduction in the comedy

itself of a reference to Southerne's own work, a sort of premonition of Shavian methods of self-advertisement[1].

In *The Maid's Last Prayer, or, Any rather than Fail* (D.L.
c. Feb. 1692/3), the title of which, like that of the last-mentioned play, is both ironical and explanatory, Southerne sinks
below even the level of *The Wives Excuse*. The "maid" in
question is an old maid, Lady Susan. Apart from the song by
Congreve[2], the most noticeable thing in the comedy is the
scene in the last act where Lady Malapert discovers she has
had an assignation with Gayman instead of with Valentine,
a theme handled with not a little skilful, if a trifle indelicate,
humour[3]. All along, indeed, Southerne gives us these witty
scenes in his plays, but he just fails of great dramatic triumph
through a certain inability to sustain his highest flights. Some
of those individual scenes are worthy of Congreve himself,
but they are buried in a mass of uninteresting padding which
the author seemed unable to refine.

The atmosphere of the school of manners, of course, in its
most perfect form, is to be found in the works of Congreve.
Congreve is not a courtier of the age of Charles: he is rather
a city beau of the age of Anne, a companion of Pope, a friend
of Walsh: yet he has inherited to the full the spirit of Etherege.

His first comedy, *The Old Batchelor*, appeared at D.L. in
March 1693, when its author was but twenty-one, a truly
wonderful production for a young man just upon his majority.
It had a brilliant cast—Betterton playing the title-part,
Powell Bellamour, Williams Vainlove and Doggett Fondle-
wife, with Mrs Barry, Mrs Bracegirdle and Mrs Mountfort
to bear them company—and with such a cast, a play so witty
could hardly fail of success[4]. Brilliancy characterises the
whole of it: the wit rises and falls with a continual vivacity,
so that we overlook the artificiality of the plot and the sometimes too grievous lack of individuality in some of the
characters[5]. With a racy prologue spoken by Mrs Bracegirdle,

---

[1] III. ii.
[2] In v. Malone thinks this was the poet's first acknowledged work.
[3] The situation appears with variations in *The Mall* (D.L. 1674).
[4] It had a run of over fourteen nights.
[5] Such as Wittol and Bluffe.

with the sharp nervous dialogue, it must have seemed to that *fin de siècle* audience, so rapidly to become hypocritical in its theatrical pleasures, as a last banquet of wit, as the last joyous and flagrant outburst before a dark and lowering storm. Wholly immoral as it is, it yet clothes that immorality with a profusion of wit that assuredly disarms, as it must in that age have disarmed, what one can only style the moral sense. There is no pain in this world, only wit and laughter and freedom, and wit and laughter and freedom, divorced from emotion, can never kill.

After this glorious success, Congreve must have received an unpleasant surprise at the cool reception given to *The Double Dealer* (D.L. Oct. 1693). Hardly a comedy in the full sense of the term, it strikes the evil note, and because of that, had our emotions been in any way aroused, we might have styled it a tragi-comedy. As it is, although the love of Mellefont and Cynthia is good and true—suggesting pre-Restoration standards—and although wit, but not in such rich profusion, does permeate the whole, we are left with a feeling of dissatisfaction. We have neither the pathos which, for example, Southerne in his serious plays was able to call into being, nor have we the sense of over-abundant intellect spent in conversation of the most airy and the most delicate kind, as we have when we read *The Way of the World* or even *Love for Love*. It is just possible that here Congreve was misled by his age. His spirit is the spirit of free gallantry: the scenes of Mellefont and of Cynthia, striving to call up a picture of honest love, appear artificial and forced. There are even touches of a definitely sentimental sort, as in that passage in Act III where Cynthia, thinking of the follies of Sir Paul and his confrères, looks into her heart and finds a moralisation. "Why should I call them Fools?" she asks, showing that in her the barriers between the emotions and the intellect had been shattered.

This slightly sentimental touch, visible in *The Double Dealer*, has vanished entirely in Congreve's following play, *Love for Love*, acted at the new theatre in L.I.F. in April 1695. Although it was a glorious success, as a dramatic production it falls just below *The Way of the World* precisely because, as Dr Johnson pointed out, it is more realistic, in the ordinary meaning of that term. The sailor Ben, a finely drawn type in its way and one of the causes of the success of the comedy, seems out of place, and the immorality of the piece, although not so flagrant as that of *The Old Batchelor*, is drawn more closely to our notice. In this drama Congreve has come nearer to the spirit of Shadwell than he has done in any other of his four works, and the Miss Prue and Tattle scenes, imitated from that antagonist of Dryden, raise in us the same distaste which must be felt on reading *The Squire of Alsatia*. Congreve was no moralist, such as Wycherley was, but the rapidly changing spirit of the age, leading here to a semi-hypocritical sentimentalism, here to a coarser realism, had laid its impress upon him: even he could not escape entirely.

The triumph of Congreve in *The Way of the World*, which appeared at L.I.F. in the last year of the century, derives from the fact that he was able to shake off for once all grosser ties. It was not a success, a cool reception which did not seem to surprise the author. He knew well enough, as he expressed it in his dedication, that "but little of it was prepared for that general Taste which seems now to predominate in the Palates of our Audience." It was, in fact, too rarefied, too refined for the spirit of its time. There is no sentiment in it, no realism, no coarseness. Mirabell and Millamant, about whom the plot, such as it is, gyrates continually, are not complete figures: they are merely automata, devised as mouth-pieces for the poet. The theme is artificial and the conclusion is artificial, if we test it by the standards of everyday life: yet both have a brilliancy and a truth which make of *The Way of the World* the master-creation of the school of manners.

With Etherege, Wycherley and Congreve the comedy of manners is seen at its best, although in the two last mentioned there are already visible the elements of decay and of disintegration. Those elements of decay and of disintegration become more pronounced as we pass to the two other writers whose names are usually associated with the greater three, Vanbrugh and Farquhar. A study even of those few comedies which the former presented to the seventeenth century theatre must display at once the complete disseverance which exists between the works of Congreve and the works of his followers. There is no finesse about Vanbrugh's work. However much he accepted the manners convention, he yet lies as far from Congreve and from Etherege as do D'Urfey and Mrs Behn. The majority of his pieces are but glorified farces: and, although he is as wantonly indecent as his predecessors, he seems to have appreciated to the full the emotions that were gathering round him, and by bringing sensibility into his themes and feeling into his wit, he served, along with others, to hasten the break-away of comedy from the Etheregian model.

His first three plays all appeared in the years 1696–1697, two at D.L. and one at L.I.F. The first of these, *The Relapse, or, Virtue in Danger* (D.L. Nov. 1696) is a good play, the preface to which is exceedingly instructive for our knowledge, not only of the writer's aims, but of the audience and of the stage conditions of the period. Fairly immoral, it seems to have met with considerable censure, although the author, with an airy kind of dissimulation, professes himself duly innocent. In this play Cibber carried on his enduring success in the character of Sir Novelty Fashion, now Lord Foppington, "a Man whom Nature has made no Fool" but "who is very industrious to pass for an Ass"—a definition which reminds us strongly of the critical precepts of Shadwell, presented several decades previously.

Aesop, the second comedy given by Vanbrugh to the Theatre Royal (Part I, *c.* Dec. 1696; Part II, *c.* March, 1696/7) is confessedly but little more than a translation of Boursault. It is rather a poor performance in two parts, by no means brilliant at its best, and in places excessively dull. The whole is composed, of course, to display the aphorisms and the apologues of Aesop, who proves a very objectionable and cynical personage in his stage existence.

In *The Provok'd Wife* (L.I.F. May, 1697), however, we

reach one of the masterpieces of Vanbrugh's art. There is not in it the sparkle of Congreve, but there is throughout a show of wit, adorning a very definite plot, well contrived and well executed. The characters, too, are well, if roughly, drawn. Sir John Brute, indeed, is one of the living figures in Restoration dramatic literature. There are violent attempts in almost every act on the part of the author to capture the manners style, but in the main his strength lies far apart from that. The succession of ludicrous incidents, the continual wave to and fro of action never for a moment still, the assignations and the discoveries and the fears and the explanations, all keep our attention focussed on a scene, slightly satirical, but always instinct with life.

Of Vanbrugh much has been said by the critics, both laudatory and condemnatory. He stands, it is true, much below Congreve, lacking his wit and his finesse; at the same time he has other qualities, lower in degree, but stamping him as a true son of the theatre. "His best jokes are practical devices," says Hazlitt in his fourth lecture on *The English Comic Writers*, "Not epigrammatic conceits.... He has more nature than art: what he does best, he does because he cannot help it." Although various critics disagree, it would seem to be this "nature," involving passion, that renders his work less artistically satisfying than that of Congreve[1]. One might suspect, indeed, that Vanbrugh owed in his art two masters, Congreve and Shadwell. He differed from both, yet he had some of the qualities of both. Shadwell is sometimes heavy: Congreve is airy: Vanbrugh is buoyant— buoyant with a sort of uproariousness, upheld by wine.

The companion of Vanbrugh, George Farquhar, hardly had made his début in this century. His first play, *Love and a Bottle*, appeared at D.L. only in 1698, at the time when its author was but twenty-one. Its plot is but poor and artificial with manifest tendencies towards the degeneration of the pure manners style by the introduction of a species of spurious

---

[1] Paul Mueschke and Jeanette Fleisher have "A Re-evaluation of Vanbrugh" (*PMLA*, 1934, XLIV. 848–89)—an exceedingly interesting and acute examination of the subject.

sentimentalism. Already in his first comedy he showed exactly
where he stood, the heir of Congreve breathing the spirit of
the changing age.

About a year later, in November 1699, was performed at
D.L. his second play, *The Constant Couple, or, A Trip to the
Jubilee*, a play which had a considerable success in its own
time. Although much of the plot is borrowed, and a certain
amount of the wit strained, *The Constant Couple* is well
wrought out and not all of its contemporary triumph was due,
as Farquhar himself modestly declared, to the acting of Wilks
as Sir Harry Wildair. In spite of the fact that the prologue
tells us

> *...Here's no slander,*
> *No Smut, no lewd-tongued beau, no double entendre,*

the whole is as licentious as any play of earlier times. What
is Wildair if not a "lewd-tongued beau" in the scene where,
under a misapprehension, he offers Angelica money as he
would have offered it to a courtesan? The statement in the
prologue, however, is valuable in considering the temper of
the age. Farquhar owes, undoubtedly, much of his success
to his inimitable portraiture of this age. He had, moreover,
learnt at least sufficient of Congreve's wit to make his comedies
amusing and piquant.

Beyond those comedies already mentioned, the school of
manners in these forty years is hardly represented. There
are a few plays, such as *The She-Gallants* (L.I.F. *c.* Dec.
1695) of George Granville, Lord Lansdowne, which can
definitely be placed in the Etherege school of comic production: and there are a number of comedies, such as those
of Mrs Behn, where the impress of Etherege and of Wycherley
is to be traced; but in the main only the chief figures stand
out. Altogether these five major dramatists have not given,
in the seventeenth century, more than a score of works, and
several of these were not very successful on the stage. They
had not, that is to say, the force and the influence which we
of to-day postulate for them. They have given us what is
finest in the Restoration age, but they by no means dominated
the theatre of their time. Not only had they to battle for

supremacy with the exponents of humours and of Spanish intrigue, but they were surrounded by a mass of popular dramatists who, in the early days, filled the T.R. and L.I.F. with rude tempestuous works, and who, in the last years of the century, provided D.L. and D.G. with farce and with sentiments. The chief things to remember about the development of the comedy of manners are, that it was not the principal fare of the theatres from 1664 to 1700, and that it was not even distinctively of the Restoration age at all. Some of its principal exponents live after the death of Charles.

VII. *Farce and Sentimentalism*

The gradual growth of a fine and well-nigh perfect comic expression in the last years of the century appears all the more strange when we consider that these last years display, alongside of the growth of the comedy of manners, a decided weakening of the true comic spirit. In two distinct directions is this weakening to be observed. More and more, farce was coming to dominate the theatres, and from 1680 onwards may be traced the slowly gathering force of sentiment, the incursion of feeling and of emotion, spurious and sincere, into the world of the intellect. Sentiment was destined to be a force guiding and altering all types of literature for over two centuries to come, but it killed the spirit of Congreve. Farce was destined to weaken and to destroy the finer expression of the comic muse.

The elements of both, of course, can be noted from the very first years of the Restoration period. There were farcical elements in the comedies of Dryden, of Wilson and of Mrs Behn. *The Man's the Master* of D'Avenant (L.I.F. March 1667/8), founded on *Jodelet, ou, Le maistre valet* and *L'héritier ridicule*, was but a farcical comedy of intrigue with many characteristics of the pre-Commonwealth minor drama[1]. The

---

[1] Leo Hughes ("Attitudes of some Restoration Dramatists towards Farce," *Philological Quarterly*, 1940, XIX. 268–87) shows that, while farce found apologists in Lacy and Aphra Behn, many dramatists (e.g. Dryden, Edward Howard and Shadwell) opposed it both on aesthetic and patriotic grounds. The same author has an interesting essay on "The Early Career of Farce" (*University of Texas Studies in English*, 1940).

same author's *The Play-House to be Lett* (L.I.F. *c.* 1663) with its skits at opera, its presentation of a "*Monsieur*" and his farce, and its "*Travesti*" of a tragedy, is nothing but a set of farces and burlesques loosely pinned together in one framework[1].

This latter play of D'Avenant's is to be connected with several other burlesques of a later decade, burlesques which must have had some influence on the development of farce proper after 1680. At D.G. about Sept. 1673 appeared *The Reformation*, a comedy attributed to Arrowsmith, not un-humorously satirising the heroic tragedy of the time. At T.R. in December two years before had been acted *The Rehearsal* of Villiers, Duke of Buckingham. *The Rehearsal* had first been penned in 1663; it had been ready by 1665: and had been laid aside owing to the closing of the theatres during the time of plague. It was taken up again after 1667, and thus presents a continuous and all-embracing burlesque of the heroic species. The original "hero" was Bilboa, none other than Sir Robert Howard. This gentleman, however, had soon to cede place to Bayes—John Dryden himself—or, at least, a combination of Dryden, Howard and D'Avenant, the holy trinity of the heroic muse. That Villiers was assisted in its composition seems not now to be doubted, and Butler probably took more than an equal share in it. Whatever its authorship, however, and whatever its success as a reforming medium, it is a work that deserves far more attention, even, than it receives at the present day. Less finished than Sheridan's masterpiece, it is yet a fine and uproarious ex-posure of contemporary Love and Honour follies. It is, too, the first of its kind. The plays ridiculed are numerous enough, extending from *The Conquest of Granada* to *The Indian Emperour*, *The Siege of Rhodes*, *Tyrannick Love*, *The Villain*, *The Slighted Maid* and *Love and Friendship*. Besides these, one or two comedies, also, of the heroic writers were satirised —notably *The Wild Gallant*, *The Assignation* and *The Play-*

---

[1] For an examination of this play, *The Rehearsal* and other similar works, see Dane Farnsworth Smith, *Plays about the Theatre in England* (1936), especially pp. 1–37.

House to be Lett. Much of what must have had keen contemporary savour is, of course, now insipid. Bayes is but a
lay figure for us, not a living model: but the main wealth of
sometimes academic, but always pointed, ridicule remains
imperishable. It is unfair often, often not in good taste: but
as a brilliant piece of burlesque it is, for the student of the
stage no less than for the student of the times, invaluable[1].

A few years later, farcical burlesque, in the hands of
Thomas Duffett, took on an even more decided form[2]. *The
Empress of Morocco* (D.L. *c.* Dec. 1673), *The Mock
Tempest, or, The Enchanted Castle* (D.L. Nov. 1674) and
Psyche Debauch'd (D.L. *c.* May 1675) presented in a coarse
way travesties of popular successes at D.G. Possibly Duffett's
earlier comedy in heroic verse, *The Spanish Rogue* (L.I.F.
c. March 1673) was also intended as a burlesque. If it was
not, it was a very poor production. None of Duffett's plays
is valuable. To a contemporary audience each must have
had some piquancy, but the fun is strained and only too often
descends to the very depths of vulgarity. The best part of
any is the *Epilogue spoken by Witches after the Mode of
Macbeth*, appended to *Psyche Debauch'd*.

To the early farcical strain as expressed in Dryden's *The
Wild Gallant* and in the plays of Wilson, and to this burlesque
expressed in the plays of D'Avenant, Villiers and Duffett,
came, in increasing waves throughout the reign of Charles,
the influence of the *commedia dell' arte* tradition. Italian,
apparently, was sufficiently well known among the courtly
audiences of 1660–1680 for plays to be presented by native
performers in that language. Even in regular English plays
we find its appearance. In Act III, Sc. i of Mrs Behn's *The
Feign'd Curtizans* (D.G. 1679) occurs a song in "Italian,"
commencing,

> *Crudo Amore, Crudo Amore,*
> *Il mio Core non fa per te,*

---

[1] See E. L. Avery, "The Stage Popularity of *The Rehearsal*" (*Research
Studies of the State College of Washington*, 1939, VII. 201–23).

[2] For Duffett see Downes. The title-page of *Psyche Debauch'd* declares
that play was written by "T. D." For the ascription to Duffett, see
Appendix C.

whilst a stage direction in Southerne's *The Wives Excuse*
(D.L. 1691) instructs the characters "*After an* Italian *Song*"
to "*Advance to the Front of the Stage*[1]." An "*Italian* Song
by Mr *Pate*" is referred to in Act II of *The Female Wits, or,
The Triumvirate of Poets at Rehearsal* (D.L. 1697). As
early as Oct. 22, 1660, the King had granted a patent to
Giulio Gentileschi to build a theatre for Italian musicians,
and, no doubt, for Italian players as well[2]. "Opere musicali,
con machine mutationi di scene et altre apparenze" are
specifically mentioned and leave is given him to build a
theatre[3]. By 1668, troupes of Italian comedians appear to
have been well enough known to give point to a phrase in the
prologue to *Tarugo's Wiles* (L.I.F. 1667)—"A *Trivolino*, or a
Skaramuchio that's dextrous at making of mouths will sooner
raise a Clap then a high flown Fancy." On Nov. 11, 1672,
Charles issued through the Lord Chamberlain an order
signifying his royal pleasure "That Antonio di Voto Doe sett
forth Exercise & Play all Drolls and Interludes, He not
receiuing into his Company any person belonging to his
Ma[tes] or Royal Highnesse Theatres Nor Act any Play usually
acted at any of y[e] said Theatres Nor takes peeces or Sceenes
out of y[e] Playes Acted at y[e] said Theatres[4]." This order is
entered in the books to "Antonio Divoto punchenello." On
April 21, 1673 another troupe had but "newly arrived[5]":
these were seen by Evelyn on May 29 and on September 4
the King ordered "to be prepared & deliuered vnto Scara-
mouchi and Harlekin vnto each of them a Medall & Chayne
of Gold" as well as a chain and medal for four others of their
company[6]. Some days later, on Sept. 12, 1673, twenty ounces
of white plate were sent as a present for one of the company[7].
On Sept. 11 they were granted a warrant of £52 for a stage,
which sum was advanced to them by St Albans. Shortly
after, they left England[8]. This band, under Tiberio Fiorilli,

[1] I. ii. [2] *Cal. State Papers, Dom. Series*, 1660/1, p. 319.
[3] S.P. 29/19, no. 16, quoted by Eleanore Boswell, *op. cit.* p. 115.
[4] P.R.O., L.C. 5/140, p. 129. Di Voto was a shower of puppets; see
Adams, J. Q., *Dramatic Records of Sir Henry Herbert*, pp. 138–9.
[5] A warrant to the customs officers to admit their properties was issued
on that date (*Cal. State Papers, Treasury Books*, 1672–75, 119).
[6] P.R.O., L.C. 5/140, p. 328. [7] *Id.* p. 329.
[8] *Cal. State Papers, Treasury Books*, 1672–75, pp. 392 and 837. The
£52 was not repaid until June 6, 1676 (*id.* 1676–79, p. 234). For the
warrant to export their goods see *id.* 1672–75, p. 826.

or Fiorelli, a famous Scaramuccio, performed apparently at Whitehall, and returned about June 1675 to act in the Hall Theatre, accepting money for admission and thereby giving great offence to some honest citizens of London[1]. Marvell, for example, in a letter dated July 24, 1675, speaks of "Scaramuccio acting daily in...Whitehall, and all sorts of people flocking thither, and paying their money as at a common play-house; nay, even a twelvepenny gallery is builded for the convenience of his Majesty's poorer subjects[2]." Marvell probably reflected the sentiments of a fair number in the London of that day, and there were doubtless many who appreciated to the full his satire of the Italians in his poem *The Statue at Charing Cross*, where he refers to the former booth erected for the foreign troop in that locality:

> 'Twere to *Scaramouchio* too great disrespect
> To limit his troop to this theatre small;
> Besides the injustice it were to eject
> That mimic so legally seized of *Whitehall*[3].

Satire of the Italians and their fare may also be found in Dryden's reference to the "*Italian* Merry-*Andrews*" in his epilogue "to the University of Oxford." Their presence probably caused the introduction of Punch into the *Oenone* of 1673[4]. Another troupe, through the good offices of the Duke of Modena, reached London in Nov. 1678, and left in Feb. 1678/9[5], after what seems to have been a poor season[6]; in the summer of 1683 an Italian company was playing again at Windsor[7]. From this date references to the *commedia*

[1] Apparently Fiorilli was back in England in 1674, when a special theatre was built for his use at Windsor (Eleanore Boswell, *op. cit.* pp. 59–60). In 1675 he left England in October (*id.* pp. 121–2). *The King's Musick* (1900), edited by H. C. de Lafontaine, presents a document of July 1675 in which mention is made of songs "that were played at Scaramoucha."

[2] Grosart's edition, vol. II. p. 467.

[3] Muse's Library edition, vol. II. p. 98. Evelyn saw these Italian players on Sept. 29, 1675.

[4] In the earlier *Acteon and Diana, With the Pastorall Story of the Nymph Oenone* (n.d.), Punch makes no appearance. He was introduced only into the enlarged edition of this pastoral printed in Kirkman's *The Wits, or, Sport upon Sport* (1673), edited by J. J. Elson (1932).

[5] *Cal. State Papers, Treasury Books*, 1676–9, pp. 1160 and 1230.

[6] A. L. Bader writes on "The Modena Troupe in England" (*Modern Language Notes*, 1935, L. 367–9) and other material is given in the present writer's *Masks, Mimes and Miracles* (1933).

[7] See Eleanore Boswell, *op. cit.* pp. 60–1.

dell' arte are frequent. Ravenscroft's *Scaramouch a Philo-sopher, Harlequin a School-Boy, Bravo, Merchant and Magician. A Comedy after the Italian Manner* appeared at D.L. in May 1677. Mrs Behn in the second part of *The Rover* (D.G. 1681) apparently introduced a real Italian harlequin[1], and in 1686 Mountfort felt the taste of the time sufficiently to produce his *The Life and Death of Doctor Faustus, Made into a Farce.... With the Humours of Harlequin and Scaramouche* (D.G. 1685). Dryden has a reference to the same characters in his *A Discourse concerning the Original and Progress of Satire* (1693), while in the same year Tate saw fit to increase what had been but a page and a half of preface to his *A Duke and no Duke* into a full-blown discourse "concerning Farce" in which he elaborately proves the genesis of Harlequin and of Scaramouch from "the *Personae* and *Larvae*...of the Ancient THEATRE." "Two *Scaramouch* Men, and two *Scaramouch* Women" as well as "two *Harlaquin* Men and Women" "*Enter and Dance*" in Powell's *New Opera: called, Brutus of Alba* (D.G. 1696) while, in the following year, Motteux made the last act of *The Novelty. Every Act a Play*, "*A Farce after the Italian Manner*" entitled *Natural Magic*.

Nor, in thus dealing with the influence of the *commedia dell' arte*, must we forget the presence in England of French as well as Italian comedians. As early as Aug. 30, 1661, Pepys was at a "French comedy," given by continental players, at the Cockpit in Drury Lane. Evelyn records their presence at court on Dec. 16 of the same year and on the 2nd of that month Jean Channouveau had received £300 for their services[2], among which was certainly a performance of an *Andromède* and probably a performance of *The Descent of Orpheus into Hell*[3]. On Aug. 25, 1663, another band received a licence to come over[4]. On Oct. 26, 1669, an order was issued signifying the King's pleasure "That ye french Comoedians haue liberty to Act and Play And that noe Persons p^{r}sume to molest or disturbe them in theire Acting & playing[5]." Early

---

[1] In this play Harlequin speaks "In *Italian*" (IV. iv) probably extempore.
[2] *Cal. State Papers, Treasury Books, 1660–67*, p. 311.
[3] See *supra*, p. 41. For the *Andromède* (or *Andromeda*) see Ethel Seaton, *Literary Relations of England and Scandinavia in the Seventeenth Century* (1935), p. 333.
[4] *Cal. State Papers, Dom. Series, 1663–64*, p. 253.
[5] P.R.O., L.C. 5/12, 252.

in 1672 they returned, much to Dryden's disgust, the laureate writing a prologue (that to Carlell's *Arviragus and Philicia*, 1672) against them and their customs. The precise movements of the French companies during the following months are a trifle hard to determine. One troupe seems to have arrived in December 1672[1], apparently leaving in May 1673, but once more little is known of their doings. French opera was given in 1673 and in 1674 while early in 1677 there came a new band which was satirised by Porter in the epilogue to *The French Conjurer* (D.G. 1677). Another troupe arrived in November[2]; they did not leave London till April of the following year[3]. Besides a visit of the Prince of Orange's French players in 1684[4], and another in 1688[5], we may note the considerable influence which must have been exerted indirectly through the visits of our actors, Betterton and Haynes, to the Parisian theatres. The French and the Italian improvised comedy in all ways left an indelible mark upon our dramatic productivity.

The chief figure in the acclimatisation of farce in England was Edward Ravenscroft, one of those many lawyers who turned from the Bar to the stage. He is really the first of a new set of writers, who, following after D'Avenant and Dryden, continued their work to the end of the century.

[1] On Dec. 17, 1672, they were allowed to import their properties (*Treasury Books*, 1672–5, p. 14). On Jan. 1, 1672/3, those properties were ordered to be sent from Portsmouth to London (*id.* p. 24) and arrived on Jan. 9 (*id.* p. 29). On May 1, 1673, was issued an order to inspect their goods at York House (*id.* p. 127). On June 1, 1674, some French actors were allowed to export their goods (*id.* p. 533); they left England on August 19 (*id.* p. 571). Eleanore Boswell suggests (1) that "export" may be an error for "import" and (2) that possibly the "French" comedians were really Fiorilli and his Italians.

[2] *Id.* 1676–9, p. 803.

[3] A warrant was issued on April 12, 1678, to examine their goods before exportation to France (*id.* p. 962).

[4] Cf. letter from B. Grenville to W. L. Gower, June 10, 1684 (*HMC*, 5th Report, Part I. p. 186). On Sept. 29, 1684, an order was issued to prepare a theatre at court for them (P.R.O., L.C. 5/145, p. 90). For this whole question, see W. J. Lawrence on French players in England in *An Elizabethan Play-House, and other Studies* (Series I. p. 125 ff.). From this several of the references above are quoted. It is possible that for some of these references the terms "French" and "Italian" are interchangeable.

[5] The French players arrived on Aug. 13 and stayed at Windsor till Sept. 22 (P.R.O., 5/17). A licence was issued to them on Aug. 11 (*id.* 65), and the theatre was being got ready for them on July 25 (*id.* p. 60).

Without any very marked qualities to stamp him as a poet, Ravenscroft was yet superior to Langbaine's contemptuous dismissal of him—"one who with the Vulgar passes for a Writer." A plagiary undoubtedly he was, but a plagiary who not always failed of success. His great claim to fame lies in the particular type of farcical drama which he adopted and popularised. He knew exactly what the audiences of the later Restoration period desired, and, with a ready pen, he set himself to supply that want. In the creation of this particular form of farce he has, as is natural, borrowed from many sources. Jonson, occasionally, supplied him with humours: Dryden's "Wild Gallant" couples provided the model for Careless, Lovell and Hillaria in *The Careless Lovers*: Spanish intrigue he employed with effect: but, above all, he looked to France and Italy. Molière he went to again and again, reducing his comedies to the meagre limits of the farcical show. The *commedia dell' arte* provided him with one definitely "Italian" piece, and with many a hint for other plays.

With Molière and hints from Dryden he started his dramatic career. *The Citizen turn'd Gentleman*[1] (D.G. July, 1672) and *The Careless Lovers* (D.G. March 1672/3) were taken bodily from *Le bourgeois gentilhomme* and from *Monsieur de Pourceaugnac* respectively, and display well the forces that were working towards the reduction of the Molière comedy to mere farce, the weakening of Molière's humour and the running together of two or three of his comedies so as to increase the incident at the expense of the characterisation and of the wit. *The Wrangling Lovers, or, The Invisible Mistress* followed at D.G. about Sept. 1676. In this play Ravenscroft first essayed another style of comic writing, that of intrigue, and again its inspiration was derived from across the Channel: its plot and characters came partly from French, partly from Spanish originals[2]. In it the "wrangling lovers," Don Diego and Octavia, as well as Sancho, the inevitable

---

[1] Republished in 1675 as *Mamamouchi*.
[2] See *supra*, p. 192.

servant, are characters quite well sustained, but are not supported sufficiently by the rest.

Ravenscroft's most interesting play, however, is none of these. In *Scaramouch a Philosopher. Harlequin a School-Boy, Bravo, Merchant and Magician. A Comedy after the Italian Manner* (D.L. May, 1677) the author realised that he was introducing a novelty on the London stage. "*The Poet*," says the prologue,

> *The Poet does a dang'rous Trial make,*
> *And all the common Roads of Plays forsake...*
> *(He) rather chose in new attempts to fail*
> *Than in the old indifferently prevail.*

Scaramouch a Philosopher is partly to be traced to *Le mariage forcé* and to *Les fourberies de Scapin* of Molière, but its immediate inspiration is undoubtedly to be sought for in some of the unrecorded improvised comedies performed by Fiorilli and his troupe at Whitehall. The snatches of Italian phrasing scattered throughout, as well as the typical characters of the *commedia dell' arte*, prove that by this time the popular comedy of Italy had become a definite part of English theatrical life. Punch and Scaramouch and Harlequin had been thoroughly acclimatised

Ravenscroft's later plays all follow the lines laid down in these his first essays in the drama. If we omit the tragi-comedy of *King Edgar and Alfreda* and the alteration of *Titus Andronicus*, we find five plays of his produced between 1677 and 1697. Of these, *The English Lawyer* (D.L. *c.* Dec. 1677) is merely a popular adaptation of the Latin *Ignoramus* of Ruggles, performed at Trinity College Hall in 1614/5[1]. The flagrant *London Cuckolds* was not produced at D.G. until Nov. 1681. This notorious piece, with a perfectly immoral plot, descending, because of its workmanship, to utter vulgarity, was followed at D.G. about June 1683 by a more or less pure *Dame Dobson, or, The Cunning Woman*. These two plays are interesting when considered together. The success of the first was of a somewhat scandalous nature, it having

---

[1] A translation of the same play, by Ferdinando Parkhurst, appeared in 1662: see *infra* p. 302 and Appendix C.

the honour of being played every Lord Mayor's day until in
1751 Garrick stopped it at his theatre[1]. Its wit is purely
tomfoolery and its satire ugly. *Dame Dobson*, on the other
hand, pays tribute to the growing force of moral sentiment
rising after 1682.

"*No Line in this*," says the prologue,

> *will tempt your Minds to Evil,*
> *It's true, 'tis dull, but then 'tis very Civil.*

Probably no better instance could be given of the rapid
change in the spirit of the age, and of the conflicting ideals
which hardly gave the dramatists a suggestion as to where
they stood.

By this time Ravenscroft's activity was nearly over. There
follows in his career a lengthy period of silence, his return
to the theatre coming not until a decade had passed by. *The
Canterbury Guests, or, A Bargain Broken*, his next comedy,
was not produced at D.L. until Sept. 1694. This was followed by *The Anatomist, or, The Sham Doctor*, given at
L.I.F. about November 1696. Both are fairly amusing pieces
of work, with touches of rather superficial wit. There is a
"mad couple" in the first, imitations of the pair in *The
Careless Lovers*, and *The Anatomist* presented Underhill with
a fine acting part.

In general, I believe, no writer had more of an influence
on the usual fare of the theatre than had Ravenscroft.
A third-rate dramatist, he yet divined what was desired by
the public, and in meeting that desire he set a fashion which
many others were only too happy to follow.

Of these, Nahum Tate merits perhaps first attention. Tate
had started his dramatic career in 1678 with tragedy. Two
original pieces and three adaptations of Shakespeare had
brought him some fame. In 1682 he continued with Dryden
the second part of *Absalom and Achitophel*. Later, in 1692,
he became poet-laureate, continuing in that office until 1715.
His work was diverse. In 1686 he had written a free rendering
of Fracastoro's Latin poem, entitling it *Syphilis: A Poetical*

---

[1] It continued for another year, till 1752, at Covent Garden.

History of the French Disease: in 1696 he translated the *Psalms* with Dr Brady[1].

This popular and varied writer did not turn to comedy until his reputation was well made. At D.L. in Nov. 1684, he brought out his *A Duke and No Duke*, merely an alteration of Cockain's *Trappolin creduto principe* (1658), but altered so that it proved popular on the stage until the end of the eighteenth century. This comedy has interest for us only because it contains a song written by Sir George Etherege, and because the 1693 edition has a lengthy preface in defence of farce "With an Account of the *Personae* and *Larvae* etc. of the Ancient THEATRE." By 1693, even earlier, farce was finding champions to defend it on the grounds of classical antiquity. *Cuckold's Haven, or, An Alderman no Conjurer* (D.G. *c.* June 1685) is also an adaptation, being based on Jonson's *Eastward Hoe!* and *The Devill is an Asse*. It shows, as clearly as Ravenscroft's plays show, the weakening of the spirit of Molière, the deliberate reduction of the comedy of humours to a slight and unexalted form.

Both before and after Ravenscroft and Tate, farce found many supporters, and it is noticeable that many of them were men connected with the theatre, men who best of all could know what was demanded by the audience.

Roger Boyle, Earl of Orrery, who is better known as the originator of the heroic tragedy, presented at L.I.F. in April 1669 his comedy of *Guzman*, borrowed from a Spanish source and farcical in spirit. As a play it would seem not to merit the whole-hearted condemnation which Pepys and Sir A. W. Ward[2] have seen fit to bestow on it, although certainly its main interest for us to-day lies in its lengthy and elaborate stage-directions. *Mr Anthony* (D.G. *c.* March 1672) is of the same type of comic drama, the duel scene in Act III resembling in many ways scenes of more pronounced farces.

Amateurish and evidently harking back to Elizabethan

---

[1] An excellent study of this author against the background of his time is provided by H. F. Scott-Thomas in "Nahum Tate and the Seventeenth Century" (*ELH*, 1934, I. 250–75). He shows how characteristic was Tate of his age.

[2] *Op. cit.* III. 345.

predecessors is *Love in the Dark, or, The Man of Bus'ness* (D.L. May, 1675) by Sir Francis Fane. There is a fair song in the first act:

> *Let us turn Usurers of Time,*
> *And not mispend an Hour...*

but otherwise, with its long dull intrigues, it is not over-remarkable.

Of the type of the more modern farces is Otway's *The Cheats of Scapin* (D.G. *c.* Dec. 1676)[1] which derives wholly from Molière and probably was of some influence in the later development of the species. It is Otway's only attempt at this class of writing, his three other comedies being more Elizabethan in structure and in plot, with a fair infusion of Restoration vulgarity. Of these, *Friendship in Fashion* (D.G. April, 1678) met with applause in its own day[2], but was hissed off the stage on its revival at D.L. in 1750[3]. For *The Souldier's Fortune* (D.G. March, 1679/80) Otway went back to Molière for a theme (that of the husband agent) which, as old as Boccaccio, had appeared already in *The Fawne*, in Rhodes' *Flora's Vagaries*, and in Fane's *Love in the Dark*. The characters are negligible save the person of Sir Jolly Jumble, a figure probably suggested by Dryden's Pandarus in *Troilus and Cressida*, one of those types which display in all their fulness the horror and the degradation of certain aspects of Restoration life. The *dénouement* of this play, however, is decidedly interesting, presenting as it does the forced renunciation of a young wife to a youthful lover by an old and betrayed husband, the last of whom is treated by Otway towards the close of the play in an almost pathetic manner. *The Souldier's Fortune* was continued in *The Atheist* (D.G. *c.* July 1683) but not in a very satisfactory way.

Another farcical adaptation of Molière was fathered upon the world by Matthew Medbourne in *Tartuffe, or, The French*

---

[1] It appeared along with *Titus and Berenice*.
[2] Gildon, p. 108.
[3] It has a very cynical prologue:
I' th' next place, Ladies, there's no Bawdy in't,
No, not so much as one well-meaning Hint.

Puritan[1] (T.R. in B.St. *c.* May 1670). The original play had appeared in Paris three years previously, and Medbourne's was the first rendering into English of the ever-popular French comedy. It follows the original fairly closely, but descends, as is usual in these plays, frequently into buffoonery.

The actor-authors of this period are well headed by Thomas Betterton. Of his comedies, one, *The Woman made a Justice*, is non-extant. All we know of it is that the female justice was taken by Mrs Long[2]. Of the others, *The Counterfeit Bridegroom, or, The Defeated Widow* (D.G. *c.* Sept. 1677), if that play be indeed by Betterton[3], is but a farcical adaptation of Middleton's *No Wit, no Help, like a Woman's*. *The Amorous Widow, or, The Wanton Wife* (L.I.F. *c.* 1670), however, was, save for its indebtedness to Molière's *George Dandin, ou, Le mari confondu,* entirely written by the actor, and received praise in its own day[4]. It is a fairly well-wrought play, and although it has no brilliant wit in it, it has interesting characters in the figures of Cunninghame and Philadelphia, the amorous Lady Laycock and Barnaby Brittle. It does much to prove to us the all-round excellence of that great and deservedly honoured actor of a youthful stage[5].

The comedies of Lacy, half of the type of humours, half farces, have already been noted, but Lacy was not the only actor who stood alongside of Betterton as an actor-dramatist. Thomas Jevon, originally a performer of low-comedy parts, who assumed later on as one of his favourite characters the type of Scaramouch, presented at D.L. about March, 1686, *The Devil of a Wife, or, A Comical Transformation*, in which he himself acted the part of Jobson the Cobbler[6]. This comedy, which was exceedingly popular in its own and in later times, is purest of pure farce, and the manner in which

---

[1] The running title is "*or, The* French *Zealot.*" It was "rendered into *English* with much Addition and Advantage."

[2] *History of the English Stage,* p. 92.

[3] Montague Summers has a short article on "The Comedies of Thomas Betterton" (*NQ*, June 27, 1936, CLXX).

[4] *A Comparison between the Two Stages,* p. 11.

[5] It was frequently reprinted in the eighteenth century.

[6] It ran to seven editions by 1735 and continued on the eighteenth century acting list in Coffey's alteration as *The Devil to Pay.*

it was issued showed that the author had no great thoughts of his own abilities as a writer[1]. Jevon's friend, William Mountfort, is much more interesting and important. About December 1685 appeared at D.G. the latter's *The Life and Death of Doctor Faustus, Made into a Farce...with the Humours of Harlequin and Scaramouche*[2]. This play is an admixture of the Italian *commedia dell' arte* and the tragedy of Marlowe. Somewhat less than a half of its dialogue is from the Elizabethan play, with omissions to suit the Restoration taste. On the stage the conjuring Harlequin and the silly Scaramouche, who, by using the name of God, is for ever scaring away the spirits that the other has raised, must have been laughable enough.

Win her and Take her, or, Old Fools will be Medling (D.L. *c.* 1691), attributed to John Smyth[3], but put on the market by another low comedian, Cave Underhill, was probably indebted mainly to the comic ideas of the latter. In style it is similar to the work of Jevon. It is practically pure farce, with, as its main figures, the clownish characters of Dulhead and Waspish. Beyond a little stage hilarity, it has nothing to recommend it. Among stage writers, also, may be numbered Thomas Wright, machinist at the T.R., whose one play, *The Female Vertuoso's* (D.L. April, 1693) was confessedly an adaptation from Molière's *Les femmes savantes*, with the addition of one new character, most probably designed for Doggett. The five acts of the French piece are reduced to three in the English, which, on the whole, are not as worthless as some other renderings from the continental literatures.

Doggett himself gave to L.I.F. in April 1696 a single

---

[1] Cf. epilogue. The motto on the title-page is "*Veni, Vidi, Vici!*"

[2] It was printed in 1697, but acted between 1684 and 1688 (see Genest, I. 451).

[3] See Anthony à Wood, *Athenae Oxonienses* (ed. Bliss), IV. 601. This was not the John Smith who was the author of *Cytherea* (unacted, 1677); see Wood, *op. cit.* II. 228 and *Biographia Dramatica*, III. 411, also Coxeter's notes to Gildon, pp. 171 and 134. *Cytherea, or, The Enamouring Girdle, A New Comedy*, was licensed May 30, 1677. From the dedication it seems to have been refused at L.I.F. Coxeter's note on it is: "He tells, that it had not been presented publickly upon the stage before 'twas printed: I refer it to the impartial reader whether 'tis likely it has ever been since."

comedy called *The Country Wake*, a play which falls in with
the other farces of the period. It may be noted, however,
as an indication of the taste of this age and of that which
followed, that *The Country Wake*, although to our minds
very loose in talk and in action, was not only successful on
its first appearance but was frequently revived in the eighteenth century[1].

The last actor-dramatist of the period to be considered is
George Powell, to whom three comedies are due. The first
of these, *A Very Good Wife* (D.L. March 1692/3) is almost
negligible because of its many borrowings[2]. It seems however to have been a success in its own time[3], and for that,
and for the prologue written by Congreve for Haynes, it
deserves attention. *The Imposture Defeated, or, A Trick to
Cheat the Devil* (D.L. *c.* Sept. 1697), which he himself considered but "a triffle of a Comedy...only a slight piece of
Scribble, purely design'd for the Introduction of a little
Musick, being no more than a short week's work[4]," is hardly
worth the noting save that it represents very well a certain
type of play which was becoming more and more popular as
the century drew to its close. *The Cornish Comedy* (D.G. *c.*
June 1696), the third play given to Powell, although he possibly had a share in its composition, would seem to be not
wholly by him. The attribution appears to be due to the
fact that he published the drama. Written in the Shadwellian
style, it introduces a vast amount of singing and dancing[5],
being of the same school as *The Imposture Defeated*. The
only character worth noticing, and that purely from an
historical point of view, is Swash, the hunting squire.

The other farces of this period present a somewhat varied
collection of theatrical pieces. Mrs Behn, as has been already
noted, adopted this type of comedy in two of her productions.
The False Count, or, A New Way to play an old Game (D.G.

---

[1] In an altered form as *Flora, or, Hob in the Well*.
[2] There is much imitation of Brome's *The City Wit* and *The Court
Beggar*, besides scenes and names from *Hide Park* and *No Wit, no Help,
Like a Woman's*.
[3] See the dedication.   [4] Preface.
[5] See the "*Dialogues*" between Acts II and III, and between III and IV.

c. Nov. 1681) is a farce of the older school, laughable enough,
but weak in characterisation[1]. It is of considerable interest
only because of the final renunciation of Julia to Carlos, a
conclusion similar to that of *The Souldier's Fortune* and of
The Mall. Much more valuable historically is *The Emperor
of the Moon* (D.G. *c.* March 1686/7) which, of the newer type,
may be classed alongside of Ravenscroft's and of Mountfort's
pieces. Derived directly from *Arlequin Empereur dans le
Monde de la Lune* (1684), a comedy itself taken from the
Italian, it introduces the typical figures of the *commedia
dell' arte*—Harlequin, Scaramouch and Dr Baliardo. As a
farcical experiment, it is exceedingly interesting, especially
when considered with other similar dramas of the time: but
of intrinsic value it has none.

The sole comedy by Dryden's son, *The Husband his own
Cuckold* (L.I.F. *c.* Feb. 1695/6) is confessedly a "Hotch-
podge" "*un pasticcio* Inglese." It is a fair piece of farcical
work, and probably deserved greater success than it actually
received. Another play of the same school, Wilson's *Belphegor, or, The Marriage of the Devil* (D.G. *c.* June 1690) has
a certain interest, as being derived from the "Matchiavellian"
source which had already given *Grim, the Collier of Croydon*
(1662) and Jonson's *The Devill is an Asse.* In Wilson's hands
the story is well treated, with a mixture of the serious and
the farcical. The characters of Roderigo and of Imperia are
particularly noticeable. Finally, before we leave farce to the
neglect which intrinsically it deserves, we must turn from
Wilson, representative of an older age, and pass to Pierre
Antoine Motteux, representative of the age to come. Motteux
is one of the most interesting figures of his period, one of
the men who connects the seventeenth century with the age
of Anne. An able translator and a fine linguist, he was a
French Huguenot who had come over to London at the
Revocation of the Edict of Nantes. His chief play was a
rendering of *Don Quixote*, but he was probably more famous
in his own day for his work in acclimatising the Italian
commedia dell' arte and in furthering the development of opera.

---

[1]   This owed considerably to Molière's *Précieuses ridicules.*

His first comedy, *Love's a Jest* (L.I.F. *c.* June 1696), was an extraordinary success. It owes confessedly its main theme to an Italian play, the authorship of which is unknown. It is a fair piece of work, although lacking, as all Motteux' plays lack, brilliancy of dialogue. For us, *The Novelty, Every Act a Play, Being a Short Pastoral, Comedy, Masque, Tragedy, and Farce after the Italian Manner* (L.I.F. *c.* June 1697) is more interesting even if it is a "Hotch-podge," including as it does a poor pastoral—in octosyllabic couplets—entitled *Thyrsis*, written by Oldmixon: a comedy translated from the French by Motteux: a worthless masque of *Hercules* by the same author: an act from Filmer's *The Unnatural Brother*: and the "*Farce after the Italian Manner*," entitled *Natural Magic*. This last introduces the regular Italian characters, Pantalone, Pasquarel, Mezzetin and Columbina, and undoubtedly forms the most important part of the whole collection.

These last plays, indeed all the farces of the period, have had to be run over in a somewhat cursory fashion. As acting pieces they may have had success, but, in reading, their wit seems remarkably dull. They are all of importance, however, as showing the rapid disintegration of the late seventeenth century stage. They must be taken in consideration with the "musical" plays so speedily coming into fashion, and with the sentimental drama. The dramatic movement in France of the eighteenth century which led towards the *drame* and the *comédies à ariettes* found its counterpart here, first in the introduction of farce, sentiment and "dialogues," later in the fuller development of the "ballad opera" of the eighteenth century.

The fact that the sentimental drama is older than is usually thought must be duly emphasised. Sir A. W. Ward has stated that Steele's *The Lying Lover* (D.L. 1704) is the first sentimental comedy[1]. Ernest Bernbaum goes back nearly a decade to Cibber's *Love's Last Shift* (D.L. 1696)[2] but neither of these two plays marks the upward limits of the species. A certain allowance, of course, has to be made for the particular definition given for this unclassifiable type, and, in general,

[1] *Op. cit.* III. 493.   [2] *The Drama of Sensibility* (1915), pp. 10 and 17.

critics are not agreed upon the main characteristics of the school. Sir A. W. Ward has found its root in "pity[1]," Ernest Bernbaum in a certain "confidence in the goodness of human nature[2]." Probably neither has quite included all the varieties of the type. Pity and this confidence in the goodness of human nature are, moreover, rather characteristics of the particular drama of sentiment which arose after 1740 in imitation of the French school of Didérot. Even Cibber and Steele do not display much appreciation of either.

At bottom, the sentimental drama, early and late, appears to be distinguished rather by the presentation of a moral problem. Neither the comedy of humours nor the comedy of manners asks any questions: both exist solely for laughter, and, if both lash vice as their defenders warmly averred they did, it was not for the purpose of lashing that they had their being, but purely and simply for the sake of the ridiculous and the witty. Lack of any moral code is the real, if not the theoretical, characteristic of the intrigue, humours and manners schools, as the presence of a definite "moral," even if it was only a seventeenth or an eighteenth century moral, is of the sentimental[3].

All through the Restoration period sporadic attempts had been made to chasten the drama but the more pronounced "moral" works did not make their appearance in any numbers until after 1680. Tuke's *The Adventures of Five Hours* (L.I.F. 1663), Stapylton's *The Slighted Maid* (L.I.F. 1663) and *The Stepmother* (L.I.F. 1663), Porter's *Carnival* (T.R. in B.St. 1663), Flecknoe's *Love's Kingdom* (1664), Shadwell's *The Royal Shepherdess* (L.I.F. 1669), Leanerd's *The Country Innocence* (D.L. 1677) and *The Counterfeits* (D.G. 1678)—all profess to have moral aims, to present no "bawdy," to indulge in no loose wit, and in none of them are those professions cynical or hypocritic. During the last years of the century such plays increase in number. Mrs Behn and D'Urfey, as we shall see, produced many. Ravenscroft paid tribute to the new style in *Dame Dobson* (D.G. 1683), Southerne in *The*

---

[1] *Op. cit.* III. 495.　　　　　　　　[2] *Op. cit.* 2 and 144 n.
[3] This agrees with J. Harrington Smith's "exemplary comedy" (*op. cit.* pp. 230-1).

Disappointment (D.L. 1684), Shadwell and Motteux in not a few dramas. From without, too, the attacks on the drama, which had been going on spasmodically since ever the theatres opened, found their culmination in the last years of the century. From 1690 onwards we can trace, in critical dicta, the growing moral sense, a moral sense that was not aroused by, but rather only given full expression in, Collier's outburst of 1698.

At the same time, it must be observed that the age was passing through a period of extremes. If, in some ways, Restoration licence was being cloaked over or attacked, a new viciousness was arising more ugly than any flagrancies of Rochester or of Sedley. In many ways the later seventeenth and the early eighteenth centuries had about them precisely the same immoral elements which the Restoration period proper had: they only clothed those elements a little better in sophisticated phrase and in easy philosophy. Whatever fifth-act repentances they may have had in the hands of Cibber or of Steele, the rakes of the age of William and of Anne were as hardened, heartless sinners as any of the days of Charles. In this way, sentimentalism was but the artistic clothing assumed to counter puritan prudery: it was a piece of hypocritical deceit. The comedy of sentiment, save in the case of a very few authors, was but a palliation used to cover an even greater callousness and viciousness in the age.

This callousness and viciousness are nowhere better to be seen than in the notorious and ugly "girl epilogues" and child "dialogues" which gave, in the last years of the century, piquancy to many a play. The men and the women of 1685–1700 who professed to abhor the immoralities of Charles' court appeared to love hearing the enunciation by lisping infants of sexual ideas not usually referred to even by adults in polite society. Many of the dialogues introduced into the comedies of 1680–1700 were intended for girls not in their teens. The instances, which I have already mentioned, from D'Urfey's *The Comical History of Don Quixote* are neither worse nor better than scores of others. Children, too, made up for the comparative innocence of the body of the play,

18   NED

by uttering the most filthy obscenities in the licence of the epilogue. In Powell's *Bonduca* (D.L. 1695) particularly objectionable verses are "spoken by Miss *Denny Chock*, But Six Years Old." The next year this Miss Chock spoke the epilogue to the same author's *The Cornish Comedy* (D.G. 1696), uttering there the most atrocious sentiments: and two years later (when she was eight years of age) she delivered the epilogue to *The Revengeful Queen* (D.L. 1698) by William Phillips. A Miss Howard similarly closed off Dilke's *The Lover's Luck* (L.I.F. 1695) and a Miss Bradshaw Mrs Manley's *The Royal Mischief* (L.I.F. 1696) as well as *The Deceiver Deceiv'd* (L.I.F. 1697) of Mrs Pix. Miss Cross, too, who ran off in her girlhood to France, came in useful for many a dramatist wanting something *risqué* wherewith to spice the dullness of his work. Young girls, of course, had appeared on the early Restoration stage, but, for the most part, the early Restoration drama is an adult drama: the actresses were nearly all women of an age capable of looking after themselves. The girl epilogue as a regular addition to comedy or to tragedy did not come in until after 1680, the writer of the *Lenten Prologue refus'd by the Players* (1682) informing us that

> '*Tis now no Jest to hear young Girls talk Baudy.*

The very expression of such a fact proves to us that the presence of young girls in the theatre was somewhat of an innovation.

Such a brief consideration as this of the age as being probably more immoral than before and yet full of moral sentiment, and of the sentimental comedy itself as presenting a genuine moral problem, as being a hypocritical cloak put over vice and as giving rise to violent reactions, may well lead us to an analysis of the growth of the species.

Peculiarly enough Mrs Behn was the first in this age to raise her voice against the fashionable vices of the time, to preach a return to more natural modes of life, and to present a genuine problem in her comedies. *The Amorous Prince, or, The Curious Husband* (L.I.F. *c.* May, 1671) and *The Young*

King, or, The Mistake (D.G. *c.* Sept. 1679) both urge the delight of sinless nature:

> How much more charming are the works of Nature
> Than the Productions of laborious Art!

cries a character in I. ii of the latter. This tendency away from the civilised world, and towards an untutored freedom, so premonitory of the ideas of Rousseau in the eighteenth century, is expressed again in the character of the Indian queen in *The Widow Ranter* (D.L. 1689). Her cry was to be taken up in later years: even in the seventeenth century itself Dryden in *King Arthur* (D.G. 1691) could call out:

> O artless Love, where the Soul moves the Tongue,
> And only Nature speaks what Nature thinks!

and Shadwell could present to us the figure of Eugenia in *The Volunteers* (D.L. 1692).

In Mrs Behn's *The Forc'd Marriage, or, The Jealous Bridegroom* (L.I.F. Dec. 1670) we are confronted with the second aspect of the incipient sentimental school. *The Forc'd Marriage* is a romantic serio-drama, scened in an Arcadian France. It is not its scene, however, or its characters that interest us, but its purpose. That purpose is a solemn one. The play is written about a moral problem, a problem of social life which evidently weighed heavily upon the authoress. The plot deals mainly with the forced marriage of Erminia, loved by Philander, to Alcippus. The last-mentioned, stung by jealousy, strangles her, but not, as he thinks, fatally. In the end she reappears, to wed Philander, Alcippus being paired off a second time with Galatea, Philander's sister. Crude as this plot is, we can see below it a strain of thought which was later to be developed more clearly and more realistically both in the English theatre and in the eighteenth century *drame* of France.

The same, or a similar, theme appeared in *The Town-Fopp, or, Sir Timothy Tawdrey* (D.G. *c.* Sept. 1676) and in *The Luckey Chance, or, An Alderman's Bargain* (D.L. *c.* April, 1686). The former of these is a comedy of intrigue, largely derived from Wilkin's *The Miseries of Inforst Marriage*. It like *The Forc'd Marriage*, is chiefly interesting, not for its dialogue or its plot, but for this attempt to relate a moral problem to the real life of the day.

> "Till then," says Bellmour, "I'll let mistaken Parents know
> The mischiefs that ensue a broken vow."

The Luckey Chance is more farcical, but again it reproduces that peculiar kind of moral seriousness which was so marked a trait of Mrs Behn. Love, with her, is something more than simple sensual passion, and mere cuckolding does not suffice for her lovers. Her women, however, are, for the most part, much weaker in constancy than her men, although Bellmour in *The Town-Fopp* is a noticeable example to the contrary. Bellmour of *The Luckey Chance*, on the other hand, returns from abroad to find Leticia, his former love, about to marry Sir Feeble Fainwou'd, the thought of which sends him into despair. Gayman, his friend, advises him to let the marriage go through, and then renew his protestations to the lady, to which Bellmour's reply is decidedly interesting:—"Oh Heavens! Leticia marry him! and lie with him!" The very phrase, rough as it is with Restoration roughness, betokens a feeling which in the majority of the contemporaries of Mrs Behn was entirely lacking[1]. In this play, moreover, Lady Fulbank is made the mouthpiece for the theories of the authoress against forced marriages. "Oh how fatal," she cries,

> Oh how fatal are forc'd Marriages!
> How many Ruins one such Match pulls on!
> Had I but kept my Sacred vows to *Gayman*,
> How happy had I been—how prosperous he!
> Whilst now I languish in a loath'd Embrace,
> Pine out my Life with Age—Consumptions, Coughs[2]...

thus emphasising the Bellmour-Leticia plot more keenly.

The figure of the Indian queen in *The Widdow Ranter, or, The History of Bacon in Virginia* (D.L. *c.* Nov. 1689) has already been drawn attention to, but the play as a whole is

---

[1] Apart from this, the comedy is largely of the style of manners and intrigue. The scene of Lady Fulbank and the reference to a "canvas Bag full of wooden Ladles" is very reminiscent of Otway's *The Souldier's Fortune*.

[2] I. ii, reading "Consumptions" for "Consumptious."

not so sentimental as are those others I have mentioned above. As a play, too, it hardly seems to merit the praise which Genest gives to it. It is a peculiar admixture of farce and intrigue, tricked out with some stale humours and a dash of the sentimental in that one pathetic figure. Mrs Behn's last play, *The Younger Brother, or, The Amorous Jilt* (D.L. *c.* Feb. 1695/6) is also a poor piece of writing, but again has interest for its serious, and in places almost bitter, character. It reveals, as do the others, the real worth and spirit of this authoress, an authoress who unfortunately prostituted her gifts in many an intrigue play for the purpose of achieving success in a licentious theatre[1].

Noticeable as being produced about the same time as Mrs Behn's first plays are the three comedies of John Leanerd, all "moral" in tone, although not so pronouncedly sentimental as the dramas just considered. *The Country Innocence, or, The Chamber-Maid turn'd Quaker* (D.L. March, 1677), which is but a slight adaptation of Brewer's *The Country Girl*, is a mediocre piece of work, but has value for its theme. *The Rambling Justice, or, The Jealous Husbands. With the Humours of Sir John Twiford* (D.L. *c.* March 1677/8) is more valuable intrinsically. Although part of it is taken from Middleton's *More Dissemblers besides Women*, it works out its intrigue theme with a strange mixture of the flagrantly indecent and of the moralistic sentimental. *The Counterfeits* (D.G. May, 1678) is only ascribed to this author, and is notable as being the precursor, in plot at least, of Cibber's *She Wou'd and She Wou'd Not* (D.L. 1702). This play, too, has a decidedly moral tone and again presents hints of the sentimental.

Along with Leanerd's three comedies might be mentioned *Sir Salomon, or, The Cautious Coxcomb* (L.I.F. *c.* 1669) of John Caryl, a surprisingly moral play containing a well-drawn psychological study in Sir Salomon Single, as well as Revet's *The Town Shifts, or, The Suburb-Justice* (L.I.F. *c.* March, 1670/1), already mentioned for its Elizabethan re-

---

[1] On "moral" qualities in Mrs Behn and other early writers see De Witt C. Croissant, "Early Sentimental Comedy" (*Parrott Presentation Volume* (1935), pp. 47–72).

miniscences, which has been singled out as an early sentimental comedy[1].

At as early a date as this, however, there were many who
were following along the lines of embryonic sentimentalism.
In 1675 Crowne was putting into the mouths of his characters,
in the very midst of Restoration licence, sentimental thoughts
not unlike many later ones of the eighteenth century. Crowne,
indeed, is as symptomatic a dramatist of the age as any
Although he had started his dramatic career fully four years
before, his first comedy was *The Countrey Wit*, which appeared at D.G. about Jan. 1675/6. Based on *Le Sicilien, ou
L'amour peintre* of Molière, and scened in contemporary
London ("*Pall Mall*, 1675") it gives a realistic picture of
fashionable life in the seventeenth century. The plot hinges
around a favourite Restoration theme—the love of a girl
(Christina) for a debauched rake (Ramble), and their combined cheating of the girl's formal fiancé (Sir Mannerly
Shallow). In the course of his courtship of Christina, Ramble
falls in with not only one or two other and more dubious love
adventures. He is the typical hero of the comedy of manners,
save that he is a trifle more brutal and sensual than they: yet
on occasion he can suddenly fall into moralisation: "How like
a barbarous Villain do I use that divine Creature Mrs
Christina!" he cries. "If I were fifty *Rambles* bound together, I had not merit enough for her Love, and I, though
I am but one, yet parcel myself out every minute to fifty
Women; yet 'tis not for want of Love to her, for the enjoyment of other Women, give (sic) me not so much Delight as
a Smile from her." That is the sentiment of a hero of 1750,
and, even though it is followed here by the cynical thought,
"And yet, I'gad, the enjoyment of her would not keep me
from the chase of other Women," we realise that it is highly
premonitory of moral sentimentalism to come.

Crowne was not destined to attempt comedy for another
ten years, he engaging himself with heroic tragedies and with
adaptations of Shakespeare, and when he did return to the

---

[1] For references relating to this play and giving an analysis of its
sentimental qualities see *supra*, p. 216.

comic theatre it was to present purely political plays, framed
mostly in the manners style, and permitting of moralisations
only on occasion. *City Politiques* (D.L. Jan. 1682/3)[1] is
closely to be related to D'Urfey's and to Mrs Behn's plays
of the same date. Its whole *raison d'être* lies in a bitter attack
upon Shaftesbury, and to a modern palate its semi-incestuous
attachments and its presentment of Florio, one who counterfeits "Disease his Vices brought upon him" make it not very
pleasant reading. Equally political is *Sir Courtly Nice, or,
It Cannot Be* (D.L. May, 1685) fashioned at Charles' request
from the *No puede esser* of Augustin Moreto, a play that had
served nearly twenty years previously as a model for the
Tarugo's Wiles of Sir Thomas St Serfe[2], but here the loose
atmosphere of the preceding comedy has given place to a
strictly moral atmosphere. Farewel is a pure character, and
the women, Leonora and Violante, are less mobile than their
contemporary sisters on the stage. Satire of "this corrupt
Age" shows clearly enough the tendency of the play as a
whole. About March, 1689/90, again after an incursion into
tragedy, came *The English Frier, or, The Town Sparks* (D.L.),
another violently political drama. It is a fairly good comedy,
with a truly excellent scene in the fifth act between Pansy
and Father Finical (bishop *in partibus infidelium*). The sentimental tone is here seen somewhat strengthened, as for
example in Lord Wiseman's remarks in the first act concerning Young Ranter. *The English Frier* was Crowne's last
noticeable work, *The Married Beau, or, The Curious Im-*

---

[1] Until recently only a guess at the date of this play could be made.
Biographia Dramatica gives it as 1675: Maidment and Logan as 1688:
Sir A. W. Ward as 1682. All doubt is set at rest by three entries in the
Lord Chamberlain's books. On June 15, 1682, a "new Comedy" of
Mr Crowne's was licensed (L.C. 5/144, p. 247). Eleven days later, how-
ever, on June 26, the Lord Chamberlain wrote a hurried order to Betterton:
"Whereas I did signifie His Ma^tes pleasure in my Order dated ye 15th of
June instant that a New Play of Mr Crownes called (blank) should be
lyncensed & Acted at His Royall Highnesse Theatre I doe now againe
signifie His Ma^tes pleasure that you forbeare acting ye said play vntill
further Order." The further order did not come until Dec. 18, 1682,
when leave was given to act *The City Politiques*, banned on June 26. In
all probability it did not appear until the commencement of the new year.

[2] Which Dennis believes Crowne did not see until he was well through
with his comedy (*Original Letters*, 1721, I. 52).

pertinent, which followed at D.L. about April 1694, being but a light farce taken from the ever-popular tale of Cervantes.

Crowne's value as a writer of comedy will rest on his wit, which, if not so refined as that of Congreve, is yet akin to that of the manners school, and on those touches of sentiment which bind him to the new school of dramatists.

So far we have traced the very faintest glimmerings of sentimentalism in the first decades of the Restoration period. By 1680, however, the new movement was growing in strength. By that year Otway had produced *The Orphan*, a play the extraordinary success of which during the following century shows clearly enough its tendency, while Lee in *The Princess of Cleve*[1] (D.G. *c.* 1681) and Banks in *Vertue Betray'd* (D.G. 1682) and in *The Unhappy Favourite* (D.L. 1681) accompanied him in the realms of tragedy by devising tearful and sentimental situations replete with that pity-moving and thought-moving quality inherent in the sentimental drama. Comedy, too, was rapidly moving along the same lines. More and more "moral" plays were being produced. Mrs Behn's experiments and Ravenscroft's *Dame Dobson* (D.G. 1683) have already been noticed. In 1689 Shadwell contributed something to the species in *Bury Fair* and later in *The Scowrers*, and he was only one of many who, belonging to other schools of drama, felt the impress of the sentimental. Chief of these undoubtedly was Thomas D'Urfey. He more than anyone else aided in urging forward the progress of the new style.

Thomas D'Urfey truly holds a most peculiar position in the history of Restoration drama. Endowed with considerable ability, he eschewed the wit of Congreve for external farce. Gifted with originality, he based nearly all his works on other plays, English or foreign, earning thus the contempt of Langbaine. "He is accounted by some," says that critic with disdain, "For an Admirable Poet, but it is by those who are not acquainted much with Authors, and therefore are de-

---

[1] T. B. Stroup ("*The Princess of Cleve* and Sentimental Comedy," *Review of English Studies*, 1935, XI. 200–3) stresses the sentimental quality of this play: his argument is, however, regarded as exaggerated by J. Harrington Smith (*op. cit.* pp. 98 and 104).

ceiv'd by Appearances[1]." A French Huguenot, he attached himself mostly to the Tory interest, and, besides his thirty odd plays, produced an innumerable number of songs and ditties, mostly of an ephemeral, because of a contemporary and political, interest. Broad farce as most of his comedies are, they are not wholly negligible, Farquhar, even, not disdaining to appropriate ideas from some of them for his more finished productions.

So far as plot is concerned, all of D'Urfey's plays are adaptations of earlier theatrical material. *Madam Fickle, or, The Witty False One* (D.G. Nov. 1676) can thus be laid aside as being nothing more than a series of incidents borrowed from Marmion, Marston, Mayne, and Rowley, sometimes, it is to be confessed, rather skilfully put together. Suggestions from Elizabethan plays occur also in D'Urfey's second comedy, *The Fool turn'd Critick* (D.L. Nov. 1676). This is a quite readable farce, marred by an over use of the theatrical disguise device. Largely Jonsonian in its characters, it possesses, even more than the former play, a certain amount of somewhat pawky humour. *A Fond Husband, or, The Plotting Sisters* followed at D.G. in May 1676, and was well received. This might be taken as a specimen of the intrigue play veering to farce. It is humorous enough, but, like the majority of this species, artificial in character-drawing and in plot-weaving alike. D'Urfey was a prolific writer, one of the most prolific, indeed, of the whole period, and other comedies followed fast on the appearance of these his first endeavours. *Trick for Trick, or, The Debauch'd Hypocrite* (D.L. *c.* March 1677/8) was, certainly, but an alteration of Fletcher's *Monsieur Thomas*, but with *Squire Oldsapp, or, The Night Adventurers* (D.G. *c.* June 1678) he turned, with

---

[1] Kathleen M. Lynch ("Thomas D'Urfey's Contribution to Sentimental Comedy," *Philological Quarterly*, 1930, IX. 249–59) interestingly discusses this author's position as an early exponent of what was to become a dominant dramatic form—particularly in *The Virtuous Wife, Love for Money, The Richmond Heiress* and *The Campaigners*. His anticipation in non-dramatic verse of later Gothicism is examined by W. Lee Ustick ("Tom D'Urfey and the Graveyard," *Modern Philology*, 1939, XXXVI. 303–6). For a general account of his work see R. S. Forsythe, *A Study of the Plays of Thomas D'Urfey* (1916–17).

his usual borrowings in the subordinate portions, to an individual main plot, much involved, and, with the possible exception of Welford, "*a wild, debauch'd Town-Spark*," practically wholly peopled by Jonsonian characters. It is decidedly weaker than *A Fond Husband* or *The Fool turn'd Critick.*

The Virtuous Wife, or, Good Luck at Last (D.G. *c.* Sept. 1679) goes for inspiration to more modern sources. Its plot was quite evidently inspired by Dryden's *Marriage a la Mode* (L.I.F. 1672) and its main theme, dealing with the marriage of Olivia to Beverley under the impression that he was Beauford, has reminiscences of the conceptions of Mrs Behn. The play is farcical, but there is an incipient problem underlying the fun, a problem not fully expressed, but showing the tendency of D'Urfey's art[1]. It is from this time indeed that we note a change in his comic plays. In September two years later (1681)[2] appeared at D.L. *Sir Barnaby Whigg, or, No Wit like a Woman's*, a purely party play, Sir Barnaby being a "*Phanatical Rascal, one of* Oliver's *Knights.*" It is, however, not so farcical as his earlier works, and in a way marks a progress on the part of D'Urfey towards presentation of characters of the manners type—particularly in the persons of Wilding, Townly and Livia—in another, as I shall endeavour to indicate, it marks a step towards the elaboration of sentiment.

This political comedy was followed up in Jan. 1681/2, with *The Royalist*, a violent outburst against the Whigs which Genest says was well received[3], contrary to the hint in the preface. It is written in blank verse and in prose, the scene being London in Commonwealth times with members of the Sequestration Committee in the cast. It is a fair production, but very loose in morals, looser indeed in our eyes when we remember that D'Urfey was trying to hold up a duly white-washed picture of the Cavaliers. Like Mrs Behn again, D'Urfey, after those political dramas, kept silent for a year or two, his next comedy, *The Banditti, or, A Ladies*

---

[1] Apparently it was a huge success: cf. among other references that in the anonymous *Wit for Money* (1691, p. 12).

[2] There is no edition of 1679, as has been stated.

[3] I. 355.

Distress (D.L. *c.* Feb. 1685/6) not appearing till nearly four years had elapsed. Based partly on the novel of *Don Fenise* which had already been utilised by Mrs Behn, one part of it, that dealing with Don Antonio, Elvira, Laura and Don Ferdinand, is closely allied to *The Dutch Lover*. It is a true comedy of Spanish intrigue, with rather much matter in it and hence unduly complicated. This may have been the reason why, although it is well-written, it was unsuccessful on the stage[1]. A similarly cold reception was given to *A Fool's Preferment, or, The Three Dukes of Dunstable* (D.G. *c.* April, 1688), the songs of which were set by Purcell. Based partially on Fletcher's *The Noble Gentleman*, it introduces a "Bassett scene" or two, professedly designed to satirise the noble art of gaming.

With this play fitly closes the second period of D'Urfey's art. It shows him tentatively feeling at a new species of dramatic expression which was to lead him later to attempts in the sentimental comedy proper. The relation between his career and that of Aphra Behn is one which, for an understanding of the age, must be kept closely in mind. Not only do their dramatic productions peculiarly coalesce, but a study of those productions proves to us the correspondence that undoubtedly exists between the political excitement of 1681–2 and the rise of the sentimental drama. Both of the writers mentioned, about the same year, 1681, drew comedy from the pure realms of intrigue and of wit, down to the arena of politics, thus more or less relating it to life's affairs. Politics have little enough to do with morals or moralisations, but once comedy had taken it as its mission to "puff" opposing parties, or to take sides on national issues, it was but a short step ere it came to treat of social and hence of domestic questions and aims.

Practically all D'Urfey's last plays show traces, greater or less, of sentimentalism. *Love for Money, or, The Boarding School* (D.L. *c.* Dec. 1690) was a fair success in its time[2],

---

[1] See the dedication.
[2] In the eighteenth century it was revived in 1708 and in 1718. It was altered by Coffey in 1733 as *The Boarding House Romps, or, The Sham Captain*.

and has peculiar value for us in connection with the points referred to above. It is one of the first of our Restoration plays to exhibit an interest in "local colour"[1] and it is decidedly modern in revealing through the romantic Merriton and Mirtilla plot elements of a melodramatic kind as well as distinct features of the sentimental comedy[2]. The former of the two characters just mentioned is the regular serious, emotional, philosophic young man of the later drama, just as Mirtilla is the typically pure and misused heroine, rendered happy at the end[3].

In *The Richmond Heiress, or, A Woman once in the Right* (D.L. *c.* April 1693) we find the sentimental note so apparent in the last-mentioned play even deeper and more pronounced[4]. The last speeches of Fulvia and of Sophronia might have come from a drama of 1750, and the former's rejection of mankind has something in it of the later temper. As a work of art, however, it lacks the individuality of *Love for Money*.

When taken into consideration with these sentimental productions, D'Urfey's other works of the same period have a decided interest as showing the lack of fixity in the age, the continual complication of diverse ideals. *The Marriage-Hater Match'd* (D.L. Jan. 1691/2) is, certainly, of interest for little more than its Elizabethan, and particularly for its Shakespearian reminiscences[5], but the three parts of *Don Quixote* and *The Campaigners* deserve more thorough atten-

---

[1] In the preface D'Urfey stated he lived all the summer at a boarding school in order to get his ideas and atmosphere.

[2] Particularly in v. iii; Merriton, hearing that Mirtilla has become rich, has scruples about marrying her, for fear he should be accused of intriguing after her money. J. Harrington Smith (*op. cit.* pp. 131–2, 139), however, believes that D'Urfey was not writing this scene seriously.

[3] This play in particular and D'Urfey in general, came in for a fairly severe attack in *Wit for Money, or, Poet Stutter: A Dialogue Between Smith, Johnson, and Poet Stutter. Containing Reflections on some late Plays; and particularly on Love for Money, or, The Boarding School* (1691). This accuses D'Urfey of plot-stealing and of general folly and conceit. He is styled there "a conceited, touchy, illiterate, pragmatical Nothing" (p. 30). This piece is interesting in many ways, but is too bitter to be taken very seriously.

[4] It was well received (Gildon, pp. 51–2).

[5] Cf. Forsythe, *op. cit.* p. 86. In iv. iii Lady Subtle declares: "I'll wear thee here, here next my Heart, where thou shalt grow for ever" —an obvious echo of Duncan's words in *Macbeth*.

tion[1]. Peculiarly, when we consider the movement of D'Urfey's art as expressed in these latter plays, *The Comical History of Don Quixote* (Parts I and II, D.G. May 1694; Part III, D.L. *c.* Nov. 1695) was so licentious that it was given a slightly doubtful reception on the stage. I have already referred to certain scenes and songs in that play, or series of plays, and have indicated my belief that the Mary Buxome scenes were objected to on hypocritical grounds, while nothing but pleasure was gained by the contemporary audiences from the indecent ditties song by Miss Cross. These three parts Collier saw fit to pillory in his famous invective and D'Urfey was actually prosecuted for profanity in May, 1698[2]. As a series of plays, the set is a failure. D'Urfey has done as much as he could possibly have done with his material, but a fantastic novel does not present fit matter for a play. One might as well think of dramatising *Tristram Shandy* as of making the novel of Cervantes into a comedy.

The Intrigues at Versailles, or, A Jilt in all Humours[3] (L.I.F. *c.* Feb. 1696/7) is not a particularly interesting work, either for plot or for language, but *The Campaigners, or, The Pleasant Adventures at Brussels* (D.L. *c.* June 1698) has points of value. It contains, in the first place, D'Urfey's reply to Collier in the shape of *A Familiar Preface upon a Late Reformer of the Stage*, which, as an attempt at critical defence, is certainly a weak enough affair. In the second place, we cannot regard *The Campaigners* as anything else but a flagrant outburst on the part of the author in opposition to the attack made upon him. The play is immoral, indecent, vulgar: scene after scene of crudest realism is put before the eyes of the spectators: and yet even here the author has had to succumb to the new forces at work. Back as we are in the graceless atmosphere of earlier Restoration days, there is, particularly in the words of Colonel Dorange, sure evidence of the altered tone. If comedy sinned now, it sinned, not

---

[1] An analysis of the relations between the novel and the plays may be found in Forsythe, *op. cit.* I. 101.

[2] E. Gosse, *Life of Congreve* (1888), p. 119.

[3] Not "*In all her Humours*," as Genest gives it (II. 119).

unconsciously as Etherege had done, but with a full realisation of its errors, with a guilty glance around as if it feared the blow that was about to fall.

By this time, of course, Cibber had appeared and with him the acknowledged reign of the sentimental comedy. *Love's Last Shift* (D.L. Jan. 1695/6) is typical, not only of the whole personality of the actor-author, but of what were to be the main characteristics of this type of drama for several years to come. Undoubtedly the most penetrating criticism passed upon it was that of Congreve who declared that it "had only in it a great many Things that were like Wit, that were in reality not Wit[1]." This comedy inaugurated definitely the Cibberian epoch of comedy, although it was, as we have seen, not alone in owing a great part of its success to "the mere Moral Delight receiv'd from the Fable." Like some comedies of D'Urfey and others it merely aided in standardising that special code of dramatic morals which set a superficial veneer over manners not far removed from those of the court of Charles. The fifth act conversion atoned for all. Such superficial, and, to our eyes, hypocritical, methods of morality are hardly likely to please a modern public, and often we feel more annoyed, as Fielding felt annoyed, with the sham of virtue than with the most flagrant exhibition of vice. The age still enjoyed its evil, gallant heroes, as Cibber himself confesses in a somewhat apologetic epilogue to this particular play, where he refers to the unlooked-for conversion of his sinning lover:

> *But then again,*
> *He's lewd for above four Acts, Gentlemen!*

Possibly no other quotation so aptly sums up the thought of the age[2].

Cibber's genius was by no means of the quality of Etherege or of Congreve. Less deep, less artistic, apt to be fluttered by praise and ever with abundant self-conceit, he was not

---

[1] Lowe's *Cibber*, I. 220.

[2] *Love's Last Shift* was acted on the recommendation of Southerne. It was last revived at Covent Garden in 1763. Dennis in his *Original Letters, Familiar, Moral, and Critical* (1721), pp. 138–143, casts doubt upon the authorship of this comedy, but apparently without any just cause.

content with the few carefully-worked masterpieces of those authors; on the success of his first play he had naught to do but rush into hasty productivity, a productivity which extended to the age of Anne and after. His other seventeenth century piece, however, *Woman's Wit, or, The Lady in Fashion* (D.L. *c.* Dec. 1696) is a poor piece of work[1]: his best plays belong to the later age.

With Cibber we are in the company of a new race of authors, authors who, like Pierre Antoine Motteux, were to drive forward the sentimental drama on its triumphal career during the eighteenth century, were to inaugurate, too, that dramatic era of song, dance and show, weaker, more trivial and less entertaining, than the song and show of the heroic tragedy or of the Restoration comedy. Everywhere in the theatrical world the elements of disintegration are only too evident. Pantomime had already begun, and the comic opera. It required only a little to send comedy careering like a mad country girl along that slightly vulgar and certainly very inartistic path of noise and spectacle which includes the ballets and the pasticcios of the eighteenth century. Cibber and Farquhar and Vanbrugh, each in his own way, kept the spirit of humour alive for a little, as did later Fielding and Moore and Sheridan and Goldsmith, but the free expression of pure laughter, untouched by thought or by conscience, unfed by musical novelties, had passed away for ever. The halcyon days of the comedy of wit were gone.

---

[1] This owes to Mountfort's *Greenwich Park* and to Carlisle's *The Fortune Hunters*. It was apparently suppressed by the author in later years. The original contract with Rich for its acting is given in Appendix B.

SUPPLEMENTARY TO
CHAPTER THREE

The volume of critical investigation devoted to Restoration tragedy and heroic drama has, naturally, been far exceeded by that devoted to the comedy of the time—partly because this form of theatrical expression more harmoniously agreed with the temper of its age and therefore succeeded in coming nearer to perfection of utterance, partly because the present century has witnessed a remarkable rehabilitation on the stage of Etherege, Wycherley and Congreve. While it is true that at least one critic has been bold enough to condemn all these plays as dull[1], evidence of the esteem in which the late seventeenth-century comedies are now held needs no stressing.

The recent studies of this subject have undoubtedly aided us considerably towards assessing rightly what the Restoration dramatists sought to accomplish[2]. On the comic spirit in general as it is exemplified in these plays much has been written, and, in addition, particularly useful surveys have been provided concerning the playwrights' attitude towards such basic topics as youth and age[3]. The surveys confirm our

[1] See *supra*, p. 1, and also Basil Williams ("Artificial Comedy," *TLS*, Jan. 12, 1928).

[2] Bartholow V. Crawford ("High Comedy in Terms of Restoration Practice," *Philological Quarterly*, 1929, VIII. 339–47) attempts to determine the contemporary definition and suggests that the comedy of manners was seen in this time as determined by (1) concentration on high society, (2) uniformity of tone with respect to the social code, and (3) emphasis upon wit. Henry Ten Eyck Perry, in *The Comic Spirit in Restoration Drama* (1925), studies the work of the major dramatists in terms of their attitudes towards the social world in which they lived. From another point of view, with special reference to the attack upon the stage at the close of the century, this is also the theme of Joseph Wood Krutch's *Comedy and Conscience after the Restoration* (1924). Bonamy Dobrée's *Restoration Comedy* (1924) is more concerned with comic style. J. Palmer's older study, *The Comedy of Manners* (1913) still has prime value, and there are good sections on this subject in Ashley H. Thorndike's *English Comedy* (1929).

[3] Elizabethan Mignon, *Crabbed Age and Youth: The Old Men and Women in the Restoration Comedy of Manners* (1947), and John Harrington Smith, *The Gay Couple in Restoration Comedy* (1948).

knowledge of the narrow interests displayed by the dramatic authors, their callous contempt of anything outside their own world of youth and their constant battle to maintain their code. It is now clear that the Restoration period started with what was in effect a parity of the sexes, with the young mistress a fit challenger to the young gallant, but that by about 1675 the latter, becoming ever more libertine, had assumed such prominence as to induce the ladies to reconsider their attitude[1]. Taking the cue from *The Amorous Widow* (L.I.F. *c.* 1670), the playwrights thereafter tended to make their treatment of sex-comedy ever more and more cynical while the feminine part of the audience struggled to impose new standards.

This consideration of the comedy of manners in relation to the life from which it arose raises in a fresh aspect the long-debated problem concerning the "realism" or the "artificiality" of the scenes and characters set upon the stage[2]. It has not been difficult to demonstrate that many among the involved and complex comic scenes may easily be paralleled by similar situations in real life[3]. The situations may seem to our eyes to be far removed from what might happen in actuality, yet events of a similar kind did occur. On the other hand, there is equally good evidence to show that, in using such situations, the dramatists treated them freely, always subserving a theatrical purpose; and it seems likely that the whole comic scene depicted for us in these plays may be regarded in the same way—as a theatricalising or idealising

---

[1] In addition to the book by J. Harrington Smith cited above, see his article "Shadwell, the Ladies, and the Change in Comedy" (*Modern Philology*, 1948, XLVI. 24–33).

[2] W. Heldt has a useful "Chronological and Critical Review of the Appreciation and Condemnation of the Comic Dramatists of the Restoration and Orange Periods" (*Neophilologus*, 1923, VIII. 39–59, 109–28, 197–204).

[3] G. M. Trevelyan ("Artificial Comedy," *TLS*, Jan. 5, 1928) quotes from a contemporary trial in which both the events and the language show how "artificial" (by our standards) was the conduct of society at that time: similar evidence is added by T. A. Lacey (*id.* March 15, 1928). Still ampler proof has more recently been provided by Gellert Spencer Alleman in *Matrimonial Law and the Materials of Restoration Comedy* (1942).

of the real[1]. This fundamentally is the truth seen by Charles Lamb: since the comedy is an idealising or intellectualising of life, the world of emotion is left behind us and we are permitted for a space to put all moral values aside[2]. The truth is well expressed by an author who has devoted a special study to the Restoration wits and whose knowledge of their lives and works well qualifies him to distinguish the real and the ideal[3]:

Here is no question of realism; Etherege seized upon and embodied in his play not the real, day by day life of Whitehall, but the life which Whitehall was pleased to imagine it led. Individual items may be factual, but the total picture is a comic illusion.

On the other hand, the licences taken by Restoration comedy were responsible for the very general attack upon it which came at the end of the century, and this attack has of late been more fully examined than it had been in the past[4]. At one time it

---

[1] Elmer Edgar Stoll has been the most emphatic champion of the anti-realistic interpretation of Restoration comedy: see his "The Beau Monde at the Restoration" (*Modern Language Notes*, 1934, XLIX. 425–32) and "The 'Real Society' in Restoration Comedy: Hymeneal Pretenses" (*id.* 1943, LVIII. 175–81), as well as his chapter on "Literature and Life" in *Shakespeare Studies* (1927) and his essay, "Literature and Life Again" (*PMLA*, 1932, XLVII).

[2] An excellent analysis and defence of Lamb's views appear in an article by Walter E. Houghton, Jr., "Lamb's Criticism of Restoration Comedy" (*ELH*, 1943, X. 61–72). The same quality in the drama of the time is traceable in the use the dramatists made of apparently real settings. Richard H. Perkinson ("Topographical Comedy in the Seventeenth Century," *ELH*, 1936, III. 270–90) shows that men like Brome freely exploited the actual as a background of their plays, that this tendency was developed further during the Restoration period, but that the tendency was rather "to use topography for technical ends." These settings were not realistic transcripts from what was seen.

[3] John Harold Wilson, *The Court Wits of the Restoration* (1948), p. 164.

[4] Joseph Wood Krutch's *Comedy and Conscience after the Restoration* (1924) has this subject as its central theme, and a more detailed analysis of *The Jeremy Collier Stage Controversy, 1698–1726* (1937) has been prepared by Sister Rose Anthony. G. F. Lamb ("A Short View of Jeremy Collier," *English*, 1949, VII. 270–5) has a brief impressionistic essay on the subject, and Kathleen Ressler endeavours to rehabilitate Collier in an article on "Jeremy Collier's Essays" (*Seventeenth Century Studies: Second Series*, ed. Robert Shafer, 1937, pp. 179–285). In "Dr James Drake and Restoration Theory of Comedy" (*Review of English Studies*, 1939, XV. 180–91), E. E. Williams takes *The Antient and Modern Stages Survey'd* (1699) as typical of a large body of moderate opinion.

was believed that Jeremy Collier was almost wholly responsible for a violent revulsion of feeling with regard to contemporary comedy: now it is seen that his famous condemnatory volume owed its enormous success and led to attempts at practical "reformation" precisely because it stated more trenchantly what many men had been thinking (and in part saying) during the years immediately before its appearance. Just before the turn of the century arrived the stage was ripe for a change in style and in orientation. The fortune of the sentimental drama is a subject more appropriate for treatment in an account of the eighteenth-century theatre, but, as has been demonstrated by several scholars, its beginnings are unquestionably to be found in the decades immediately following the year 1680. There is an ironic piquancy in the reflection that the characteristic comedy-drama of the reign of good Queen Victoria was thus being fashioned within the reign of good King Charles[1].

[1] Reference should here be made to a suggestive study recently published—Clifford Leech's "Restoration Comedy, The Earlier Phase" (*Essays in Criticism*, 1951, I. 165–84).

APPENDIX A

History of the Playhouses
1660–1700

IN September 1642 playing had been stopped by the new Puritan government, "while these sad Causes and set times of Humuliation doe continue," and later ordinances in 1647 and 1648 were issued for the purpose of maintaining the prohibition[1]. The impoverished actors petitioned in vain, and officially those whose hearts had not been made sour by the prevailing austerity had to content themselves with imaginary performances as they read their dramas in printed text. Of such play-lovers there must indeed have been many if we are to judge by the truly extraordinary wealth of tragedies and comedies that came flooding from the printing houses during these eighteen years. Even if the parliamentary regulations had been strictly enforced, we may be sure that when the theatres reopened in 1660 their fare would have been well known to at least a large part of the eager audiences who flocked to their doors[2].

But the regulations were not strictly enforced, and recent studies of the drama during the Commonwealth have easily demonstrated that surreptitious performances were given at various theatres whenever the old actors were able to gather a company and an audience—and this was frequently[3]. No doubt the players risked

[1] These Puritan orders are reprinted in J. P. Collier, *A History of English Dramatic Poetry* (1879), II. 36, 41 and 44–6 and in H. C. Hazlitt, *The English Drama and Stage under the Tudor and Stuart Princes* (1869), pp. 63, 64 and 65–70.

[2] This is well dealt with by Louis B. Wright in an interesting article on "The Reading of Plays during the Puritan Revolution" (*Huntington Library Bulletin*, No. 6, 1934, pp. 73–108).

[3] Many documents relating to performances during this time are printed or cited by Hyder E. Rollins in "A Contribution to the History of the English Commonwealth Drama" (*Studies in Philology*, 1921, XVIII. 267–333), as well as in his supplementary study, "The Commonwealth Drama: Miscellaneous Notes" (*id.* 1923, XX. 52–69) and by Leslie Hotson in *The Commonwealth and Restoration Stage* (1928)—cited hereafter under the author's name. Apparently quasi-dramatic performances were never completely suppressed at the great Fairs (Bartholomew Fair and Southwark Fair). In this connection very considerable interest attaches to a

imprisonment and the spectators a fine, yet the severity of the punishment could not prevent either from indulging in these now forbidden joys. Erratic though the shows may have been, they definitely provide a direct link between the new and the old; many of the actors of 1660 had had the opportunity of exercising their skill during the dark years and by no means all of the older members of the audience had to search their memories beyond the year 1642 for records of performances they had seen in the past.

I. *D'Avenant's "Operas," 1656–1659.*

By far the most interesting of all stage activities between 1642 and 1660, however, are those associated with the name of Sir William d'Avenant, the one man who, albeit through a subterfuge, actually succeeded in breaking the ban and in securing official sanction for his shows[1]. The subterfuge was, in effect, threefold: where others had striven to present performances of the earlier Caroline tragedies and comedies as entertainments, D'Avenant continually emphasised that he was intent only on "opera," wrote his own pieces (thus uncontaminated by the stain of production during the reign of Charles I) and adroitly cultivated a moral patriotic note. It is entirely possible that his theatrical activities were considerably more extensive than has generally been supposed—a satirical ballad written before the beginning of April 1656 actually suggests that he had shows in no less than four theatres— but even if we accept only such presentations as are attested by firm documentary evidence the importance of his pre-Restoration management is made amply clear. In Feb. 1655/6 he was engaged in raising a sufficient sum of money for his ventures. On May 23 *The First Day's Entertainment*, given "by Musick and Declamations after the manner of the Ancients," was put before an audience at Rutland House—the declamations being in effect a debate concerning the virtues of opera, subtly combined with patriotic praise

bill for puppet-plays at John Harris' booth, which William Van Lennep thinks is "The Earliest Known English Playbill" (*Harvard Library Bulletin*, 1947, I. 382–5). As is well known, only a few scattered bills are known before the eighteenth century. W. J. Lawrence reproduces four hand-bills of 1692–94 in *The Elizabethan Playhouse and Other Studies, Second Series* (1913), pp. 240–1, and Eleanore Boswell ("A Playbill of 1687," *Library*, 4th ser., 1931, XI. 499–500) draws attention to another, recording *A King and No King* on Feb. 22, 1687.

[1] On D'Avenant's Commonwealth theatrical efforts Leslie Hotson (pp. 139–62) has published much new material. Other records of these efforts appear in A. H. Nethercot, *Sir William D'Avenant* (1938), Alfred Harbage, *Sir William Davenant* (1935) and Montague Summers, *The Playhouse of Pepys* (1935).

of England. D'Avenant's next step seems to have been the publication of *The Siege of Rhodes*[1], a copy of which he sent to his influential friend Bulstrode Whitelocke on Sept. 3: a production of the piece no doubt followed later the same month. Despite the cramped quarters both for actors and for spectators, a proscenium and five scenes were designed for the opera by John Webb, inheritor of the art of Inigo Jones: the originals of these are still extant in the Duke of Devonshire's collection at Chatsworth[2]. The small stage of Rutland House, however, was far too narrow for his ambitious projects, and early the following year D'Avenant is found presenting a memorandum to Secretary Thurloe, arguing the virtues of his operatic ventures: apparently he was successful in obtaining official approval for more public performances than those at Rutland House, and before July 25, 1658, *The Cruelty of the Spaniards in Peru*, "exprest by Instrumentall and Vocall Musick, and by the Art of Perspective in Scenes," was being "represented daily at the *Cockpit* in *Drury-Lane*, At Three after noone punctually."

This house, known variously as The Phœnix and The Cockpit, had been established by Christopher Beeston in 1616[3]. Various contemporary records tell of its surreptitious use by actors during the early years of the Commonwealth period and, even although its interior was "pulled downe" in March 1649[4], it was evidently still fit for the staging of plays. Precisely who had it in control in 1658 is uncertain, but the probability is that D'Avenant rented it from John Rhodes, a "bookseller" and, according to John Downes, a former wardrobe-keeper at Blackfriars, who had been resident there since 1644[5].

The Cruelty of the Spaniards in Peru was obviously designed to win favour by its patriotic tone, and it was soon followed by a companion piece, *The History of Sir Francis Drake*: perhaps, too,

[1] The preface is dated Aug. 17, 1656.

[2] They were originally identified by W. G. Keith, "The Designs for the First Movable Scenery on the English Public Stage" (*Burlington Magazine*, 1914, XXV. 29–33, 85–9). See also the same author's "John Webb and the Court Theatre of Charles II" (*Architectural Review*, 1925, LVII. 50–55). Other work of Webb's is dealt with by Hamilton Bell, "Contributions to the English Playhouse" (*Architectural Record*, 1913). Even during the earlier part of the Commonwealth there were men interested in experimenting with new scenic devices (see the present writer's note on "Scenery between Shakespeare and Dryden," *TLS*, Aug. 15, 1936).

[3] On the early history of this theatre see J. Q. Adams, *Shakespearean Playhouses* (1917), pp. 348–67 and Leslie Hotson, pp. 88–100.

[4] Leslie Hotson, pp. 43 and 77.

[5] On Rhodes see *infra*, p. 289.

a second part to *The Siege of Rhodes* also appeared during the year 1659[1]. By this time, however, D'Avenant's ventures were receiving an unwelcome share of critical official scrutiny. The probability is that previously he had somehow managed to secure support for his projects from Oliver Cromwell, and when the Protector died, on Sept. 3, 1658, those who looked upon these operas as evil things, felt free to express themselves more freely than hitherto they had dared. Nevertheless, as Evelyn testifies, the "opera" was still active as late as May 6, 1659.

II. *The "Old Actors" at the Red Bull, 1659–1660.*

Political events by this time were moving rapidly. General George Monk marched down to London early in the new year, and by May Charles II had come back to his own again. No men more than the actors rejoiced in the change of the atmosphere, and almost at once there was feverish theatrical activity. D'Avenant hurried off to France, receiving his pass on March 17, 1660, just after arranging for the lease of Lisle's Tennis Court[2]. At the same time, while he was thus flying a higher pitch, various remnants of the theatrical companies which had flourished during the reign of Charles I hastily set up their stages.

Already on May 12, 1659, Anthony Turner and Edward Shatterall[3] were in trouble over premature performances at the Red Bull, recognisances for their appearance before the Middlesex justices being given by William Wintershall and Henry Eaton[4]. This theatre, established in 1605 and of old notorious for the "popular" nature of its shows, was one of the last open-air or public playhouses, and during the Commonwealth it had witnessed not a few surreptitious performances[5]. The facts that Wintershall's and Shatterall's names are here associated together and that the same names appear in Downes' list of the actors who, as "the scattered Remnant of several" pre-Commonwealth troupes, "Fram'd a Company who acted at the Bull[6]" suggest that already

---

[1] Although not printed until later, this was entered in the Stationers' Register on May 30, 1659.

[2] Leslie Hotson, pp. 124 and 162. On the tennis court as a theatre see *infra*, p. 301.

[3] Turner is known to have been acting at the Cockpit in 1622, and he was in Beeston's company there in 1637 (Gerald E. Bentley, *The Jacobean and Caroline Stage* (1941), II. 607–8: this work is cited hereafter as "G. E. Bentley." For Shatterall see *infra*, p. 288.

[4] *Middlesex County Records* (ed. J. C. Jeaffreson), III. 279.

[5] Leslie Hotson, pp. 34, 38, 44.

[6] Pp. 1–2, Downes' "William Shatterel" is probably a mistake for "Edward".

this group had been formed into a theatrical organisation. Unfortunately it is impossible to determine with any assurance precisely which actors in Downes' list were original members of the Red Bull men and which were brought in during the course of the year 1660, but reasonable guesses may be made. Certainly on August 14, 1660, when they came to an agreement with Sir Henry Herbert, Master of the Revels[1], they included, besides Wintershall, Michael Mohun, Robert Shatterall, William Cartwright, Walter Clun, Charles Hart and Nicholas Burt. For most of these there is clear evidence of pre-Commonwealth histrionic activities. "Major" Mohun, who headed the troupe, is recorded as a boy apprenticed to Beeston, he was certainly at the Cockpit between 1637 and 1640, and in 1658 he was exercising his art at Antwerp[2]; Wintershall seems to have been one of Queen Henrietta's men[3]; Robert Shatterall, Edward's brother, was at the Cockpit in 1639 and seems to have been a boy under Beeston[4]; Cartwright, born about 1606, had been in Queen Henrietta's company just before the closing of the theatres and was concerned with illegal performances in 1648[5]; Wright declares that both Clun and Hart were boys at the Blackfriars[6]; Burt is recorded as a boy under Shank at the same theatre[7]. It is also likely that original members of the group were Richard Baxter[8], John Lacy[9] and Thomas Loveday[10], all of whom

---

[1] Leslie Hotson, p. 202. See *infra*, p. 316.

[2] G. E. Bentley, II. 511–12. He died in October 1684, and did not act after 1682.

[3] *Id.* II. 623–4. The "Key" to *The Rehearsal* states that he died in July 1679.

[4] *Id.* II. 571–2. He left the stage probably about 1679. Edward Shatterall may be the Edward Schottnel who was acting at The Hague in 1644.

[5] *Id.* 404–5. He died in Dec. 1686. On this actor see Eleanore Boswell, "Young Mr Cartwright" (*Modern Language Review*, 1929, XXIV. 125–42).

[6] *Id.* II. 405. Clun was killed in Aug. 1664. Hart left the stage in 1682 and died in Aug. 1683.

[7] *Id.* II. 397. He seems to have retired about 1679.

[8] *Id.* II. 360–2. Born in 1593, he served first at the Red Bull and later joined the King's Men. He died probably before 1667.

[9] *Id.* II. 495–6. Aubrey asserts he had been John Ogilby's apprentice; he was at the Cockpit in 1639. He died in Sept. 1681. As portraits of Restoration actors are few in number, attention may here be drawn to the interesting examination devoted by Charles W. Cooper to "The Triple-Portrait of John Lacy" (*PMLA*, 1932, XLVII. 759–65). He shows that, while the usual identification of one figure (Galliard in *The Variety*) is correct, the second cannot be either Teague in *The Committee* or Sauny in Lacy's alteration of *The Taming of the Shrew*, and the third may well not be Scruple in *The Cheats*. Cooper hazards the suggestion that it may be Obadiah in *The Alchemist*.

[10] *Id.* II. 498. He was acting at Norwich in 1635, and in 1644 at The Hague. Peculiarly his name does not appear in Downes' list.

had had previous histrionic experience and whose names appear along with the others cited above in an order dated Oct. 6, 1660[1]. A record of their repertoire has been preserved for us[2]. Most of the plays are from the "Beaumont and Fletcher" series—*The Humorous Lieutenant, The Beggar's Bush, The Tamer Tamed, Wit Without Money, The Maid's Tragedy, Philaster, Rollo, The Elder Brother, A King and No King*, but there are also a few of Shakespeare's—*Henry IV, The Merry Wives of Windsor* and *Othello*—besides Shirley's *The Traitor, The Wedding*, and *Love's Cruelty*, Killigrew's *Claracilla*, Jonson's *Epicœne*, Chapman's *Bussy D'Ambois* ("Dumboys"), D'Avenant's *The Unfortunate Lovers* and Middleton's *The Widow*.

III. *The " Young Actors" at the Cockpit, 1659–1660.*

While these older actors were thus endeavouring to recapture the glories of by-gone days, another and a younger group was vying with their efforts. Already on Feb. 4, 1659/60 Thomas Lillieston was arrested for wrongfully acting at the Cockpit or Phoenix[3]. This house, Downes informs us, was taken over by a group of players under the direction of "Mr *Rhodes* a Bookseller being Wardrobe-Keeper formerly (as I am inform'd) to King *Charles* the First's Company of Comedians in Black-Friars[4]." His assertion that it presented plays under a licence from General Monk (*i.e.* between Feb. 4 and March 24, 1659/60) is not supported but rather contradicted by contemporary evidence[5]. On the other hand, Lillieston was a member of Rhodes' company, while there is a record that on July 28, 1660 the manager had to pay a fine of £4. 6s., twopence for every day his troupe had then performed at the Cockpit[6]. Downes lists his group as consisting of Thomas Betterton, Thomas Sheppey, Thomas Lovel, Lillieston, Cave Underhill, Robert Turner, James Dixon and Robert Nokes, as well as another six who "commonly Acted Women's Parts"—Edward Kynaston, James Nokes, Edward Angel, William Betterton, John Mosely and one Floid[7]. Nearly all of these men seem to have been young and new to the stage; only for Lovel do we

---

[1] See *infra*, p. 294.
[2] Herbert, p. 82.
[3] *Middlesex County Records*, III. 282.   [4] P. 17.
[5] Leslie Hotson, p. 197.
[6] *Id.* 198: Hotson suggests that "2*d.*" is a mistake for "2*s.*", but perhaps we ought to take the document as it stands.
[7] P. 18.

have sure evidence of pre-Commonwealth experience[1]. Rhodes himself presents a puzzle[2]. Records relating to "John Rhodes" come from as early as 1624, but if they all refer to the same man he must indeed have had a busy and variegated career—an actor-musician in the King's Men, a bookseller, a part-owner of the Fortune Theatre, a member of the Drapers' Company and now the manager of one of the two theatrical troupes established at the Restoration. We may be concerned with more than a single man here, although such diverse activities are just within the bounds of possibility[3].

IV. *Beeston of Salisbury Court, 1660.*

Certain documents tempt us at first to believe that, in addition to these two companies—Mohun's at the Red Bull and Rhodes' at the Cockpit—still a third acting troupe had been set up at Salisbury Court. This theatre[4], about the same size as the Cockpit and, like it, a "private" roofed playhouse, was set on a plot of

---

[1] G. E. Bentley, II. 498. He is recorded at Norwich in 1635. Betterton, born in 1635, continued in active career until after 1700; he died in 1710. Not much is known about Sheppey, but he was still acting in 1688. Lovel disappears from our knowledge within a short time, as does Lillieston, but Underhill performed as late as 1710. Turner may soon have taken to strolling; Dixon proved undistinguished, and soon vanishes from our ken; Robert Nokes, less famous than his brother, James, is not heard of after 1663. After winning fame in the interpretation of women's roles, Kynaston pursued a distinguished career in male parts until about 1698; similarly James Nokes passed from young heroines to more mature parts, becoming one of the most popular comic actors of the age; he acted up to 1689 and died in 1696. Angel, too, won success in comedy, acting up to the time of his death, about 1673. The other three mentioned by Downes were of no importance.

[2] See G. E. Bentley, II. 544–6, and Leslie Hotson, pp. 99–100.

[3] A. H. Nethercot, *Sir William D'Avenant*, p. 339, suggests that *Lady Alimony*, printed in 1659, may have been one of the plays given by Rhodes' men, but we have no sure record of their repertoire. There is a peculiar prologue to a revival of *The Alchemist* which probably may be dated in 1660: although this play was later, in 1661, being given by the "old actors," the allusion here to "young Beginners" suggests that this performance was by Rhodes' company (Autrey Nell Wiley, *Rare Prologues and Epilogues, 1642–1700* (1940), pp. 13–17). Pepys saw *The Loyal Subject* at the Cockpit on Aug. 18, 1660. A. C. Sprague, *Beaumont and Fletcher on the Restoration Stage* (1926), pp. 10–11, takes the list given by Downes (p. 18) as belonging to Rhodes' company. If so, then in addition to *The Loyal Subject* we have the following titles: *The Maid in the Mill, The Wild Goose Chase, The Spanish Curate, The Mad Lover, A Wife for a Month, Rule a Wife and Have a Wife, The Tamer Tamed, Pericles, The Unfortunate Lovers, Aglaura, The Changeling* and *The Bondman*.

[4] See Leslie Hotson, pp. 100–14.

ground some 140 feet long by 42 feet wide[1]. In 1652 it was bought by William Beeston, who proceeded to repair, and partly to reconstruct it. This William Beeston was the son of Christopher Beeston; born not later than about 1606[2], he had presumably been trained as an actor by his father and was later concerned with the management both of Salisbury Court and of the Cockpit. Two things concerning him are of particular interest. First, he seems to have been among the most active members of his profession in endeavouring to keep the idea of dramatic performances alive during the period of the Commonwealth; and, secondly, no other actor has received such direct praise as a theatrical "coach." Francis Kirkman, in 1652, called him "the happiest interpreter and judg of our English Stage-Playes this Nation ever produced" and declared that "the chief, and most ingenious of-them acknowledg their Fames & Profits essentially sprung from" his "instructions, judgment and fancy[3]." Two years later, Richard Flecknoe, in a postscript to *Love's Dominion*, made over the rights in this play, if ever it were to be acted, to "Mr Will. Beeston, who by Reason of his long Practice and Experience in this way, as also for having brought up most of the Actors extant, I think the fittest Man for this Charge and Imployment."

The document which appears to establish him as the manager of a third company is a licence issued to him by Sir Henry Herbert, authorising him to set up Salisbury Court as a playhouse[4]. This order, however, is both unsigned and undated; the attribution to it of the date 1660 is based only on a guess by Edmund Malone[5]. Since we do not know when the order was issued or what particular use Beeston made of it, no theory can be built on its contents. There is no record of any actors belonging at this date to a Beeston company, and the probability is no such company then existed: no doubt Beeston merely acted as theatre-owner and sat hoping for tenants. Despite the common belief (which I once shared) that three companies were acting in London during the first part of the year 1660, we may be content with merely the two groups of "old" and "young" players performing under the management of Mohun and Rhodes respectively, with Beeston anxiously looking round for actors to occupy his playhouse.

[1] J. Q. Adams, *Shakespearean Playhouses*, p. 372.
[2] "Some Notes on William Beeston" (*TLS*, Nov. 22, 1923). On his activities see G. E. Bentley, II. 370–4.
[3] *The Loves and Adventures of Clerico and Logis* (1652), epistle dedicatory.
[4] Herbert, p. 81.
[5] "Historical Account of the English Stage" in his *Variorum Shakespeare* (1821), II. 243.

At the same time, it seems certain that by the summer of 1660 Beeston must have secured the tenants he sought. On Aug. 20, when Herbert appointed a certain John Rogers to guard the "playhouses from all Molestations and Injuries[1]," his order was addressed "To the Actors of the Playhouses called the Red Bull, Cockpitt, and Theatre in Salesbury Court." This was only a few days after Herbert had, according to his statement of July 11, 1662[2], succeeded in forcing agreements on the Red Bull players ("the Kinges Company"), Beeston and Rhodes. From a letter of the 30th, addressed by H. Moseley to Herbert[3], we are definitely told that three companies were then operating—"the gentlemen actors of the Red Bull," "Mr Rhodes, of the Cockpitt playhouse" and "the Whitefryers playhouse and players[4]."

The absence of any information concerning the personnel of any body of "Beeston's men" tends, however, to suggest that the actors at Salisbury Court in Aug. 1660, were a visiting company rather than a troupe of his own, and the strong likelihood is that they formed a troupe under the redoubtable George Jolly[5]. This interesting and fiery character was certainly acting in 1640[6], and from 1648 to 1660 his career, as director of a company of English players on the Continent, can easily be traced. The first sure record concerning him after the Restoration is a licence, dated Dec. 24, 1660, granting him leave "to erect one company" and "to purchase, build or hire a theatre[7]." From this document it has generally been assumed that Jolly did not start activities in England until the year 1661, but a more probable hypothesis is that he had already been appearing under Beeston's aegis and that his application for an individual licence in December was motivated by other events in the theatrical world[8].

[1] Herbert, pp. 83–4.
[2] *Id.* pp. 120–2.   [3] *Id.* p. 90.
[4] Whitefriars was an alternative name for Salisbury Court.
[5] W. J. Lawrence, in an essay entitled "A Forgotten Restoration Playhouse" (*Englische Studien*, 1905, xxxv. 279–89), first called attention to the importance of this manager. New documents presented in the first edition of the present volume and in Leslie Hotson, pp. 167–96, more clearly outlined his activities, and further records of his strolling career have materially added to our knowledge of his work. It is possible he may have been concerned with the performance of Tatham's *The Rump* at "Dorset Court" (Salisbury Court) about June, 1660.
[6] G. E. Bentley, II. 483–4.
[7] Leslie Hotson, pp. 177–8.
[8] See *infra*, pp. 308–13.

V. *The Establishment of Theatrical Monopoly, 1660.*

Such events had resulted mainly from the ardent courtiership of Sir William D'Avenant and of Thomas Killigrew[1]. D'Avenant already held a patent for a theatre, issued by Charles I in 1639[2], but any hopes he may have had for authority to set up a single monopoly were blasted by Killigrew's importunacy: he too wanted a share in theatrical profits, and on July 9, 1660, his influence with the King enabled him to secure an order for a royal warrant— a warrant which not only gave him permission to set up a playhouse but also provided a monopoly for D'Avenant and himself[3]. No doubt the pair of scheming adventurers hurried into consultation immediately, and ten days later (July 19) D'Avenant had completed a draft for a final joint patent and this was approved on Aug. 21[4].

The next task of the patentees was naturally to see their privileges realised in actuality, and apparently their first step towards this goal was to secure, through royal command, united control over the two companies directed by Mohun and Rhodes. An actors' petition, signed by several of the Red Bull players[5], informs us that, "according to your Majesty's approbation from all the companies we made election of one company," and the truth of this statement is proved by a declaration later made by Herbert, to the effect that on Oct. 8 Killigrew and D'Avenant set up a company of twenty players and caused them to perform until at

---

[1] References to the former appear *supra*, p. 4. Alfred Harbage has a biography of the latter—*Thomas Killigrew: Cavalier Dramatist, 1612–83* (1930).

[2] A. H. Nethercot, *Sir William D'Avenant*, p. 170.

[3] Leslie Hotson, p. 199.

[4] *Id.* pp. 199–200. Hotson shows (pp. 200–2) that a document dated Aug. 20, ordering the suppression of all other theatres, is merely a draft in D'Avenant's handwriting, and was no doubt never issued. The patent, after noting that many plays performed "doe containe much matter of prophanation and scurrility" and "for the most part tende to the debauchinge of the manners of such as are present at them," although they might be used to "serue as innocent and harmlesse divertisement for many of our subjects," declares that the King is pleased to grant a licence to Killigrew and D'Avenant for the setting up of two companies and for the erection of two theatres, granting them leave to fix prices of entrance "as either haue bin accustomely giuen...or as shall be reasonable in regard of the great expences of scenes, musick, and such new decorations as haue not been formerly used." It is also agreed that no other companies should act in London and that the two patentees should peruse all plays before acting and cut out any offensive passages.

[5] Herbert, p. 95.

least the 16th of that month[1]. No doubt this explains why a list of His Majesty's Comedians, dated Oct. 6, 1660, gives the names not only of several "Red Bull" actors (Burt, Hart, Mohun, Robert Shatterell, Lacy, Wintersell, Clunne, Cartwright, Edward Shatterell, Baxter, Loveday) but also of Kynaston and Betterton, members of the Rhodes' troupe[2].

Performances were thus given at the Cockpit, since on the very day of the combined operations, Oct. 8, Herbert addressed a peremptory order to Rhodes at that theatre, demanding under what authority the house was being used as a playhouse[3]. Rhodes' answer was "that the Kinge did authorize Him."

By this time the two patentees were nearly ready to carry out their real object—the establishing of two independent theatres. No doubt after some discussion among themselves, D'Avenant elected to take over the younger men of Rhodes' company, while Killigrew chose the older players of the Mohun group. There is a suggestion in the actors' petition referred to above[4] that even before the commencement of the united performances the latter had entered into a covenant with the "Red Bull" men that they should "act with woemen, a new theatre, and habitts according to our sceanes." Both courtier-managers started activities at the same time, the beginning of Nov. 1660, just a month after the temporary setting up of the united players at the Cockpit.

VI. *The King's Men, 1660–1665.*

Killigrew's company came under the direct patronage of the King and as a temporary Theatre Royal the manager chose Gibbon's Tennis Court in Vere-street, Clare Market. This house had already been used for play performance: indeed, there is a record of its having witnessed in March 1653 a production of Killigrew's own *Claracilla*[5]. Although Pepys enthusiastically praised it as "the finest playhouse, I believe, that ever was in

---

[1] Leslie Hotson, p. 205. On Oct. 16 Pepys saw *Wit without Money* and on Oct. 30 *The Tamer Tamed*, both at the Cockpit.

[2] L.C. 5/137, p. 332. In giving these lists I have retained the spellings of the names of actors. In the first edition of the present book I had endeavoured to argue against the theory that such an amalgamation was effected, but Hotson's findings prove that R. W. Lowe (*Thomas Betterton* (1891), pp. 67–9) was right in his original interpretation of the evidence.

[3] Herbert, p. 93.

[4] See *supra*, p. 293. Herbert, p. 95.

[5] Leslie Hotson, pp. 49–50 and 118.

England[1]," it cannot have been very commodious and certainly was not equipped to make use of that scenery which Killigrew had promised his actors. Presumably because the house was not quite ready, the King's Men started playing, on Monday, Nov. 5, 1660, at the Red Bull, moving into their new quarters on the Thursday (Nov. 8) of the same week[2].

In addition to the actors already listed as members of the Mohun company[3], another six are mentioned by Downes[4]. Peculiarly, one of them, "Mr *Kynaston*," had belonged to the rival group under Rhodes and we can only assume that by some special arrangement he was permitted to seceded from D'Avenant's chosen company. Theophilus Bird, although not apparently mentioned in any of the early documents relating to Mohun's men, may possibly have been one of their original members, since he had been a Blackfriars actor as early as 1635, but it is entirely possible that during these first months of theatrical activity he had been busily occupied with his brother-in-law, William Beeston, for whom we find him serving as agent in 1652[5]. A third name on Downes' list is that of "Mr *Duke*," Marmaduke Watson, who is first found associated with Killigrew's men in a document of July 29, 1661[6]. After a moderately undistinguished career, he seems to have retired about the year 1678. Of Thomas Hancock we know little, and the fact that he is mentioned in a livery warrant for the first time on May 30, 1662[7], leads us to guess that he joined the company later: the same is possibly true of Nicholas Blagden[8], while there is every likelihood that the sixth of Downes' additional actors, Thomas Bateman, did not associate himself with Killigrew's company until the beginning of the year 1665[9].

From an early date, too, Killigrew had his actresses—Mrs Corey, Mrs Ann Marshall, Mrs Eastland, Mrs Weaver, Mrs Uphill, Mrs Knepp and Mrs Hughes—and, as Pepys amply shows, several of these won both fame and notoriety.

---

[1] Nov. 20, 1660. It is just possible that Pepys was, in fact, referring to the company rather than to the building. His words are: "And so we went in and saw it [*The Beggar's Bush*], it was well acted: and here I saw the first time one Moone, who is said to be the best actor in the world... and indeed it is the finest playhouse, I believe, that ever was in England."

[2] Leslie Hotson, p. 177; A. H. Nethercot, *Sir William D'Avenant*, p. 349.

[3] See *supra*, p. 288.

[4] P. 2.

[5] G. E. Bentley, II. 377; Leslie Hotson, p. 103. He died in 1664.

[6] See *infra*, p. 297.

[7] See *infra*, p. 363.

[8] But see *infra*, p. 297.

[9] He is presumably the "Thomas Bateston" recorded on March 16, 1664/5 (see *infra*, p. 299).

Fortunately, the combined records of Pepys and Herbert, supported by some other scattered documents, enable us to make up what was, no doubt, the larger part of this company's repertoire. Shakespeare is represented here by *Henry IV[1], *The Merry Wives, *Othello, A Midsummer Night's Dream, Jonson by *Epicoene, The Alchemist, Bartholomew Fair and Volpone, but by far the greater proportion of the offerings come from the "Beaumont and Fletcher" series—here are *Wit without Money, *The Beggar's Bush, *The Maid's Tragedy, The Scornful Lady, *The Elder Brother, The Chances, *The Humorous Lieutenant, *A King and No King, *Rollo, The Loyal Subject, The Mad Lover, The Wild Goose Chase, The Maid in the Mill, A Wife for a Month, The Spanish Curate, *The Tamer Tamed, Monsieur Thomas, *Philaster, Rule a Wife and Have a Wife, The Little Thief, The Knight of the Burning Pestle. Among miscellaneous "Elizabethan" works appear Shirley's *The Traitor, The Wedding, The Changes, The Imposture, The Brothers, The Young Admiral, *Love's Cruelty, The Cardinal and The Opportunity, Middleton's *The Widow, Massinger's The Virgin Martyr, The Bondman and The Renegado, Rowley's All's Lost by Lust, Brome's The Jovial Crew, The Northern Lass and The Antipodes, Dekker's The Merry Devil of Edmonton, Webster's The White Devil, Chapman's *Bussy D'Ambois, D'Avenant's *The Unfortunate Lovers, Killigrew's *Claracilla and The Princess, Berkeley's The Lost Lady, Glapthorne's Argalus and Parthenia, Suckling's Aglaura and Brennoralt, Newcastle's The Country Captain and The Variety—together with several new pieces[2].

Very soon after the occupation of the theatre in Vere-street, Killigrew set about making plans for a more commodious building. On Dec. 20, 1661 a plot of ground was leased from the Earl of Bedford[3] by Killigrew and Sir Robert Howard, acting in conjunction, eight actors[4], William Hewett and Robert Clayton. The plot itself, situate between Drury Lane and Bridges-street, was 112 feet by about 58 feet, the rent £50 a year, and the agreement called for the expenditure, before the end of 1662, of £1500 on a theatre to be erected on the site. A month later, on Jan. 28,

---

[1] An asterisk marks those plays already recorded in the Red Bull list: see supra, p. 289.

[2] Downes, pp. 8–9, adds several others of uncertain date: Julius Caesar, Titus Andronicus, Catiline, The Devil's an Ass, Every Man in His Humour, Every Man out of His Humour, Sejanus, and The Example. W. Van Lennep, in "Thomas Killigrew Prepares his Plays for Production," Adams Memorial Studies, 1948, pp. 803–8; examines the cut texts of several plays.   [3] Leslie Hotson, p. 243.

[4] Hart, Burt, Lacy, Mohun, Robert Shatterell, Clun, Cartwright and Wintershall.

1661/2, Hewett and Clayton, as trustees, made over the ground to the company, the shares being divided into 36 parts. Nine each went to Killigrew and Howard, while two were apportioned to each of the actors[1] save Lacy, to whom four were appointed[2]. The same day (Jan. 28, 1661/2) witnessed another agreement between the actors and the building sharers[3]. Here the company is made up of the eight players mentioned above, together with Theophilus Bird, Richard Baxter, Edward Kynaston, Nicholas Blagden and Thomas Loveday[4]. By May 1662, it seems as though Loveday had temporarily left the company, while then or shortly after Hancock, Thomas Gradwell and Tanner had joined it. From that date until 1665 the personnel of the troupe evidently remained largely the same[5].

Perhaps the actresses did not come into the privilege of receiving a "livery" until 1666. On June 30 of that year comes the first known such warrant, issued to Mrs Weaver, Mrs Marshall, Mrs Rutter, Mrs Yates, Mrs Nepp, Mrs Dalton, Mrs Ellen Gwyn, Mrs Elizabeth Hall, Mrs Francis ["ffransis"] Davenport and Mrs Anne Child, authorising them to receive "foure yards of bastard scarlet cloath and one quarter of a yard of veluett for their liueryes[6]." On Feb. 8, 1667/8 Mrs Weaver, Mrs Yates, Mrs Dalton, Mrs Hall and Mrs Child are cancelled, while Mrs Elizabeth Hall and Mrs Jane Davenport are added[7].

[1] Mohun, Hart, Burt, Shatterell, Clun, Cartwright and Wintershall.
[2] Leslie Hotson, p. 243.   [3] *Id.* pp. 243-4.
[4] In the livery warrant of July 29, 1661, neither Blagden nor Bird is mentioned, while Betterton's name is tantalisingly added, as well as those of Watson and both the Shatteralls. We can assume only that Betterton's inclusion is a clerical mistake, due to his presence in the united company of Oct. 1660. A second list, probably of Feb. 5, 1661/2, omits the names of Betterton, Lacy and Edward Shatterall; a third, dated May 30, 1662, includes Lacy but omits Loveday, and adds Hancock, Edward Shatterall and Gradwell. On Nov. 4, 1662, a further livery warrant omits Gradwell and Loveday, but adds Thomas Tanner (see *infra*, pp. 363-4).
[5] See the livery warrant of Feb. 25, 1665/6 (*infra*, p. 364). Erroneously this includes the name of Clun; he was murdered on Aug. 2, 1664. An order of March 16, 1664/5 also bears his name as well as Loveday's: this, as noted above, also includes "Thomas Bateston" (*infra*, p. 295). That these lists were apt to be copied out, rather carelessly, from earlier warrants seems proved by that of Feb. 8, 1667/8, where the names of Bird, Clunn, Blagden and Edward Shatterell were in the original list and then deleted, and where the names of Loveday and Batiman were inserted (*infra*, p. 364).
[6] See *infra*, p. 364.
[7] See *infra*, p. 364. Shortly after, on Oct. 2, 1669, the names are Mrs Marshall, Mrs Cory, Ellin Gwynn, Mrs Kneepe, Mrs Rutter, Mrs Hues, Mrs Davenport and Mrs Yackley (see *infra*, p. 365). On Nell Gwynn see Clifford Bax, *Pretty Witty Nell: An Account of Nell Gwyn and Her Environment* (1932).

Not without disturbances and confusions the company moved towards the building of their new theatre. Killigrew does not seem ever to have won the confidence of the players, and even when Mohun, Hart and Lacy were appointed as deputy managers trouble still reigned[1]. Sometimes we can tell the reason why this trouble arose, sometimes we merely know of its occurrence[2]. On April 25, 1662, a new, individual patent was issued to Killigrew[3], but money was not so easy to come by. The estimated cost of the new building was far below the £2400 which eventually had to be expended[4] and this sum did not cover the additional heavy payments needed for fresh costumes and still fresher scenery. Before the Theatre Royal was opened, Killigrew had put his nine shares in the hands of trustees[5].

At last the playhouse was occupied by the company, on May 7, 1663[6], and the "old actors" at last were established in a moderately convenient home of their own[7]. Downes gives a list of new actors who "came not into the Company, till after they had begun in *Drury-Lane*," but we know that these admissions must have been spread over many years. Joe Haines, after being at the "nursery," did not join the company until the beginning of 1668[8]; probably Philip Griffin and Cardell Goodman did not enter it till then or later; the first record of Lyddall or Lydal seems to be in Dryden's *An Evening's Love* (1668); Charleton and Sherley are recorded elsewhere only in 1669. Indeed, the only one of Downes' list of whom early references are extant is George Beeston; he was certainly at the Theatre Royal at the beginning of 1663. In addition, four players "Bred up from Boys, under the Master ACTORS" are mentioned—Richard Bell, who appeared in *Catiline* during Dec. 1668, Reeves, who had a part in the same play, William Hughes and William Harris. The fact that the names of Bell, Hughes, Harris, Haines, Shirley and Liddall are first listed in a livery

---

[1] Leslie Hotson, pp. 244–5.

[2] As, for example, the following order of Sept. 9, 1661: "To the Company of his Maties Comoedians at the new Theatre These are to will and require you vpon sight hereof to forbeare to act any more playes or showes as you will answer the Contrary at your perills giuen vnder my hand this nynth day of September 166j To his Maties Comadians or Actors at the new Theater."

[3] It is presented in full in P. Fitzgerald, *op. cit.* I. 77.

[4] Leslie Hotson, pp. 249, 254–5.

[5] The complicated story of the financial arrangements made by Killigrew and his relatives is told by Hotson.

[6] Downes, p. 3, gives April 8, but the opening date of May 7 is fully substantiated by Pepys.

[7] P. 2.   [8] See *infra*, p. 313.

warrant of Oct. 2, 1669, suggests that they all came into the company about the same time[1]. Downes' note, therefore, is likely to be highly deceptive. The same caution must be observed in dealing with his list of the actresses who are said to have joined the company during these years—Mrs Boutell, Nell Gwyn, Mrs James, Mrs Rebecca Marshall, Mrs Margaret Rutter, Mrs Verjuice and Mrs Anne Reeves.

At Bridges-street Killigrew and his company were free to make use of scenic display, and no doubt they began with high hopes—although not without problems. Thus, on March 16, 1664/5, disputes between the manager and his players are suggested in an official "Sumons for ye Comoedians" issued from the Lord Chamberlain's office[2]. But all such bickerings were as nothing to the great disaster that came to them, as to the whole of London, not long after the opening of their playhouse. The year 1665 was the year of the great plague, and on June 5 the playhouse had to shut its doors by force of a royal order decreeing the cessation of all dramatic performances[3].

During the two years that they had used the new Theatre Royal, several fresh plays came into their repertoire, and we have the titles of some older dramas in addition to those already recorded for the company. From various sources we know that, within this time, they gave *The Humorous Lieutenant, The Brothers, Epicoene, Bartholomew Fair, The Alchemist, The Night Walker, The Traitor, Love's Mistress, Rule a Wife and Have a Wife, Volpone, The Maid's Tragedy, Rollo, The Scornful Lady, The Elder Brother, The Faithful Shepherdess, Othello, Henry IV, Julius Caesar*, as well as Killigrew's own *The Parson's Wedding*.

[1] See *infra*, p. 364.
[2] L.C. 5/186: "These are to require you to giue notice vnto his Mates Comoedians Nicholas Burt [Charles Hart *deleted*] Michaell Mohun Robert Shatterell John Lacy William Wintersell Walter Clun William Cartwright Edward Shatterell Edward Kinnaston Richard Baxter Thomas Loueday Thomas Bateston Marmaduke Watson Thomas Hancock Nicholas Blagden & Thomas Gradewell That I doe hereby Comand them to attend mee at my Lodgings at Whitehall vpon Saterday Morning the Eighteenth day of this Instant March And that they bring with them the Articles that were made betweene [them *deleted*] Thomas Killegrew Esqr and them."
[3] L.C. 5/138, p. 417: "Whereas it is thought Dangerous that soe greate resort of People should be permitted at yor Theatre in this tyme of Infection of the Plague These are therefore to require you that you forbeare Acting any more Playes vntill you shall receive further Order from mee."

VII. *The Duke's Men, 1660–1665.*

On the same day that found Killigrew commencing operations, D'Avenant signed an agreement with his actors, to be known as the Duke's Men, and began performances at Salisbury Court[1]. The agreement[2] is a particularly interesting one, and it provides us with the names of the principal members of the D'Avenant Company—Thomas Betterton, Sheppey, Robert Nokes, James Nokes, Lovell, Moseley, Underhill, Turner and Lillieston[3].

The same day, Nov. 5, performances started at Salisbury Court, while D'Avenant hastily went ahead with plans for his new theatre. At their temporary home, Pepys saw them give Beaumont and

---

[1] It is to be suspected that Jolly was pushed out of this theatre and that this was the cause of his pleading for a special licence. See *supra*, p. 292, and *infra*, pp. 308–13.

[2] Herbert, pp. 96–100. It is an agreement tripartite between D'Avenant, the actors and "Henry Harris, of the citty of London, Painter." In brief the articles are as follow: (1) D'Avenant agrees to constitute the actors into a company, which will give performances under his patent, at Salisbury Court or elsewhere until he provides them with a "newe theatre with scenes." (2) Until that theatre is opened, D'Avenant is to have 4 shares out of a total of 14, Betterton, James Nokes and Sheppey acting as the manager's deputies in the overseeing of the accounts, and the cost of music is to be defrayed, at a total of not more than 30s. a day, out of the gross receipts. (3) At a week's notice the actors are to hold themselves ready to join D'Avenant, Harris "and other men and women provided or to be provided by the said Sir Wm. Davenant" at the new theatre. (4) At this new theatre the shares are to be 15 in all, of which 2 shares are to go to D'Avenant for house-rent, building and frames for scenes, with a further single share for scenes and costumes. (5) The remaining 12 shares are to be divided into 7 and 5, D'Avenant to have the 7 for maintaining the actresses and 5 to go to the Company, Harris having a portion equal with the highest. (6) The receipts are to "bee by ballatine, or tickettes sealed for all doores and boxes." (7) D'Avenant is to provide three men to receive the money for these tickets, the actors appointing some of themselves to supervise the accounts. (8) He is to appoint half the number of doorkeepers, the wardrobe-keeper and the barber, their salaries to be deducted from the general receipts. (9) D'Avenant is to appoint the successor to any actor-sharer deceased and to settle the wages of the "hirelings." (10) He is not to provide among the costumes "eyther hatts, feathers, gloues, ribbons, sworde-belts, bandes, stockinges, or shoes, for any of the men actors aforesaid, unless it be a propertie." (11) A private box, holding 6 persons, is to be provided for Killigrew. (12) The actors are to enter into a bond of £500 each for the keeping of these articles. (13) Harris is to enter at a week's notice and enter into the same bond. (14) D'Avenant is to be sole "Master and Superior" of the Company.

[3] This agrees with Downes' list, p. 18, except that he adds the name of Dixon as well as those of some boy actors. See *supra*, p. 289.

Fletcher's *The Maid in the Mill*[1], *The Mad Lover*, *The Spanish Curate*, *Rule a Wife and Have a Wife* and *The Little Thief*, Middleton's *The Changeling*, Massinger's *The Bondman*, Heywood's *Love's Mistress*, and an anonymous *Love's Quarrel* (possibly an alternative title for an old play).

At last, some time in June 1661, the new theatre was ready—and its importance lies in the fact that here D'Avenant, with his abiding interest in opera and scenery, set the model for the modern stage[2]. Not without difficulties had it been brought to completion. In order to raise money for the reconstruction of Lisle's Tennis Court in Lincoln's Inn Fields, D'Avenant sold, in March, half a share to Richard Alchorne and a whole share to Sir William Russell[3]. Within a few months expenses were accumulating so steadily that in June further shares were disposed of and some more followed during the following year[4]. Nevertheless, by dint of patient effort, the manager-adventurer found his dream realised. Downes gives us the names of his actresses—Mrs Davenport, Mrs Saunderson (later the wife of Betterton), Mrs Davies, Mrs Long, Mrs Anne Gibbs (later the wife of Shadwell), Mrs Norris, Mrs Holden and Mrs Jennings[5]. Along with these, according to Downes, D'Avenant engaged some other actors "*to Compleat the Company he had from Mr* Rhodes." The first of these is the Henry Harris, who signed the agreement of Nov. 1660; he won considerable fame and continued acting up to 1682. Joseph Price, who died in 1671, was less notable; John Richards seems to have been an undistinguished but capable performer of small parts[6].

[1] His reference to "Blackfriars" on Jan. 29, 1661, is almost certainly a slip for "Whitefriars" (i.e. Salisbury Court). See Hazelton Spencer, "The Blackfriars Mystery" (*Modern Philology*, 1926, xxiv. 173–80).

[2] Leslie Hotson, pp. 120–7.

[3] *Id.* p. 220.   [4] *Id.* p. 220–1.

[5] Mrs Davenport, born in 1642, known as "Roxalana," became the mistress of the Earl of Oxford and retired in 1662. Mrs Saunderson married Betterton in 1662. Mrs Davies became one of Charles' mistresses in 1668, and Mrs Long the mistress of the Duke of Richmond. The marriage of Anne Gibbs to Shadwell took place between 1663 and 1666; she acted until about 1685 (but see the correspondence by D. M. Walmsley and Montague Summers in *TLS*, April 16, May 7, 14 and 21, 1925). Probably Mrs Norris was the wife of the actor Henry Norris; she continued playing until 1682. About Mrs Holden and Mrs Jennings little is known, save the recording of a few parts.

[6] In Aug. 1662, this actor was lured away to Ogilby's theatre in Dublin (Leslie Hotson, p. 213). He returned in 1676. Not as much as could be wished is known of this Smock Alley theatre. William Van Lennep ("The Smock Alley Players in Dublin," *ELH*, 1946, pp. 216–22) shows that a manuscript of Wilson's *Belphegor*, now preserved in the Folger Shakespeare Library, was made for it about 1675: the names of actors include

"The Five following," adds Downes, "came not in till almost a Year after they begun"—and he lists Smith, Sandford, Medburn, Young and Norris. The famous William Smith and Samuel Sandford, both of whom continued acting until the middle nineties, are recorded elsewhere as members of the company in 1662[1]. Matthew Medburne was active until just before his death in 1679. Young's name appears in numerous cast-lists of the sixties and seventies; Henry Norris, already engaged in 1662, was an unimportant performer. To these must be added, from another document, Francis Pavy, not otherwise mentioned until many years later, in 1688[2]; Joseph Williams, who was still performing in 1705; John Crosby; Revet, who may be Edward Revet, author of *The Town Shifts*; and Mrs Brown. And evidently the worthy John Rhodes, who had originally been responsible for gathering the company together, was continued for a time as D'Avenant's deputy[3].

those of Margaret Osborne, John Freeman, George Bright, Will Peer and Pinkethman. For *Julius Caesar* they used, before 1676, the text printed in 1719 and attributed to D'Avenant and Dryden. In 1677 the troupe were at Oxford and in 1681 they performed in Edinburgh. Another article by R. C. Bald, "Shakespeare on the Stage in Restoration Dublin" (*PMLA*, 1941, LVI. 369–78), also discusses the *Julius Caesar* and *Belphegor* texts. The former gives us the names of Wamsley, Williams, Lysle, Cotts, Cudworth, Smith and his wife, Richards and his wife, Ashbury and Baker. See also J. G. McManaway, "Additional Prompt-Books of Shakespeare from the Smock Alley Theatre" (*Modern Language Review*, XLV. 1950, 64–5).

[1] Leslie Hotson, p. 212, gives a list of various actors who were tried for an assault on one of the messengers of the Revels Office on July 4, 1662: this includes the names of Betterton, the two Nokes, Turner, Lillieston, Medburne, Underhill, Sandford, Dixon, Price, Harris and Francis Pavy.   [2] See *infra*, p. 332.

[3] A warrant in L.C. 5/138, p. 91, orders the Treasurer of the Chamber "to pay or cause to be p̄d vnto John Rhodes the sume of Twenty pounds for acting of the play called Ignoramus or the Accademicall Lawyer at Court before his Matie." The manuscript of this play is discussed both by Leslie Hotson, pp. 214–15, and by Bernard M. Wagner ("John Rhodes and *Ignoramus*," *Review of English Studies*, 1929, V. 43–8). The author was Ferdinando Parkhurst, and it is stated that the play was "acted at the Cockpit in Drury Lane, and also before the King and Queen's Majesty at Whitehall on Saturday night, 1 Nov. 1662." Presumably this comedy, then, had been in Rhodes' repertoire before D'Avenant received his patent. Certainly the cast in 1662 points to a performance by D'Avenant's actors. It is true that "Pegg" and "Mrs Margaret" might seem to refer to similarly named players at the Theatre Royal, but the list consists mainly of known members of the D'Avenant troupe—Lillieston, Smyth, Underhill, the two Nokes, Norris, Medburne and Sandford. The other names are Will, Mrs Jennings, Crosby, Mrs Norris, Angell, Mrs Brown and Revet. The prologue was spoken by Alexander Read. Another document (in L.C. 7/3) seems to show that D'Avenant's stepson, Philip Cademan, joined the company about this time.

Before six months had passed, D'Avenant succeeded in obtaining the sole right to perform certain older plays[1]. These include nine Shakespearian dramas, Webster's *The Duchess of Malfi* and Denham's *The Sophy*: in addition he had two months' liberty, from Dec. 12, 1660, to act *The Mad Lover, The Maid in the Mill, The Spanish Curate, The Loyal Subject, Rule a Wife and Have a Wife* and *Pericles*. The wording of the warrant suggests that a similar (but now non-extant) list of plays had been prepared for Killigrew, and no doubt the two months' provision to D'Avenant was made because these plays, mostly from the Beaumont and Fletcher series, had been in his repertoire but were now being given over to the rival patentee[2]. Even the incomplete records of performances up to the time when the theatres were closed, by the plague, in 1665 show that D'Avenant made full use of his privilege. Of Shakespeare's works he produced *Hamlet, Twelfth Night, The Law against Lovers* (a mixture of *Measure for Measure* and *Much Ado about Nothing*), *Romeo and Juliet, Henry VIII, Lear* and *Macbeth*. *The Duchess of Malfi* is recorded several times. In addition, apart from new plays and some early performances of *The Mad Lover, The Maid in the Mill* and *The Spanish Curate*, the company presented the manager's own *The Wits, Love and Honour, The Unfortunate Lovers* and *The Siege of Rhodes*, Massinger's *The Bondman*, Shirley's *The Grateful Servant*, Glapthorne's *Wit in a Constable, The Valiant Cid* (probably Rutter's play), Middleton's *A Trick to Catch the Old One*, Brome's *Sparagus Garden* and Cooke's *Greene's Tu Quoque*[3]. During this time, from the opening of the new theatre in 1661 to its temporary closing in 1665, D'Avenant, like Killigrew, had consolidated his position. An exemplification of the patent he had

---

[1] See *infra*, pp. 352–4. Previously I had sought to suggest that D'Avenant's claim to at least some of these was based on his possession of early prompt-books ("The Rights of Beeston and D'Avenant in Elizabethan Plays," *Review of English Studies*, 1925, I. 84–91), but I now agree that Hazelton Spencer ("The Restoration Play Lists," *id.* 1925, I. 443–6) seems to be justified in arguing against this hypothesis—although it is peculiar that the King's men of the Restoration appear to have regarded themselves as descendants of the pre-Commonwealth King's men, and it is difficult to determine why just a few Globe-Blackfriars plays came to D'Avenant after 1660.

[2] The specific reference to Blackfriars would seem to be needless had Killigrew not been endeavouring to make a claim to all plays formerly in the possession of the pre-Commonwealth King's Men.

[3] On Aug. 20, 1668, another list of plays is given to D'Avenant and about Jan. 12, 1668/9, a third list records Killigrew's holdings (see *infra*, p. 353). It has been suggested that these repeat similar documents issued in 1660 or 1661, but for this there is no evidence.

received in 1639 from Charles I was granted him on May 16, 1661, but obviously something firmer and more in keeping with changed theatrical conditions was required. On Aug. 14, 1662, he secured a warrant for a licence on the surrender of his former patent[1], and in November the grant was officially approved[2]. The patent eventually came to his hands as signed on Jan. 15, 1662/3[3]. This gave to him, and to Killigrew, apparently full and complete monopoly, but both these managers found that they had many problems, within and without their theatres, to solve.

[1] *Cal. State Papers, Dom. Series, 1661/2*, p. 460.
[2] *Id.* p. 577.
[3] P. Fitzgerald, *op. cit.* I. 73; Leslie Hotson, pp. 217–18. It recites the patent given to D'Avenant by Charles I, mentions the grant made by Charles II in 1660, notes that D'Avenant has surrendered his former patents, grants him full liberty to erect one theatre in London, authorises him to style his company by the title "the servants of our dearly-beloved brother, James, Duke of York," determines "that the said company shall be under the sole government and authority of the said Sir William Davenant...and all scandalous and mutinous persons shall from time to time be ejected, and disabled from playing in the said theatre." The patent then refers to the fact that certain unauthorised companies are presuming to play in London, reiterates the King's will that none shall be tolerated save those of D'Avenant and Killigrew, and makes certain other arrangements for these two troupes. "To preserve amity and correspondence betwixt the said companies and that the one may not encroach upon the other by any indirect means, we will and ordain that no actor or other person employed about either of the said theatres ejected by the said Sir W. Davenant and Thomas Killigrew, or either of them, or deserting his company, shall be received by the governor or any of the said other company, or any other person or persons, to be employed in acting, or in any matter relating to the stage, without the consent and approbation of the governor of the company whereof the said person so ejected or deserting was a member, signified under his hand and seal." "And forasmuch as many plays formerly acted do contain several pro-phane, obscene, and scurrilous passages, and the women parts therein have been acted by men in the habits of women, at which some have taken offence; for the preventing of these abuses for the future we do strictly charge, command, and enjoin that from henceforth no new play shall be acted by either of the said companies containing any passages offensive to piety and good manners, nor any old or revived play containing any such offensive passages as aforesaid, until the same shall be corrected and purged by the said masters or governors of the said respective companies from all such offensive and scandalous passages as aforesaid. And we do likewise permit and give leave that all the women's parts to be acted in either of the said two companies from this time to come may be performed by women, so long as these recreations, which by reason of the abuses aforesaid were scandalous and offensive, may by such reformation be esteemed not only harmless delights, but useful and instructive repre-sentations of human life, by such of our good subjects as shall resort to see the same."

VIII. *Performances at Court and in Oxford.*

Before considering these problems it may be well to note that, in addition to the public playhouses, the two companies of actors performed frequently, by command, on other and royal stages[1]. Of these court theatres the oldest was the Cockpit-in-Court which, established in 1633[2], was used for the performances of plays up to 1664. The following year, 1665, saw the setting up of the Hall Theatre, concerning which numerous documents happily provide us with intimate details[3]. It was for this playhouse that Webb prepared his *Mustapha* scene designs, including one for the special "frontispiece" or proscenium[4]. It was here that the last great masque of *Calisto* was performed, here that French and Italian comedians set up their stages. Although plays were also given in reconstructed halls in St James's and at Windsor[5], this Hall Theatre was the Restoration court playhouse *par excellence*.

When the companies gave command performances at Whitehall or when royalty attended the public playhouses sums of money were due to them from the Treasury, but apparently one of the troubles which beset the managers was the difficulty involved in securing the final warrants. In one instance, bills due for performances in 1662 remained unpaid till 1670[6].

Besides such court productions, there were other special performances for the "Act" at Oxford. On a stage established at the King's Arms in 1661, the players performed Rowley's *All's Lost by Lust*, Shirley's *The Young Admiral*, Middleton's *A Mad World, My Masters*, *The Two Merry Milkmaids of Islington*, Brome's *The City Wit*, Cooke's *Greene's Tu Quoque*, Heywood's *The Rape of Lucrece*, Daborne's *The Poor Man's Comfort*, Massinger's *A Very*

---

[1] The authoritative work on this subject is Eleanore Boswell's *The Restoration Court Stage (1660–1702)* (1932). For the prologue to the first play given at the Cockpit, *The Silent Woman*, on Nov. 19, 1660, see Autrey Nell Wiley, *Rare Prologues and Epilogues 1642–1700* (1940), p. 10.

[2] Eleanore Boswell, pp. 10–21.

[3] Nearly all of these details we owe to the researches of Eleanore Boswell (pp. 22–56). She gives a calendar of the known performances, pp. 278–93.

[4] Identified by Eleanore Boswell, pp. 37–8. This is No. 380 in the catalogue of Percy Simpson and C. F. Bell (*Designs by Inigo Jones*, 1924).

[5] *Id.* pp. 58–64.

[6] Many of these bills, or warrants for payment, were given in the first edition of the present volume, but as Eleanore Boswell (pp. 294–9) has presented a summary of payments for plays at court I have omitted the details here—except, of course, for those documents which actually give the titles and dates of performance. These appear in Appendix B, pp. 343–52.

Woman[1]. Precisely who these actors were is difficult to determine; their repertoire is a somewhat peculiar one, but the presence among them of Mrs Davenport ("Roxalana") and Anne Gibbs shows that some at least were of the D'Avenant troupe[2]. Possibly it was a composite company, although the fact that the Duke's men were the performers in 1669, 1671 and 1672[3] may suggest that those of 1661 belonged to the same tradition. The King's men started to include Oxford within the sphere of their activities in 1673, returned in 1674 and behaved so badly they were prohibited from returning the following year. They were back, however, in 1676, 1680 and 1681. After the union of the companies in 1682[4] the combined players performed at Oxford in 1686 and 1693[5].

Concerning one of these visits some extant documentary evidence gives interesting information. During the Act in 1677 the University Chancellor, the Duke of Ormonde, had brought over the actors who, under his aegis, were settled at the Smock Alley Theatre in Dublin[6]. Three years later, the King's men, who apparently had been forbidden to come to Oxford, sought royal support for a visit to the university town, and on May 15, 1680, the Lord Chamberlain dispatched a letter to the Vice-Chancellor, advising him of the proposed journey and bidding him welcome the actors[7]. This, apparently, put the poor official in a difficulty,

---

[1] On these players see R. Crompton Rhodes, "The King's Players at Oxford, 1661–1712" (*TLS*, Feb. 21, 1929), F. S. Boas, "The University of Oxford and the Professional Players" (*id.* March 14, 1929), Montague Summers, *The Playhouse of Pepys*, pp. 126 ff., and Sybil Rosenfeld, "Some Notes on the Players in Oxford, 1661–1713" (*Review of English Studies*, 1943, XIX. 366–75).

[2] W. J. Lawrence (*TLS*, Feb. 28, 1929), however, draws attention to a reference to the "Red Bull" players on this occasion (*Cal. State Papers, Dom. Series*, 1661, p. 32).

[3] W. J. Lawrence, "Oxford Restoration Prologues" (*TLS*, Jan. 16, 1930).

[4] See *infra*, p. 331.

[5] Sybil Rosenfeld, in the article referred to above, notes letters sent by the Queen to the Vice-Chancellor on behalf of her players in 1691 and 1693.

[6] An epilogue spoken by Joe Haines on this occasion is preserved in manuscript at Harvard University: see William Van Lennep, "The Smock Alley Players of Dublin" (*ELH*, 1946, XIII. 216–22).

[7] L.C. 5/143, p. 506, and 7/1.

"Windsor Castle May: 15th 1680

"Reverend S[r]

His Ma[tes] Comoedians haveing obteyned His leave to go and aire themselves in the Country, now Hee have ['have' written over 'hath'] no need of theire Attendance at Court and beleiveing no aire better than that at Oxford, having likewise prevailed with His Ma[te] to command mee to recommend them to your Protection, That they may represent some of

since Ormonde had urged his support for another visit from his own Irish troupe. The players made further appeal to the highest authority, their royal master; and accordingly on June 5 the Lord Chamberlain was forced to issue a final, if, on his part, reluctant command[1].

Besides these performances at Oxford and before royalty at court, the players were called upon to grace special functions at the Inner Temple, and a valuable record of their performances has been preserved[2]:

Nov. 2, 1663.	*The Brothers*	(King's men).
Feb. 2, 1663/4.	*Epicoene*	(King's men).
Nov. 1, 1664.	*The Night Walker*	(King's men).
Feb. 2, 1664/5.	*The Changes*	(King's men).
Feb. 2, 1667/8.	*The Comical Revenge*	(Duke's men).
1668/9.	*Secret Love*	(King's men).
	The Little French Lawyer	(King's men).
Nov. 1, 1670.	*Sir Martin Mar-all*	(Duke's men).

theire good Playes, for some convenient time before the University: I do very heartily do it, assuring my selfe, that for the Character and Previledge they have of being His Ma[tes] sworne Servants, and for being men of letters, you will be pleased to afford them all the favour that shall bee necessary towards theire security, whilst they are there, which they promise they shall not abuse in any degree I am with much truth

Reverend S[r]

Yo[r] most Affectionate and humble Servant,

Arlington.

For the Reverend D[r] Timothy Haughton Vice Chancell[r] of the University of Oxford."

[1] L.C. 7/1. "I wrote to you on May the 15th recommending to yo[r] favour and protection His Ma[tes] Comoedians, who haveing since complained to him, that there is another Company of the same Profession, whose admittance in the University will frustrate them of the Proffitt they promised themselves under His Ma[tes] name His Ma[te] hath comanded mee to lett you know His Pleasure that Hee would have His owne Comoedians onely gratified with this favour they needing such an Extraordinary Encouragement to repaire them for some misfortunes lately befallen them, and perswadeing himselfe they can singly afford the University as much divertisement as theire vacancie from theire studies will admitt off." Leslie Hotson, *op. cit.* pp. 263–4, shows that on May 16, Ormonde wrote on the subject to the Bishop of Oxford and that the Vice-Chancellor, on May 30, communicated with Sir Leoline Jenkins, telling him of a visit by Ormonde's son, the Earl of Ossory, to the Lord Chamberlain. In the end the King's servants, as was natural, ousted the Chancellor's. Other documents relating to this affair, including an interesting letter quoted from J. R. Magarth, *The Queen's College* (1921), II. 64, are noted by Sybil Rosenfeld in the article referred to above.

[2] *A Calendar of the Inner Temple Records,* edited by F. A. Inderwick (1901), vol. III.

Feb. 2, 1670/1.   *The Committee* (King's men).
Nov. 1, 1671.   *Philaster* (King's men).
Feb. 2, 1675/6.   *The Spanish Curate* (King's men).
Nov. 1, 1675.   *The Scornful Lady* (King's men).
Feb. 2, 1681/2.   *The London Cuckolds* (Duke's men).
Nov. 1, 1682.   *Rule a Wife.*
Nov. 1, 1683.   *The Plain Dealer.*
Nov. 1, 1684.   *A Fond Husband.*
Nov. 4, 1685.   *The Souldier's Fortune.*
Feb. 2, 1685/6.   *The Committee.*
Nov. 1, 1686.   *The Spanish Curate.*
Feb. 2, 1686/7.   *The Spanish Fryar.*
Nov. 1, 1687.   *The Cheats of Scapin.*
Nov. 1, 1689.   *The Squire of Alsatia.*
Nov. 1, 1690.   *Amphitryon.*
Nov. 1, 1697.   *Love for Love.*
Feb. 2, 1697/8.   *The Spanish Fryar.*

IX. *George Jolly, the Nursery and the Strollers.*

This summary of court and academic performances has, of course, taken us far ahead of the plague year, and it will be necessary now to return to a consideration of two rivals who early confronted the patentees and with whom they were forced to compromise.

The first of these was George Jolly. Already it has been suggested that, during the summer of 1660, this trouper had been acting at Salisbury Court; probably because he was ousted from that house by D'Avenant, he sought, in November, for an individual licence, and this, surprisingly, was granted him on Dec. 24, 1660, notwithstanding the sole authority given to the patentees[1]. From this time on to 1662 considerable uncertainty attaches to his activities, and perhaps the best plan is to present briefly such facts as are known. Presumably towards the end of Oct. 1661, Beeston presented a petition against Jolly[2], and, after both parties had been summoned before the Lord Chamberlain, an order was addressed to "George Jolly and his Company actors or Commoedians at the Cockpitt," ordering him to cease performances until the difference with Beeston had been settled. Later, on

---

[1] *Cal. State Papers, Dom. Series, 1660–1,* p. 423. The greater part of the text is given in Leslie Hotson, pp. 177–8.
[2] L.C. 5/184.

Nov. 26[1], a formal decision was promulgated, settling the rent that Jolly was to pay Beeston for the use of Salisbury Court and apparently commanding him not to use any other theatre. We have thus two of the older houses—the Cockpit and Salisbury Court—mentioned late in 1661. At Salisbury Court Pepys saw Ford's *'Tis Pity She's a Whore* on Sept. 9 that year, and probably in 1662, Edward Browne attended performances there of *The Maid in the Mill*, *The Spanish Curate* and *The Bondman*[2]. In addition we know that the Red Bull was still being used, since on March 23, 1660/1, Pepys saw *All's Lost by Lust* at that theatre, and on May 26, 1662, Marlowe's *Dr Faustus*; record of a performance of Daborne's *The Poor Man's Comfort* has also been recorded on May 28, 1661[3]; *Den nieuwgemaakten Adelman* was seen by two foreign visitors on Jan. 22, 1661/2[4], and for the year 1662 there are listed *The Two Merry Milkmaids* and *A Mad World, My Masters*[5].

From these facts we find that Salisbury Court, which had been used by D'Avenant's men up to June 1661, housed a company in September of that year and possibly later in 1662, the Cockpit was Jolly's home in November, the Red Bull had performances in March and May, 1661, as well as in Jan. and May, 1662. Beeston probably had no company of his own[6]; the only regular troupe of players we know of in London during these two years, apart from D'Avenant's men and Killigrew's, is that captained by Jolly. The most probable hypothesis, therefore, appears to be that Jolly used all of these older houses at various times. If he did this, then he utilised the Red Bull for the first half of 1661, when Salisbury

---

[1] L.C. 5/137, p. 333: "Whereas his Ma{t}{ie} Ordered George Jollyes Company of Players should act at Wm Beestons Theater in Salisbury Court And for that the said George Jolly & Wm Beeston have refered themselves to mee wt he the said George Jollye shall giue for his said Company of Players to Act stage playes in the Theatre belonging to Wm Beeston in Salisbury Court and not elsewhere with such priveledges & the vse of such Roomes to dress themselues and reherse in as formerly were allowed Sr Wm Davenants Players I thus Declare the said George Jolley shall pay vnto ye said Wm Beeston for ye vse of his Theater in Salisbury Court for stage playes once aday with ye vse of such roomes & priveledges as were formerly graunted to Sr William Davenants men the sume of thirty shillings Currant money euery day there shalbe stage acting in any Theater in or about ye Cyty of London."

[2] W. W. Greg, "Theatrical Repertories of 1662" (*Gentleman's Magazine*, 1906, XXXI. 69–72). The original document is in B.M. MS. Sloane 1900.

[3] Jordan, *A Royal Arbor of Loyal Poesie*.

[4] Ethel Seaton, *Literary Relations of England and Scandinavia in the Seventeenth Century* (1935), p. 333.

[5] W. W. Greg, *loc. cit.*

[6] See *supra*, p. 291.

Court was occupied by D'Avenant's players, shifted over to become Beeston's tenant, and then, quarrelling with the owner about the rent, moved to the Cockpit, was ordered back to Salisbury Court in November and finally gave some shows at the Red Bull early in 1662. If we assume that the performances at Salisbury Court in 1662 were presented by D'Avenant's men while the opera was being refitted[1], then only one series of troublesome records remains unaccounted for. These concern the Cockpit in 1662. On Oct. 21, two foreign visitors saw *Friar Bacon* there[2], and presumably during that year Browne attended nine performances at the "Cock Pit in Drewry Lane." Opposite the first of these (*The Silent Woman*) he put the symbol "K.P.," certainly the King's Players. The next seven pieces[3] are all recorded earlier as produced by the "old actors" at the Red Bull or by Killigrew's men at the Theatre Royal, and we may presume that these also were given by this "K.P." troupe. Then comes the final title, "Dr Fostos" and opposite it are the words "Licens: Players[4]." If the dates of Browne's visits to the Cockpit indeed fall within the year 1662, then, it would seem, we must assume that for some reason Killigrew's men found it convenient, temporarily, to make use of this house, perhaps only for the course of a week or two; and at the same time we may believe that during part of this year (certain in October) Jolly was making use of its stage[5].

Although such evidence as is provided for us seems to suggest that Jolly confined himself, or was forced to confine himself, to a repertoire of lesser-known or then largely ignored Elizabethan

[1] This is suggested by A. C. Sprague (*Beaumont and Fletcher on the Restoration Stage*, 1926, p. 23).

[2] Ethel Seaton, *op. cit.* p. 333.

[3] *The Elder Brother, Bussy D'Ambois, Othello, The Chances, The Tamer Tamed, Wit Without Money* and *The Opportunity*.

[4] W. W. Greg, *loc. cit.* reads this as "Quens(?) Players," but undoubtedly "Licens: Players" is in the original. In any case there was not any company known as the Queen's men—although no one has so far discussed the peculiar livery orders for "the Queenes Comoedians" on Dec. 17, 1661 (L.C. 5/137, p. 333), Feb. 5, 1661/2, Nov. 4, 1662, Dec. 29, 1663, Feb. 25, 1665/6, and Oct. 2, 1669 (see *infra*, p. 364). In each case the list of actors is the same as that given in corresponding warrants for the King's men. J. G. McManaway ("Philip Massinger and the Restoration Drama," *ELH*, 1934, I. 276–304) alone has noted the unexplained nature of these references. The problem of *Dr Faustus* is discussed by Richard H. Perkinson in "A Restoration 'Improvement' of *Doctor Faustus*" (*ELH*, 1934, I. 305–24).

[5] Leslie Hotson, pp. 178–9, argued strongly for Jolly's company being Browne's "Licens: Players," and, although I once dissented from this identification, I am now convinced he is right in his interpretation of the evidence.

plays[1], it goes without doubt that his performances in London must have been an irritation and an ever-present threat to the two monopoly-holders: at the same time, he himself no doubt found that London's small potential audience tended to flock to the Theatre Royal and to Lincoln's Inn Fields rather than to the stages occupied by his probably undistinguished troupe. Accordingly we need feel no surprise in finding him agreeable, on Dec. 30, 1662, to the leasing of his warrant to the two patentees in return for a sum of £4 a week[2]—presumably after he had made sure of obtaining Herbert's licence for provincial performances, the royal grant for which he received on Jan. 29, 1662/3[3]. Happily, Jolly then set off for pastures new; on April 15, 1663, he was at Norwich and perhaps remained there until August[4]. Perhaps the pieces by Edward Browne in 1662-3 were of their repertoire—*Greene's Tu Quoque, Ignoramus, The Pinner of Wakefield, A Girl Worth Gold, 'Tis Pity She's a Whore, The Little Thief, A New Way to Pay Old Debts, The Fair Quarrel* and "*Muliasses*" (*i.e.* Mason's *The Turk* or *Muleasses*).

During his absence the patentees represented to the King that he had sold (not leased) his licence; they asked permission for the erection of a third theatre, to be used as a "nursery" or training

[1] Many plays acted in the provinces also were of the rarer sort. Thus, for example, the Troutbeck players acted *The Fair Maid of the West* at Rydal Hall on Dec. 27, 1661, and *Gorboduc* was similarly given by the Longsleddall players on Dec. 30, 1662 (F. G. Blair, "Restoration Plays," *TLS*, March 29, 1923). [2] Leslie Hotson, pp. 179-82.

[3] *Cal. State Papers. Dom. Series, 1663-4*, pp. 1 and 27. Herbert's control over provincial playing is interestingly illustrated by the licence issued from his office on April 14, 1662, to George Bayley, who, with a company of eight men, proposed to present a play called *Noah's Flood* (Clifford Leech, "A Restoration Touring Company," *TLS*, May 31, 1934).

[4] Bernard M. Wagner, "George Jolly at Norwich" (*Review of English Studies*, 1930, VI. 449-52). The Norwich records earlier give us information about a company headed by Thomas Knowles (Dec. 29, 1660), of another, bearing a commission from Herbert, including Robert Williams, Samberlain Harvey and Nicholas Calvert (Jan. 7, 1660/1), of an unnamed group, who took in a boy, John Taylor by name, as an apprentice (Jan. 19, 1660/1), and of a company, also bearing a commission from Herbert, captained by Gabrael Shad (Feb. 20, 1660/1). It is just possible that, in his wanderings, Jolly returned to the Continent. On Feb. 1, 1662/3, "the Comedians of the King of England"—"de Commedianten van den Coninck van Inghelandt"—were paid £4 at Ghent for a performance. Harry R. Hoppe ("English Actors at Ghent in the Seventeenth Century," *Review of English Studies*, 1949, XXV. 305-21), who publishes this record, shows, however, that other documents make any definite identification of this company either with Killigrew's men or with Jolly's somewhat difficult. On the whole, Jolly's seems to be the more probable.

school. Jolly's grant was therefore revoked, on July 23, 1663, and a new licence drafted for Killigrew and D'Avenant[1]. Before this licence was formally issued, however, on March 30, 1664, the pair of monopolistic intriguers had made arrangements with a Col. William Legge, by which he became the nominal licensee[2]. Meanwhile, it is probable that Jolly hurried back to London, had a stormy scene with the patentees, set up his company in conjunction with Beeston, got into trouble with the authorities but somehow managed to keep his flag flying until 1665[3]. In or about that year a visiting Frenchman, Chappuzeau, mentions, besides the two patent theatres, "une troisième en Drury Lane qui a grand abord" —presumably the Cockpit under Jolly's management[4]. After the plague, Jolly must have recommenced operations, and no doubt through the representations of the patentees a stern order was issued to him from Whitehall in March, 1666/7[5]. Presumably he remained obdurate, for on April 2 his licence was revoked[6], on the 8th his arrest was ordered[7].

In an attempt to forestall him, the patentees now proceeded to implement their plans for a "nursery." The prologue to John Dover's *The Roman Generalls*, licensed for printing on Nov. 7, 1667, specifically speaks of "both the Houses *Nursery*," which certainly means the nursery owned by both the houses; Pepys attended performances at it on Jan. 7 and Feb. 24, 1667/8; in 1667 Shirley's *The Constant Maid* was printed "As it is now Acted at the new Playhouse called the Nursery in Hatton-Garden." Nominally, this third theatre was licensed to Captain Edward Bedford.

It would appear that Jolly made one last endeavour to assert

---

[1] *Cal. State Papers. Dom. Series, 1663-4*, p. 214.

[2] *Id.* p. 539. It is likely that Jolly returned to London towards the end of August and endeavoured, in conjunction with Beeston, to establish his claim. At any rate a warrant to arrest Beeston "for acting stage playes without leaue" was issued on Aug. 29, 1663, followed by another the next day calling for the arrest of "all persons acting playes without Authority" (L.C. 5/185). The following year saw another "Warr^t to app Wm Beeston or any other acting Stage playes by his authority Sept 7^t 1664" (L.C. 5/186).

[3] Leslie Hotson, pp. 184-5.

[4] W. J. Lawrence, "A Forgotten Restoration Playhouse" (*Englische Studien*, 1905, XXXV. 279).

[5] *Cal. State Papers. Dom. Series, 1666-7*, p. 602; printed in Leslie Hotson, p. 186.

[6] *Cal. State Papers. Dom. Series, 1667*, p. 51; Leslie Hotson, p. 187.

[7] L.C. 5/186. "Whereas George Jolliffe p^{r}sumeth to Act Playes by an old Warr^t granted by his Ma^te which his Ma^te hath since recalled & made voyd & that he hath noe new Lycence These are therefore to require you to App^{r}hend the said George Jolliffe & bring him before me to answere ye said Offense."

his liberty, but on Jan. 20, 1667/8, still another order for his arrest was promulgated[1]. No doubt after this, according to his own later statement, he accepted the patentees' proposal that he should act as their deputy at the nursery, raising a company which would receive two-thirds of the receipts[2]. From the fact that Jolly and Bedford appear in the Lord Chamberlain's papers associated in money matters, the probability is that these two men worked together, Bedford as licensee and Jolly as manager. One of its earliest actors must have been the famous Joe Haines who received his training there and later joined the Theatre Royal[3].

A new nursery was set up some years later in the old Theatre Royal in Vere-street[4], and in 1669–71 a certain John Perin came into the picture[5]. In April, 1671, apparently after performances had ceased at Vere-street, he set up "a booth or playhouse" in Finsbury Fields and acted there for nine weeks[6]. On its demise, plans were made (Oct. 1671) for still another nursery in the Barbican; the inhabitants of the parish of St Giles without Cripplegate anxiously presented petitions against it, the aldermen protested—only to receive the King's contemptuous reply, "That Playhouses should be pulled down when the Meeting houses were[7]." The nursery in the Barbican, with which Jolly was associated as late as 1673, certainly existed up to the time when Dryden described it in his *MacFlecknoe*[8]:

> "An ancient fabrick raised t'inform the sight,
> There stood of yore, and Barbican it hight...
> Near these a Nursery erects its head,
> Where Queens are formed, and future Hero's bred;
> Where unfledged Actors learn to laugh and cry,
> Where infant Punks their tender voices try,
> And little *Maximins* the Gods defy."

---

[1] L.C. 5/186. "A Warr^t to App George Jolliffe John Russell Paul Ryemes & Peter Green for acting playes Erecting Stages & publishing dumb shewes."   [2] Leslie Hotson, pp. 184–5.

[3] Tobyas Thomas, *The Life of the Famous Comedian Jo Haines* (1701); on March 7, 1668, Pepys notes that Haines was "only lately come thither from the Nursery." Since Thomas says that the comedian remained at the nursery "whilst the Play House in Hatton Garden lasted," it is possible that this theatre's run was a short one. It may be noted here that shortly after this date Haines made theatrical history by giving entr'acte entertainments at the first performance of Molière's *Le bourgeois gentilhomme* (see W. J. Lawrence, "An English Comedian at the Court of Louis XIV," *NQ*, 12th ser., May 21, 1921, VIII). This was in the summer of 1670.

[4] Pepys mentions it on April 23, 1669.

[5] Sir Henry Herbert had a case against Perin, Jacob Hall and Robert Turner in May, 1669 (L.C. 5/187), and on April 22, 1671, Bedford sued against him for a debt of £6 (L.C. 5/188).

[6] Leslie Hotson, pp. 189–90.   [7] *Id.* pp. 190–2.   [8] I. 65–79.

The Norwich records, along with other documents, suggest that the income of the nursery was materially added to by tours of the company, and that during such tours the group was known as the Duke of Monmouth's men. On Sept. 22, 1669, Jolly was in Norwich and the licence under which he acted, although not formally issued until later in the year, was probably that ordered for Bedford on Nov. 25[1]. Three years later, on Aug. 6, 1672, John Coysh arrived in the city and, since on March 12, 1683, he was described as the successor to Jolly's patent, presumably he was using Jolly's authority on his earlier visit[2]. On Dec. 10, 1673, however, John Perin was the bearer of the Monmouth patent. For Feb. 10, 1685, and Oct. 16, 1686, Henry Gaine appeared as "servant" to Coysh, although by this time that actor-stroller had seemingly changed his allegiance and entered the service of the Duke of Norfolk: at least he was in Norwich on Sept. 23, 1696, with that lord's "patent[3]."

Beside this nursery group of Monmouth's men, we have record of several other provincial companies. Some who appeared early at Norwich have been noted above[4]. On Jan. 2, 1663/4, an order was issued for a touring licence to be prepared in the name of John Rhodes[5]. A Newmarket company, apparently controlled by

---

[1] L.C. 5/12, p. 185. "Whereas his Mate hath appoynted & authorized Edward Bedford his Mates sworne servant together with his Grace the Duke of Monmouths Company from tyme to tyme to practize & Exercise the Quality of playing of Comedies...within his Mates Kingdome of England & Dominion of Wales (the Citty of London & Westmr Excepted) These are to signifie vnto you his Mates pleasure that you forthwith prpare a bill fitt for his Mates Royall Signature to Lycence & Authorize the said Edward Bedford with his Grace the Duke of Monmouths said Company." Sybil Rosenfeld, *Strolling Players and Drama in the Provinces, 1660–1765* (1939), pp. 35–7, after examining the Norwich records, endorses the view that the nursery and the Duke of Monmouth's men were one.

[2] He had entered the nursery at the same time as Haines: see *supra*, p. 313. The fact that he had been a regular member of the Theatre Royal company between 1674 and 1681 seems to indicate that sometimes the nursery company carried older players with them on tour.

[3] Tony Aston joined this company in Coysh's time and travelled with him, Doggett, Booker and Mins. On Oct. 13, 1697, Sept. 24, 1698, and Sept. 29, 1699, Doggett presented Norfolk's "patent" at Norwich.

[4] See *supra*, p. 311.

[5] *Cal. State Papers. Dom. Series, 1663–4*, p. 462, and L.C. 5/138, p. 387. "Whereas his Matie hath appoynted & Authorized John Rhodes his Mates sworne Servant together with his Company from tyme to tyme to practize & exercise ye Quality of playinge of Comedyes Historyes Tragedyes Enterludes Morralls Pastoralls Stage Playes Maskes & Showes within his Mates Kingdome of England & dominions of Wales ye Cytyes of London & Westmr excepted These are to signifie vnto you his Mates Pleasure that you forth with prpare a Bill fitt for his Mates Royall Signature

Robert Parker, is recorded at Norwich in the autumns of 1676, 1678 and 1680[1]; he was back in the city at Easter, 1684; three years later, in the spring of 1687, John Power was the manager of this troupe, which performed also in 1691, 1692 and 1694. By the beginning of the eighteenth century, if not before, these actors were seemingly known as the Duke of Grafton's men[2]. Concerning Cornelius Saffery, who acted at Norwich in 1672 and 1676, and Moundford Ballydon, who was there in 1687[3], we know nothing more. Nor do we know much about the Duchess of Portsmouth's men, to whom allusion is made in a prologue and epilogue written by Duffett for *The Indian Emperour*[4]. Obviously the old traditions remained, and even until the end of the century the acting companies moved about, theoretically at least, in the liveries of their lords.

One further comment may be made concerning the nurseries. That public performances were given in these houses is certain, but, as has lately been demonstrated[5], care must be taken to avoid confusion between such productions and those given by the "young actors" at the patent houses. These "young actors" were those outside of the sharers, including performers no longer young in years but still in the status of "hirelings." It may be added, however, that when these "young actors" were given permission to present plays for their own benefit some of the sharers occasionally seem to have come to their aid. Such productions certainly occurred in the period of Lent, but at the same time it must not be forgotten that they came also at other seasons—the summer particularly, and perhaps at Christmas as well. During the period

to Lycence & Authorize the said John Rhodes...to practise yᵉ Art & Quality of playinge...within any Town Halls Motehalls Guldhalls Schoolehowses or other convenient places," all local bye-laws notwithstanding.

[1] In L.C. 5/188 appears a warrant to apprehend Robert Parker and Samuell Tanton for acting without a licence (Feb. 25, 1670); such a licence they must have obtained later.   [2] Sybil Rosenfeld, pp. 39–45.

[3] *Id.* pp. 38 and 41. See also J. S. Finch, "Sir Thomas Browne and the Strolling Players in Norwich" (*Review of English Studies*, 1939, xv. 468–70).

[4] Summers, *Playhouses*, p. 125, identifies "Mr Poel" as Martin Powell and asserts that Coysh was the manager of this company. The prologue and epilogue appear in Duffett's *New Songs* (1676), p. 96. It seems just possible that the nursery company may temporarily have been known as the Duchess of Portsmouth's servants. On strolling players generally see Alwin Thaler, "Strolling Players and Provincial Drama after Shakespeare" (*PMLA*, 1922, XXXVII. 243–80).

[5] Philip H. Gray, Jr., "Lenten Casts and the Nursery: Evidence for the Dating of Certain Restoration Plays" (*PMLA*, 1938, LIII. 781–94)— cited later as "Gray, 'Lenten Casts'."

from July 6 to Oct. 10, 1695, for example, no less than 68 performances were sponsored by the "young people"; there were 57 in the corresponding months of 1696, 58 in 1687, 24 in 1698 and 27 in 1699[1]. Assuredly, not all of these were "benefit" shows, but among them must have been several at least belonging to this category. While, therefore, a scrutiny of the casts may well aid us towards the dating of certain plays, it would be an error to assume that all the "young actors" plays were produced in the Lenten season.

Examination of the works of individual dramatists suggests that at least some of the professional writers gained their first hearing by having their apprentice efforts accepted for such productions, and there is also the possibility that, during the eighties and nineties, the "young" players found treasure-trove in the collection of earlier dramatic manuscripts which had come down from Elizabethan times[2]. At this time many actors came forward with plays, and it is perhaps not impossible that several of them are based on manuscript originals and that they were presented for the double benefit of the "young people" and of their "authors" or sponsors.

X. *Sir Henry Herbert and the Mastership of the Revels.*

If Jolly was a rival to the patentees in one way, Sir Henry Herbert was very definitely their dangerous rival in another. Herbert, who had been appointed Master of the Revels in 1623 and through whose skilled management that post had been turned into a most lucrative office, fiercely sought to re-establish his control over the playhouses. On June 20, 1660, he was sworn into the Mastership under Charles II and his papers give full testimony to the frantic struggles he made in an endeavour to assert his supremacy. On Aug. 14, 1660, he came to an agreement with the Mohun group, who promised to pay him £10 immediately, £2 for every new play and £1 for every revived play, as well as £4 a week[3]. After apparently keeping to their bargain for a few weeks, however, the actors, knowing of the pending monopoly for D'Avenant and Killigrew, decided that they no longer owed him allegiance.

---

[1] Leslie Hotson, p. 308.
[2] This suggestion is made by Alfred Harbage in "Elizabethan-Restoration Palimpsest" (*Modern Language Review*, 1940, XXXV. 311–12).
[3] Leslie Hotson, p. 202. This document is certainly the one to which Herbert referred in 1662, giving it the date of Aug. 11, and which had hitherto been thought to be non-extant:

In the patent given to the two courtier-managers Herbert naturally saw a complete blow to his authority, for the warrant evidently gave to them his most cherished prerogatives—the "correcting" and approving of plays and the right to licence acting companies. Accordingly he addressed anxious complaints to the Attorney-General[1], and at the same time despatched a peremptory order to Rhodes, demanding under what authority his house was being used as a playhouse[2]. Rhodes' answer was that he derived his authority from the King. Undeterred, the indefatigable Master of the Revels addressed, on Oct. 13, a letter to Mohun "and the rest of the actors of the Cockpitt play-house," demanding a lowering of their rates and the right to censor their plays[3]. Later he filed suit against Killigrew and D'Avenant on account of the dramas performed by the united company. After long delays this was decided in their favour (Feb. 3, 1661/2)[4]. In another suit brought against D'Avenant alone, however, judgment was given against the defendant (June 20, 1662), whereupon quite naturally D'Avenant submitted a petition to the King, begging for a clarification of the position[5]. In the meantime, Herbert had secured a writ against Betterton for having illegally presented new and old plays between Nov. 5, 1660, and May 6, 1662, and had actually despatched one of his messengers, Edward Thomas, to the theatre with a demand that productions should cease. On this occasion the irate players seized the unfortunate messenger, beat and maltreated him[6].

Presumably the result was one dictated by higher authority, so that both Herbert and the pair of patentees had to give way on certain points. At any rate, on June 4, 1662, articles were signed between Killigrew and the Master of the Revels, evidently after a private "deal" by which the former rather deserted his colleague D'Avenant[7]. By this agreement Killigrew agreed to pay £2 for every new play and £1 for every revived play acted by the company since Aug. 11, 1660, to settle the costs of such suits as Herbert had brought against the actors, to give him a present of £50, to assist Herbert in establishing the Office of the Revels even to the extent of leaving D'Avenant to his fate. That Killigrew kept to his bargain, at least temporarily, is proved by the Worcester

---

[1] Herbert, pp. 85-7.   [2] Id. p. 93.
[3] Id. pp. 93-4.
[4] Leslie Hotson, pp. 211-12.   [5] Id. pp. 211-12.
[6] Id. p. 212. The actors were Betterton, the two Nokes, Robert Turner, Lilleston, Medburne, Underhill, Sandford, Dixon, Price, Harris and Pavy. They were all duly fined.
[7] Herbert, pp. 113-15.

College manuscript of *The Cheats*, duly endorsed by Herbert on March 3, 1662/3[1]. Precisely what happened to D'Avenant we cannot tell. Herbert complained that it was hard that such a person as himself, ever devoted to the interest of the King, should "bee ousted of his just possession, rightes and proffittes, by Sir William Davenant, a person who exercised the office of Master of the Revells to Oliuer the Tyrant, and wrote the First and Second Parte of Peru, acted at the Cockpitt, in Oliuer's tyme, and soly in his favour." Evidently he was pleased with the way things were going, for he told Edward Hayward that "Great matters are to bee expected from the Duke of Yorks playhouse[2]."

To this Edward Hayward and to Captain John Poyntz it seems that Herbert now leased out the Mastership[3]—not, however, without promising Killigrew the reversion of the office[4]. On Herbert's death, April 27, 1673, the manager of the King's men immediately advertised in *The London Gazette*[5] his accession to the vacant chair, and he exercised his duties until his son superseded him on Feb. 24, 1676/7[6]; under Charles the Mastership remained until 1725.

XI. *Actors' Troubles.*

The close connection between theatre and court is marked nowhere more strongly than by the fact that the players, being liveried servants of royalty, were immune from arrest unless by warrant from the Lord Chamberlain[7]. Such being the case, it is

---

[1] On this see the edition by Milton C. Nahm (1935). The struggle of Herbert to maintain his authority is summarised by Arthur F. White in "The Office of Revels and Dramatic Censorship during the Restoration Period" (*Western Reserve Bulletin*, N.S. 1931, XXXIV. 5–115).

[2] Herbert, p. 128. The other relevant documents appear in this volume.

[3] *Id.* pp. 126–31.

[4] A. F. White, *loc. cit.* p. 7.

[5] May 1–5, 1673.

[6] L.C. 7/1. "Charles Killigrew Esq. Master of the Revells in Mr Thomas Killigrews place resigned, Feb. 24: 1676/7." In the same volume appears an order from the Lord Chamberlain, dated Feb. 12, 1678/9, commanding the two companies to "obey such orders and directions as they shall from time to time receive from Mr Charles Killegrew Master of the Revells, to His Ma^{te}."

[7] Thus on Dec. 20, 1669, the Lord Chamberlain reprimanded a couple of bailiffs for having "arrested or caused to bee arrested Thomas Creek one of His Royal Highnesse the Duke of Yorkes Servants without leaue" (L.C. 5/187). On the other hand, the actors, being servants of the court, were "on duty." On April 26, 1670, a bailiff was instructed: "Whereas Jeremiah Lisle One of his Royall Highnesse ye Duke of Yorks Comoedians hath absented him selfe from his duty & otherwise Misbehaued him selfe...These are to require you to Apprehend and take into Custody the

not surprising that the order-books of this hard-worked and harassed official[1] should be full of petitions and complaints from the numerous persons who were owed money by the spendthrift "Comoedians." Some perhaps took up this profession for ulterior motives, as is hinted in a complaint of one Henry Dobson against Mrs Weaver[2]. Whether the accusation be true or not, the actors certainly seem to have been born borrowers. Henry Harris, who knew so well how to drink ale with Shadwell and the Earl of Dorset[3], and the facetious Joe Haines[4] were easily the worst

body of the said Jeremiah Lisle And bring him before mee to answere vnto such things as shalbe Objected ag^t him" (L.C. 5/188). So we find "A Warr^t to App   Adams & Allenson for absenting themselfes from ye Dukes house Theatre" (L.C. 5/188, dated about Aug. 12, 1670). On Dec. 9, 1669, Sandford and Medbourne were similarly ordered to be arrested for having been "refractory & disorderly" (L.C. 5/12, p. 302), while on Dec. 5, 1670, Mrs Norton, of the Theatre Royal, was in the same kind of trouble (L.C. 5/188).

[1] Although it is characteristic of the age that the Earl of Dorset, who was Lord Chamberlain under William and Mary, was one of the most noted among Restoration rioters. In June 1678 Nell Gwyn reported that "My lord of Dorseit apiers wonse in thre munthe, for he drinkes aile with Shadwell the dramatist and Mr Haris [i.e. Henry Harris, the well-known actor] at the Dukes house all day long" (*Camden Miscellany*, v. 25–6).

[2] "To the Right Honro^ble &c The humble petition of Henry Dobson Humbly sheweth that one Eliz. Farley hath [by, *deleted*] gone by the name of Eliz: Weauer wife to a Gent of Grayes Inne to defraud her Creditors and now being discouered that she is none of his Wife although she hath had a child by him and haueing noe other shift for the defrauding of her said Creditors but meerely being sworne one of his Maties servants she oweing yor pet^r the summe of 25! 11^s 06^d whereof she hath paid 14! soe there remaines due 11! 11^s 06^d which hath beene thirty tymes demanded and bids defyance to yor pet^r yor pet^rs most humble request is that your Hono^r wilbe pleased to grant leaue to yor pet^r to take his course at Law ag^t her" (L.C. 5/184, about Sept. 30, 1662). Mrs Weaver was ordered, on June 13, 1663, to appear on account of a petition by Robert Kerby, and on May 24, 1665, Mrs Anne Hame was allowed to go to law against her (L.C. 5/185 and 5/186).

[3] See *supra*, note 1. Harris was ordered to be arrested on June 29, 1663 (L.C. 5/185); Thomas Halfpenny was permitted to go to law against him on Nov. 30, 1667, Robert Bird on Jan. 8, 1667/8, Richard Snow on Feb. 27, 1667/8, Sir Henry Herbert on March 21, 1667/8, Levett on March 27, 1668, Mary Inglesby on Dec. 15, 1668, William Keene on Jan. 9, 1668/9. Harris also was being constantly sued by his wife for maintenance: she petitioned on Jan. 25, 1675/6 and again on Nov. 2, 1677. He was sued for £8 lent to his wife on May 19, 1677 (L.C. 5/185–190).

[4] Haines was petitioned against by Thomas Jennings on Feb. 1, 1667/8, by Martin Powell on Jan. 9, 1668/9, by William Matthews on the same day, by John Tummins on Sept. 3, 1674, by one Tinder on Jan. 26, 1674/5, by Hannah Barton, widow, of Gutter-lane, Cheapside, "for dyet & Lodging & part engaged for him which she is likely to pay," on Feb. 10, 1674/5. Haines was arrested on March 30 of the same year. The list of petitions could be almost indefinitely extended.

offenders, but others, including Lacy[1], Blagden[2], Loveday[3], Clun[4], Shatterell[5], Coysh, Martin Powell[6], Wintersell[7], Kent[8], Underhill[9], Goodman[10] and Sheppey[11] shared in their delinquencies.

No doubt the picture of debts and disturbances presented in these documents must be set alongside the other picture of rivalries and confusions in the management of the playhouses.

XII. *The King's Men, 1666–1682.*

During the enforced closing of the theatres after June 1665 Killigrew appears to have engaged in some improvement of his Theatre Royal. Pepys, on March 19, 1665–6, passed the playhouse and noticed it all dirt owing to the widening of the stage. He opined that God alone knew "when they will begin to act again." By the end of the year, however, the actors were once more at work. It would appear that the first performances were in the

[1] A petition of Edward Man against Lacy appears on March 1, 1660/1; at the desire of one Serle he was arrested on or before Nov. 28 of that year.

[2] Blagden appears as defendant against Bedford on Oct. 15, 1663; against Anthony Wood in 1662; against Sir William Clarke on March 26, 1664; against Letchfield on July 8, 1664; and against Robert Toplady on Sept. 17, 1664.

[3] Loveday is associated with Blagden in the last-mentioned petition. Matthew Harris sought for payment from him of a ten-guinea debt on July 20, 1663, and there was a petition against him on April 16, 1664.

[4] On Sept. 14, 1663, Mary Meggs petitioned against Clun. This Mary Meggs was fruit-woman at the theatre. There was issued "A Warr^t to App Mary Meggs for abuseing Mrs Rebecca Marshall one of his Mat^{es} Comoedians to ye disturbance of his Mat^{es} Actors and Comitting other Misdemeanours" on Nov. 5, 1669 (L.C. 5/187). On this lady, better known as "Orange Moll," see Leslie Hotson, pp. 291–2. Clun was associated with other players in petitions against the company in general. Thus we find "The humble petition of Edward Dicket and his wife late Wright ag^t Walter Clunn and the other Comoedians" on March 1, 1663/4 (L.C. 5/185).

[5] Shatterell was petitioned against by William Phillipps on Sept. 17, 1664; by George Hewett on May 21, 1666; by Bartholomew Barker on Oct. 16, 1667; by Thomas Tunman on March 21, 1670/1; by Jean Assevedo on Feb. 3, 1674/5; and by Cecily Smith on Feb. 15, 1676/7.

[6] Both Coysh and Powell were petitioned against by Thomas Burry on March 16, 1675/6.

[7] Edward Gavile claimed £34 for goods from him on May 23, 1677.

[8] Kent was associated with the last-mentioned claim against Shatterell.

[9] Anne Allen agreed to accept yearly instalments from Underhill on Jan. 17, 1683/4.

[10] Alice Price, "widow...for lodginge & mony lent in Great Russell Streete in Bloomesbury," petitioned against Goodman on Dec. 15, 1677.

[11] For Sheppey see *infra*, p. 332.

nature of charity shows and were stopped[1], but Charles gave the lead by calling for plays at court. On Thursday, Oct. 11, it seems that *Wit without Money* was presented at Whitehall[2] and Evelyn records a production of *Mustapha* there a week later (Oct. 18). Pepys had been told by Mrs Knepp that both houses would begin again on the 29th, but on that day he was forced to go to the court playhouse, where he saw *Love in a Tub*. On Friday, Dec. 7, however, he was able to enter the Theatre Royal for *The Maid's Tragedy* and noted that the companies had been performing for about a fortnight.

From this time on troubles, trivial and great, attended the King's house. In 1667 a stir seems to have been caused by some rather outspoken passages uttered on the stage. *The Change of Crownes* was silenced on Tuesday, April 16, and Lacy was sent to prison[3]. Shortly after the reopening of the theatre we read of another arrest, this time of Pepys' friend, Mrs Knepp[4]. Other complications seem to have disturbed the equanimity of the Theatre Royal during this time. Anne Quynn, who had joined the company probably only a short time before this date, had evidently quarrelled with the management because some other actress had taken her parts. She left the house, petitioned the Lord Chamberlain, and an order was issued to Hart that he should immediately reinstate her[5]. Lord Buckhurst, Pepys heard on Saturday, July 13,

---

[1] *Cal. State Papers, Dom. Series, 1666–7*, pp. 232 and 299.

[2] Eleanore Boswell, *op. cit.* p. 282.

[3] Pepys, Saturday, April 20, 1667. He tells us that on his release Lacy abused Howard, and the warrant for his re-arrest is extant: "Whereas John Lacy hath both in abusive words and actions abused the Honoble James Howard Esqr These are to require you to take into Custody the said John Lacy and him safely [keepe *deleted*] to deliver into the Custody of the [Marshall of the Marshalsey *deleted*] Knight Marshall or the Deputy...Aprill 20t 1667." The order for Lacy to be brought before the Lord Chamberlain is dated April 25, so that the letter in the *Hist. MSS. Commission Reports* which states he was freed on the 23rd, would not seem to be correct. (Documents in L.C. 5/186.) See the edition of *The Change of Crownes* prepared by F. S. Boas (1949). On the arrest of Henry Killigrew after the affair of July 20, 1667 (*supra*, p. 18) see Carl Niemayer, "Henry Killigrew and the Duke of Buckingham" (*Review of English Studies*, 1936, XII. 326–8).

[4] "A Warrt to App Mrs Nepp One of his Mates Comoedians & to deliuer her to his Mates Knt Marshall Dated ffeb: 12: 1667" (i.e. 1667/8; in L.C. 5/186). She was arrested again on April 23, 1668.

[5] L.C. 5/138, p. 376. The order bids the actress be taken on again, commands that she be given all her old parts, none daring to act these without her express consent, and closes by bidding "yt you Assigne her a dressing roome with a chymney in it to be only for her vse & whom she shall admitt." It is dated May 4, 1667.

1667, had got Nell Gwyn away from the company and on Monday, Aug. 26, he was informed that she had been cast off by that gay nobleman and that Hart, her former admirer, now hated her. From an order dated Dec. 14 it is clear that Mohun for some time had not been acting[1].

For some reason both of the theatres had stopped performances in October, 1669[2]. The most interesting record of this year is the Chancery suit discovered by Leslie Hotson which involves John Dryden and a scene-painter Isaac Fuller[3]. Dryden had just finished *Tyrannick Love* (April, 1669) and the players engaged Fuller to execute "a new Scene of an Elysium." Apparently they attempted to cheat him of his fee and the case went in his favour. Apart from showing that *Tyrannick Love* was produced in June, 1669, and that it ran for a fortnight, the suit is particularly interesting because it reveals that this single set, which occupied the artist for six hard weeks, was valued at the very large sum of £335.

In the midst of these and other disturbances came the great disaster, the complete demolition by fire, on Jan. 25, 1671/2, of the Theatre Royal in Bridges-street[4]. For fully a month the company must have ceased acting, but on Monday, Feb. 26, 1671/2, they started again in the old Duke's theatre in Lincoln's Inn Fields (vacated because D'Avenant's men were now housed in the ornate Dorset Garden playhouse[5]), presenting *Wit without Money*, a title which without doubt expressed their own condition. Here they continued until midsummer, 1673, as is made plain by a L.C. warrant on June 7 of that year[6].

Whether the company temporarily ceased acting after that date seems to be uncertain. All we know is that plans went ahead for a new structure, with the actors in such dire straits that they

---

[1] L.C. 5/138, p. 411: "If Mr Mohun hath received any money for the tyme that he was absent from playeing that you deteyne soe much in your hands out of the next share he is to haue."

[2] All we know of this is an order in L.C. 5/12, p. 251, declaring that the two companies are allowed "to Act & play againe vpon Monday next & soe to continue Acting." It is dated Oct. 16, 1669. The Theatres were closed again, because of the Duchess of York's death, in April, 1671 (L.C. 5/12, p. 302: order dated April 1, 1671).

[3] *Op. cit.* pp. 250–2.

[4] The fire is described in a contemporary ballad and also in a letter of Jan. 27, 1671/2 (see *HMC*, 11. 22). It caused great damage in Russell-street and one actor, Bell, lost his life.

[5] See *infra*, p. 330.

[6] L.C. 5/140, p. 263. "It is his Ma^tes pleasure that there shall not bee acted any playes at the Theatre in Lincolnes Inne ffeilds after Midsummer day next ensueing vntill further order." This is addressed to Killigrew.

appealed for a gift from the King—who characteristically provided them with a letter addressed to the parish churches asking for contributions on their behalf[1]. The sharers, who now included John Dryden in their number, entered into a covenant with certain building investors[2]; money was raised by divers means and the actors were levied for the cost of the "scene-house[3]." At last the new playhouse was ready and on Thursday, March 26, 1673/4, opened its doors. In all probability Sir Christopher Wren's cross-section preserved in All Souls, Oxford, represents this Theatre Royal in Drury Lane, while its proscenium is at least suggested in the engraved frontispiece to *Ariane*[4].

Apart from their lack of money and the accumulated debts that weighed upon them, two particular troubles afflicted the actors. The first was that Thomas Killigrew seems to have been hopeless as a manager, and the players were restive under his control[5]. A very peremptory order against any actor or actress leaving either company without due notice was issued by the Lord Chamberlain on May 16, 1674[6]. Early the following year Killigrew was complaining that members of his troupe were appropriating monies due to him[7], and the difference between the players and the master, after being adjudicated by the Lord Chamberlain, was finally settled in an agreement undated but probably drawn up about the middle of the month[8].

---

[1] T. N. Bushfield, "Church Brief for a London Theatre" (*NQ*, 8th ser., Oct. 10, 1896, x). Contributions were made in many parishes.

[2] Leslie Hotson, p. 254.

[3] *Id*. p. 255. Since Hotson deals with the complex financial negotiations at this time and later, the details are omitted here.

[4] Wren's cross-section, originally discussed by Hamilton Bell ("Contributions to the History at the English Playhouse," *Architectural Record*, 1913, XXXIII. 359–68) is reproduced in *The Development of the Theatre* (new edition, 1947), Fig. 194; the *Ariane* frontispiece appears in the same book, Fig. 195.

[5] Leslie Hotson, pp. 256–8.   [6] See *infra*, p. 360.

[7] L.C. 5/141, p. 100 and 7/1, p. 4: "Whereas Complaint is made unto mee by M[r] Thomas Killigrew Master of the Revells and Master of yo[r] Company that some of you haue violently taken and shared Money against an Agreement betweene you and his positive order to the Contrary I do hereby appoint Friday Morninge next at my Lodgeings at Whitehall to heare the matter in difference And require you whose Names are underwritten to appeare before mee at that tyme And in the meane time that you continue Acting without any disturbance." The names given are those of Kynaston, Mohun, Lacy, Burt, Shatterell, Wintersell and Carterett (i.e. Cartwright). This is dated Jan. 11, 1674/5.

[8] L.C. 5/141, p. 114 and 7/1: "It is agreed and consented by M[r] Thomas Killegrew and by M[r] Mohun, M[r] Kynnaston, M[r] Wintersell, M[r] Shatterell, M[r] Cartwright for themselues and theire Company That halfe the

Still, however, perplexity reigned. On Dec. 9 of the same year articles were drawn up for the better regulating of the Theatre Royal, and these were approved on Dec. 14[1]. Despite this, some of the leading actors absented themselves from the playhouse, so

proffitt of the House shall go towards the payment of the debts of the House The Company alleadgeing Mr Killegrew had resigned His Power, which hee had by His Patent as Master of theire Company unto the Company Mr Killegrew produces a Resignation back againe unto him by the Company of all his Power as formerly Except intermedling with the proffitts and shares, which is to be done according to Articles betweene them which Agreement concerning the proffitts and shares Mr Killegrew declares he will observe and not any waies breake or contradict And according to that Agreement Mr Killegrew expects onely his two shares, And the rest to be divided according to the Articles and Consent of the Company." It is dated merely "Jan: 1674/5."

[1] L.C. 5/141, p. 307. "Articles of Agreem^t for the Better Regulateing theire Ma^tes Servants the Comoedians at the Royall Theatre humbly presented to yor Lord_pp Consideraĉon by the Master & Company yor Lord_pp being Our Superior Officer. December 9: 1675.

"1 That noe man or Weoman shall dispose of theire parts without the consent of the Company Subpoena 20 shillings

"2 That neither Man or Weoman shall refuse any part the Company shall thinke them fitt for Subpoena a weekes wages

"3 That noe hired man or Weoman neglect rehearsall vpon forfeiture as formerly

"4 Whereas by Experience Wee find Our Cloathes Tarnished & Imberelled by frequent Weareing them out of the Playhouse It is thought fitt noe Weoman presume to goe out of the House with the Play House Cloathes or Properties vpon Penalty of theire Weekes pay

"5 That neither Man or Weoman make vse of either Scenes or Cloathes without the Generall consent of the whole Company

"6 Vpon Complaynt of People of Quality of Mrs Meggs Severall Maydes offending them in the Pitt besides offending the Stage with theire Noise & treading vpon theire Cloathes & other affronts wee desire she may be obliged to strictly observe her Covenants

"7 That noe Hired Man or Weoman quitt the Company without three Monethes warninge, & that giuen to Mr Thomas Killegrew vnd^r theire hands

"8 That noe Man or Weoman be entertained in the Company with[out] the Generall Knowledg & consent of the Company for the future & that they play three Monethes without Sallary by Way of Approbation Acording to ancient Articles

"9 That neither Feathers nor Clothes nor Ribbons nor any thing relating to the Stage be taken vp without the Consent of the Company vpon penalty of paying for them themselves

"10 To p^rvent the Disorders of the shareing Table by an Inundation of People that presse vpon them in theire businesse Henry Hayles is appoynted to stand at the Dore & there to admitt them as they are called and by one to deliuer vp theire charge & soe dismisse them

"11 To avoyd the future inconveniency of strangers frequent Egresse & regresse when a play is done in ye House, it is thought fitt that some one or two be appoynted to stand at the Tyring house Dore till the House is discharged the persons appoynted are David Middleton and Brittaine

that on Feb. 14, 1675/6 the King had to step in to compel them to act again[1]. Two months later Killigrew, promising to make over his patent to his son Charles, persuaded that young man to seek a settlement: by giving what amounted to bribes to Hart and Kynaston the latter succeeded, on May 1, 1676, in getting the actors to enter into a new agreement[2]. Thereafter, however, the elder Killigrew backed down from his promise to hand over the patent to his son. A violent quarrel ensued. On Aug. 3, the manager was ordered not to act until further order[3], and on Sept. 9, the Lord Chamberlain, assuming command, set up Mohun, Kynaston, Hart and Cartwright as a committee of control[4] and later, for some reason, appointed Hart as sole director[5]. On Jan. 23, 1676/7 Charles Killigrew brought the case against his father to Chancery, and, shortly after, the latter handed over his authority. Charles became master of the Theatre Royal on Feb. 22, 1676/7[6] and Master of the Revels on the 24th[7].

"12   That noe persons Vnconcerned in the Businesse of the Play be admitted to stand betweene the Scenes

"13   Henry Hales is ordered to take vp all fforfeits"

This document is signed by Lacy, Kynaston, Shatterell, Hart, Wintersell, Killegrew, Mohun, Cartwright and Burt.

[1] L.C. 7/1, p. 5: "His Mate understanding That His Company of Comoedians have left off actinge upon private differences and disagreements betweene themselues is very much displeased thereat And hath commanded mee to require and order the said Company forthwith to act and play as formerly And that none of the said Company presume to leave off Acting."

[2] Leslie Hotson, p. 259.   [3] L.C. 5/141, p. 433.

[4] L.C. 7/1: "Whereas His Mate hath commanded mee to take upon mee the Governement and direction of His Company of Comoedians during the difference betweene Mr Killegrew and His Sonne to which the said Company haue submitted thmselues according to a writeing signed by them I do hereby nominate and appoint Mr Michaell Mohun, Mr Charles Hart, Mr Edward Kynnaston, and Mr William Cartwright under mee from tyme to tyme to order and direct all things whatsoever belonging to the well orderinge of the said Company"—dated Sept. 9, 1676.

[5] L.C. 7/1. An order dated Feb. 22, 1676/7 recites that the Lord Chamberlain had established the four men as managers "and by a second Order I did appoint Mr Hart alone."

[6] L.C. 7/1: "Now whereas the Father and the Sonne are agreed, and that the Father hath certified the same to mee under his hand writeinge, that hee hath resigned and delivered up all his right power and authority with his two voyces as Master of the Company of His Mates Comoedians unto his sonne Mr Charles Killegrew I do therefore...hereby order that the said Company do in all things conforme themselues to the orders and directions of Mr Charles Killegrew."

[7] L.C. 7/1: "Charles Killigrew Esq. Master of the Revells in Mr Thomas Killigrews place resigned. Feb. 24: 1676/7." Orders regarding his authority are to be found scattered throughout the L.C. books: e.g. 7/1, dated

During all this time minor worries attended the theatre. Haynes was silenced on Nov. 4, 1675[1], and Mrs Slade on Nov. 25 of the same year[2]. What with silencings, voluntary abstentions and internal differences Drury Lane was indeed in a bad way. Nor did matters improve after Charles Killigrew assumed control. The actors were no better pleased with the son than with the father. The King, on July 30, expressed himself dissatisfied with the management of the Theatre Royal and declared that he would allow the actors self-government[3]. In an attempt to maintain his hold on the playhouse, Charles Killigrew adopted new tactics: on Sept. 28, 1677, he associated himself with others who owned 20 out of the 36 shares and got them to enter into a new contract with a number of the "young" actors—Philip Griffin, Cardell Goodman, Martin Powell, Carey Perin, Thomas Disney, Marmaduke Watson and Sarah Cooke[4]. The dissentions continued and there seem to have been several occasions when, as a result of these, the theatre was closed[5]. Accusations were made of thefts of the playhouse properties: the treasurer, James Gray, declared that Charles Killigrew and Shatterell clandestinely mortgaged the

Feb. 12, 1678/9: "I do hereby order that His Ma^{tes} Comoedians, and His Royall Highnesse Comoedians do obserue and obey such orders and directions as they shall from time to time receive from Mr Charles Killegrew Master of the Revells, to His Ma^{te}." Leslie Hotson, *op. cit.* pp. 261 and 279, notes that the passing over of the Mastership was recorded in the *Gazette* for Feb. 1–5, 1676/7.

[1] L.C. 7/1 and 5/141, p. 287: "Whereas Joseph Haynes hath with ill & scandalous language, & insolent carriage abused Sr Edmund Windham" is the reason given.

[2] L.C. 5/141, p. 294.

[3] L.C. 5/142, p. 98 and 7/1. "His Ma^e being dissatisfied with the Governement of the Players His Servants at the Royal Theatre, upon theire humble petition which I here send you is pleased to gratify them in theire proposition of governeing themselves but withall, that Mr Killegrews right to his shares and proffitts may bee preserved and that he may haue also security given him to indempnify him from those Articles and debts, which hee alleadges hee is lyable unto, as you will see in his Answeare to theire petition which I here alsoe send you His Ma^{es} desires it may be dispatcht by you with all conveniency That the Company may begin to play to support themselues because they suffer every day they lye still." The letter is addressed from Arlington to Sir William Jones, the Attorney General. Killigrew seems to have been sparing of his money. The dismissal of the musicians has already been noted (*supra*, p. 62) and on May 12 Robert Baden was petitioning for £135. 12s. due for properties delivered (L.C. 5/190). This was ordered to be paid by Jan. 10, 1677/8 (L.C. 5/191). On April 5, 1678, Thomas Jolly sued the company for £54 "for makeing cloathes for ye vse of ye Company" (L.C. 5/191).

[4] Leslie Hotson, pp. 261–2.

[5] *Id.* p. 262.

stock, a statement endorsed by Charles' half-brother, Henry Killigrew, and by Griffin; Kynaston later made a similar charge against Henry Killigrew and Wintershall[1]; while the Lord Chamberlain was forced on April 19, 1678, to forbid the actors from removing any costumes outside the theatre or wearing any theatrical garments out of acting hours[2].

In 1678 or 1679, at one of the times when the playhouse had been involuntarily closed, the treasurer, James Gray, Cardell Goodman and Thomas Clarke set off for Scotland[3], but very soon after the arrival of the troupe in Edinburgh, Killigrew demanded their return, promising to pay their travelling expenses: they were back in London some time in February 1679/80, but no money was refunded them—whence a long-drawn out suit which was not finally settled until Feb. 8, 1683/4[4].

[1] *Id.* pp. 262–3 and 268.

[2] This order and another restraining Charles Killigrew from disposing of the stock (the latter dated Oct. 30, 1679) are in the L.C. books. The first appears in 5/143, p. 69 and 7/1: "Whereas Michaell Mohun, Nicholas Burt, and Robert Shatterell three of His Mates Comoedians haue given Bond of fiue hundred pounds unto Charles Killegrew Esq....to returne the Stock of Clothes and Scenes belonging to the Royal Theatre entire at the end of three yeares...and whereas I am informed that some of the said Clothes hath beene carried out of the House, and embezelled by some of the Company These are therefore to require all His Mates Company of Comoedians both men and women that none of them presume to go out of the House in theire acting Clothes."

L.C. 5/143, p. 399 and 7/1. "His Mate being informed that you are going about to dispose of the Players Stock of Clothes, Bookes, and other Properties belonging to His Mates Theatre Royall, His Mate hath comanded mee to require you And I do hereby require you not to dispose of any of the said Clothes, or other properties belonging to the said Playhouse, but that you cause them safely to bee kept, and that you take an Inventory of the same, and deliuer a Copy of the said Inventory to Major Mohun to bee by him kept for the rest of the Company that are concerned therein."

[3] Leslie F. Casson, in "Notes on a Shakespearean First Folio in Padua" (*Modern Language Notes*, 1936, LI. 417–23), suggests that this annotated copy may have been the one used by this group. If so, Carlisle was one of their number.

[4] Leslie Hotson, pp. 262–3. The following appears in L.C. 7/1: "Whereas His Mate hath comanded mee to examine a Complaint of Mr Gray Mr Goodman, and Mr Clarke, against Mr Charles Killegrew concerning monies taken up for defraying theire charges in comeing out of Scotland: I haue called Mr Charles Killegrew, Mr Gray, Mr Clarke and Mr Goodman before mee, and they haveing submitted the whole matter to my determination, And Mr Gray haveing made it appeare, that he with Mr Goodman, and Mr Clarke are bound in a Bond of Twenty pounds to Mr Morley, which was taken up for the use of some of the Comoedians there in Scotland, towards the bringing of them back to act in His Mates Theatre at London and that he hath beene sued upon that

Difficulties with their chief poet, too, harassed the actors. As has been noted above, John Dryden was included among the sharers when Drury Lane was being built, and apparently the inclusion of his name in their midst was due to the fact that some time about the year 1668 he contracted to write three plays annually in return for one and a quarter shares. By January or February, 1677/8, however, the poet had deserted the company and given a play to the Duke's men[1]. The actors immediately put forward their complaint in the shape of a petition, with what result we can, now,

Bond by Mr Charles Killegrew to whom that Bond was assigned by Mr Morley, In the charges of which suite he makes appeare That by Bills, Answeares, Injunctions in Chancery and Comõn Law he hath expended the sume of Twenty Six pounds Sixteen Shillings, and haveing heard all parties, and examined the whole matter, do find that Mr Gray ought to bee freed from the said Bond, and paid his charges by the whole Company, that was then in being for whome hee did that service, and for as much as that Company is dissolved These are therefore to signify His Ma[tes] Pleasure, that out of the monies that is in yo[r] present possession, or that shall first bee received by you, ariseing out of the Bookes, Scenes, and Cloths, either of the old or new stock belonging to the said former Company at the Royall Theatre, you cause the said Bond of Twenty pounds to bee discharged, and M[r] Gray freed from the same and alsoe that you satisfy M[r] Gray his charges of 26[ll]: 16[s]: 00[d]: occasioned by the suite upon the said Bond." In the same entry book is another document, dated March 3, 1683/4 identically similar to the above down to "dissolved." The following is then added: "And the said M[r] Charles Killegrew is allowed three shares out of yo[r] Company, for the Bookes, Scenes, and Clothes, that did belong to them, and ought to haue discharged the debts of that Company, These are therefore to signify His Ma[tes] Pleasure that out of the said three shares payable to the said M[r] Killegrew in consideration of the said Bookes, Scenes and Clothes, you cause the said Bond of twenty pounds to be discharged and M[r] Gray freed from the same And alsoe that you satisfy the said M[r] Gray his charges of twenty six pounds sixteene shillings occasioned by the suite upon the said Bond." Both of these are addressed to D'Avenant and Betterton. This money was not paid by Dec. 8, 1684, when another order was issued to have the payment made immediately. A reference is made to this Scotch visit in Dryden's Prologue to the University of Oxford (ed. Sargeaunt, p. 239):

"Our House has suffered in the Common woe,
We have been troubled with *Scotch* Rebels too.
Our brethren are from *Thames* to *Tweed* departed,
And of our Sisters all the kinder hearted
To *Edenborough* gone, or coached or carted."

It may be noted here that Goodman had been arrested on April 4, 1678 "for Certaine abuses & misdemeanors by him Comitted" (L.C. 5/188). On June 18, 1677 Haynes had been similarly arrested "for reciteinge... a Scurrilous & obscoene Epilogue" (L.C. 5/188).

[1] In the prologue to Duffett's *The Mock-Tempest* (D.L. Nov. 1674) the audience are chided because they have "forc'd a reverent Bard to quit our House." This cannot apply to Dryden, but shows that he was not alone in abandoning the Theatre Royal.

only surmise. At any rate, Dryden's next plays were performed by the rivals of the King's men[1].

Unquestionably Dryden's action was motivated by his realisation of the wretched state into which Drury Lane theatre had sunk. On July 30, 1680, a new agreement was drawn up by Griffin, Shatterell, Clarke, Goodman, Powell, Watson, Sheppey and Charles Killigrew[2]. This was a sorry remnant of a once brave troupe. The epilogue to *Mithridates*, the first play produced in 1681, no doubt summed up general feeling when it exclaimed: "Pox on this Playhouse, 'tis an old tir'd jade[3]." By the beginning of Feb. 1680/1,

[1] On this see James M. Osborn, *John Dryden: Some Biographical Facts and Problems* (1940), pp. 184–9.

The petition was originally printed in Malone's *Life of Dryden*, but Osborn reproduces the original document and presents a transcript which includes certain phrases that had been deleted: "Whereas, upon Mr Drydens binding himselfe to write 3 Playes a yeare, Hee the said Mr Dryden was admitted & continued as a Sharer in the Kings Playhouse for divers yeares; and received for his Share & a quarter, 3 or 4 hundred pounds, Comunibus annis, but though he received the monyes, we received not the Playes, not one in a yeare. After which, the House being burnt, the Company in building another contracted great debts, so that the Shares fell much short of what they were formerly. Thereupon Mr Dryden complaining to the Company of his want of proffit, The Company was so kind to him, that they not onely did not presse him for the Playes which he so engag'd to write for 'em, (and for which he was paid before hand[]) But they did also at his earnest request give him a third day for his last new Play call'd All for Love [Hee promiseing before most part of the Company That they should have the refuseall of all his Playes thenceforward,] and at the receipt of the money of the said third day, he acknowledg'd it as a guift, & a particular kindnesse of the Company, Yet notwithstanding this kind proceeding Mr Dryden has now jointly with Mr Lee (who was in Pension with us to the last day of our Playing, & shall continue) Written a Play call'd Adipus, and given it to the Dukes Company, contrary to his said agreem^t, his promise, and all gratitude and to the great prejudice, and almost undoing of the Company, They being the onely Poets remaining to us. Note—Mr Crowne being under the like agreem^t with the Dukes house writt a Play call'd the Destruction of Jerusalem, and being forced by their refusall of it to bring it to us, the said Company compell'd us after the studying of it, & a vast expence in Scenes and Cloathes, to buy off their clayme, by paying all the pension he had received from them Amounting to One hundred & twelve pounds paid by the Kings Company, Besides neare forty pounds he the said Mr Crowne paid out of his owne Pocket.

These things consider'd, if notwithstanding Mr Drydens said agreem^t, promise, & moneys freely given him for his said last new Play, & the many titles we haue to his Writeings, this Play be Judg'd away from us, We must submit."

This is signed by Charles Killigrew, Hart, Burt, Goodman and Mohun.

[2] Leslie Hotson, p. 264.

[3] Autrey Nell Wiley, *Rare Prologues and Epilogues, 1642–1700* (1940), p. 44.

profits sank so far that performances ceased; half-rent was accepted by the building sharers, but after a few days the miserable houses compelled dismissal of audiences[1]. Finally, in April, 1682, all attempts to keep up the struggle were abandoned and on May 4 articles of union with the rival company were signed by Charles Killigrew, Betterton, Charles D'Avenant and Smith[2]. Thus, for a time, ended the career of Drury Lane as an independent theatre.

XIII. *The Duke's Men, 1666–1682.*

The Duke's men had suffered a severe blow shortly after their recommencement of activities late in 1666. In April 1668 Sir William D'Avenant died. Thereafter until June 1673 Lady D'Avenant held control for her son, Charles D'Avenant, then only a boy, assigning the practical management to Betterton and Harris[3]. Carrying on their earlier manager's tradition, however, the company eagerly pursued their plans for the erection of a magnificent new theatre. In August 1670 a plot of ground in Dorset Garden was leased, the sharers agreeing to raise among themselves a sum of £3000 for building operations[4]; but, as generally happens in such affairs, the initial estimate of cost fell sadly below the actual £9000 eventually paid out. Introduced by a prologue specially written by Dryden[5], the Duke's Theatre[6] in

[1] From the L.C. books we know that the theatre was closed by command from the 19th to the 29th of January, 1680/1.

[2] On Oct. 14, 1681 an agreement was signed between Charles D'Avenant, Betterton, Smith, Hart and Kynaston. Given in Gildon's *Life of Betterton*, it is reprinted in P. Fitzgerald, *op. cit.* I. 148. By this Hart and Kynaston, in return for 5s. on every day when the Duke's men played, agreed to hand over their shares in the Theatre Royal, to try to free themselves for service in the rival company, to promote a union of the companies and, if necessary, to go to law with Charles Killigrew. The final agreement of union is also given by Fitzgerald (*op. cit.* I. 154). By this Killigrew and D'Avenant became managers of a joint company, the Theatre Royal plays being given over. It is quite obvious that here, as in the financial arrangements, Killigrew was behaving in a high-handed manner (Leslie Hotson, pp. 270–2). Lawsuits immediately started and on Dec. 14, 1682, he was finally deprived of his rights (*id.* p. 267).

[3] Leslie Hotson, pp. 227–8.

[4] The full story is told in Leslie Hotson, pp. 229 ff. It is clear that very soon the shares gradually were concentrated in the hands of a few men. In 1674 the sharers included Harris, Betterton, William Smith, James Nokes and Underhill.

[5] *Poetical Works*, ed. Sargeaunt, p. 216.

[6] On the accession of James II it was also known as The Queen's Theatre.

Dorset Garden presented London with a playhouse far more ornate than anything the city had known in the past. About 140 feet long by 57 feet wide, it had a richly embellished proscenium frame, the appearance of which has been preserved for us in the illustrations accompanying *The Empress of Morocco*[1]. Even foreign visitors could not restrain their admiration. Describing a visit to Dorset Garden, François Brunet[2] declares that

> "le lieu ou l'on joue est incomparablement plus beau et plus propre que ceux de nos Comediens, on est assis dans le parterre qui est en Amphitheatre ou l'on entend jamais de bruit, il ny a que Sept Loges qui peuvent contenir chacun Vingt personnes. Il y a encore pareil nombre au dessus et un paradis plus haut."

Here the company settled down to a repertoire partly composed of such older plays as they had given in the past, partly of new pieces many of which tended towards the spectacular and operatic[3]. While these involved the expenditure of large sums of money, it is fairly clear that, although burdened, the Duke's men were in a better way than their rivals when the Union came in 1682. Charles D'Avenant, who had taken over control in June 1673, may have been a better manager than Charles Killigrew, and in any case Dorset Garden's position was strengthened by the commanding figure of honest and astute Thomas Betterton. At any rate, it was the Duke's company which initiated the process which led to the amalgamation of the two troupes; indeed, it might almost be said that the one incorporated the other.

XIV. *The United Companies, 1682–1695.*

The joint companies started acting on Nov. 16, 1682, with Betterton indisputably the master of the theatrical world. Hart, Harris, Burt, and Mohun were retired or about to retire[4]. Wintershall and Lacy were gone. Among the "remnant" of the King's

---

[1] These have been frequently reproduced and give what is presumably a reasonably faithful representation of the stage and proscenium. See W. J. Lawrence, "The Plates in Settle's *The Empress of Morocco*" (*TLS*, July 11, 1935).

[2] *Voyage d'Angleterre* (1676), quoted in Leslie Hotson, pp. 234–5.

[3] Ned Bliss Allen, in *The Sources of John Dryden's Comedies* (1935), p. 124, conjectures that the audiences which went to Dorset Garden may have been composed largely of citizens, and that this explains the kind of fare provided at that theatre.

[4] That Mohun's retirement was not voluntary is shown in the interesting document printed *infra*, pp. 365–6.

men who still were active Downes[1] lists Wiltshire[2], Cartwright,
Kynaston, Griffin, Goodman, Watson, Powell, Mr Corey, Mrs
Boutell, Mrs Cook and Mrs Mountfort; to these he adds the names
of Mountford and Carlisle, members of the Duke's company who
"were grown to the Maturity of good *Actors*."

Troubles were not stopped by the Union. There were debates
among the sharers and minor annoyances must have worried the
actors[3]. At the same time, performances seem to have been given
fairly regularly until the death, in Feb. 1684/5, of Charles, the
great patron of the drama. Thereafter, the theatres were closed
until an order was made for their starting again on April 20, 1685[4].
Less than two years later, on Jan. 12, 1687/8, James constituted
a fresh band of royal comedians, including "Thomas Betterton
Wm Smith James Noke Cave Vnderhill Anthony Leigh Edward
Kinaston Phillip Griffin Joseph Williams Tho: Jevon John
Downes John Verbroggell [*sic*] John Bowman Samuell Sandford
Francis Baker Martin Powell George Bright William Monfort
John ffreeman Francis Pauy George Powell Henry Bowtell and
John Barr[5]," to whom were added, on May 19, Thomas Sheppey[6]
and, on May 23, Thomas Sympson and Arron Darby[7]. The
women in the royal company are also enumerated: "Elizabeth
Barry Sarah Cooke Margrett Osborne Francis Mariaknight [*sic*]
Katherine Davies and Anne Bracegirle [*sic*][8]." Like Charles,
James attended the public playhouse and ordered a certain number
of plays at court[9]. On several occasions there are records of payments made out of the Privy Purse to Mrs Barry[10]; Crowne was
paid £20 for *Sir Courtly Nice* on Jan. 9, 1687/8 and £20 for *Darius*
on May 8, 1688[11].

As before, small things and great bothered the management.
Here was Mrs Lacy, claiming 3s. 4d. daily from the takings of the

---

[1] P. 39.

[2] He seems to have left the Theatre Royal about 1680, but acted with
the united company until 1685.

[3] Leslie Hotson, pp. 282–4.

[4] L.C. 5/145, p. 184. [5] L.C. 5/148, p. 66.

[6] *Id.* p. 204. [7] *Id.* p. 205.

[8] *Id.* p. 66.

[9] On some occasions, it would seem, the actors were not on time. On
Oct. 5, 1687, the Lord Chamberlain bade Charles Killigrew, as Master
of the Revels, to "take care the Comoedians do come in good time"
(L.C. 7/1 and 5/148, p. 19).

[10] There are three separate entries of such payments: on April 10, 1686,
£40 (L.C. 5/147, p. 112, deleted), on April 21, 1687, £35 (*id.* p. 321),
May 8, 1686 (*id.* p. 136) and Dec. 20, 1687, £20 for her acting in *The
Emperor of the Moon* (L.C. 5/148, p. 59).

[11] See *infra*, p. 356.

house[1], and here was a reshaping of the forces governing the playhouse. On Nov. 30, 1675, Alexander D'Avenant had entered the Duke's theatre as treasurer, and this post he held until May, 1683. Four years later, in May, 1687, he started negotiations for the purchase of the shares held by Charles D'Avenant, and on Aug. 30, 1687, the deal was completed by a payment of £2400. Subsequently, however, it was revealed that, in reality, the greater part of this sum (£2000 in all) had been provided by Sir Thomas Skipwith, and it is in the record of these negotiations that the lawyer Christopher Rich enters into the theatrical picture[2]. Skipwith, on Sept. 12, 1687, allowed Alexander D'Avenant to farm his shares, while in March, 1689/90, the latter sold his smaller share to Rich, who likewise handed it over to him to "farm." It was these negotiations which started trouble for the future, since Alexander D'Avenant set up his young brother, Thomas, as director of the playhouse, and something of the same inner disturbance afflicted the Theatre Royal now as had afflicted it in the time of Charles Killigrew, while the break in the Union was precipitated when, in Dec. 1693, Rich and Skipwith, taking charge of the theatre, offended Betterton by giving his best parts to Powell. The theatrical world had indeed sunk low when the single theatre of the metropolis came under the ageis of Rich—"an old snarling Lawyer...a waspish, ignorant pettifogger in Law and Poetry[3]."

Meanwhile, on Feb. 13, 1688/9, William and Mary came to the throne. The Catholic atmosphere of the preceding years vanished, and a slightly more chastened tone is to be observed in the theatre. Still royalty paid a certain attention to the drama: for command performances monetary recompense was provided (although after delays)[4], and on Aug. 23, 1689, a band of royal comedians in ordinary was formed[5]. Notwithstanding all this, however, the old intimacy between court and stage was gone.

During this reign, records of clashes between management and actors recommence. On March 11, 1689, Mrs Corey had been petitioning the Lord Chamberlain because she was banished from

---

[1] This claim was made on the strength of a loan made years ago by her actor-husband. There are nearly a dozen references to her petitions in the Lord Chamberlain's books.

[2] Leslie Hotson, pp. 284–8.

[3] *A Comparison between the Two Stages*, ed. S. B. Wells (1942), p. 11.

[4] See *infra* p. 352.

[5] L.C. 5/149, p. 219. These included John Hodgson, John Freeman, Aaron Darby, Powell, Bright and Trefusis: to these were added on July 5, 1690, Francis Pavy (L.C. 5/150, p. 119), on March 2, 1691/2, Joseph Harris (L.C. 5/151, p. 35) and on April 2 Michael Lee (*id.* p. 51).

the playhouse[1], and beneath this petition lay a story of disruption[2]. Apparently Henry Killigrew, engaged in perpetual quarrel with his half-brother Charles, engaged with Leigh, Nokes, Momford (Mountfort), Mrs Corey and other actors to launch a new company. This project came to nothing, and the actress, self-described (and correctly) as "the first and...the last of all the Actresses that were constituted by King Charles the Second at His restauration," had not been granted readmission to the united company.

The abortive effort to establish a second company was a signpost to the future. Unrest within the theatre was accompanied by dwindling audiences, and by a consequent managerial attempt to make ends meet by cutting casts. Already in 1690 the actor Powell tells us[3] that "*the Poets lay dormant; and a new Play cou'd hardly get admittance, amongst the more precious pieces of Antiquity, that then waited to walk the Stage.*" At the same time the managers sought to reduce the players' salaries, with consequent friction[4]. Quarrels between the management and the actors must have been frequent, and matters had grown to such a state by September, 1691, that Betterton himself abandoned his share and went on salary. On Dec. 7 Killigrew and Betterton were in the Court of Chancery over various differences[5]. A few days later, from Dec. 16 to 19, the theatres were closed, because of an affront, so it is said, to a peer[6]. In August, 1692, Williams left the playhouse for several months, probably because of internal differences, and on Sept. 26, Betterton, Mountfort, Leigh and Bowman, no doubt after a great amount of arguing, drew up a document setting forth the rights of the sharing actors[7]. After this, Betterton came into

[1] L.C. 5/149, p. 16.

[2] Albert S. Borgman, "The Killigrews and Mrs Corey" (*TLS*, Dec. 27, 1934) and his *The Life and Death of William Mountfort* (1935), pp. 47–8.

[3] *The Treacherous Brothers*, preface.

[4] Leslie Hotson, p. 290. The following order appears in L.C. 5/192: "Mr Montfort Mr Charles Killiegrew Mr Thomas D'Avenant or Mr Alexander Mr Betterton Mr Powell Junior Mr Bray Danceing Master The Book Keeper The Property Maker Mr Ashbun Mr Trefusis Gentlemen Mr Haynes complaineing against Mr Montfort, my Lord Chamberlaine hath appointed to heare the Controversy upon Friday morning next And His Lordpp desires the Gentlemen above named to be at His Lodgeings at the Cock pitt at Whitehall at that time Octobr 15th 1689 Yor humble Servant Rich: Colinge." Early the following year Nicholas Burt petitioned against Killigrew "for deteyneing his share of Cloathes, Scenes, and Bookes belonging to the Theatre Royall" (Feb. 10, 1689/90). The same month Elizabeth Currer was complaining against Killigrew and D'Avenant.

[5] See P.R.O. Chancery Affidavit Register, vol. 30, Hilary Term, 1691–2, Nos. 911–3. The question, as usual, was one of money and debts.

[6] L.C. 5/150, pp. 340 and 345.   [7] See Appendix B.

share again. In December, 1692, the theatres lost by death two of their best men, Mountfort and Leigh, although Williams returned to the theatre sometime in January, 1692/3. Going from bad to worse, the company was probably losing heavily, so that on Jan. 16 of this year, Betterton and Bowman went on salary again. All this time, Alexander D'Avenant, acting in an underhand manner, had been cheating and defrauding the actors, until, when the discovery of his impostures was imminent, he fled in October, 1693[1]. A month later, Doggett, Bowen, and others mutinied, but were brought to reason by Betterton and the patentees.

It was too late to patch up quarrels, however, and in December, 1694, Betterton, at the head of a great body of the finest actors, laid a lengthy petition before the Lord Chamberlain[2]. On the 10th of the month, after Rich and the other patentees had filed a series of answers to the various counts, the contending parties were ordered to attend at the house of Sir Robert Howard on Monday, Dec. 17.

For a month or two, matters dragged on. On Feb. 11, 1694/5, the patentees made advances to Betterton, advances which were indignantly refused. In the beginning of March, the Lord Chamberlain drew up a series of proposals to which the patentees agreed on March 19[3], but Betterton, trusting to get a licence, proceeded to make active plans for the reopening of the old theatre in Lincoln's Inn Fields[4]. Evidently no more could be done, and on March 25, 1694/5 a fresh licence was granted to the revolting

---

[1] See Appendix B.   [2] Given in Appendix B.

[3] L.C. 7/3. "A copy of patentees Submission to the Lord Chamberlaines Proposall....Haveing considered of the Differences between ye Patentees & Adventurers & the Comedians at the Theatres by the Papers on both sides delivered to me; I doe propose it as a thing reasonable That the shares of the profitts and Aftermoney should be diuided into ten Equall parts, ffiue Shares to goe to the patentees and ffiue Shares to the Actors, to be diuided among them, and some of the Cheife Actors to be Sharers the others to haue Sallairey The Lord Chamberlaine reserveing ye Governem^t of the Kings Servants to himselfe as allwayes was practiced by his Predecessors, or to whom he should appoint." This is signed by Killigrew, Skipwith and Rich "In Confidence yor Lordshipp will vnite us & Compose all disputes & differences between us."

[4] L.C. 7/3. "Wee the Patentees of the Theatres in Order to an amicable composure of matters, haveing severall times, & pticularly on the 11th of ffebruary last, sent to Mr Betterton & other Comedians in Combinačon with him, to meet us, They Refused soe to doe, declareing that haueing putt themselues under your Lorpps Jurisdiččon & reserved all matters in difference to your Lorpps determinačon, They could doe nothing without your Lorpps Order.

That Wee haueing submitted to yor Lorpps Proposalls In Confidence That yor Lorppe would vnite us, and Settle all matters in difference

actors[1]. The newly converted playhouse was opened on April 29, with the result that the Theatre Royal found itself in such a position that

> "'twas almost impossible to muster up a sufficient number to take in all the Parts of any Play; and of them so few were tolerable, that a Play must of necessity be damn'd that had not extraordinary favour from the Audience. No fewer than *Sixteen* (most of the old standing) went away; and with them the very beauty and vigour of the Stage; they who were left behind being for the most part Learners, Boys and Girls, a very unequal match for them who revolted[2]."

XV. *The Theatre Royal and Lincoln's Inn Fields, 1695–1699.*

The year 1695 was not precisely a propitious time for the opening of two playhouses. The autumn was a black season for England financially[3], and "the Town" was not "able to furnish out two good Audiences every day[4]." The result was, that, when the pair of houses started operations, rivalry was intense. "Between us and the other Theatre," says Powell in the prologue to *Bonduca* (D.L. 1695),

> "There is proclaim'd, and still maintain'd a War,
> And all, but knocking out of Brains, is fair."

between vs, yet Wee find that they proceed in Converting the Tennis Court in Lincolnes Inn ffeilds to a Playhouse.

Wee therefore now humbly pray your Lordshipp That you will be pleased

1 To order a Stopp to be putt thereunto.

2 To require the said Comedians to Act under the Patents at such Sallaires as they had when they left off acting on the 22th of Dec last vntill such tyme as ye matters in difference shall be Composed, To the facilitateing whereof

3 Wee humbly propose That as to such matters in difference as are too tedious & troublesome for yor Lorpes Examinacon That it may (if yor Lorppe thinke fitt) be referred to Mr Henry Harris & Mr Wm Smith who were formerly for many Yeares Shareing Actors & Managers of ye Theatres, and by that meanes well acquainted with the Rules & Methods of the Company That they make their Report to yor Lopppe."

[1] A copy of this licence is contained in L.C. 7/1. The authority is given to Betterton, Mrs Barry, Mrs Bracegirdle, Bowman, Williams, Underhill, Dogett, Bowen, Mrs Verbruggen, Mrs Leigh and Bright.

[2] *A Comparison between the Two Stages*, p. 7.

[3] Noted by E. H. Sloane, *Robert Gould* (1940), p. 37, quoting W. Cunningham, *The Growth of English Industry and Commerce* (1912), II. 436-8.

[4] *A Comparison between the Two Stages*, p. 10.

There are indications that plays were stolen by the one house from the other; similarly titled dramas appearing almost at the same time at Drury Lane and Lincoln's Inn Fields tell their own story; apparently in order to repay an "obligation" to Skipwith, no less a person than Vanbrugh saw fit, in the second part of his *Æsop* (D.L. 1697), to ridicule the seceding actors by putting them on the stage and by depicting them as lazy, ignorant and stupidly contemptuous of the good offered to them by the worthy patentee[1].

For the sake of completeness, and for comparison with other lists of performances given elsewhere in the present volume, there may be recorded here the basic facts contained in a record of productions at the Theatre Royal from 1696 to the end of the century[2]:

1696:	Nov.	6.	*Oroonoko.*
	,,	25.	*The Relapse.*
	Dec.	28.	*Love's Last Shift.*
1697:	Jan.	2.	*Timon of Athens.*
	,,	22.	*Æsop.*
	Mar.	9.	*The Prophetess.*
	,,	13.	*The Indian Queen.*
	,,	27.	*The Libertine.*
	Apr.	5.	*Cynthia and Endimion.*
	,,	8.	*Psyche.*
	,,	23.	*Oroonoko.*
	May	8.	*A Plot and No Plot*
	,,	24.	*Æsop.*
	,,	25.	*The Tempest.*
	,,	26.	*Don Sebastian.*
	,,	27.	*The Lancashire Witches.*
	,,	31.	*The Sham Lawyer.*
	June	5.	*The Indian Queen.*
	,,	12.	*Oroonoko.*
	,,	18.	*Marriage a la Mode.*
	Nov.	19.	*The Scornful Lady.*
	,,	26.	*Timon of Athens.*
	Dec.	4.	*The Prophetess.*
	,,	9.	*Æsop.*

[1] On this see Dane Farnsworth Smith, *Plays about the Theatre in England* (1936), pp. 59–64.

[2] This document was discovered by Leslie Hotson (*op. cit.* pp. 377–9). He gives the full details, together with a list of performances up to June 1701. Here are presented only the dates and titles of the plays.

1698:	Jan.	5.	*The Relapse.*
	,,	18.	*The Country House.*
	Feb.	7.	*King Arthur.*
	,,	25.	*King Arthur.*
	Mar.	19.	*King Arthur.*
	Nov.	19.	*Alexander.*
	,,	26.	*Œdipus.*
	,,	28.	*The Little Thief.*
1699:	Jan.	28.	*Bonduca.*
	Feb.	2.	*The Spanish Wives.*
	,,	3.	*King Lear.*
	,,	7.	*The Island Princess.*
	Mar.	25.	*The Island Princess*
	June	29.	*The Jovial Crew.*
	Oct.	24.	*The Committee.*
	,,	28.	*The Traitor.*
	Nov.	11.	*Caius Marius.*
	,,	21.	*The Orphan.*
	,,	28.	*The Constant Couple.*
	Dec.	14.	*The Marriage Hater.*
	,,	16.	*The Earl of Essex.*

The presentation of this list of plays anticipates, of course, the progress of events. Performances require actors, and during the first few months after Betterton's secession there was a scramble for the available players. The Theatre Royal, on April 10, 1695, seized on Verbruggen and his wife. Foreseeing trouble, the Lord Chamberlain commanded, on April 16, that no actor should quit either house, and this decree was confirmed on July 25[1]. In spite of this, by April 3, 1696, Doggett was making preparations

---

[1] L.C. 7/1 and 7/3. "Whereas Thomas Betterton Elizabeth Barry Anne Bracegirdle John Bowman Joseph Williams Caue Underhill Thomas Doggett William Bowen Elinor Lee George Bright are by my Warrant sworne and admitted His Mates servants & Comoedians in Ordinary and have His Mates Leave and Authority Signified under hand and Seale dated ye 25th day of March [over April deleted] 1695 to act Comoedyes Tragedyes Playes Enterludes and Opera's and to performe all other Theatricall and Musicall Entertainements but so as to be alwayes under my Government & regulation from time to time as hath been Exercised by my predecessors To prevent therefore any disorder or disturbance which may happen among them by ye deserting & quitting ye Company without due notice and my leaue first obtayened as hath been alwayes accustomed I do hereby order that none of His Mates Comoedians aboue named, nor any that shall be admitted hereafter into ye said Company by me do presume to desert or quitt ye said Company to act or play in any other place or company whatsoever without my leaue first had." The second order, also in L.C. 7/1, is even more explicit: "To prevent all

to leave Betterton[1], and on Oct. 26 was acting at D.L. Verbruggen, similarly, had been enticed from the patentees and was performing at L.I.F.[2] What exactly happened we do not know. The Lord Chamberlain, according to this document, distinctly ordered that Verbruggen should continue with the D.L. company until Jan. 1, 1696/7; on October 27 the latter entered into an agreement with the L.I.F. house, deciding to start there at the beginning of the new year[3]. Why Doggett was left free we do not know. The order against any actor's leaving either theatre was reiterated

disorders & [the last two words added above the line] disturbances which may arise & happen by reason of ye Actors or any Servants hyred by ye Two Companyes of His Ma^tes Comoedians who shall desert & Quitt either of ye said Companyes & goe from one Company to ye other at Theire owne Pleasure after They haue been hyred & Entertained by Either Company I do hereby order in further Confirmation of my former Order dated ye Sixteenth day of Aprill Last That no Actor Actress or Servant hyred & Entertained by either of ye Companyes do presume to desert Quitt or Leaue ye Company wherein hee or shee is hyred & Entertained to goe & Act and be Entertained in ye other Company untill ye time is Expired wherein They haue Giuen Bond or Articles to giue Warning to Quitt ye Company And then to haue ye discharge of ye Company wherein hee or shee was or is first hyred & Entertained and my Leaue under my hand for approbation of ye same at Theire perrills of being punished."

[1] On this date he entered into an agreement with the managers of the T.R., arranging to start at that house on Oct. 10. He was to receive £4 per acting day from Skipwith, the patentee, or have a share "up to the heighth as shall be paid to Mr George Powell or Mr John Verbruggen," as well as a benefit of an old play to be acted on a Wednesday or Friday in Lent, the actor paying the charges of the house. Bonds of £500 were given by both the management and the actor.

[2] L.C. 7/1. "Haveing heard ye differences between ye Comoedians of both Theatres it appeared that both ye Companies had seduced Actors Mr Doggett from ye Theatre in Lincolns Inne feilds and Mr Vanbruggen from the pattentees Contrary to Theire owne Articles and my Orders pursuant thereunto I doe therefore hereby Order for this time onely that Mr Vanbruggen shall remaine to act with the pattentees untill the first day of January next (that they may in the meane time provide themselues of others to Act his Parts) and that after the first day of Jan^r next Mr Vanbruggen hath free Liberty to Act [the last two words added] at which Theatre he will...and for ye future my Orders of ye 16th of Aprill 1695 and of ye 25 of July 1695 shall be punctually obserued." This is dated Oct. 26, 1696.

[3] L.C. 7/3. Unfortunately an order in L.C. 5/192 does not give the Theatre at which Verbruggen was playing; it is incomplete and breaks off half finished: "Whereas Mr Van Bruggen one of His Ma^tes Comoedians hath violently assaulted   Boyle Esqr and Broke him ag^t ye publique peace and hath with reproch full of scandalous words & speeches abused Sr Thomas Skypwith Barr^t I doe hereby discharge Mr Van bruggen from Acting in yor Theatre, or any other untill I giue further directions herein And I require."

on May 27, 1697[1], and Doggett, who had got tired of the D.L. management and had abandoned that company, was ordered to be arrested on Nov. 23 of that year[2]. Probably the comedian acquiesced for the moment, but in October, 1700, he had entered into an agreement with the L.I.F. house[3].

Other orders and agreements of these five years all point to the same thing, a state of unrest and of uncertainty in theatrical affairs, a tyrannical government at the D.L. and D.G. houses, a mixed republic at L.I.F. A lengthy and important settlement of the affairs of the latter company is preserved in the Public Record Office[4]. This evidently was found unsatisfactory, as on Nov. 11, 1700, Betterton was appointed sole manager of the theatre[5]. The D.L. troupe had its own troubles arising out of the domineering tone of the patentees. Doggett, who had but newly joined that company, headed a petition (undated, but probably about 1697)[6] against the management. Rich and Skipwith tried in all ways, legitimate and otherwise, to crush their rivals. They introduced buffoonery, rope-dancing, tumbling, dancing. Betterton petitioned against these, we must suppose in vain[7]. The years were rapidly approaching when pantomime was to banish legitimate drama from the stage. The years, too, were coming when Collier's outburst was to startle London's theatre-goers and players. On Jan. 24, 1696, the Lord Chamberlain had issued an order that

---

[1] L.C. 5/152, p. 15.

[2] L.C. 5/152, p. 40.

[3] L.C. 7/1. This is not dated. "Mr Doggett is to be wth ye Company in Little Lincoln's Inn ffields & to continue acting with them from ye 12 day of October next Ensuing, to ye 21 day of May following, & have for his Salary three pounds a week certain, except in case of any publick Calamity, or prohibition from acting He is also to have ye whole profits of one play acted for his benefit" without any charge: if the sum does not reach £100 "Ye Company shall be oblig'd to make up to him ye aforesd sum of 100ll for ye first play to be acted for his Benefit, namely the first play that shall be acted for him this present year 1700." In later years it was arranged that he should have one benefit, with a minimum income of £60, "provided that Mr Dogget shall not choose to be acted for his benefit any new or reviv'd play during ye first run."

[4] Given in Appendix B.   [5] L.C. 5/153, p. 22.   [6] L.C. 7/3.

[7] L.C. 7/3. This "sheweth that it appears by the Receipts and constant Charges of the Theatres for some Years past, that the Town will not maintain two Playhouses. That the two Company's have by their bidding against each other for Singers, Dancers &c who are generally Strangers, rais'd the Prices so high that both are impoverisht by it, and most of their Profitts cary'd away by Forreigners. That both Companys have been forc'd for their Subsistance to bring on the Stage, Dancers on the Ropes, Tumblers, Vaulters, Ladder dancers &c and thereby debas'd the Theatre, and almost levell'd it with Bartholomew ffaire."

all plays should be fully licensed[1]. On June 4, 1697 he commanded all scurrilous sentiments and expressions of profanity to be deleted from dramas[1]. In spite of this, the old tone continued, and a more peremptory order was issued on Feb. 18, 1698/9. It becomes increasingly obvious, as we examine the records of these last years of the century, that a new theatrical world was in process of formation. Fundamentally, this new theatrical world was marked by the substituting of an upper-middle-class morality for the moral code of the aristocrats, and by the supplanting of the brilliantly witty amateurs by the professionals. The Lord Chamberlain's preoccupation with "Obsenityes & other Scandalous matters & such as any wayes Offend against ye Lawes of God & Good manners" was motivated by the awareness of the court that the gracefully graceless manners which had ruled during the reign of Charles II were giving way to a decorous but duller code of behaviour sponsored by an increasingly merchant society. It is convenient to mark the change as coming at the turn of the century; at the same time we must not ignore the premonitory signs so evident during the latter years of the 'Restoration' age. The audience was now demanding a reformation in stage dialogue; although Congreve's *The Way of the World* was to come just as the old century gives way to the new, the professional and middle-class Colley Cibber had produced his first play five years previously and had already shown how he was to exploit the moralising strains so appealing to this changing audience. Sentimentalism is rightly to be considered a prime characteristic of the eighteenth-century stage, yet it is certain that the conditions out of which the later sentimental movement developed were being shaped during the last decade of the seventeenth century. This indeed is the

---

[1] L.C. 7/1 and 7/3. "Whereas Severall Playes &c are Acted & Prologues spoken wherein many things ought to be struck out and Corrected And ye playes approued & Licensed by ye Master of the Revells according to ye Antient Custome of His place and upon the Examination of the said Master I find that he Complaines that of Late severall new & revived playes haue been Acted at ye Theatres of Drury Lane & Dorsett Gardens without any Licence And that of Late ye Managers of that Company haue refused to send such playes to be perused Corrected & allowed by ye Master of ye Revells I doe therefore Order and Command that for ye future noe playes shall be Acted but such as shall first be sent (and that in due time) to Charles Killegrew Esqr Master of ye Revells by him to be perused and diligently Corrected & Licensed....And I doe further Order & Command the said Master to be very Carfull in Correcting all Obsenityes & other Scandalous matters & such as any wayes Offend against ye Lawes of God & Good manners or the knowne Statutes of this Kingdome...."

[2] L.C. 5/152, p. 19.   [3] L.C. 5/152, p. 162.

principal cause of the confusion so amply apparent in stage affairs during that time.

We may well leave the theatres at this point: the Puritan conscience reasserted, the patentee house veering towards buffoonery, the L.I.F. theatre struggling on with a divided management, and the one man who had made dignified the actor's art in Restoration times growing old and weak, ready to retire, just before his death, in the reign of Queen Anne.

APPENDIX B

Documents Illustrative of the History of the Stage

[The following records are taken from documents or books in the Lord Chamberlain's department of the Public Record Office. As not all of these are of equal importance, I have condensed a few; actual wording is indicated by inverted commas. Hitherto extracts have been given only from two books in this collection (L.C. 7/1 and L.C. 5/138), first by R. W. Lowe in his *Life of Betterton* and later by E. Thaler in *Shakespeare to Sheridan*. These books, however, are by no means the most important, the highly interesting play-lists not starting till a date covered by other warrant volumes.]

I. Lists of Plays performed before Royalty.

1. *Plays given by the T.R. Company.*

(*a*) Warrant dated Aug. 29, 1668, for plays acted from Dec. 10, 1666 to July 31, 1668 (L.C. 5/139, p. 129), and similar warrants (L.C. 5/12, p. 17) carrying on list of performances to May 6, 1669. (In these lists I have condensed the long entries of payments which usually take the form "20: 00: 00," and have added the £ marks.)

"His Ma^te...hath had presented before him those following Comoedies & Tragoedies at Court and at the Theatre Royall.

Dec:	10 1666	The Silent Weoman at Court			£20
		[The second list reads "Scornefull Lady."]			
	20	The Humorous Leiv^t at the Theatre the Queenes Ma^te there			20
Jan:	22	The Indian Emperour at the Theatre Royall		...	10
ffeb:	14	fflora's Vagaries at Court		...	20
		[The second list reads "Rule a Wife and have a Wife."]			
March	2:	The Mayden Queene at the Theater		... ...	10
	5	The Mayden Queene at the Theatre		... ...	10
1667					
Ap:	15:	The Change of Crownes his Ma^te and the Queene were at the Theatre		...	20
	18	The Mayden Queene at Court		...	20
	27	Bartholomew fayre at the Theatre		... ...	10
May	13:	The Comittee at the Theatre		...	10
		[Here the second list adds "16 Auglaura at Court." 20]			

	18	The Country Capt. at ye Theatre £10
Aug:	17	The Troubles of Queene Elizabeth at the Theatre 10
		[The second list reads "7" for "17."]
Aug:	28:	The fox at Court 20
		[This is omitted in the second list.]
Sep^t:	27	The Sea Voyage His Ma^{te} had two boxes at y^e
		Theatre 20
		[The second list reads for "27," "25th."]
Octo:	7	The Poetesse at the Theatre 10
	19	The Black Prince at the Theatre 10
	29	The English Monsier at ye Theatre 10
Nov:	11	The Indian Emperour at the Theatre 10
	16	Philaster at the Theatre 10
	21	The Goblins at ye Theatre 10
	23	The Maydes Tragedie at ye Theatre 10
Jan:	04:	The Mayden Queene at the Theatre 10
	20:	The Indian Emperour King & Queene at the
		Theatre 20
	27	The Mayden Queene at Court 20
ffeb:	20:	The Duke of Lerma at ye Theatre 10
March 20		The Virgin Martyr at the Theatre 10

[The second list reads "2" for "20," has no date opposite The
      Mulbery Garden, and writes Jan. 12 for June 12.]

	1668	
May	18	The Mulbery Garden His Ma^{te} and the Queene
		at the Theatre 20
June	12	An Evening Loue his Ma^{te} and the Queene at the
		Theatre 20
July	14	Hide Parke at the Theatre 10
	31	Monsr Raggou at ye Theatre ... ... 10 "

The second list runs as follows:—

"Sep^t	14:	The Damaseiles A la Mode ye King here £10
Sep^t	28:	The Citty Match the King here 10
Nov:	6:	The Island Princesse King & Queene 20
	9	The Tamer tamed at Court 20
	21	The Scornefull Lady at Court 20
Dec:	3^d: 1668.	The Vsurper King here 10
	7:	The Vsurper at Court 20
	18:	Cattalines Conspiracie Knig (sic) here 10
Jan:	2^d:	Cattalines Conspiracie King & Queene here ... 20
	7	The Island Princesse King here 10
	13	Cattalines Conspiracie King here 10
	16:	Horace The King here 10
	21:	Horace The King & Queene 20
	29:	The Heiresse The King here 10
ffeb:	8th	The Comittee at Court 20
	22	Bartholomew ffayre at Court 20
March 23:		The Coxcombe ye King here 10
Ap. 17: 1669		The Alchymist The King here 10
May 6: 1669		The King & Noe King ... ... 10 "

(b) Warrant dated Nov. 26, 1674, for plays acted from Mar. 26,
1674 to Nov. 10, 1674 (L.C. 5/141, p. 73).

"1674.

March	26:	The Beggers Bush	...	£10
	30	The ffrench Opera	...	10
Ap:	23	Marriage a la mode	...	10
May	11	Loue in a Maze	...	10
	12	Indian Emperor	...	10
	16	Nero	...	10
Octo	20	The Traytor ...	...	10
	24	Philaster	...	10
Nov.	9	Rollo Duke of Normandy		10
		A box for yᵉ Queene	...	10
	10	Indian Emperor	...	10"

(*c*) Warrant dated Jan. 27, 1674/5, for plays acted from Nov. 12, 1674 to Jan. 15, 1674/5 (*id.* p. 116).

"Nouember	12:	The Alchymist ...	...	£10
	16	Aglaura the King & Queene		20
	19	The Mock Tempest	...	10
	24	Loue in a Mase ...	...	10
	30	Bartholomew fayre	...	10
Dec	8	The Tamer tamed	...	10
	17	The Island princesse	...	10
	21	The Rehearsall ...	...	10
	28	The Rehearsall ...	...	10
Janʳʸ	12	The Country Wife	...	10
	15	The Country Wife	...	10"

(*d*) Warrant dated June 14, 1675, for plays acted from Jan. 25, 1674/5 to June 7, 1675 (*id.* p. 215).

"Jan:	25.	The Moore of Venice The King & Queene			£20
March	8	Catalins Conspiracye the Kings Maᵗᵉ		...	10
Aprill	19	Rollo Duke of Normandy ...	...	...	10
Ap.	23	King & No King, King & Queene		...	20
Ap.	30	Sophinisba		...	10
May yᵉ	4ᵗʰ	Sophinisba King & Queene	...	...	20
May	7ᵗʰ	Sophinisba King & Queene	...	...	20
May	10	Loue in yᵉ Darke		...	10
June	7	The Island Princesse at Whitehall		...	20"

(*e*) Warrant dated Feb. 16, 1675/6, for plays acted from June 19, 1675 to Jan. 29, 1675/6 (*id.* p. 359), and warrant dated June 1, 1677, for plays acted from June 19, 1675, to May 5, 1677. The first is given to Jan. 29, and the list is continued from the second.

"June	19	Marriage ala Mode	...	...	£10
Octo:	26	The Alchymist	...	...	10
Nov:	6	Sophonisba ...	...	...	10
	11	The Comittee ...	...	...	10
	17	Aureng-Zebe ...	...	...	10
	20	Aureng-Zebe ...	...	...	10
Dec:	17	Merry Wives of Windsor		...	10

NED

	21	Granada I part	£10		
	29	Sophonisba both theire Ma[tes]	20		
Jan:	12	Moor of Venice	10		
	17	The ffox	10		
	29	Augustus Caesar	10		
May	16	The Country Wife	10		
1676.	18	Tyranick Loue or y[e] R Martir	20		
	23	Phylaster	10		
May	29	Aurengzebe at Court	20		
June	13:	Noe foole like y[e] old foole ...	10		
Nov:	18:	A foole turned Critick ...	10		
	27:	Haniballs overthrow	10		
Dec:	4:	Julius Caesar	20		
	5	The Mayden Queene	20		
	11	The playne dealer	10		
	13	The playne dealer	10		
Jan	1st	A shoemaker a Gent.	10		
	12	1 p[t] of y[e] destruction Jerusalem	20		
	18	2[d] pr[t] Jerusalem	10		
March	17	The Rivall Queene	10		
Aprill	2[d]	The Capt or Towne Misse ...	10		
1677.					
May	5	Scaramucha & Harlakyn ...	10"		

2. *Plays given by the Duke's Company.*

(*a*) Warrant dated Aug. 31, 1668, for plays acted from Oct. 29, 1666 to Aug. 9, 1668 (L.C. 5/139, p. 125).

"Oct.	29:	Loue in a Tub at Court	£20
1666		Mustopha at Court	20
Nov:	26:	Worse & Worse at Court	20
Dec	3[d]	Adventure of fiue houres at Court ...	20
	17	Mackbeth at Court	20
	28	Hen: fifth at Court	20
Jan	1	The Villaine at Court	20
March	3	The English princes at y[e] Theatre ...	10
	28	Humorous Louers	10
Aprill	9.	Loue in a Tubb	10
May	2	The Witts at Court	20
	6	The Humorous Lovers at the Theatre	10
	9.	The Schoole of Complements at Court	20
May	21	The Seige of Rhodes at y[e] Theatre ...	10
Aug.	15	S[r] Martin	10
	21	S[r] Martin	10
Oct	4.	S[r] Martin	10
	8	The Coffee house	10
	15	The Coffee house	10
	22	Mustapha	10

[The date 22 here seems to have been written over 27.]

Nou.	5	S[r] Martin	10
	7	The Tempest	10
	14	The Tempest	10

	19	The Rivalls £10
Dec	26	The Tempest 10
Dec	16	Tu Quoque 10
	28	Loue in a Tubb 10
Jan	8	Sr Martin 10
ffeb	3	Sr Martin at Court 20
	6	She would if she could at ye Theatre 10
	22	Albumazer 10
	25	She would if she could 10
March	7	She would if she could 10
	14	The Tempest 10
	26	The Mans ye Master 10
April	13.	The Tempest 10
	18	Sr Martin 10
	20	She woud if she coud 10
	23	The Mans ye Master 10
May	2	The Sullen Louers 10
	4	The Sullen Louers 10
	29	She woud if she coud at Court ... 20
Aug: 9, 1668		The Guardian 10

£540"

(*b*) Warrant dated Sept. 11, 1674, for plays acted from Mar. 9, 1671, to Mar. 12, 1672/3 (L.C. 5/141, p. 2).

"March 9: 1671		Haniball £10
	13	Romantick Lady ... 10
	28	Pompey 10
Nov.	14	Sr Solomon at Co^{rt} ... 20
Ap	20 72.	Adventure 5 houres... 10
May	17	Charles 8 10
July	4	Cittizen turned Gent. 10
	8	the same 10
	17	the same 10
Aug	3	ffatall Jealosie ... 10
	16	Cittizen turned Gent. 10
Aug:	17:	Loue in a Tubb ... 10
	21	The Witts 10
	29	Cittizen turned Gent. 10
	31	Sr Martin Marall ... 10
Sept.	3	King Hen: 8: ... 10
	17	Charles 8 10
Oct^o.	3	Cittizen turned Gent. 10
Nov.	4:	Y^e Morning Ramble 10
	17	Y^e Gaurdian ... 10
Dec:	2:	Epsom Wells ... 10
	4:	Epsom Wells ... 10
	27	Epsom Wells at Court 20
Jan:	10:	Y^e Amorous Widow 10
ffeb	4	Y^e Amour Widow ... 10
	6	Y^e Dutch Lovers ... 10
	18	Mackbeth 10
March 12 167⅔		Y^e Careless lovers ... 10"

(*c*) Warrant dated June 14, 1675, for plays acted from July 3, 1673, to Mar. 2, 1674/5 (*id.* p. 216).

"July 3: 1673   Morocco £10
Aug: 3 (or 9?) Yᵉ Mans yᵉ Master   ...   10
Sepᵗ. 27   Yᵉ Rectory   10
Oct: 21:   Sʳ Martin Marall   10
    28:    Herod & Meriamne   10
Dec: 5   Epsom Wells   10
Jan 31:   Adventure 5 houres   10
Mar: 18:   Yᵉ Sea Captaines   10
Nov: 2:   Constantenople   10
    1674
    3   Cittizen turned Gent at Court   20
    1674
Nov   9   Love & Revenge   10
    17   Yᵉ Tempest double price   ...   20
    18   Tempest double price   ...   20
    26   Tryvmphant Widdow   ...   10
    28   Tempest   20
Dec: 2:   Hamlett K: & Q: 20
    30:    She would if she could   ...   10
Jan. 8   Yᵉ Gaurdian K & Q: ...   20
    21.   Sʳ Martin Marall   10
Jan: 22 1674 Sʳ Martin Marall K & Q   ...   20
ffeb: 27   Psyche first Acting   ...   30
Mar: 2 :   Psyche   ...   .   20"

(*d*) Warrant dated June 29, 1677, for plays acted from May 28, 1675, to May 12, 1677 (L.C. 5/142, p. 81).

"His Maᵗˢ Bill from His Royall Highnesse Theatre.

1675.
May   28   At the Conquest of China £10
June   15   At the Libertine   10
Sept   28   At Dʳ ffaustus   10
    22   King and Queene at Alcibiades and a box for the
        Mayds of Honoʳ   25
Jan.   10   At the Country Witt   10
March 11   At the Man of Mode   10
Aprill 1676   At the Man of Mode and Box for the Mayds of
    18   Honoʳ   15
May   25   At the Virtuoso   10
Jan   8   At Don Carlos   10
Nou.   4   At Madam ffickle   10
ffeb   12   At Anthony & Cleopatra   10
    24   At the 2ᵈ part of the Seige of Rhodes   10
March 24   At the Rouer   10
[May 12]   At Circe double price   ...   .   20"

(*e*) Warrant dated Aug. 19, 1678, for plays acted from May 31, 1677, to May 28, 1678 (L.C. 5/143, p. 162).

"His Ma[tes] Bill From His Royall Highnesse Theatre
1677

May	31th:	At the Fond Husband ... £10
June	8th:	At the ffond Husband ... 10
July	28th:	At the Impertienents ... 10
Nov:	15th:	At the Tempest ... 20
Nov:	17th:	At the Polititian ... 10
Jan:	17th:	At S[r] Patient ffancy ... 10
March	11th:	At M[r] Lymberham ... 10
1678.		
Aprill	5th:	At ffriendship in ffashion 10
May	28th:	At the Counterfeits ... 10"

3. *Plays given by the United Companies.*

(*a*) Warrant dated Jan. 10, 1684/5, for plays acted from Nov. 5, 1677, to Jan. 2, 1684/5 (L.C. 5/145, p. 120). To the end of 1681, of course, the entries refer to plays given by the Duke's actors at D.G.

"1677. Nov: 5. The King at y[e] Tempest, double price £20

17. at S[r] Popler Wisdome	10
Jan: 17: at S[r] Patient ffancy	10
March: 11 at Lymberham	10
78 Aprill 25th at friendship in fashion	10
May 25. at y[e] Counterfeits	10
March 1st at y[e] Soldiers fortune	10
8. at y[e] Spanish fryer	10
80 Aprill 4: at y[e] 2[d] part of y[e] Rover	10
81: Ap: 18: at y[e] Soldiers fortune with y[e] Q: & a Box for y[e] Maides of Hono[r]	20
Nov: 22. At y[e] London Cuckolds	10
June 24 at y[e] Royalist	10
ffeb: 11 at Venice P[r]served	10
1682 Nov: 9th. at the Soldiers fortune wth y[e] Q: & a box for y[e] Maides of Hono[r]	20
Nov: 25. at y[e] London Cuckold with y[e] Queene & a box for y[e] Maides of hono[r]	20
Decemb[r] 1st 82. at y[e] Duke of Guise with y[e] Q: & a box for y[e] Maides of hono[r]	20
14: at y[e] London Cuckolds	10
30: at y[e] Chances with y[e] Q: & a box for y[e] Maides of hono[r]	20
Jan: 11th at y[e] Wanton Wife with y[e] Q. & a box for y[e] Maides of hono[r]	20
18 At Othelo with y[e] Queene & a box for y[e] Maydes of Hono[r]	20
ffeb: 11th. at Valentinian	10
23. At y[e] Scornfull Lady	10
1684 Nov: 3[d]. At a Duke & No Duke with y[e] Queene & a box for the Maydes of hono[r]	20
29: At y[e] Spanish fryar	10
Dec: 9: Att a Duke & No Duke	10
Jan: 2[d] At y[e] Leivtenant	10

For Acting at Whitehall
1680. February 11th

	The King at yᵉ Rover	£20
13.	at yᵉ Wanton Wife	20
17.	at Sʳ ffopling	20
20.	at Epsom Wells	20
27.	at She woud if she coud	20
March 6.	at Nights intregue	20 "

(*b*) Warrant dated Dec. 28, 1685, for plays acted from Jan. 13, 1684/5, to Dec. 14, 1685 (L.C. 5/147, p. 68).

"His Maᵗⁱᵉˢ Bill from the Theatre

1685

Janu:	13	The Queene at Jerusalem ye secd part	£05
This was	15	The King & Queene at the Silent Weoman	05
before yᵉ	20	The Queene at Rolo	05
late Kinges	22	The King and Queene at yᵉ Rover	05
death	27	The King & Queene at yᵉ Disapoyntmᵗ	05
1685 Aprill	28	The King & Queene & a Box for yᵉ Maydes of Honoʳ at Rolo	15
May	11ᵗʰ	The King & Queene & a Box for yᵉ Maydes of Honoʳ at Sʳ Courtley Nice	15
May yᵉ	30	The Queene at Othelo	10
June	3ᵈ	The King and Queene & a Box for yᵉ Maydes of Honoʳ at the Opera	30
Octobʳ	29	The Rover at Whitehall	20
	20	The Queene & a Box for yᵉ Maydes of honoʳ at A King & noe King	15
Nov:	4ᵗʰ	Rule a Wife at Whitehall	20
	9	Sʳ Courtley Nice at Whitehall	20
	16	The Citty Politiques at Whitehall	20
	24	yᵉ Moore of Venice at Whitehall	20
	30	Sʳ Phoplyn att Whitehall	20
Dec:	14:	The playne Dealer at Whitehall	20 "

(*c*) Warrant dated May 15, 1686, for plays acted from Dec. 30, 1685, to May 10, 1686 (*id.* p. 125 and L.C. 5/16, p. 124).

"1685 The Kings Bill from yᵉ Theatres.

Dec:	30ᵗʰ	The King & Queene & a Box for yᵉ Maydes of Honoʳ at yᵉ Comittee	£15
Jan:	13:	The Dutches of Malfey at Whitehall	20
	20:	All for Love at Whitehall	20
	27:	The Chances at Whitehall	20
ffeb:	3:	The Scornfull Lady at Whitehall	20
	8:	The King & Queene & a Box for yᵉ Maydes of honoʳ at Mackbeth	15
	10:	The Humorous Lievtenant at Whitehall	20
	11:	The King & Queene & a Box for yᵉ Maydes of honoʳ at yᵉ French Opera	25
	16:	The Mock Astrologer at Whitehall	20

[The list of 5/16 seems to give " 26 " as the date.]

Aprill 8:   The King & Queene & a Box for ye Maydes
              of hono^r at ye Com̄ittee   £15
        30   Hamlett at Whitehall   20
1686: May 6: The King & Queene & a Box for ye Maydes
              of hono^r at ye Rehearsall   15
       10:   The K: & Q: & a Box for ye Maydes of hono^r
              at Sr Courtly Nice   15 "

(*d*) Warrant dated Dec. 30, 1686, for plays acted between
Oct. 6 and Dec. 15, 1686 (L.C. 5/147, p. 260).

"1686.
Octo. 6:   The King & Queene & a Box for ye Maydes
              of hono^r at Mustapha   £15
       13   The King & Queene & a box for ye Maydes
              of Hono^r at ye Mock Astrologer   15
       20   Sr Martin Marall at Whitehall   20
       27   Alexander ye Greate at Whitehall   20
Nov: 3   Sr Courtly Nice at Whitehall   20
       10   Othelo ye Moor of Venice at Whithall   20
       17   The Committe at Whitehall   20
       24   The Humorouse Leiv^t at Whitehall   20
Dec: 1.   The Beggars at Whitehall   20
        9   A King & no King at Whitehall   20
       15   the Mayden Queene at Whitehall   20 "

(*e*) Warrant dated June 30, 1687, for plays acted from Jan. 3,
1686/7 to May 16, 1687 (*id*. p. 361).

"1686   His Ma^{tes} Bill from ye Theatres
January 3   The fond Husband at Whitehall   £20
       10   The Orphan at Whitehall   20
       19   The Rover at Whitehall   20
       20   The King & Queene & a Box for ye Maydes
              of Hono^r at ye Rehearsall   15
       26   Rolo at Whitehall   20
1687
Aprill 6:   The King & Queene & a Box for ye Maides
              of Hono^r at ye Maides Tragedy   15
       11   The Spanish Curate at Whitehall   20
       18   Julius Caesar at Whitehall   20
       25   The Island Princes at Whitehall   20
May ye 9   King Lear at Whitehall   20
       12   The King at ye Mistress   10
       16:   Valentinian at Whitehall   20 "

(*f*) Warrant dated April 3, 1688, for plays acted from Jan. 31,
1687/8, to Feb. 27, 1687/8 (L.C. 5/148, p. 145).

"1687
January 31:   The Villaine at Whitehall   £20
February 6.   The Double Marriage at Whitehall   20
       13   The Beggars Bush at Whitehall   20
       20   The History of King Lear at Whitehall   20
       27   The Humerous Leivetenant at Whitehall   20 "

(g) Warrant dated Jan. 2, 1689/90, for plays acted in May, Nov. and Dec. 1689 (L.C. 5/149, p. 368).

"1689.   Theire Ma^es Bill from the Theatres.

May the 28th:	The Queene a Box, and a Box for the Maids of Hono^r at the Spanish Fryer	£15
31	Sr Courtly Nice Acted by the Queenes Command	10
Novr the 7	The Queen a Box & a Box for the Maids of Hono^r at ye Masacre of Paris	15
15	The Joviall Crew acted at Whitehall	20
Dec^r: the 4th	The Queen a Box, and a Box for the Maids Hono^r at Don Sebastian King of Portugall	15"

(h) Warrant for plays acted in Jan. 1689/90, April, Oct. and Nov 1690, Feb. 1690/1, Jan. and Feb. 1691/2, Nov. 1692 and Jan 1692/3 (L.C. 5/151, p. 369).

"168 9/90

Jan^r 16th	ye Queen a Box & a Box for ye Maids Hon^r Alex^d	£15
(cancelled) 1690 Apr. 30th	Y^e Queene a Box & a Box for ye Maids Hono^r Amphytrion	
Apr 30 1690	Acted at White-hall Sr Courtley	20
Octo^r 21	Y^e Q: a Box & a Box for ye Maids Hon^r Amphitrion	15
Nov. 4th	at Whitehall Rover	20
17th	ye Q a Box & a Box for ye Maids Hono^r Prophetess	30
Feb^r 4th	ye Q a Box & a Box for ye Maids Hon^r Edward 3	15
Jan^r 169½ 7th	ye Q a Box & a Box for ye Maids Hon^r K Arthur	30
Feb 9th	ye Q a Box & a Box for ye Maids Hon^r Orphan	15
Nov: 14th	ye Q: a Box & a Box for ye Maids Hon^r Henry 2	15
Feb 16	ye Q a Box & a Box for ye Maids Hon^r Fairy Queen	31
1693 Jan^r 13	ye Q a Box & a Box for ye Maids of Hon^r double dealer	15"

II. PLAYS BELONGING TO THE COMPANIES.

1. *Plays allotted to D'Avenant* (Dec. 12, 1660). In margin "Sr Will. Dauenant Acting Playes."

"Whereas Sr William Davenant, Knight hath humbly p^rsented to us a proposition of reformeinge some of the most ancient Playes that were playd at Blackfriers and of makeinge them, fitt, for the Company of Actors appointed vnder his direction and Com̃and, Viz: the playes called the Tempest, Measures, for Measures, Much adoe about nothinge, Rome and Juliet, Twelfe night, the Life of Kinge Henry the Eyght, the Sophy, Kinge Lear, the Tragedy of Mackbeth, the Tragedy of Hamlet prince of Denmarke, and the Dutchesse of Malfy, Therefore wee haue granted vnto the sayd Sr William Dauenant, liberty to represent the playes aboue named by the Actors vnder his comand, notwithstandinge any Warrant to the contrary, formerly granted." The warrant proceeds to forbid any but D'Avenant's actors to present these plays, and declares that he should also have the right in his own works. A note is then inserted regarding the passing over of actors from one company to another, and the warrant closes by granting D'Avenant two months right in "The Mad Lover, The Mayd in ye Mill, the Spanish Curate the Loyall Subject Rule a Wife and haue a Wife and Persiles prince of Tyre." (L.C. 5/137, p. 343.)

2. *Plays allotted to D'Avenant* (Aug. 20, 1668).

"Playes allowed to be acted by his Royall Highnesse ye Duke of Yorkes Comoedians

The Poetaster	Bird in a Cage
Cupids Reuenge	Chabot Admirall of ffranse
Timon of Athens	ffaithfull Shepheard (Shepheardesse
Troyolus and Crisseida	in L.C. 5/12)
Three parts of H: ye 6:	Herod and Antipater
The honest mans fortune	Humor out of breath
Woemen pleas'd	Jealous Louers
Witt at Seuerall Weapons	Loues Melancholy
The Woemen Hater or The hungry	Muliasses the Turke
Courtier	Queene of Arragon
All fooles	Reuenge of Bussy D'Ambois
Birons Conspiracy	Reuenge for Honor
Broken heart	

This is the list of the playes allowed to His Royall Highnesse Actors and none other has right to them Aug. 20th 1668." Signed, Manchester. (L.C. 5/139, p. 375.)

3. *Plays allotted to Killigrew* (*c*. Jan. 12, 1668/9).

"Plays Acted at the Theatre Royall.

A Catalogue of part of His Ma^{tes} Servants Playes as they were formerly acted at the Blackfryers & now allowed of to his Ma^{tes} Servants at ye New Theatre

Everyman in his Humour	The Captaine
Everyman out of his Humour	The Chances
Cyntheas Revells	The Coxcombe
Sejanus	The Double Marriage
The ffox	The ffrench Lawyer
The Silent Weoman	The ffalse One
The Alchymist	The fayre Mayd of ye Inn
Catalin	The Humorous Leiv^t
Bartholomew ffayre	The Island Princes
Staple of Newes	The Knights of Malta
The Devills an Asse	The Loyall Subject
Magnitick Lady	The Lawes of Candye
Tale of a Tubb	Loves Progresse
New Inn	The Winters Tale
Beggers Bush	King John
Bonduca	Richard the Second
Custome of ye Country	Loues Cure

Loues Pilgrimage
The Noble Gentlemen
The Nice Valour
The Prophetesse
The Marshall Mayd
The Pilgrim
The Queene of Corinth
The Spanish Curate
The Sea Voyage
Valentinian
The Weomans Prize
A Wife for a Moneth
The Wyd Goose-Chase
The Elder Brother
The ffaythfull Shephardesse
A King & noe King
The Maydes Tragedie
Phylaster
Rollo Duke of Normandy
The Scornefull Lady
Thiery & Theodorat
Rule a Wife & haue a Wife
The Gentlemen of Verona
The Merry Wives of Windsor
The Comoedy of Errors
Loves Labour Lost
Midsomer Nights Dreame
The Merchant of Venice
As you like it
The Tameing of ye Shrew
Alls well y^t ends well
Henry ye fourth
The Second part
The Royall Slaue
Richard ye Third
Coriolanus
Andronicus

Julius Ceaser
The Moore of Venice
Anthony & Clopatra
Cymbelyne
The Doubtfull Heire
The Impostor
The Brothers
The Sisters
The Cardinall
The Duke of Lerma
The Duke of Millan
Alphonso
The vnnaturall Cumbat
The Gardian
Aglaura
Arviragus & Philitia 1st pt.
Arviragus & Philitia 2d pt.
The Spartan Ladyes
The Bashfull Lover
Bussy D'Amboys
Brenoralt
Country Captaine
The Variety
The Emperour of ye East
The Deserveing ffavorett
The Goblins
The ffatall Dowry
The Lost Lady
The Devell of Edmonton
More Desemblers then Weomen
The Mayor of Quinborough
The Northen Lasse
The Novella
Osmond ye Great Turke
The Roman Actor
The Widdow
The Widdows Teares"

(L.C. 5/12, p. 212.)

III. References to Particular Performances.

1. For the warrant for payment of £20 to John Rhodes in respect of a performance of *Ignoramus* at Court, Nov. 1, 1662, see Appendix A, p. 302. The original warrant is in A.O. 3/130.

2. "A Warrant to the Master of the Great Wardrobe to prouide and deliuer to Thomas Killigrew Esqr to the value of forty pounds in silkes for to cloath the Musick for the play called the Indian Queene to bee acted before their Maties Jan. 25th 1663" (*i.e.* 1663/4; L.C. 5/138, p. 15).

3. Order to deliver, to Monsieur Grabut "such of the Scenes remayning in the Theatre at Whitehall as shalbe vsefull for the

french Opera at the Theatre in Bridges Street." These Grabut is ordered to return within fourteen days, Mar. 27, 1674 (L.C. 5/140, p. 456).

A letter to Killigrew demanding the return of the scenes is in L.C. 5/140, p. 471, dated April 27, 1674.

Statement regarding dancers: "In his Ma^tes Letters Patents for erecting the two Theaters There is a Clause That One house shall not entertaine any person that are before entertained in the other House without leaue or a discharge giuen by ye house where they were first entertained

It was affirmed by Mr Lacy that he had agreed with Mr Grabu that the ffrench Danceing Masters should dance at ye Kings Theatre & that they should haue Tenn Shillings a day for every day they did dance

It is further affirmed by Mr Killegrew Mr Hart & Mr Lacy that they did agree with ye Six dancers for fiue shillings aday whether they did dance or not, & this agreem^t Testified by two Wittnesses ready to take theire Oathes

That Accordingly for two Monethes together they practiced theire Dances, had in ye end theire Clothes made fitt for them & theire Money carryed to them according to ye agreem^t.

The Dancers did not accept of theire Money alledging they had made noe binding agreem^t nor could, by reason of a former one they had with Mr Grabu which did not leaue them at Liberty to make any They farther say that when they treated with Mr Killegrew, they Gaue an Intimacōn of this agreem^t but prove it not & those on Mr Killegrewe's side vtterly deny that any such thing was alleaded

Mon^sr Grabu was often at theire practising, &...therefore very probably not Ignorant of ye agreem^t that had beene made betweene them & Mr Killegrew. May ye Second 1674" (L.C. 5/140; in index at end among letters NOPQ).

Order regarding these: "I doe hereby Order that Mr Pecurr M^r Le Temps Mr Shenan and M^r D'muraile ffrench Dancers in the late Opera doe attend Mr Killegrew Master of His Ma^tes Comoedians in His Ma^tes Theatre Royall & observe & performe his Comands according to agreem^t betweene them...6: day of May 1674" (L.C. 5/140, p. 472).

4. Order to musicians to attend at the Theatre in Whitehall "at such tymes as Madam Le Roch & Mr Paisible shall appoynt for ye practiceing of such Musick as is to be in ye ffrench Comedy to be acted before His Matie on ye Nyne & twentieth of May instant," May 22, 1677. (L.C. 5/142, p. 38.)

The Theatre was ordered to be prepared for a play on this day; it may be that the French opera, *Rare en Tout*, was performed then. (L.C. 5/142, p. 40.)

5. "It is his Ma^{tles} pleasure that Mr Turner & Mr Hart or any other Men or Boyes belonging to His Ma^{tles} Chappell Royall that sing in ye Tempest at His Royall Highnesse Theatre doe remaine in Towne all the Weeke (dureing his Ma^{tles} absence from Whitehall) to performe that service, only Saterdayes to repaire to Windsor & to returne to London on Mundayes if there be occacōn for them And that (they) also performe ye like Service in ye Opera in ye said Theatre or any other thing in ye like Nature where their helpe may be desired." May 16, 1674. (L.C. 5/15, p. 3.)

6. Order for *Rule a Wife and Have a Wife* to be given at Court on Nov. 15, with command that the actors and the music should be ready "That ye King may not stay for them." Nov. 11, 1682. (L.C. 5/144, p. 303.)

7. "These are to require you to Act the Play called the Tragedy of Valentinian at Court before His Ma^e upon Munday night next being the Eleaventh of this moneth." Feb. 6, 1683/4. Addressed to actors of T.R. (L.C. 7/1; and L.C. 5/145, p. 14.)

"These are to signify unto you His Ma^{es} Pleasure That you give order for Candles, & all other usuall Allowances of Bread, Beere, Wine and Coales to bee deliuered unto John Clarke Keeper of the Theatre in Whitehall for the use of His Ma^{es} Comoedians who are to act a Play at Court on Munday night next being the Eleaventh of ffebruary instant And that you give order for Coales for ayreing the Play house the day before." Feb. 9, 1683/4; to the Duke of Ormond, Lord Steward. (L.C. 7/1.)

8. Order to pay Betterton £20 for "the King & Queenes Ma^{tles} Seeing the Play called Alexander at the Theatre Royall." Dec. 19, 1685. (L.C. 5/147, p. 52.)

9. Order to pay Mrs Barry £20 "for the Play called the Emperour of the Moone acted before His Ma^{te}." Dec. 20, 1687. (L.C. 5/148, p. 59.)

10. Order to pay Crowne £20 "as a quift from His Ma^{te} for His Play called Sr Courtley Nice." Jan. 9, 1687/8. (L.C. 5/148, p. 64.)

11. Order to pay Crowne £20 "as a quift from His Ma^{te} for seeing His Play called Darius King of Persia." May 8, 1688. (L.C. 5/148, p. 195.)

12. Order to pay Mrs Barry £25 for "the Spanish Fryar, or the double discovery" acted before Her Majesty. June 8, 1689. (L.C. 5/149, p. 154.)

13. Order for a large looking glass to be employed in *Sir Courtley Nice* that evening. April 30, 1690. (L.C. 5/150, p. 74.)

14. Order to pay Mrs Barry £25 for "Circe" acted by command. Nov. 7, 1690. (L.C. 5/150, p. 170.)

[An order had been given on Oct. 18 to get the Theatre ready for a play on Nov. 4, the King's birthday (*id.* p. 156); on this occasion a new orange colour curtain was provided (*id.* p. 164) and eight cane stools (*id.* p. 164).]

15. Order to pay William "Monfort" £10 for "Edward ye Third acted before Her Ma^te." Oct. 10, 1691. (L.C. 5/150, p. 306.)

16. Order to pay Mrs Barry £25 for "ye Orphan or ye Unhappy Marriage." Mar. 3, 1691/2. (L.C. 5/151, p. 30.)

17. Order to pay Mrs Barry £25 for *Caius Marius*. June 10, 1693. (L.C. 5/151, p. 242.)

18. Order to pay Mrs Barry £25 for "ye old Batchelor." April 16, 1694. (L.C. 5/151, p. 352.)

19. Documents relating to the Court Masque of *Calisto*.

(*a*) Order to deliver to Henry Harris, Yeoman of the Revels, "Two Habitts or dresses for two Shepheardes: Eight Habitts or dresses for Eight Satyrs: Eight habitts or dresses to represent ye Winds: Six habitts for Six Soldiers," the masque to be given at Christmas. Sept. 27, 1674. (L.C. 5/141, p. 74.)

(*b*) Order to give Phillipp Kinnersley, Yeoman of the Wardrobe, "a Curtaine of Blew Red & White in Breadthes of Stuffe of what kind you thinke fitt to fall downe before the Stage in ye Theatre in Whitehall." Nov. 3, 1674. (*Id.* p. 77.)

(*c*) Order to set lights in the Theatre, and to heat the tiring rooms and pit for rehearsals on Saturday, Tuesday and Thursday nights. Nov. 28, 1674. (*Id.* p. 74.)

(*d*) Order to provide to same "Eight Dozen of Wall Tynn Sconces for His Ma^tes Service in ye Theatre in Whitehall And also that you cause Lattices to looke through to be made in ye Curtaine that is to fall downe before the Stage there." Dec. 7, 1674. (*Id.* p. 77.)

(*e*) Order for fire shovels for masque. Dec. 15, 1674. (*Id.* p. 82.)

(*f*) Order to deliver to Henry Harris "Habitts to represent the foure parts of the world, habitts for foure Aeriall spiritts habitts for foure glorious spiritts habitts to represent the Thames, peace, and plenty one habitt for the Genius of the Countrey, one habit for Mrs Blake habitts for fiue Shepheards habitts for Eight Bacchusses habitts for Eight Affricans habitts for Two Shepheards and two Shepheardesses for the Chorus, ffiue habitts for ffiue

Baskes habitts for fiue Sea Gods, a habitt for one shepheardesse that sings, Six sleight habitts for boyes in the Clouds, habitts for foure Cupids Twelue habitts more for Countrey workemen to fitt twelue dancing Misters." Dec. 15, 1674. (*Id.* p. 83.)

(*g*) Warrant for "fferrett Ribbon to Hang the Curtaine vpon in the Theatre" at Whitehall. Jan. 15, 1674/5. (*Id.* p. 102.)

(*h*) Order to provide for the masque "A coppy of the play for the Queene, a coppy for the Lady Mary, A coppy for the Lady Mary and the Lady Anne, A coppy to correct vpon all occasions, a coppy of the prologue, and all the songs for Mr Staggins, and also...soe many printed bookes of the Maske and bound after such manner as Mr Crowne who is the Auther shall giue you an account shalbe necessary." These to be delivered to Crowne and distributed by him. Feb. 13, 1674/5. (*Id.* p. 127; and p. 556, where the words "for the Lady Mary" are deleted.)

(*i*) Ladyes in the Maske. 1674

	Attendants	
Lady Mary	4	[The names of the attendants are given in the MS. but it was thought necessary to give only the numbers of them here.]
Lady Anne	4	
Pages of ye Backstairs	2	
Lady Pembrooke	4	
Lady Henrietta Wentworth	3	
Lady Mary Mordant	2	
Lady Derby	2	
Lady Dacy	1	
Lady Herbert	2	
Mrs Blake	2	
M^rs ffrasier	3	
Mrs Jenings		

Lords and Gentlemen

Duke of Monmouth	2	and a "Barber" and "two footemen"
Lord Deincourt	1	
Lord Donblayne	1	
Mr Orpe	2	
Mr Lane	2	
Mr Trevor	1	
Mr Leonard	1	
M^r ffranshaw	1	

Singers

Mrs Davies	I	
Mrs Knight	I	
Mrs Butler	I	
Mrs Blunt		
Mrs Masters		
Mr Price		
Mr Hart	Maxfield	
Tanner	Preston	
Richardson	Letelier	(4) boyes
Marsh	Bopins	
fford	Bury	
Robert	—	
Degrang	—	
Shepheard	—	

2 Harpiscalls 2 Theorboes 3 Base Violls 4 Recorders 4 Gittars 4 Trumpetterrs 33 Violins

Dancers

St Andre	Motley
Isaacke	Berto
Delisle	Letang
Herriette	Muraile
Dyer	Le Roy
Smyth	Le Duke

(L.C. 5/141, p. 546.)

(*j*) Orders giving places for people of "good quality," those of "lesser quality" to go to the gallery (*id.* p. 549).

(*k*) For the order regarding the stage and scenery (*id.* p. 551), see *supra*, p. 43.

(*l*) Various orders: for "twenty garlands" and 20 habits for 20 violins "like Indian gownes" but not so full (Jan. 26, 1674/5; *id.* p. 553); for two presses for clothes (Jan. 28; *id.* p. 553); for 37 cases of flannel to wrap up "the rich habitts" (Feb. 9; *id.* p. 554); for 10 brasiers to warm the actors (Feb. 9; *id.* p. 554); for habitts for some of the musicians (Feb. 12; *id.* p. 555); for custody of clothes (Feb. 15; *id.* p. 555); for bread and wine during rehearsals (Jan. 28; *id.* p. 555); for 60 yards of cherry-coloured "Avinion," 30 yards of white, 130 yards of "Auraina," 30 yards of Green, 1 yard of sky-coloured, 84 yards of "silver Gawes," 6 yards of "gold gawes" and 4 pieces of "Tinsey Ribon" (Jan. 19; *id.* p. 556); for a shepherd's costume for Mr Richardson (April 13; *id.* p. 556).

(*m*) Accounts for *Calisto* "Pro diversis necessarijs pro usu et servitio....Regis in Le Maske apud Whitehall" are preserved in L.C. 9/112.

IV. ROYAL ORDERS RELATING TO THE GOVERNING OF THE THEATRES.

1. *Entrance to Playhouses.*

(*a*) "Whereas Wee are informed that diverse persons doe rudely presse and with evill Language and Blows force theire wayes into the two Theatres at the times of theire publique Representations, and Acting w^{th}out paying the prizes established, to the greate disturbance of Our Servants lycenced by Our Authority....Our Will and pleasure therefore is...that no person of what Quality soever presume rudely or by force to come into either of the two Theatres till the Playes are quite finished... notwithstanding theire pretended previledge by custome of forceing theire Entrance at the fourth or fifth Acts without Payment." Dec. 7, 1663. (L.C. 7/1; and L.C. 5/138, last page.)

(*b*) A printed order regarding entrance, dated Feb. 2 in the 26th year of Charles II, is contained in L.C. 7/3. This reiterates the order regarding payment, and commands "(to avoid future Fraud) That none hereafter shall enter the *Pit, First*, or *Upper Gallery*, without delivering to the respective Door-keeper the Ticket or Tickets which they received for their Money paid at the first Door." No person shall be allowed to sit on the stage or come "within the scenes."

(*c*) "It is His Ma^{es} Pleasure that no person whatsoever presume to come betweene the Scenes at the Royall Theatre dureing the time of Actinge....And that in no case whatsoever any person do presume to sitt upon the Stage or stand there dureing the time of Actinge." Jan. 18, 1686/7. (L.C. 7/1.)

2. *General Orders relating to Actors, etc.*

(*a*) "It is His Ma^{es} pleasure according to a Clause in His Ma^{es} Letters patents for erecting the two Companies for the two Theatres That no person whatsoever that are hired or anywaies entertained by any Bargaine or Agreement or hath acted or practiced either in His Ma^{es} Theatre or His Royal Highnesses Theatre shall depart from either the said Theatres without giving three Moneths warninge And that neither of the said Theatres do entertaine hire or desire to act or practice any person that hath beene soe entertained in any waies as aforesaid at the other Theatre." May 16, 1674. (L.C. 7/1 and L.C. 5/15, p. 2.)

(*b*) For the later orders of 1695, see *supra*, Appendix A, pp. 300–4.

3. *Particular Orders relating to the Conduct of Actors.*

(*a*) A complaint made to the House of Lords that an affront had been offered to a peer in the playhouse; consequent suspension of players until the pleasure of the House of Lords be known. Dec. 16, 1691. (L.C. 5/150, p. 340.)

Order for re-commencement of acting. Dec. 19, 1691. (*Id.* p. 345.)

(For other orders regarding suspension of actors see Appendix A.)

(*b*) Order to Betterton and patentees: "Severall persons of Quality having made Complaint to me that the Musick belonging to yor Theatre behave themselves disrespectfully towards them, by wearing their Hats on both in the Playhouse and upon the Stage; These are therefore to Require you, to give orders that for ye future they take care to be uncovered." Feb. 20, 1698/9. (L.C. 5/152, p. 163.)

4. *Licences to various Companies.*

(*a*) For Rhodes' licence (L.C. 5/138, p. 387) see *supra*, Appendix A, p. 278; and for Bedford's (L.C. 5/12, p. 185) see *supra*, Appendix A, p. 279.

(*b*) "On Sealed paper of forty shillings Charles Earle of Dorsett and Midds Lord Chamberlaine of His Ma^tes Houshold one of His Ma^tes most hono^le Privy Councill & Knight of ye most Noble Order of the Garter &c. In pursuance of His Ma^es Pleasure & Comand giuen vnto mee herein, I doe hereby give and grant full Power Lycence and Authority vnto Thomas Betterton, Elizabeth Barry, Anne Bracegirdle, John Bowman, Joseph Williams, Cave Vnderhill Thomas Doggett, Wm Bowen, Susan Verbruggen, Eilanor Leigh, George Bright, His Ma^es Sworne Servants & Comoedians, in Ordinary, and the Major part of them, their Agents, & Servant, from time to time, in any convenient place or Places, to Act and represent, all and all manner of Comedyes, & Tragedyes, Playes Enterludes, & Opera's, and to performe all other Theatricall & Musicall Enterteynments, of what kind soever, But so as to bee allwayes vnder my government & Regulation, from time to times as hath been Exercised by my p^rdecessors." Mar. 25, 1695. (L.C. 7/1; also in 7/3.)

Order relating to the government of L.I.F. This recites the granting of the Licence to the actors mentioned above and proceeds

"And Whereas ye said Thomas Betterton Eliz: Barry Anne

Bracegirdle John Verbrugen John Bowman Caue Underhill George Bright and Elizabeth Leigh haue taken ye Tennis Court in Little Lincolns Inne Feilds and paid a greate fine and doe pay a Great rent for ye same and at an Extraordr Charge & Expence haue converted ye same into a Theatre or Playhouse where they now act Comedies Tragedies &c

And further the said parties being necessited to provide every thing anew for the Carrying on soe Great an undertakeing as all variety of Cloath's Forreigne-habitts Scoenes properties &c which must be paid out of the publique *Receipts* by the Persons aboue named *proportionable* to the severall Shares & proportions each of them haue in ye proffitts of the said playhouse

It is therefore resolued and agreed by the Concent of ye whole Company that the Shares doe never exceed the number of Tenn

It is further Resolued and agreed that every whole sharer dyeing or quitting the Company fairely shall after ye Expiration of fiue yeares from the Establishmt of the Company haue the summe of One hundred payd him or his Executor after his Death by the rest of the Sharers at Two Equall payments within the space of Three month's after his Death or Quitting the Company as Theire interest and due for theire Shares in Cloaths Scenes Properties &c That is to say the summe of Twenty pounds to a whole sharer for the first yeare, Twenty pounds more for ye second Yeare and soe on to One hundred pound's at ye fiue Yeares End And soe to all other parts of shares in proportion to a whole share

But in Consideration of the great Expences ye first three yeares being more then reasonable can be supposed for the like Terme to come It is agreed that any whole Sharer dyeing at or after the Expiration of Three Yeares shall haue the summe of One hundred pounds payd His Executor as well & fully as if the whole Terme of Fiue yeares was Expired so in proportion to every under Sharer That is to say this payment to be made upon no other account but the Death of the party

If any sharer be made incapable of His Business in the Company by sickness or any other accident every whole sharer so disabled shall haue forty shillings p week allowed him every Week the Company shall Act And every Person under the degree of a whole sharer shall haue an allowance in proportion to his part of a Share he then enjoyed when he was so disabled.

If any Sharer shall hereafter be receiued into any proportion of Share he shall be obliged to signe the said Articles....

If any sharer be adjudged incapable of acting he shall not be obliged to acquitt his share and take the Salary provided in that

Case above mentioned before a Twelue Month be Expired in which space [written over "place"] of a Twelue month if he recover so as to attend his Business as formerly he shall then enjoy his share as formerly

If any hyred Servant whose Salary Exceeds Twenty Shillings the Week be made incapable of his Business by sickness or any other accident on the Stage he shall haue such a Weekly allowance proportionable to his Salary as the Majority of the Sharers shall Settle upon him.

If any Actor in Share or Sallary shall Quitt this Company and afterwards shall by Acting or otherwise assist any other Company he shall be incapable of receiueing any Benefitt of these Articles And alsoe every Actor Quitting the said Company shall be obliged to giue sufficient Security for his performing the Conditions of this Article before he shall receiue his proportion of Cloaths &c

It is further agreed by the Concent of ye whole Company that as the number of Sharers are not to Exceed Tenn so no person shall haue any proportion of aboue one share in consideration of Acting." Signed by Betterton, Verbruggen, Bowman, Underhill, Bright, Mrs Barry, Mrs Bracegirdle, Mrs Leigh.

(L.C. 7/1; and 7/3.)

V. Warrants for granting Livery to Actors.

(The substance of the following is given in Appendix A.)

1. "A Warrant to the Master of the Greate Wardrobe to provide and deliver unto His Maes Players whose names follow (vizt) Nicholas Burt Charles Hart Michaell Mohun Robert Shatterell, John Lacy, William Wintershall Walter Clunn William Cartwright Edward Shotterell Eduard Kynnaston Richard Baxter Thomas Loveday, Thomas Batterton and Marmaduke Watson to each of them foure yards of Bastard Scarlett for a Cloake and to each of them a quarter of a yard of Crimson Velvett for the Cape of itt being the usuall Allowance of every second yeare to commence at October last past." July 29, 1661. (L.C. 7/1; and L.C. 5/137, p. 31.)

2. Warrant for liveries to Clun, Cartwright, Wintersell, Mohun, Robert Shatterell, Hart, Baxter, Blagden, Loveday, Kinaston, Burt, and Bird, as Queen's actors. Feb. 5, 1661 (probably 1661/2). (L.C. 5/137, p. 43.)

3. Warrant as above for liveries to Hart, Mohun, Lacy, Bird, Birt, Robert Shatterell, Clunn, Wintersell, Cartwright, Kinaston, Blagden, Watson, Hancock, Baxter, Edward Shatterell,

Gradwell as His Majesty's players. May 30, 1662. (L.C. 5/138, p. 10.)

The same as Queen's players. Dec. 29, 1663. (*Id.* p. 10.)

4. Warrant for liveries to Hart, Mohun, Lacy, Birt, Burt, Robert Shatterell, Clunne, Wintersell, Cartwright, Kinaston, Blagden, Watson, Hancock, Baxter, Edward Shatterell and Thomas Tanner, as Queen's actors. Nov. 4, 1662. (L.C. 5/137, p. 173.)

The same as His Majesty's players, same date. (*Id.* p. 173.)

5. Warrant for liveries to Hart, Mohun, Lacy, Bird, Birt, Robert Shatterell, Clunn, Wintersell, Cartwright, Kinnaston, Blagden, Watson, Hancock, Baxter, Edward Shatterell and Gradwell, as His Majesty's players. Feb. 25, 1665/6. (L.C. 5/138, p. 65.)

The same as the Queen's actors, same date. (*Id.* p. 65.)

6. Warrant for liveries for Hart, Loueday, Mohun, Lacy, Batiman [Bird, deleted, Loveday and Batiman insertions], Birt, Robert Shatterell [Clunn deleted], Wintersell, Cartwright, Kinnaston [Blagden deleted], Watson, Hancock, [Baxter and Edward Shatterell deleted], Gradewell. Feb. 8, 1667 (probably 1667/8; the month is written over "May July 18" deleted). (L.C. 5/138, p. 271.)

7. Warrant for liveries to Hart, Mohun, Wintersell, Cartwright, Kinnaston, Robert Shatterell, Lacey, Bird, Bell, Hughes, Harris, Haynes, Wattson, Shirley, Liddall, Graydon, as Queen's actors. Oct. 2, 1669. (L.C. 5/119.)

The same as His Majesty's players, same date. (*Id.*)

8 (*a*) Warrant for liveries to 16 actors as His Majesty's players, and to the same as Queen's players. Oct. 23, 1673. (L.C. 5/140, p. 353.)

(*b*) The same as King's and Queen's players. Mar. 29, 1675. (L.C. 5/141, p. 147.)

(*c*) The same as King's and Queen's players. April 30, 1678. (L.C. 5/143, p. 72.)

9. "A warrant to prouide and deliuer to Mrs Weauer, Mrs Marshall Mrs Rutter Mrs Yates Mrs Nepp Mrs Dalton Ellen Gwyn Eliz: Hall ffransis Dauenport and Anne Child Weomen Comoedians in his Ma^tties Theatre Royall vnto each of them foure yards of bastard scarlet cloath and one quarter of a yard of veluett for their liueries." June 30, 1666. (L.C. 5/138, p. 71.)

10. Warrant for liveries to [Mrs Weaver deleted] Mrs Marshall Mrs Rutter [Mrs Yates deleted] Mrs Nep [Mrs Dalton deleted]

Ellen Gwyn [Elizabeth Hall deleted] ffrancis Davenport [in margin, Elizabeth and Jane; Anne Child deleted]. Feb. 8, 1667 (probably 1667/8; the date is written over "July 22ᵗʰ"). (L.C. 5/138, p. 271.)

11. Warrant for liveries to Mrs Marshall, Mrs Cory, Ellin Gwynn, Mrs Kneepe, Mrs Rutter, Mrs Hues, Mrs Davenport, and Mrs Yackley. Oct. 2, 1669. (L.C. 5/119.)

12. (a) Warrant for liveries to 11 "Weomen Comoedians." Oct. 23, 1673. (L.C. 5/140, p. 353.)

(b) The same to 11 women comedians. Mar. 29, 1675. (L.C. 5/141, p. 147.)

(c) The same to 11 women comedians. April 30, 1678. (L.C. 5/143, p. 72.)

13. "It is His Maᵉˢ pleasure that Mʳ Mohun Mʳ Hart, and Mʳ Kynnaston bee continually furnished at the charge of the Master and Company of His Maᵉˢ Comoedians with the perticulers following unto each of them in such proportion as they are here sett downe (vizt)

Two perruques to begin with for the first yeare

One perruque yearely afterwards to begin a yeare hence

Two Cravatts yearely

One Lace or point Band in two yeares the first band to be now provided.

Three paire of Silke Stockins yearely

Four paire of Shooes yearely

Three Hatts yearely

Two plumes of feathers yearely

Three Shirts with Cuffs to them yearely." Mar. 6, 1671/2. (L.C. 7/1; and L.C. 5/140, p. 5.)

VI. Documents relating to the Articles of Union.

Most of the entries relating to this are given in Appendix A. The following Petition of Mohun is the only interesting one omitted.

"Mʳ Mohun   To the Kings most Excellent Maᵗᵉ
    pet.   The humble petition of Michaell
             Mohun, One of yoʳ Maᵗᵉˢ Actors at
             the Theatre Royall

Sheweth

That yoʳ petʳ hath faithfully served yoʳ Maᵗᵉ & Father (of ever Blessed Memory) 48 yeares in yᵉ quality of an Actor, and in all yᵉ Warrs in England & Ireland & at yᵉ Seege of Dublin was desperately wounded & 13 monethes a Prisoner, and after that yo[r] pet[r] served yo[r] Mate in ye Regm[t] of Dixmea[d] in Flaunders & came over with yo[r] Mate into England where yo[r] Sacred Pleasure was that he should Act againe, as he hath ever since vpon all Occasions continued That it being yo[r] Mates Pleasure to reduce the two companyes into one yo[r] pet[r] is depriued of his share and quarter in ye Scenes Clothes & playes (that cost about 4000[ll] by M[r] Charles Killegrew who has rented them to M[r] Davenant for a share (as yo[r] pet[r] is informed) and tells him if yo[r] pet[r] hath any right theirto he must gett it by law. And instead of a share & quarter w[ch] yo[r] pet[r] had formerly in yo[r] Mates Company for Acting he is now only proffered 20[s] a day when they haue occasion to vse him, soe that they haueing not studyed Our Playes nor yo[r] pet[r] therein he cannot conceaue the same will amount to aboue 20[ll] p an[o] Wherefore yo[r] pet[r] most humbly prayes That yo[r] Mate will be graciously pleased to Order the p[r]sent Company to allow him the same Conditions as M[r] Hart and M[r] Kinaston haue, (whos Shares were all equall before) whereby he may be enabled to support himselfe & 5 children And yo[r] pet[r] shall as in duty bond pray &c.

M[r] Mohun   It is His Ma[tes] pleasure & Comand, That ye
Order   Persons concerned in Mannageing the concernes
& proffitts of the playes at ye Royall Theatre & His Royall High-nesse Theatre (being now Vnited into one Company) Doe giue and allow vnto M[r] Michell Mohun, the same Conditions which they allow vnto M[r] Hart & M[r] Kinniston (theire shares haueing beene equall formerly   Arlington Whitehall November 23. 1682

M[r] Mohun   Vpon the former Petition of M[r] Mich: Mohun
Order   it was againe thus Ordered.
It is His Ma[tes] pleasure That theire Ma[tes] Comoedians doe giue an allowance to M[r] Michaell Mohun the same allowance for his Weekely Pension, and for his Acting, as is allowed & giuen vnto M[r] Charles Hart the same to Comence from the three & twentieth day of November last & to be imployed p[r]sently, & to haue his owne parts to Act: This Order to be without Consequence to any others Given vnder my hand this 5[th] day of December 1682 in the 34[th] yeare of His Ma[tes] Reigne." (L.C. 5/191.)

VII. Documents relating to Particular Actors.

(For the warrants creating several actors and actresses His Majesty's Servants, see Appendix A, pp. 293-8.)

1. Order for warrant granting the place of Yeoman of the Revels to Henry Harris, payment to commence on June 24, 1663. Feb. 20, 1663/4. (L.C. 5/138, p. 388; there seems to have been some doubt as to his actual appointment as in L.C. 5/138, p. 280, is an order for a warrant for the same post, dated Mar. 3, 1667. On April 4, 1667, an order was issued stopping payment to him until further notice (L.C. 5/138, p. 369). In L.C. 7/1 appears a list of officers of the Revels; in which appears "Henry Harris Yeoman in Mr Caryes place sworne Aug: 6: 1663:)

2. Certificate that Haynes and Mrs Elizabeth Roch are His Majesty's servants. Apr. 14, 1679. (L.C. 5/143, p. 305.)

(A similar certificate was issued on July 10, 1682; L.C. 5/16, p. 97.)

3. Letter to Betterton:

"May: 7th: 1681

Mr Betterton

I did yesterday signify unto you that Mrs Norris should bee received into yor Company againe And this is to explaine that order That it is His Ma^{tes} Pleasure that shee reconcile her selfe unto her adversary, and submit herselfe to the rules and Governement of the Company and upon this condition shee is to bee admitted as formerly." (L.C. 7/1; and 5/16, p. 28.)

4. "The Case of Philip Cademan Gent." (c. 1696):

Recites the fact that Sir William D'Avenant was granted a patent "At wch time S^r W^m stood indebted to Mr Cademan in a Bond of 100^{li} and in Consideration that Mr Cademan woud acquit S^r W^m of ye s^d debt and Act as a Player S^r W^m promised to settle upon him 30^s ℔ Week to be paid out of ye proffitts arising from ye playhouse W^{ch} Mr Cademan did accordingly and received 30^s ℔ Week during Sr W^{ms} Life and several years after his Death. And in ye year 1673 as he was Acting his Part upon ye Stage, he received a Wound from the late Mr Harris ye player wth a foyle under his right Eye, wch touch'd his Brain by means whereof he lost his memory his speech and the use of his right side, wch made him incapable of acting any more Notwithstanding wch his Salary was continu'd until Mr Rich had ye management of ye playhouse (as indeed all persons had it for their Lives that were disabled from acting by Sickness or other Misfortunes...)

and then M.ʳ Rich thought it reasonable that M.ʳ Cademan shoud do something for his Salary, and orderd him to sit and deliver out Tickets w.ᶜʰ he did until he was disabled by Sickness in y.ᵉ year 1695 But after he was restord to his health he offerd to serve in y.ᵉ same Capacity he did before But M.ʳ Rich refusd to suffer him and has ever since denyd to pay him his Salary." (L.C. 7/3.)

5. Whereas John Powell of Dorset Garden was lately committed prisoner in the Gatehouse by warrant of the Right Hon. Mr Secretary Vernon for breach of peace and "for his Insolence in Affronting and drawing his Sword upon Collonell Stanhop and M.ʳ Davenant," and whereas the patentees have admitted him again, a warrant is issued to suspend them from acting. May 3, 1698. (L.C. 5/152, p. 80.)

VIII.

1. *Petition of the Players, c.* Dec. 1694. (L.C. 7/3.)

"Sheweth That your Pet.ʳˢ whose names are here subscribed being noe longer able to suffer & Support themselves under the unjust oppressions & Violations of almost all the By lawes Customes & usage that has been established among us from y.ᵉ beginning & which remained unviolated till after D.ʳ Davenant sold his patent & shares to his Brother Alexander under whome and by whome severall Titles have been claimed by diverse persons And sometimes a Trust in him onely pretended whereby many have been defrauded, with other pretences & Combinaċons whereby severall persons have been Lett in who seek after their owne Interest to recover their Debts." (The petition proceeds to remark that all things in the playhouse have been changed and beg the Lord Chamberlain to appoint a day for hearing their complaints. The document is signed by Betterton, Underhill, Kenniston (*i.e.* Kynaston), Bowen, Williams, Doggett, Bright, Sandford, Mrs Barry, Mrs Bracegirdle, Mrs Verbruggen, Mrs Bowman, Mrs Betterton, Mrs Ellen Leigh and John Bowman. Inclosed with it are the articles of grievance, as below.)

(1) Dr D'Avenant sold his share in the patent "as he thought" to his brother Alexander for £2300. Sir Thomas Skipwith and Rich, since Alexander D'Avenant's flight, have produced deeds to prove that Alexander D'Avenant's name was but made use of: the payment for the share came from them. According to these, Alexander D'Avenant farmed the profits for them at £6 a week for five years, during which time Skipwith and Rich never revealed the secret of their ownership of the patent. This gave

Alexander D'Avenant credit among the actors, and by means of the cheat he was advanced by Mrs Barry some £600 to £800, and deceived others of the company in a like manner.

(2) When Dr D'Avenant came of age he made a promise that in consideration of the share in the costumes and scenery in the theatre each whole sharer who left off playing or was disabled should be paid the sum of £100. This, according to the petitioners, was actually given to Smith. It had been confirmed since, but the payment was not forthcoming to the whole sharers who now intended to leave.

(3) The actors have been persuaded to part with their interest in the after-money "which is the money recēd for the 4ᵗʰ & 5ᵗʰ Acts which brings in 400 or 500ˡˢ ℘ ann which they were to have for 16 Yeares for the payment of 1000ˡˢ Debt & now they have ingrossed soe Considerable a part of the profitts they would force us into Shares againe—threatning some they will shutt up the doores if they will not Consent to it."

(4) The profit money arising from "mulcts" and fines is now claimed by the patentees.

(5) The present patentees forbid continuous acting.

(6) Many good actors have been turned away and "ignorant insufficient fellowes putt in their places." The players under the new management are treated as slaves.

(7) Mrs Barry made an agreement with Dr D'Avenant, Killigrew, Smith and Betterton for 50s. a week and one benefit every year. Later she made an agreement with Thomas Betterton that if, after the expenses had been met, her profits from the benefit did not come to £70, that amount should be made up to her. This agreement was carried out for many years, but now the patentees not only refuse to make up the £70 but claim third profits in the benefit.

(8) When Betterton left his share, a quarter and half a quarter, he agreed with Killigrew and Alexander D'Avenant to act for £5 a week and an annual present of 50 guineas. Now that the patentees have "ingrossed" the after money they want to drag him into share again and "lessen him a quarter & halfe a quarter tho' he prsumes he is not lessen'd in his Acting." Betterton likewise is not supplied with a "Perruck" as he ought to be.

(9) At the Union of the Stages it was agreed that 5s. per acting day should be paid to Lady D'Avenant for fruit money: this was to be given by Killigrew who had received £50 from D'Avenant, Smith and Betterton. Lady D'Avenant had sold her right to

this 5s. and Rich had not paid it to them: these are now threatening Betterton.

(10) Rich refuses to pay £20 for an organ in St Bride's Church which had been subscribed by order of Killigrew and Thomas D'Avenant.

(11) Williams had an agreement for £4 a week from Killigrew and Thomas D'Avenant. The patentees had offered him £10 to sign a certain paper: he refused and they took £1 off his salary.

(12) Mrs Bracegirdle demands one annual benefit, the charges to be paid by the patentees.

(13) Mrs Verbruggen demands an extra 5s. weekly.

(14) Killigrew, about six months before the lodging of this petition, had promised to raise Doggett's salary to equal that of any under Betterton: this was revoked by the patentees who merely offered him an extra 10s.

(15) Bright had studied many of Leigh's parts, and for this, and for dancing, he demands 5s. a week extra.

2. *The Reply of the Patentees*, Dec. 10, 1694. (L.C. 7/3.)

"10 Dec****94 Sr Thos Skipwiths et al Answ^{re} to the... aligacōns—before Lord Dorset.

p̱ Seci: Darwell.

Betterton et al Skipwith Bar^t et al. To attend Lord Dorset at Sr Robt Howards at Westm^r Munday 17 Decr 94. betweene 10 & 11 a Clock.

The Answere to ye Peticon & Articles of P^{r}tended Greivances P^{r}sented to the right Honorable The Earle of Dorsett Lord Chamberlayn of their Maties Houshold by Mr Thomas Betterton & others by name of their Maties Servants & Comedians.

The p^{r}sent Patentees of the Theatres saving their Right &c—say' (Here follows an analysis of their right to speak as patentees of the theatres. They mention the patent given to D'Avenant by Charles II, giving him full power "to gather together Enterteyn Governe Priviledge & keep such & so many Players & p̱sons to Act Plays as he or they from time to time should think meete." They emphasise the fact that he was given authority to "make such allowances to the Actors and other Persons Imployed in Acting as he or they should think fitt." On April 25 of the same year Charles granted to Killigrew the patent in a theatre to be the King's and Queen's company, "both wch Patents were by Ind^r Dated ye 4th of May 1692 made between Charles Killigrew Esqr of ye one p̱te And Dr Davenant Thomas Betterton & William

Smith of ye other pte United. And all ye benefitts Priviledges Powers & Authoritys before mencōnd are covenanted & Agreed to be as one from thenceforth for ever Subject to ye Provisoes condicons & Agreem^ts therein conteyned. And that all Plays then after to be Acted should be acted by the Company then Employed or after to be Employed at the Dukes Theatre & by such other pson & psons as Mr Killigrew & Dr Davenant their heirs & Assigns should from time to time direct & appoint **** And by ye s̄d Ind^r Mr Killigrew was & is to have 3 shares in Twenty of ye Cleere Pffitts & to disperse & dissolve ye Kings Company of Players forthw^th as by ye s̄d Ind^r amongst divers covenants & Agreem^ts therein conteyned may more at large appear." The patentees then proceed "to give your Lordp an Acco^t how matters stand in a Cause in Chancery now depending before ye Right Honōble Sr John Sommers Kn^t Lord Keeper of ye Great Seale of England Wherein Mr Killigrew is Plf: And Dr Davenant Mr Betterton & others are ye Defts And then wee shall pceed to Answere ye Articles wch Mr Betterton & his Mutinous Companions (as ye Patent is pleased to term them) have p^rsented unto Your Lordp, The End of Mr Killigrews Bill is to have a true Account of all ye Receipts of ye Theatres from May 1682 And alsoe of all Paym^ts and disbursem^ts & to have his pporcōn thereof being 3 shares in 20 of ye Cleere Pffitts And alsoe an Equall Power in ye Governm^t & Managem^t And touching Paym^t to sharing Actors Ground Rent of ye Dukes Theatre now called ye Queens Theatre Taxes Reparacōns, ye 2 ffront houses there, fforfeit Mony, ffruite Mony, & 3^s-4^d a day, pd to Mrs Lacy & other matters.

To which Bill Dr Davenant Mr Betterton & sev^ll other Defts did putt in their Answers which are very long & have submitted to ["have" deleted] an account & have referred themselves to ye Judgem^t of ye Co^rt Whereupon divers Witnesses were Examined on both sides And upon hearing ye Cause the 7th of Decemb^r 1691 It was referred to Sr Robert Legard One of ye Masters in Chancery to take & state ye said Account And therein [written over "also"] to certifie ye State of ye Governm^t—Sr Robert Legard after further Depositions taken before him made his Report And therein reported sev^ll things Specially to ye Co^rt & in pticular ye Government & Managem^t of ye Theatres & how he found it to stand on ye Deeds & pffes taken in ye Cause—To which report both sides have filed Excepcōns wch are not yett argued.

Having stated this matter of ffact as 'tis truely Lyeing before my Lord Keeper & by him (un)Determined Wee shall now pceed

to Answ.ͬ yᵉ Articles by M.ͬ Betterton Exhīted before your Lordp."
(Here the patentees proceed to discuss point by point the allega-
tions of Betterton and his companions.)

"And ffirst ["may it please yo.ͬ Lordp" written and deleted
after "ffirst"] as to M.ͬ Bettertons alledging yᵗ S.ͬ Thomas Skipwith & M.ͬ Rich by letting yᵉ World beleive yᵉ Right of yᵉ Patent
& Shares was in Alexand.ͬ Davenant gave him Creditt & Authority
to lay yᵉ ffoundacōn ffor all yᵉ Cheats and fforgeries yᵗ Alex:
Davenant was found Guilty of by Couzening M.ͬˢ Barry of 6 or
800ˡˢ & others of sev.ˡˡ Thousands.

Answere May it please yo.ͬ Lordp M.ͬ Alexand.ͬ Davenant fled
in Octob.ͬ 1693 And it has not appeared to us yᵗ any Cheats or
fforgeries have been p.ͬtended to be done by him till ab.ᵗ ½ a Year
before he fled whereas yᵗ D.ͬ Daven.ᵗ (by reason y.ᵗ M.ͬ Bolesworth
one of his Wives Trustees had not Executed yᵉ Conveyances of
yᵉ Patent & Shares as well as M.ͬ Betterton yᵉ other Trustee had
done) did in July 1690 enter into a Bond of 3000ˡˢ penalty to M.ͬ
Rich yᵗ M.ͬ Bolesworth should Execute yᵉ same wᵗ.ʰin 3 Moneths
then next (tho he hath not yett done it) And tis Well known yᵗ S.ͬ
Thomas Skipwᵗʰ & M.ͬ Rich when the rent [the last three words
added] was behind spoke of this concerne to divers psons in so
much yᵗ M.ͬ Davenant compleined of yᵉ unkindness in soe doeing
And M.ͬ Betterton may Remember yᵗ yᵉ Writings tho' ["tho'"
written above the line] drawn & Ingrossed at M.ͬ ffolkes Chamber
yᵉ same were sealed at M.ͬ Serj.ᵗ Pembertons Chamber (who was
of Counsell for S.ͬ Thomas Skipwith) And M.ͬ Rich p̄d M.ͬ Betterton 2000ˡˢ of yᵉ Purchase Mony by a Note on S.ͬ ffrancis Child
when all yᵉ Writings were putt into M.ͬ Riches Custody (& never
were out of his Custody) And M.ͬ Davenant never had them one
Minute whereby to Cheate or Countenance a cheat Nor doth
M.ͬ Betterton or M.ͬˢ Barry or any other pson that we have heard of
p.ͬtend to have any Mortage or Grant of yᵉ sd Patent or those Shares
or any pte of them but she hath declared yᵗ she lent M.ͬ Davenant
400ˡˢ [written originally 4000 but deleted] in Aprill 1693 upon a
share granted or supposed to be granted by S.ͬ William Davenant
to one Cheston & 200ˡˢ more in May 1693 of some Rent Issueing
out of yᵉ Dukes Theatre yᵗ M.ͬ Ashburnham gave to M.ͬ Thomas
Davenant And yᵗ as for yᵉ other 200ˡˢ yᵗ she hath yᵉ Do.ͬˢ Bond
for it as well as his Brothers.

Tis true yᵗ M.ͬ Alexand.ͬ Davenant farmed yᵉ s̄d Patent & 2
Shares as he farmed yᵉ Shares of divers other psons p.ͬtended yᵗ
he best Understood wᵗʰ yᵉ Assistance of M.ͬ Betterton to Manage
yᵉ Affaires of yᵉ Theatres to yᵉ Best Advantage & yᵗ S.ͬ Thomas

Skipwith & M.ʳ Rich were Obliged to sell yᵉ same Patent & Shares
for 2400ˡˢ to M.ʳ Alexand.ʳ Davenant as they Cost but M.ʳ Davenant
was not ["not" added] Obleiged to repurchase yᵉ same The 6ˡˢ p̱
Weeke was often p̄d at yᵉ office at yᵉ Playhouse and it was well
known to diverse p̱sons: but M.ʳ Rich lent more Monys to M.ʳ
Alexand.ʳ Davenant then he recēd for his p̱te of the Rent insomuch
yᵗ M.ʳ Davenant when he went off owed M.ʳ Rich on Bonds & a
Note above 600ˡˢ And to S.ʳ Thomas Skipwith & his late ffather
to whom he is sole Executor by Bonds & other securitys above
700ˡˢ wᶜ.ʰ is still oweing & S.ʳ Thomas Skipwith & M.ʳ Rich have
declared themselves Willing to sell yᵉ s̄d Patent & 2 shares to
D.ʳ Davenant or any other for yᵉ s̄d principall sūms of 2400ˡˢ—
600ˡˢ & 700ˡˢ wᵗ.ʰ Interest for yᵉ same respectively at 6ˡˢ p̱ Cent
p̱ Ann & their Charges & ["that" deleted] they [deletion] will
discount what M.ʳ Alex: Davenant p̄d upon yᵉ ffarm aforesd or
otherwise eversince [the last word added]. And S.ʳ Tho: Skipwith
ever since 1687 hath sent Notes for p̱sons to see plays Gratis
wᶜ.ʰ tis beleived M.ʳ Betterton could not be Ignorant off now May
it please yo.ʳ Lordp for M.ʳ Betterton to charge S.ʳ Thomas Skipwith
& M.ʳ Rich in such a Scandalous manner to have layd the ffoundacōn of M.ʳ Alexand.ʳ Davenants Cheats & fforgeries & for M.ʳ Betterton to gett divers other p̱sons as he has done to signe to [last
word added] yᵉ same when sev.ˡˡ of them hath since declared that
[last word added] they neither read nor heard read yᵉ Paper
annexed to yᵉ s̄d Petition wherein those scandalous words are
mencōnd shews wᵗ sort of a Man M.ʳ Betterton is."

(The patentees here have a long preamble in which they express
the hope that Betterton will be ordered to make some kind of
satisfaction. They state that they do not wish to brand Betterton
"for a Cheat or Couzener tho' he did really conceal from yᵉ
World yᵉ Mortgageing of his Rent of 6ˡ.ˢ p̱ Weeke in the Queens
Theatre for many years." Betterton and D'Avenant, say the
Patentees, declare that £6 a weeke for five years must have given
Skipwith considerable profit: as a matter of fact he received only
one per cent. for the last two years and Betterton has forgotten
the £600–£700 taken by Alexander D'Avenant and Betterton's
own 20 per cent. per annum on moneys laid out for the building
of Dorset Garden playhouse.)

Article 2. This concerns the alleged promise of Dr D'Avenant
to give £100 to every wholesharing actor leaving the company for
his share in "Cloaths Scenes Bookes & p̱pertyes." The patentees
reply that they have not any knowledge of this promise. £100
was certainly given to Smith but that "was upon an other con-

sideracon well known to M.ʳ Betterton who can tell whether M.ʳ
Tho: Sheppy Robert Nokes James Nokes Thomas Lovell John
Mosely Henry Turner & Thomas Lilleston who were formerly
sharing Actors who had any such sūms pd them upon yᵉ Account
aforesd but wee are Informed if a sharer went off or dyed S.ʳ
William Davenant putt another in his Roome & such new Sharer
was to give 500ˡˢ security for his good behaviour...& when
M.ʳ Betterton went out of share in January 1692 he did not desire
any such thing nor did M.ʳ Betterton M.ʳ Mountfort M.ʳ Leigh
or M.ʳ Bowman when they settled yᵉ priviledges of sharing Actors
& came into share on 26 September 1692 make any such Demand
And if Mʳ Thomas Davenant deputy Mannager appointed by
Word of Mouth onely hath p.ʳtended to grant any such thing he
might as well w.ᵗʰ submission to your Lordp grant away other
psons shares of Rent or pffitts." Following this is an interesting
statement that Sir William D'Avenant had sold most of his shares
in his lifetime "before he could carry on yᵉ Management of yᵉ
Playhouse And yᵗ D.ʳ hath since sold yᵉ patent & some of yᵉ
Shares."

Article 3. Aftermoney. The patentees express their surprise
that Betterton should raise this point now after he has acted with
Alexander D'Avenant for nearly a year. They affirm that Betterton
and the others asked the patentees to take the aftermoney for
£1000 to pay a debt of that amount on the theatres. They offer
Betterton that if he will forfeit salaries and gratuities since he parted
with his sharing rights, they will take him in once more as a sharer.

Article 4. Forfeits. This, the patentees say, is merely a trick
of Betterton's to curry favour with his companions. "M.ʳ Betterton knows yᵗ by yᵉ Decree in yᵉ Co.ʳᵗ of Chancery it is & hath
been brought into yᵉ Receipt & divided as other Monys are." This
very fact, they say, was decided on 26 September, 1692, after the
long discussions on the part of Betterton, Mountfort and Leigh
concerning the rights of the sharing actors.

Article 5. "As to Acting so many Days a Week & takeing yᵉ
bad w.ᵗʰ yᵉ good &c." The patentees affirm that the company
acted the previous year more frequently than they did when
Betterton was in control. They suggest that Betterton is here
inspired by mean spite "ffor he was greatly displeased to think
yᵉ Young People Acted yᵉ last vacacōn near 30 Days without
M.ʳ Betterton M.ʳ Williams M.ʳ Bright M.ʳ Kinaston M.ʳ Sandford
or M.ʳˢ Betterton." The young actors by this means got enough to
keep them over the vacation. However, as Rich has to pay £3
every acting day at the Theatre Royal and £7 every acting day

at the Queen's Theatre, he cannot afford to keep the doors always open, the receipts often being under £20 per diem, whereas the full expenses come to £30. There follows a hint that Betterton went on salary in 1692 because theatrical conditions were bad.

Article 6. The taking away of sharers' rights. Betterton and Bowman, it is affirmed, "soon after y⁰ Death of M⁰ Mountfort & M⁰ Leigh to witt on y⁰ 16ᵗʰ of Janʳʸ 1692 requested to be in Sallary untill y⁰ beginning of y⁰ then next vacacōn onely but they have kept in Sallary ever since altho M⁰ Betterton hath often ꝑmised yᵗ he would be Willing at any time to come into share again." Alexander D'Avenant, say the patentees, would not do anything without Betterton: from 1687 till he "went off in 1693 all things were done as M⁰ Betterton would have it & he gave out wᵗ Plays he would during yᵗ time as well as y⁰ last Year by wᶜʰ means very little could be Divided or thrown off to pay Debts out of y⁰ Receipts & on y⁰ 14ᵗʰ of July last above 189ˡˢ was runne in Debt." They suggest that Alexander D'Avenant started his underhand methods in 1687 by (a) adding a quarter and half a quarter to Betterton's share, (b) giving him a vacation present of 50 guineas, (c) "allowing him to brow beate and discountenance young Actors as M⁰ Giloe Carlisle Mountfort & others." "Wee allow," declare the patentees, "sallarys to y⁰ ꝑsons yᵗ now complayn beyond wᵗ was over formerly p̄d to any Man or Woman belonging to y⁰ Kings Theatre & M⁰ Betterton for his & his Wives Acting have for y⁰ 2 last years received out of y⁰ Playhouse after y⁰ rate of 10ˡˢ ꝑ Weeke (besides 6ˡˢ ꝑ Weeke) for Rent" whereas Rich and Skipwith who expended fully £3600 on the patent did not get clear £30 last year.

Article 7. Concerning Mrs Barry. "May it please your Lordp That M⁰ Betterton himselfe took notice yᵗ M⁰ˢ Barry made so great Advantage of a Play given her one day in y⁰ Year that y⁰ same wᵗʰ her Sallary was more then his 5ˡˢ ꝑ Weeke And wee Observing yᵗ although y⁰ receipts of late had been lesse then Usuall yett y⁰ Constant & Incident Charges are higher & consequently needfull to be Retrencht & M⁰ˢ Barry having declared yᵗ M⁰ Tho: Davenant had released her of her bargain And yᵗ she would not be Obleiged to Play unless she came to a new Agreemᵗ wᵗʰ us Itt was ꝑossed yᵗ she would continue at her Usuall Sallary of 50ˢ ꝑ Weeke & remitt one 3ᵈ of y⁰ ꝑffitts of y⁰ Days Play to M⁰ˢ Bracegirdle wᶜʰ we beleived would by y⁰ Addicōn of M⁰ˢ Bracegirdles ffriends so Increase y⁰ Receipts as yᵗ M⁰ˢ Barry would not be a great looser."

Article 8. Concerning Betterton's quitting his share, quarter and half a quarter for £5 a week and a vacation present of 50 guineas, and being taken back on one share only. Betterton, say the patentees, "never had upon Account of his Acting when he was at ye best any more then one Actors share till Dr Daven^t sold his Patent for from May 1682 to 1687 by pffe in Chancery it appears y^t he had but one share & ½ a q^r & this ½ q^r was in pte of satisfacōn for his care in ye Managem^t And Mr Smith had ye like when he was an Actor & Joint Manager wth Mr Betterton but when Mr Smith went out of ye house And Mr Tho: Davenant in 1687 came into ye Managem^t & had 3^{ls}–10^s for his trouble then Mr Betterton had a q^r & ½ a q^r of a share Added to him by Alex: Davenant for w^t private Consideracōn is unknown to us wch was continued to Mr Betterton till ab^t ffeb^{ry} 1689 then Mr Betterton was in Sallary in Sepr 1691 at 5^{ls} p Weeke & a Vacōn p^rsent of 50^{ty} Guineas for his generall care then he came into share again & had but one Acto^{rs} share till ab^t Septr 1692 when ye Agreem^t ab^t ye After Mony & ye Acting sharers priviledges were settled he came into one share and a q^r but Mr Mountfort & Mr Leigh dyeing in Decemb^r followeing Mr Betterton on ye 16th January 1692 came into Sallary again at 5^{ls} p Weeke & 50^{ty} Guineas for his generall Care by name of a Vacacōn p^r sent but Mr Betterton well knows why he was then pmitted to leave his share & q^r & go into Sallary onely for y^t Year wch wee shall not now discover unless he pleases It is true Mr Betterton doth not think himselfe lessen'd in his Acting but ye Patentees & Adventurers to their sad Experience find y^t a Man at 60 is not able to doe That wch he could at 30 or 40 he hath put himselfe into all great pts in most of ye Considerable plays Especially in ye Tragedys & yett wⁿ he Acts a great pte we must be forced to Act an Ordinary Play one or 2 days after as Scapin Monsr Rogou & such like to ease him & soe loose w^t wee gott on ye day he played Whereas there are Act^{rs} enough in ye House to Act good plays Allways & Mr Betterton himselfe could formerly have Acted a great pte 4 or 5 dayes in a Weeke wⁿ he was a Sharer & before he became so Aged." They then declare that Betterton should be the last to complain. He had received £50 for his care in attending rehearsals etc "And alsoe he has had 50^{ls} for his care & trouble to gett up ye Indian Queen tho he hath not yett done itt wth wch summs & w^t he & his Wife hath received for Acting & his Rent of 1^l p diem amounts to above 16^{ls} p Weeke for every Weeke ye Company Acted ye last Year." His complaints are the more unexpected and strange "because ye last Year when Mr Doggett Bowen & others Mutinied Mr Betterton declared they ought to be Ejected ye House & by his pswasions they were denyed to be received till they Quitted yᵉ Combinaçõn & each Man treated onely for himselfe." As regards the perruck "Mᵣ Betterton was told that as for yᵉ Perruck something should be considered to be given him in Leiw thereof tho' this of a Perruck is an Innovaçõn & may pve of great Inconvenience by reason all others will graft upon it to have yᵉ like Allowance." Betterton did not carry out his duties carefully. "Wee very often attended ourselvs & treated wᵗʰ yᵉ Poets." Later it is stated that "Mᵣ Betterton for yᵉ Care he tooke as Principall Actor in yᵉ Nature of a Monitor in a Schole to looke after rehearsalls...had a Gratificaçõn of 50 Guineas besides yᵉ Complimᵗ of his Wifes 50ˢ a Week."

Article 9. Concerning 5s. a day for fruit money. Sir William D'Avenant, it is affirmed, "Immediately after yᵉ King granted him his Patent not knowing otherwise how to carry on yᵉ Charge of Acting wᵗʰout great summs of Money to buy Apparell Habitts & ppertys Machins & other decoraçõns sold out to yᵉ Honoble Mᵣ Ashburnham late Cofferer of his Matie Houshould yᵉ Hounoble John Harvey Esqᵣ yᵉ Lord Lonnolly & sevˡˡ other psons diverse [the last word added] pts & shares in yᵉ pffitts thereof all wᶜʰ Interested psons or yᵉ psons Clayming undᵣ them ought to have been made ptys to yᵉ Granting of yᵉ sd 5ˡ p diem & to have some consideraçõn as well as yᵉ Lady Davenant Dᵣ Davenᵗ Mᵣ Killigrew Mᵣ Betterton tis true Mᵣ Killigrew acknowledges yᵗ he had 50ˡˢ wᶜʰ he is ready to bring into Cash & my Lady Davenant we hear had 400ˡˢ wee would faine [the last word added] know wᵗ Dᵣ Davenᵗ & Mᵣ Betterton had."

Article 10. Concerning Rich's refusal to pay £50 "for yᵉ Organs in Sᵗ Brides & alsoe Mᵣ Atterbury yᵉ Lecturer wᵗ has been allowed to his pᵣdecessors." Betterton also ought to pay his share. "Mᵣ Betterton lives in one of yᵉ ffront Houses & has done for many Years & has not yett pd any Rent for it." He, therefore, ought to pay the parish duties, and the patentees hope that he will pay rent for his house before he is forced by law.

Article 11. Williams' claim for £4 a week salary. The patentees reply that when Mountfort and Leigh were alive Williams never had more than £3 a week or ¾ of a share. "Abᵗ August 1692 Mᵣ Williams left yᵉ house for abᵗ ½ a year but Mᵣ Mountfort & Mᵣ Leigh both dyeing in Decembᵣ 1692 Mᵣ Williams was asked to act again & he being pretty sensible of our necessity of him at yᵗ time Imposed upon us & would not come in to Act unless he had 4ˡˢ p Weeke for yᵗ Year wᶜʰ Mᵣ Thomas Davenᵗ agreed to give him for yᵗ Year." After the year was over they offered him ¾ of a share and £10 in consideration of some clothes: he refused and accordingly they reduced him to £3 per week. This, say the patentees, is all he deserves "for he knows yᵗ yᵉ last year Mʳ Powell & Mʳ Verbruggen did Act his pts above 30 times."

Article 12. "As to Mʳˢ Bracegirdle pposicōn of having pts of yᵉ Cleere pffitts of an Old Play." The patentees answer that before she asked for it they offered her third part of the profits of a benefit, and they trust that Dorset will leave this matter for them to arrange.

Article 13. Concerning Mrs Verbruggen's salary. The patentees consider that 50s. is quite enough for her: her demand of 5s. extra was simply due to their proposal to Mrs Bracegirdle.

Article 14. Doggett's demand. Doggett, say the patentees, was taken into the playhouse in 1690 at 10s. a week "from being a Stroler & in ffebʳʸ 169⅔ he entered into Articles undʳ hand & seale to serve yᵉ Playhous at 40ˢ ℔ Weeke & to give 9 Acting Months notice undʳ hand & seale when he should have a Mind to leave yᵉ Company." At the request of Betterton and Mrs Barry the patentees had since allowed him 10s. a week more: but about three weeks ago he had written demanding for himself £3 a week for a year.

Article 15. "Mʳ Brights studing up many pts of Mʳ Leigs & what he saveth yᵉ Company by dancing desires an Addicon of 5ˢ a Weeke to his Sallary." Bright, declare the patentees, signed on for 40s. a week, but already he had been promised this extra 5s.

The patentees then point out that regarding the other signatories to the petition—Bowman, Underhill, Kynaston, Sandford, Bowen, Mrs Betterton, Mrs Leigh and Mrs Bowman—no complaint has been stated, and proceed to summarise their treatment of these actors and actresses. Three weeks previously Bowman had signed on for £3 per week or ¾ share "wᶜʰ was wᵗ he had when he last went out of share in Janʳʸ 169⅔." Before that date he never had more than £3 weekly salary. Underhill received a weekly salary of £3 although he acted but seldom. Kynaston received the same, but likewise acted only infrequently. Sandford got £2. 10s. per week but "by reason of his Indisposition & his Voice often failing he is able to Act but seldom." Bowen signed on for 40s. weekly, but was advanced 10s. a week the previous year. This Betterton himself declared was more than he deserved. Although this actor is easily drawn to mutiny "yett he studys his pts very quickly & Acts wᵗʰ vigour." Mrs Betterton was in receipt of 50s. a week "constantly pd her in Complemᵗ to Mʳ Betterton She not appears in any pts to yᵉ satisfaction of yᵉ Audience." Mrs Leigh since the death of her husband had been raised 10s., so that her salary was now 30s. This, say the patentees, is all that the popular Mrs Cory received. Mrs Bowman's salary had been raised 5s. a week since 18 October last (1694). She was now getting 30s. though she had signed on for 25s. "She being a Child-bearing Woman some other must learn some of her pts or else those Playes she is in cannot be acted." She certainly, in the opinion of the patentees, had no cause to complain. Finally, the patentees draw the attention of the Lord Chamberlain to the fact that there were still a number of actors who did not sign Betterton's petition: namely: Powell, Verbruggen, Trefuse, Lee, Horden, Harland, Cibber, Harris, Pinkethman, "Young Kent," Mrs Aylyffe, Mrs Hodgson, Mrs Knyght, Mrs Rogers, Mrs Perryn, Mrs Lawson, Mrs Kent, Mrs Lucas, and Mrs Temple.

IX. Miscellaneous.

1. *Documents relating to the Cockpit, the Theatre in Whitehall, etc.*

(*a*) Warrant to deliver to George Johnson, Keeper of the Royal Cockpit in St James's Park "such a quantitie of Greene Bayes as will couer the Stage...and to hange ouer ouer (sic) the doores there." Nov. 13, 1662. (L.C. 5/137, p. 175.)

(That this was for the performance of a play seems proved by a later warrant, dated Nov. 15, 1689 (L.C. 5/149, p. 318), for "Greene bayes" to cover the stage for a play to be acted there "on Friday next.")

(*b*) Warrant to deliver 110 yards of green baize for the upper tyring rooms of the Cockpit, which in their present state are unfit for rich clothes, a looking glass, 20 chairs and stools and 3 tables. Dec. 10, 1662. (L.C. 5/119.)

(*c*) Warrant "to make vp Habitts of seuerall coloured Silkes for foure and Twenty violins twelue of them being for his Maties service in the Theatre Royall and the other twelue Habitts for His Maties service in His Highnesse the Duke of Yorkes Theatre and also foure and Twenty Garlands of seuerall coloured flowers"; all these to be delivered to Killigrew, Mar. 20, 1664/5. (L.C. 5/138, p. 45; the same warrant, with minor deviations, is repeated in L.C. 5/119.)

(*d*) Warrant "to make vp Habitts of seuerall coloured rich Taffataes for fower and Twenty violins like Indian Gownes but not soe full with short sleeues to the Elbow and trymmed with Tinsell about the neck and bottome and at the sleeues after the fashion as Sr Henry Herbert...shall informe yor Lopp and to bee deliuered to Sʳ Henry Herbert for his Maᵗˢ extraordinary service and also fowr and twenty Garlands of seuerall coloured floures to each of them." Mar. 18, 1664/5. (*Id.* p. 46.)

(*e*) Warrant to deliver for use in the Theatre "One large long Cushion of Gold Coloured Damaske trymed with silke fringe and Tassells and a table Carpett of the like Damaske four foote long and two foot three Inches broad trymed suteable to the Cushion And one Pewter Standish." April 10, 1665. (*Id.* p. 49.)

(*f*) Warrant to deliver "three large trunks bound with Iron to keepe clothes for his Maᵗᵗᵉˢ Service in the Theatre at Whitehall." April 17, 1665. (*Id.* p. 49.)

(*g*) (Cancelled order.) Warrant to deliver for use in the Theatre in Whitehall "Six Turky worke chayres for yᵉ Stage two Spanish Tables Six tynne Candle sticks Six Little tynne Candlesticks for sizes one greate Chayre to bee vsed vpon yᵉ stage." Dec. 31, 1666. (*Id.* p. 261; deleted there, re-entered p. 264 and dated February 28, 1666/7.)

(*h*) Order "to cause yᵉ Stage in yᵉ Theatre in Whitehall to be altered and made in such fashion as it was for Scaramouch's Acting And his Maᵗᵗᵉˢ Seate to be placed & made as then it was. And that yᵉ doore be opened as the Actors then went in at" and to prepare "such boxes & partitions as the ffrench Comoedians shall desire you for theire Accomodation." Feb. 5, 1676/7. (L.C. 5/141, p. 528.)

(A further order for altering the stage for the French comedians, dated Dec. 4, 1677, appears in L.C. 5/142, p. 160.)

(*i*) Warrant to provide "vnto Monsʳ Cabin fiue Habitts to be made of such fashion & of such particulers as he shall giue you informacōn," to be ready for Friday, Feb. 5, 1677/8. (L.C. 5/143, p. 32.)

(*j*) Warrant "to require you to rayle in two benches betweene yᵉ Lord Stewards box and yᵉ Scenes in yᵉ Theatre for yᵉ Ambassadors." Oct. 14, 1685. (L.C. 5/17, p. 20; and L.C. 5/146, p. 27.)

(*k*) "These are to pray and require you to cause the Seates in the Theatre, in the Pitt, only to bee new matted, they being soe dirty, and vnfitt to place any Person of Quality on for whome they are appoynted." Oct. 27, 1685; Lord Chamberlain to Sir Christopher Wren. (L.C. 5/147, p. 1.)

2. *Agreements of Actors and Playwrights.*

(For the petitions of several scene-painters, see *supra*, p. 42.)

(*a*) "Articles of Agreement Indented, and made ye 29th Day of October 1696, By, and between Colley Cibber Gent. on the One Parte, and Christopher Rich Esq., one of the Patentees of the Theatres on the other Parte as followeth

Impri^s The said Colley Cibber in consideration of one Shilling to him now Paid, and for the farther Considerations herein after mentioned doth Bargain, and sell unto ye said Christopher Rich his Heires and Assignes A Certain New Play written by the s^d C: Cibber, and stiled Woman's Witt or ye Devill to Dealt with to bee Acted only by the Company of Actors under the Goverment of the s^d Chr: Rich his Heires, or Assignes within a Month after the Parts of the said Play shall bee Distributed to the said Company of Actors Item: In Consideration whereof it is Agreed that Mr Cibber shall have all the Mony Receiv'd on the Third day of acting such Play Paying out of the same all the Charges of the House Constant and Incident: But if the Receipts on the fourth Day shall amount to 55^li or upwards then the said Charges of such Third Day shall bee returned to Mr Cibber

And in case the Receipts on such fourth Day shall Amount to 40^li or upwards, then the said Play shall bee acted the next Day Following: And if the fift days Receipts shall amount to 40^li or upwards, then the said Play shall bee acted again the next day, and the said Mr Cibber shall have all the Receipts of such sixt Day Paying out [of] the same all the Charges of the House Constant, and Incident. And if the Receipts on such sixt Day shall not amount to the Full Charges of the House Constant, and Incident then Mr Cibber is to make it up at his own Costs, and Charges: And if the Receipts on such sixt Day shall amount to 40^li then the said Play shall bee acted on the next day following. And if the Receipts on such seaventh Day shall amount to 50^li or Upwards, then the said Charges of such sixt Day shall bee return'd to Mr Cibber

And the said Mr Cibber is to have the sole Benefitt of Printing such Play: But he is not to suffer it to bee Printed till a month next after it shall bee first acted

Item it is agreed between the Parties to these Presents, that the said Colley Cibber shall bargain and sell unto the said Mr Rich his Heires, or Assignes all such other Play, and Plays as the said Mr Cibber shall hereafter write to bee acted only by the Company under the Goverment of the said Mr Rich his Heires, or Assignes, upon the like Termes, and Considerations aforesaid during the said Mr Cibbers being an Actor in this Company aforesaid, and that the said Mr Cibber shall not During his being an Actor in such Company write any Play, or other thing whatsoever for any other Company: In wittness whereof the said Parties to thes Articles of Agreement have thereunto Interchangeably sett their hands, and seales the Day, and Year first above written.

Sign'd Seal'd, and Deliver'd   Colley Cibber [seal]
by ye said C Cibber a six-
Penny stamp then Appearing
on this Paper."

(L.C. 7/3; witnessed by G. Perrill and J. Shore.)

(b) Contract with Robinson for scenes:

"Whereas Mr Robert Robinson has this day Undertaken to paint, or Cause to be painted well, & in Workmanlike manner ye Severall Sets of scenes, & Machines, for a New Opera Written by Mr Settle, & to Be forthwith, & wth all ye Expedition that may be, perform'd At ye Theatre Royall, wch sayd Scenes, & Machines are to be The whole paintings that are to belong to ye sayd Opera according To Such Measures as ye sayd Robert Robinson, hath agreed & Concerted wth ye sayd Mr Settle. Now therefore we whose names are Underwritten Doe hereby agree, & promise to pay, or Cause to be payd, from ye Office of ye say'd Theatre Royall Unto ye sayd Mr Robinson or his order ye full Summ of one hundred & thirty Pounds Sterling in full Sattisfaction of, & for ye sayd Paintings, in manner following Vizt: Ten Pounds p^r Week Dureing [ye deleted] such time as he shall be working, & Painting of ye sayd Scenes, & Machines, & ye Remainder on ye first, Second, & fourth days of ye Acting ye sayd Opera, or w^thin fourteen days after ye sayd Paintings shall be finish'd. Wittness our hands ye 18th day of March. 1699

Fra: M: Knight   Geo: Powell
Jane Rogers   Robt Wilks
                     John Mills
                     Will: Pinkethman

Mem^r That Mr Robinson on his part doth agree, & promise to finish the Scenes & Work w^thin [deletion] Mention'd, w^thin Seauen Weeks of ye date hereof. Wittness my hand

Robt Robinson."

(L.C. 7/3.)

(c) Articles of Agreement between Verbruggen and Skipwith, April 10, 1695.

1. For three years Verbruggen will "with his best care & skill Sing Dance Act Rehearse and Rep[r]sent."

2. Skipwith will give him £4 out of every £20 to be divided among the adventurers; all debts contracted since Oct. 17, 1694, to be paid out of the general receipts.

3. Skipwith gives a bond of £300.

4. Verbruggen does likewise.

Witnessed by Philipp Griffin and Hild. Horden. A note is appended "That because a Share produced nothing, S[r] Thomas Skipwith advanced 4[l] a weeke to M[r] Verbruggen." (L.C. 7/3.)

(d) Articles of Agreement between John and Susanna Verbruggen and Skipwith, April 10, 1695:

1. John Verbruggen agrees that, for a payment of £75, his wife will act in the theatre.

2. Susanna Verbruggen to have £4 out of £20 (as above); if this does not amount to £105 per year (i.e. £3 a week for 35 acting weeks) this sum shall be made up to her. At the end of every 6 acting days (except when the young actors play for their own benefit) she shall have £3 till the whole £105 is completed. If, on the other hand, her share comes to more than £105 she shall be allowed to keep it. (L.C. 7/3.)

(e) Articles of Agreement between Doggett and Skipwith, April 3, 1696:

1. Doggett to start acting on Oct. 10, and to perform nowhere else.

2. Skipwith to give him £4 for every six acting days "or else share up to the heighth as shall be paid to M[r] George Powell or M[r] John Verbruggen."

3. Doggett to get the benefit of one old play to be acted on a Wednesday or Friday in Lent after Christmas, he to pay the charges of the house.

4. Doggett and Skipwith give bonds of £500. (L.C. 7/3.)

Another document of date April 3, 1696, refers to the fact that Skipwith has given Doggett £50, with a promise of another £50 on Oct. 12. Should Doggett die or should "not before that time leave off acting with the Company of Actors in Lincolns Inn ffieilds" the whole £100 would be forfeited. Skipwith is to bear all charges save 10s. of a benefit play, but this must not be an opera or a recently revived drama. If Doggett leaves off acting at L.I.F. by July 20 "& shall from that time travell in the Vacation to Improve himselfe in Acting" and learns five parts, Skipwith shall pay him £10. If Doggett gives notice within 3 weeks and travels "to Improve himselfe in Acting & makeing Observa͞cons

for yᵉ benefitt of this Company" Skipwith shall give him
£20.

(*f*) Articles of Agreement between "William Bullock of
Sᵗ Giles Cripplegate" and Skipwith, April 15, 1695:

1. Bullock to act only with the D.L. company.
2. Skipwith to give Bullock 20s. a week; the contract being
terminable only on 9 months' notice. Signatures of Bullock,
Verbruggen and Griffin (copy; L.C. 7/3).

(*g*) Articles of Agreement between Sorin, a dancing master,
and Betterton, July 25, 1696:
Sorin to receive 30s. a week with augmentation, if necessary.
Witnessed by John Baptist Draghi. (L.C. 7/3.)

(*h*) Letter of notice, June 17, 1699; Erasmus Evans and Susanna
Evans, his daughter, give notice that the latter will dance at L.I.F.
for only one month longer. (L.C. 7/3.)

(*i*) Warrant for discharge, Dec. 10, 1680. "Whereas John
Dowson was Entertained Dancing Master in his Maᵗᵉˢ Theatre
Royall but Entered not into Articles for his Continuance there
And the said John Dowson desireing to be discharged from yᵉ
said Theatre I doe hereby discharge him." (L.C. 5/144, p. 22;
Lord Chamberlain's warrant.)

3. *Various Documents relating to Theatres, and Actors' Petitions.*

(*a*) Petition of Verbruggen (*c.* 1697/8 or later). Summary:
Smith, one of the chief actors and sharers of L.I.F., died in
Michaelmas, 1696, and the company was in distress to find a
substitute. Verbruggen thereupon withdrew "by the Ld Chamber-
lains Leave" from the D.L. company and entered L.I.F. as a
sharing actor and manager. By articles of Oct. 27, 1696, between
Betterton, Mrs Barry, Mrs Bracegirdle, Mrs Bowman, Underhill,
Bright, Mrs Leigh on the one part and Verbruggen on the other,
Verbruggen was to get one share. Betterton at that time had
1½ shares, but quitted a ¼ share in favour of the Petitioner. Verbruggen was also to have 20s. a week. He was informed then that
the debts were not above £200, and was surprised at the smallness
of his income from the share. The other parties to the agreement
declared that Betterton, Mrs Barry and Mrs Bracegirdle, who
would not let the books be seen, were making huge profits. About
Michaelmas last Verbruggen was told that the debts were about
£800; after an attendance before the Lord Chamberlain it was
agreed that there should be no benefits and that all spare money
should go to pay off these debts. During this winter the receipts
have been specially large "especially ever since the Italian Woman

hath sung." Yet Betterton and the others pretended the debts were not yet settled, even although they had stopped Verbruggen's 20s. a week. Betterton has ordered bills, announcing *Othello* to be acted on Friday next with singing by the Italian woman, for his own benefit. Verbruggen hears she is to sing also at benefits of Mrs Barry and Mrs Bracegirdle, and then to leave off performing. (L.C. 7/3.)

(*b*) Letter from Richard Coling to Mr Knight, Mar. 8, 1689/90; "My Lord Chamberlayne would haue you to sumon Mr Downs prompter at theire Ma^{tes} Theatre to appeare on Munday morning next by Nyne of the Clock It being the tyme His Lordpp hath appoynted to heare the difference betweene Mr Killigrew & Mrs Currer." (L.C. 5/150, p. 366.)

(*c*) Order to Sir Christopher Wren to inspect the Duke's Theatre in Salisbury Court as the King has heard that there is a wall defective. Nov. 29, 1671. (L.C. 5/14, p. 73.)

APPENDIX C

Hand-list of Restoration Plays
[1660–1700]

THE Hand-list aims at registering all known plays of the Restoration period, including those whose titles only have been recorded. In general, all works published before 1660 have been disregarded, the sole exceptions being such dramas (*e.g.* those by D'Avenant) which have a definite connection with the later stage. The arrangement is as follows:

1. The title is given usually according to the form it assumes in the earliest printed text, preceded by an indication of the type of play concerned. The contractions employed are:

T.	Tragedy.	M.	Masque.
C.	Comedy.	Ent.	Entertainment.
Hist.	History Play.	D.O.	Dramatic Opera.
T.C.	Tragi-comedy.	O.	Opera.
F.	Farce.	Past.	Pastoral.
F.C.	Farcical Comedy.	Pol.	Political Play.

2. In brackets is then given the theatre, month and year of performance, known or conjectured: if no such information is presented, the play did not appear on the stage. The contractions for the theatres are as follow:

T.R. in V.St.	Theatre Royal in Vere Street.
T.R. in B.St.	Theatre Royal in Bridges Street.
D.L.	Theatre Royal in Drury Lane.
L.I.F.	Lincoln's Inn Fields.
D.G.	Dorset Garden.

The dates following are those of separate editions, quartos unless otherwise indicated. Indication of any known manuscripts is also included here; most of these are recorded by Alfred Harbage in "Elizabethan and Seventeenth-century Play Manuscripts" (*PMLA*, 1935, L. 687–99) and "Elizabethan and Seventeenth-Century Play Manuscripts: Addenda" (*PMLA*, 1937, LIII. 905–7) —cited as "Manuscripts" and "Addenda" respectively.

4. In the notes are presented, in brief, such evidence as serves to date the plays, with references. Where an exact date of first performance has been recorded, or where there is a recorded date

which in all probability is close to the première, this is given with a reference: L.C. here stands for an entry in one of the play-lists given in Appendix B. "Imprimatur" means that there is a licence for printing in the published play (usually on the title-page). S.R. refers to an entry recorded in the *Transcript of the Registers of the Worshipful Company of Stationers from 1640–1708* (ed. G. E. Briscoe Eyre, 1913, 3 vols.) and T.C. to a similar entry in *The Term Catalogues* (ed. Edward Arber, 1906, 3 vols.). The citation of references to advertisements in newspapers is based largely on Sybil Rosenfeld's "Dramatic Advertisements in the Burney Newspapers, 1660–1700" (*PMLA*, 1936, LI. 123–52) and "The Restoration Stage in Newspapers and Journal, 1660–1700" (*Modern Language Review*, 1935, XXX. 445–59): where there are several newspaper entries of approximately the same date only one has been selected for inclusion here. For earlier works by Restoration playwrights references are given to W. W. Greg's *A List of English Plays written before 1643 and printed before 1700* (1900)—cited as "Greg, *List*"—and to *A Check List of English Plays, 1641–1700* compiled by Gertrude L. Woodward and James G. McManaway (1945)—cited as "Woodward-McManaway, *Check List*." The latter is, of course, the nearest approach we have to a "bibliography" of Restoration drama, and is an invaluable guide. References to Philip H. Gray, Jr., "Lenten Casts and the Nursery: Evidence for the Dating of Certain Restoration Plays" (*PMLA*, 1938, LIII. 781–94) are given as "Gray, 'Lenten Casts'." All the other contractions used are mentioned earlier in this volume.

For many plays only an entry in the *Term Catalogues* remains as a guide towards a determination of the production date. In general, it would appear from the scanty evidence available that plays were issued shortly after their performance, with a tendency towards a gap of two or three months gradually narrowing towards the end of the century. Where no other definite facts are to be found I have usually allowed for about two months between the dates of theatrical representation and of publication, with modifications if there appear to be any slight or even inconclusive indications of performance at a particular period of the year (*e.g.* references suggesting summer instead of autumn with a play entered in the Stationers' Register in November). It should, however, be observed that among these conjectural dates may be several which would have to be altered considerably were we possessed of adequate records of the Restoration repertoire. Thus, for example, the Hon. James Howard's *The English Monsieur* was printed in 1674, with an entry in the *Term Catalogues* for May and his *All Mistaken* was issued in 1672, also with a May entry: yet Pepys saw the latter in 1667 while the recent discovery of a diary kept by two Dutch students proved that the former was on the stage as early as 1663. Had it not been for these two records we should certainly have considered both plays much later in date and we should have assumed that *All Mistaken* preceded *The English Monsieur*. On the other hand, the number of entries in the *Term Catalogues* which do harmonise with other references indicating performances shortly before gives us reason to believe that exceptions of the kind indicated above were probably rare.

ARROWSMITH, Rev. JOSEPH.
    C.   The Reformation (D.G. *c.* Sept. 1673) 1673 (2 issues).
        [T.C. Nov. 1673. Downes, p. 33, ascribes it to "a Master of Arts in Cambridge"; Langbaine, p. 546, gives Arrowsmith's name. The cast suggests it may have had a summer production.]

AUBREY, JOHN.
    C.   The Countrey Revell, or The Revell of Aldford (incomplete) MS. Bodl. Aubrey 21 (two scenes printed by Andrew Clark in "*Brief Lives*"...set down by *John Aubrey* (Oxford, 1898), II. 334–9).
        [Aubrey refers to this in a letter of Oct. 26, 1671 as a "very satyricall" piece he is "writing...for Thomas Shadwell" (*op. cit.* I. 52).]

BAILEY, ABRAHAM.
    C.   The Spightful Sister. A New Comedy. 1667 (2 issues).
        [Imprimatur, April 10, 1667.]

BANCROFT, JOHN.
    T.   The Tragedy of Sertorius (D.L. *c.* March 1678/9) 1679.
        [Imprimatur, March 10, 1678/9. T.C. May, 1679.]
   Hist. King Edward the Third, with the Fall of Mortimer Earl of March. An Historicall Play (D.L. *c.* Nov. 1690) 1691.
        [*London Gazette*, Jan. 19–22, 1690/1. T.C. Feb. 1690/1. There is considerable doubt concerning the authorship. The dedication is signed by William Mountfort, who was given a warrant of £10 with respect to a performance of the play before the Queen (L.C. Oct. 10, 1691); *The Gentleman's Journal* (Oct. 1692) says that it was written by the same author as *Henry the Second*, which Gildon, p. 5, gives to Bancroft; Coxeter declares Bancroft "made a present of it to *Mountfort* the Actor" (*The Companion to the Play-House*, 1764). Alfred Harbage, "Elizabethan-Restoration Palimpsest," pp. 310–18, makes it reasonably certain that the play is an adaptation of a pre-Commonwealth original, possibly *The Politic Queen*, a manuscript of which was in the possession of Humphrey Moseley.]
   Hist. Henry the Second, King of England; with the Death of Rosamond (D.L. Nov. 1692) 1693.
        [Presumably Tuesday, Nov. 8, 1692 (a playbill for the second day, Nov. 9, is extant and is confirmed by a letter dated Nov. 9; W. J. Lawrence, *Elizabethan Playhouse*, 2nd ser. (1913), p. 240, and *HMC*, 12th Report, App. Part v, p. 124). *London Gazette*, Nov. 24–28, 1692. *The Gentleman's Magazine*, Oct. 1692 (issued probably in November). Performed before the King, Mon. Nov. 14,

1692 (L.C.). For the authorship see under *King Edward the Third*. Alfred Harbage, *loc. cit.*, believes it is an adaptation of *Henry II*, a manuscript of which was in Moseley's possession.]

BANKS, JOHN.
T. The Rival Kings: or The Loves of Oroondates and Statira (D.L. *c.* June, 1677) 1667 (3 issues).
    [S.R. July 26, 1678 (entered and then deleted; probably the year should be 1677). T.C. Nov. 1677. The cast suggests a performance in Lent (Gray, "Lenten Casts," p. 791), or more probably in the summer.]
T. The Destruction of Troy (D.G. *c.* Nov. 1678) 1679.
    [Imprimatur, Jan. 1678/9. S.R. Feb. 26, 1678/9. T.C. May, 1679. Medbourne, one of the cast, was arrested on Nov. 26, 1678, and died shortly after in prison. November, therefore, is the latest date for the première.]
T. The Unhappy Favourite: or the Earl of Essex (D.L. *c.* Sept. 1681) 1682; 1685; 1693; [1699]; 1702; 1712.
    [T.C. Nov. 1681; Feb. 1684/5; May 1699. *Flying Post*, March 11–14, 1698/9.]
T. Vertue Betray'd: or, Anna Bullen (D.G. *c.* April 1682) 1682; 1692; 1715.
    [T.C. Nov. 1682; June 1696. Summers (Downes, p. 226) gives April 5, 1682, as the date, but without any evidence.]
T. The Island Queens: Or, The Death of Mary, Queen of Scotland.... Publish'd only in Defence of the Author and the Play, against some mistaken Censures, occasion'd by its being prohibited the Stage. 1684.
T. The Innocent Usurper; or, The Death of the Lady Jane Gray. 1694.
    [Dedication signed Oct. 5, 1693, where it is stated that the play was written ten years before. T.C. June 1694. It was banned by the censor, according to a statement in the dedication.]
T. Cyrus the Great: or, The Tragedy of Love (L.I.F. *c.* Dec. 1695) 1696.
    [T.C. June 1696. The prologue declares it was written before *The Unhappy Favourite* (*i.e.* before Sept. 1681) and speaks of it as "A banish'd Play." As William Smith, who had a part in this tragedy, died of a chill caught during performance in Dec. 1695, the piece presumably was first acted in that month. Downes, p. 44, names it *The Grand Cyrus*.]
T. The Albion Queens: or the Death of Mary Queen of Scotland (D.L. March 1703/4) 1704.
    [Mon. March 6, 1703/4. This is an altered version of *The Island Queens*.]

BARNES, JOSHUA.
C. The Academie or The Cambridge Dunns (Emmanuel College, Cambridge, 1675). MS. Emmanuel College, III. i. 4.
    [Wed. June 26, 1675 (G. C. Moore Smith, *College Plays performed in the University of Cambridge* (1923), p. 72).]
T. Englebert (Cambridge). MS. Emmanuel College, III. i. 2.
T. Landgartha or The Amazon Queen of Denmark and Norway (Cambridge, 1683). MS. Emmanuel College, III. i. 2.
C. Plautus his Trinummi Imitated. MS. Emmanuel College, III. i. 4.

BARTLEY, Sir WILLIAM.
T.   Cornelia (T.R. in V.St., June 1662).
[Herbert, p. 118, dates the play June 1, but Avery, p. 239, points out that this was a Sunday: quite possibly the year should be 1663 instead of 1662. Herbert gives the author's name as "sir W. Bartleys," again a possible error: Berkeley may be intended.]

BAYLIE, SIMON.
The Wizard. MSS. (1) Durham Cathedral Library; (2) B.M. Add. 10,306.

BEDLOE, WILLIAM.
Pol.   The Excommunicated Prince: or, The False Relique. A Tragedy. As it was Acted by His Holiness's Servants. Being the Popish Plot in a Play. 1679.
[Prefatory note dated July 16, 1679. *Domestick Intelligence*, Oct. 31, 1679. Anthony à Wood (*Fasti Oxonienses*, ed. P. Bliss (1813–20), 11. 373) declares that "tho' the name of Capt. Will. Bedloe is put as author, yet" Thomas Walter "wrote all, or the most part of it."]

BEHN, APHRA or ASTRAEA.
T.C.   The Forc'd Marriage, or the Jealous Bridegroom (L.I.F. *c.* Dec. 1670) 1671; 1688; 1690.
[T.C. Feb. 1671, May 1688.]
C.   The Amorous Prince, or, The Curious Husband (L.I.F. *c.* May 1671) 1671.
[T.C. July, 1671.]
C.   The Dutch Lover (D.G. Feb. 1672/3) 1673.
[Th. Feb. 6, 1672/3 (L.C.). T.C. Nov. 1673.]
T.   Abdelazer, or the Moor's Revenge (D.G. *c.* Sept. 1676) 1677; 1693.
[T.C. Nov. 1676. The prologue shows that it came out in the early autumn. An adaptation of Marlowe's *Lust's Dominion.*]
C.   The Town-Fopp: or Sir Timothy Tawdrey (D.G. *c.* Sept. 1676) 1677; 1699.
[Imprimatur, Sept. 20, 1676. T.C. Feb. 1676/7. *Post Boy*, March 11–14, 1698/9.]
C.   The Debauchee: or, The Credulous Cuckold (D.G. *c.* Feb. 1676/7) 1677.
[Imprimatur, Feb. 23, 1676/7. T.C. May, 1677. S.R. Aug. 20, 1677. *London Gazette*, Aug. 6–9, 1677. Langbaine, p. 529, says it "is by some ascrib'd to Mrs Behn." The play is an adaptation of Brome's *Mad Couple Well Match't.*]
C.   The Rover: Or, The Banish't Cavaliers (D.G. March 1676/7) 1677; 1697; 1709.
[Sat. March 24, 1676/7 (L.C.). Imprimatur, July 2, 1677. S.R. July 7, 1677. *London Gazette*, Aug. 6–9, 1677; *Post Boy*, Feb. 4–6, 1696/7. T.C. Nov. 1677; May, 1697.]
C.   The Counterfeit Bridegroom: or the Defeated Widow (D.G. *c.* Sept. 1677). See under *UNKNOWN AUTHORS.*
C.   Sir Patient Fancy (D.G. Jan. 1677/8) 1678.
[Th. Jan. 17, 1677/8 (L.C.). Imprimatur, Jan. 28, 1677/8. T.C. Feb. 1677/8.]
C.   The Feign'd Curtizans, or, A Nights Intrigue (D.G. *c.* March 1678/9) 1679 (2 issues).

[Imprimatur, March 27, 1679. T.C. May 1679. The prologue refers to the Popish plot. It is just possible that this play is the same as *Midnight's Intrigues* (1677) and that the prologue is of later vintage: see under *UNKNOWN AUTHORS*.]

T.C. The Young King: or, The Mistake (D.G. *c.* Sept. 1679) 1683; 1698.

[T.C. Nov. 1682; Nov. 1698. *Post Boy*, April 30–May 3, 1698. The epilogue, spoken at the Duke of York's "*second Exile into Flanders*," points to a performance between Sept 24 and Oct. 14, 1679.]

C. The Revenge: or, A Match in Newgate (D.G. *c.* June 1680) 1680.

[T.C. Nov. 1680. W. Van Lennep ("Two Restoration Comedies," *TLS*, Jan. 28, 1939) notes that Narcissus Luttrell has put on his copy the date July 6, 1680, and "Mrs Ann Behn." This attribution strongly confirms the note by Langbaine, p. 547, that it "is ascribed to Mrs *Behn*." On the other hand, the author of *A Comparison between the Two Stages*, p. 11, gives it, under the variant title of *The Vintner trick'd: Or, a Match in Newgate*, to THOMAS BETTERTON. It is, however, to be observed that this author was ignorant of the fact that the play had been printed and consequently he may have had inadequate information about the composition of the piece.]

C. The Second Part of the Rover (D.G. *c.* April 1681) 1681.

[There is a record of a performance before royalty on April 4, 1680 (L.C.) but, as Avery, p. 262, shows, this was a Sunday. It is likely that the play actually was not given until April, 1681. T.C. June 1681.]

C. The False Count, or, A New Way to play an Old Game (D.G. *c.* Nov. 1681) 1682; 1697 (reissue).

[That this play must have appeared about Nov. 1681 is demonstrated by W. Van Lennep (*loc. cit.*).]

C. The Roundheads or, The Good Old Cause (D.G. *c.* Dec. 1681) 1682 (2 issues); 1698.

[*Domestick Intelligence*, Feb. 2–6, 1681/2. T.C. Feb. 1681/2, Nov. 1698. *Post Boy*, April 30–May 3, 1698. The prologue contains a reference to the "Ignoramus" jury (Nov. 24, 1681). This is an alteration of Tatham's *The Rump*.]

C. The City-Heiress: or, Sir Timothy Treat-all (D.G. *c.* March 1681/2) 1682; 1698.

[*Domestick Intelligence*, June 22–26, 1682. T.C. June 1682; Nov. 1698. *Post Boy*, April 30–May 3, 1698.]

C. Like Father, like Son (D.G. March 1682).

[Only the prologue and epilogue of the adaptation of Randolph's *The Jealous Lovers* survive (see Autrey N. Wiley, *Rare Prologues and Epilogues, 1642–1700* (1940), pp. 92–9, and G. Thorn-Drury, *A Little Ark* (1921), pp. 43–5). Summers, *Bibliography*, p. 25, gives the date March 30, 1682, but without citing his evidence.]

C. The Luckey Chance, or An Alderman's Bargain (D.L. *c.* April 1686) 1687.

[S.R. May 8, 1686, with April 23 as date of licence, under the title of *The Disappointed Marriage, or, ye Generous Mistris*. T.C. Feb. 1686/7.]

F.   The Emperor of the Moon (D.G. *c.* March 1686/7) 1687; 1688.
 [S.R. May 24, 1687, with date of licence April 6. T.C. June, 1687; Feb. 1687/8.]

T.C.   The Widdow Banter or, The History of Bacon in Virginia (D.L. *c.* Nov. 1689) 1690.
 [Prologue and epilogue in S.R. Nov. 20, 1689. T.C. Feb. 1689/90.]

C.   The Younger Brother: or, The Amorous Jilt (D.L. *c.* Feb. 1695/6) 1696. MS. Bodl. Rawl. poet. 195.
 [*Post Man*, Feb. 29–March 2, 1695/6. T.C. May 1697; Nov. 1697.]

BELON or BELLON, PETER.
 C.   The Mock-Duellist, or, The French Vallet (D.L. *c.* May 1675) 1675.
 [Imprimatur, May 27, 1675. T.C. Nov. 1675. Attributed to Belon by Langbaine, p. 517.]

BETTERTON, THOMAS.
 T.   Appius and Virginia, Acted...under the name of The Roman Virgin or Unjust Judge (L.I.F. May 1669) 1679.
 [Wed. May 12, 1669 (Pepys). Langbaine, p. 509, declares it "was alter'd (as I have heard by Mr Carthwright) by Mr *Betterton*."]
 C.   The Amorous Widow, or, the Wanton Wife (L.I.F. *c.* 1670) 1706 (2 issues). 8° 1710 (in *The Life of Mr Thomas Betterton*); 12° 1714; 12° 1725 (Dublin, fuller text).
 [The only record regarding date is in Downes, p. 29, who gives it to Betterton and says it was acted before 1670; the attribution is confirmed by *A Comparison between the Two Stages*, p. 11.]
 C.   The Woman made a Justice (L.I.F. *c.* 1670).
 [Here Downes, p. 30, is the only authority for authorship and date.]
 C.   The Counterfeit Bridegroom (D.G. *c.* Sept. 1677). See under *UNKNOWN AUTHORS.*
 C.   The Revenge: or, A Match in Newgate (D.L. *c.* June 1680). See *APHRA BEHN.*
 D.O.   The Prophetess: or, the History of Dioclesian (D.G. June 1690). See *JOHN DRYDEN.*
 [For his other works see the Handlist of Plays, 1700–1750.]

BLOW, JOHN.
 M.   Venus and Adonis (1680–87). MSS. (1) B.M. Add. 22,110; (2) Christ Church, Oxford; (3) Westminster Chapter Library. (First published by G. E. P. Arkwright, 1902; also by A. Lewis, 1939.)

BOOTHBY, FRANCES.
 T.C.   Marcelia: or the Treacherous Friend (T.R. in B.St. *c.* Aug. 1669) 1670.
 [Imprimatur, Oct. 9, 1669. T.C. Nov. 1669.]

BOURNE, REUBEN.
 C.   The Contented Cuckold, or the Womans Advocate. 1692.
 [Imprimatur, April 26, 1692.]

BOYER, ABEL.

T. Achilles; or, Iphigenia in Aulis (D.L. *c.* Dec. 1699) 1700; 12° 1714 (as *The Victim; or Achilles and Iphigenia in Aulis*).
    [Dedication dated Jan. 10, 1699/1700. *Post Boy*, Jan. 20–23, 1699/1700.]

BOYLE, ROGER, Earl of ORRERY.

T.C. The Generall (Thomas Court, Dublin, Oct. 1662, as *Altamira*; T.R. in B.St. Sept. 1664). MS. Worcester College, Oxford.
    [William S. Clark (*The Dramatic Works of Roger Boyle Earl of Orrery* (1937), I. 101–64 and 23–35) prints the manuscript and argues, with justification, that this play was composed early in 1661. It was presented for the author's friends in Dublin, Fri. Oct. 18, 1662 and appeared in London, Wed. Sept. 14, 1664. Licensed by Herbert (list headed Nov. 3, 1663; Herbert, p. 138).]

T.C. The History of Henry the Fifth (L.I.F. Aug. 1664) F. 1668 (*bis*); F. 1669; F. 1672; F. 1677; F. 1690. MSS. (1) Bodl. Rawl. poet. 2; (2) Bodl. Rawl. poet. 180; (3) Huntington Library, HM 20; (4) Huntington Library, EL 11, 642; (5) Huntington Library, HM 599; (6) Folger Shakespeare Library, 1110. 2.
    [Sat. Aug. 13, 1664 (Pepys). Summers gives Aug. 11 as the première, but without authority. Pepys' reference to "the new play" suggests that the 13th was not the first performance. Licensed by Herbert (in same list as above, headed Nov. 3, 1663). S.R. Nov. 2, 1664.]

T. Mustapha, Son of Solyman the Magnificent (L.I.F. April 1665). Printed with *The History of Henry the Fifth*; see above. MSS. (1) Bodl. Rawl. poet. 5; (2) Bodl. Rawl. poet. 27; (3) B.M. Add. 29,280; (4) Huntington Library, EL 11, 641; (5) Folger Shakespeare Library, 1110. 2.
    [Mon. April 3, 1665 (Pepys). S.R. Aug. 7, 1667.]

T.C. The Black Prince (T.R. in B.St., Oct. 1667) F. 1669 (in *Two New Tragedies*); F. 1672.
    [Sat. Oct. 19, 1667 (Pepys and L.C.). S.R. June 8, 1669. T.C. Nov. 1669.]

T.C. Tryphon (L.I.F. Dec. 1668). Printed with *The Black Prince*. See above. MSS. (1) Bodl. MS. Rawl. poet. 39; (2) Bodl. Malone 11.
    [Tues. Dec. 8, 1668 (Pepys). S.R. June 8, 1669. T.C. Nov. 1669. This and the preceding three dramas were published as *Four New Plays*, F. 1670.]

C. Guzman (L.I.F. April 1669) F. 1693.
    [Fri. April 16, 1669 (Pepys). S.R. Oct. 27, 1692 (imprimatur, Oct. 25). *London Gazette.* March 9–13, 1692/3.]

C. Mr Anthony (D.G. *c.* March 1672) 1690 (2 issues).
    [For evidence dating the first performance between January and July 1672 see W. S. Clark, *op. cit.* II. 515–16. Imprimatur, Aug. 27, 1689. T.C. Nov. 1689.]

T. Herod the Great. F. 1694 (2 issues).
    [Apparently prepared for the stage in 1672 (see W. S. Clark, *op. cit.* II. 586–7). *London Gazette*, June 18–21, 1694. The *Six Plays*, F. 1694, includes the contents of *Four New Plays*, together with *Guzman* and *Herod the Great*.]

T. Zoroastres (? 1675). MS. B.M. Sloane 1828.
[Probably written about 1675. Printed by W. S. Clark, *op. cit.*
II. 643–99.]

T. The Tragedy of King Saul. 1703.
[Attributed to Orrery by W. S. Clark, *op. cit.* I. 57–8.]

T.C. Altemira (L.I.F. Dec. 1701) 1702.
[This is *The Generall*, revised by the Hon. Charles Boyle. *Post Man*, Dec. 20, 1701.]
[A letter, dated May 4, 1665, from Henry Savile to his brother,
Sir George Savile (*Savile Correspondence*, Camden Society, 1858,
p. 4) mentions "my Lord of Orrery's new play called The Widow."
W. S. Clark, *op. cit.* I. 40–1, justly denies the correctness of this
statement and suggests that it refers to a revival of Middleton's
The Widow.]

BRADY, NICHOLAS.
T. The Rape: or, The Innocent Impostors (D.L. Feb. 1691/2) 1692
(4 issues).
[On Jan. 19, 1691/2, Shadwell asked the Lord Chamberlain's
support to get it performed as the next new play at D.L. and a
copy was apparently sent to the latter on May 2, 1692 (*HMC*,
4th Report, App. 280–1). *Gentleman's Journal*, March 1691/2.
T.C. June 1692.]

BROWN, THOMAS.
C. Physick lies a Bleeding, Or The Apothecary turned Doctor.
A Comedy, Acted every Day in most Apothecaries Shops in
London. 1697.
[For a later work see the Handlist of Plays, 1700–1750.]

BULTEEL, JOHN.
Pageant. London's Triumph. 1656.
C. Amorous Orontus: or the Love in Fashion (T.R. in B.St. 1664)
1665; 1675 (as *The Amorous Gallant; or, Love in Fashion. A Comedie,
in Heroick Verse, As it was Acted*).
[*Newes*, April 27, 1665. S.R. July 1, 1665. T.C. June, 1675.
The ascription in *Biographia Dramatica* (1812), II. 25, is confirmed
by the note in S.R., "by John Bolteele." Among miscellaneous
plays of various dates, but misleadingly described as "About the
time" of Shadwell's *The Squire of Alsatia* (D.L. 1688), Downes,
p. 41, lists *Love in, and Love out of Fashion*, probably this piece
under its second title.]

BURKHEAD, HENRY.
Pol. The Tragedy of Cola's Fury: or, Lirenda's Misery. 1645 (Kilkenny).
T.C. The Female Rebellion. MSS. (1) Bodl. Tanner 466; (2) MS.
Hunterian Museum, Glasgow, 635 (published by Alexander Smith,
1872).
[This is given as by Henry Birkhead; Alfred Harbage (*TLS*,
Nov. 8, 1934) suggests that the author is Burkhead, author of
Cola's Fury. See also Bernard M. Wagner in *TLS*, Oct. 4, 1934.]

CARLELL, LODOWICK.
[For his earlier plays see Greg, *List*, pp. 16–17, and Woodward-
McManaway, *Check List*, pp. 20–21.]

T. Heraclius Emperour of the East. 1664.

[Imprimatur, March 9, 1663/4. S.R. March 10, 1663/4. *Intelligencer*, May 9, 1664. On Sat. March 8, 1663/4, Pepys saw a *Heraclius* acted, but from the "Advertisement" to the printed play apparently this was not Carlell's.]

CARLETON, R.

Past. The Concealed Royalty, or The May Queen (amateur, 1674) MS. Bodl. Eng. poet. d. 2.

— The Martial Queen (amateur, 1675). MSS. (1) Bodl. Rawl. poet. 126; (2) Bodl. Eng. poet. d. 2.

CARLISLE, JAMES.

C. The Fortune-Hunters: or, Two Fools well met (D.L. *c.* March, 1688/9) 1689.

[*London Gazette*, June 24–27, 1689. T.C. June 1689.]

CARPENTER, RICHARD.

Pol. A New Play Call'd The Pragmatical Jesuit New-leven'd.

[1661 or 1665.]

CARR, WILLIAM.

Pol. Pluto Furens & Vinctus; or, The Raging Devil Bound. A Modern Farse. Per Philocomicum. 1669 (Amstelodami, presumably London).

[Harrison Gray Platt ("An Author for *Pluto Furens*," *Modern Language Notes*, 1930, XLIV. 507–10) identifies the writer. Apparently this is the "*Pluto*" mentioned in a newsletter of Jan. 5, 1668/9, as intended for acting in the prison of King's Bench and suppressed (for the letter see F. G. Blair, "Restoration Plays," *TLS*, March 29, 1923, where the reference is supposed to be to Randolph's *Plutus*).]

CARTWRIGHT, GEORGE.

T. The Heroick-Lover, or, The Infanta of Spain. 8° 1661.

[*Mercurius Publicus*, Nov. 15–22, 1660.]

CARY, HENRY, Viscount FALKLAND.

C. The Mariage Night (L.I.F. *c.* Sept. 1663) 1664.

[Imprimatur, Oct. 16, 1663. *Intelligencer*, Nov. 23, 1663. On March 21, 1666/7, Pepys calls it, presumably by a slip, *The Wedding Night*.]

CARYLL, JOHN.

T. The English Princess, or, The Death of Ricard the III (L.I.F March 1666/7) 1667 (2 issues); 1673; 1674.

[Th. March 7, 1666/7 (Pepys). The date March 3 in the L.C. list is probably an error, since this fell on a Sunday. Imprimatur, May 22, 1667. S.R. June 1, 1667. T.C. Nov. 1673. Langbaine, p. 530, definitely ascribes the play to "Mr *John Carel*." On the authority of Alan Keen, Woodward-McManaway, *Check List*, p. 148, records a copy in the Cardiff Library dated 1666; the Librarian informs me that his copy is dated, as above, 1667.]

C. Sir Salomon: or, The Cautious Coxcomb (L.I.F. *c.* 1669) 1671; 1691.

[Downes, p. 29, puts this among plays of 1669. S.R. Feb. 9, 1670/1. T.C. May 1671. *London Gazette*, Oct. 19–21, 1691. Langbaine, p. 549, ascribes it to "*John Carell*." On the printing

of the second edition see Fredson Bowers, "Bibliographical
Evidence from a Resetting in Caryll's *Sir Salomon* (1691)"
(*Library*, 5th ser. 1948, III. 134–7). Acted later as *Sir Salomon
Single*, and as *The Cautious Coxcomb*.]

CAVENDISH, MARY, Duchess of NEWCASTLE.
— Playes written by the Thrice Noble, Illustrious and Excellent
Princess, The Lady Marchioness of Newcastle. F. 1662.
    [*Kingdoms Intelligencer*, Feb. 3–10, 1661/2. The volume con-
tains: (1) *Loves Adventures* (2 parts); (2) *Several Wits: The wise
Wit, the wild Wit, the cholerick Wit, the humble Wit*; (3) *Youths
Glory and Deaths Banquet* (2 parts); (4) *The Lady Contemplation*
(2 parts); (5) *Wits Cabal* (2 parts); (6) *The Unnatural Tragedie*;
(7) *The Public Wooing*; (8) *The Matrimonial Trouble* (2 parts);
(9) *Natures Three Daughters, Beauty, Love, and Wit* (2 parts);
(10) *The Religious*; (11) *The Comical Hash*; (12) *Bell in Campo*
(2 parts); (13) *The Apocriphal Ladies*; (14) *The Female Academy*.]
— Plays, Never before Printed. F. 1668.
    [This contains: (1) *The Sociable Companions; or, The Female
VVits*; (2) *The Presence*; (3) *The Bridals*; (4) *The Convent of a
Pleasure*; (5) "A Piece of a Play."]

CAVENDISH, WILLIAM, Duke of NEWCASTLE.
  C. The Country Captaine, and The Varietie, Two Comedies. 12°
1649.
  C. The Humorous Lovers (L.I.F. March 1667) 1677; MS. B.M.
Harl. 7367.
    [Th. March 28, 1667 (L.C.). Imprimatur, Nov. 27, 1667. T.C.
Feb. 1676/7.]
  C. Sr Martin Mar-all, or the Feign'd Innocence (L.I.F. Aug. 1667).
See *JOHN DRYDEN*.
  C. The Heiress (T.R. in B.St., Jan. 1668/9).
    [Fri. Jan. 29, 1668/9 (L.C.). On Mon. Feb. 1, Pepys says it was
first acted "on Saturday last"; Avery, p. 253, points out that this
Saturday was the fast-day for Charles I and suggests a slip on
Pepys' part.]
  C. The Triumphant Widow, or The Medley of Humours (D.G. Nov.
1674) 1677.
    [Th. Nov. 26, 1674 (L.C.). Imprimatur, Nov. 27, 1676. T.C.
Feb. 1676/7. Apparently, the original draft of at least part of this
play was written by Newcastle and the final comedy prepared by
THOMAS SHADWELL. The manuscript of several among
Newcastle's scenes, entitled "A Pleasante & Merrye Humor off
A Roge," written probably shortly before 1660, is in the possession
of the Duke of Portland: it is described and partly printed by
John D. Jump ("The Merry Humour of a Rogue," *Journal of the
Gypsy Lore Society*, 3rd ser., 1938, XVII. 24–30.]

CHAMBERLAYNE, WILLIAM.
  T.C. Love's Victory, 1658.
  T.C. Wits Led by the Nose: or, A Poet's Revenge (D.L. *c.* July 1677)
1678 (2 issues).
    [Imprimatur, Aug. 16, 1677. T.C. Nov. 1677. Gray, "Lenten
Casts," pp. 781–94, notes that the cast indicates a "young actors"

play and places the first performance in Lent: quite possibly, however, the première was in the summer. The play is an alteration of *Love's Victory*, but not necessarily by Chamberlayne.]

CIBBER, COLLEY.

C. Love's Last Shift; or, The Fool in Fashion (D.L. Jan. 1695/6) 1696; 1702.

[Dedication signed Feb. 7, 1695/6. *London Gazette*, Feb. 10–13, 1695/6. T.C. Feb. 1695/6. Textual alterations in the copy used for Cibber's collected plays in 1721 are discussed by Dougald MacMillan ("The Text of *Love's Last Shift*," *Modern Language Notes*, 1931, XLVI. 518–19).]

C. Womans Wit: or, The Lady in Fashion (D.L. *c.* Dec. 1696) 1697.

[The original contract, dated Oct. 29, 1696, is given in Appendix B. *Post Man*, March 20–23, 1696/7.]

T. Xerxes (D.L. *c.* Feb. 1698/9) 1699 (3 issues).

[*Post Boy*, April 25–27, 1699. T.C. June 1699.]

T. The Tragical History of King Richard III (D.L. *c.* Dec. 1699). [1700.]

[Dedication dated Feb. 1699/1700. T.C. Feb. 1699/1700.]

[For his later works see the Handlist of Plays, 1700–1750.]

CLARK, WILLIAM.

T.C. Marciano; or, The Discovery (Holyrood House, Edinburgh, Dec. 1662) 1663 (Edinburgh).

[The title-page gives the precise date of acting, Sat. Dec. 27, 1662.]

COCKAIN or COKAYNE, Sir ASTON.

[For his earlier works see Greg, *List*, pp. 22–3, and Woodward-McManaway, *Check List*, p. 26.]

T. The Tragedy of Ovid Intended to be Acted shortly. 8° 1662 (added to a reissue of his *Poems*, originally published 8° 1658); 8° 1669 (reissue, with new general title, *Choice Poems of Several Sorts*).

CODRINGTON, ROBERT.

C. Ignoramus. 1662.

[A translation of Ruggles' Latin play.]

CONGREVE, WILLIAM.

C. The Old Batchelour (D.L. March 1692/3) 1693 (several issues); 1694 (reissued thrice); 1697; 1707; 1710.

[Originally written in 1689. There are references to it in *The Gentleman's Journal*, Jan. and Feb. 1692/3, but these issues were not published till March and April: a reference in the epilogue shows that the play was not produced earlier than Lent. *London Gazette*, March 23–27, 1693 (third edition). See John C. Hodges, "The Composition of Congreve's First Play" (*PMLA*, 1943, LVIII. 971–6) and R. G. Howarth, "The Date of 'The Old Batchelor'" (*TLS*, June 13, 1936).]

C. The Double Dealer (D.L. Oct. 1693) 1694; 1706; 1711.

[*London Gazette*, Dec. 4–7, 1693. The première came in late Oct. or early Nov.: the eighth performance is noted in a letter addressed during the latter month from Dryden to Walsh. A royal performance was given on Sat. Jan. 13, 1693/4 (L.C.).]

C. Love for Love (L.I.F. April 1695) 1695 (4 editions); 1697; 1704; 1711.
> [Tues. April 30, 1695 (Downes, pp. 43–4). *London Gazette*, May 9–13, 1695.]

T. The Mourning Bride (L.I.F. Feb. 1696/7) 1697 (3 editions); 1703.
> [Emmett L. Avery ("The Première of *The Mourning Bride*," *Modern Language Notes*, 1942, LVII. 55–7) demonstrates that the first performance was in all probability on Sat. Feb. 20, 1696/7. *London Gazette*, March 11–15, 1696/7.]

C. The Way of the World (L.I.F. March 1699/1700) 1700 (2 editions); 1706.
> [Probably Tues. March 5, 1699/1700 (date conjectured by Lucyle Hook in *Huntington Library Quarterly*, 1944–5, VIII. 309); certainly acted before March 12 (letter of that date in *HMC*, 15th Report, I, Dartmouth MSS., III. 145).]
> [For his later works see the Handlist of Plays, 1700–1750.]

COOKE, EDWARD.
T. Love's Triumph, or, The Royal Union. 1678.
> [T.C. May 1678.]

CORYE, JOHN.
C. The Generous Enemies or the Ridiculous Lovers (T.R. in B.St. *c.* July 1671) 1672.
> [Imprimatur, Aug. 30, 1671. T.C. May 1672.]

C. A Cure for Jealousie (L.I.F. *c.* Dec. 1699) 1701.
> [*Post Man*, May 27, 1701. The preface shows that it came out during the run of *The Constant Couple*.]
> [For his later work see the Handlist of Plays, 1700–1750.]

COTTON, CHARLES.
T. Horace, A French Tragedy of Monsieur Corneille. Englished by Charles Cotton. 1671.
> [Dedication dated Nov. 7, 1665; address to the reader, Oct. 8, 1670. T.C. May 1671; Nov. 1677.]

COWLEY, ABRAHAM.
> [For his earlier work see Greg, *List*, pp. 23–5 and Woodward-McManaway, *Check List*, pp. 30–2.]

C. The Guardian. 1650 (2 issues).
C. Cutter of Coleman-Street (L.I.F. Dec. 1661) 1663; 1693.
> [Mon. Dec. 16, 1661 (Pepys). *Mercurius Publicus*, April 23–30, 1663. An alteration of *The Guardian*.]

COX, ROBERT.
> [For his association with *The Wits* (1662, 1673) see *FRANCIS KIRKMAN*.]

CROWNE, JOHN.
> [See G. P. Winship, *A Bibliography of the Restoration Dramatist John Crowne* (1922).]

T. Juliana or the Princess of Poland (L.I.F. *c.* Aug. 1671) 1671.
> [Imprimatur, Sept. 8, 1671. The dedication, dated Oct. 4, 1671, shows it was produced in the summer. T.C. Nov. 1671.]

T. The History of Charles the Eighth of France, or the Invasion of Naples by the French (D.G. *c.* Dec. 1671) 1672; 1680 (reissue).

[Downes, p. 32, says this was the first new play at D.G.; if he is correct, it may have appeared as early as Nov. 1671. S.R. Jan. 4, 1671/2, as *Charles the Great*. T.C. Nov. 1672; June 1680.]

T. Andromache (D.G. *c*. Aug. 1674) 1675.

[T.C. Feb. 1674/5. The dedicatory epistle shows it was a summer play and that it was mainly the work of a "young gentleman," which Crowne revised.]

M. Calisto: or, The Chaste Nimph (Court, early in 1675) 1675.

[Prologue, T.C. June 1675; masque, Nov. 1675. The elaborate *Prologue to Calistho, with the Chorus's between the Acts* was published separately, 1675. On the dating of the masque see Eleanore Boswell, *Restoration Court Stage*, pp. 179–82: there were rehearsals in Dec. 1674 and certainly performances on Mon. Feb. 15 and Tues. Feb. 16, 1674/5.]

C. The Countrey Wit (D.G. Jan. 1675/6) 1675; 1693.

[Mon. Jan. 10, 1675/6 (L.C.). T.C. May 1676. A list of plays seen by Nell Gwyn (Harvard University Library) has *The Country Knight* on March 19, 1673/4: the title would fit Crowne's play, but the agreement between the L.C. and T.C. dates makes it dangerous to hazard a declaration that the two pieces are the same. Acted later as *The Country Wit; or, Sir Mannerly Shallow*.]

T. The Destruction of Jerusalem by Titus Vespasian. In Two parts (D.L. Jan. 1676/7) 1677; 1693; 1703.

[Part I, Fri. Jan. 12. Part II, Th. Jan. 18, 1676/7 (L.C.). On Jan. 19, Lady Chaworth mentions both parts in a letter to Lord Roos (*HMC*, 12th Report, App. v, Rutland MSS., 36). T.C. May 1677.]

T. The Ambitious Statesman, or the Loyal Favourite (D.L. *c*. March 1678/9) 1679; 1681 (reissue).

[T.C. June 1679.]

T. The Misery of Civil-War (D.G. *c*. March 1679/80) 1680; 1681 (as *Henry the Sixth, The Second Part. Or the Misery of Civil War*).

[T.C. May 1680; Nov. 1681. The head-title is *The Miseries of Civil War*.]

T. Thyestes (D.L. *c*. March 1680/1) 1681.

[T.C. May 1681.]

T. Henry the Sixth, The First Part. With the Murder of Humphrey Duke of Glocester (D.G. *c*. Sept. 1681) 1681.

[T.C. Nov. 1681.]

C. City Politiques (D.L. Jan. 1682/3) 1683; 1688.

[Summers, *Bibliography*, p. 47, and Hugh Macdonald, *John Dryden, A Bibliography* (1939) give Sat. Jan. 20, 1682/3 as the date of first performance, but this seems to be a guess based on a manuscript "20 Jan. 168⅔" on the Huntington Library copy of the prologue and epilogue. The play was licensed June 15, 1682; preparations for performance were stopped by an order dated June 26; final approval did not come until Dec. 18 (L.C. entries). T.C. May 1683.]

C. Sir Courtly Nice: or, It Cannot Be (D.L. May 1685) 1685; 1693 (2 issues); 1703.

[Mon. May 11, 1685 (L.C.). This may not have been the first performance: Summers (*Downes*, p. 239) gives May 4, apparently on the basis of a manuscript notation. T.C. Nov. 1685.]

T. Darius King of Persia (D.L. April 1688) 1688 (2 issues).

[This play had been acted shortly before May 5 (news-letter in *HMC*, 5th Report, App. p. 197). S.R. June 12, 1688. T.C. July 1688.]

C. The English Frier: or, The Town Sparks (D.L. *c.* March 1689/90) 1690.

[Prologue and epilogue, imprimatur, March 17, 1689 (*i.e.* 1689/90). *London Gazette*, April 28–May 1, 1690. T.C. May 1690.]

T. Regulus (D.L. June 1692) 1694.

[*Gentleman's Journal*, June 1692, dated June 17, says it was "acted last week." *London Gazette*, Nov. 9–13, 1693. T.C. Nov. 1693.]

C. The Married Beau: or, The Curious Impertinent (D.L. *c.* April 1694) 1694.

[*London Gazette*, June 14–18, 1694. T.C. June 1694.]

T. Caligula (D.L. *c.* March 1697/8) 1698.

[*Flying Post*, March 29–31, 1698. T.C. May 1698.]

C. Justice Busy; or, The Gentleman Quack (L.I.F. 1699).

[The only information extant on this play is in Downes, p. 45, and in a separate printing of the *Songs*, set by John Eccles.]

DANCER, DAUNCER or DAUNCY, JOHN.

Past. Aminta: The Famous Pastoral. 8º 1660.

[S.R. Nov. 8, 1659.]

T.C. Nicomede (Smock Alley, Dublin) 1671.

[Imprimatur, Dec. 16, 1670. T.C. July 1671.]

T.C. Agrippa King of Alba: or, The False Tiberinus (Smock Alley, Dublin) 1675.

[T.C. Nov. 1674.]

D'AVENANT, CHARLES.

D.O. Circe (D.G. May 1677) 1677; 1685; 1703.

[Songs, imprimatur, May 7, 1677. Songs, S.R. May 11, and opera, June 19, 1677. Opera, imprimatur, June 18, 1677. T.C. Songs, May 1677; opera, July 1677. *The Songs in Circe* were printed separately, 1677. In an L.C. list a performance of *Circe* is recorded without date, but as it is the last item of a bill giving plays from May 28, 1675 to May 12, 1677, presumably the day was May 12. If so, this was probably not the first performance.]

D'AVENANT, Sir WILLIAM.

[For his pre-Commonwealth plays see Greg, *List*, pp. 27–30, and Woodward-McManaway, *Check List*, pp. 35–9.]

Ent. The first days Entertainment at Rutland House (Rutland House, May 1656) 8º 1657.

[Fri. May 23, 1656 (Leslie Hotson, p. 150).]

O. The Siege of Rhodes Made a Representation by the Art of Prospective in Scenes, And the Story sung in Recitative Musick (Rutland House, Sept. 1656) 1656; 1659.

[Dedication dated Aug. 17, 1656. Copy sent to Bulstrode Whitelocke, Sept. 3, 1656. The 1659 edition says performed at the Cockpit (*i.e.* in 1658 or 1659).]

O. The Siege of Rhodes: The First and Second Part (probably Cockpit, 1658; L.I.F. June 1661) 1663; 1670.

[Fri. June 28, 1661 (Pepys, saying that Tues. July 2 was the fourth day). Part II, S.R. May 30, 1659.]

O. The Cruelty of the Spaniards in Peru. Exprest by Instrumentall and Vocall Musick, and by Art of Perspective in Scenes, &c. (Cockpit, 1658) 1658.
[MS. date in B.M. copy (E 756) July 25, 1658.]

O. The History of Sʳ Francis Drake (Cockpit, 1658) 1659.
[MS. date in B.M. copy (E 764) June 16, 1659.]

T. The Tragedy of Hamlet Prince of Denmark (L.I.F. ? Aug. 1661) 1676 (bis); 1683; 1695 (reissue); 1703.
[The precise date of D'Avenant's (or Betterton's) cut version is not known. Downes, pp. 20–21, says that L.I.F. put on The Siege of Rhodes, then The Wits and after these Hamlet. The first was being presented on July 2 and 4, 1661; The Wits followed on Aug. 15, 17 and 23. On Sat. Aug. 24 Pepys saw Hamlet, and probably D'Avenant's alterations were made for this production. T.C. Feb. 1676. H. N. Paul ("Players' Quartos and Duodecimos of Hamlet", Modern Language Notes, 1934, XLIX. 369–75) argues that certain alterations in the quarto of 1683 came from Dryden's hand.]

T.C. The Law against Lovers (L.I.F. Feb. 1661/2) F. 1673 (in The Works).
[Sat. Feb. 15, 1661/2 (Ethel Seaton, Literary Relations of England and Scandinavia in the Seventeenth Century, 1935, pp. 324–6). Summers, Bibliography, p. 52, gives no evidence for his date of Feb. 10, 1661/2. The Works were entered in the S.R., Oct. 31, 1672.]

C. The Play-House to be Lett (L.I.F. c. Aug. 1663) F. 1673 (in The Works).
[Licensed by Herbert (entry in list headed Nov. 3, 1663; Herbert, p. 138). Internal evidence suggests that it appeared during the summer (A. H. Nethercot, D'Avenant, pp. 377–8). André de Mandach (Molière et la comédie de mœurs en Angleterre (Neuchâtel, 1946), pp. 40–42) endeavours to prove that it first came out in the autumn of 1662.]

C. The Rivals (L.I.F. before Sept. 1664) 1668; 1669 (reissue).
[Imprimatur, Sept. 19, 1668. S.R. Nov. 9, 1668. T.C. Nov. 1668. Pepys saw it on Sat. Sept. 10, 1664, but it was not new then. This alteration of Fletcher's Two Noble Kinsmen is ascribed to D'Avenant by Langbaine, p. 547, and Downes, p. 23.]

C. Greene's Tu Quoque (Sept. 1667).
[Th. Sept. 12, 1667 (Pepys). Pepys notes that this was the première, "with some alterations of Sir W. D'Avenant's."]

C. The Tempest; or, The Enchanted Island (L.I.F. Nov. 1667) 1670 (2 issues); F. 1701 (in Dryden's Works).
[Th. Nov. 7, 1667 (Pepys and L.C.). S.R. Jan. 8, 1669/70. T.C. Feb. 1669/70. The dedication is signed by JOHN DRYDEN and dated Dec. 1, 1669. This is the original Dryden-D'Avenant adaptation; for the later "operatic" version see THOMAS SHADWELL.]

C. The Man's the Master (L.I.F. March 1668) 1669.
[Th. March 26, 1668 (Pepys). S.R. June 8, 1669. T.C. June 1669.]

D.O. Macbeth....With all the Alterations, Amendments, Additions, and New Songs (D.G. Feb. 1672/3) 1674 (bis); 1687 (2 issues); 1695; 1710.
[Tues. Feb. 18, 1672/3 (L.C.) T.C. May 1673. This seems to

have been the first production of the operatic version chronicled by Downes, p. 33, as "The Tragedy of *Macbeth*, alter'd by Sir *William Davenant*...being in the nature of an Opera." D'Avenant, however, had died in 1668 and, since Pepys noted "divertisements" and "variety" in the performances he saw in 1664 and 1667, it is to be presumed that many of the alterations date back long before 1673. There is a 1673 quarto which included some of the additions of the quarto of 1674; this may represent the earlier acting version although it is possibly only a publisher's venture (see Hazelton Spencer, *op. cit.* pp. 79 and 152–7). The music was composed by Locke, Channel and Priest.]

T. The Tragedy of Julius Caesar...alter'd by Sir William Davenant and John Dryden (before 1676) 8° 1719 (in *A Collection of Plays by Eminent Hands*, vol. 1).

[This version was being used at the Smock Alley Theatre, Dublin, before 1676: see William Van Lennep, "The Smock Alley Players of Dublin" (*ELH*, 1946, XIII. 216–22). In general, the ascription to D'Avenant and Dryden has been rejected, but certainly this version was in existence much earlier than had previously been supposed. It should be noted, however, that *Julius Caesar* seems to have been the property of the King's men.]

[J. Frank Kermode ("A Note on the History of Massinger's *The Fatal Dowry* in the Eighteenth Century," *NQ*, May 3, 1947, CXCII) draws attention to the fact that about 1750 there existed a manuscript, said to have been in D'Avenant's hand and "suppos'd to have been one of his," *The Guiltless Adulteress; or, Judge in His Own Cause*—an adaptation of *The Fatal Dowry* (see *The Works of Aaron Hill*, 1753, II. 332). In "The Session of the Poets" (*Poems on Affairs of State*, 1703, p. 210) is a peculiar reference to what seems to have been a play called *The Secrets*: nothing more is known of this.]

DENHAM, Sir JOHN.

T. The Sophy. F. 1642; 8° 1667 (in *Poems*); 8° 1671 (in *Poems*); 8° 1684 (in *Poems*).

[S.R. Feb. 9, 1667/8.]

T. Horace (Court, Feb. 1667/8). See *KATHERINE PHILIPS.*

DENNIS, JOHN.

C. A Plot, and No Plot (D.L. May 1697) [1697].

[Sat. May 8, 1697 (Morley list in Leslie Hotson, p. 377). *Post Man*, May 25–27, 1697.]

T. Rinaldo and Armida (L.I.F. *c.* Nov. 1698) 1699.

[*London Gazette*, Dec. 19–22, 1698. Songs. *Flying Post*, Dec. 6–8, 1698.]

T. Iphigenia (L.I.F. *c.* Dec. 1699) 1700.

[*Post Man*, Dec. 21–23, 1699. Downes, p. 45, lists this after *The She-Gallants*, acted in 1695, and before *The Fate of Capua* and *The Way of the World* (both of which probably appeared early in 1700). But his entries are not strictly chronological.]

[For his later works see the Handlist of Plays, 1700–1750.]

DIGBY, GEORGE, Earl of BRISTOL.

C. Elvira: or, The Worst not always true (L.I.F. 1662–1665) 1667;

1677. [A manuscript formed No. 25 in the H.F.House sale, 1924.]

[Imprimatur, May 15, 1667. T.C. Nov. 1677. Langbaine, p. 530, declares that "the Person of Quality" who wrote this play is "suppos'd to be the Lord *Digby*." There is no evidence as to when precisely it appeared.]

C. The Adventures of Five Hours (L.I.F. Jan. 1662/3). See *Sir SAMUEL TUKE.*

C. 'Tis better than it was (L.I.F. 1662–5).
[Downes, p. 26, gives the title and author.]

C. Worse and Worse (L.I.F. *c.* July 1664).
[Downes, p. 26, gives the title and author. Pepys saw it on Wed. July 20, 1664, hearing it was by the same hand as wrote *The Adventures of Five Hours.*]

DILKE, THOMAS.
C. The Lover's Luck (L.I.F. *c.* Dec. 1695) 1696 (2 issues).
[*London Gazette*, Jan. 20–23, 1695/6. T.C. Feb. 1695/6.]

C. The City Lady: or, Folly Reclaim'd (L.I.F. *c.* Jan. 1696/7) 1697.
[Dedication dated Jan. 15, 1696/7. *Post Man*, Jan. 21–23, 1696/7. T.C. June 1697. Music by John Eccles.]

C. The Pretenders: or, The Town Unmaskt (L.I.F. *c.* March 1697/8) 1698.
[Songs, *Post Boy*, March 29–31, 1698; play, *Post Man*, April 14–16, 1698.]

DOGGETT, THOMAS.
C. The Country-Wake (L.I.F. *c.* April 1696) 1696; [?1697].
[*London Gazette*, May 7–11, 1696.]

DOVER, JOHN.
T. The Roman Generalls: or the Distressed Ladies. 1667.
[Imprimatur, Nov. 7, 1667.]

C. The Mall: or, the Modish Lovers (D.L. *c.* Jan. 1673/4) 1674.
[Dedication signed J. D., probably John Dover. T.C. May 1674.]

D'OYLEY, E.
T. Brittanicus, or The Man of Honour (dated 1695). MS. Folger Shakespeare Library, F. 10. 16. 42.

DRAKE, JAMES.
C. The Sham Lawyer: or the Lucky Extravagant (D.L. May 1697) 1697.
[The title-page adds "As it was *Damnably* ACTED at the Theatre-Royall." Th. May 31, 1697 (Morley list in Leslie Hotson, p. 377). *Post Boy*, June 26–29, 1697.]

DRYDEN, JOHN.
[See Hugh Macdonald, *John Dryden: A Bibliography of Early Editions and Drydeniana* (1939); James M. Osborn, "Macdonald's Bibliography of Dryden" (*Modern Philology*, 1941–2, XXXIX. 69–98, 197–212, 313–19); Fredson Bowers, "Variants in Early Editions of Dryden's Plays" (*Harvard Library Bulletin*, 1949, III. 278–88).]

C. The Wild Gallant (T.R. in V.St. Feb. 1662/3) 1669 (*bis*); 1684; 1694.
[Th. Feb. 5, 1662/3 (Evelyn). S.R. Aug. 7, 1667. T.C. May

1669; Feb. 1683/4. Alfred Harbage, "Elizabethan-Restoration Palimpsest," pp. 307–9, argues that Dryden's play is based on a lost comedy by Brome.]

T.   The Indian-Queen (T.R. in B.St. Jan. 1663/4). See *Sir ROBERT HOWARD*.

T.C.   The Rival Ladies (T.R. in B.St. *c.* June 1664) 1664; 1669; 1675; 1693.

[S.R. June 27, 1664. *Newes*, Nov. 3, 1664. See Roswell G. Ham, "Dryden's Epilogue to *The Rival Ladies*, 1664" (*Review of English Studies*, 1937, XIII. 76–80).]

T.   The Indian Emperour, or, The Conquest of Mexico by the Spaniards. Being the Sequel of the Indian Queen (T.R. in B.St. *c.* April 1665) 1667; 1668 (2 issues); 1670 (3 editions); 1681; 1686; 1692; 1694; 1696 (3 editions); 1703. MSS. (1) Trinity College, Cambridge, R. 3. 10; (2) Public Library, Douai, 787.

[S.R. May 26, 1665. Newly published Oct. 28, 1667 (Pepys).]

T.C.   Secret-Love, or the Maiden Queen (T.R. in B.St. March 1666/7) 1668; 1669 (*bis*); 1679 (some misdated 1675); 1691; 1698 (2 issues).

[Sat. March 2, 1666/7 (Pepys and L.C.). S.R. Aug. 7, 1667. Newly printed Jan. 18, 1667/8 (Pepys). T.C. Nov. 1691.]

C.   Sᵣ Martin Mar-all, or the Feign'd Innocence (L.I.F. Aug. 1667) 1668 (*bis*); 1669 (reissue); 1678; 1691; 1697.

[Th. Aug. 15, 1667 (Pepys and L.C.). S.R. June 24, 1668. T.C. Nov. 1668. In the S.R. entry the play is given to *WILLIAM CAVENDISH, Duke of NEWCASTLE*, who no doubt provided the original draft of the play; Downes, p. 28, says he gave "Mr *Dryden* a bare Translation of it, out of a Comedy of the Famous *French* Poet *Monseur Moleire.*" Dryden's name does not appear on any title-page before that of 1691.]

C.   The Tempest, or, The Enchanted Island (L.I.F. Nov. 1667). See *Sir WILLIAM D'AVENANT*.

C.   An Evening's Love, or the Mock-Astrologer (T.R. in B.St. June 1668) 1671 (*bis*, some misdated 1675); 1675 (reissue); 1691.

[Fri. June 12, 1668 (L.C.). S.R. Nov. 20, 1668. T.C. Feb. 1670/1; Nov. 1691.]

T.   Tyrannick Love, or, the Royal Martyr (T.R. in B.St. *c.* June 1669) 1670 (2 issues); 1672; 1677; 1686; 1694; 1695 (reissue); 1702.

[S.R. July 14, 1669. T.C. Nov. 1670. See Leslie Hotson, pp. 250–3, for a suit which shows that, although planned for April, the play was not performed until June.]

T.   The Conquest of Granada by the Spaniards: In Two Parts (T.R. in B.St., Part I, *c.* Dec. 1670; Part II, Jan. 1670/1) 1672; 1673; 1678; 1687; 1695; 1704.

[The head-title reads *Almanzor and Almahide, Or, the Conquest of Granada*. A letter of Jan. 2, 1670/1, from Lady Mary Bertie gives the première of Part II as either Tues. Jan. 3 or Tues. Jan. 10, probably the latter (*HMC*, 12th Report, App. v, Rutland MSS. 22). S.R. Feb. 25, 1670/1. T.C. Feb. 1671/2.]

C.   Marriage A-la-Mode (L.I.F. *c.* April 1672) 1673; 1684; 1691; 1698.

[The date of first performance is uncertain. The dedication declares that the King was shown the manuscript at Windsor (*i.e.* between the end of May and the middle of July 1671) and one might have thought that the King's men would have been anxious to present it as early as possible in the autumn. On the other hand, the prologue's reference to the absence of gallants in the playhouse because of their serving in the fleet points to a later date: the Third Dutch War was formally declared on March 17, 1671/2, and although there had been some skirmishes before that time it is unlikely that any large body of gentlemen were in service much earlier. It is possible, but not probable, that the prologue was not that used for the première (see Charles E. Ward, "The Dates of Two Dryden Plays," *PMLA*, 1936, LI. 786–92). If the play is alluded to in *The Rehearsal*, it must, of course, have appeared before the end of 1671, but the supposed allusion is by no means certain. That it was acted before the beginning of June 1672 seems proved by the S.R. entry on June 3 of *Westminster Drollery*, a work that prints the song "Whilst Alexis lay prest." No one knows what, if any, authority Summers had for his often repeated statement that the comedy was given first at Easter 1672. S.R. March 18, 1672/3, as *Amorous Adventures or Marriage a la Mode. London Gazette*, May 29–June 2, 1673. T.C. June 1673; Feb. 1683/4; Nov. 1691.]

C.   The Assignation: or, Love in a Nunnery (L.I.F. *c.* Nov. 1672) 1673; 1678; 1692.

    [S.R. March 18, 1672/3. *London Gazette*, May 29–June 2, 1673. T.C. June 1673. The prologue refers to Ravenscroft's *The Citizen turn'd Gentleman*, D.G. July 1672.]

T.C. Amboyna (L.I.F. *c.* May 1673) 1673 (2 issues); 1691.

    [The head-title reads *Amboyna, or the Cruelties of the Dutch to the English Merchants*. S.R. June 26, 1673. T.C. Nov. 1673; Nov. 1691. This may have been acted earlier. Charles E. Ward, *loc. cit.* pp. 786–92, presents several items of evidence for a date in 1672, but unfortunately none of these is conclusive: (1) a reference to "Amboyna" in a prologue printed in *Westminster Drollery* (entered S.R. June 3, 1672); (2) the fact that, if the play is propaganda, it would have been more effective in 1672 than in 1673; (3) the performance of a piece called "The Dutch Cruelties at Amboyna" by Anthony Devo at a Charing Cross booth in November of the former year (*Cal. State Papers. Dom. 1672–3*, p. 148). The thought of Amboyna was much in the air then and for many decades previously, hence the allusion in the prologue may well be to the event and not to the play; propaganda does not by any means stop towards the beginning of hostilities during a war; the piece given at the booth is likely to have been quite independent of Dryden's work. While, therefore, *Amboyna* may have been produced as early as June 1672, it is impossible to hazard a guess with any assurance.]

C.   The Mistaken Husband (D.L. *c.* Sept. 1675). See under *UNKNOWN AUTHORS*.

T.   Aureng-Zebe (D.L. Nov. 1675) 1676; 1685; 1690; 1692; 1694; 1699; 1704.

    [Wed. Nov. 17, 1675 (L.C.). S.R. Nov. 29, 1675. *London Gazette*, Feb. 17–21, 1675/6. T.C. May 1676.]

D.O. The State of Innocence, and Fall of Man.   1677; 1678; 1684 (*bis*); 1690; 1692; 1695 (*bis*); 1703. MSS. (1) B.M. Add. 37,158;

(2) Bodl. Rawl. *c.* 146; (3) Harvard University Library; (4) Huntington Library, EL 11, 640; (5) Folger Shakespeare Library.
[S.R. April 17, 1674 as *The Fall of Angels. London Gazette,* Feb. 8–12, 1676/7. T.C. Feb. 1676/7; Nov. 1684.]

T. All for Love: or, The World well Lost (D.L. Dec. 1677) 1678; 1692; 1696; 1703; 1709.
[Wed. Dec. 12, 1677 (account reproduced in *The Theatrical Inquisitor,* July 1816). S.R. Jan. 31, 1677/8. *London Gazette,* March 21–25, 1678.]

C. The Kind Keeper; or, Mr Limberham (D.G. March 1677/8) 1680; 1690; 1701.
[Mon. March 11, 1677/8 (L.C.). T.C. Nov. 1679; June 1690; Nov. 1691.]

T. Oedipus (D.G. *c.* Nov. 1678) 1679; 1682; 1687; 1692; [1696]; 1701; 1711.
[Imprimatur, Jan. 3, 1678/9. *London Gazette,* March 10–13, 1678/9. T.C. May 1679; Feb. 1686/7. Written in collaboration with *NATHANIEL LEE.*]

T.C. Troilus and Cressida, or, Truth Found too Late (D.G. *c.* April 1679) 1679; 1695 (some misdated 1679).
[S.R. April 14, 1679. T.C. Nov. 1679.]

C. The Spanish Fryar, or, The Double Discovery (D.G. March 1679/80) 1681 (2 issues); 1686; 1690; 1695; 1704; 1717.
[Mon. March 8, 1679/80 (L.C.) *Observator,* June 9, 1686; *True Protestant Mercury,* March 9–12, 1690/1. T.C. June 1681.]

T. The Duke of Guise (D.L. Nov. 1682) 1683; 1687; 1699 (2 issues).
[Fri. Dec. 1, 1682 (L.C.); Lady Newdigate-Newdigate, in *Cavalier and Puritan in the Days of the Stuarts* (1901), p. 250, records, apparently from a contemporary document, a performance on Sat. Nov. 18, but no authority is given; nor is there authority for the statement that it was given first on Nov. 30 (Edmond Malone, *Critical and Miscellaneous Prose Works of John Dryden* (1800), I. i. 120), except that Luttrell has "30 Nov." (and also "4 Dec. 1682") on the separately printed prologue. The play was banned on July 18, 1682 (L.C.) and received final approval from the King on Oct. 29. *Observator,* Feb. 13, 1682/3. *Flying Post,* April 4–6, 1699. T.C. May 1699. Written in collaboration with *NATHANIEL LEE.*]

D.O. Albion and Albanius (D.G. June 1685) F. 1685; F. 1687 (2 issues); 1691.
[On Wed. June 3, 1685 there is a record of "The Opera," presumably this work, but Sat. June 6 is given by Macdonald, p. 127, on the basis of a manuscript note by Luttrell (Edmund Malone, *op. cit.* I. i. 188): in all probability the latter was a date of purchase. *Observator,* June 8, 1685. Music by Louis Grabut.]

T, Don Sebastian, King of Portugal (D.L. *c.* Dec. 1689) 1690; 1692.
[Wed. Dec. 4, 1689 (L.C.): but the first performance may have been earlier in the season. The play was written many years previously. S.R. Dec. 17, 1689. T.C. Feb. 1689/90. *London Gazette,* Jan. 2–6, 1689/90.]

D.O. The Prophetess: or, the History of Dioclesian (D.G. *c.* June 1690) 1690 (3 issues).
[*London Gazette,* June 12–16, 1690. Downes, p. 42, and Gildon,

p. 60, attribute this alteration of Fletcher's play to *THOMAS BETTERTON*; Langbaine, p. 214, gives it to Dryden. Probably both collaborated in the work; Dryden's share is attested to by the fact that in B.M. MS. Stowe 755 the dedication to the music (printed as by Purcell) appears in the poet's own hand (see Roswell G. Ham, "Dryden's Dedication for *The Music of the Prophetesse,* 1691," *PMLA,* 1935, L. 1065–75, and R. P. McCutcheon, "Dryden's Prologue to *The Prophetess,*" *Modern Language Notes,* 1924, xxxix. 123–4).]

C. Amphitryon; or, The Two Socia's (D.L. Oct. 1690) 1690; 1691 (reissue); 1694; 1706.

> [Tues. Oct. 21, 1690 (L.C.). *London Gazette,* Oct. 30–Nov. 3, 1690.]

D.O. King Arthur; or, The British Worthy (D.G. *c.* May 1691) 1691 (2 issues); 1695.

> [*London Gazette,* June 4–8, 1691. Music by Henry Purcell.]

T. Cleomenes, the Spartan Heroe (D.L. April 1692) 1692.

> [On Feb. 12, 1691/2 the play was reported as due to appear shortly (*Gentleman's Journal,* Feb. 1691/2); it was ready for production on Sat. April 9, 1692, but was stopped by order of Queen Mary (*id.* April, and Narcissus Luttrell, *A Brief Relation of State Affairs* (1857), II. 413); finally it was presented before Sat. April 16. *London Gazette,* May 2–5, 1692. Apparently half of the last act was written by *THOMAS SOUTHERNE* (dedication to *The Wives Excuse,* D.L. Dec. 1691).]

T.C. Love Triumphant; or, Nature will Prevail (D.L. *c.* Jan. 1693/4) 1694.

> [On Jan. 11, 1693/4 Evelyn observed that it was "now shortly to be acted." *London Gazette,* March 12–15, 1693/4.]

M. The Secular Masque (D.L. April 1700) 1700 (in Vanbrugh's *The Pilgrim*).

> [Dryden is said to have died on the third night, which would put the première on April 29, 1700.]

DRYDEN, JOHN Jnr.

C. The Husband his Own Cuckold (L.I.F. *c.* Feb. 1695/6) 1696.

> [Dedication dated from Rome Aug. 20, 1695. *London Gazette,* July 9–13, 1696.]

DUFFETT, THOMAS.

C. The Spanish Rogue (L.I.F. *c.* March 1672/3) 1674.

> [Acted by the King's men, certainly at L.I.F. and probably during Lent (Gray, "Lenten Casts," pp. 791–2).]

Burlesque. The Empress of Morocco. A Farce (D.L. *c.* Dec. 1673) 1674.

> [T.C. May 1674.]

C. The Amorous Old-woman: or, 'Tis Well if it Take (D.L. *c.* March 1673/4). See under *UNKNOWN AUTHORS.*

Burlesque. The Mock-Tempest: or The Enchanted Castle (D.L. Nov. 1674) 1675.

> [Th. Nov. 19, 1674 (L.C.). T.C. Feb. 1674/5.]

Burlesque. Psyche Debauch'd (D.L. *c.* May 1675) 1678.

> [Since this was designed to ridicule Shadwell's *Psyche,* it probably appeared either during Lent or summer 1675.]

M. Beauties Triumph; a Masque. Presented by the Scholars of Mr Jeffery Banister, and Mr James Hart....At Chelsey (amateur, ?1675) 1676.

DUNTON, JOHN.
Religious Play. The Visions of the Soul. 8° 1692.

D'URFEY, THOMAS.
T. The Siege of Memphis, or The Ambitious Queen (D.L. *c.* Sept. 1676) 1676.
   [T.C. Nov. 1676.]
C. Madam Fickle: or the Witty False One (D.G. Nov. 1676) 1677; 1682; 1691.
   [Sat. Nov. 4, 1676 (L.C.). Imprimatur, Nov. 20, 1676. T.C. Feb. 1676/7; Nov. 1691.]
C. The Fool Turn'd Critick (D.L. Nov. 1676) 1678.
   [Sat. Nov. 18, 1676 (L.C.). T.C. June 1678. In the press early 1677 (advertisement in Crowne's *The Destruction of Jerusalem*, T.C. May 1677).]
C. A Fond Husband: or, The Plotting Sisters (D.G. May 1677) 1677; 1678; 1685; 1711.
   [Th. May 31, 1677 (L.C.). Imprimatur, June 15, 1676. T.C. Nov. 1677. The MS. in Bodl. Rawl. poet. 52 of *A Fond Husband* is not this play but an anonymous work of about 1723 (Alfred Harbage, "Addenda.") Acted later as *The Fond Husband; or, The Doating Sisters.*]
C. Trick for Trick: or, The Debauch'd Hypocrite (D.L. *c.* March 1677/8) 1678.
   [Imprimatur, April 30, 1678. T.C. June 1678.]
C. Squire Oldsapp: or, The Night-Adventurers (D.G. *c.* June 1678) 1679.
   [Imprimatur, June 28, 1678. T.C. Dec. 1678.]
C. The Virtuous Wife; or, Good Luck at last (D.G. *c.* Sept. 1679) 1680.
   [T.C. Nov. 1679.]
C. Sir Barnaby Whigg: or, No Wit like a Womans (D.L. *c.* Sept. 1681) 1681.
   [T.C. Nov. 1681.]
C. The Royalist (D.G. Jan. 1681/2) 1682.
   [Tues. Jan. 24, 1681/2 (L.C.). The list reads "June 24" but this is certainly a mistake for January. Two newsletters dated Jan. 26 say that the King attended the play "yesterday" and one states that this was "the poet's day" (*HMC*, 12th Report, App. v, 64, and 10th Report, App. IV, 175), so that the "24" of the list may be a further error for "25". T.C. May 1682.]
T.C. The Injured Princess, or The Fatal Wager (D.L. *c.* March 1681/2) 1682.
   [The head-title reads *The Unequal Match or The Fatal Wager.* T.C. May and Nov. 1682.]
Play. A Common-Wealth of Women. A Play (D.L. *c.* Aug. 1685) 1686; 1688.
   [Imprimatur, Sept. 11, 1685. T.C. Nov. 1685; Dec. 1868. Summers, *Bibliography*, p. 64, gives the date Th. Aug. 20, 1685,

apparently on the basis of a manuscript note, but this may be the
purchase-day of the separately printed prologue and epilogue, not
the day of performance.]

Play. The Banditti, or, A Ladies Distress. A Play (D.L. *c.* Feb.
1685/6) 1686.
 [Imprimatur, March 1, 1685/6. T.C. Dec. 1686.]

C. A Fool's Preferment, or, The Three Dukes of Dunstable (D.G.
c. April 1688) 1688.
 [Imprimatur, May 21, 1688.]

C. Love for Money: or, the Boarding School (D.L. *c.* Dec. 1690)
1691 (2 editions); 1696.
 [S.R. April 4, 1691. *London Gazette*, April 6–9, 1691. T.C.
May 1691. A reference in the text to "1690" seems to indicate
that the play was presented in that year.]

T. Bussy D'Ambois, or the Husbands Revenge (D.L. *c.* March
1690/1) 1691.
 [S.R. April 4, 1691. T.C. May 1691. *London Gazette*, April
27–30, 1691. The allusion to a "*Lenten Dish*" puts the first performance in March.]

C. The Marriage-Hater Match'd (D.L. *c.* Jan. 1691/2) 1692 (2 issues);
1693.
 [T.C. Feb. 1691/2; Nov. 1693. *Gentleman's Journal*, Feb.
1691/2.]

C. The Richmond Heiress: or, A Woman Once in the Right (D.L.
c. April 1693) 1693 (2 issues).
 [Dedication dated May 6, 1693. *Gentleman's Journal*, April 1693.
London Gazette, May 15–18, 1693. T.C. June and Nov. 1693.]

C. The Comical History of Don Quixote (D.G. *c.* May 1694) 1694 (*bis*).
 [This play and the songs in Part II, *London Gazette*, July 2–5,
1694. T.C. Nov. 1694.]

C. The Comical History of Don Quixote...Part the Second (D.G.
c. May 1694) 1694.
 [The prologue speaks of "*This Soutlry* [sic] *Season.*" *Gentleman's Journal*, June 1694 (which also refers to the hot weather).
London Gazette, July 19–23, 1694. T.C. Nov. 1694.]

C. The Comical History of Don Quixote. The Third Part. With the
Marriage of Mary the Buxome (D.G. *c.* Nov. 1695) 1696.
 [*London Gazette*, Dec. 12–16, 1695.]

C. A Wife for Any Man (acted 1695–7).
 [Two songs from this lost play were published in 1699 (see
Cyrus L. Day, "A Lost Play by D'Urfey," *Modern Language
Notes*, 1934, XLIX. 332–4).]

D.O. A New Opera, call'd Cinthia and Endimion: or, The Loves of
the Deities (D.L. *c.* Dec. 1696) 1697 (*bis*).
 [*Post Man*, Jan. 14–16, 1696/7. The opera was "Designed to
be Acted at Court before the late Queen." Presumably it had been
publicly acted shortly before the end of December.]

C. The Intrigues at Versailles: or, A Jilt in all Humours (L.I.F.
c. Feb. 1696/7) 1697 (*bis*).
 [T.C. June 1697. *Post Man*, June 24–26, 1697.]

C. The Campaigners: or, The Pleasant Adventures at Brussels (D.L.
c. June 1698) 1698.
 [*Post Man*, July 7–9, 1698. The preface answers Collier's *Short*

View (May) and the cast suggests a summer production.]

T. The Famous History of the Rise and Fall of Massaniello. In Two
    Parts (D.L. *c.* May 1699) 1700.
       [The second part has the title: *The Famous History and Fall of
       Massaniello: or, A Fisherman a Prince. The Second Part...1699.*
       T.C. June (Songs) and Nov. 1699. Songs in both parts, *Post Boy*,
       June 24–27, 1699; play, *London Gazette*, Oct. 2–5, 1699, and *Post
       Boy*, June 28–July 1, 1700.]
       [For his later works see the Handlist of Plays, 1700–1750.]

ECCLESTONE, EDWARD.
    D.O. Noah's Flood, or, The Destruction of the World. 1679; 1685
          (as *The Cataclysm, Or General Deluge of the World*); 1690 (as
          The Deluge: or, The Destruction of the World).
             [T.C. Nov. 1679; Feb. 1685; June 1690. See J. R. Baird,
          "Milton and Ecclestone's *Noah's Flood*," *Modern Language Notes*,
          1940, LV. 183–7.]

ECHARD, LAWRENCE.
    — Plautus's Comedies. Amphitryon, Epidicus and Rudens made
       English. 8º 1694.
          [S.R. June 26, 1693.]
    — Terence's Comedies, made English (unacted, save for *Eunuchus*,
       D.L. 1717) 8º 1694; 8º 1698.
          [S.R. June 26, 1693.]

ETHEREGE, Sir GEORGE.
    C. The Comical Revenge; or, Love in a Tub (L.I.F. March 1664)
        1664 (*bis*); 1667; 1669 (*bis*); 1689; 1690 (reissue); 1697.
           [Wed. April 27, 1664 (Evelyn). S.R. July 8, 1664. *Newes*,
        Nov. 3, 1664.]
    C. She wou'd if she cou'd (L.I.F. Feb. 1667/8) 1668; 1671; 1693.
           [Th. Feb. 6, 1667/8 (Pepys and L.C.). S.R. June 24, 1668.
        T.C. Nov. 1668.]
    C. The Man of Mode, or, Sʳ Fopling Flutter (D.G. March 1675/6)
        1676; 1684 (2 issues); 1693.
           [Sat. March 11, 1675/6 (L.C.). Imprimatur, June 3, 1676.
        S.R. June 15, 1676. *London Gazette*, July 3–6, 1676. T.C. Nov.
        1676; Feb. 1683/4.]

FANE, Sir FRANCIS.
    C. Love in the Dark, or The Man of Bus'ness (D.L. May 1675)
        1675 (some misdated 1671).
           [Mon. May 10, 1675 (L.C.). S.R. June 29, 1675. T.C. Feb.
        1675/6.]
    M. A Masque Made at the Request of the late Earl of Rochester, for
        the Tragedy of Valentinian (D.L. Feb. 1683/4) 8º 1685 (in Tate's
        Poems by Several Hands).
    T. The Sacrifice. 1686; 1687 (2 issues).
           [Imprimatur, May 4, 1686. T.C. May 1686.]

FANSHAWE, Sir RICHARD.
    Past. Il Pastor Fido. The Faithfull Shepheard. 1647; 1648 (reissue);
           1664; 1676; 1692 (reissue).

[*Intelligencer*, May 9, 1664. Probably this was *The Faithful Shepherd* seen by Pepys at the Nursery on Tues. Feb. 25, 1667/8.]

C. Querer Por Solo Querer: To Love only for Love Sake. 1670; 1671 (reissue). MS. B.M. Add. 32,133.
   [S.R. July 20, 1670. T.C. Nov. 1671.]

FARQUHAR, GEORGE.
   C. Love and a Bottle (D.L. *c.* Dec. 1698) 1699.
      [*Post Man*, Dec. 27–29, 1698.]
   C. The Constant Couple or a Trip to the Jubilee (D.L. Nov. 1699) 1700 (*bis*); 1704.
      [Tues. Nov. 28, 1699 (Morley list in Leslie Hotson, p. 378). *Post Man*, Dec. 7–9, 1699. For revisions in the second edition see G. W. Whiting, "The Date of the Second Edition of *The Constant Couple*" (*Modern Language Notes*, 1932, XLVII. 147–8); see also Alfred Jackson, "Play Notices from the Burney Newspapers 1700–1703" (*PMLA*, 1933, XLVIII. 817–8).]
      [For his later works see the Handlist of Plays, 1700–1750.]

FILMER, EDWARD.
   T. The Unnatural Brother (L.I.F. *c.* Jan. 1696/7) 1697.
      [*Post Boy*, Jan. 21–23, 1696/7. T.C. May 1697.]
   T. The Unfortunate Couple (L.I.F. *c.* June 1697). See *PETER ANTHONY MOTTEUX.*

FILMER, Sir EDWARD.
   T. Pompey the Great (L.I.F. *c.* Dec. 1664). See *EDMUND WALLER.*

FISHBOURNE, CHRISTOPHER.
   — Sodom. MSS. (1) B.M. Harley 7312; (2) Bibliothèque Nationale; (3) Hague; (4) Victoria and Albert Museum, Dyce 43; (5) Hamburger Staats- und Universitäts-Bibliothek.
      [This scandalous piece, usually ascribed to *JOHN WILMOT, Earl of ROCHESTER*, is said to have been printed in 1684 and 1689 but no copy of this edition is extant. The evidence for Rochester's authorship is given by Johannes Prinz (*John Wilmot*, 1927, pp. 82–3, 166–77) but Rodney M. Baine ("Rochester or Fishbourne: A Question of Authorship," *Review of English Studies*, 1946, XXII. 201–8) gives good reason for believing that Christopher (not John) Fishbourne was responsible.]

FLECKNOE, RICHARD.
      [For his earlier plays see Woodward-McManaway, *Check List*, p. 63.]
   T.C. Love's Kingdom. A Pastoral Trage-Comedy. Not as it was Acted at the Theatre near Lincolns-Inn, but as it was written and since corrected (L.I.F. *c.* March 1663/4) 8° 1664; 8° 1674 (reissue).
      [Imprimatur, April 22, 1664. An alteration of the same author's *Love's Dominion*, 8° 1654.]
   T.C. Erminia. Or, The fair and vertuous Lady (unacted?) 8° 1661; 8° 1665.
   C. The Damoiselles a la Mode (T.R. in B.St. Sept. 1668) 1667.
      [Mon. Sept. 14, 1668 (Pepys). Imprimatur, May 15, 1667. This is presumably *The Ladies a la Mode* seen by Pepys on Sept. 15, attributed by him to Dryden.]

FLEMING, ROBERT.
Religious Play. Monarchical Image. 8º 1691 (in *The Mirrour of Divine Love*).

FORDE, THOMAS.
T.C. Loves Labyrinth: A Tragi-Comedy. 8º 1660 (in *Virtus Rediviva*).
[The separate title-page to the play has a sub-title: *or, The Royal Shepherdess*.]

FOUNTAIN, JOHN.
C. The Rewards of Vertue. 1661.

GILDON, CHARLES.
T. The Roman Bride's Revenge (D.L. *c.* Nov. 1696) 1697.
  [*Post Man*, Dec. 22–24, 1696.]
T. Phæton: or, The Fatal Divorce (D.L. *c.* March 1697/8) 1698.
  [*Post Boy*, April 28–30, 1698.]
  [For his later works see the Handlist of Plays, 1700–1750.]

GODOLPHIN, SIDNEY.
T. Pompey the Great (L.I.F. *c.* Dec. 1664). See *EDMUND WALLER.*

GOULD, ROBERT.
T. The Rival Sisters: or, The Violence of Love (D.L. *c.* Oct. 1695) 1696.
  [*London Gazette*, Nov. 7–11, 1695.]
T. Innocence Distress'd: or, The Royal Penitents. 8º 1737.
  [Posthumously printed; possibly written before 1700. See Eugene H. Sloane, *Robert Gould* (1940).]

GRANVILLE, GEORGE, Lord LANSDOWNE.
C. The She-Gallants (L.I.F. *c.* Dec. 1695) 1696.
  [*Post Boy*, Feb. 27–29, 1695/6. T.C. Feb. 1695/6. The preface declares that this had been written in France twelve years before. In the author's *Works*, 8º 1726, the play appears as *Once a Lover, Always a Lover*.]
T. Heroick Love (L.I.F. *c.* Dec. 1697) 1698.
  [*London Gazette*, Feb. 17–21, 1697/8. T.C. Feb. 1697/8.]
  [For his later works see the Handlist of Plays, 1700–1750.]

GREEN, ALEXANDER.
C. The Polititian Cheated. A New Comedy. 1663.

HARRIS, JOSEPH.
T.C. The Mistakes, or, The False Report (D.L. *c.* Dec. 1690) 1691.
  [The preface shows this came out about Christmas, probably a "young actors" play. T.C. Feb. 1690/1. One scene was written by *WILLIAM MOUNTFORT*.]
C. The City Bride: or, The Merry Cuckold (L.I.F. *c.* March 1695/6) 1696.
  [*Post Boy*, April 25–28, 1696.]
C. Love's a Lottery, and a Woman the Prize. With a New Masque, call'd Love and Riches Reconcil'd (L.I.F. *c.* March 1698/9) 1699.
  [*Post Man*, May 25–27, 1699. T.C. June 1699.]

HAYNES or HAINES, JOSEPH.
T. A Fatal Mistake: or, The Plot Spoil'd. 1692; 1696.
[The play reads like a burlesque; the statement on the title-page
—"A Tragedy, As it was lately ACTED, &c."—suggests that it never
appeared on the stage.]

HEAD, RICHARD.
C. Hic et Ubique; or, The Humours of Dublin. 1663.

HIGDEN, HENRY.
C. The Wary Widdow: or, Sir Noisy Parrat (D.L. *c.* March 1692/3)
1693.
[*Gentleman's Journal,* Feb. 1692/3 (but not issued till March)
London Gazette, May 29–June 1, 1693.]

HOLDEN, JOHN.
C. The German Princess (L.I.F. April 1664).
[Fri. April 15, 1664 (Pepys). The attribution to Holden appears
in "The Session of the Poets" (*Poems on Affairs of State,* 1703,
p. 211.]
C. The Ghosts (L.I.F. April 1665).
[Mon. April 17, 1665 (Pepys). Ascribed to Holden by Downes,
p. 26.]

HOOLE, CHARLES.
— Comoediae sex Anglo-Latinae. 1663; 1667; 1676.
[A translation of Terence's plays.]

HOPKINS, CHARLES.
T. Pyrrhus, King of Epirus (L.I.F. *c.* Aug. 1695) 1695.
[The prologue indicates a summer production. *London Gazette,*
Aug. 22–26, 1695.]
Play. Neglected Virtue: or, The Unhappy Conquerour (D.L. *c.* Dec.
1695). See *HILDEBRAND HORDEN.*
T. Boadicea Queen of Britai𝑟 (L.I.F. *c.* Nov. 1697) 1697.
[For the date of performance see Baldwin Maxwell, "Notes on
Charles Hopkins' *Boadicea*" (*Review of English Studies,* 1928, IV.
79–83).]
T. Friendship Improv'd; or, The Female Warriour (L.I.F. Nov.
1699) 1700.
[The play is referred to in one of Dryden's letters, dated Nov. 7
(see Baldwin Maxwell, *loc. cit.* pp. 79–83). Dedication dated
Nov. 1, 1699. *Post Man,* Feb. 17–20, 1699/1700.]

HORDEN, HILDEBRAND.
Play. Neglected Virtue: or, The Unhappy Conqueror (D.L. *c.* Dec.
1695) 1696.
[The preface is signed by Horden, who, however, does not claim
the play as his. It is sometimes ascribed to *CHARLES HOP-
KINS.*]

HORNE, JOHN.
Past. Fortune's Task, or The Fickle Fair one (1684). MS. Huntington
Library, H.M. 11.

HOWARD, Hon. EDWARD.
T. The Usurper (T.R. in B.St. Jan. 1663/4) 1668.
[Sat. Jan. 2, 1663/4 (Pepys). S.R. Feb. 4, 1663/4. Imprimatur,
Aug. 2, 1668.]

T.C. The Change of Crownes (T.R. in B.St. April 1667). MS. in possession of Austen-Leigh (printed by F. S. Boas, 1949).
   [Mon. April 15, 1667 (Pepys and L.C.). S.R. Aug. 7, 1667. The MS. has a licence note by Herbert dated April 13.]

C. The London Gentleman (unacted?).
   [Nothing is known of this play save the entry in S.R. Aug. 7, 1667.]

T.C. The Womens Conquest (L.I.F. *c.* Nov. 1670) 1671.
   [S.R. Nov. 18, 1670. T.C. May 1671.]

C. The Six days Adventure, or the New Utopia (L.I.F. *c.* March 1670/1) 1671.
   [T.C. July 1671.]

C. The Man of Newmarket (D.L. *c.* April 1678) 1678.
   [Imprimatur, April 13, 1678. T.C. Dec. 1678.]

HOWARD, HENRY.

T. The United Kingdoms (? Cockpit, 1663/4).
   [The only knowledge we have of this play is from "The Key to *The Rehearsal*" (1704), which states that "it was acted at the Cockpit in Drury Lane soon after the Restoration." If this statement is correct, it might have been given either by the King's men during some time when they were temporarily using that house or (less probably) by Jolly's company.]

HOWARD, Hon. JAMES.

C. The English Monsieur (T.R. in B.St. *c.* July 1663) 1674; 8° 1679.
   [Th. July 30, 1663 (seen by Dutch students: Ethel Seaton, *Literary Relations of England and Scandinavia in the Seventeenth Century* (1935), p. 337). T.C. May 1674.]

T.C. Romeo and Juliet (L.I.F. before 1665).
   [The only record of this alteration is in Downes, p. 22.]

C. All Mistaken, or the Mad Couple (T.R. in B.St. Sept. 1667) 1672; 1710.
   [Fri. Sept. 20, 1667 (Pepys). T.C. May 1672.]

HOWARD, Sir ROBERT.

C. The Blind Lady. 8° 1660 (in *Poems*), 8° 1676 (reissue).
   [S.R. April 16, 1660. *Mercurius Publicus*, Nov. 15–22, 1660.]

C. The Surprisal (T.R. in V.St. April 1662) F. 1665 (in *Four New Plays*); 1692 (in *Five New Plays*; 3 issues); 1700 (reissue).
   [Wed. April 23, 1662 (Herbert, p. 118: Malone giving the date as April 25). S.R. Feb. 4, 1663/4. *Four New Plays*, imprimatur, March 7, 1664/5. S.R. March 7, 1664/5. *Five New Plays*, second edition, *London Gazette*, May 26–30, 1692.]

C. The Committee (T.R. in V.St. *c.* Nov. 1662) F. 1665 (in *Four New Plays*); 1692 (in *Five New Plays*; 3 issues); 1700 (reissue).
   [Th. Nov. 27, 1662 (Evelyn; Court performance). S.R. March 7, 1664/5. Acted later as *The Committee; or, The Faithful Irishman*.]

T. The Indian-Queen (T.R. in B.St. Jan. 1663/4) F. 1665 (in *Four New Plays*); 1692 (in *Five New Plays*; 3 issues); 1700 (reissue).
   [Mon. Jan. 25, 1663/4 (L.C.). S.R. Feb. 4, 1663/4. In B.M. MS. Add. 31,449 is an operatic version of this play, with music by Henry Purcell.]

T. The Vestal-Virgin, or, The Roman Ladies (T.R. in B.St. before 1665) F. 1665 (in *Four New Plays*); 1692 (in *Five New Plays*; 3 issues); 1700 (reissue).

[Nothing is known of the acting of this play save a passing reference in Downes, p. 15. S.R. March 7, 1664/5.]

T.   The Great Favourite, Or, the Duke of Lerma (T.R. in B.St. Feb. 1667/8) 1668; 1692 (in *Five New Plays*; 3 issues); 1700 (reissue).

[Th. Feb. 20, 1667/8 (Pepys and L.C.). S.R. June 24, 1668. Alfred Harbage ("Elizabethan-Restoration Palimpsest," pp. 297–304) gives good reason for believing that this is an alteration of a manuscript play by Ford, *The Spanish Duke of Lerma*.]

C.   The Country Gentleman (probably not completed, 1669).

[On March 4, 1668/9 Pepys speaks of a satirical play being written by Howard and *GEORGE VILLIERS, Duke of BUCK-INGHAM*. A letter in B.M. MS. Add. 36,916 gives the title as above. It would seem that this could hardly be *The Country Knight* recorded in 1675: see *UNKNOWN AUTHORS* and *JOHN CROWNE*.]

T.   The Conquest of China by the Tartars. See *JOHN WILMOT, Earl of ROCHESTER*.

HUGHES, JOHN.

T.   Amalasont, Queen of the Goths (1696).

[Halliwell, p. 13, declares that a manuscript existed in 1860 and that he had seen a copy of a song in *Amalasont, Queen of the Goths: or, Vice Destroys Itself*.]

JEVON, THOMAS.

C.   The Devil of a Wife, or, A Comical Transformation (D.G. March 1685/6) 1686; 1693; 1695 (3 editions).

[Th. March 4, 1685/6 (*HMC*, 12th Report, App. v, Rutland MSS. 106). Imprimatur, March 30, 1686. S.R. March 31, 1686. T.C. May 1686.]

JOHNS, WILLIAM.

Moral Interlude. The Traitor to Himself, or Mans Heart his greatest Enemy. A Moral Interlude in Heroic Verse...As it was Acted by the Boys of a Publick School. 1678.

[T.C. June 1678.]

JORDAN, THOMAS.

[For his early works see Greg, *List*, p. 58 and Woodward-McManaway, *Check List*, pp. 74–7.]

Ent. Bacchus Festival: or, A New Medley: being a Musical Representation at the Entertainment of his Excellency the Lord General Monk at Vintners Hall, 12 April 1660. 1660.

[Although by no means a "play," this is included as an interesting record of semi-dramatic activities immediately before the arrival of Charles.]

C.   Money is an Asse. 1668; 1668 (reissue, with title *Wealth outwitted: Or, Money's an Asse*).

[Jordan says this was written when he was fifteen years of age, and the actors' names suggest an original performance about 1635: but the author is notorious for his deliberate inexactitudes.]

Pageants:

London's Resurrection to Joy and Triumph. 1671 (*bis*).

[T.C. Nov. 1671].

London Triumphant: or, The City in Jollity and Splendor. 1672 (2 issues).

London in its Splendor. 1673.
The Goldsmiths Jubilee: or, London's Triumphs. 1674.
The Triumphs of London. 1675.
London's Triumphs. 1676.
Londons Triumphs. 1677.
The Triumphs of London. 1678.
London in Luster. 1679.
London's Glory. 1680.
London's Joy. 1681.
The Lord Mayor's Show. 1682.
The Triumphs of London. 1683.
> [S.R. Oct. 26, 1683.]

London's Royal Triumph. 1684.

JOYNER, WILLIAM.
   T.   The Roman Empress (T.R. in B.St. *c.* Aug. 1670) 1671. MS.
Worcester College, Oxford (as *Aurelia*).
> [S.R. Sept. 12, 1670. T.C. Nov. 1670.]

KILLIGREW, THOMAS.
> [For his earlier works see Greg, *List*, p. 59 and Woodward-McManaway, *Check List*, pp. 77–8.]

 ―-   Comedies and Tragedies. F. 1664. (A MS. of *Cicilia and Clorinda*
is in the Folger Shakespeare Library, 4458. A MS. of "*Clarasilla*"
is in Harvard University Library.)
> [S.R. Oct. 24, 1663. *News*, Jan. 28, 1663/4. This volume con-
tains: (1) *The Prisoners* (printed 1641); (2) *Claricilla* (printed 1641);
(3) *The Princesse: Or, Love at first Sight*; (4) *The Parson's Wedding*;
(5) *The Pilgrim*; (6) *Cicilia and Clorinda, Or, Love in Arms* (2 parts);
(7) *Thomaso, Or, The Wanderer* (2 parts); (8) *Bellamira her Dream:
Or, The Love of Shadows*. All of these seem to have been written
before or during the Commonwealth period. After 1660 there is
information concerning the production of *Claricilla* (T.R. in V.St.,
Sat. Dec. 1, 1660—Herbert, p. 117), *The Princesse* (T.R. in V.St.,
Fri. Nov. 29, 1661—Pepys), *The Parson's Wedding* (T.R. in B.St.,
Wed. Oct. 5, 1664—Pepys). This last comedy is listed by Herbert
(p. 138) among other plays headed by the date Nov. 3, 1663.]

KILLIGREW, Sir WILLIAM.
   T.C.   Selindra (T.R. in V.St., March 1661/2) 8º 1665 (in *Three Playes*;
reissued 1674); F. 1666 (in *Four New Playes*).
> [Mon. March 3, 1661/2 (Herbert, p. 118). Imprimatur, Aug. 23,
1664. *Three Playes*, S.R. Oct. 21, 1664; *Intelligencer*, Nov. 21,
1664.]

   T.C.   Pandora (or, The Converts) (L.I.F. *c.* April 1664) 8º 1665 (in
Three Playes; reissued 1674); F. 1666 (in *Four New Playes*).
> [Imprimatur, May 3, 1664. S.R. May 21, 1664. *Intelligencer*,
May 23, 1664. Downes, p. 26, says this was acted at L.I.F.,
although one would have expected a performance by the King's
men.]

   T.C.   Ormasdes (acted? 1664) 8º 1665 (in *Three Playes*; reissued 1674);
F. 1666 (in *Four New Playes*, as *Love and Friendship*).
> [Imprimatur, Aug. 23, 1664.]

   T.C.   The Seege of Urbin (T.R. in B.St. 1665?) F. 1666 (in *Four New
Playes*). MS. Bodl. Rawl. poet. 29.

[W. J. Lawrence (*TLS*, Oct. 18, 1928) shows that the cast given in the Bodleian manuscript points to a performance early in 1665; but this list may, of course, be only a tentative one. On the manuscript see also Bernard M. Wagner (*TLS*, Nov. 1, 1928).]

T.   The Imperial Tragedy. Taken out of a Latin Play, And very much altered. F. 1669.

[T.C. May 1669. Langbaine, p. 315, attributes this play to Killigrew and, since it appears frequently bound up with the *Four New Playes*, it most probably is by him. It is an adaptation of *Zeno* by Joseph Simeons (see W. H. McCabe in *Philological Quarterly*, 1936, xv. 311–14). Langbaine, p. 535, adds that it "has been acted (if I mistake not) at the Nursery in *Barbican*."]

KIRKMAN, FRANCIS.

Pol.   The Presbyterian Lash. Or, Noctroff's Maid Whipt. 1661.

[Preface signed F.K. The attribution to Kirkman may be erroneous, although Narcissus Luttrell, who gives it to him, is a good authority. Langbaine, p. 545, also takes F.K. to stand for Francis Kirkman.]

—   The Wits, or, Sport upon Sport....Part 1. 8° 1662; 8° 1672.

[John James Elson, in his excellent edition of this and the following work (1932), shows that the attribution of the drolls to *ROBERT COX* cannot be supported, even although the contents of his *Actaeon and Diana* (printed without date and in 1656) are included here. The probability is that, despite the fact that Part 1 was published by Marsh, both volumes are largely the work of Francis Kirkman, no doubt for a reading public. The contents of this first part, with the plays from which the drolls were taken, are as follow (details from J. J. Elson): (1) *The Bouncing Knight, or, The Robers Rob'd* (from *1 Henry IV*); (2) *Jenkin's Love-Course and Perambulation* (from Shirley's *Love-Tricks*); (3) *The False Heire and Formal Curate* (from Beaumont and Fletcher's *The Scornful Lady*); (4) *The Lame Common-wealth* (from Beaumont and Fletcher's *Beggars' Bush*); (5) *The Sexton, or The Mock-Testator* (from Beaumont and Fletcher's *The Spanish Curate*); (6) *A Prince in Conceit* (from Shirley's *The Opportunity*); (7) *An Equall Match* (from Beaumont and Fletcher's *Rule a Wife and Have a Wife*); (8) *The Stallion* (from Beaumont and Fletcher's *The Custom of the Country*); (9) *The Grave-Makers* (from *Hamlet*); (10) *The Loyal Citizens* (from Beaumont and Fletcher's *Cupid's Revenge*); (11) *Invissible Smirk, or the Pen Combatants* (from *The Two Merry Milkemaids*); (12) *The Three Merry Boyes* (from Beaumont and Fletcher's *The Bloody Brother*); (13) *The Bubble* (from Cooke's *Greenes Tu Quoque*); (14) *The Club-men* (from Beaumont and Fletcher's *Philaster*); (15) *Forc'd Vallour* (from Beaumont and Fletcher's *The Humorous Lieutenant*); (16) *The Encounter* (from Beaumont and Fletcher's *The Knight of the Burning Pestle*); (17) *The Humour of Simpleton* (condensed version of Cox's *Simpleton the Smith*); (18) *The Humour of Bumpkin* (the text from *Actaeon and Diana*, possibly a "jig" of the sixteenth century); (19) *The Humours of Simpkin* (text from *Actaeon and Diana*); (20) *The Humour of Hobbinal* (text from *The Rurall Sports on the birthday of the Nymph Oenone* in *Actaeon and Diana*); (21) *The Humour of John Swabber* (shortened text from *Actaeon and Diana*); (22) *The Humours of*

Monsieur Galliard (from William Cavendish's *The Variety*); (23) *The Landlady* (from Beaumont and Fletcher's *The Chances*); (24) *The Testy Lord* (from Beaumont and Fletcher's *The Maid's Tragedy*); (25) *The Imperick* (from Jonson's *The Alchemist*); (26) *The Surprise* (from Beaumont and Fletcher's *The Maid in the Mill*); (27) *The Doctors of Dull-head College* (from Beaumont and Fletcher's *Monsieur Thomas*).]

— The Wits; or Sport upon Sport. 8° 1673 (*bis*).

[This collection, published by Francis Kirkman, assures the reader that the drolls contained therein had been acted, and considerable reference is made to the actor *ROBERT COX*. The contents are as follow: (1) *The Black Man* (apparently an early "jig"); (2) *Venus and Adonis, or The Maid's Philosophy* (possibly of sixteenth-century origin); (3) *Philetis and Constantia* (based on a poem by Cowley, published in 1633); (4) *King Ahasuerus and Queen Esther*; (5) *King Solomon's Wisdom*; (6) *Diphilo and Granida*; (7) *Wiltshire Tom* (text from *The King and Queenes Entertainement at Richmond*); (8) *Oenone* (an extended version of no. 20 in the first series); (9) *Bottom the Weaver* (from *A Midsummer-Night's Dream*); (10) *The Cheater Cheated* (from Marston's *The Dutch Courtezan*). T.C. May 1673.]

LACY, JOHN.

C. The Old Troop: or, Monsieur Raggou (T.R. in V.St. *c.* 1663) 1672; 1698.

[T.C. June 1672; Feb. 1697/8. *Post Boy*, Jan. 25–27, 1697/8. A performance before 1665 is proved by a reference in the epilogue to Sir Robert Howard's *The Vestal-Virgin*, itself recorded in Downes as performed before the Plague. *The Old Troop* was revived on Fri. July 31, 1668 (Pepys and L.C.).]

C. Sauny the Scott: or, The Taming of the Shrew (T.R. in B.St. April 1667) 1698; 1708; 1714.

[Tues. April 9, 1667 (Pepys). *Post Boy*, Nov. 20–28, 1697. T.C. May 1698.]

C. The Dumb Lady, or, The Farriar Made Physician (T.R. in B.St. *c.* 1669) 1672.

[T.C. May 1672. The precise acting date is uncertain.]

C. Sir Hercules Buffoon, or, The Poetical Squire (D.G. *c.* Sept. 1684) 1684.

[T.C. Nov. 1684. Summers, *Bibliography*, p. 83, puts this play in April–May 1682. It is possible that it may belong to this time, since Lacy died in 1681, but there would appear to be no other evidence extant.]

LEANERD, JOHN.

C. The Country Innocence: or, The Chamber-maid turn'd Quaker (D.L. March 1676/7) 1677.

[Imprimatur, April 6, 1677. S.R. April 13, 1677. T.C. May 1677. This adaptation of Brewer's *The Countrie Girl* probably was a Lent production (Gray, "Lenten Casts," pp. 781–94).]

C. The Rambling Justice, or the Jealous Husbands (D.L. *c.* March 1677/8) 1678 (2 issues); 1680 (reissue as *The Jealous Husbands... with the Humours of Sir John Twiford and the Rambling Justice*); 1694 (reissue, as *The Rambling Justice*).

[Imprimatur, March 13, 1677/8. T.C. June 1678; Nov. 1679. The prologue specifically calls it a "*Lenten Play.*"]

C. The Counterfeits (D.G. May 1678) 1679.

[Tues. May 28, 1678 (L.C.). Imprimatur, Aug. 29, 1678. T.C. Dec. 1678.]

LEE, NATHANIEL.

T. The Tragedy of Nero, Emperour of Rome (D.L. May 1674) 1675; 1696 (*bis*).

[Sat. May 16, 1674 (L.C.). T.C. June 1675.]

T. Sophonisba, or Hannibal's Overthrow (D.L. April 1675) 1676; 1681; 1685; 1691 (2 issues); 1693; 1697 (*bis*); 1704; 1709; 1712.

[Fri. April 30, 1675 (L.C.). T.C. Nov. 1675; Nov. 1691.]

T. Gloriana, or the Court of Augustus Caesar (D.L. Jan. 1675/6) 1676; 1699.

[Sat. Jan. 29, 1675/6 (L.C.). T.C. May 1676; May 1699. *Flying Post,* May 2–4, 1699.]

T. The Rival Queens, or the Death of Alexander the Great (D.L. March 1676/7) 1677; 1684; 1690; 1694 (*bis*); 1699; 1702; 1704.

[Sat. March 17, 1676/7 (L.C.), confirmed as first performance in a newsletter (*HMC*, 12th Report, App. IX, 66). T.C. Nov. 1677; Feb. 1685; June 1690; Nov. 1691; June 1699. *Flying Post,* June 1–3, 1699.]

T. Mithridates, King of Pontus (D.L. Feb. 1677/8) 1678; 1685 (2 issues); 1693; 1697; 1702; 1711. MS. Public Library, Douai, 787.

[Imprimatur, March 28, 1678. T.C. June 1678; Feb. 1684/5.]

T. Oedipus (D.G. *c.* Nov. 1678). See *JOHN DRYDEN.*

T. Caesar Borgia: the Son of Pope Alexander the Sixth (D.G. *c.* Sept. 1679) 1680; 1690 (reissue); 1696; 1711.

[T.C. Nov. 1679. The epilogue suggests that it followed Settle's *The Female Prelate.*]

T. Theodosius; or, The Force of Love (D.G. *c.* Sept. 1680) 1680 (2 issues); 1684; 1692; 1697; 1708.

[T.C. Nov. 1680; Feb. 1684/5.]

T. Lucius Junius Brutus, Father of his Country (D.G. Dec. 1680) 1681; 1708.

[The title-page states that it was prohibited on Dec. 11, 1680; T.C. June 1681 declares that this was after six performances, but Gildon, in the preface to *The Patriot* (1703), gives the number as three.]

T. The Princess of Cleve (D.G. *c.* Sept. 1681) 1689 (2 issues); 1697.

[On the original date of acting see Roswell G. Ham, *Otway and Lee* (1931), pp. 165–7. *London Gazette,* May 13–16, 1689. T.C. May 1689; June 1697. *Post Boy,* Aug. 7–10, 1697.]

T. The Duke of Guise (D.L. Nov. 1682). See *JOHN DRYDEN.*

T. Constantine the Great (D.L. *c.* Nov. 1683) 1684.

[Apparently, from manuscript notations, the play appeared about Nov. 12, 1683 (see Hugh Macdonald, *John Dryden, A Bibliography,* 1939, p. 160, and Autrey N. Wiley, *Rare Prologues and Epilogues, 1642–1700* (1940), p. 182). Roswell G. Ham, *op. cit.* pp. 206–8, argues that this was written some time before its production.]

T. The Massacre of Paris (D.L. Nov. 1689) 1690.

[Th. Nov. 7, 1689 (L.C.). Apparently written in 1679 (see Roswell G. Ham, *op. cit.* pp. 165–7). T.C. Nov. 1689.]

LESLEY or LESLY, GEORGE.

— Divine Dialogues. Viz. Dives's Doom. Sodom's Flames, and Abraham's Faith. 8⁰ 1684.

[This is marked "Second Edition" and there are two dedications dated 1675. No earlier printing, however, has been recorded.]

LOWER, Sir WILLIAM.

[For his earlier works see Greg, *List*, pp. 62–3 and Woodward-McManaway, *Check List*, pp. 83–4.]

T.C. The Amourous Fantasme. 12⁰ 1660 (the Hague); 12⁰ 1661.

[Reissue, and forming part of *Three New Playes*, the other two pieces being *The Noble Ingratitude* (1659) and *The Enchanted Lovers* (1658).]

MAIDWELL, LEWIS.

C. The Loving Enemies (D.G. *c.* March 1679/80) 1680.

[*True News*, May 12–15, 1680. T.C. May 1680. The prologue refers to Dryden's Rose Street adventure (Dec. 18, 1679).]

MANLEY, MARY DE LA RIVIERE.

C. The Lost Lover; or, the Jealous Husband (D.L. *c.* March 1695/6) 1696.

[*London Gazette*, April 20–23, 1696. T.C. June 1696.]

T. The Royal Mischief (L.I.F. *c.* April 1696) 1696.

[*Post Man*, June 4–6, 1696. T.C. June 1696.]

[For her later works see the Handlist of Plays, 1700–1750.]

MEDBOURNE, MATTHEW.

T. Saint Cecily or The Converted Twins. A Christian Tragedy. 1666; 1667 (reissue as *The Converted Twins*).

[Imprimatur, June 11, 1666. The title-page ascribes it to "E.M."; the dedication is signed by Medbourne.]

C. Tartuffe; or, The French Puritan (T.R. in B.St. *c.* May 1670) 1670; 1707.

[S.R. June 28, 1670. T.C. June 1670. The running title is "*or, The* French *Zealot*." An allusion in the prologue to the arrival of French royalty at Dover shews that it must have come out in May or June.]

MILTON, JOHN.

T. Samson Agonistes. 8⁰ 1671 (in *Paradise Regained*); 8⁰ 1680; F. 1688; F. 1695 (in *Poetical Works*).

[S.R. Sept. 10, 1670. T.C. Nov. 1670.]

MOTTEUX, PETER ANTHONY.

[See R. N. Cunningham, "A Bibliography of Peter Anthony Motteux" (*Oxford Bibliographical Society, Proceedings and Papers,* 1931–33, III. 317–37).]

C. Love's a Jest (L.I.F. *c.* June 1696) 1696.

[*Post Man*, July 7–9, 1696. T.C. Nov. 1696.]

M. The Loves of Mars and Venus (L.I.F. Nov. 1696) 1696; 1697 (reissue).

[Acted with Ravenscroft's *The Anatomist*. *Post Man*, Dec. 10–12, 1696. T.C. May and Nov. 1697.]

C. The Novelty. Every Act a Play (L.I.F. *c.* June 1697) 1697.

[*Post Man*, June 8-10, 1697. Summers, *Bibliography*, p. 90, gives a performance date of June 8 but without mentioning his authority. This play includes *Thyrsis* by *JOHN OLDMIXON* and *The Unfortunate Couple* by *EDWARD FILMER*, an altered version of his own *The Unnatural Brother*, besides Motteux' own *All Without Money, Hercules* and *Natural Magic*.]

M. Europe's Revels for the Peace (L.I.F. Nov. 1697) 1697.

[Dialogue from *Post Boy*, Nov. 30–Dec. 2, 1697. Songs, T.C. Feb. 1697/8. The B.M. copy has a manuscript date, Nov. 29. Music by John Eccles.]

T. Beauty in Distress (L.I.F. *c.* April 1698) 1698.

[*London Gazette*, June 16–20, 1698. T.C. June 1698.]

O. The Island Princess, or the Generous Portuguese (D.L. *c.* Jan. 1698/9) 1699; 1701. MS. BM. Add. 15,318.

[This includes a masque, set by Jeremiah Clarke, entitled *The Four Seasons or Love in Every Age*, printed separately in 1699. Masque, *Post Boy*, Feb. 7–9, 1698/9; Opera, *Flying Post*, March 7–9, 1698/9. Masque, T.C. Feb. 1698/9. T.C. May 1699.]

[For his later works see the Handlist of Plays, 1700–1750.]

MOUNTFORT, WILLIAM.

F. The Life and Death of Doctor Faustus. Made into a Farce.... With the Humours of Harlequin and Scaramouche (D.G. *c.* Dec. 1685) 1697.

[The 1697 edition is definitely marked as a revival at L.I.F.; formerly it had been played at D.G. There is no external evidence regarding the date; internal evidence suggests a performance about 1685, although there is a record of a *Dr Faustus* on Sept. 28, 1675 (L.C.) and possibly another on Sept. 24 preceding (list of plays seen by Nell Gwyn, Harvard University Library). These may refer to Mountfort's farce.]

T. The Injur'd Lovers: or, The Ambitious Father (D.L. *c.* Feb. 1687/8) 1688.

[Imprimatur, March 8, 1687/8. T.C. May 1688. Luttrell dates the separate prologue and epilogue Feb. 6, 1687/8.]

T.C. The Successfull Straingers (D.L. *c.* Dec. 1689) 1690; 1696 (reissue).

[Imprimatur, Jan. 27, 1689/90. S.R. Jan. 27, 1689/90. T.C. Feb. 1689/90. *London Gazette*, Feb. 3–6, 1689/90. T.C. May 1696.]

T. Distress'd Innocence: or, The Princess of Persia (D.L. *c.* Oct. 1690). See *ELKANAH SETTLE.*

Play. King Edward the Third (D.L. *c.* Nov. 1690). See *JOHN BANCROFT.*

T.C. The Mistakes, or, The False Report (D.L. *c.* Dec. 1690). See *JOSEPH HARRIS.*

C. Greenwich Park (D.L. *c.* May 1691) 1691.

[*London Gazette*, May 21–25, 1691. T.C. May 1691.]

T. Henry the Second, King of England (D.L. Nov. 1692). See *JOHN BANCROFT.*

[For a possible later work see the Handlist of Plays, 1700–1750.]

NEVILE, ROBERT.

C. The Poor Scholar. 1662.

NORTON, RICHARD.
- **T.** Pausanias, the Betrayer of his Country (D.L. *c.* April 1696) 1696.
  [*Post Boy*, May 9–12, 1696. This play was introduced to the stage by Thomas Southerne.]

OGILBY, JOHN.
- **Pageant.** The Relation of His Majestie's Entertainment passing through the City of London. F. 1661; 1661 (Edinburgh).
- **Pageant.** The Entertainment of His Most Excellent Majestie Charles II in his passage through the City of London to his Coronation. F. 1662; F. 1685; 1685.

OLDMIXON, JOHN.
- **Past.** Thyrsis (L.I.F. *c.* June 1697). See *PETER ANTHONY MOTTEUX.*
- **Past.** Amintas (D.L. 1698) 1698.
  [For his later works see the Handlist of Plays, 1700–1750.]

OTWAY, THOMAS.
- **T.** Alcibiades (D.G. Sept. 1675) 1675 (*bis*); 1687.
  [Wed. Sept. 22, 1675 (L.C.; but something is wrong with the list and this exact date must be accepted with caution). T.C. Feb. 1688.]
- **T.** Don Carlos; Prince of Spain (D.G. June 1676) 1676; 1679; 1686; 1695; 1704.
  [Th. June 8, 1676 (L.C.; the list gives "Jan. 8" but this seems to be an error). Imprimatur, June 15, 1676. S.R. June 15, 1676. T.C. Nov. 1676; Dec. 1678.]
- **T.** Titus and Berenice....With a Farce call'd the Cheats of Scapin (D.G. *c.* Dec. 1676) 1677 (2 issues); 1701.
  [Imprimatur, Feb. 19, 1676/7. T.C. Feb. 1676/7.]
- **F.** The Cheats of Scapin (D.G. *c.* Dec. 1676). See last entry.
- **C.** Friendship in Fashion (D.G. April 1678) 1678 (3 issues).
  [Fri. April 5, 1678 (L.C.). Imprimatur, May 31, 1678. T.C. June 1678.]
- **T.** The History and Fall of Caius Marius (D.G. *c.* Sept. 1679) 1680; 1692 (*bis*); 1696; 1703.
  [The prologue refers to the King's serious illness, *i.e.* late August or early September. T.C. Nov. 1679.]
- **T.** The Orphan: or, the Unhappy Marriage (D.G. *c.* March 1679/80) 1680; 1685; 1691; 1696; 1703; 1705; 1711.
  [The prologue refers to the return of the Duke and Duchess of York from Scotland, *i.e.* late February or early March. Aline Mackenzie ("A Note on the Date of *The Orphan*," *ELH*, 1945, XII. 316–26) argues that it was written between 1676 and 1678. T.C. May 1680; Feb. 1684/5; Nov. 1691.]
- **C.** The Souldiers Fortune (D.G. March 1679/80) 1681; 1683; 1687; 1695.
  [Mon. March 1, 1679/80 (L.C.; almost certainly the year is 1679/80, although the list is a trifle ambiguous). T.C. Nov. 1680; June 1696.]
- **T.** Venice Preserv'd; or, A Plot Discover'd (D.G. Feb. 1681/2) 1682; 1696 (*bis*); 1704.
  [Th. Feb. 9, 1681/2 (date given in separately printed prologue). Prologue and epilogue, *Observator*, April 27, 1682. T.C. May 1682.]

C. The Atheist. Or, the Second Part of the Souldiers Fortune (D.G.
  c. July 1683) 1684.
  [*Observator*, Aug. 8, 1683. T.C. Nov. 1683.]
  [The *Observator*, Nov. 27 and Dec. 4, 1686, had an advertisement from the T.R. about a lost play of Otway's. Apparently this
  was never recovered. *Heroick Friendship*, published under his
  name in 1719, is generally regarded as spurious.]

PARKHURST, FERDINANDO.
C. Ignoramus (Court Nov. 1662). MS. in possession of the Duke of
  Westminster.
  [Sat. Nov. 1, 1662 (L.C.; performance at Court). It is not
  absolutely certain what company was concerned, probably
  D'Avenant's men.]

PAYNE, HENRY NEVIL.
T. The Fatal Jealousie (D.G. Aug. 1672) 1673 (2 issues).
  [Sat. Aug. 3, 1672 (L.C.). Imprimatur, Nov. 22, 1672. T.C.
  May 1672.]
C. The Morning Ramble, or, The Town-Humours (D.G. Nov. 1672)
  1673 (2 issues).
  [Mon. Nov. 4, 1672 (L.C.). T.C. May 1673.]
T. The Siege of Constantinople (D.G. Nov. 1674) 1675.
  [Mon. Nov. 2, 1674 (L.C.). S.R. Nov. 29, 1674. T.C. Feb.
  1674/5.]

PERRIN, PIERRE.
O. Ariadne, or, The Marriage of Bacchus...Ariane, ou le Mariage de
  Bacchus (D.L. March 1674) 1674.
  [Mon. March 30, 1674 (L.C.; listing "The French Opera").
  Originally composed by Robert Cambert, this piece failed to be
  produced in Paris. There is a puzzle in that the title-page to the
  London text gives it to Louis Grabut: probably he undertook a
  revision of the score.]

PHILIPS, KATHERINE.
T. Pompey (Smock Alley, Dublin, Feb. 1662/3). 1663 (Dublin);
  1663; 1664; F. 1667 (in *Poems*); F. 1669 (in *Poems*); F. 1678 (in
  Poems).
  [*Mercurius Publicus*, June 25–July 2, 1663. Poems, S.R. Nov. 25,
  1663.]
T. Horace (amateurs at Court, Feb. 1667/8; T.R. in B.St. Jan. 1668/9)
  F. 1667 (in *Poems*); F. 1669 (in *Poems*); F. 1678 (in *Poems*).
  [This translation was left unfinished by the authoress and was
  completed by *Sir JOHN DENHAM*. Tues. Feb. 4, 1667/8
  (Evelyn, confirmed by record in Ethel Seaton, *Literary Relations
  of England and Scandinavia in the Seventeenth Century*, 1935,
  pp. 337–8). Sat. Jan. 16, 1668/9 (L.C.; professional performance).]

PHILLIPS, WILLIAM.
T. The Revengeful Queen (D.L. *c.* June 1698) 1698.
  [*Post Man*, July 2–5, 1698.]
  [For his later works see the Handlist of Plays, 1700–1750. Early
  catalogues give a play *Alcamenes and Menalippa*, which Chetwood
  dates 1668, possibly a mistake for 1698.]

PINKETHMAN, WILLIAM.
C. Love without Interest; or, The Man too hard for the Master (D.L. *c.* April 1699) 1699.
> [*Post Boy*, May 2–4, 1699. The dedication is signed by Pinkethman, who, however, was probably not the author.]

PIX, MARY.
T. Ibrahim the Thirteenth Emperour of the Turks (D.L. *c.* June 1696) 1696.
> [*Post Boy*, June 27–30, 1696.]
F.C. The Spanish Wives (D.L. *c.* Sept. 1696) 1696.
> [*Post Boy*, Oct. 15–17, 1696. T.C. Nov. 1696.]
C. The Innocent Mistress (L.I.F. *c.* June 1697) 1697 (2 issues).
> [*Post Boy*, July 29–31, 1697. T.C. Nov. 1697.]
C. The Deceiver Deceived (L.I.F. *c.* Dec. 1697) 1698; 1699 (reissue as *The French Beau*).
> [*Post Boy*, Dec. 18–21, 1697. T.C. Feb. 1697/8. This was originally given to D.L. and withdrawn. There is the suggestion that Powell's *The Imposture Defeated* was stolen from it (see G. Thorn-Drury, "An Unrecorded Play-title," *Review of English Studies*, 1930, VI. 316–18. Included in the text are two dialogues, by *THOMAS D'URFEY* and *PETER ANTHONY MOTTEUX* respectively.]
T. Queen Catharine or, the Ruines of Love (L.I.F. *c.* June 1698) 1698.
> [*Post Boy*, July 26–28, 1698. T.C. Nov. 1698.]
T. The False Friend: or, The Fate of Disobedience (L.I.F. *c.* May 1699) 1699.
> [*Post Boy*, July 6–8, 1699.]
> [For her later works see the Handlist of Plays, 1700–1750.]

POLWHELE, ELIZABETH.
C. The Frolick; or, The Lawyer Cheated (1671).
> [J. O. Halliwell, *A Dictionary of Old English Plays* (1860), p. 105, records a manuscript of this play.]

PORDAGE, SAMUEL.
T. Troades. 8º 1660 (in *Poems upon Several Occasions*).
T. Herod and Mariamne (D.G.? Oct. 1673) 1673; 1674 (reissue).
> [Tues. Oct. 28, 1673 (L.C.). There is a puzzle here. The title-page refers to the Duke's Theatre, whereas the prologue is given as "Spoken at the *Theatre* in *Lincolns-Inn-Fields*." Probably Gray ("Lenten Casts," pp. 787–8) is right in suggesting that this was a "young actors" production at L.I.F., later transferred to Dorset Garden. If so, it must have been, not in Lent, but after midsummer, since the King's men had been using L.I.F. during the first half of the year. See also William S. Clark, "Pordage's *Herod and Mariamne*" (*Review of English Studies*, 1929, V. 61–4). The dedication is signed by Elkanah Settle; the prologue suggests the play had been written many years before its production. S.R. Feb. 18, 1673/4. T.C. Feb. 1673/4.]
T. The Siege of Babylon (D.G. *c.* Sept. 1677) 1678.
> [Imprimatur, Nov. 2, 1677. T.C. Nov. 1677.]

PORTER, THOMAS.
T. The Villain (L.I.F. Oct. 1662) 1663; 1670; 1694.
    [Sat. Oct. 18, 1662 (Pepys). S.R. June 15, 1663.]
T.C. A Witty Combat: or, the Female Victor. 1663.
    [The statement on the title-page, "As it was *Acted* by Persons
    of Quality in *Whitsun*-Week with great applause," is not, of course,
    to be taken as implying a theatre performance.]
C. The Carnival (T.R. in B.St. *c.* 1663) 1664.
    [*Intelligencer*, May 2, 1664.]
C. The French Conjurer (D.G. *c.* March 1676/7) 1678.
    [Imprimatur, Aug. 2, 1677. T.C. Nov. 1677. Gray ("Lenten
    Casts," pp. 789-90) points out that this seems to have been a
    "young actors" play and suggests a first performance in Lent:
    allusions in the prologue and text seem to refer to this season.]

POWELL, GEORGE.
T. The Treacherous Brothers (D.L. *c.* Dec. 1689) 1690; 1696 (reissue).
    [S.R. Feb. 13, 1689/90. *London Gazette*, Feb. 20–24, 1689/90.
    T.C. May 1696.]
T. Alphonso King of Naples (D.L. *c.* Dec. 1690) 1691.
    [*London Gazette*, Feb. 12–16, 1690/1. T.C. Feb. 1690/1.]
C. A Very Good Wife (D.L. *c.* March 1692/3) 1693; 1703.
    [*Gentleman's Journal*, April 1693 (really May). *London Gazette*,
    June 15–19, 1693. T.C. Nov. 1693.]
D.O. Bonduca; or, The British Heroine (D.L. *c.* Sept. 1695) 1696.
    [*London Gazette*, Oct. 24–28, 1695. T.C. June 1696.]
C. The Cornish Comedy (D.G. *c.* June 1696) 1696.
    [*Post Boy*, Aug. 25–27, 1696. Gildon, p. 158, says this was
    actually written by a Cornish attorney.]
D.O. A New Opera: called, Brutus of Alba: or, Augusta's Triumph
    (D.G. *c.* Oct. 1696) 1697 (2 issues).
    [The dedication is signed by George Powell and Jack Verbruggen
    and dated Oct. 16, 1696. T.C. Nov. 1696.]
C. The Imposture Defeated: or, A Trick to Cheat the Devil (D.L.
    c. Sept. 1697) 1698.
    [This includes a masque, *Endimion; The Man in the Moon*. *Post
    Boy*, Nov. 16–18, 1697. T.C. Nov. 1697; Feb. 1697/8; May 1698.]
T. The Fatal Discovery; or, Love in Ruines (D.L. *c.* Feb. 1697/8).
    See under *UNKNOWN AUTHORS.*

QUINAULT, PHILIPPE.
O. Cadmus et Hermione (D.G. *c.* Feb. 1685/6).
    [A performance of this opera (music by J. B. Lully and libretto
    by Philippe Quinault) has been almost certainly proved by W. J.
    Lawrence ("The French Opera in London: A Riddle of 1686,"
    TLS, March 28, 1936). The allusion appears in the prologue to
    Jevon's *The Devil of a Wife*.]

RANT, HUMPHREY.
C. Phormio (*c.* 1674). MS. B.M. Sloane 1145.
    [Recorded by Alfred Harbage, "Manuscripts," p. 694.]

RAVENSCROFT, EDWARD.
C. The Citizen turn'd Gentleman (D.G. July 1672) 1672; 1675
    (reissued as *Mamamouchi*).

[Th. July 4, 1672 (L.C.). Imprimatur, Aug. 9, 1672. T.C. Nov. 1672; Nov. 1675.]

C. The Careless Lovers (D.G. March 1672/3) 1673.

[Wed. March 12, 1672/3 (L.C.). It is confessedly a "young actors" play, performed in Lent. T.C. Nov. 1673 (as *The Careless Lovers; or, The Conceited Travellers*). See James G. McManaway, "The Copy for *The Careless Lovers*" (*Modern Language Notes*, 1931, XLVI. 406–9).]

C. The Wrangling Lovers: or, The Invisible Mistress (D.G. *c.* Sept. 1676) 1677 (2 issues).

[Imprimatur, Sept. 25, 1676. T.C. Nov. 1676.]

F. Scaramouch a Philosopher, Harlequin A School-Boy, Bravo, Merchant and Magician. A Comedy After the Italian Manner (D.L. May 1677) 1677.

[Sat. May 5, 1677 (L.C.). T.C. July 1677.]

T.C. King Edgar and Alfreda (D.L. *c.* Oct. 1677) 1677.

[*London Gazette*, Oct. 29–Nov. 1, 1677. T.C. Feb. 1677/8.]

C. The English Lawyer (D.L. *c.* Dec. 1677) 1678 (2 issues).

[S.R. Jan. 16, 1677/8. T.C. May 1678.]

T. Titus Andronicus, or the Rape of Lavinia (D.L. ? 1678 or 1679) 1687.

[Imprimatur, Dec. 21, 1686. *Observator*, March 2, 1686/7. T.C. Feb. 1686/7. The preface states that this appeared at the time of the Popish Plot; in corroboration there is only Downes' listing of *Titus Andronicus* among plays given by the King's men before 1682.]

C. The London Cuckolds (D.G. Nov. 1681) 1682; 1683; 1688; 1697.

[Tues. Nov. 22, 1681 (L.C.). T.C. Feb. 1681/2; May 1683.]

C. Dame Dobson: or, The Cunning Woman (D.G. *c.* June 1683) 1684.

[Summers (Downes, p. 233) gives the date June 1, 1683, apparently on the basis of a manuscript notation. T.C. Nov. 1683.]

C. The Canterbury Guests, or, A Bargain Broken (D.L. *c.* Sept. 1694) 1695.

[T.C. Nov. 1694. *Gentleman's Journal*, Oct./Nov. 1694. *London Gazette*, Dec. 17–20, 1694. The play may have appeared on the stage as early as May (see Genest, II. 58).]

C. The Anatomist: or, the Sham Doctor (L.I.F. Nov. 1696) 1697 (2 issues).

[Sat. Nov. 14, 1696 (a letter of Nov. 19 speaks of its having been acted "four or five days together"—*HMC*, 12th Report, Part II, Cowper MSS. II. 367). With this play was given the masque, *The Loves of Mars and Venus*, for which see *PETER ANTHONY MOTTEUX. Post Man*, Dec. 10–12, 1696. T.C. May 1697.]

T. The Italian Husband (L.I.F. *c.* Nov. 1697) 1698.

[Dedication dated Dec. 16, 1697. *Post Man*, Dec. 14–16, 1697. The text includes a masque, *Ixion*.]

RAWLINS, —.

C. Tom Essence: or, The Modish Wife (D.G. *c.* Aug. 1676) 1677.

[Imprimatur, Nov. 4, 1676. T.C. Nov. 1676. Ascribed by Langbaine, p. 552, to "One Mr Rawlins." The cast suggests a young actors' vacation play.]

C. Tunbridge-Wells: or, A Day's Courtship (D.G. *c.* March 1677/8) 1678.

[T.C. May 1678. The title-page says that it was "Written by a Person of Quality." Langbaine, p. 554, states he had "been told it was writ by Mr *Rawlins*."]

RAYMES, WILLIAM.
— Selfe Interest, or The Belly Wager (*c.* 1680–90). MS. Folger Shakespeare Library, 1008. 1.

REVET, EDWARD.
C. The Town-Shifts, or, the Suburb-Justice (L.I.F. *c.* March 1670/1) 1671.
[Imprimatur, May 2, 1671. T.C. July 1671. Gray ("Lenten Casts," p. 787) puts it in March because of its cast of "young actors."]

RHODES, RICHARD.
C. Flora's Vagaries (T.R. in V.St. *c.* Jan. 1662/3) 1670 (2 issues); 1677.
[Tues. Nov. 3, 1663 (Herbert, p. 138; but whether the date of licence or that of performance is uncertain). S.R. Feb. 4, 1663/4. Imprimatur, July 28, 1669. T.C. Nov. 1669.]

RIVERS, Rev. ANTONY.
T. The Traytor...with Alterations (D.G. March 1691/2) 1692.
[T.C. May 1692. A revised version of Shirley's play. *Gentleman's Journal*, April 1692. Acted later as *The Traitor; or, The Tragedy of Amidea*.]

ROCHE-GUILHEN, Mme LA.
C. Rare en Tout (Court, May 1677) 1677.
[Tues. May 29, 1677 (L.C.).]

RYMER, THOMAS.
T. Edgar, or the English Monarch: an Heroick Tragedy. 1678; 1691 (reissue as *The English Monarch*); 1693 (reissue with original title).
[Imprimatur, Sept. 13, 1677. T.C. Nov. 1677; Nov. 1690; June 1693.]

SACKVILLE, CHARLES, Earl of DORSET.
T. Pompey the Great (L.I.F. *c.* Dec. 1662). See *EDMUND WALLER.*

SADLER, ANTHONY.
Pol. The Subject's Joy for the King's Restoration. 1660.

ST SERFE, Sir THOMAS.
C. Tarugo's Wiles, or, the Coffee-House (L.I.F. Oct. 1667) 1668.
[Sat. Oct. 5, 1667 (Pepys).]

SANDYS, G.
Religious Play. Christ's Passion. 8° 1687; 1698 (reissue).
[A translation from Hugo Grotius.]

SAUNDERS, CHARLES.
T. Tamerlane The Great (D.L. *c.* March 1680/1) 1681.
[T.C. May 1681.]

SCOTT, THOMAS.
C. The Mock-Marriage (D.G. *c.* Oct. 1695) 1696.
[*London Gazette*, Oct. 10–14, 1695.]

T. The Unhappy Kindness: or, A Fruitless Revenge (D.L. *? c.* July 1697) 1697.

[There is no evidence regarding the date of production. It may merely be guessed that this was a summer piece.]

SEDLEY, Sir CHARLES.

T. Pompey the Great (L.I.F. *c.* Dec. 1662). See *EDMUND WALLER.*

C. The Mulberry-Garden (T.R. in B.St. May 1668) 1668; 1675.

[Mon. May 18, 1668 (Pepys and L.C.). The play seems first to have had as a provisional title *The Wandering Ladies* (Pepys, Jan. 11, 1667/8).]

T. Antony and Cleopatra (D.G. Feb. 1676/7) 1677; 1696.

[Mon. Feb. 12, 1676/7 (L.C.). Imprimatur, April 24, 1677. S.R. May 4, 1677. T.C. May 1677. *London Gazette*, Jan. 14–17, 1677/8.]

C. Bellamira, or the Mistress (D.L. May 1687) 1687.

[Th. May 12, 1687 (L.C.). S.R. June 17, 1687, recording imprimatur of May 24. T.C. June 1687.]

T. Beauty the Conqueror; or, the Death of Marc Antony. 8° 1702 (in *Miscellaneous Works*).

[An alteration of his *Antony and Cleopatra*.]

T. The Tyrant King of Crete. 12° 1722 (in *Works*).

[An alteration of Henry Killigrew's *Pallantus and Eudora*.]

C. The Grumbler. 12° 1722 (in *Works*, with separate title-page dated 1719).

SETTLE, ELKANAH.

T. Cambyses King of Persia (L.I.F. *c.* Jan. 1670/1) 1671; 1672; 1675; 1692.

[Imprimatur, March 6, 1670/1. T.C. May 1671; Feb. 1671/2; Feb. 1675/6. W. J. Lawrence ("Oxford Restoration Prologues," *TLS*, Jan. 16, 1930) shows that it cannot be earlier than the close of 1670 and that it was acted at Oxford, July 12, 1671.]

T. The Empress of Morocco (D.G. July 1673) 1673 (2 issues); 1687; 1698.

[Th. July 3, 1673 (L.C.). T.C. Nov. 1673; Nov. 1698. *Post Man*, Oct. 1–4, 1698. T.C. Nov. 1673. Apparently produced first at Court.]

T. Love and Revenge (D.G. Nov. 1674) 1675 (2 issues). MS. B.M. Harl. 6903.

[Mon. Nov. 9, 1674 (L.C.). T.C. May 10, 1675.]

T. The Conquest of China, By the Tartars (D.G. May 1675) 1676.

[T.C. 1675/6. Summers, *Bibliography*, p. 107, gives (without evidence) the date Th. May 20, 1675; the play was seen by the King on Fri. May 28 (L.C.).]

T. Ibrahim The Illustrious Bassa (D.G. *c.* March 1676) 1677; 1694.

[Imprimatur, May 4, 1676. S.R. July 7, 1676. T.C. Nov. 1676.]

Past. Pastor Fido: or, The Faithful Shepherd (D.G. *c.* Dec. 1676) 1677; 1689; 1694. MS. Bodl. Rawl. poet. 8.

[Imprimatur, Dec. 26, 1676. S.R. Jan. 22, 1676/7. T.C. July 5, 1677; May 1689.]

T. The Female Prelate: Being The History of the Life and Death of Pope Joan (D.L. *c.* Sept. 1679) 1680; 1689 (3 issues).

[T.C. Nov. 1680; May 1689. The epilogue to Lee's *Caesar Borgia* (T.C. Nov. 1679 and presumably acted about Sept.) suggests that that play was acted shortly after *The Female Prelate*.]

T. Fatal Love: or, The Forc'd Inconstancy (D.L. *c.* Sept. 1680) 1680.
[T.C. Nov. 1680.]

T. The Heir of Morocco, with the Death of Gayland (D.L. *c.* March 1681/2) 1682; 1694.
[Sat. March 11, 1681/2 (L.C.), confirmed by the separately printed prologue (where the title appears as *The Emperor of Morocco*). T.C. May 1682.]

T. Distress'd Innocence: or, The Princess of Persia (D.L. *c.* Oct. 1690) 1691.
[S.R. Nov. 11, 1690. *London Gazette*, Dec. 11–15, 1690. T.C. Feb. 1690/1. The dedication acknowledges that one scene was written by *WILLIAM MOUNTFORT*.]

Pageant. The Triumphs of London. 1691.

Pageant. The Triumphs of London. 1692.

O. The Fairy-Queen (D.G. May 1692) 1692 (several issues); 1693 (reissue).
[Mon. May 2, 1692 (Luttrell, *A Brief Relation of State Affairs* (1857), II. 435). S.R. Nov. 2, 1691. *London Gazette*, May 5–9, 1692. *Gentleman's Journal*, May 1692. For the arguments in favour of ascribing this to Settle see F. C. Brown, *Elkanah Settle* (1910). The music was composed by Henry Purcell. See Paul. S. Dunkin, "Issues of *The Fairy Queen*, 1692" (*Library*, 4th ser., 1946, XXVI. 297–304).]

C. The New Athenian Comedy. 1693.

Pageant. The Triumphs of London. 1693.

Pageant. The Triumphs of London. 1694.

T. The Ambitious Slave: or, a Generous Revenge (D.L. March 1693/4) 1694.
[Wed. March 21, 1693/4 (letter quoted by Edmund Malone, *Shakespeare* (1821), III. 162–3). *London Gazette*, April 12–19, 1694. Leslie Hotson, pp. 274–6, shows that the plot for this play was provided by Elizabeth Leigh in 1682, and that it was written before the union of the companies.]

Pageant. The Triumphs of London. 1695.

T.C. Philaster, or Love lies a-bleeding (D.L. *c.* Dec. 1695) 1695.
[T.C. June 1696.]

D.O. The World in the Moon (D.G. June 1697) 1697.
[*Post Boy*, June 22–24, 1697. T.C. June 1697. *Post Boy*, June 29–July 1, 1697, says "The New Opera will be Acted this day." Summers, *Bibliography*, p. 108, gives, without evidence, the date Th. June 17, 1697. The music was by Daniel Purcell and Jeremiah Clarke.]

Pageant. Glory's Resurrection; Being the Triumphs of London Revived. F. 1698.

Pageant. The Triumphs of London. F. 1699.
[For his later works see the Handlist of Plays, 1700–1750.]

SHADWELL, THOMAS.
C. The Sullen Lovers: Or, the Impertinents (L.I.F. May 1668) 1668; 1670; 1693. MS. in the possession of the Duke of Portland.

[Sat. May 2, 1668 (Pepys and L.C.). S.R. Sept. 9, 1668. T.C. Nov. 1688.]

T.C. The Royal Shepherdess (L.I.F. Feb. 1668/9) 1669; 1691.
[Th. Feb. 25, 1668/9 (Pepys). S.R. June 8, 1669. T.C. Nov. 1669.]

C. The Hypocrite (L.I.F. ? 1670).
[All that is known of this play is the reference in the preface to Settle's *Ibrahim* and in Dryden's *MacFlecknoe*.]

C. The Humorists (L.I.F. *c.* Dec. 1670) 1671; 1691. MS. in the possession of the Duke of Portland.
[S.R. Feb. 9, 1670/1. T.C. May 1671.]

C. The Miser (T.R. in B.St. *c.* Jan. 1671/2) 1672 (3 issues); 1691.
[T.C. June 1672. The preface declares it was produced before the burning of the theatre (*i.e.* Jan. 25, 1671/2.]

C. Epsom-Wells (D.G. Dec. 1672) 1673; 1676; 1693; 1704.
[Mon. Dec. 2, 1672 (L.C.). S.R. Feb. 17, 1672/3. Imprimatur, Feb. 17, 1672/3. *London Gazette*, May 29–June 2, 1673. T.C. May 1673.]

D.O. The Tempest, or the Enchanted Island (D.G. April 1674) 1674; 1676 (*bis*); 1690; [" 1676," but about 1692]; 1695; 1701.
[Th. April 30, 1674 (see Hazelton Spencer, *Shakespeare Improved*, p. 94). The opera was in preparation by Aug. 22, 1673 (*Letters to Sir Joseph Williamson at Cologne*, ed. W. D. Christie, Camden Society, I. 180) and must have been in rehearsal in March 1673/4 (reference to "Tempests and Operas" in a MS. prologue spoken at the opening of D.L. on March 26, 1674 (Helen M. Hooker, "Dryden's and Shadwell's *Tempest*," *Huntington Library Quarterly*, 1942–3, VI. 224–8). There has been more controversy over this than any other Restoration play. The claimants are: (1) *Shadwell*: recorded by Downes, p. 34, and indicated by several items of external evidence (see W. J. Lawrence, *Elizabethan Playhouse*, I. 191 ff.; M. Summers, *Shakespeare Adaptations*, 1922, introduction; D. M. Walmsley, "Shadwell and the Operatic *Tempest*," *Review of English Studies*, II. 1926, 463–6 and 1927, III. 451–3); (2) *Dryden*: claimed as author mainly because the quartos of the operatic version included Dryden's preface and because one of these quartos formed part of the conglomerate *Works* of Dryden issued in the nineties (G. Thorn-Drury, "Some Notes on Dryden" and "Shadwell and the Operatic *Tempest*," *Review of English Studies*, 1925, I. 327–30; 1927, III. 204–8); (3) *Betterton*: on the grounds that Aug. 1673 was the time when Shadwell was occupied with *Psyche* his authorship is rejected and the name of Betterton proposed as a person actively engaged with the operatic ventures of the Duke's men (Charles E. Ward, "'The Tempest': A Restoration Opera Problem," *ELH*, 1946, XIII. 119–30). Ward's is the latest and in some respects the most thorough study of the question, but the evidence for Shadwell seems fairly firm, although Betterton no doubt had a hand in the work.]

C. The Triumphant Widow (D.G. Nov. 1674). See *WILLIAM CAVENDISH, Duke of NEWCASTLE.*

D.O. Psyche (D.G. Feb. 1674/5) 1675 (*bis*); 1690. [*The English Opera; or the Vocal Musick in Psyche*, 1675.]
[Sat. Feb. 27, 1674/5 (L.C.). S.R. Aug. 1, 1674. T.C. Feb.

1674/5; Nov. 1691. The music was composed by Matthew Locke. The preface declares that this work had been completed sixteen months before the date of publication. Acted later as *Psyche; or, Love's Mistress.*]

C. The Libertine (D.G. June 1675) 1676; 1692; 1697; 1704; 1705.

    [Tues. June 15, 1675 (L.C.). The date June 12, 1675 appears in a list of plays seen by Nell Gwyn (Harvard University Library). *London Gazette*, Feb. 17–21, 1675/6. T.C. Feb. 1675/6. Acted later under the titles *The Libertine Destroyed* and *Don John; or, The Libertine Destroyed.*]

C. The Virtuoso (D.G. May 1676) 1676 (*bis*); 1691; 1704.

    [Th. May 25, 1676 (L.C.). Imprimatur, May 31, 1676. Dedication dated June 26, 1676. S.R. June 1, 1676. *London Gazette*, July 3–6, 1676. T.C. Nov. 1676.]

T. The History of Timon of Athens, The Man-Hater....Made into a Play (D.G. *c*. Jan. 1677/8) 1678 (2 issues); 1688 (2 issues); 1696; 1703.

    [Imprimatur, Feb. 18, 1677/8. S.R. Feb. 23, 1677/8. T.C. July and Dec. 1688.]

C. A True Widow (D.G. *c*. Dec. 1678) 1679; 1698 (reissue).

    [Dedication dated Feb. 16, 1678/9. T.C. May 1679; June 1689. The epilogue refers to the "troubled Times" and this may be associated with the confusion aroused by the Popish Plot. Peculiarly a reference is made in Act I to the date, March 21, 1678: it possibly was planned for production then, although the epilogue, pointing to a later date, may not have been that used for the première.]

C. The Woman-Captain (D.G. *c*. Sept. 1679) 1680.

    [T.C. Nov. 1679. This came out immediately before Otway's *Caius Marius* (reference in the prologue to the latter play). Acted later as *The Woman Captain; or, A Usurer turned Soldier.*]

C. The Lancashire Witches, And Tegue o Divelly The Irish Priest (D.G. *c*. Sept. 1681) 1682 (*bis*); 1691 (as *The Lancashire Witches. The Amorous Bigot; bis*).

    [*Domestick Intelligence*, Nov. 10–14, 1681. T.C. Nov. 1681 and May 1682.]

C. The Squire of Alsatia (D.L. May 1688) 1688 (*bis*); 1692; 1693 (reissue); 1699.

    [A. S. Borgman (*Thomas Shadwell*, p. 75) quotes letters of May 5 and May 12, 1688, to confirm his belief that the first performance was on Fri. May 4. T.C. May 1688.]

C. Bury-Fair (D.L. *c*. April 1689) 1689.

    [*London Gazette*, May 23–27, 1689. T.C. June 1689.]

C. The Amorous Bigotte: with the Second Part of Tegue O Divelly (D.L. *c*. March 1689/90) 1690; 1691.

    [Dedication dated May 5, 1690. *London Gazette*, May 12–15, 1690. T.C. May 1690. The prologue acknowledges indebtedness to a "damn'd old play."]

C. The Scowrers (D.L. *c*. Dec. 1690) 1691.

    [*London Gazette*, Feb. 19–23, 1690/1. T.C. Feb. 1690/1.]

C. The Volunteers: or The Stock Jobbers (D.L. *c*. Nov. 1692) 1693.

    [*London Gazette*, Dec. 15–19, 1692. T.C. June 1693.]

SHAW, SAMUEL.
— Words Made Visible; or, Grammar and Rhetorick accomodated
to the Lives and Manners of Men. 8° 1679 (2 issues); 8° 1680
(as *Minerva's Triumphs; or, Grammar and Rhetoric*); 8° 1683.

SHERBURNE, Sir EDWARD.
T. Medea. 8° 1648; 8° 1701.
[This and the following two plays are translations from Seneca.]
T. Troades; or, The Royal Captives. 8° 1679; 8° 1701.
[T.C. June 1679. *London Gazette*, July 10–14, 1679.]
T. Phaedra and Hippolitus. 8° 1701.

SHERWIN, THOMAS.
Religious Play. Youth's Tragedy. A Poem, drawn up by Way of
Dialogue. 1671.
Religious Play. Youths Comedy on the Souls Tryals and Triumph.
A Dramatick Poem. 8° 1680.
[T.C. Nov. 1694.]

SHIPMAN, THOMAS.
T. Henry the Third of France, Stabb'd by a Fryer. With the Fall of
the Guise (L.I.F. *c.* March 1671/2) 1678 (3 issues).
[The epilogue was spoken "soon after the Royal Theatre was
fir'd" and presumably the play came out shortly after Jan. 25,
1671/2. Imprimatur, Oct. 16, 1678. T.C. Dec. 1678.]

SMITH, HENRY.
T. The Princess of Parma (L.I.F. *c.* April 1699) 1699.
[*Post Boy*, May 20–23, 1699.]

SMITH, JOHN.
C. Cytherea: or The Enamouring Girdle. A New Comedy. 1677.
[Imprimatur, May 30, 1677. T.C. July 1677.]

SMYTHE or SMYTH, JOHN.
C. Win her and Take her, or, Old Fools Will be Medling (D.L. 1691)
1691.
[The ascription to Smythe is due to Anthony à Wood (*Athenae
Oxonienses* (ed. Bliss, 1820), IV. 601); but the epilogue seems to
suggest that *CAVE UNDERHILL* had a share in it.]

SOUTHBY, —.
T.C. Timoleon: or, The Revolution. A Tragi-Comedy. 1697.
[*Post Boy*, March 2–4, 1696/7. Bodl. Mal. 116 has a manuscript
note attributing it to Southby.]

SOUTHERNE, THOMAS.
T. The Loyal Brother: or, The Persian Prince (D.L. Feb. 1681/2)
1682 (2 issues).
[J. W. Dodds (*Thomas Southerne*, p. 28) notes that Luttrell has
a manuscript date, Feb. 7, 1681/2, on the separately printed
prologue. *True Protestant Mercury*, May 20–24, 1682. T.C. May
1682.]
Play. The Disappointment: or, The Mother in Fashion (D.L. April
1684) 1684.
[Dodds (*op. cit.* p. 48) notes a similar manuscript date, April 5,
1684, on the separately printed prologue. T.C. June 1684. On
the printing see Clifford Leech, "A Cancel in *The Disappointment*"

(*The Library*, 4th ser., 1933, XIII. 395) and R. O. Hummel, Jr.,
"A Further Note on Southerne's *The Disappointment*" (*id.* 5th ser.,
1946, I. 67–9).]

C. Sir Anthony Love: or, The Rambling Lady (D.L. *c.* Dec. 1690)
1691; 1698 (2 issues).
[*London Gazette*, Dec. 18–22, 1690. *Post Man*, Oct. 1–4, 1698.
T.C. Feb. 1690/1; June 1698.]

C. The Wives Excuse: or, Cuckolds make themselves (D.L. Dec.
1691) 1692 (2 issues).
[*Gentleman's Journal*, Jan. 1691/2. T.C. Feb. 1691/2.]

T. Cleomenes, the Spartan Heroe (D.L. April 1692). See *JOHN
DRYDEN*.

C. The Maids Last Prayer: or, Any, rather than Fail (D.L. *c.* Feb.
1692/3) 1693 (*bis*).
[*Gentleman's Journal*, Jan. 1692/3 (but issued in March). *London
Gazette*, March 9–13, 1692/3.]

Play. The Fatal Marriage: or, The Innocent Adultery. A Play (D.L.
c. Feb. 1693/4) 1694 (*bis*).
[*London Gazette* March 19–22, 1693/4.]

T. Oroonoko (D.L. Dec. 1695) 1696; 1699 (2 editions and a variant
issue).
[*Post Boy*, Dec. 12–14, 1695.]

SOUTHLAND, THOMAS.

C. Love a la Mode....Written by a Person of Honour (Middlesex
House, amateur, *c.* 1663) 1663.
[Dedication signed T.S., with declaration that the play was
written in 1660. For the author's name and family see J. O.
Halliwell [-Phillipps], *Dictionary of Old English Plays*, p. 150,
and the *Complete Baronetage* (Exeter, 1900), I. 183.]

T. The Ungrateful Favourite....Written by a Person of Honour. 1664.
[Imprimatur, May 11, 1664. The use of the same author ascription and the same motto on the two title-pages seems to indicate
that Southland was responsible for this play also.]

STAPYLTON, Sir ROBERT.

T.C. The Royal Choice (1653).
[The only record of this play is an entry in S.R. Nov. 1653.]

C. The Slighted Maid (L.I.F. Feb. 1662/3) 1663 (*bis*).
[Mon. Feb. 23, 1662/3 (Pepys). S.R. April 14, 1663. *Mercurius
Publicus*, April 23–30, 1663.]

T.C. The Step-mother (L.I.F. *c.* Nov. 1663) 1664 (2 issues).
[S.R. Dec. 26, 1663. *Newes*, Jan. 28, 1663/4. For a performance
at Court, possibly on Th. Dec. 10, 1663, see W. J. Lawrence,
Modern Language Review, 1933, XXVIII. 103.]

T. The Tragedie of Hero and Leander. 1669.
[Imprimatur, Aug. 25, 1668. T.C. Nov. 1668.]

STROUDE, —.

C. All-Plot; or, The Disguises (L.I.F. 1662–1671).
[The only record is in Downes, p. 31.]

TALBOT, J.

T. Troas. 1686.
[A translation from Seneca.]

TATE, NAHUM.
T. Brutus of Alba: or, The Enchanted Lovers (D.G. *c.* July 1678) 1678.
    [Imprimatur, July 15, 1678. T.C. Dec. 1678. The libretto of *Dido and Æneas* is ultimately based on this play: see *infra*.]
T. The Loyal General (D.G. *c.* Dec. 1679) 1680.
    [T.C. Feb. 1679/80.]
T. The History of King Richard the Second (D.L. Dec. 1680) 1681; 1691 (reissue as *The Sicilian Usurper*).
    [Sat. Dec. 11, 1680 (Avery, p. 262, notes that the play was banned, on Dec. 14, after two performances, which gives Dec. 11 as the first). T.C. June 1681; Nov. 1690.]
T. The History of King Lear (D.G. *c.* March 1680/1) 1681; 1689; 1699; 1703; 1712.
    [T.C. May 1681; Nov. 1689; May 1699. *Flying Post*, April 1–4, 1699.]
T. The Ingratitude of a Common-Wealth: Or, the Fall of Caius Martius Coriolanus (D.L. *c.* Dec. 1681) 1682.
    [T.C. Feb. 1681/2. *Loyal Protestant*, March 7, 1681/2.]
F. A Duke and No Duke (D.L. Nov. 1684) 1685; 1693 (with a preface).
    [Mon. Nov. 3, 1684 (L.C.). T.C. Nov. 1684; May 1693. Summers (*Downes*, p. 234) gives, without any authority, the date Aug. 18.]
F. Cuckolds-Haven: or, an Alderman No Conjurer. A Farce (D.G. *c.* June 1685) 1685.
    [Imprimatur, Aug. 14, 1685. T.C. Nov. 1685. The cast suggests a summer performance.]
T.C. The Island-Princess....Reviv'd with Alterations (D.L. April 1687) 1687.
    [Mon. April 25, 1687 (L.C.). T.C. June 1687.]
O. [Dido and Æneas.] An Opera Perform'd at Mr Josias Priest's Boarding School at Chelsey (amateur, *c.* Dec. 1689) [n.d.]. MS. score at St Michael's College, Tenbury.
    [For the evidence regarding date see Barclay Squire, "Purcell's Dramatic Music," *Sammelbände der internationalen Musikgesellschaft*, 1904, v. iv. 506–14. The opera was included later in Charles Gildon's *Measure for Measure* (L.I.F. *c.* 1700).]
    [For a later work see the Handlist of Plays, 1700–1750.]

TATHAM, JOHN.
    [For his earlier works see Greg, *List*, p. 114 and Woodward-McManaway, *Check List*, pp. 134–5.]
C. The Rump: or The Mirrour of The late Times, A New Comedy (Dorset Court, June 1660) 1660; 1661 (2 issues).
    [S.R. Aug. 23, 1660.]
Pageant. Londons Glory represented by Time, Truth and Fame. 1660.
Pageant. London's Tryumphs. 1661.
Pageant. Aqua Triumphalis. 1662.
    [S.R. Aug. 25, 1662.]
Pageant. London's Triumph. 1662.
Pageant. Londinium Triumphans. 1663.
Pageant. London's Triumphs. 1664.

TAUBMAN, MATTHEW.
Pageant. London's Annual Triumph. 1685.
Pageant. London's Yearly Jubilee. 1686.
Pageant. London's Triumph; or, The Goldsmiths Jubilee. F. 1687.
Pageant. London's Anniversary Festival. 1688.
Pageant. London's Great Jubilee. 1689.

TAYLOR, SILAS.
— The Serenade; or, The Disappointment (1669).
  [On May 7, 1659, Pepys read a manuscript of this play.]

THOMSON, THOMAS.
C. The Life of Mother Shipton. A New Comedy. As it was Acted
    Nineteen dayes together with great Applause. [1668–1671.]
      [No record exists to show whether this was actually performed
    or not. Summers, *Bibliography*, p. 120, says, without evidence,
    that this and the following piece were presented by Jolly's company
    at the Cockpit or Salisbury Court, but this seems unlikely. The
    title-page gives the author's initials; Langbaine, p. 504, identifies
    him by name. On the date of the printed text see J. G. McManaway,
    "Massinger and the Restoration Drama" (*ELH*, 1934, I. 293–6).]
C. The English Rogue...As it was acted before several Persons of
    Honour with Great Applause. 1668 (2 issues).
      [This also gives the author's initials.]

TROTTER, CATHERINE.
T. Agnes de Castro (D.L. *c.* Dec. 1695) 1696.
      [*London Gazette*, Jan. 27–30, 1695/6. T.C. Feb. 1695/6.]
T. Fatal Friendship (L.I.F. *c.* May 1698) 1698.
      [*London Gazette*, July 4–7, 1698. In some copies the head-title
    is said to read *The Fatal Marriage*.]
      [For her later works see the Handlist of Plays, 1700–1750.]

TUKE, RICHARD.
Religious Play. The Souls Warfare. 1672; 1672 (reissued as *The Divine
    Comedian: or, The Right Use of Plays, Improved, in a sacred Tragy-
    Comaedy*.

TUKE, Sir SAMUEL.
T.C. The Adventures of Five Hours (L.I.F. Jan. 1662/3) F. 1663;
    1664; 1671; 1704; 1712.
      [Th. Jan. 8, 1662/3 (Pepys and Evelyn). Evidently, from the
    prologue, it had been intended to have the première on Dec. 15.
    Downes, p. 22, says that it was "Wrote by the Earl of Bristol and
    Sir *Samuel Tuke*" and the latter's interest in Spanish drama
    suggests that he may have provided a first draft (see *GEORGE
    DIGBY, Earl of BRISTOL*): to be noted is the fact that on
    July 20, 1664, Pepys had heard that it was by the same author as
    wrote *Worse and Worse*. W. S. Clark (*TLS*, May 3, 1928) draws
    attention to another peculiar fact that Evelyn, on Dec. 23, 1662,
    and Jan. 8, 1662/3, speaks of Sir George Tuke as the author.
    Imprimatur, Feb. 21, 1662/3. S.R. March 2, 1662/3.]

TUTCHIN, JOHN.
Past. The Unfortunate Shepherd. 8° 1685 (in *Poems on Several
    Occasions*).

UNDERHILL, CAVE.

C. Win her and Take her, or, Old Fools Will be Medling. (D.L. 1691). See *JOHN SMYTHE.*

VANBRUGH, Sir JOHN.

C. The Relapse: or, Virtue in Danger (D.L. Nov. 1696); 1697; 1698.
[Sat. Nov. 21, 1696 (see Avery, p. 271). *Post Boy*, Dec. 26–29, 1696. T.C. May 1697; Nov. 1697; May 1698; June 1698. S.R. Sept. 21, 1697.]

C. Aesop (D.L. Part I, *c.* Dec. 1696; Part II, *c.* March 1696/7) 1697 (*bis*); 1702.
[*London Gazette*, Jan. 18–21, 1696/7. T.C. Feb. 1696/7; Part II, May 1697.]

C. The Provok'd Wife (L.I.F. *c.* May 1697) 1697; 1698; 1709.
[*Post Boy*, May 11–13, 1697. T.C. May 1697; Nov. 1698.]

F.C. The Country House (D.L. Jan. 1697/8) 8° 1715; 12° 1719; 12° 1740 (as *La Maison Rustique or the Country House*).
[Tues. Jan. 18, 1697/8 (Morley list in Leslie Hotson, p. 377). This record throws back the date of composition many years from the date of publication. Full particulars of later performances are given in the following volume.]
[For his later works see the Handlist of Plays, 1700–1750.]

VERBRUGGEN, JOHN.

O. Brutus of Alba (D.G. *c.* Oct. 1696). See *GEORGE POWELL.*

VILLIERS, GEORGE, Duke of BUCKINGHAM.

C. The Chances (T.R. in B.St., Feb. 1666/7) 1682; 1692; 1705.
[Tues. Feb. 5, 1666/7 (Pepys).]

C. The Country Gentleman (probably not completed, 1669). See *Sir ROBERT HOWARD.*

C. The Rehearsal (T.R. in B.St., Dec. 1671) 1672; 1673; 1675; 1683; 1687; 1692; 1701; 1709 [and in various editions of the *Works*].
[Th. Dec. 7, 1671 (Avery, p. 255). S.R. June 19, 1672. T.C. June 1672; Feb. 1674/5; Nov. 1683. Evidently the burlesque had been written before 1665 and was later altered.]
[The *Works* 1704 contain: (1) *The Militant Couple: Or The Husband may Thank Himself*; (2) *The Belgic Heroe Unmasked: Or the Deliverer set forth in his proper Colours*; (3) *The Battle: Or The Rehearsal at White-Hall* (also called *The Farce upon Segmoor Fight*). In the *Works* 8°,1714, appears *The Restauration: Or Right will take Place*, wrongly attributed ⌐ Buckingham.]

WALKER, WILLIAM.

T. Victorious Love (D.L. *c.* June 1698) 1698.
[*Post Man*, July 19–21, 1698.]
[For a later work see the Handlist of Plays, 1700–1750.]

WALLER, EDMUND.

T. Pompey the Great....Translated out of French by Certain Persons of Honour (St James's, amateur, *c.* Jan. 1662/3; L.I.F. *c.* Dec. 1664) 1664.
[S.R. Feb. 15, 1663/4. *Newes*, March 3, 1663/4. This was a collaborative effort in which Waller was joined by *Sir CHARLES SEDLEY, EDWARD FILMER, SIDNEY GODOLPHIN* and *CHARLES SACKVILLE, Earl of DORSET.*]

T. The Maid's Tragedy Altered. 8° 1690 (*bis*); 8° 1690 (in *The Second Part of Mr Waller's Poems*).
[S.R. Nov. 24, 1689. *London Gazette*, Feb. 16–19, 1690/1.]

WALTER, THOMAS.
Pol. The Excommunicated Prince: or, The False Relique. 1679. See *WILLIAM BEDLOE.*

WESTON, JOHN.
T.C. The Amazon Queen; or, The Amours of Thalestris to Alexander the Great. 1667.
[Imprimatur, Feb. 11, 1666/7.]

WHARTON, Lady ANNE.
T. Love's Martyr, or Witt above Crowns. MS. B.M. Add. 28,693.
[S.R. has a caveat against entering this play, Feb. 3, 1685/6.]

WHITAKER, WILLIAM.
T. The Conspiracy or the Change of Government (D.G. *c.* March 1679/80) 1680.
[T.C. May 1680.]

WILD, ROBERT.
C. The Benefice. 1689 (*bis*). MS. B.M. Lansdowne 807.
[T.C. May 1689. This play must have been written before 1660.]

WILLIAMS, JOSEPH.
C. Have at All; or, The Midnight Adventure (D.L. *c.* May 1694).
[Recorded in *Gentleman's Journal*, May 1694.]

WILMOT, JOHN, Earl of ROCHESTER.
T. Lucina's Rape: Or The Tragedy of Vallentinian. MS. B.M. Add. 28,692.
[This has a cast list that dates it not later than 1679, but whether it was acted then is not known.]
T. The Conquest of China by the Tartars (a scene for this play by Sir Robert Howard is in B.M. MSS. Add. 28,692).
[This may be dated about 1678; see J. Harold Wilson, "The Dating of Rochester's 'Scaen'" (*Review of English Studies*, 1937, XIII. 455–8) and the present writer's "Dryden, Howard and Rochester" (*TLS*, Jan. 13, 1921). Dryden, in a letter dated Sept. 3, 1697, declared he proposed to revise this play, but apparently the project was never fulfilled.]
T. Valentinian (D.L. Feb. 1683/4) 1685 (2 issues); 1691; 1696.
[Mon. Feb. 11, 1683/4 (L.C.). T.C. Nov. 1684. *London Gazette*, Feb. 16–19, 1691. A revised version of *Lucina's Rape.*]
— Sodom. See *CHRISTOPHER FISHBOURNE.*

WILSON, JOHN.
C. The Cheats (T.R. in V.St. March 1662/3) 1664; 1671; 1684; 1693 (2 issues). MS. Worcester College, Oxford.
[Licensed Fri. March 6, 1662/3 and suppressed Mon. March 22. The title-page states it was written in 1662. Dedication dated Nov. 16, 1663. Imprimatur, Nov. 5, 1663. S.R. Nov. 9, 1663. *Newes*, Nov. 26, 1663. T.C. May 1671. The manuscript has been published by Milton C. Nahm (1935).]

T. Andronicus Comnenius. 1664.

[Dedication dated Jan. 15, 1663 (*i.e.* 1663/4). *Newes*, Feb. 11, 1663/4. S.R. Feb. 15, 1664/5. Milton C. Nahm suggests that the anonymous *Andronicus* of 1661 is an early draft of this work (see "John Wilson and his 'Some Few Plays'," *Review of English Studies*, 1938, XIV. 143–54).]

C. The Projectors. 1665.

[Imprimatur, Jan. 13, 1663/4. S.R. Feb. 15, 1664/5. *Newes*, April 27, 1665. This may or may not have been acted.]

T.C. Belphagor: or The Marriage of the Devil (Smock Alley, Dublin, before 1675; D.G. *c.* June 1690) 1691 (2 issues). MS. Folger Shakespeare Library, 827. 1.

[Imprimatur, Oct. 13, 1690. T.C. Feb. 1690/1. The Prologue was spoken after a performance of *The Prophetess*. For the Dublin performance see William V. Lennep, "The Smock Alley Players of Dublin" (*ELH*, 1946, XIII. 216–22).]

WRIGHT, JAMES.

C. Malade imaginaire (translated).

[Cited by Summers, *Playhouse*, pp. 342 and 448, from a Colbeck Radford catalogue.]

WRIGHT, JOHN.

T. Thyestes...Translated out of Seneca. 1674.

[T.C. Feb. 1673/4.]

Burlesque. Mock-Thyestes. 1674 (published with above).

WRIGHT, THOMAS.

C. The Female Vertuoso's (D.G. *c.* April 1693) 1693.

(*Gentleman's Journal*, May 1693 (probably not issued until June). *London Gazette*, June 22–26, 1693. T.C. Nov. 1693.]

WYCHERLEY, WILLIAM.

C. Love in a Wood, or, St James's Park (T.R. in B.St. *c.* March 1670/1) 1672; 1693; 1694 (2 issues); 1711.

[S.R. Oct. 6, 1671. T.C. Nov. 1671. There is a reference to a Lent performance in the dedication.]

C. The Gentleman Dancing-Master (D.G. *c.* Aug. 1672) 1673; 1693; 1702.

[S.R. Sept. 18, 1672. T.C. Nov. 1672. Downes, p. 32, says this was the third new play at D.G. (opened Nov. 1671), coming after Crowne's *Charles the Eighth* and Ravenscroft's *The Citizen turn'd Gentleman*. Guessing that these plays followed each other at short intervals, several historians have assumed that this would place the première at the very end of 1671 or in January 1671/2, and this seems supported by the statement in the epilogue that "all gentlemen must pack to sea" (in reference to the Third Dutch War, formally declared on March 17, 1671/2). On the other hand, the L.C. list gives Crowne's drama in May 1672, and from the fact that three performances of Ravenscroft's comedy are recorded early in July there can seem to be no doubt but that the latter was first produced in this month. If Downes is correct, therefore, *The Gentleman Dancing-Master* must have come after July; this agrees with the S.R. entry, and also with the fact that Downes' next record is of Shadwell's *Epsom Wells*, which apparently came out towards the beginning of December.]

C. The Country-Wife (D.L. Jan. 1674/5) 1675; 1683; 1688; 1695 (*bis*).

[Tues. Jan. 12, 1674/5 (L.C.). S.R. Jan. 13, 1674/5. T.C. May 1675; Dec. 1688. There is a slight puzzle about the date of the première. The two L.C. records on Jan. 12 and Jan. 15, 1674/5, together with the S.R. entry at the same time, seem to indicate that this was the time of its first production. On the other hand, the prologue, in speaking of "the late so bafled scribler of this day" appears to refer to a not too distant failure of *The Gentleman Dancing Master*. From the fact that the T.C. advertisement (1. 205) gives the play as acted at "the Duke's Theatre Royal" George B. Churchill (in his edition of *The Country Wife and The Plain Dealer*, 1924, p. xxv) suggests that it originally came out at L.I.F. when that theatre was being used by the King's men (*i.e.* before midsummer 1673). The phrase in the T.C., however, is likely to be merely a slip.]

C. The Plain-Dealer (D.L. Dec. 1676) 1677 (*bis*); 1678; 1681; 1686; 1691; 1694; 1700; 1709.

[Mon. Dec. 11, 1676 (L.C.). Imprimatur, Jan. 9, 1676 (*i.e.* 1676/7). There is a reference to the play in the preface to Dryden's *The State of Innocence*, entered in the S.R. for April 17, 1674, but this work was not printed till 1677 and no doubt the preface was penned at that time (see George B. Churchill, "The Relation of Dryden's *State of Innocence* to Milton's *Paradise Lost* and Wycherley's *Plain Dealer*," *Modern Philology*, IV. 381-8).]

UNKNOWN AUTHORS.

Pol. The Abdicated Prince: or, The Adventures of Four Years. A Tragi-Comedy. 1690 (*bis*).

[T.C. May 1690. Second edition, *Athenian Mercury*, Sept. 29, 1694.]

C. The Amorous Old-woman: or, 'Tis Well if it Take....By a Person of Honour (D.L. *c.* March 1674) 1674; 1684 (reissue as *The Fond Lady*).

[T.C. May 1674. Langbaine, p. 526, says he had "been told this Play was writ by" *THOMAS DUFFETT*, but Duffett certainly was not "a Person of Honour."]

— Andromeda (Jan. 1661/2).

[Mon. Jan. 20, 1661/2 (Ethel Seaton, *Literary Relations of England and Scandinavia in the Seventeenth Century*, 1935, pp. 333 and 335). In all probability this was a pre-Commonwealth drama, although there is no known work that seems to fit.]

T. Andronicus: A Tragedy, Impieties Long Successe, or Heavens Late Revenge. 8º 1661.

[The preface says this was written eighteen years before at Oxford, taken to York, lost there and rediscovered in London. See *JOHN WILSON*.]

T. Anna Bullen. MS. Huntington Library, HM 973.

[Edythe N. Backus ("The MS. Play, *Anna Bullen*," *PMLA*, 1932, XLVII. 741–52) identifies this as an eighteenth-century copy of a play written about 1681.]

T. The Armenian Queen (? 1676).

[The prologue and epilogue for this play are in Thomas Duffett's

New Poems, Songs, Prologues and Epilogues, 8° 1676. It was evidently a country production.]

Ballet. Le Balet de la Paix. Dancé en presence de Monseigneur le President de Bordeaux Ambassadeur Extraordinaire du Roy de France en Angleterre. 1660.

Ballet. Ballet et Musique pour le divertissement du Roy de la Grande Bretagne. 1674.

Pol. The Banish'd Duke: or, The Tragedy of Infortunatus. 1690.
[Although the title-page says this was "Acted at the Theatre Royal," it is certain the play was never performed. T.C. Nov. 1690. *London Gazette,* Aug. 18–21, 1690.]

Pol. The Bloody Duke: or, The Adventures for a Crown. A Tragi-Comedy...Written by the Author of the Abdicated Prince. 1690.
[T.C. May 1690.]

C. The Bragadocio, or, The Bawd turn'd Puritan: A New Comedy. By a Person of Quality. 1691.
[T.C. Feb. 1690/1.]

Pol. Caledonia: or, The Pedlar turned Merchant. A Tragi-Comedy, as it was Acted by His Majesty's Subjects for Scotland in the King of Spain's Province of Darien. 1700.
[*Post Boy,* Feb. 22–24, 1699/1700.]

C. The Captain, or, Town Miss (D.L. April 1677).
[Mon. April 2, 1677 (L.C.). This may be Fletcher's *The Captain.*]

Ent. The Christmas Ordinary. A Private Show, wherein is expressed the Jovial Freedom of that Festival. Acted at a Gentlemans House among other Revels. 1682.
[By "W.R.".]

T. The Cid (1691). MS. B.M. 8,888 (said to be in the hand of William Popple, Andrew Marvell's nephew).

Past. The Constant Nymph: or, the Rambling Shepheard...written by a Person of Quality (D.G. *c.* July 1677) 1678.
[Imprimatur, Aug. 13, 1677. T.C. Nov. 1677. The dedication shows it was acted during the "vacation"—no doubt the summer.]

Play. The Coronation of Queen Elizabeth, with The Restauration of the Protestant Religion: or, The Downfal of the Pope. Being a most Excellent Play (Bartholomew and Southwark Fairs, *c.* 1680) 1680.
[Dedication signed "J.D."]

C. The Counterfeit Bridegroom: or the Defeated Widow (D.G. *c.* Sept. 1677) 1677.
[Imprimatur, Oct. 4, 1677. T.C. Nov. 1677. This alteration of Middleton's *No Wit, No Help, like a Woman's* has been variously ascribed to *APHRA BEHN* and to *THOMAS BETTERTON.*]

— The Country Knight (? D.G. March 1674/5).
[This title is recorded in a list of plays seen by Nell Gwyn (Harvard University Library), apparently on March 19, 1674/5. It may be a variant title for another play. See under *Sir ROBERT HOWARD* and *JOHN CROWNE.*]

Pol. Cromwell's Conspiracy. A Tragy-Comedy, Relating to our latter Times. Beginning at the Death of King Charles the First, And ending with the happy Restauration of King Charles the Second. Written by a Person of Quality. 1660.
[The B.M. copy (E 1038) has a manuscript date, August 8.]

T.C. The Cure of Pride. MS. Huntington Library, HM 95.

[This adaptation of Massinger's *The City Madam* seems to belong to the Restoration period.]

T. The Tragicall History of the Life and Death of Doctor Faustus (? Cockpit, or Red Bull, 1662) 1663.

[On this early stage version of Marlowe's play see Richard H. Perkinson, "A Restoration 'Improvement' of *Doctor Faustus*" (*ELH*, 1934, I. 305–24).]

T.C. Emilia. 8º 1672.

C. An Evening Adventure; or, A Night's Intrigue.

[This title, recorded in several early play lists and dated 1680, is probably a "ghost." *Biographia Dramatica* (1812), II. 203, suggests that it may be John Stevens' *An Evening's Intrigue.*]

Past. The Exposure (T.R. in B.St. Nov. 1663).

[Recorded in Herbert papers, possibly about Nov. 1663 (Herbert, p. 138).]

T.C. The Faithfull Genius. (A MS. formed no. 361 in the H.F. House sale in 1924.)

[This has no date, but seems to belong to the Restoration period.]

T. The Faithfull Virgins. MS. Bodl. Rawl. poet. 195.

[Licensed by Herbert: "This tragedy apoynted to be acted by the dukes Company of Actors only leaving out what was Cross'd by Henry Herbertt M.R." There is no evidence concerning actual performance.]

Pol. The Famous Tragedie of the Life and Death of Mris. Rump. 1660.

T. The Fatal Discovery: or, Love in Ruines (D.L. *c.* Feb. 1697/8) 1698 (2 issues).

[Preface signed by *GEORGE POWELL*. T.C. May 1698. *Post Man*, March 3–5, 1697/8.]

C. The Feign'd Astrologer. 1668.

C. Feign'd Friendship: or The Mad Reformer (L.I.F. *c.* May 1699) 1699.

[T.C. June 1699. *Post Man*, June 13–15, 1699.]

C. The Female Wits; or, The Triumvirate of Poets at Rehearsal (D.L. *c.* 1697) 1704.

[This must have been acted before Verbruggen left the T.R. for L.I.F. and shortly after *The World in the Moon* was presented (D.G. June 1697). Woodward-McManaway, *Check List*, no. 574, records an edition of 1697 at the Huntington Library, but without giving details.]

— Feniza or The Ingeniouse Mayde. (A MS. of this play formed no. 351 in the H.F. House sale in 1924.)

Pol. The Folly of Priest-Craft. A Comedy. 1690.

[T.C. Nov. 1690. *New Observator*, Oct. 24, 1690. A variant title, *The Converts*, has been recorded.]

F. The Fool's Expectation: Or, The Wheel of Fortune (D.G. 1698).

[Only the prologue and epilogue are extant (Autrey N. Wiley, *Rare Prologues and Epilogues, 1642–1700* (1940), pp. 305–10).]

— Fools Have Fortune; or, Luck's All.

[This title is given by Alfred Harbage (*Annals of English Drama*, 1940, pp. 142–3) as a play of the Duke's men about 1680 I do not know any other reference to it.]

C. The Gordian Knot Unty'd (D.L. *c.* Nov. 1690).
[Recorded in *Gentleman's Journal*, Jan. 1691/2. It is mentioned in the prologue to Bancroft's *King Edward the Third* (D.L. *c.* Nov. 1690). Dennis Arundell (*TLS*, June 18, 1925) suggests that the author may have been William Walsh, but his evidence is very flimsy.]

Pol. Hells Higher Court of Justice; or the Triall of the Three Politick Ghosts, Viz. Oliver Cromwell, King of Sweden, and Cardinal Mazarine. 1661.
[By "J.D." The B.M. copy (E 1087) has a manuscript date, April 13.]

T. Heraclius (L.I.F. ? March 1664).
[Tues. March 8, 1663/4 (Pepys; but with no mention of the theatre at which it was played).]

Pol. Hewson Reduc'd: or, the Shoemaker return'd to his Trade. 1661.

Ent. The Huntingdon Divertisement, or, an Enterlude For the Generall Entertainment at the County-Feast, Held at Merchant-Taylors Hall, June 20, 1678. 1678.
[Imprimatur, May 16, 1678. S.R. June 17, 1678.]

— The Illustrious Sclaves (1672). MS. B.M. Add. 32,094.

T. Irena. 1664.
[Imprimatur, Oct. 13, 1664.]

T.C. The Island Princess; or, The Generous Portugal (D.L. Jan. 1668/9) 1669.
[Th. Jan. 7, 1668/9 (Pepys and L.C.). T.C. Nov. 1669. An alteration of Fletcher's play.]

T. Jugurtha or The Faithless Cosen german. MS. Bodl. Rawl. poet. 195.
[The precise date is unknown, but it is stated to fall within the Restoration period: it should, however, be remembered that Henslowe records a *Jugurth* in 1600 and that Herbert re-licensed an old play called *Jugurth* in 1624.]

C. Knavery in all Trades: or, the Coffee-House. A Comedy. As it was Acted in the Christmas Holidays by several Apprentices. 1664.

T.C. The Labyrinth (T.R. in B.St. May 1664).
[Mon. May 2, 1664 (Pepys). This play is otherwise unknown unless it be *Love's Labyrinth* (1660) by *THOMAS FORDE*.]

Pol. The Late Revolution: or, The Happy Change. A Tragi-Comedy. 1690.
[T.C. May 1690. *London Gazette*, April 24–28, 1690.]

T. Love Despised (L.I.F. Aug. 1668).
[Mon. Aug. 17, 1668 (Pepys). Downes, p. 29, records a revival of Beaumont and Fletcher's *Cupid's Revenge*, and Pepys notes that *Love Despised* was the "new name" of that play: it is impossible to tell whether this was an altered version or not.]

T.C. The Lovers Stratagem or Virtue Rewarded. MS. Bodl. Rawl. poet. 18.
[The precise date is unknown, but this seems to be a Restoration play. A brief account of the plot appears in Summers, *Playhouse*, pp. 341–2.]

C. Love's Metamorphosis, or The Disguis'd Lovers.
[Summers, *Playhouse*, pp. 343 and 449, lists this play from a manuscript in a Colbeck Radford catalogue. He states that this is inscribed "Nar. Luttrell, his Book, 1682."]

— Love's Mistery (? T.R. in V.St. Nov. 1660).

> [Mon. Nov. 12, 1660 (Herbert, p. 118; but the entry is deleted). This is almost certainly not a new play; perhaps the title is an alternative name for an older drama or is given in error for Heywood's *Love's Mistress*.]

T.C. Love's Quarrel (Salisbury Court, April 1661).

> [Sat. April 6, 1661 (Pepys). Almost certainly not a new play: probably an alternative title for an earlier work newly revived.]

C. Love will finde out the Way....By T.B. 1661; 1667 (reissue as *The Constant Maid: or, Love will finde out the Way...by J.S.*).

> [This is Shirley's *The Constant Maid*. The 1667 issue describes it as acted at the Nursery in Hatton Garden.]

C. The Lyar (?1661). See, *infra, The Mistaken Beauty, or the Lyar* (D.L. *c.* Sept. 1684).

C. The Mistaken Beauty, or the Lyar (D.L. *c.* Sept. 1684) 1685.

> [Early play-lists record a quarto of 1661 with the title, *The Lyar*, but this is now unknown. That it may have once existed is suggested by the fact that Pepys saw a play called *The Mistaken Beauty* on Nov. 28, 1667: it was then "old." T.C. Nov. 1684 and May 1685.]

C. The Mistaken Husband (D.L. *c.* Sept. 1675) 1675.

> [T.C. Nov. 1675. The preface declares that one scene was written by *JOHN DRYDEN*. Alfred Harbage, "Elizabethan-Restoration Palimpsest," pp. 304–7, suggests that this play was an old manuscript comedy by Brome, altered by Dryden.]

C. Mr Turbulent: or, The Melanchollicks (D.G. *c.* Jan. 1681/2) 1682; 1685 (reissue as *The Factious Citizen, or, The Melancholy Visioner*).

> [The B.M. copy (161. d. 20) has a manuscript date, Jan. 27, 1681/2. *True Protestant Mercury*, Feb. 4–8, 1681/2.]

— The Muse of New-Market: or, Mirth and Drollery. Being Three Farces Acted before the King and Court at Newmarket (Newmarket, *c.* 1680) 1680.

> [This includes three drolls: (1) *The Merry Milkmaid of Islington, or the Rambling Gallants defeated* (from Nabbes' *Tottenham Court*); (2) *Love Lost in the Dark, or the Drunken Couple* (from Massinger's *The Guardian*); (3) *The Politick Whore or the Conceited Cuckhold* (from Davenport's *The City Night-Cap*). T.C. May 1681. *Domestick Intelligence*, Jan. 30–Feb. 2, 1681/2.]

— Music; or, A Parley of Instruments. The First Part. 1676.

C. The New-made Nobleman (Red Bull, Jan. 1661/2).

> ["*Den niewgemaakten Adelman*" seen by continental visitors, Wed. Jan. 22, 1661/2 (Ethel Seaton, *Literary Relations of England and Scandinavia in the Seventeenth Century*, 1935, p. 333). W. Van Lennep (*TLS*, June 20, 1936) believes that this was Fletcher's *The Noble Gentleman*.]

C. Midnight's Intrigues (*c.* 1677).

> [Recorded in the prologue to Chamberlayne's *Wits Led by the Nose* (D.L. *c.* July 1677). See *APHRA BEHN, The Feign'd Curtizans* (D.G. 1679).]

C. No Foole like ye Old Foole (D.L. June 1676).

> [Tues. June 13, 1676 (L.C.).]

C. The Northern Castle (T.R. in B.St. Sept. 1667).

[Sat. Sept. 14, 1667 (Pepys). Almost certainly a mistake for *The Northern Lass*.]

T. The Perjured Nun (? 1680).

[Some early play-lists record this title as a reprint or alteration of Brewer's *The Lovesick King*. No copy has authoritatively been reported.]

Pol. A Phanatique Play. The First Part, As it was Presented before and by the Lord Fleetwood, Sir Arthur Hasilrig, Sir Henry Vane, the Lord Lambert, and others, last night, with Master Iester and Master Pudding. 1660; 1660 (variant issue as *A Phanatick Play*).

[The Bodley copy (Wood 615) has a manuscript date, March 1659; in the Thomason tracts it is March 14.]

C. The Physician against his Will (*c.* 1667).

[J. O. Halliwell (*A Dictionary of Old English Plays*, 1860, p. 194) says that "there is among Flecknoe's poems a prologue, intended for a play, with this title."]

T. Piso's Conspiracy (D.G. *c.* Dec. 1675) 1676.

[T.C. Feb. 1675/6. An alteration of the *Nero* of 1624.]

— The Poetess (D.L. Oct. 1667).

[Mon. Oct. 7, 1667 (L.C.). Almost certainly an error. *The Poetaster* is a possibility, but there is no record of a Restoration production of that play, and in any case it was among the pieces given to D'Avenant in a warrant of Aug. 20, 1668.]

— The Polititian; or, Sir Popular Wisdom (D.G. Nov. 1677).

[For Sat. Nov. 17, 1677 the L.C. records have, in one list, *The Polititian* and, in the other, Sr *Popler Wisdome*: that these refer to the same play is proved by a letter, dated Nov. 17, 1677, by Andrew Marvell (see *HMC*, 14th Report, App. II. 357, and Edmond de Beer in *TLS*, March 8, 1923).]

Pol. The Puritanical Justice; or, The Beggars turn'd Thieves. By Way of Farce, as it was lately Acted in and about the City of London. 1698.

F. The Rampant Alderman, or News from the Exchange, A Farce. 1685.

[S.R. Aug. 30, 1684. T.C. Nov. 1684. This is an adaptation of Marmion's *The Fine Companion*.]

M. The Rape of Europa by Jupiter (D.G. 1694) 1694.

— The Rectory (D.G. Sept. 1673).

[Sat. Sept. 27, 1673 (L.C.).]

Pol. The Religious-Rebell, or the Pilgrim-Prince. 1671.

T.C. The Renegado. MS. Bodl. Rawl. poet. 20.

[The manuscript of this altered version of Massinger's play cannot be dated with any assurance. The only recorded performance of *The Renegado* was on June 6, 1662. See W. J. Lawrence (*TLS*, Oct. 24, 1929) and J. G. McManaway, "Philip Massinger and the Restoration Drama" (*ELH*, 1934, I. 287–8).]

C. The Rival Mother (? 8° 1678).

[Some early playlists, followed by a few more modern, confidently record this title, but no copy seems to have been authoritatively reported.]

— The Romantick Lady (T.R. in B.St. March 1670/1).

[Mon. March 13, 1670/1 (L.C.). The year is not certain but is probably as given here.]

Pol. Rome's Follies: or, The Amorous Fryars....As it was lately Acted at a Person of Qualities House. 1681.
[*Impartial Protestant Mercury*, Dec. 30–Jan. 3, 1681/2.]

T. Romulus and Hersilia: or, The Sabine War (D.G. Aug. 1682) 1683.
[Th. Aug. 10, 1682 (*True Protestant Mercury*, Aug. 12–16, 1682). T.C. Nov. 1682. *Loyal Impartial Mercury*, Nov. 14–17, 1682. Both Mrs Behn and Lady Slingsby were arrested on account of the epilogue written by the former and spoken by the latter (see Autrey Nell Wiley, *Rare Prologues and Epilogues 1642–1700* (1940), pp. 129–34). The order of arrest is in L.C. 5/191 and 5/16, p. 118.]

Pol. The Royal Cuckold: or, Great Bastard....A Tragy-Comedy. 1693.
[T.C. June 1693.]

Pol. The Royal Flight: or, The Conquest of Ireland. A New Farce. 1690.
[T.C. Nov. 1690. *New Observator*, Oct. 15, 1690.]

Pol. The Royal Voyage, or the Irish Expedition. A Tragi-comedy. 1690.
[T.C. June 1690.]

Ent. School-Play (amateur, *c.* 1663) 8º 1664.

— The Sea-Captains (D.G. March 1673/4).
[Wed. March 18, 1673/4 (L.C.).]

C. She Ventures, and He Wins. A Comedy (L.I.F. *c.* Sept. 1695) 1696.
[The dedication is signed "Ariadne." *London Gazette*, Oct. 10–14, 1695.]

Pol. The Siege and Surrender of Mons. A Tragi-Comedy. 1691.
[Imprimatur, April 23, 1691. T.C. Nov. 1691.]

Pol. The Siege of Derry. 1692.

T.C. Tamerlane the Beneficent (1692). MS. B.M. Add. 8,888 (said to be in the hand of William Popple, Andrew Marvell's nephew).

Pol. The Tragical Actors of the Martyrdome of the late King Charles wherein Oliver's late falsehood, with the rest of his gang are described in their several actions and stations. 1660 (no date on title-page, but colophon, "Printed for Sir Arthur, 1660").
[The B.M. copy (E 1019) has a manuscript date, March 30, 1660.]

T.C. The Triumphs of Virtue (D.L. *c.* Jan. 1696/7) 1697.
[*Post Boy*, April 17–20, 1697.]

C. Try Before You Trust. MS. B.M. 37,158.
[The date of this piece is unknown, but probably comes towards the end of the seventeenth century.]

C. A Pleasant Comedy called The Two Merry Milk-maids. 1661.
[A version of the comedy of 1619.]

— The Ungrateful Lovers (L.I.F. Sept. 1667).
[Wed. Sept. 11, 1667 (Pepys). This is almost certainly a "ghost" title: no doubt Pepys meant *The Unfortunate Lovers.*]

T. The Unnatural Mother....Written by a Young Lady (L.I.F. *c.* Aug. 1697) 1698.
[T.C. Nov. 1697, and Feb. 1697/8 (as *Love's Reward; or, The Unnatural Mother*). *Post Boy*, Nov. 20–23, 1697.]

Satire. Wit for Money: or, Poet Stutter. A Dialogue between Smith, Johnson, and Poet Stutter. Containing Reflections on some late

Plays; and particularly, on Love for Money, or, The Boarding School. 1691.

[T.C. May 1691. The B.M. copy (641. p. 1) has a manuscript date, April 23.]

C. The Woman turn'd Bully (D.G. *c.* May 1675) 1675.

[Imprimatur, July 5, 1675. S.R. July 8, 1675. T.C. Nov. 1675.]

For the sake of completeness there is added here a list of titles of various drolls and puppet-plays. These have not been included in the general alphabetical list of unknown plays because (1) some of the titles are vague and general (e.g. *Whittington*), (2) some probably are relics of pre-Commonwealth dramatic activity, and (3) some, although conjecturally dated before 1700, may belong rather to the early years of the eighteenth century. Most of the titles are recorded in *A Dictionary of Old English Plays* (1860) by J. O. Halliwell (J. O. Halliwell-Phillipps): references are given to this book and brief indication is given of the sources, where stated, of his information.

Puppet-plays

Bartholomew Fair (Pepys, Sept. 9, 1668).

Holofernes (Pepys, Aug. 6, 1664).

Patient Grizill (Pepys, Aug. 30, 1667).

Punchinello (Halliwell, p. 203, quoting a record of March 29, 1666, which mentions "Punchinello, the Itallian popet player" at "booth at Charing-Cross").

Whittington (Pepys, Sept. 21, 1668).

Drolls

The Boaster; or Bully-huff catch'd in a Trap (Halliwell, p. 34, with reference to *The Theatre of Ingenuity*, 1698: obviously taken from *1 Henry IV*).

The Devil of a Wife (Halliwell, p. 73).

Dives and Lazarus (Halliwell, p. 76, referring to *Wit and Drollery*, 1682, and *The Pleasant Musical Companion*, 1687).

The Dutch Cruelties at Amboyna, with the Humours of the Valiant Welshman (see *Cal. State Papers. Domestic, 1672–3*, p. 148, under date May 11, 1672).

Friar Bacon (Halliwell, p. 104).

Irish Evidence; or The Humours of Teague (Harbage, *Annals*, p. 144, under the date 1682).

Jephtha's Rash Vow; or The Virgin Sacrifice (Halliwell, p. 132, referring to "Sorbière's Journey to London" in 1698, but Sorbière's *Relation d'un voyage en Angleterre* was originally published in 1664 and translated in 1709: a droll of this title is recorded in 1703—see the Handlist of Plays, 1700–1705).

Mad Tom of Bedlam; or The Distressed lovers, with the Comical Humours of Squire Numskull (Halliwell, p. 160, but this also is firmly recorded only in the eighteenth century, an announcement of 1730 declaring that it was written by Doggett).

The Mad Wooing; or, A Way to Win and Tame a Shrew (Halliwell, p. 160, referring to *The Theatre of Ingenuity*, 1698).

Merry Andrew (presumably this is the title intended by Pepys' *Marry Andrey* of Aug. 29, 1668).

Noah's Flood (see *supra*, p. 311).

The Old Widow (Halliwell, p. 185, referring to *Wit's Interpreter*, 1662, and giving Cartwright's *The Ordinary* as the source).

The Prince's Ball; or, The Conquest of Queen Judith (Harbage, *Annals*, p. 144, under the date 1682).

St George and the Dragon (Halliwell, p. 218, referring to *The Theatre of Compliments*, 1688).

The Siege of Namur (Halliwell, p. 228, referring to "Sorbière's Journey to London", 1698).

Vienna Besieged (Halliwell, p. 265, referring to *The Theatre of Compliments*, 1688).

INDEX

[A final volume in this series will present a general comprehensive index of all the English plays catalogued in this and the other Hand-lists. Consequently the present index is concerned only with persons and subjects.]

NED